AF413365

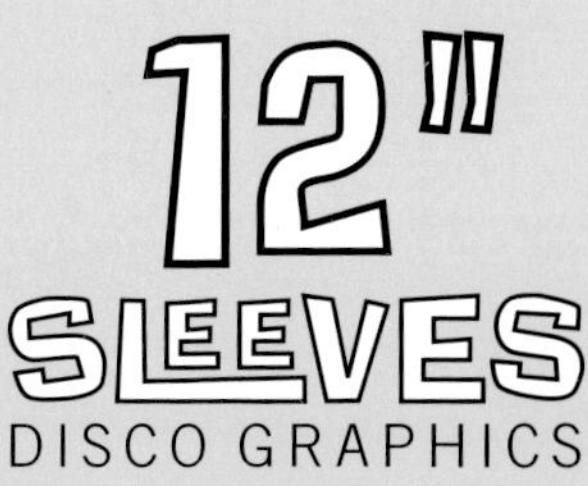
12"
SLEEVES
DISCO GRAPHICS

… So what shall I play now? Hmm, perhaps I'll pump it up
a bit, but I don't want to go too far… Hmm, but I'm sure it'll
work… Where is it? Let's see, not this one, not this either,
not that one, no… okay, yes, the image silhouetted against
a yellow background… I've got it!
For 20 years my work as a DJ has been a constant
to-and-fro between typographies, photos, collages and
music: music that in many cases I have identified by
means of graphic elements. I would even say that at times
I have felt drawn to certain discs more for their visual
image than for the actual sound. Perhaps that's why I now
work as a graphic designer.
This book sets out to bring together all those covers that
have accompanied my night-time work during these
20 years. With all the distance between the different styles,
graphic references and pieces of music.
I've already chosen my favourites.
Now it's your turn to do the same.

Toni Rubio

...¿ Y ahora qué pongo?... mmm, quizás subo el tono, pero no quiero arriesgarme mucho... mmm, aunque seguro que funciona... Voy a buscarlo. A ver..., este no, este tampoco, este no, no... ah sí, la imagen recortada sobre fondo amarillo... ¡Ya lo tengo!

Durante 20 años, mi trabajo de DJ ha sido un constante devaneo entre tipografías, fotos, collages y música. Música que tantas veces he identificado por elementos gráficos. A veces incluso diría que he sentido predilección por algunos temas más por su imagen que por la propia música. Quizá por eso ahora trabajo como diseñador gráfico.

Este libro quiere reunir todas aquellas portadas que, a lo largo de estos años, han acompañado mi trabajo nocturno. Con toda la distancia entre los diferentes estilos, referencias gráficas y piezas musicales. Yo ya he seleccionado mis preferidas. Ahora te toca a ti hacer lo mismo.

Toni Rubio

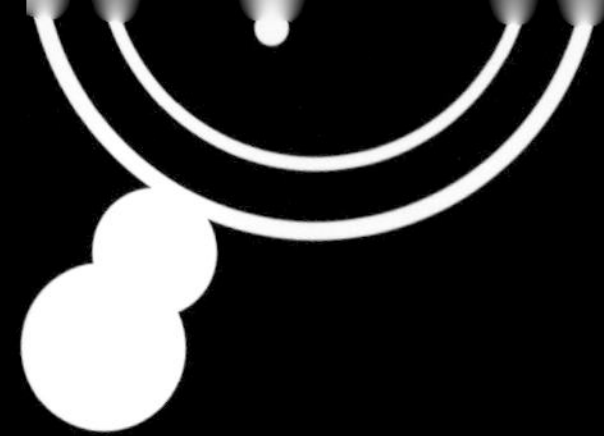

12" x 12"
The Size Matters

Jaume Pujagut

A few years ago I wrote something like this in a magazine published by Discos Castelló and edited by Mingus B. Formentor that went by the name of *Discolic* (issue 2, March 1988):
'My theory is that discoholics not only listen to music, they actually love discs, those round objects, normally black, that come in cardboard sleeves. While they listen to the music (very often on headphones) they look at the drawings or photographs on the sleeve; they learn that the TV actor Don Johnson wrote lyrics for the Allman Brothers or that the new Prince album was recorded in a studio in Philadelphia, remixed in N.Y. and then had a brass section added in Honolulu, and that the post-production was done on a little island in the far-off Caribbean. In short, the minor details of history.'
The fact is that even after all these years I still think the same: nothing can equal the magic of those 144 square inches of visual and graphic information associated with the music read off the grooves of a disc of generally black vinyl.
You have in front of you the latest contribution to a long tradition.
A tradition that was launched in 1977 with the first *Album Cover Album*, featuring the work of Hipgnosis and Roger Dean, and has continued to the present day with the reprinting of the Taschen book *1000 Record Covers* by Michael Ochs. A tradition with such

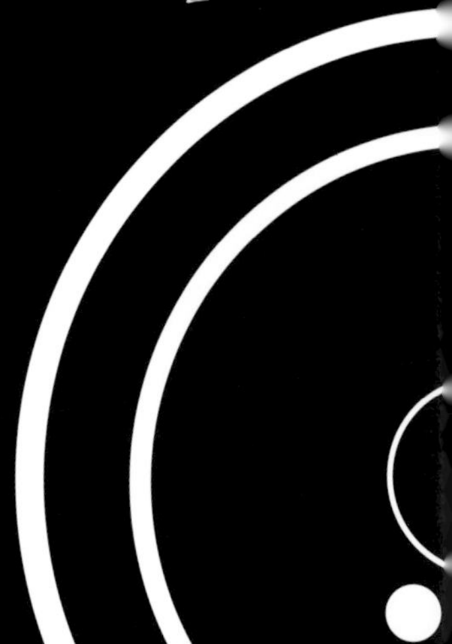

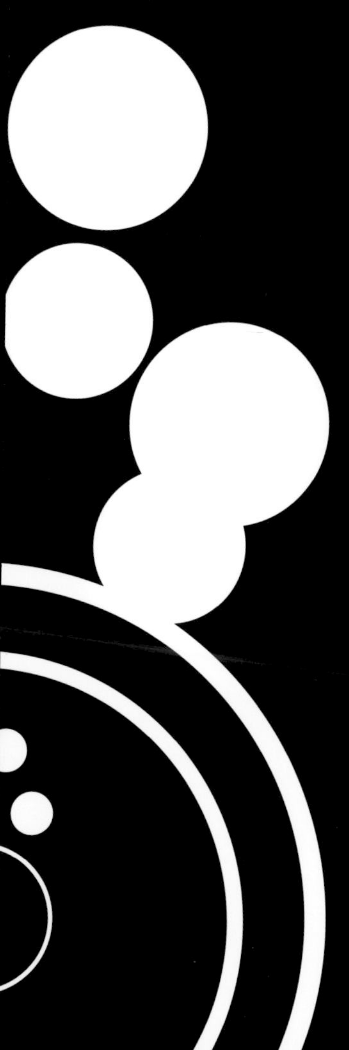

significant milestones as the compilation of Blue Note covers containing many
of Reid Miles' designs for the legendary American jazz and blues label; or the book of covers for film soundtrack albums with a foreword by the great Saul Bass, who way back in 1959 designed the sleeve for the soundtrack of *The Man with the Golden Arm* for Decca, or the beautifully produced sleeves of the Munich-based jazz label ECM. We could speak of the achievements of little-known pioneers like Colin Fulcher, alias Barney Bubbles, who created the graphic image for the progressive rock group Hawkwind and went on to work on numerous projects for Stiff and Radar Records.
If we want to bring this survey of the symbiosis between graphic design and music up to date we should not overlook Peter Saville and Factory Records, Mark Farrow, or the Berlin designer Angela Lorenz. And at the same time we can speak of innovation, because I believe that this is the first book devoted to the sleeves of the kind of dance music records known as maxi or 12" singles or Super 45s, although some of them play at 33 rpm. This selection features sleeves of records released up until the year 2000, the forerunners and early examples of what is known as club culture, or simply dance music. For the most part the emphasis is on Black music, but also on some of the more danceable rock and roll and indie pop such as 'Dance This Mess Around' by the B-52s, or the legendary 'Blue Monday' by New Order, with its famous sleeve by Peter Saville: urban myth has

it that the complexity of the sleeve design meant that Factory Records
lost money on every disc sold.

Leafing through the pages of this book will take you on a fascinating
journey through the history of dance and house music, from all-
time classics such as the contagious funk of James Brown's 'Sex
Machine' to adaptations of jazz converted into club floor-fillers such
as US3's 'Cantaloupe Island', by way of the delights of Northern Soul,
represented by Soft Cell and their inimitable version of 'Tainted Love'
with the final segue into 'Where Did Our Love Go?' You will also have
a chance to rediscover Grace Jones and her interpretation of 'La Vie
en Rose', or the early days of rap with Grandmaster Flash & The
Furious Five and their landmark hit 'The Message', and the ground-
breaking Eric B & Rakim. And who could fail to recall Tom Jones
and Mousse T doing 'Sex Bomb', a title that also applies to the singer
himself, or Jamiroquai, that white boy with a Black soul? Then there
are the entertaining Dee-Lite, the sweet and fresh De La Soul or the
Jungle Brothers; the wonderful voice of Mick Hucknall fronting Simply
Red; Basement Jaxx, and Pulp, and Prince… and Frankie Goes To
Hollywood with their gay anthem 'Relax'… and Coolio and Roger
Sánchez… and even genuine Brit pop from The Housemartins,
The The or The Style Council. And let's not forget the ladies: Mari
Wilson and her recreation of the fifties sound, Cher, The Candy Girls,
Blondie, Sister Sledge, Queen Latifah or Rose Royce.

We can recall the golden age of house with Inner City; revisit funk with

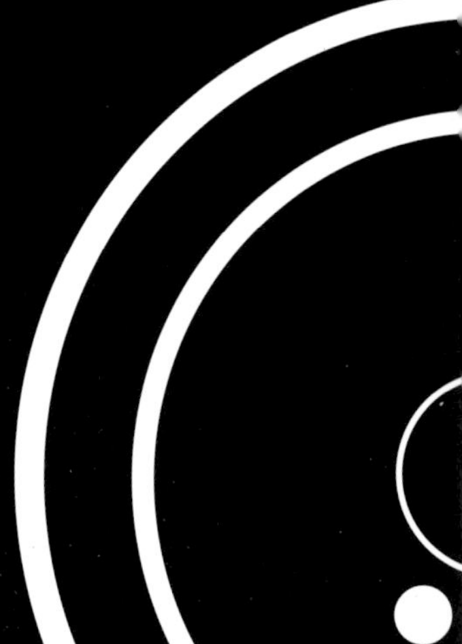

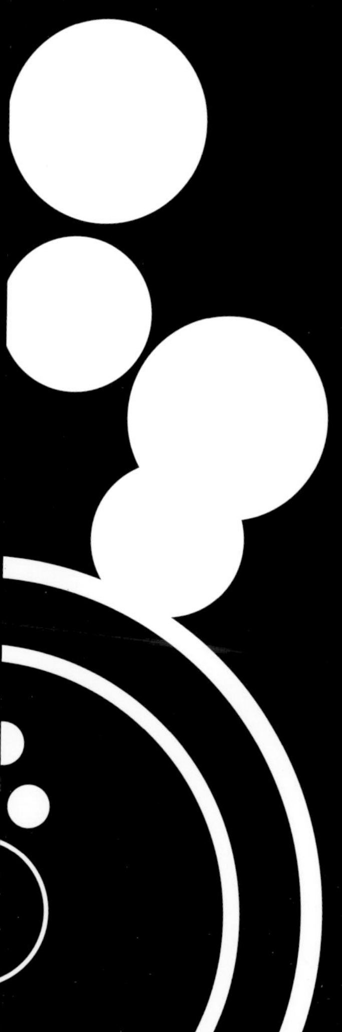

The Brand New Heavies or Soul II Soul and relive the techno
pop of Depeche Mode and Apollo Four Forty, or the music of harder-
to-classify artists like Moby, Lime or Sylvester – a fantastic tour of
dance floors all over the planet, a trip down memory lane to uniquely
magical moments, a piece of our recent history.
And if the quality of the music is impressive, the graphics are no less
so. Just a few days ago, the publisher Lars Müller said at a conference
in Barcelona that from the 1970s to the early 1990s the dream of
every up-and-coming graphic designer was to be commissioned to do
a record sleeve. I would go further and say that the dream of young
graphic designers today is still essentially the same: to design the
cover and the liner for a CD by their favourite group or singer.
If you look at the sleeves in chronological order you will have no
difficulty tracing the history of graphic design. If you sample them at
random you will pick up on a whole diversity of languages and trends
in the world of visual communication, and you will also perceive
common idioms, coincidences and chance resemblances.
Sex is an evident presence: almost explicit with Pulp, animal with
Colourbox, suggestive with Le Click sleeve or pictorially playful with
Tom Jones. There are references to the sleeves of –old?– Blue Note
jazz albums in the covers designed for Keith Sweat, Guru, Beatbox,
Philip Bent or the James Taylor Quartet. There is class
and elegance in the covers for Mari Wilson or Cher's 'One By One',
and a constructivist revival with Republica, Simply Red or the

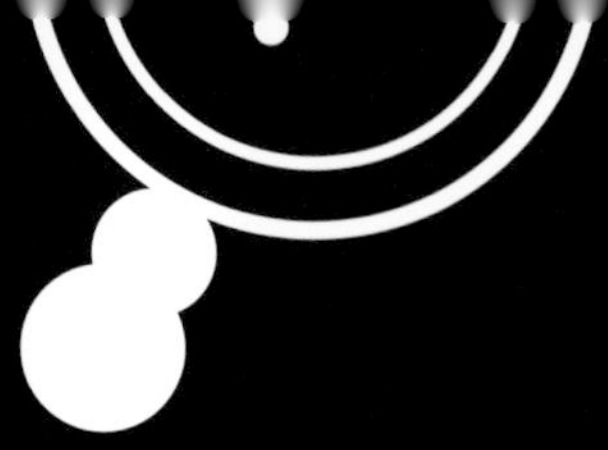

Frankie Goes To Hollywood remix of 'Two Tribes'.
The psychedelic era is represented here by Rhythm Quest and De La Soul and their 'Say No Go'. The graphic spirit of the seventies is apparent in the covers for Superstar, The Oh, 'Do Ya' by Inner City, A'lisa B and Bob Sinclair. Children's drawings feature on the sleeves for P. Lion, Andreas Dorau or Tom Tom Club. There are references to the world of the comic strip with The Snap, The Power, Tag Team or the Robbie Rivera and the Rhythm Bangers cut 'Bang'. The typography on sleeves for Lime, Lime 3, Superfunk, Paul Johnson, 'Jerk Out' by The Time, Bob Sinclair's 'Ultimate Funk', 'Plamen' by The Top or 'Peace Sign' by War. And then, of course, there is the cult of the image, the close-up photograph as used by the Pasadenas on 'Tribute', Oleta Adams, Faith Evans, Coolio or Prince. The roster of names and references is almost endless, I could go on and on mentioning covers that feature pictograms and references to architecture or to the Japanese manga comic; I could go on and on listing examples of 3-D typography or allusions to such popular icons as Chanel perfume, or minimalist images of car doors, cassette tapes, handguns, lobsters, soft drinks cans, soccer balls and superheroes… but the best thing for you to do now, dear reader, is to start turning the pages and enjoy all of these images, and just possibly –this is only a suggestion– you ought to do so with your headphones on, listening to some of your favourite songs.

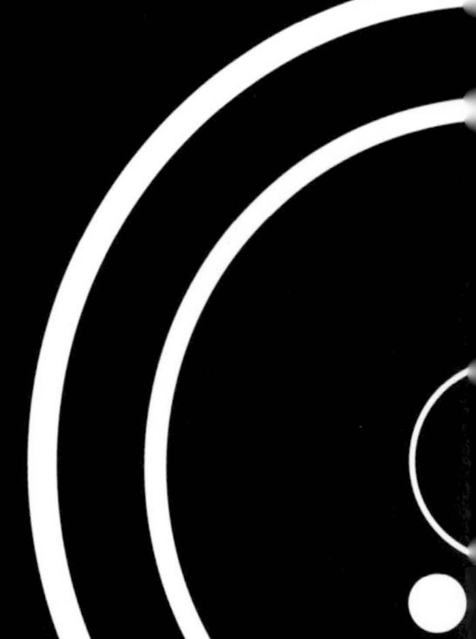

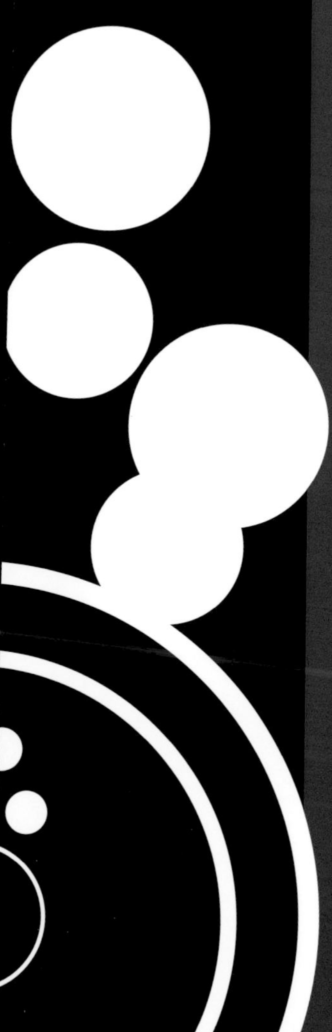

31,2 X 31,2 cm
El tamaño es importante

Jaume Pujagut

Hace algunos años escribí algo así en una revista editada por Discos Castelló, dirigida por Mingus B. Formentor y que tenía por nombre *Discolic* (número 2, marzo de 1988):

"Mi teoría es que los discolics no sólo escuchan música, sino que aman los discos, esos objetos redondos, normalmente negros, que están depositados en fundas de cartón. Mientras escuchan la música (muchas veces con auriculares) observan los dibujos de la funda o miran las fotografías; descubren que el televisivo Don Johnson era letrista con los Allman Brothers o que el nuevo disco de Prince está grabado en un estudio de Philadelphia, remezclado en N.Y., con una sección de viento añadida en Honolulu y la post-producción hecha en una lejana isla del Caribe. En fin, pequeños detalles para la historia."

Pues bien después de todos estos años sigo pensando lo mismo, nada supera la magia de esos 973,44 centímetros cuadrados de información visual y gráfica asociada a la música leída a través de los surcos de un disco de vinilo, generalmente negro.

Tienes entre las manos un nuevo ejemplo de una larga tradición. Una tradición que se inició en 1977 con la edición del primer *Album Cover Album* que recogía los trabajos de Hipgnosis y Roger Dean y que llega hasta nuestros días con la re-edición del volumen de

Taschen *1000 record covers* de Michael Ochs. Una tradición con hitos importantes como la recopilación de cubiertas de Blue Note Records que contiene muchos de los trabajos de Reid Miles para la mítica discográfica estadounidense; o el libro de cubiertas de bandas sonoras con prólogo del genial Saul Bass, que ya en 1959 había realizado la portada para la banda sonora de *The Man with the golden arm*, para Decca; o las cuidadas ediciones de la discográfica afincada en Munich, ECM. Incluso podríamos hablar de la labor de pioneros casi desconocidos como Colin Fulcher, alias Barney Bubbles, responsable de la imagen del grupo de rock progresivo Hawkwind y posteriormente el responsable de muchos de los trabajos de Stiff y Radar Records.
Si queremos actualizar esta nómina de colaboraciones entre el diseño gráfico y la música no podemos olvidar a Peter Saville y Factory Records, a Mark Farrow o a la berlinesa Angela Lorenz.
Y al mismo tiempo podemos hablar de novedad porque creo que es la primera vez que se edita un libro que selecciona portadas de vinilo dedicado a la música de baile, los conocidos como Maxi Singles o Super 45, aunque algunos de ellos deben reproducirse a 33 rpm. Una selección que recoge portadas editadas hasta el año 2000. Unos trabajos precursores de lo que se conoce como cultura de club, o simplemente música para bailar. Unos trabajos representados mayoritariamente por la black music y algo del rock and roll más bailable como el 'Dance This Mess Around' de los americanos B52,

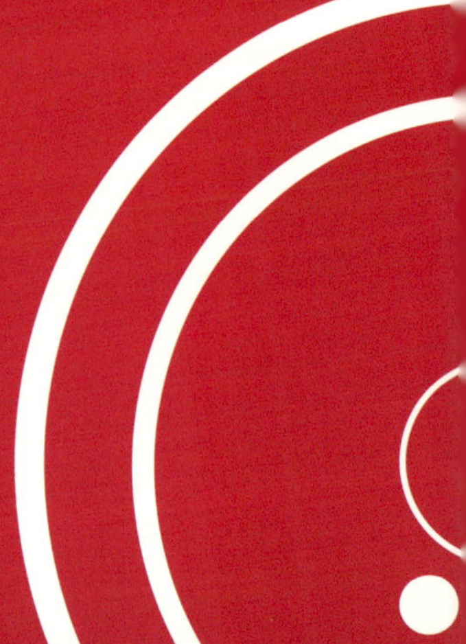

o el mítico 'Blue Monday' de New Order con una cubierta diseñada
por Peter Saville y del que las leyendas urbanas dicen que el complejo
diseño de la portada hacía perder dinero a la discográfica con
cada disco que vendía.
Mirar las páginas de este libro te llevará a un fascinante viaje a
través de la historia de la música de baile y el house. Desde clásicos
inmarchitables como el contagioso funk de James Brown y su 'Sex
Machine' hasta re-adaptaciones del jazz convertidas en "llena-pistas"
como el 'Cantaloupe Island' de los US3, pasando por las delicias
del Nothern Soul de la mano de Soft Cell y su particular versión del
'Tainted Love' con el *medley* final de 'Where did our love go?' También
podrás recuperar a Grace Jones y su versión de 'La vie en rose' o a
precursores del rap como los Grandmaster Flash & The Furious Five
con su himno 'The message'. Y quien no recuerda a los influyentes
Eric & B Rakim, a Tom Jones que con la ayuda de Mousse T nos
ofrece su 'Sex Bomb', un título de canción que también podríamos
aplicar al personaje, o a Jamiroquai, el chico blanco con alma
negra. Y los divertidos Dee-Lite, los juguetones De la Soul o los
Jungle Brothers; la maravillosa voz de Mick Hucknall al frente de
los Simply Red, los Basement Jaxx, y Pulp y Prince… y Frankie
goes to Hollywood con su proclama gay en 'Relax'… y Coolio y
Roger Sánchez. Incluso genuino pop británico de la mano de los
Housemartins, The The o The Style Council. Sin olvidar a las damas
como Mari Wilson y su rememoración de los cincuenta, a Cher,

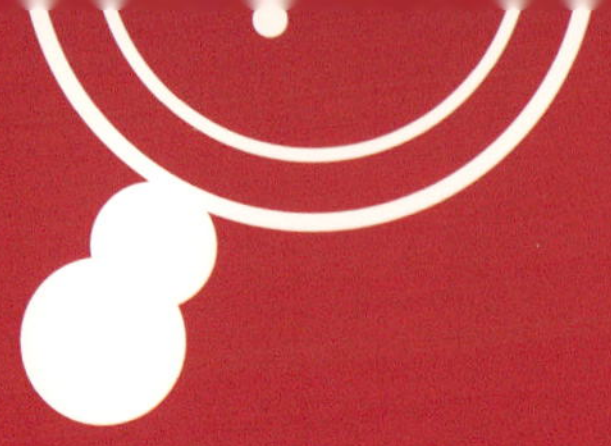

las Candy Girls, Blondie, Sister Sledge, Queen Latifah o Rose Royce.
Podemos recordar los buenos tiempos del house con Inner City; del
funk con los Brand New Heavies o Soul II Soul; el techno setentero
de Depeche Mode y Apollo Four Forty o a personajes de difícil
clasificación como Moby, Lime o Sylvester.
Un fantástico recorrido por las pistas de baile de todo el planeta,
un recuerdo de situaciones irrepetibles, un fragmento de nuestra
historia más reciente.
Y si el nivel musical es impresionante, lo mismo podemos decir de
la parte gráfica. Hace unos días, el editor Lars Müller dijo en una
conferencia celebrada en Barcelona que, a partir de los años setenta y
hasta principios de los noventa, el sueño de todo diseñador gráfico era
poder realizar una portada de disco. Yo me atrevería a asegurar que
los sueños de los nuevos diseñadores gráficos siguen siendo casi los
mismos, diseñar la cubierta y el libreto del CD de su artista favorito. Si
miráis las portadas en orden cronológico no os costará seguir la historia
del diseño gráfico. Si las miráis de forma aleatoria descubriréis todo
tipo de lenguajes y tendencias en el mundo de la comunicación visual.
También podréis ver lenguajes comunes, coincidencias y casualidades.
El sexo, casi explícito de Pulp, animal con los Colourbox, sugerente
como en la portada de Le Click o pictojuguetón con Tom Jones.
Las referencias a las ¿viejas? cubiertas de jazz de Blue Note en las
portadas de Keith Sweat, Guru, Beatbox, Philip Bent o James Taylor
Quartet. La clase y la elegancia de las cubiertas de Mari Wilson o el

'One by One' de Cher. El revival constructivista de Republica, Simply Red, o los Frankie goes to Hollywood remezclados por Two Tribes. La era psicodélica representada por the Rhythm Quest o los De la Soul y su pieza 'Say no go'. El espíritu gráfico de los años setenta presente en las cubiertas de Superstar, The Oh, el 'Do ya' de Inner City, A'lisa B o Bob Sinclair. Los dibujos infantiles para las portadas de P. Lion, Andreas Dorau o Tom Tom Club. Las referencias al mundo del cómic de The Snap, The Power, los Tag Team o Robbie Rivera y los Rhythm Bangers en 'Bang'. Las tipografías en las portadas de Lime, Lime 3, Superfunk, Paul Jonson, 'Jerk Out' de The Time, Bob Sinclair en 'Ultimate funk', 'Plamen' de The Top o el 'Peace Sign' de War. Y por descontado el culto a la imagen, las fotografías en primer plano que utilizan los Pasadenas en 'Tribute', Oleta Adams, Faith Evans, Coolio o Prince. La lista de nombres y referencias es casi interminable, podría seguir escribiendo sobre cubiertas solucionadas a base de pictogramas, referencias a la arquitectura o al manga japonés; podría seguir hablando de tipografías en 3 dimensiones o de guiños a iconos populares como el perfume Chanel, de propuestas minimalistas, de puertas de automóviles, cintas de casete, pistolas, langostas, latas de refresco, pelotas de fútbol y superhéroes… pero lo mejor que puedes hacer, querido lector, es pasar las páginas y disfrutar con todas estas imágenes y quizá, sólo es una sugerencia, podrías hacerlo con los auriculares puestos y escuchando alguna de tus canciones preferidas.

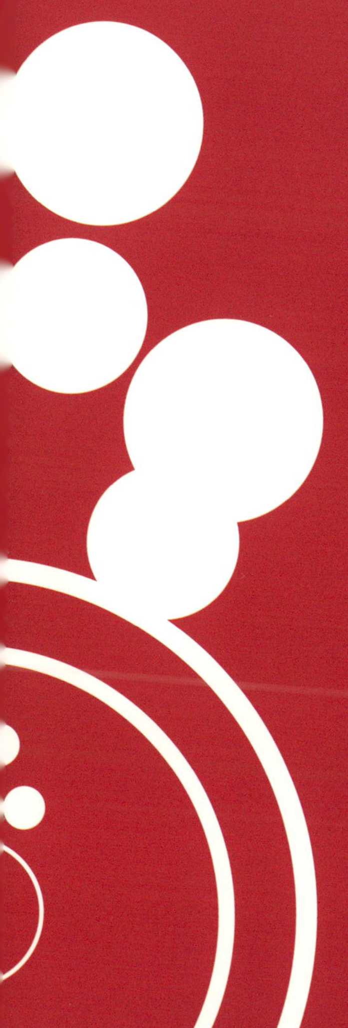

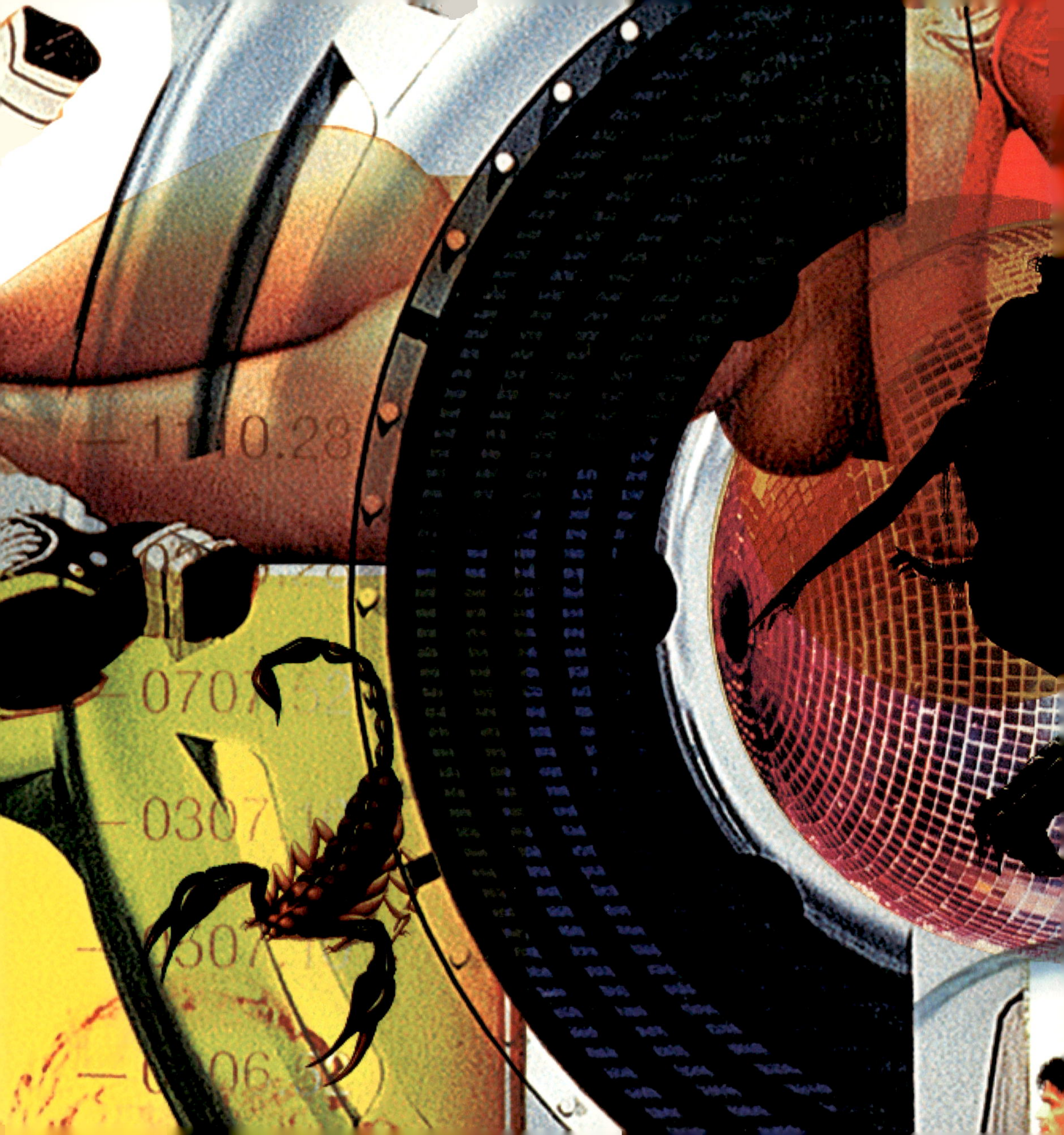

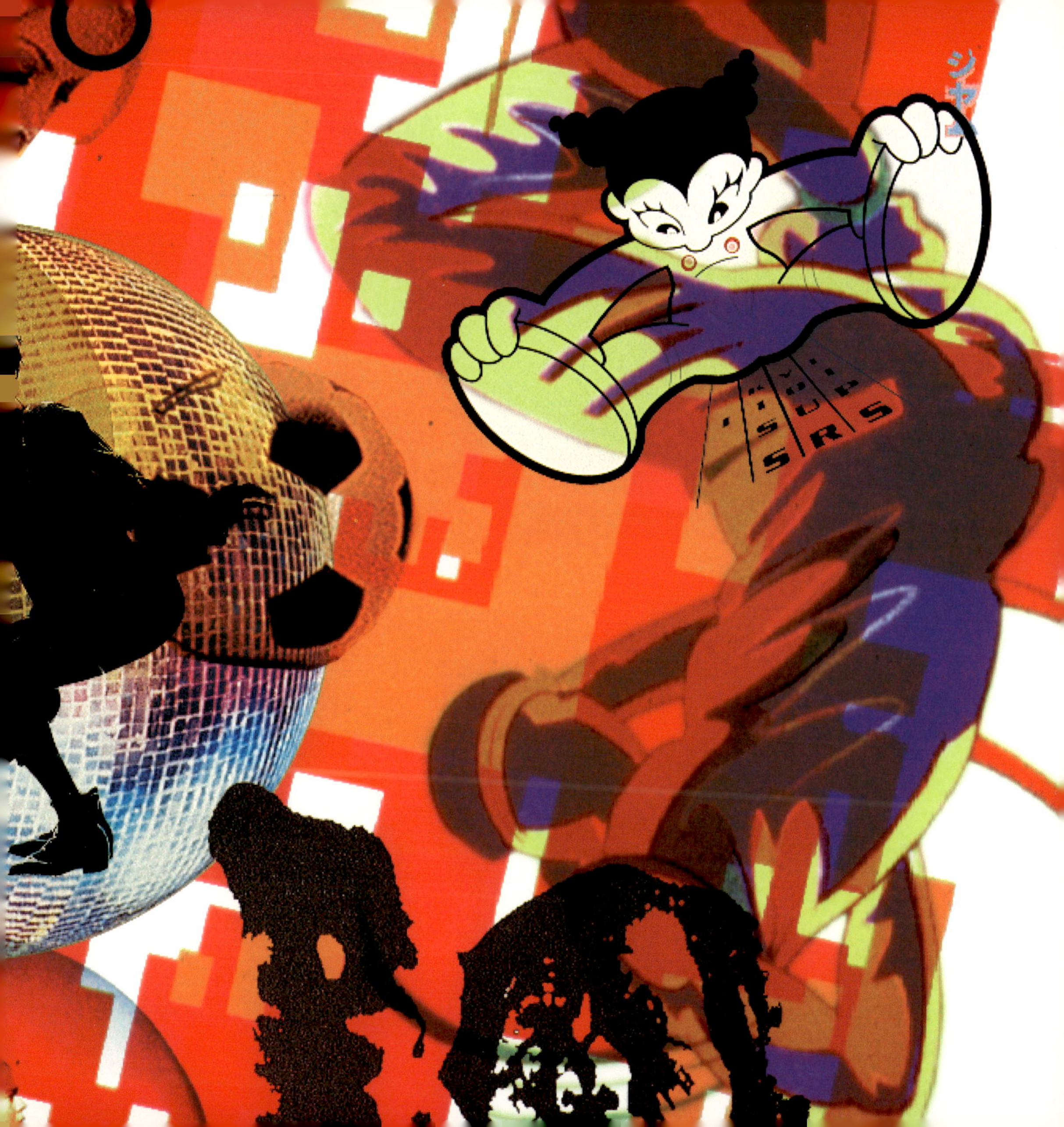
シャン

ROSE ROYCE
DO YOUR DANCE

SUPER 45

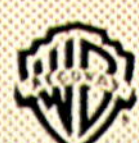

SUPERSINGLE
RCA
PC 8066
10
Laurent Voulzy
ROCKOLLECTION
LE MIROIR
PARA DISCOTECAS

SUPER SINGLE 45 RPM
SUPER SINGLE 45 RPM
SUPER SINGLE 45 RPM
SUPER SINGLE 45 RPM
SUPER SINGLE 45 RPM
SUPER SINGLE 45 RPM

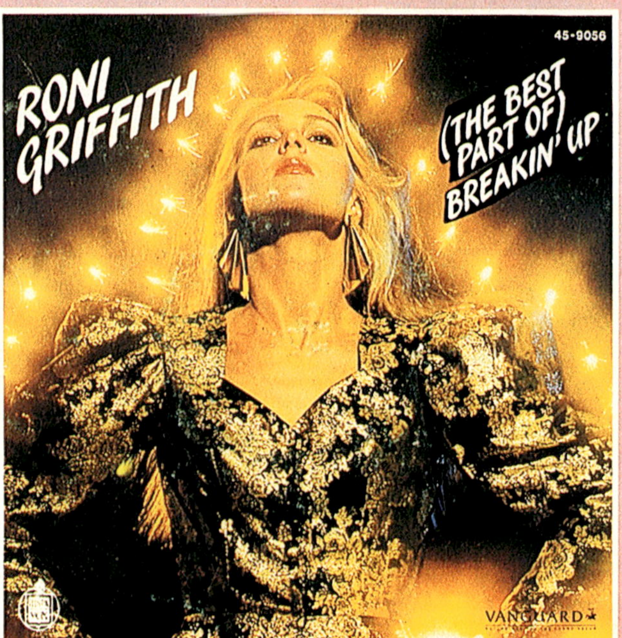
45-9056
RONI GRIFFITH
(THE BEST PART OF) BREAKIN' UP
VANGUARD
45-UP

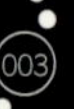

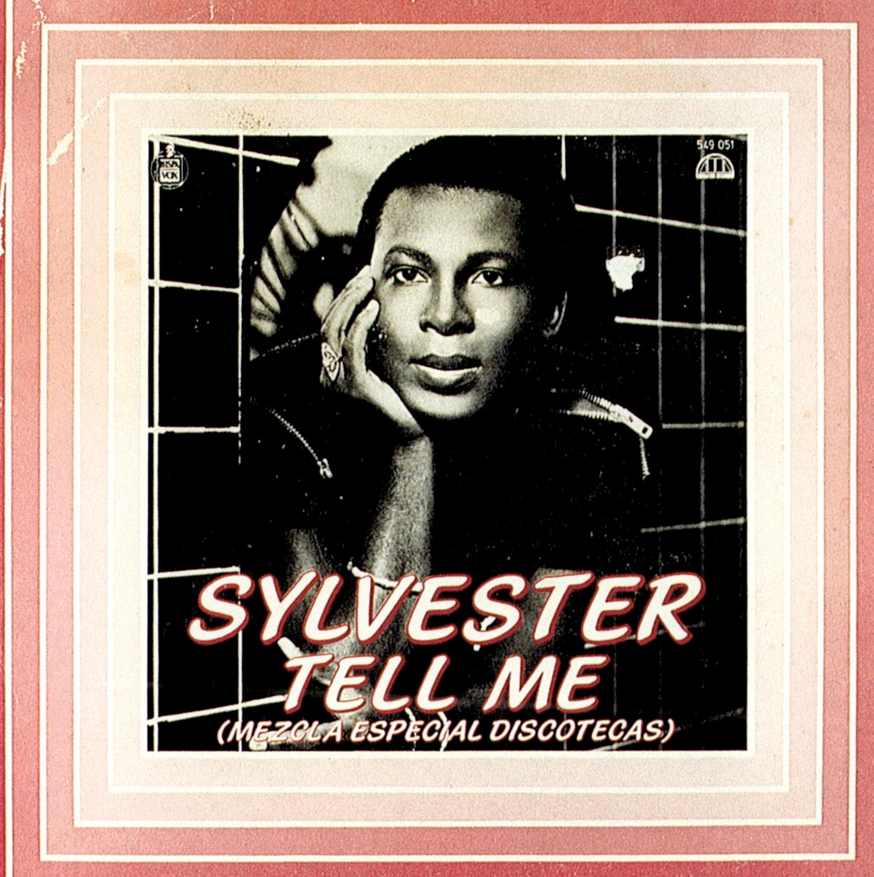
SUPER 45
549 051
SYLVESTER
TELL ME
(MEZCLA ESPECIAL DISCOTECAS)

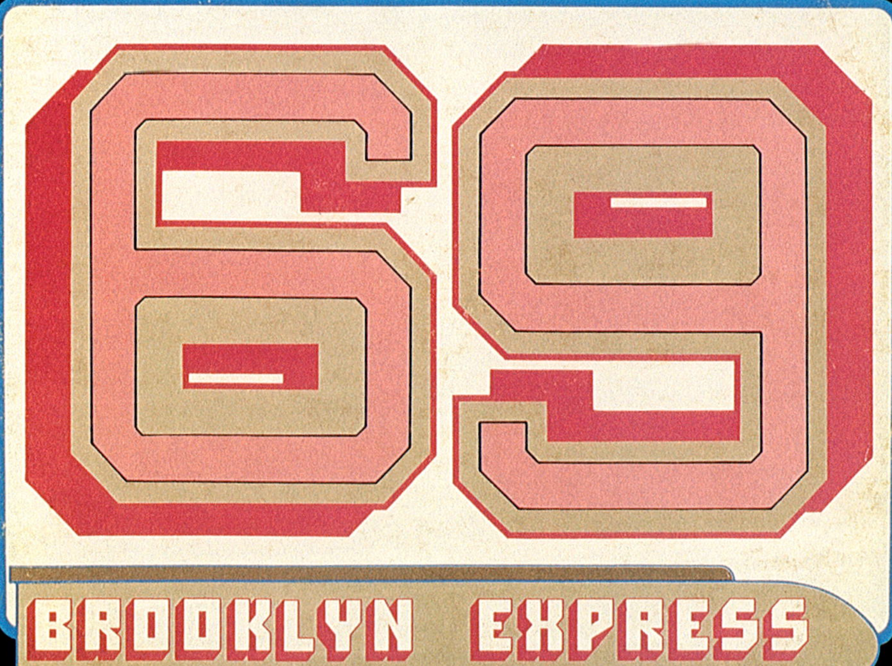

SIXTY NINE
45 R.p.m. Maxi
69
BROOKLYN EXPRESS

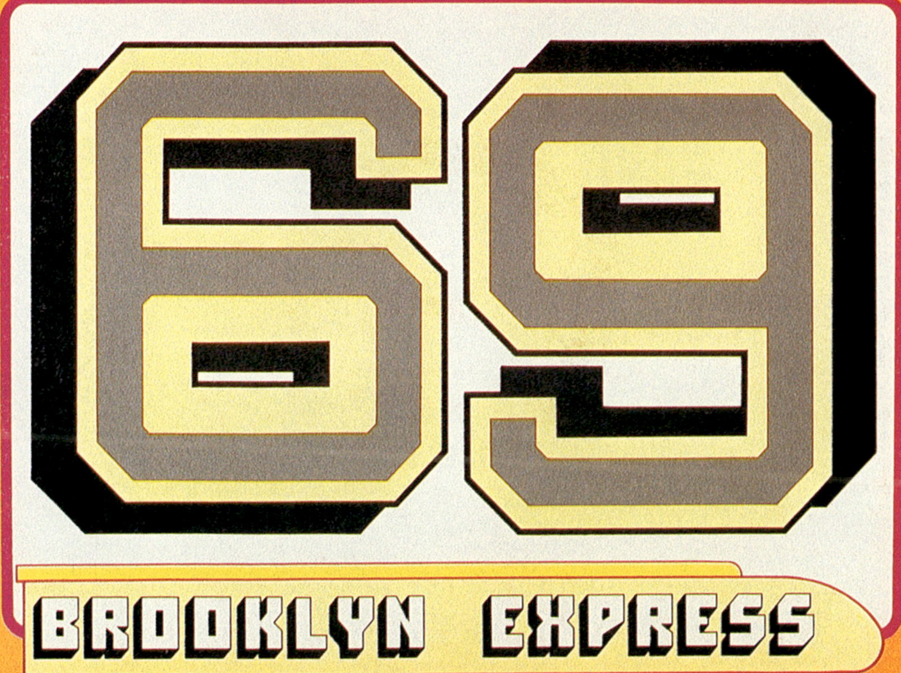
SIXTY NINE
69
BROOKLYN EXPRESS

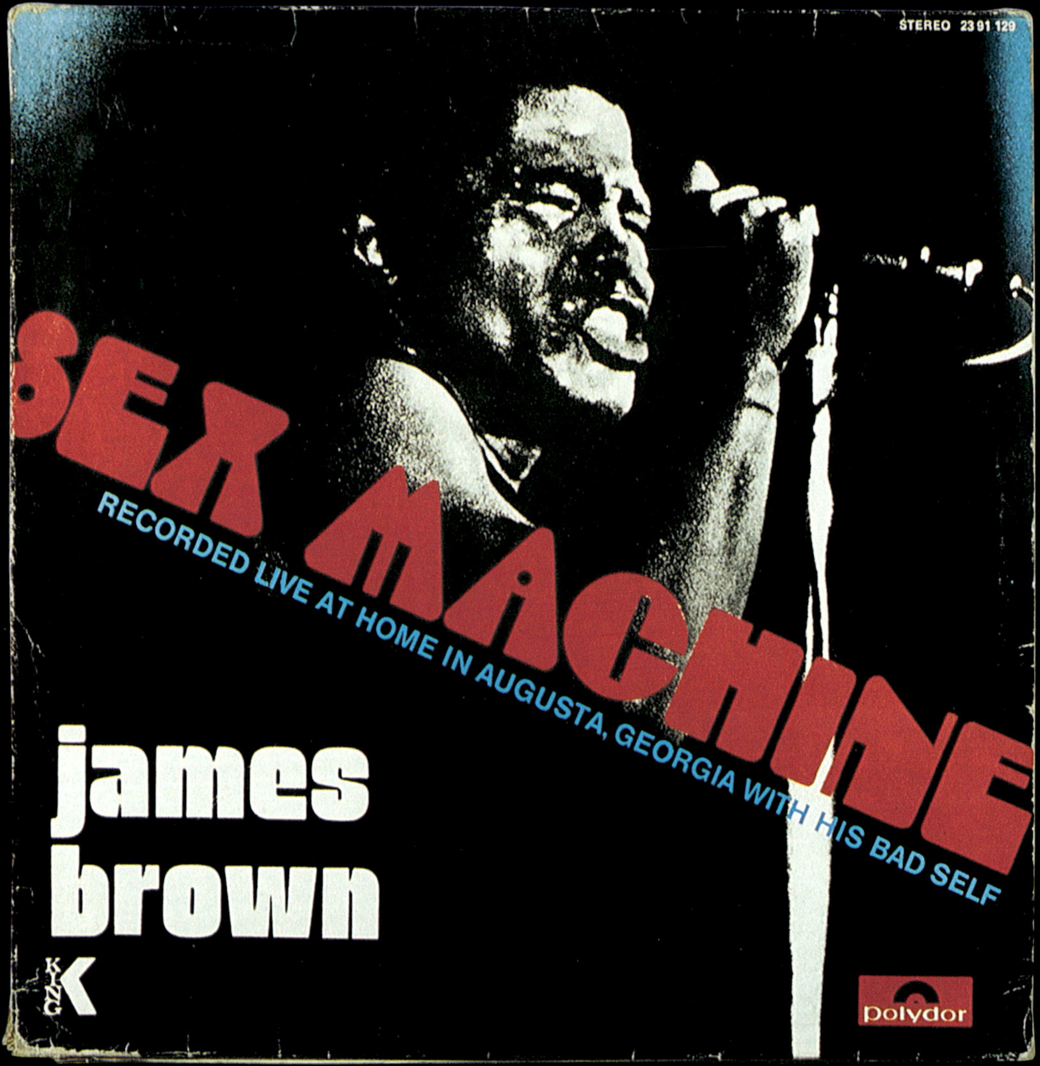

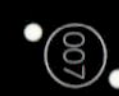
STEREO   23 91 129
SEX MACHINE
RECORDED LIVE AT HOME IN AUGUSTA, GEORGIA WITH HIS BAD SELF
james brown
KING
Polydor
Artist James Brown Title Sex Machine Record Label Polydor Date 1984

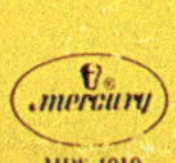
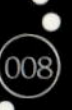

33-1/3 STEREO
KURTIS BLOW
"THE BREAKS"
VOCAL
b/w
"THE BREAKS"
(INSTRUMENTAL/Do it yourself!)
mercury
℗©1980 Phonogram, Inc., A Polygram Company, One IBM Plaza, Chicago, IL 60611.
Printed in U.S.A. Distributed by Polygram Distribution, Inc.
MDS-4010
12" SINGLE

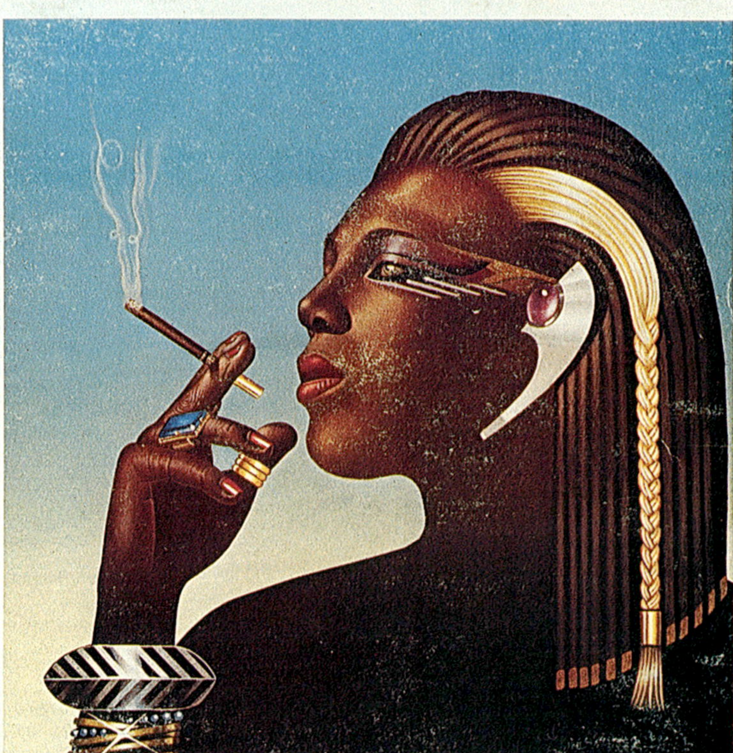
SYLVESTER
ALL I NEED

LIME
GOLD DIGGER

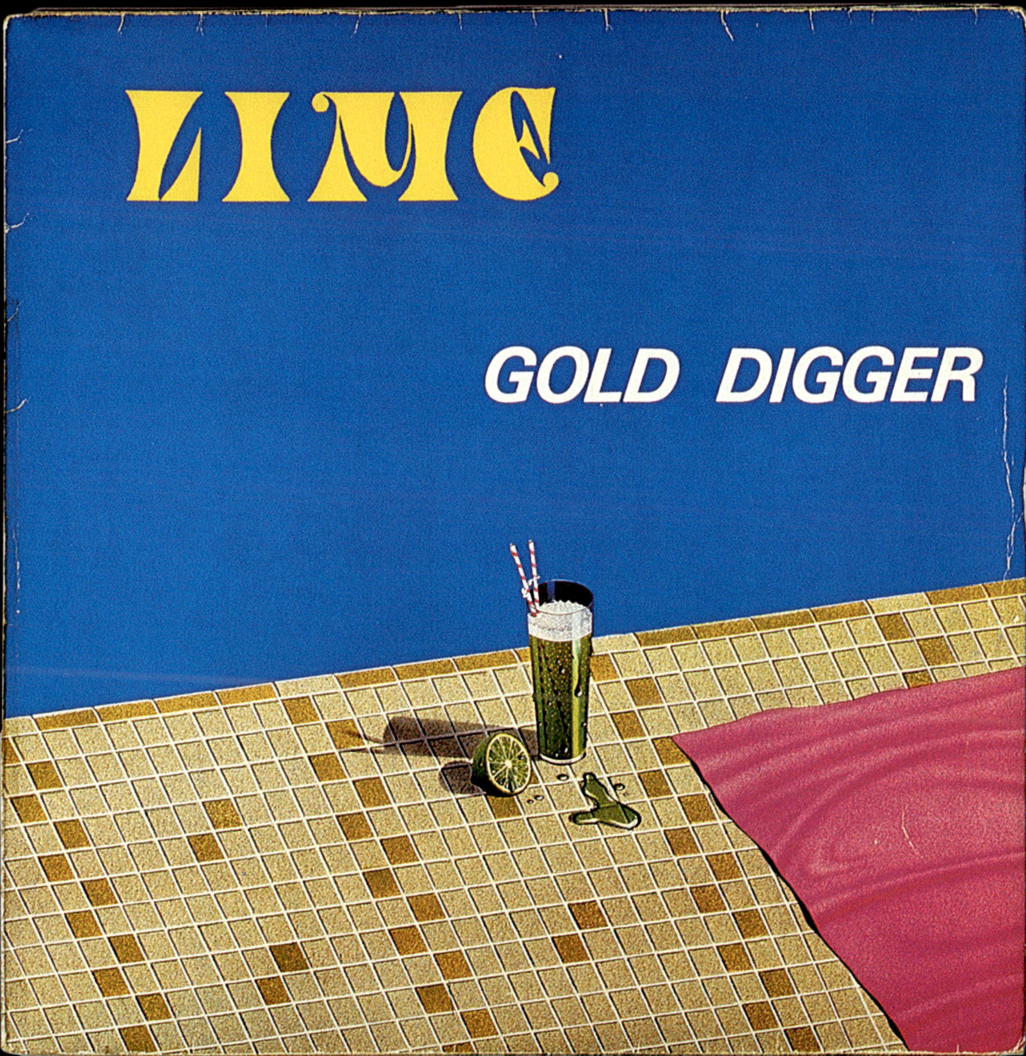

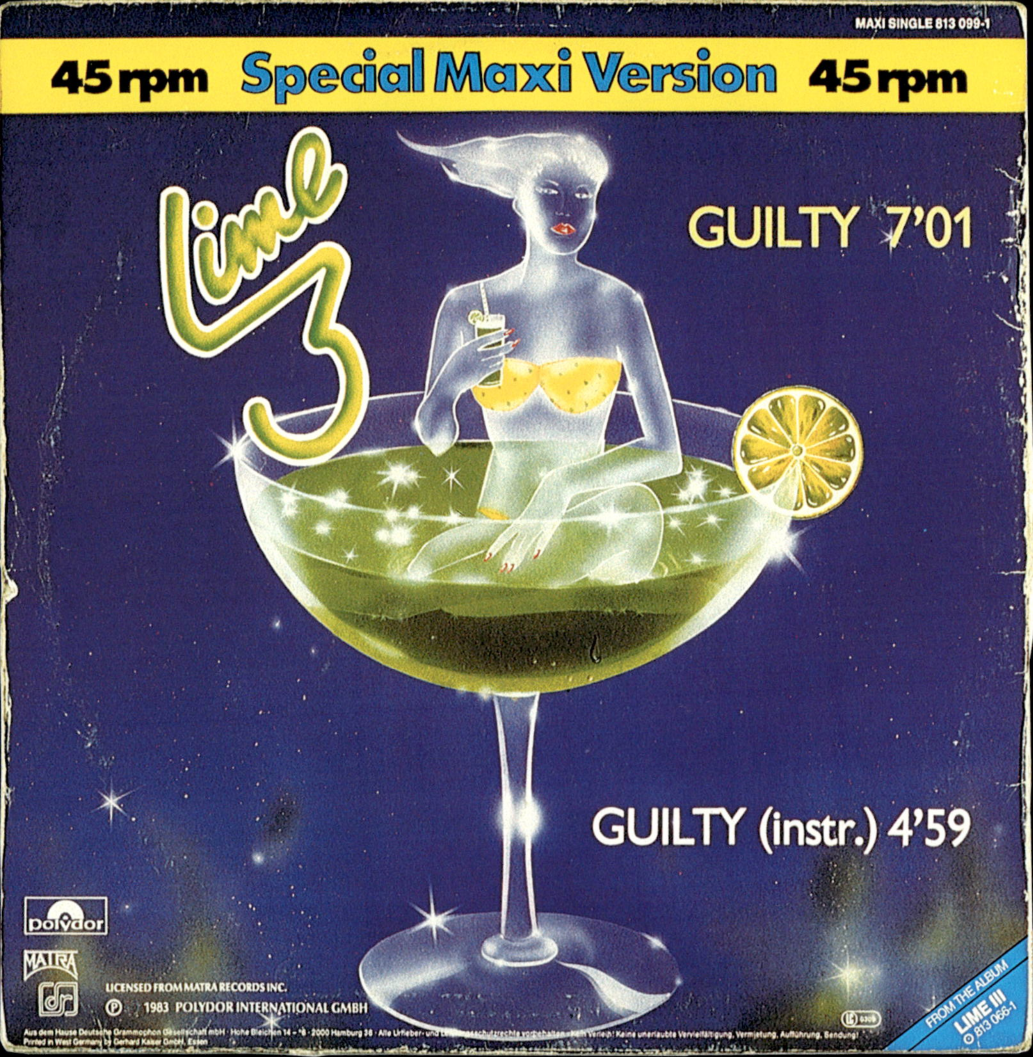

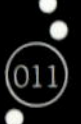

MAXI SINGLE 813 099-1
45 rpm Special Maxi Version 45 rpm
Lime 3
GUILTY 7'01
GUILTY (instr.) 4'59
Polydor
MATRA
LICENSED FROM MATRA RECORDS INC.
℗ 1983 POLYDOR INTERNATIONAL GMBH
Aus dem Hause Deutsche Grammophon Gesellschaft mbH · Hohe Bleichen 14 · ☏ 2000 Hamburg 36 · Alle Urheber- und Leistungsschutzrechte vorbehalten! Keine unerlaubte Vervielfältigung, Vermietung, Aufführung, Sendung!
Printed in West Germany by Gerhard Kaiser GmbH, Essen
FROM THE ALBUM
LIME III
© 813 066-1

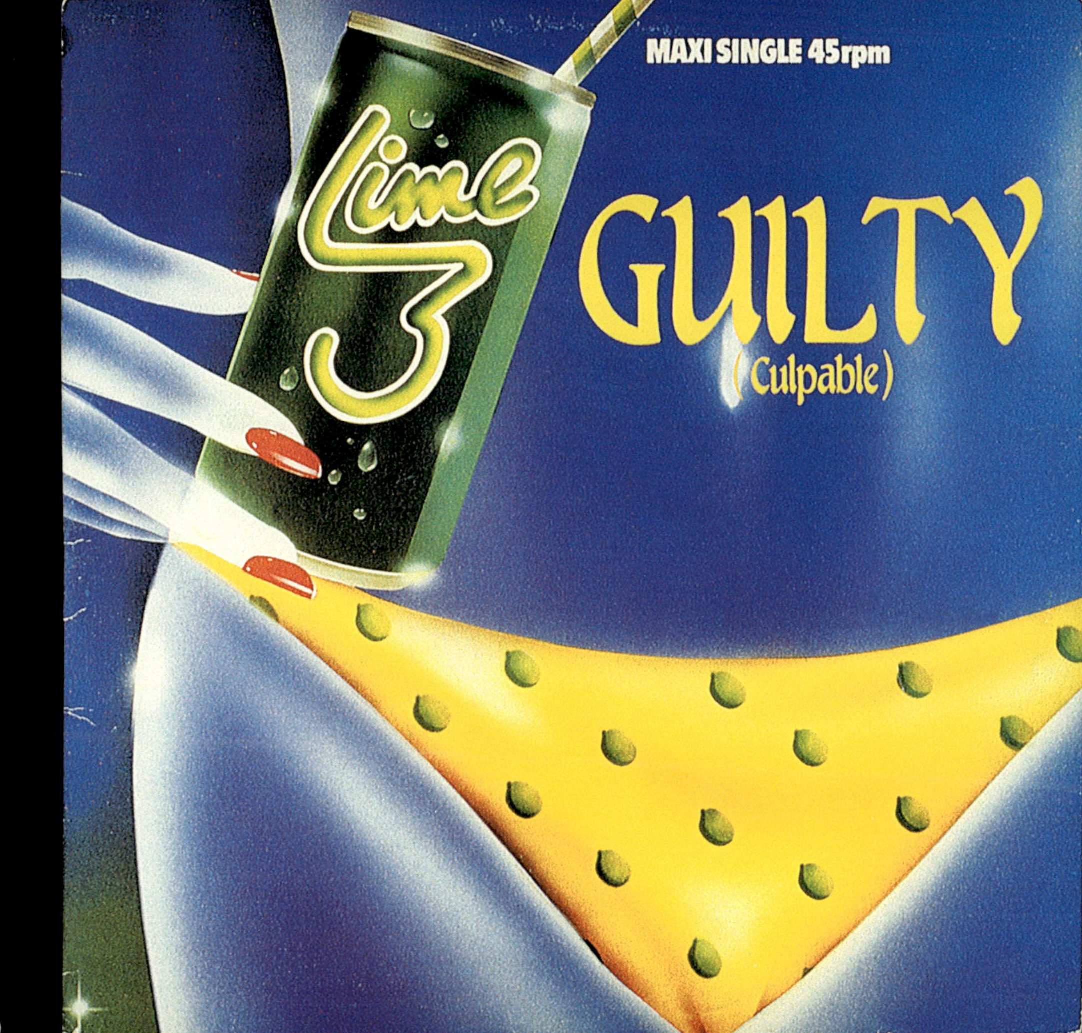

MAXI SINGLE 45 rpm
Lime 3
GUILTY
(Culpable)

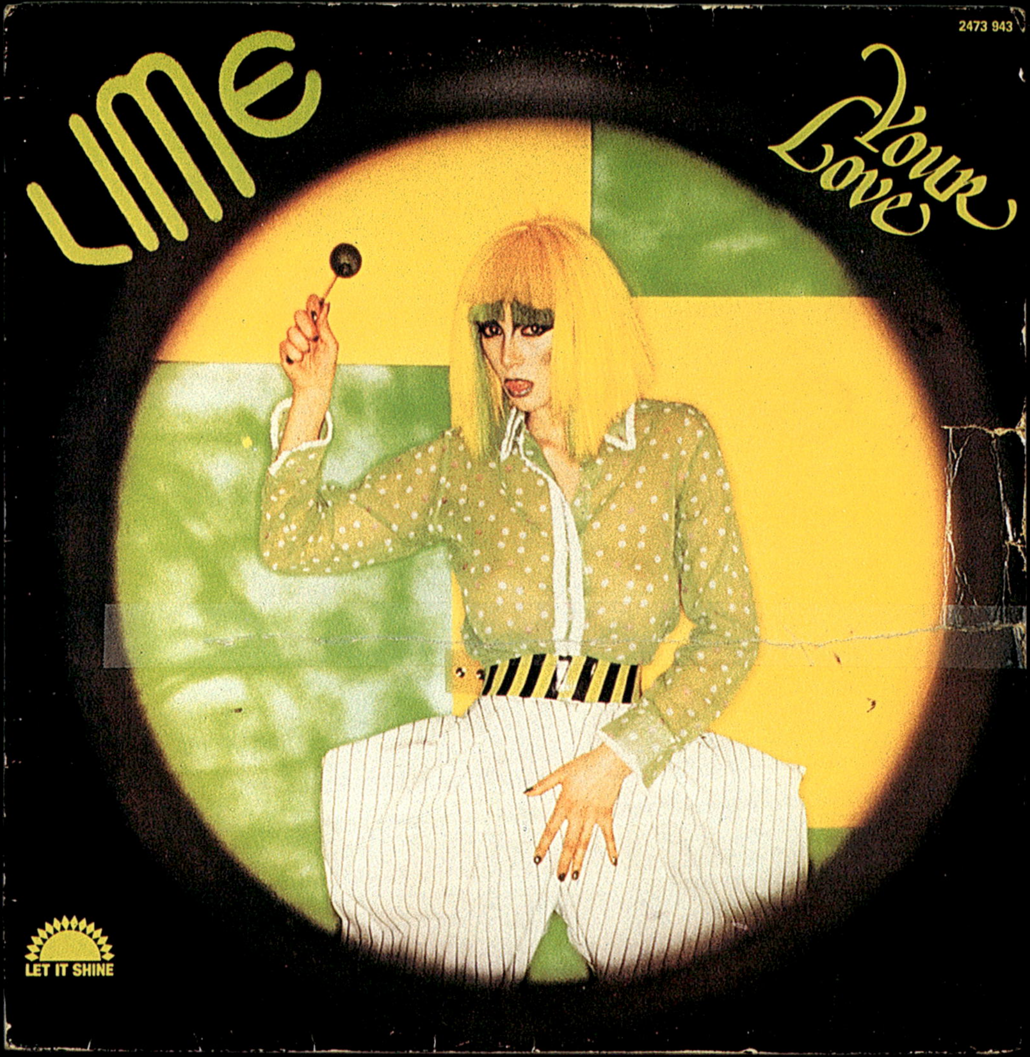

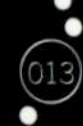

013 Artist **Lime** Title **Your Love** Design Michael Gray Photography Michael Gray Record Label **Let It Shine** Date **1981**

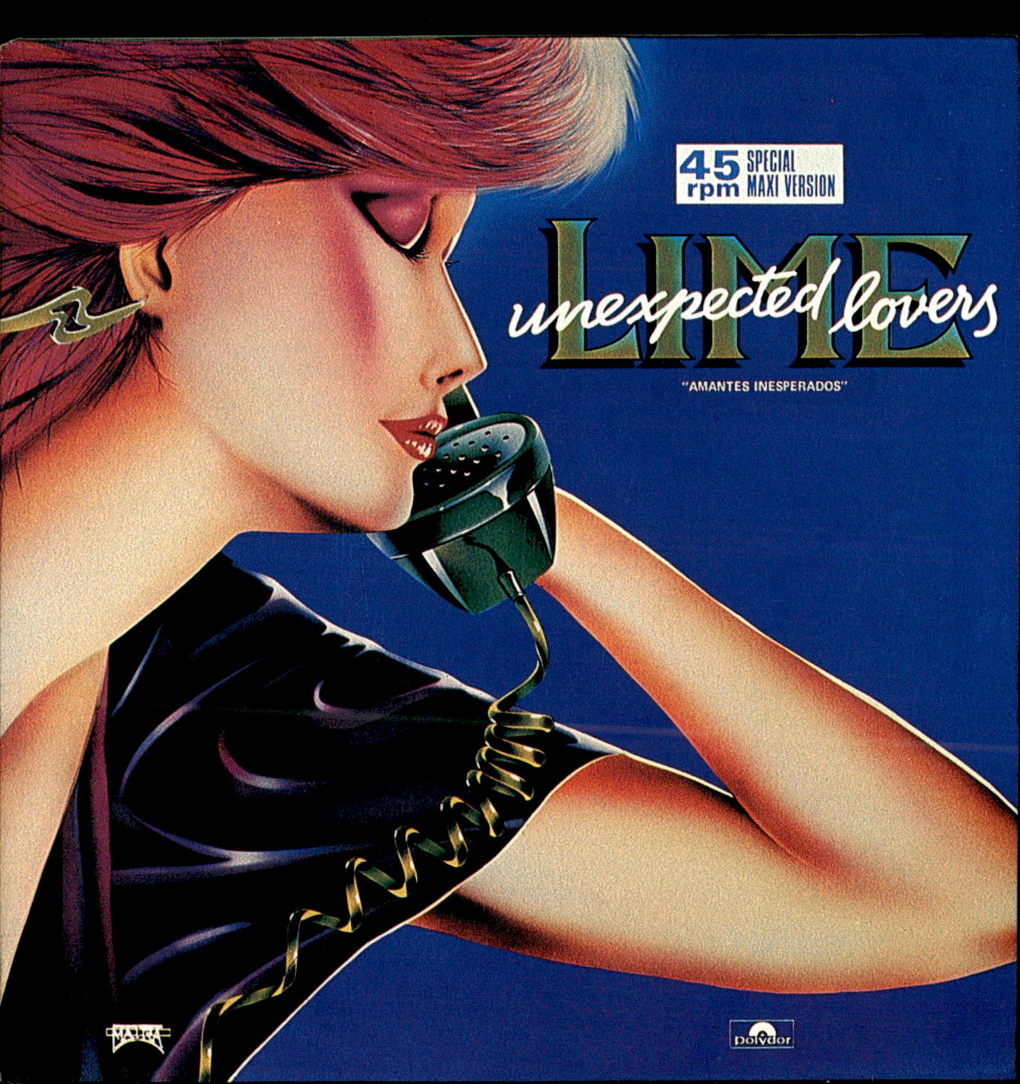
45 rpm SPECIAL MAXI VERSION
LIME
unexpected lovers
"AMANTES INESPERADOS"
polydor

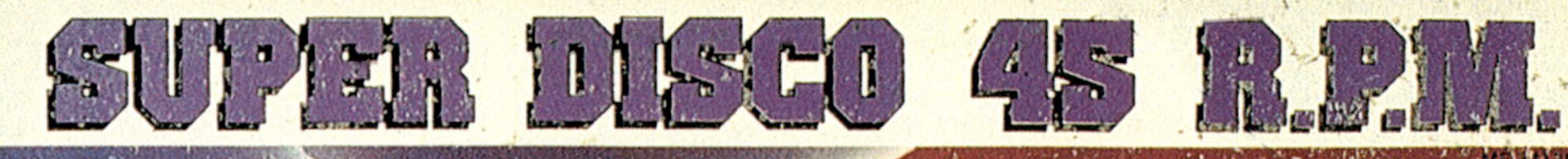
SUPER DISCO 45 R.P.M.
CAPTAIN COKE
FUTURE WORLD ORCHESTRA
CFE

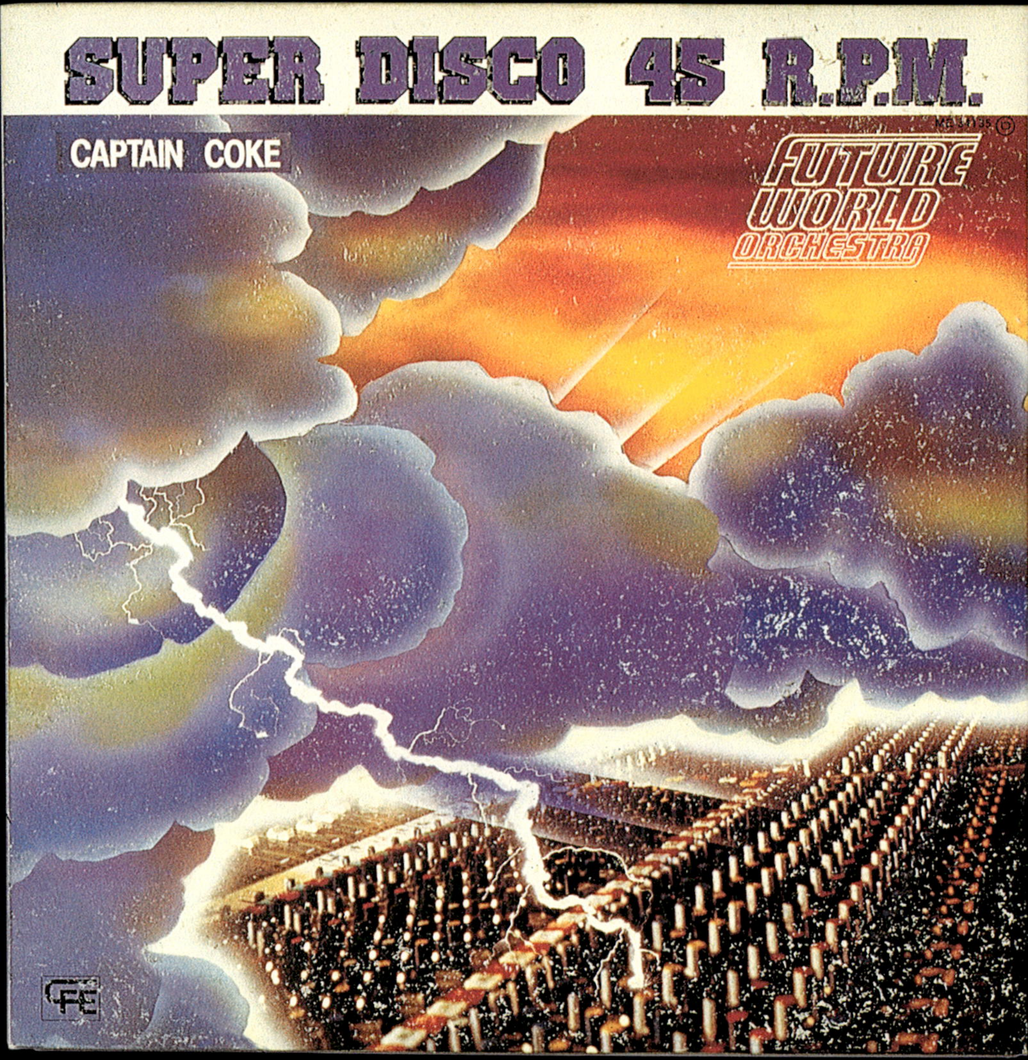

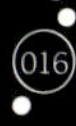

Artist The KLF Title Last Train To Trancentral Design Designland Photography Ute Klaphake
Record Label Blanco y Negro Date 1991

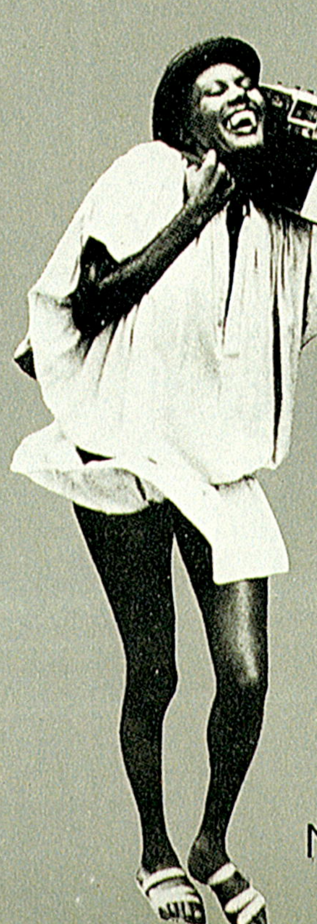

GRACE JONES
la vie en rose
MAXI~SINGLE 45r.p.m.

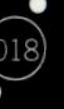

Artist **Misa** Title **Banzai** Design **Stefano Coletti** Photography **Studio Monly Shadow**
Record Label **New Music International / Vale Music** Date **1999**

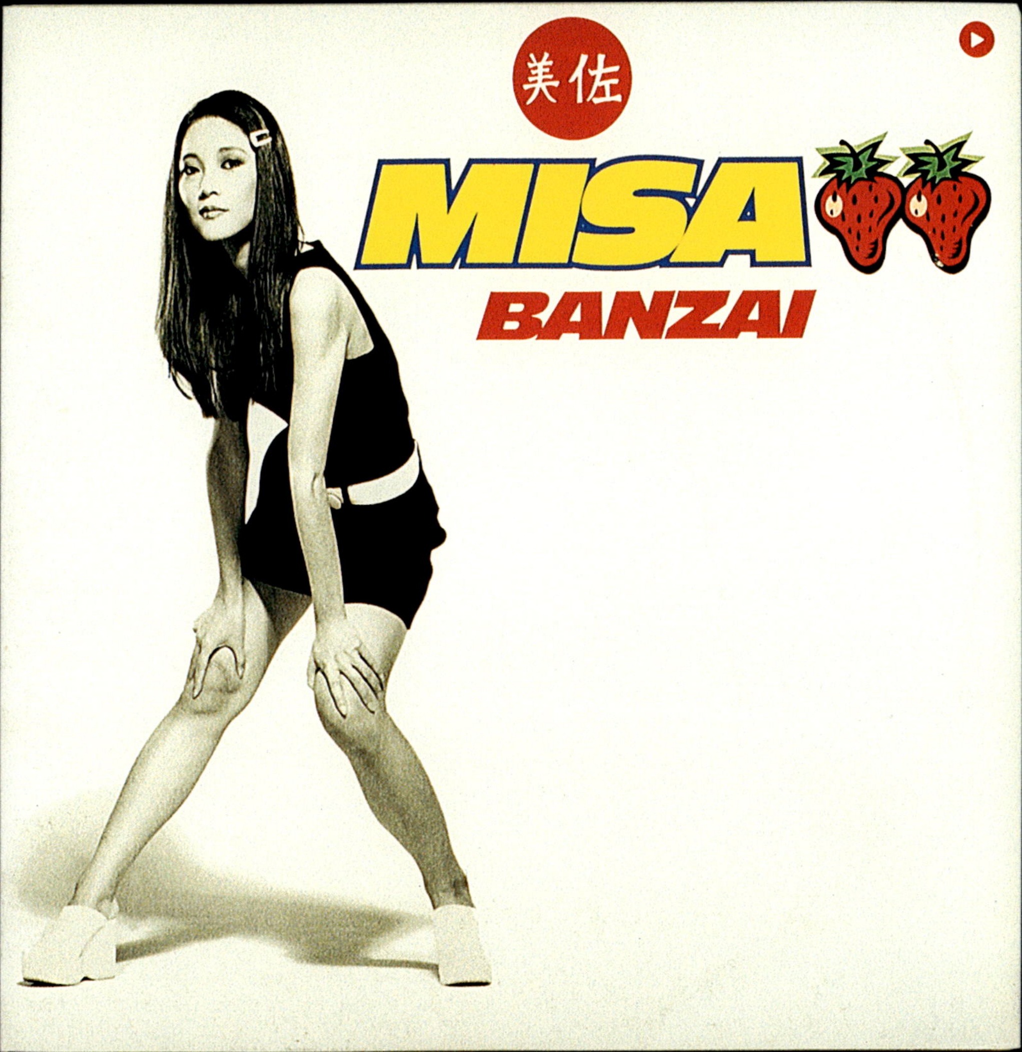

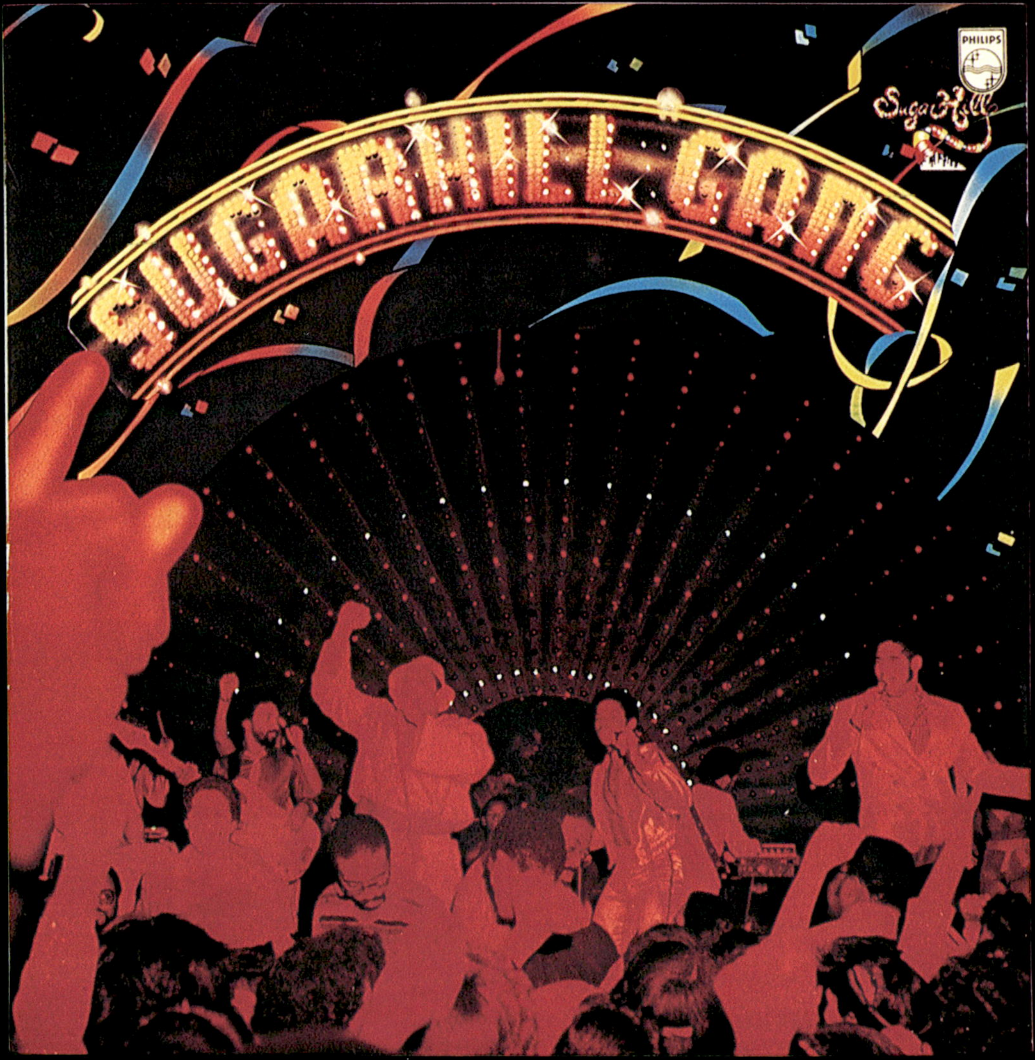

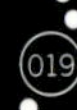

019 Artist Sugarhill Gang Title Sugarhill Gang Record Label Philips 1979

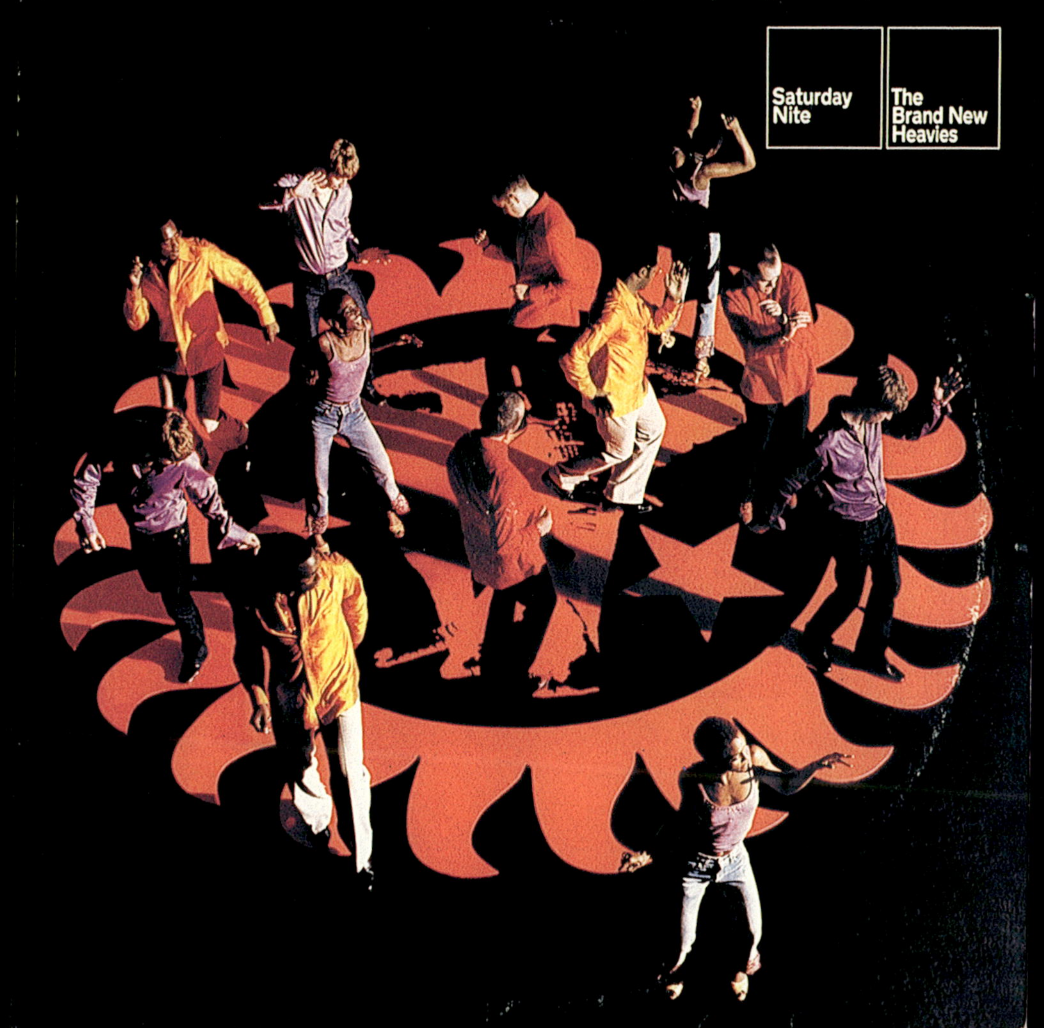

020

BOB SINCLAR
Side A
YP064
1. I FEEL FOR YOU (6:52-SACEM)
(Bob Sinclar & Pradel)
CONTAINS A SAMPLE FROM "LOOK FOR LOVE" BY CERRONE
PUBLISHING CERRONE MUSIC SACEM
COURTESY OF MALIGATOR RECORDS/F, SIDE MUSIC
PUBLISHING: MCA MUSIC LIMITED/CHRYSALIS MUSIC LIMITED
PRODUCED BY BOB SINCLAR
(P) & (C) 2000 MIGHTY BOP SESSIONS INC.

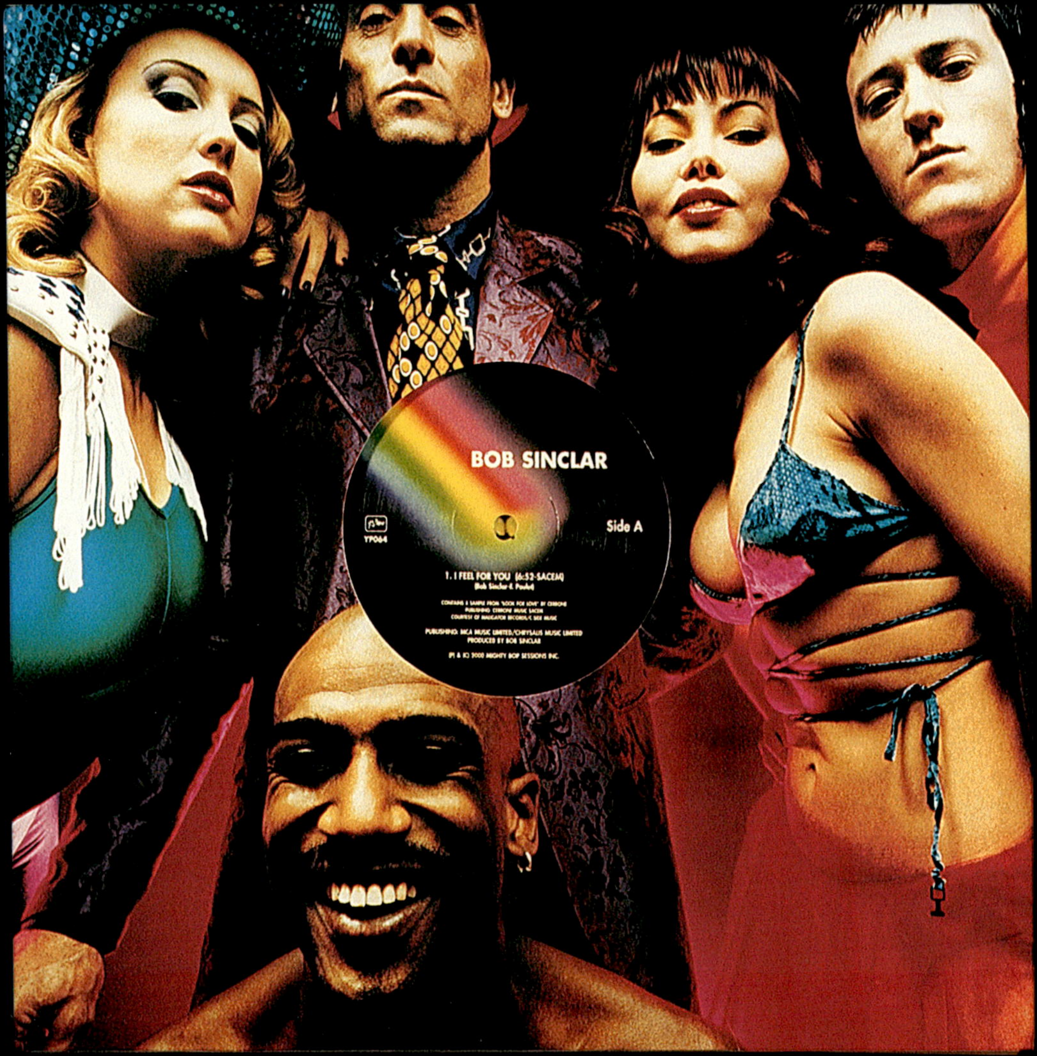

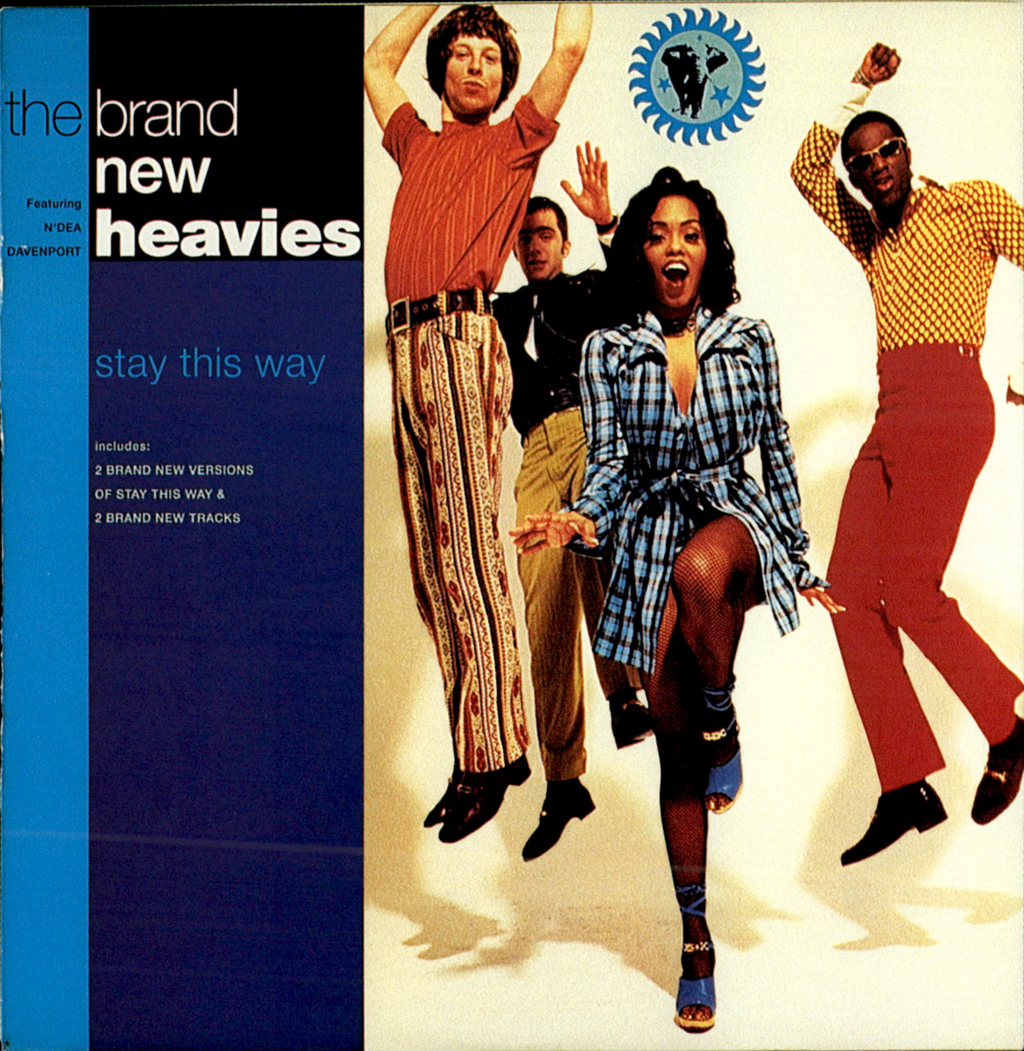

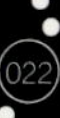

the brand
new heavies

Featuring
N'DEA
DAVENPORT

stay this way

includes:
2 BRAND NEW VERSIONS
OF STAY THIS WAY &
2 BRAND NEW TRACKS

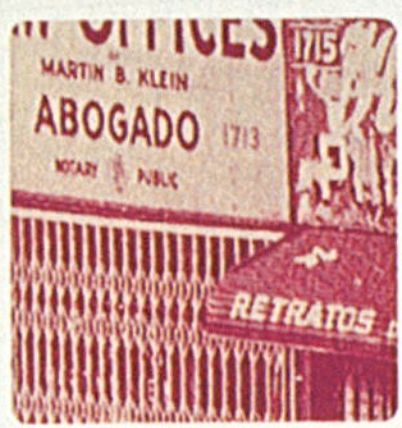

MARTIN B. KLEIN
ABOGADO 1713
NOTARY PUBLIC
RETRATOS

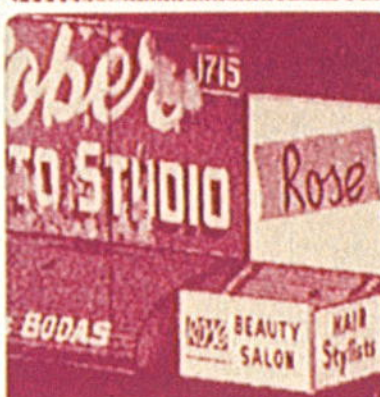
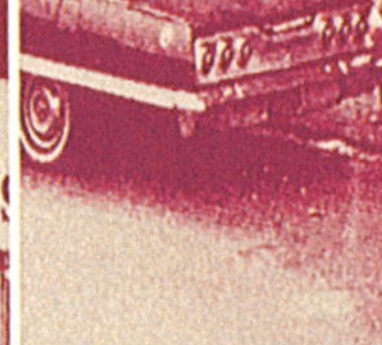
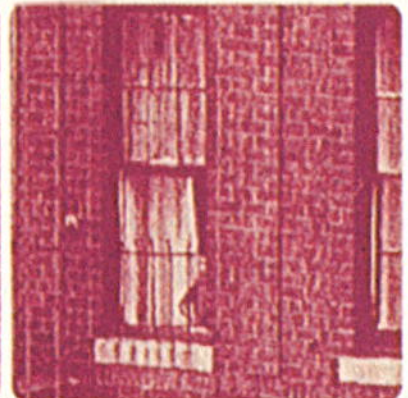
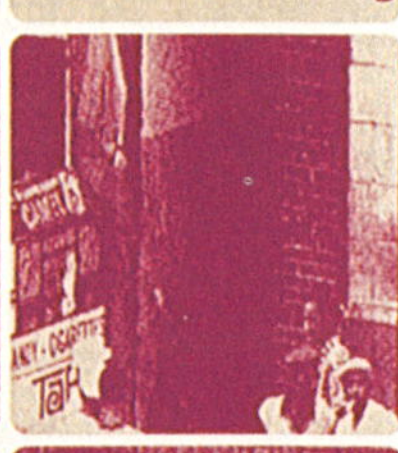

Symphonic Tonic
Street Corner Symphony
Featuring Cece ROGERS

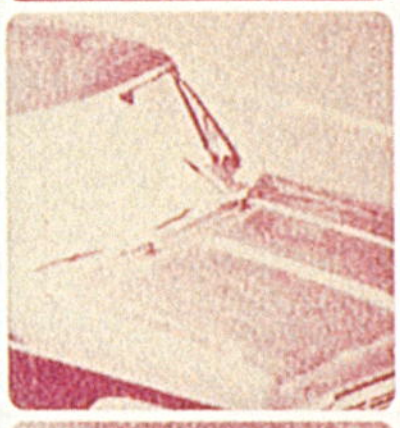
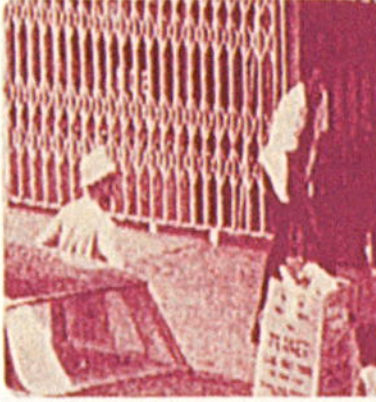
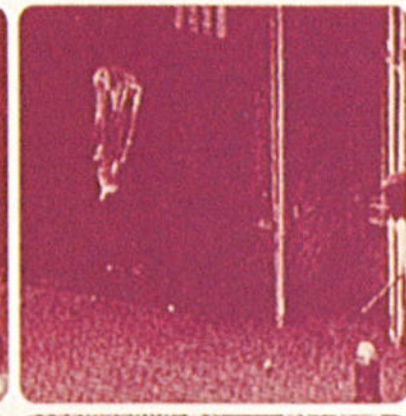
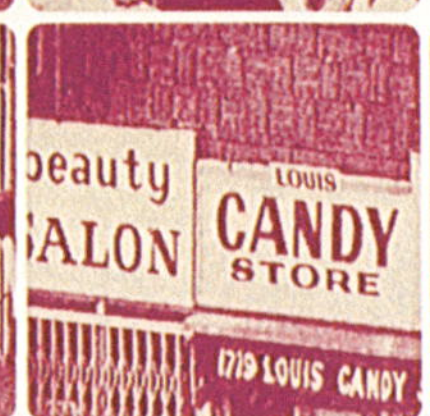
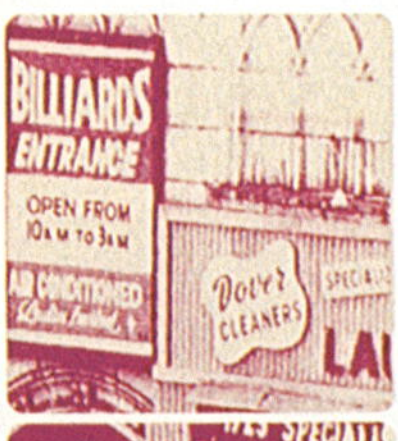

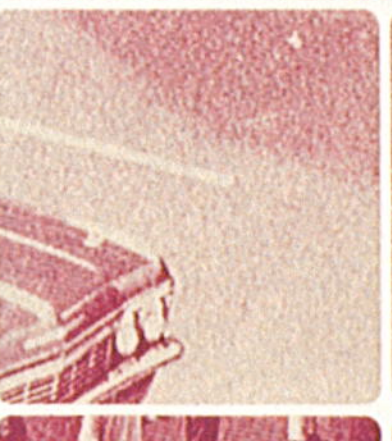
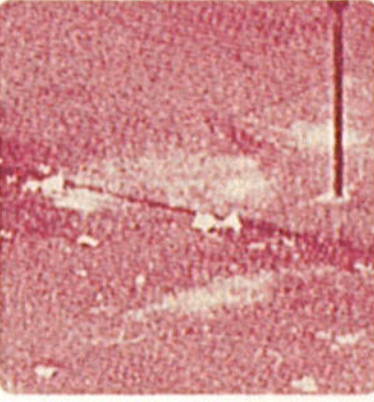
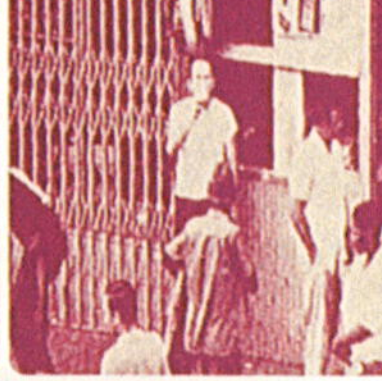
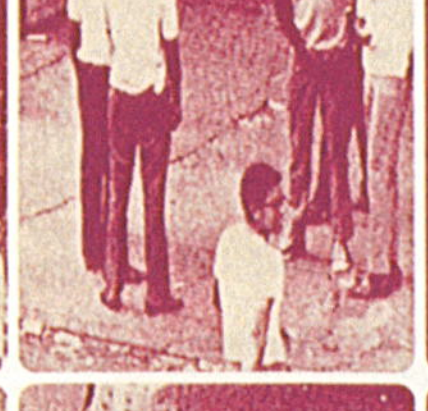
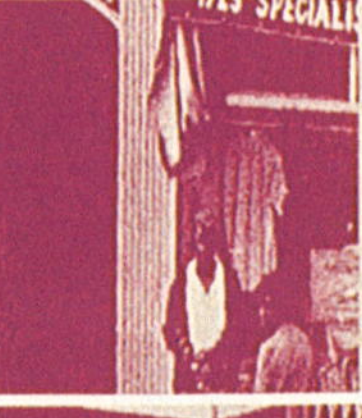

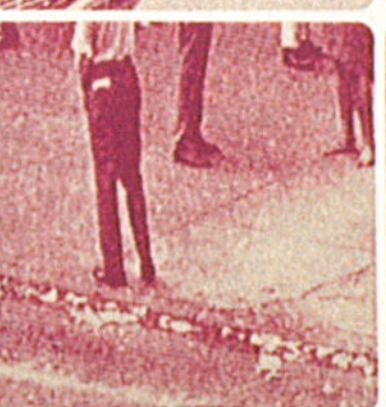
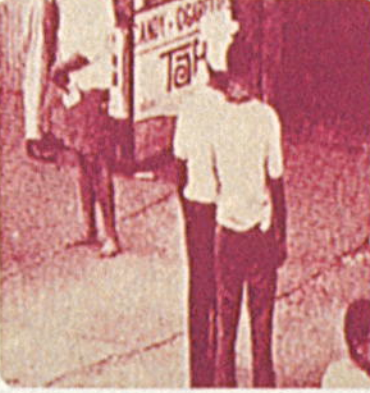
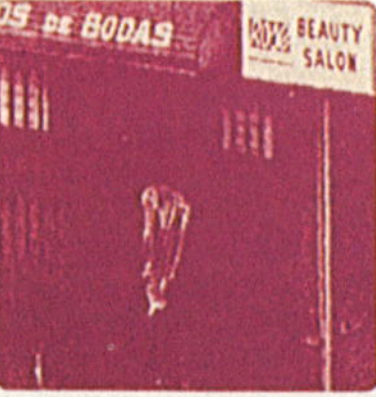
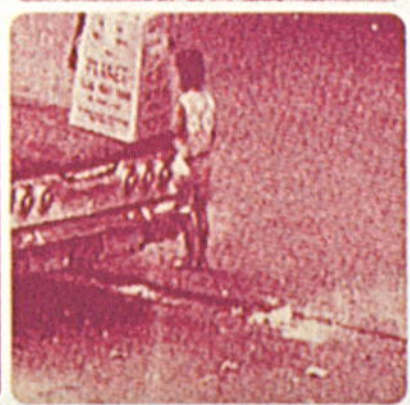
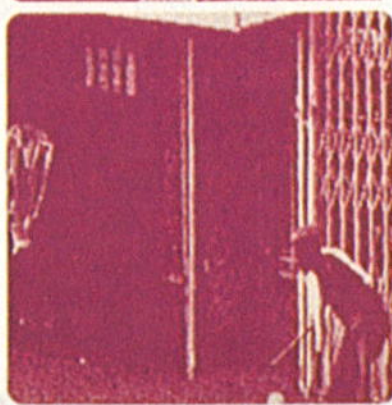

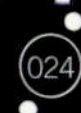

the
brand new heavies
ULTIMATE
TRUNK FUNK
the ep
Featuring
N'DEA
DAVENPORT
EASTERN
Featuring
NEVER STOP
(HEAVIES MIX)
STAY THIS WAY
(SLAM MIX)
GOT TO GIVE
(NEW RECORDING)
MR. TANAKA

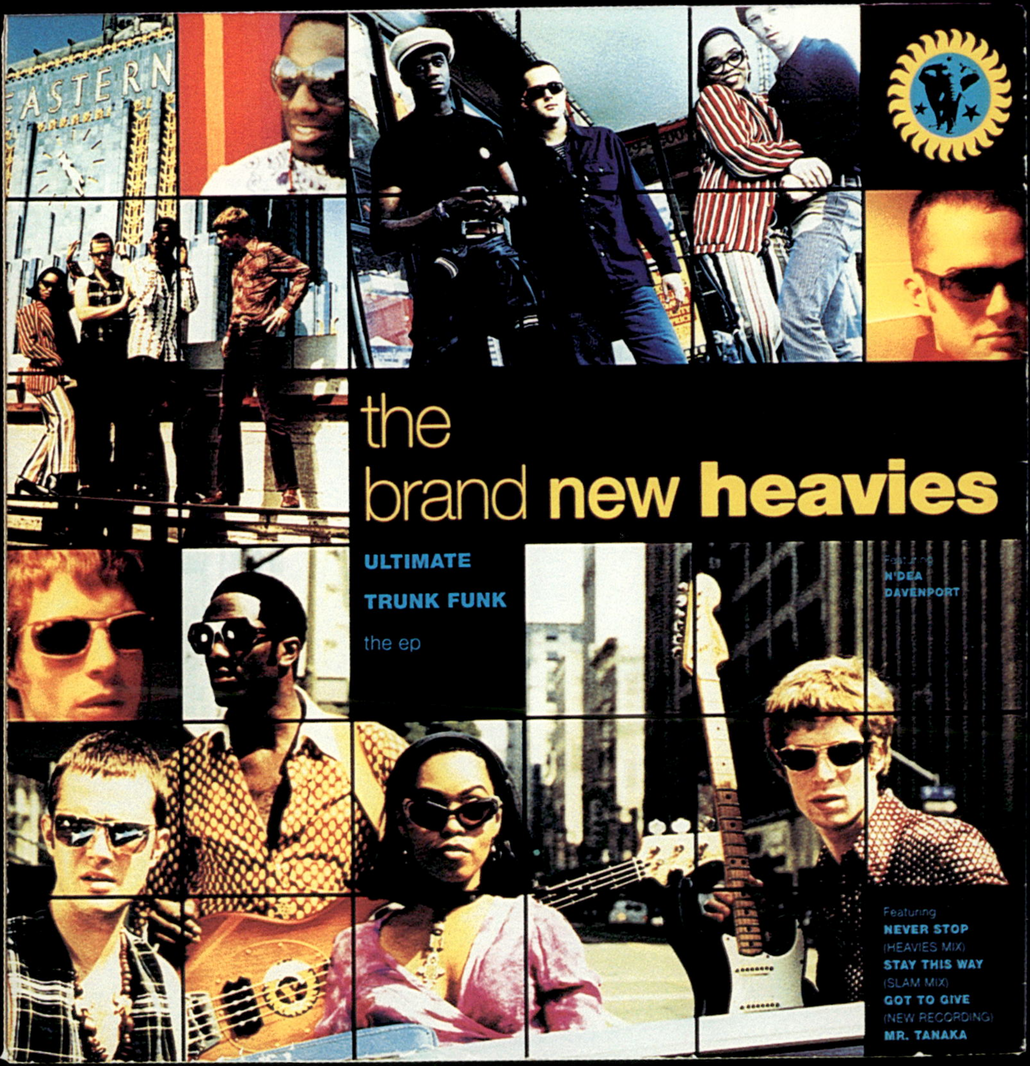

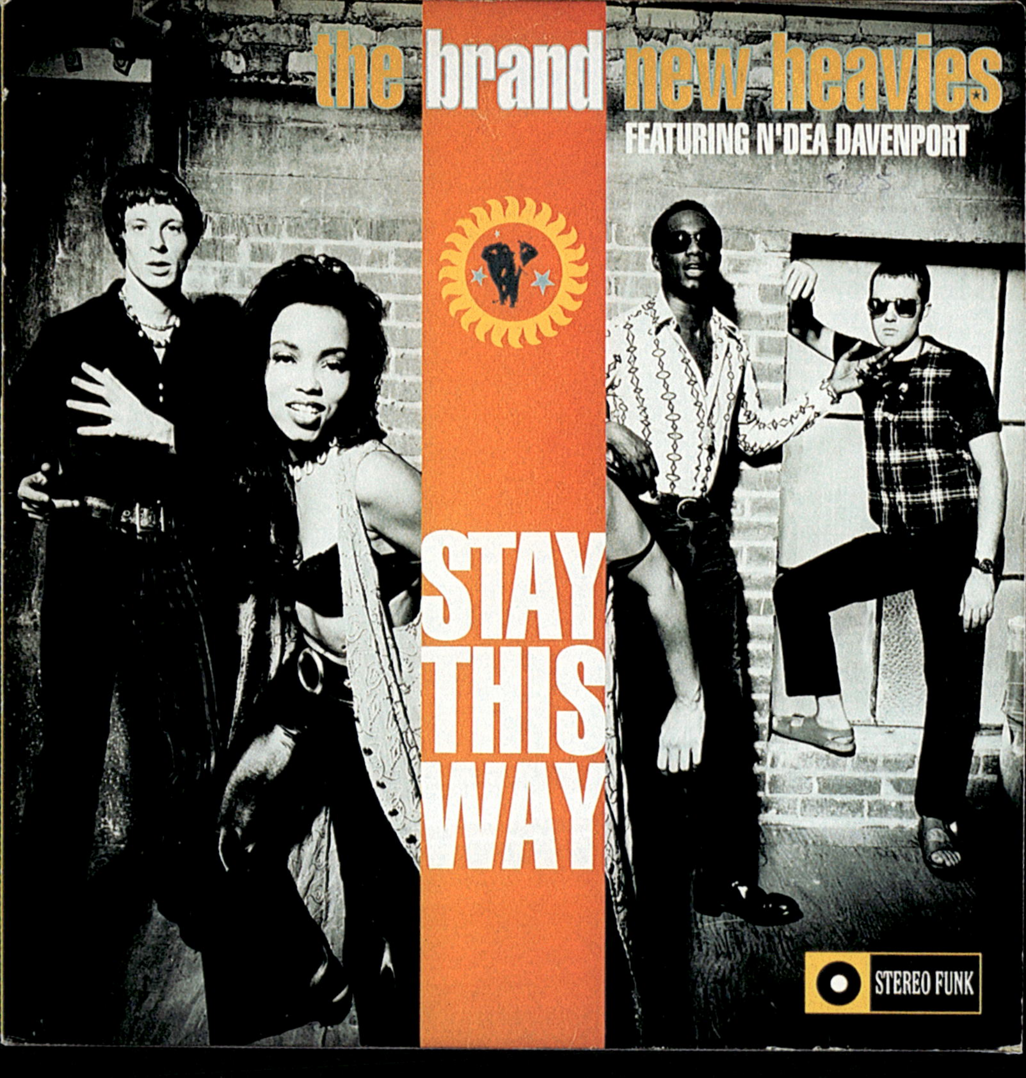

025 Artist The Brand New Heavies Title Stay This Way Record Label Delicious Vinyl Date 1991

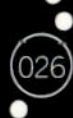 026   Artist Alliance Ethnik Title Honesty & Jalousie Design Moogly Photography Youri Lenquette
Record Label Delabel / Virgin Date 1995

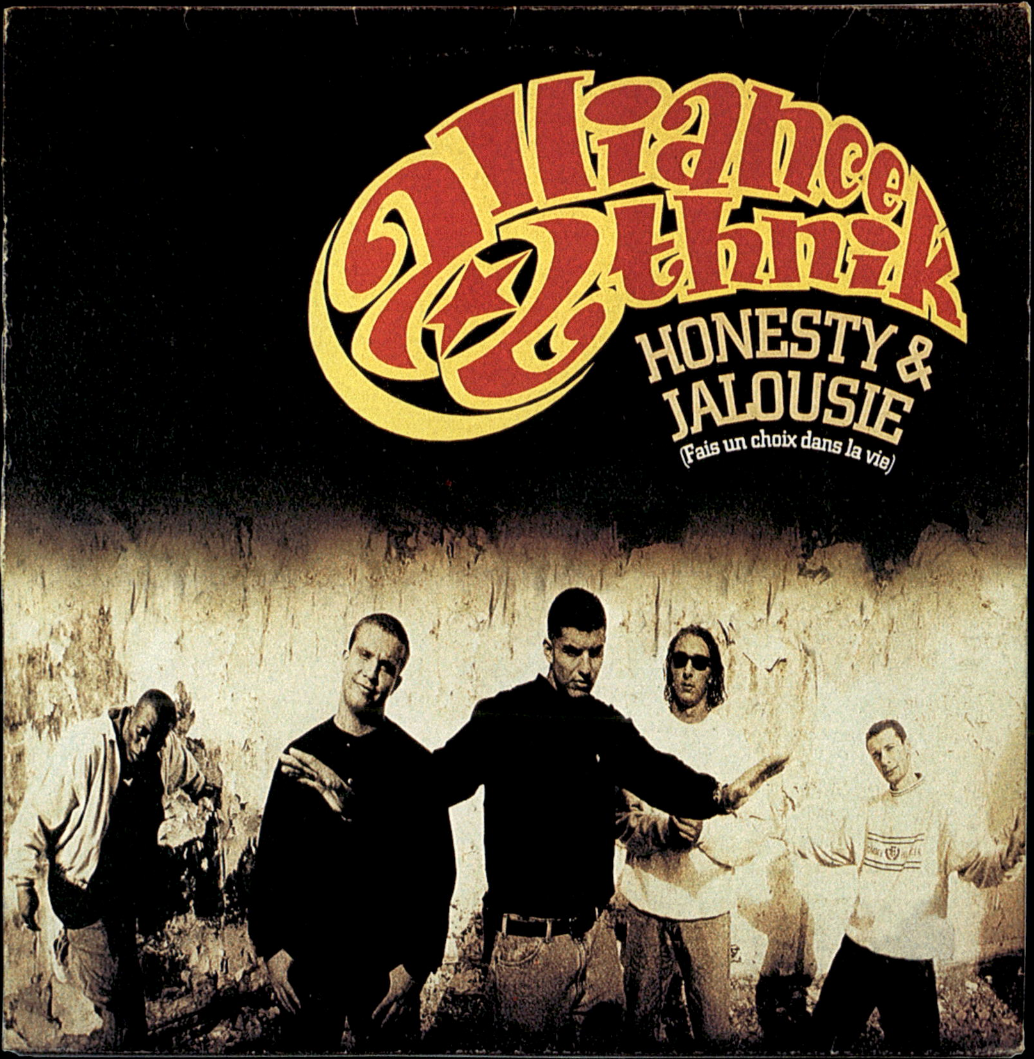

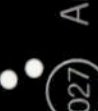

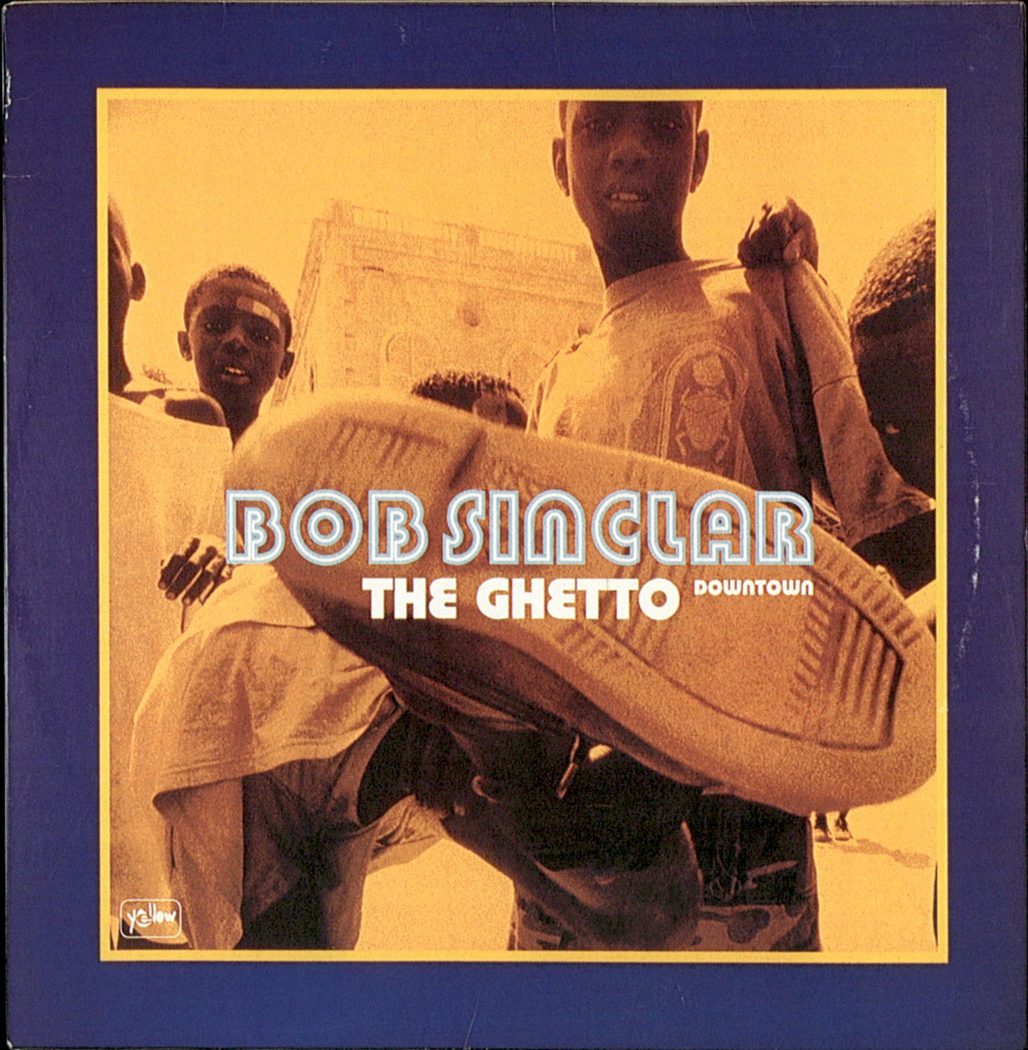

BOB SINCLAR
THE GHETTO DOWNTOWN
yellow

Artist Bob Sinclar Title The Ghetto Design Restez Vivants Photography Bernard Benant Record Label Yellow Date 1998

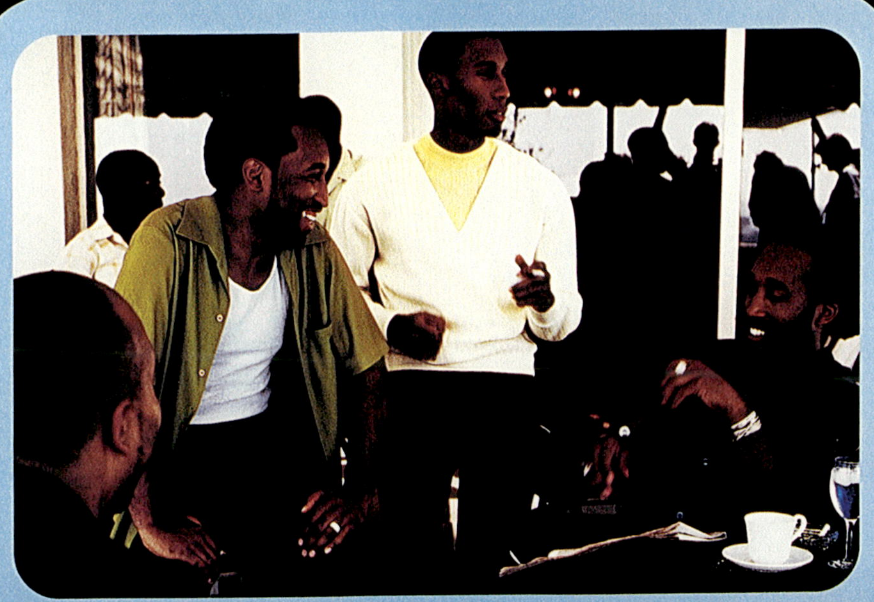

TONY TONI TONÉ
let's get down   featuring DJ Quik

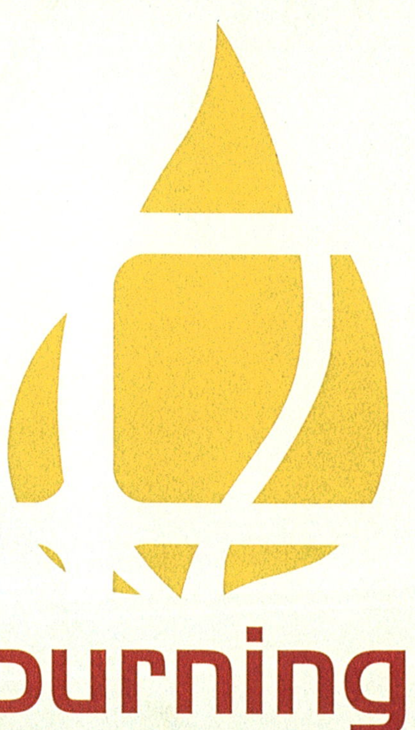

INCLUDES MIXES BY
SHARAM, KLUBBHEADS
FLEXY & DJ KRYPTONITE

mk

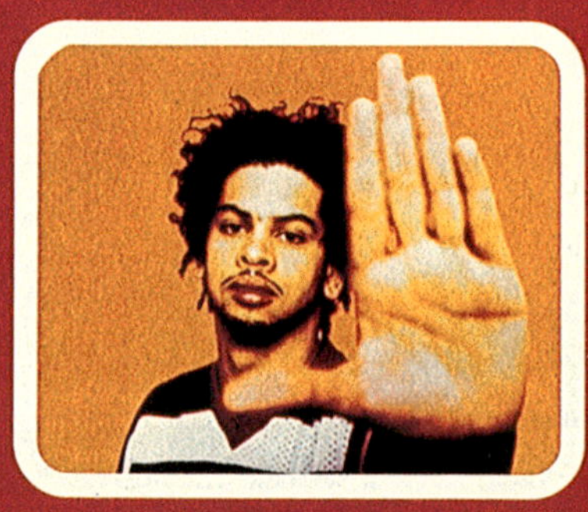

burning

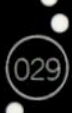

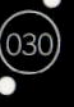

inner city
'DO YA'

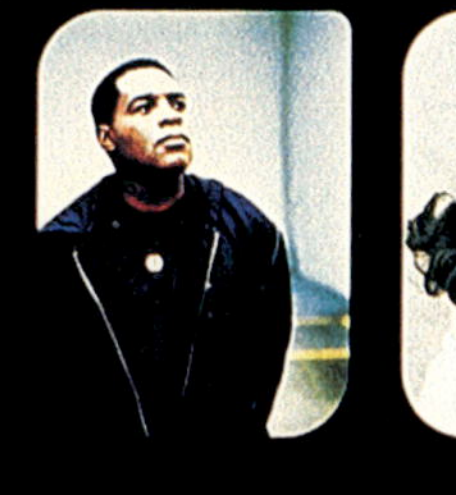
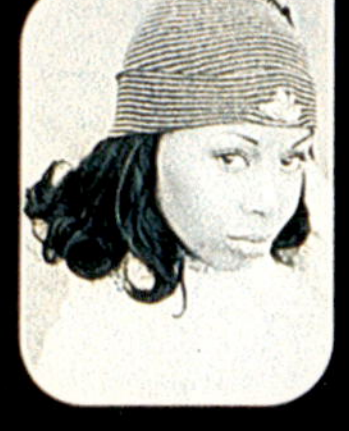
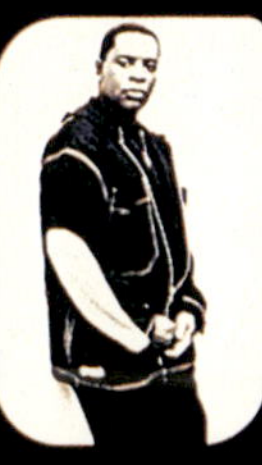
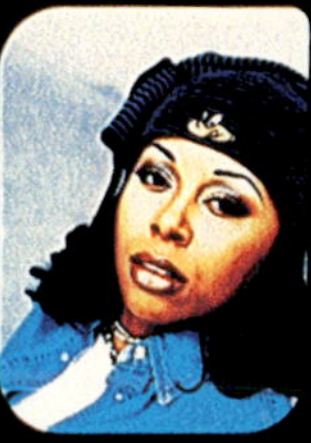
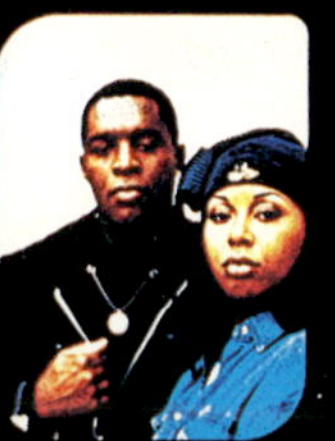

12" no.1 Includes: Reese, Chez D Trent, Sure Is Pure, Carl Craig & Claude Young remixes.

disco

DISCO - FUNK - SPEECH/RAP

SUPER SINGLE - NON-STOP-DISCOMIX

·WODKA·FLIGHT·269·

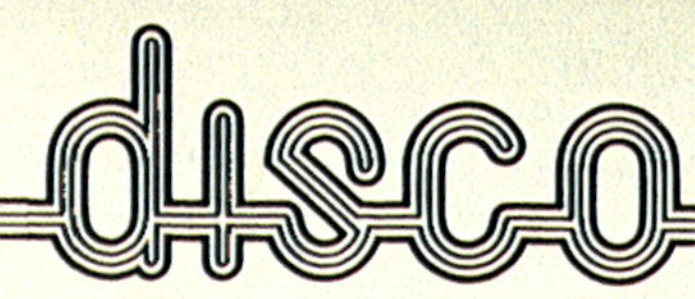

BY
DADDY COOL

ONLY LIMITED EDITION

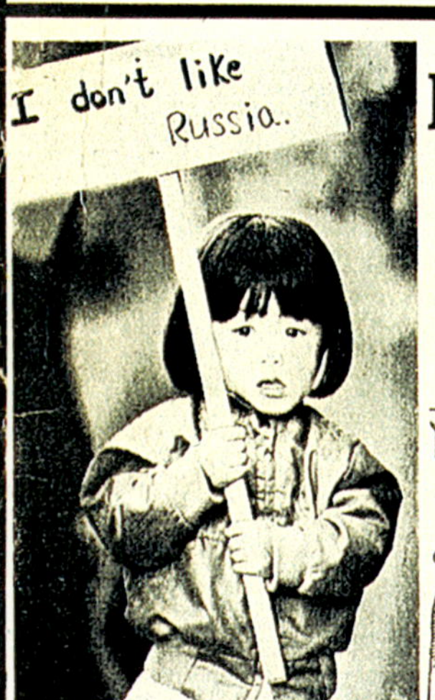

A minor's message

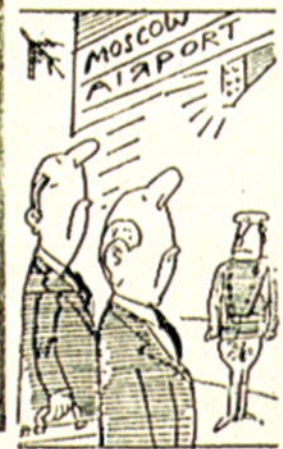

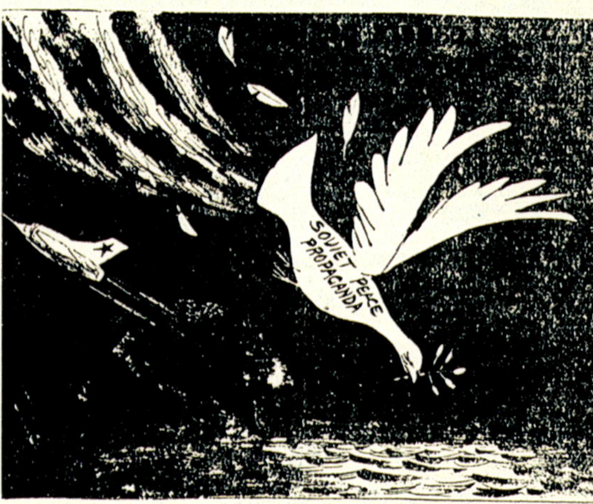

WORLD LICENCOR: RECORDED   AT   MUSIC MASTER
MUSIC MASTER BENELUX INT'L , MEERSTRAAT 8 LAARNE 9270 BELGIUM

PHONE:91.693837
91.697736
TELEX:12234 MUSICO

SKELETRONICS

YOUR LOVE IS ALLRIGHT

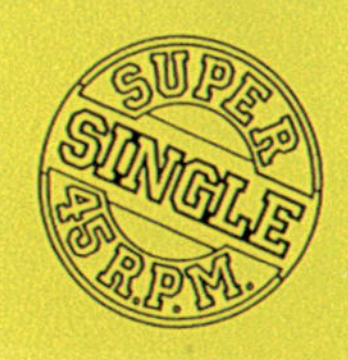

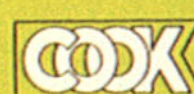

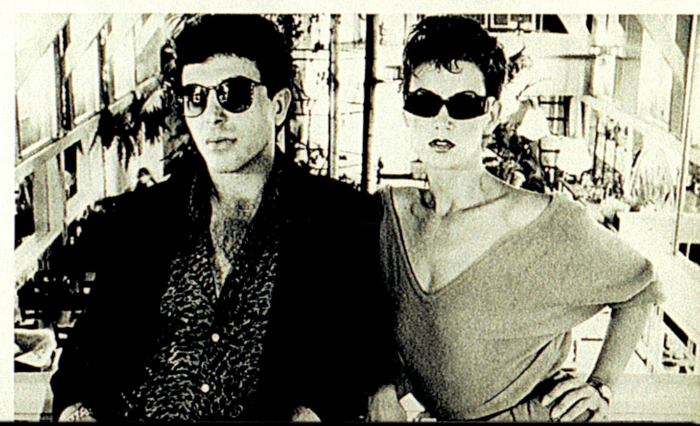

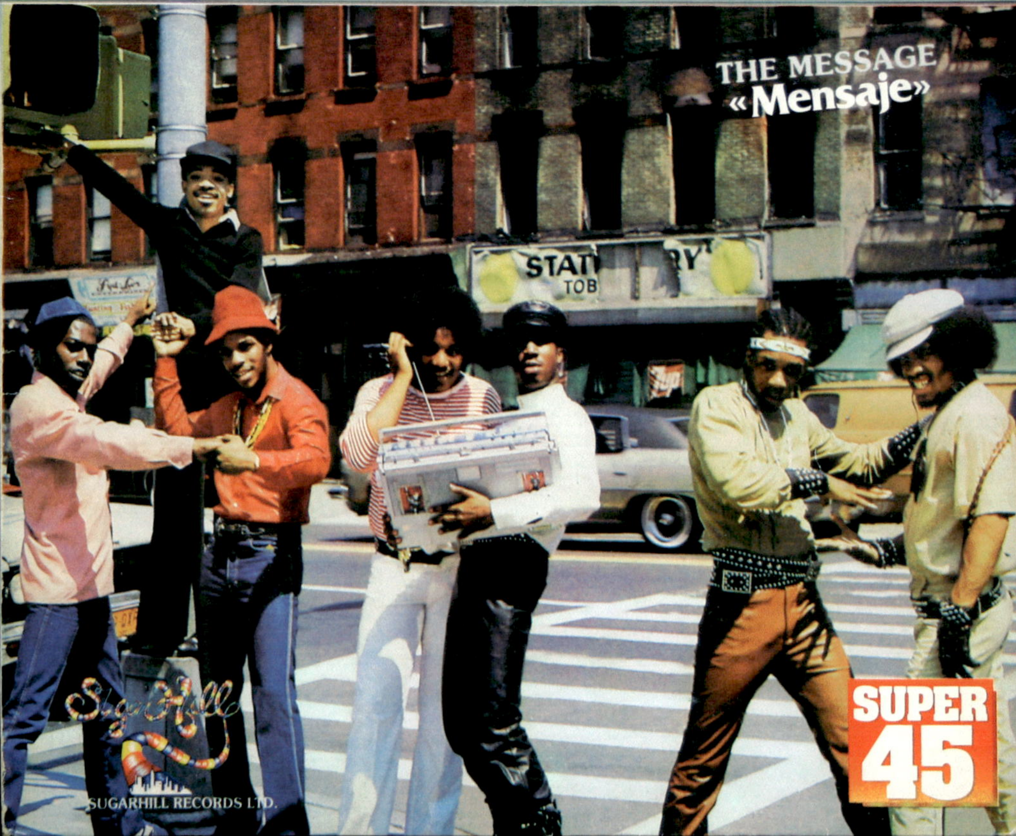
OOS-562
GRANDMASTER FLASH
& THE FURIOUS FIVE
THE MESSAGE
«Mensaje»
STAT RY
TOB
SUPER
45
SUGARHILL RECORDS LTD.

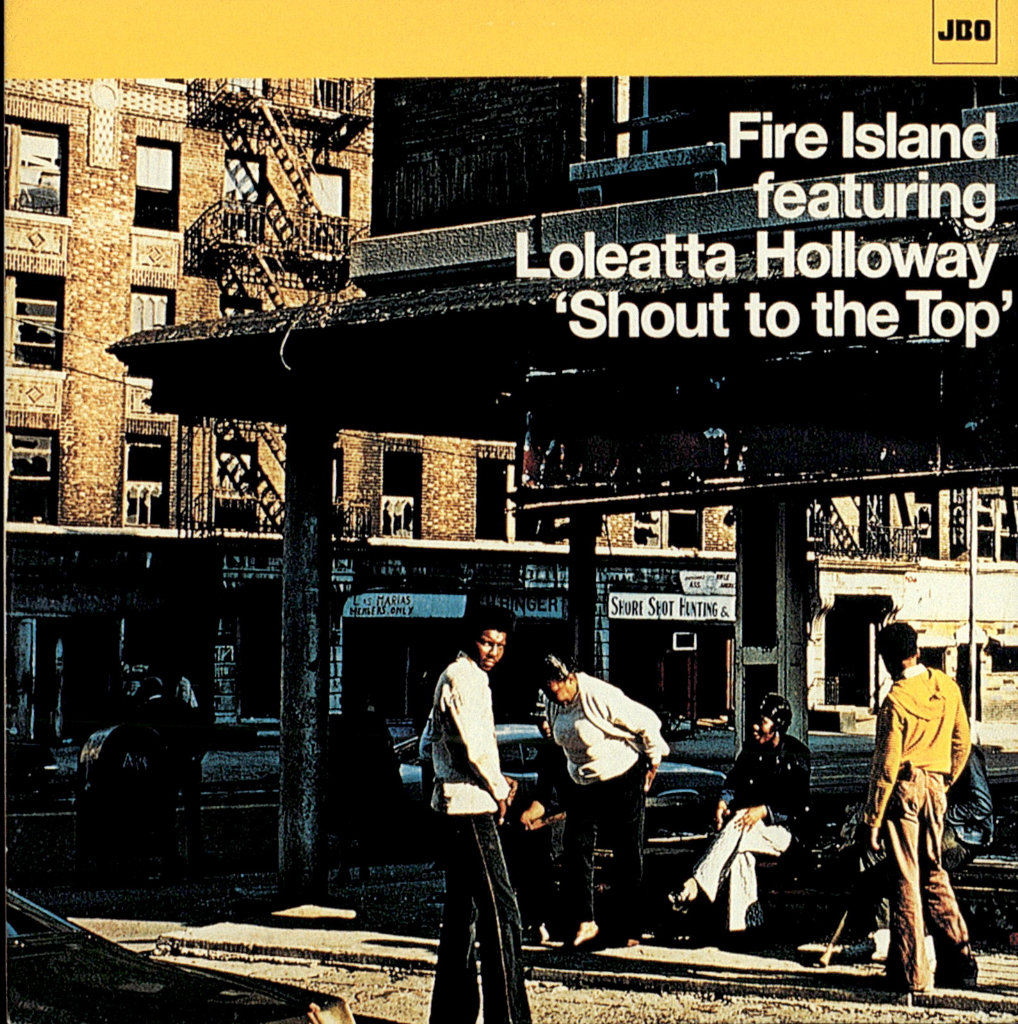

JBO
Fire Island
featuring
Loleatta Holloway
'Shout to the Top'
LAS MARIAS MEMBERS ONLY
SHORE SPOT HUNTING &
Artist Fire Island feat. Loleatta Holloway Title Shout to the Top Design Blue Source Photography Leonard Freed
Record Label JBO Date 1998

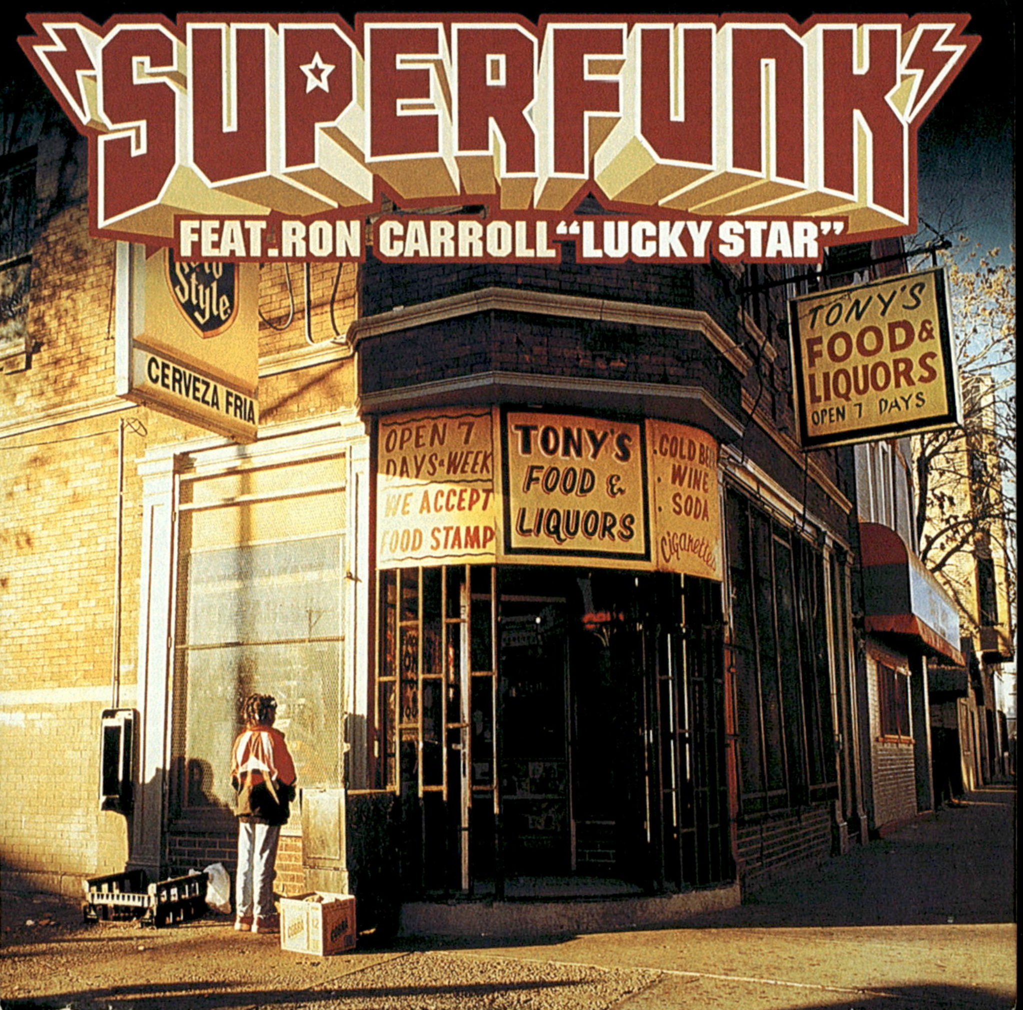
SUPERFUNK
FEAT. RON CARROLL "LUCKY STAR"
Hand Style
CERVEZA FRIA
TONY'S FOOD & LIQUORS OPEN 7 DAYS
OPEN 7 DAYS A WEEK
WE ACCEPT FOOD STAMP
TONY'S FOOD & LIQUORS
COLD BEER
WINE
SODA
Cigarettes
035
Artist Superfunk feat. Ron Carroll Title Lucky Star Record Label Rise Date 2000

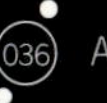

PAUL JOHNSON
get get down

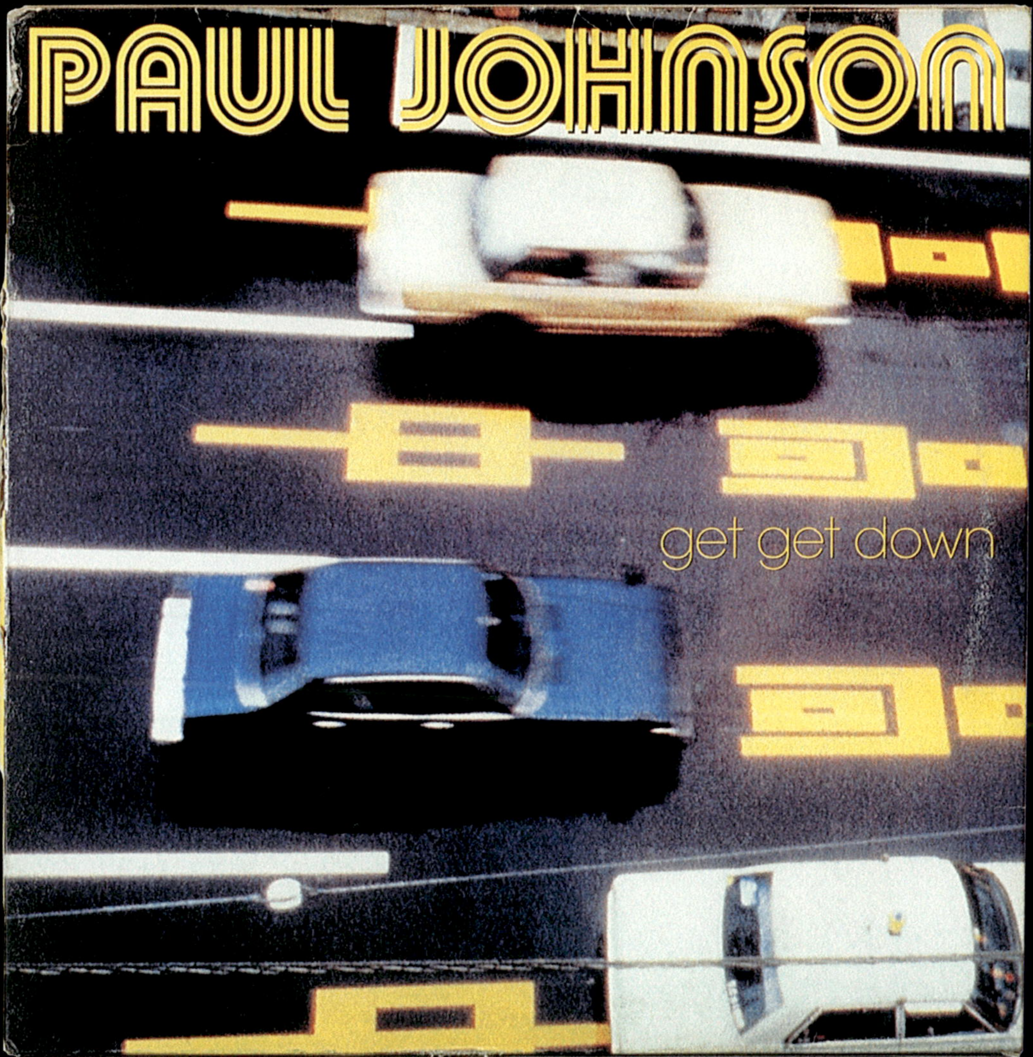

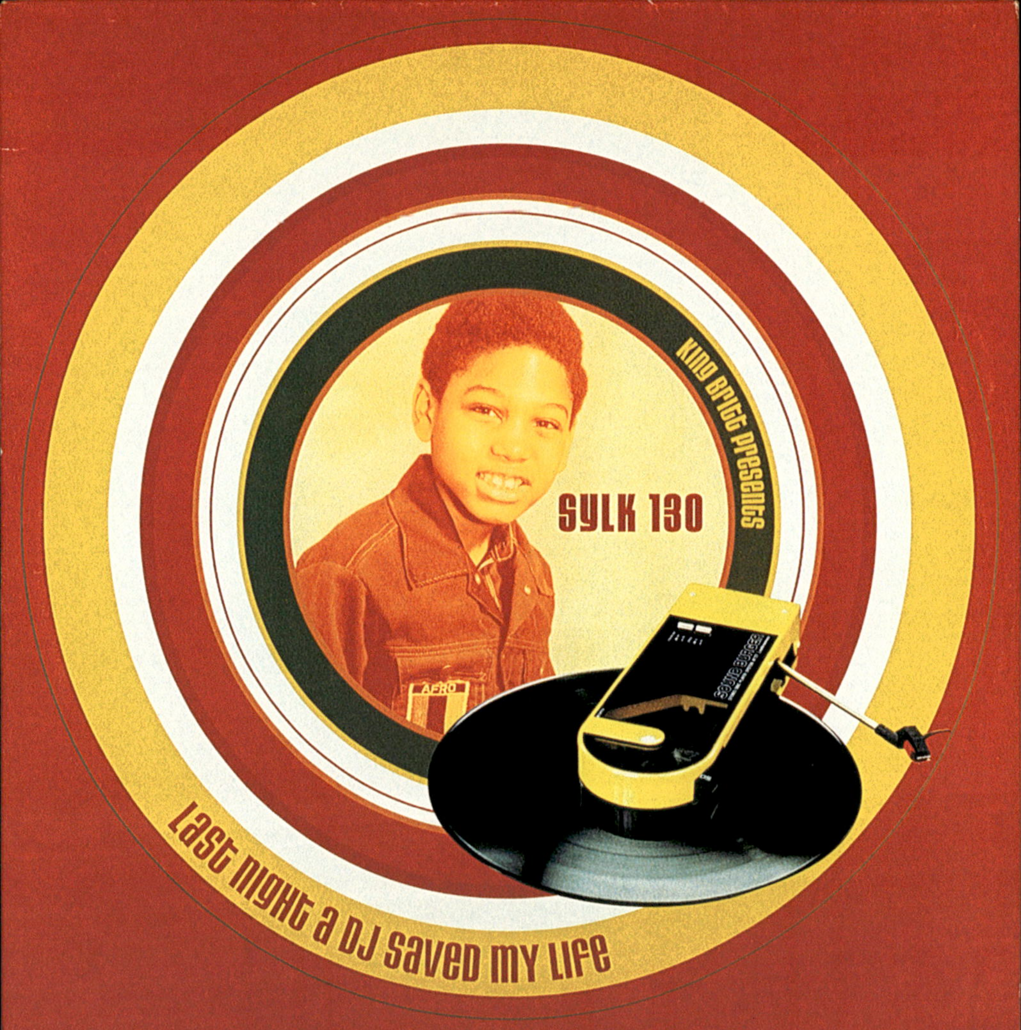

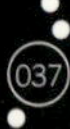

King Britt presents
SYLK 130
Last Night a DJ Saved My Life
AFRO

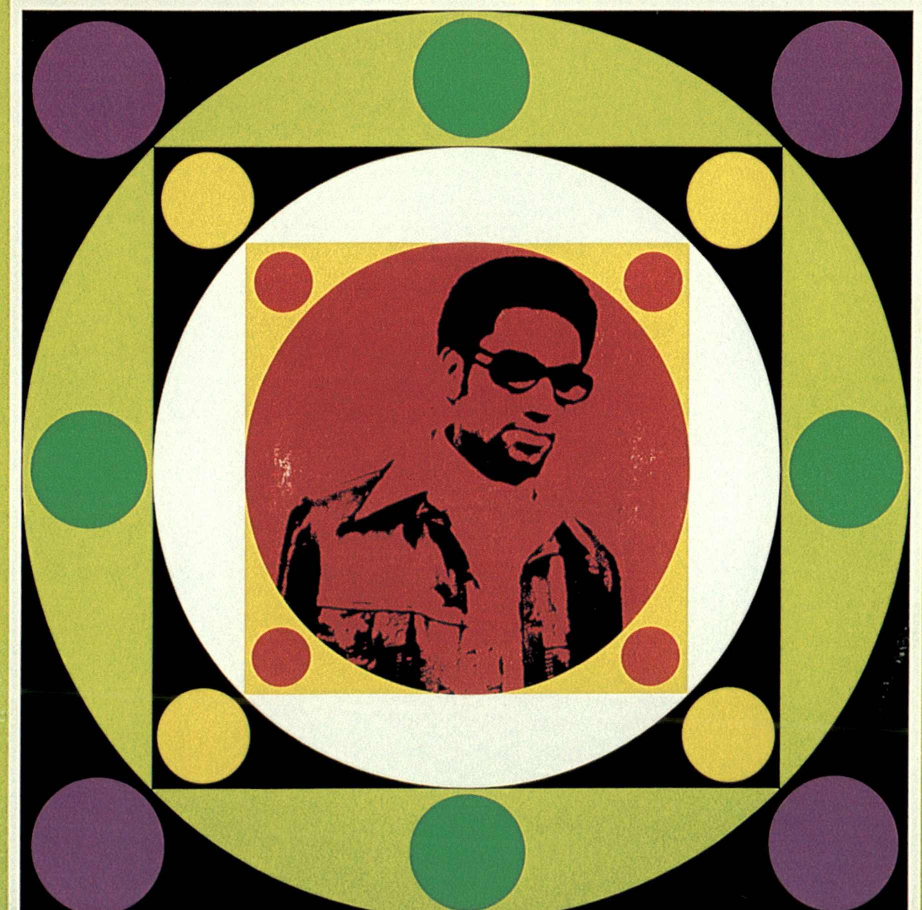
KING BRITT PRESENTS SYLK 130 THE REASON/WHEN THE FUNK HITS THE FAN
038
Artist Sylk 130 Title The Reason Record Label Sony Music Date 1996

ELECTRIX
BLAME THE MUSIC

Including mixes by
Armin van Buuren
Floris and Plastika

Artist **Groovy 69** Title **Lovestar** Design **Elestudio** Record Label **Vendetta** Date **1998**

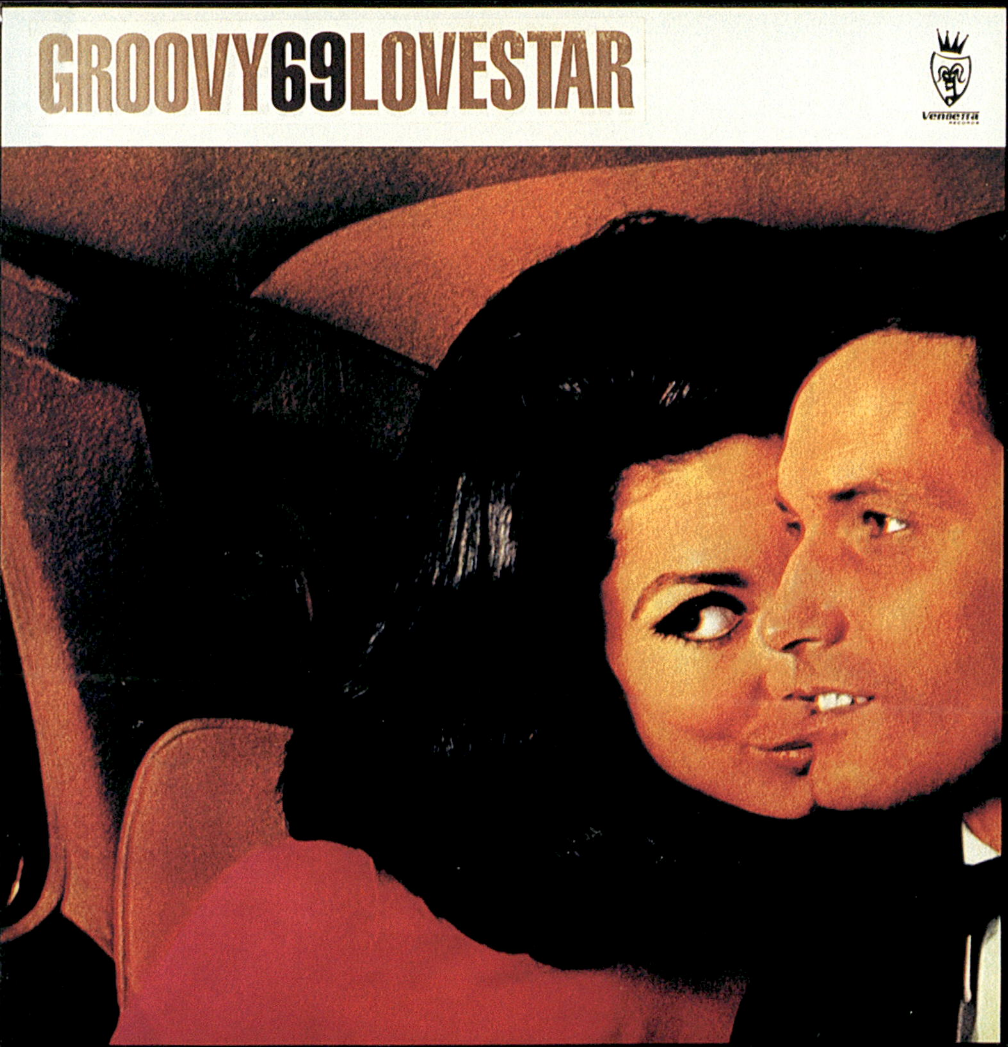

GROOVY69LOVESTAR

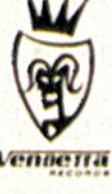

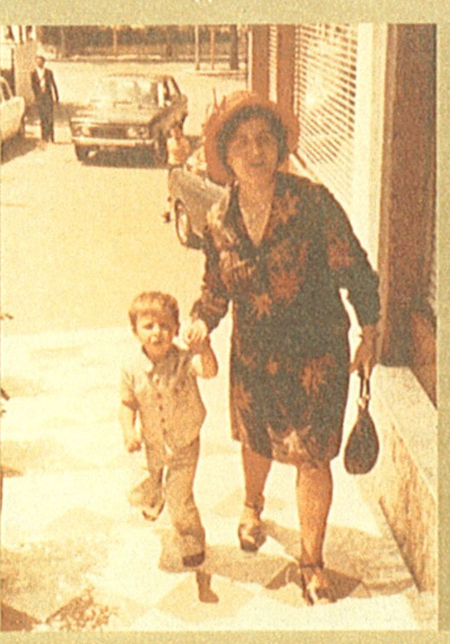
JUNIOR JACK
my feeling
Kick 'N' deep   •   At Home Mix   •   Happiness

MOUSSE T.
Ooh Song / More I Get
Part 1

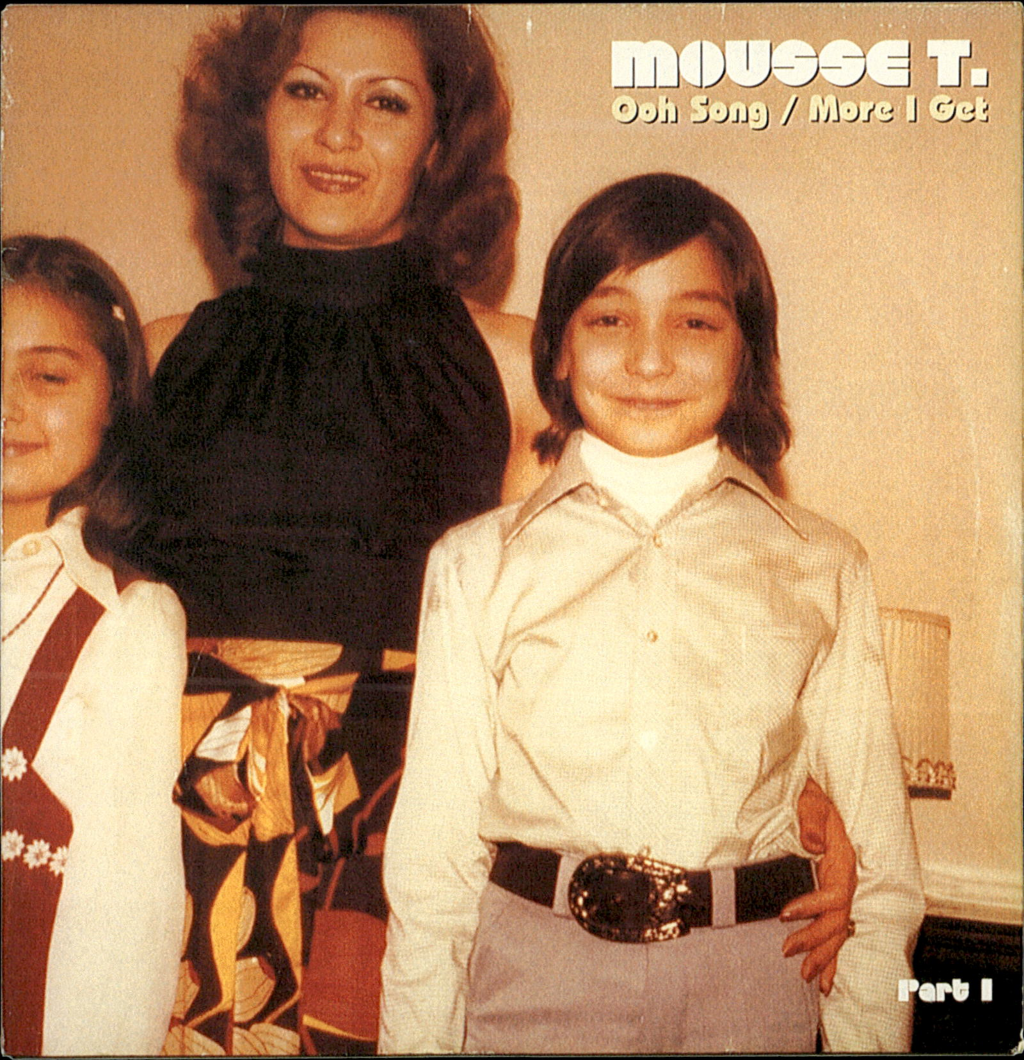

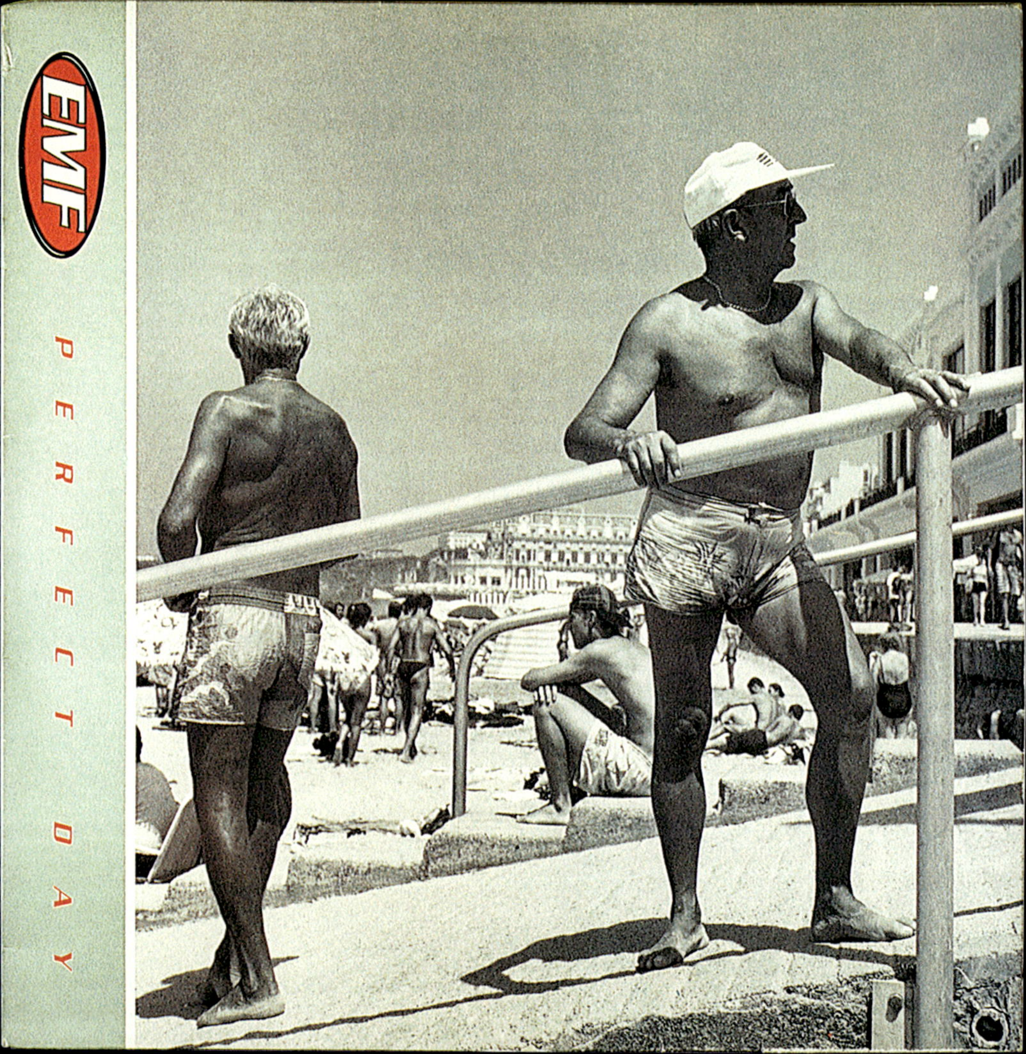

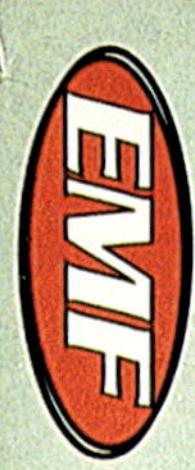

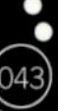

043 Artist **EMF** Title **Perfect Day** Photography **Kevin Westenberg** Record Label **EMI** Date **1995**

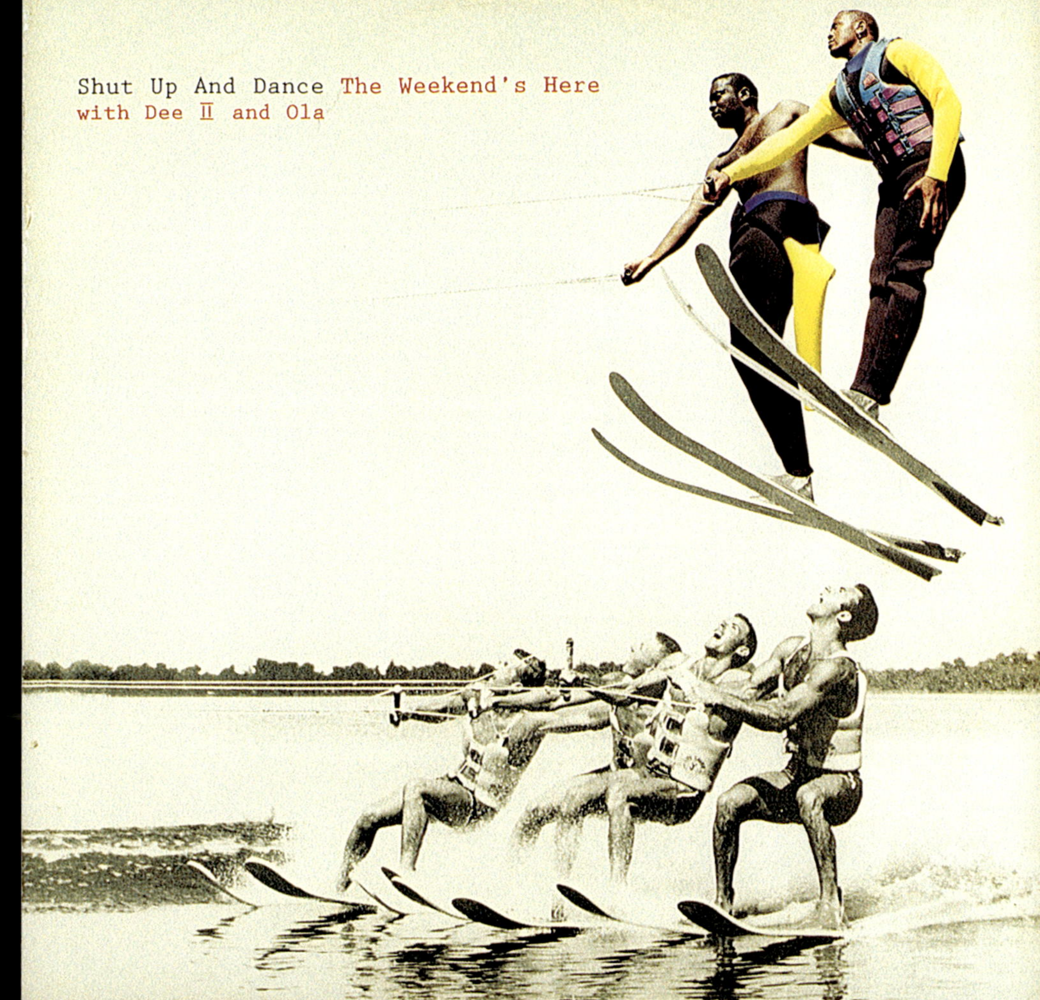

Shut Up And Dance The Weekend's Here
with Dee II and Ola

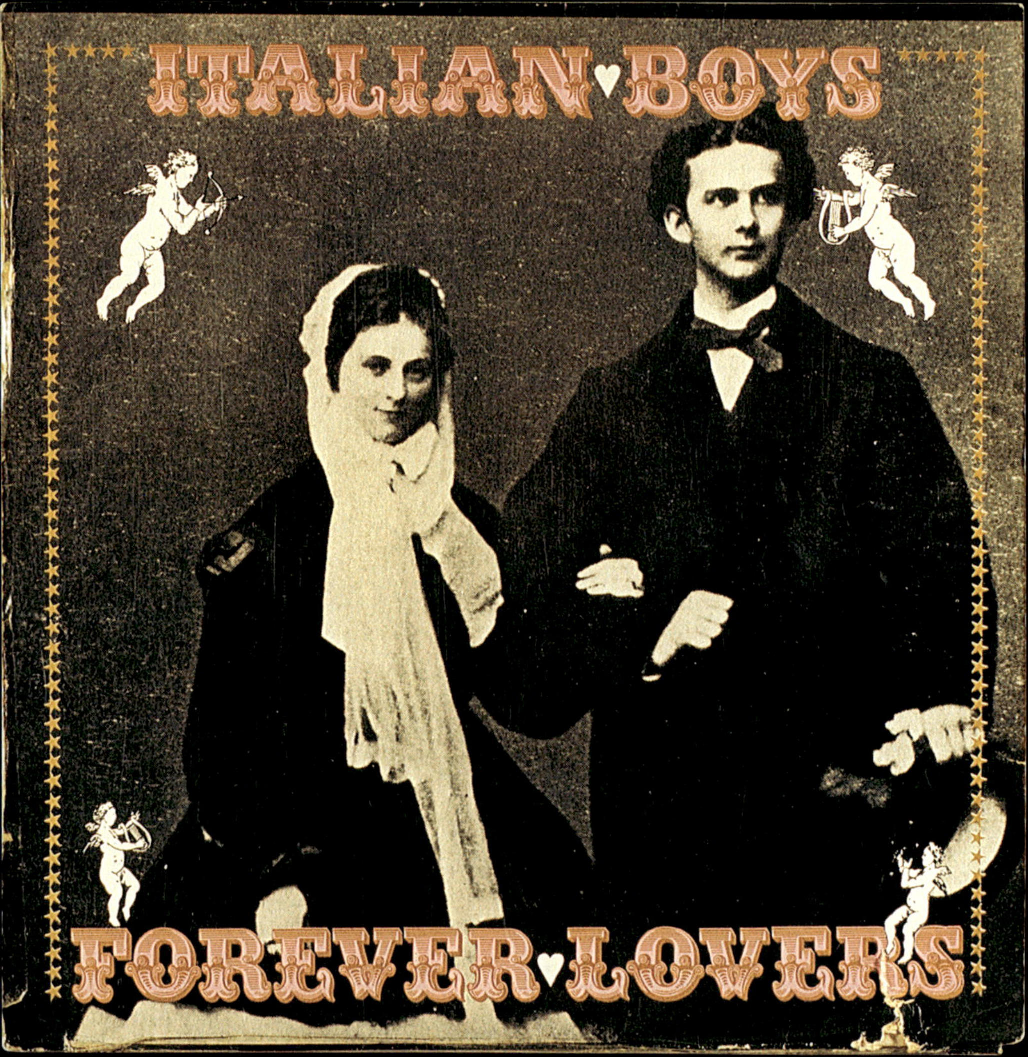

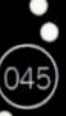

ITALIAN BOYS
FOREVER LOVERS

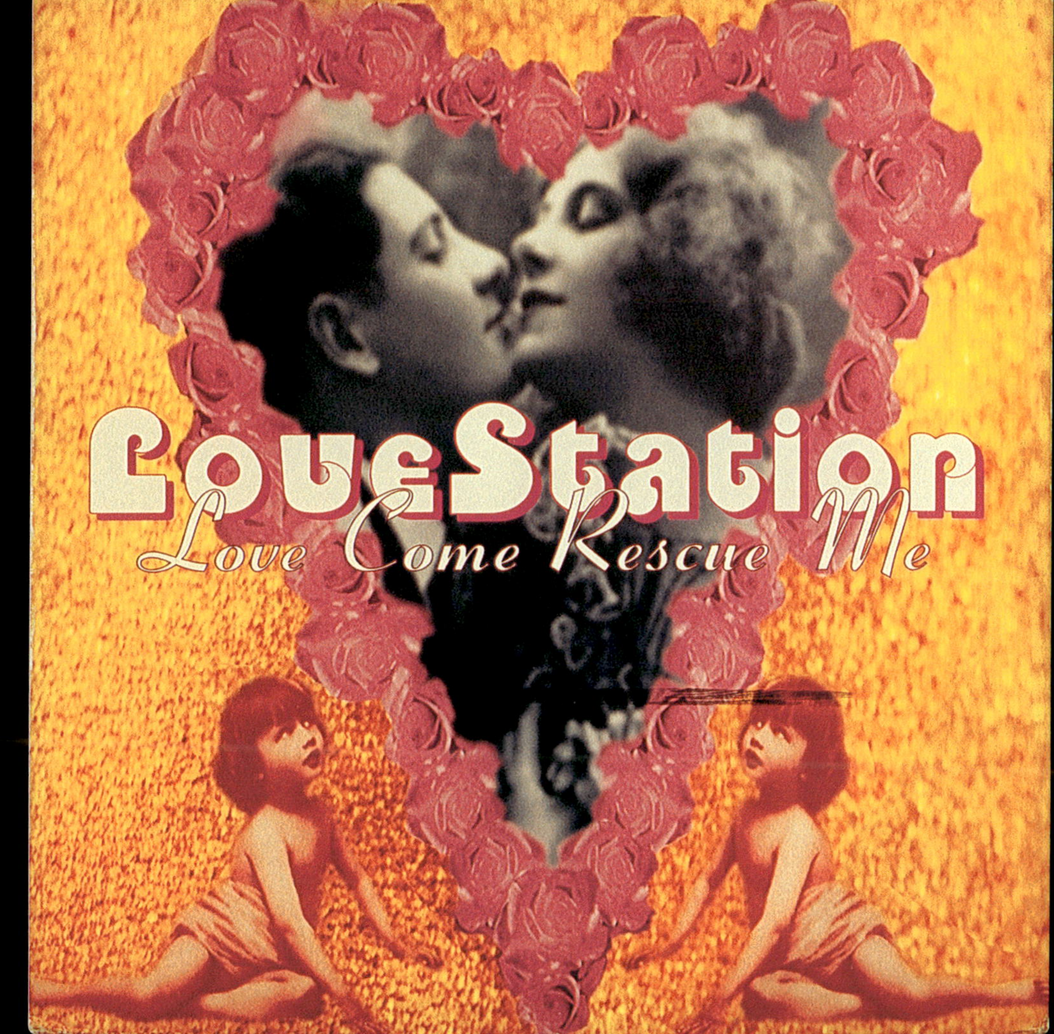
LoveStation
Love Come Rescue Me

Sunshine lady !!!

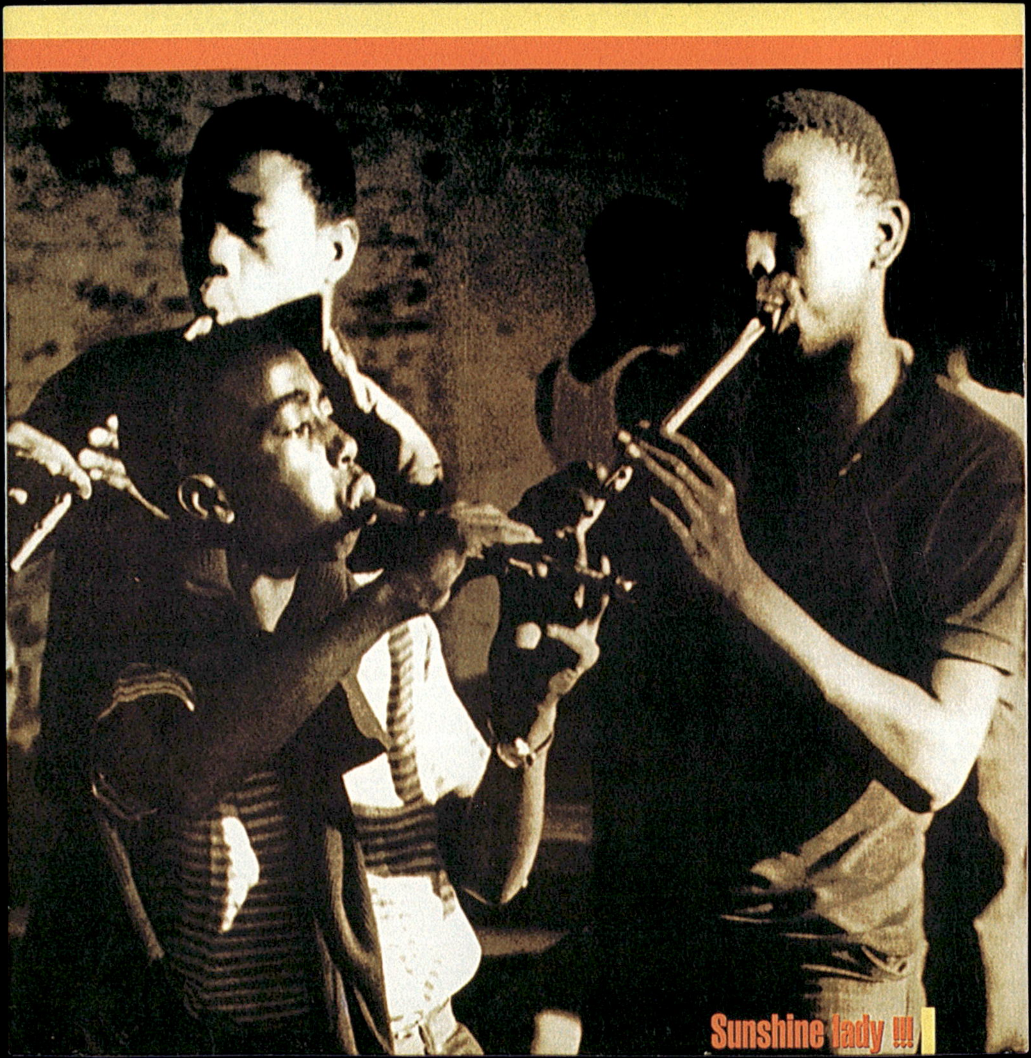

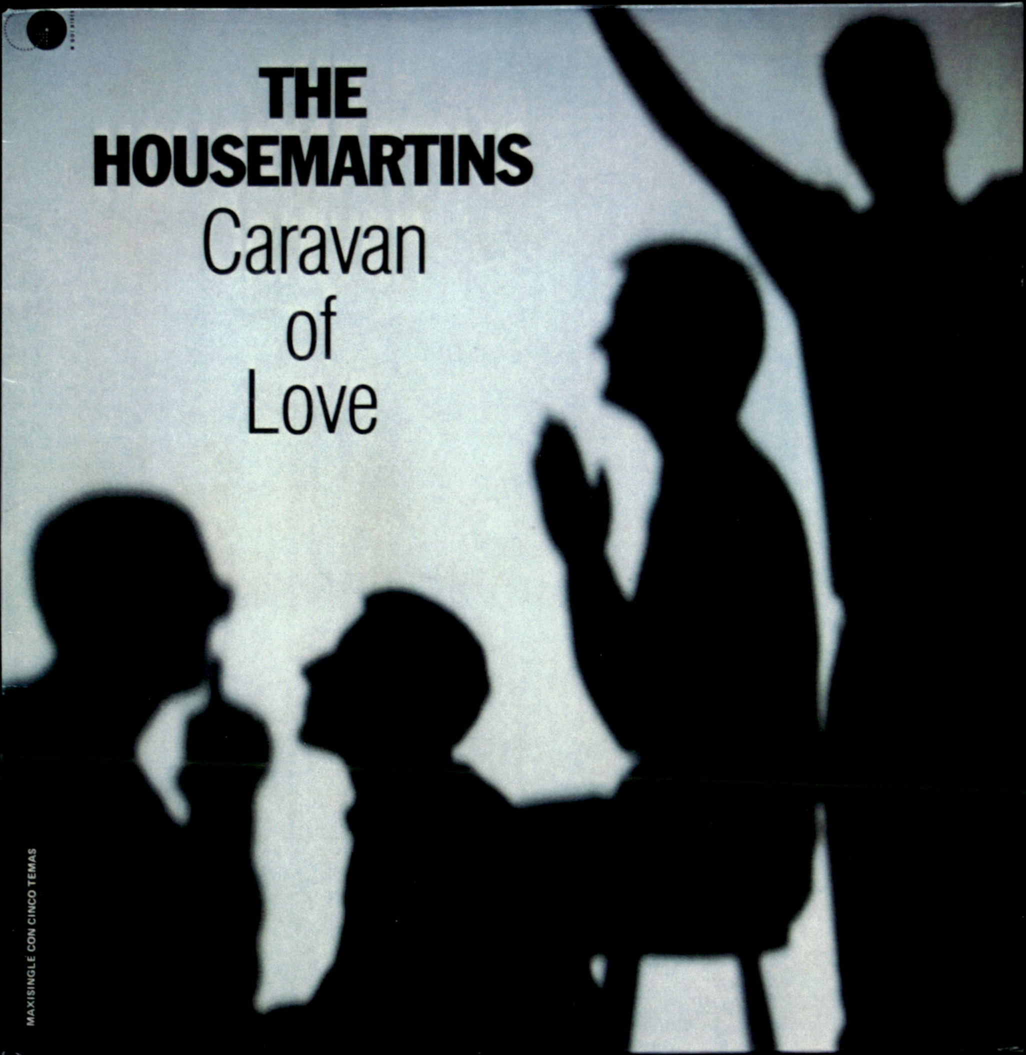

THE
HOUSEMARTINS
Caravan
of
Love
Artist The Housemartins Title Caravan of Love Design D. Storey Photography P. Cox Record Label Go Discs Date 1986
MAXISINGLE CON CINCO TEMAS
048

MTUME
JUICY FRUIT
SUPERSINGLE

WHAM!
BAD BOYS
SUPERSINGLE

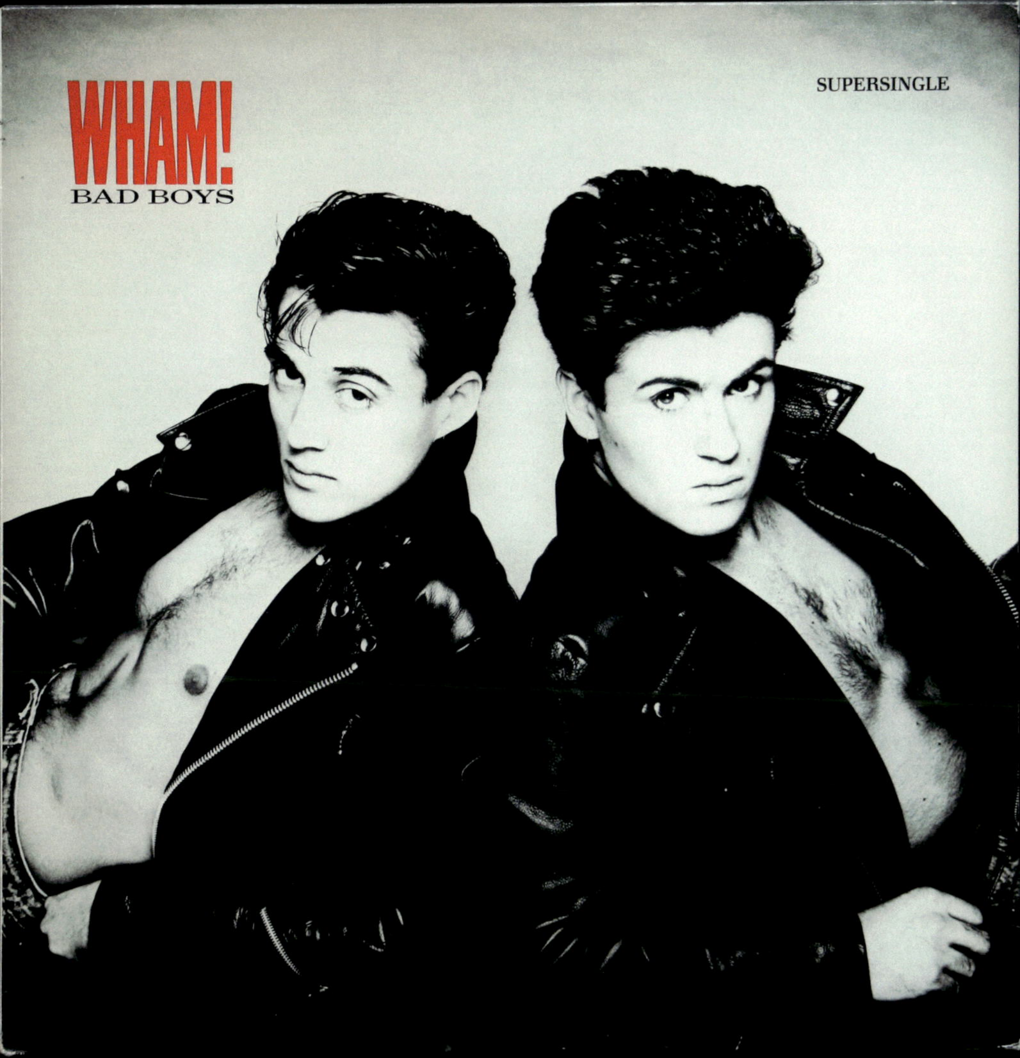

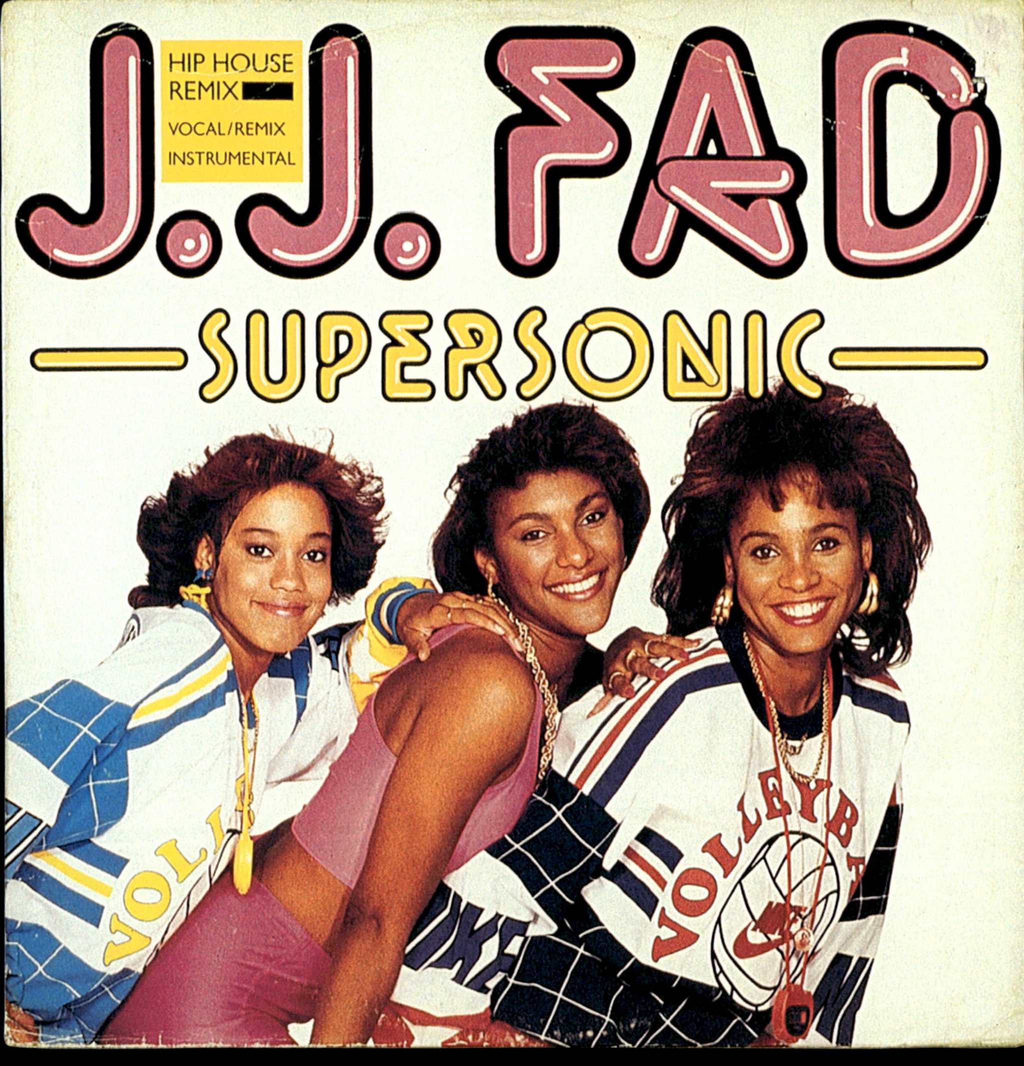

HIP HOUSE
REMIX
VOCAL/REMIX
INSTRUMENTAL
J.J. FAD
SUPERSONIC

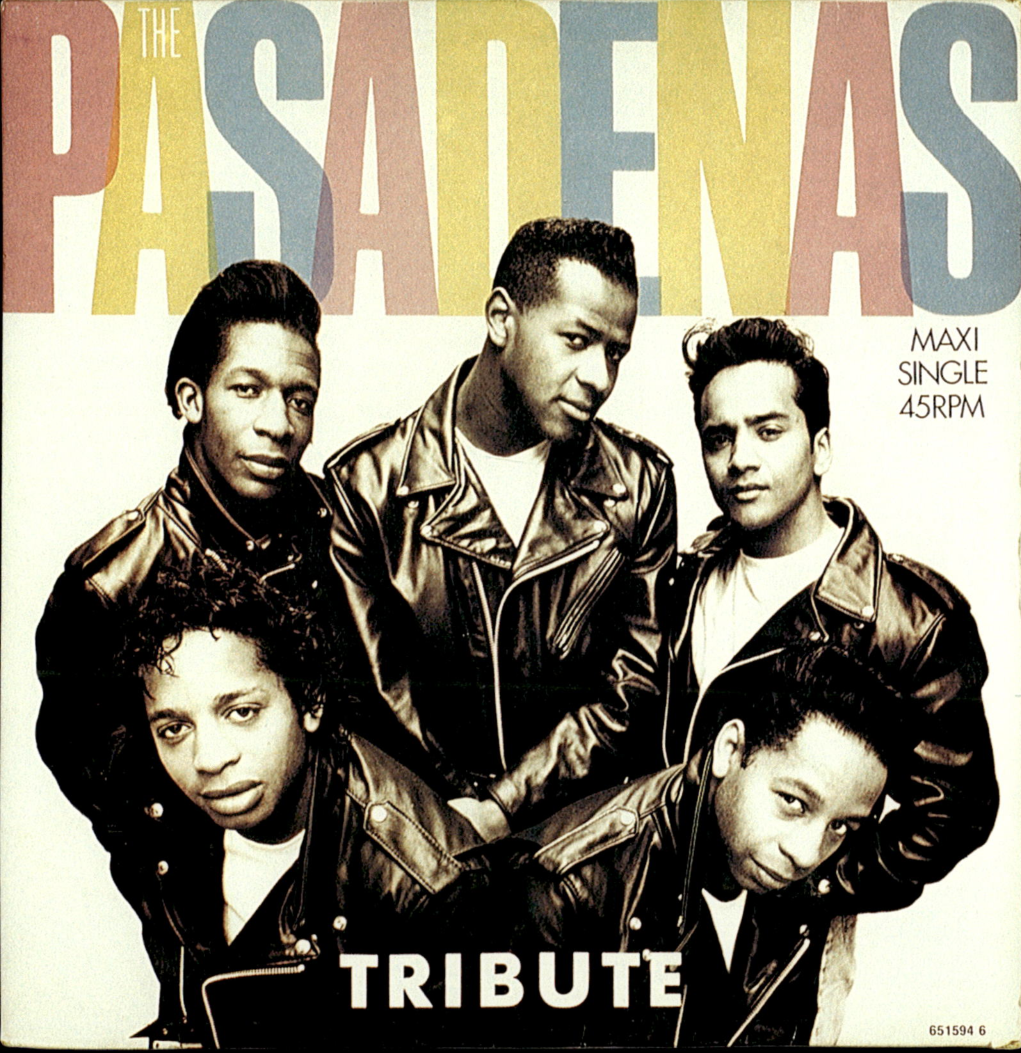
THE PASADENAS
MAXI
SINGLE
45RPM
TRIBUTE
651594 6

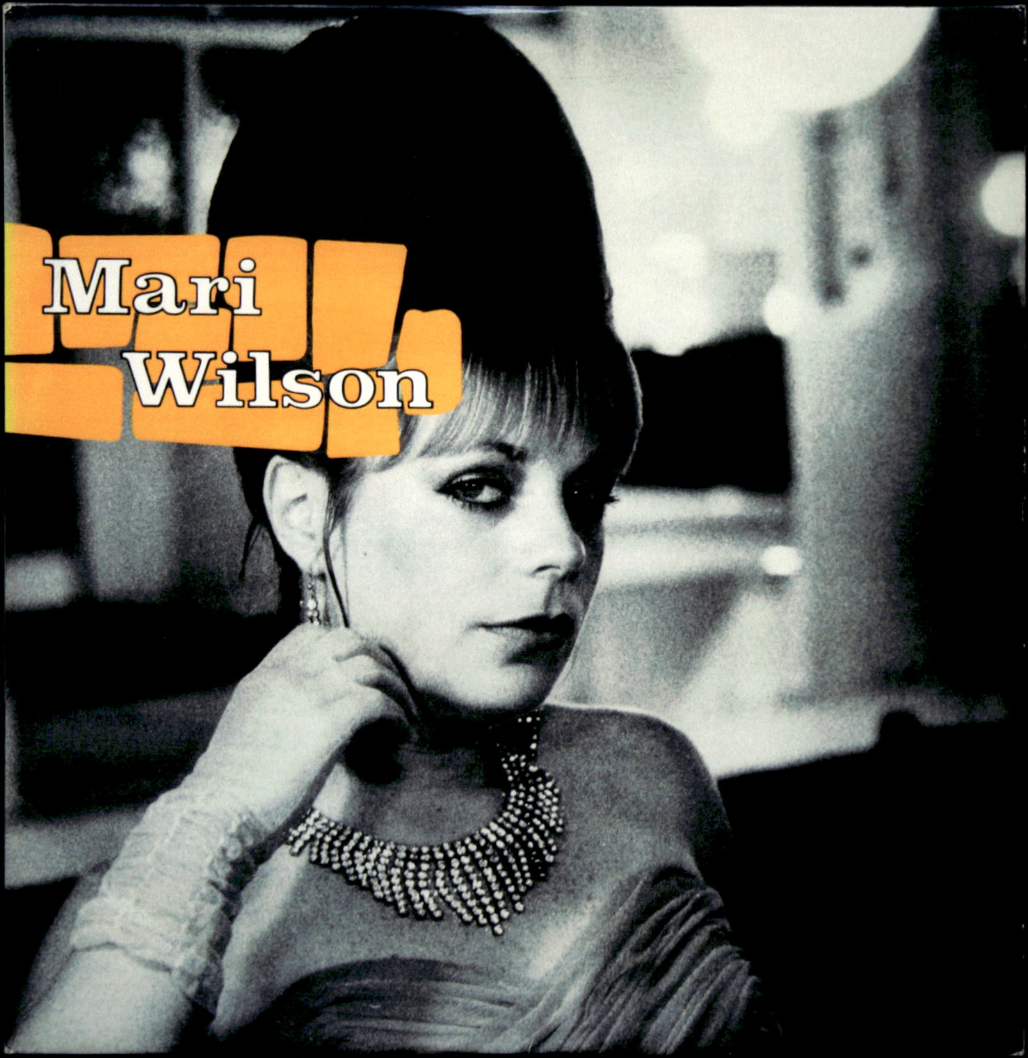

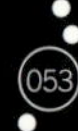

(053) Artist **Mari Wilson with the Wilsations** Title **Beware Boyfriend** Photography **Anton Corbijn**
Record Label **Compact Listeners** Date **1982**

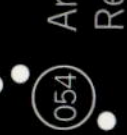

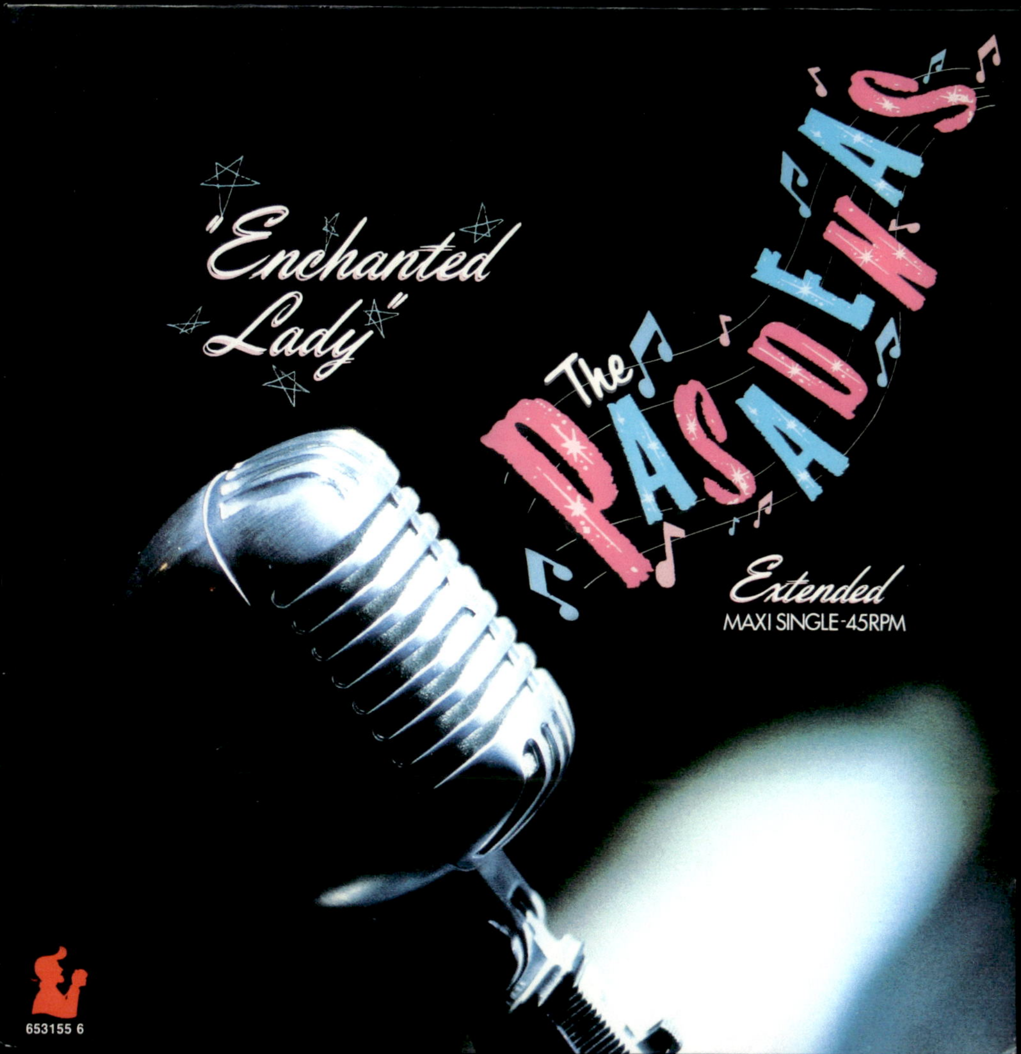

653155 6

"Enchanted Lady"

The PASADENAS

Extended
MAXI SINGLE-45RPM

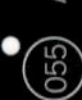

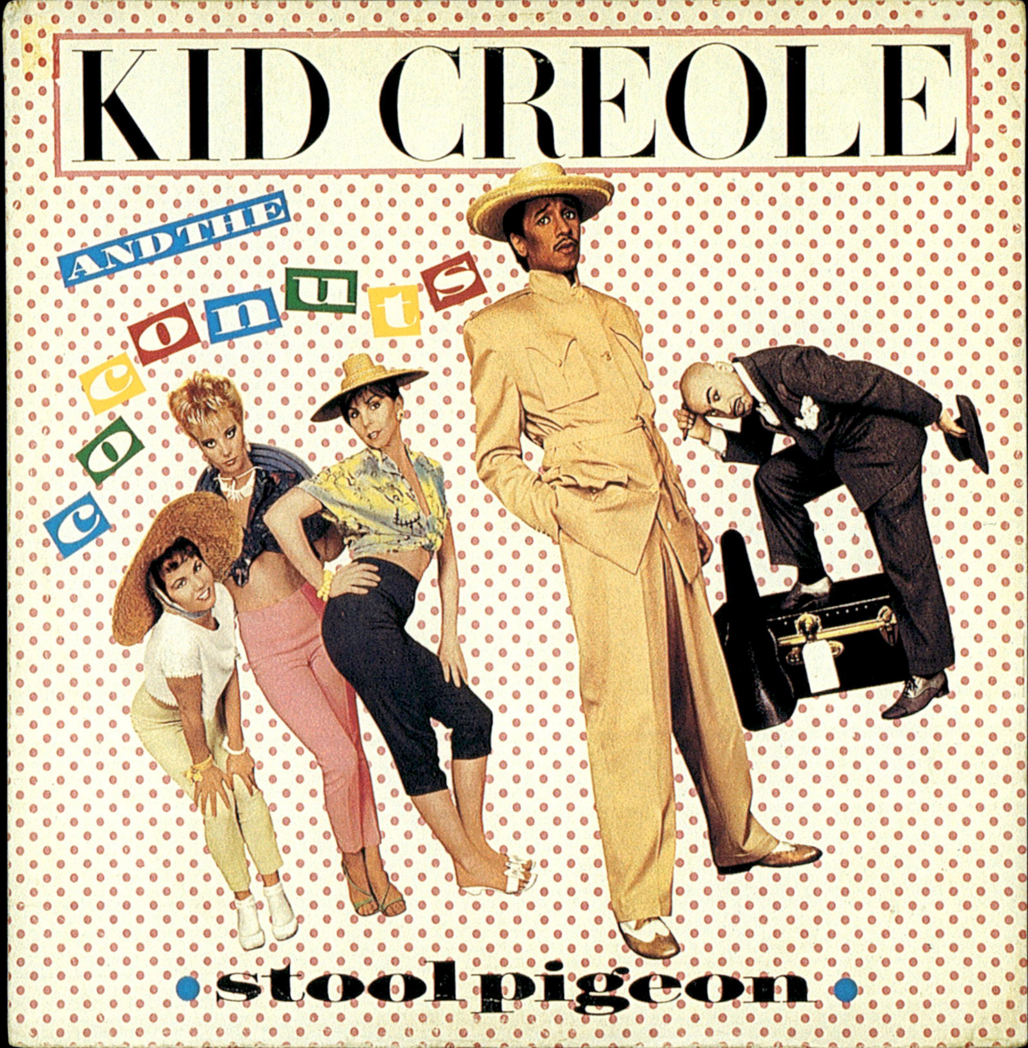

KID CREOLE
AND THE
COCONUTS
stool pigeon

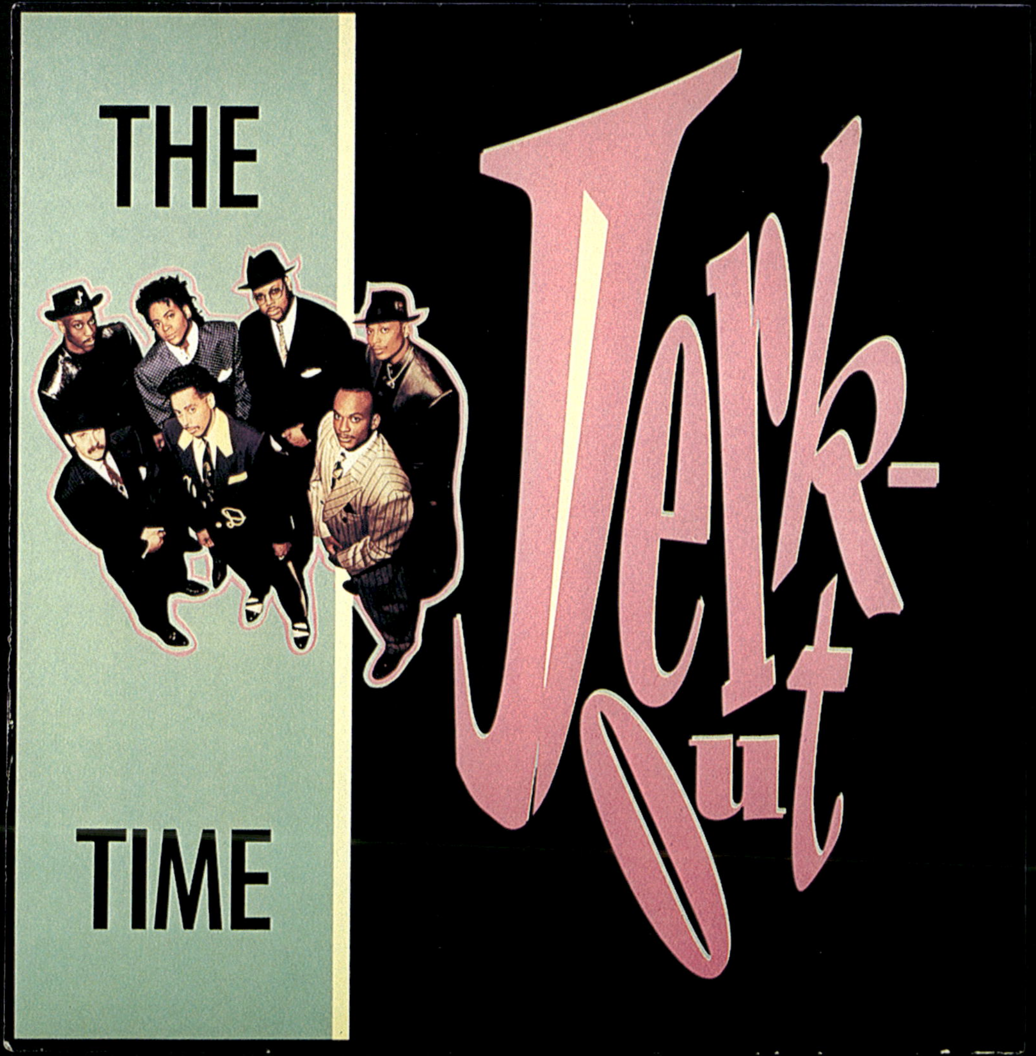

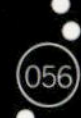

THE
TIME
Jerk-
Out

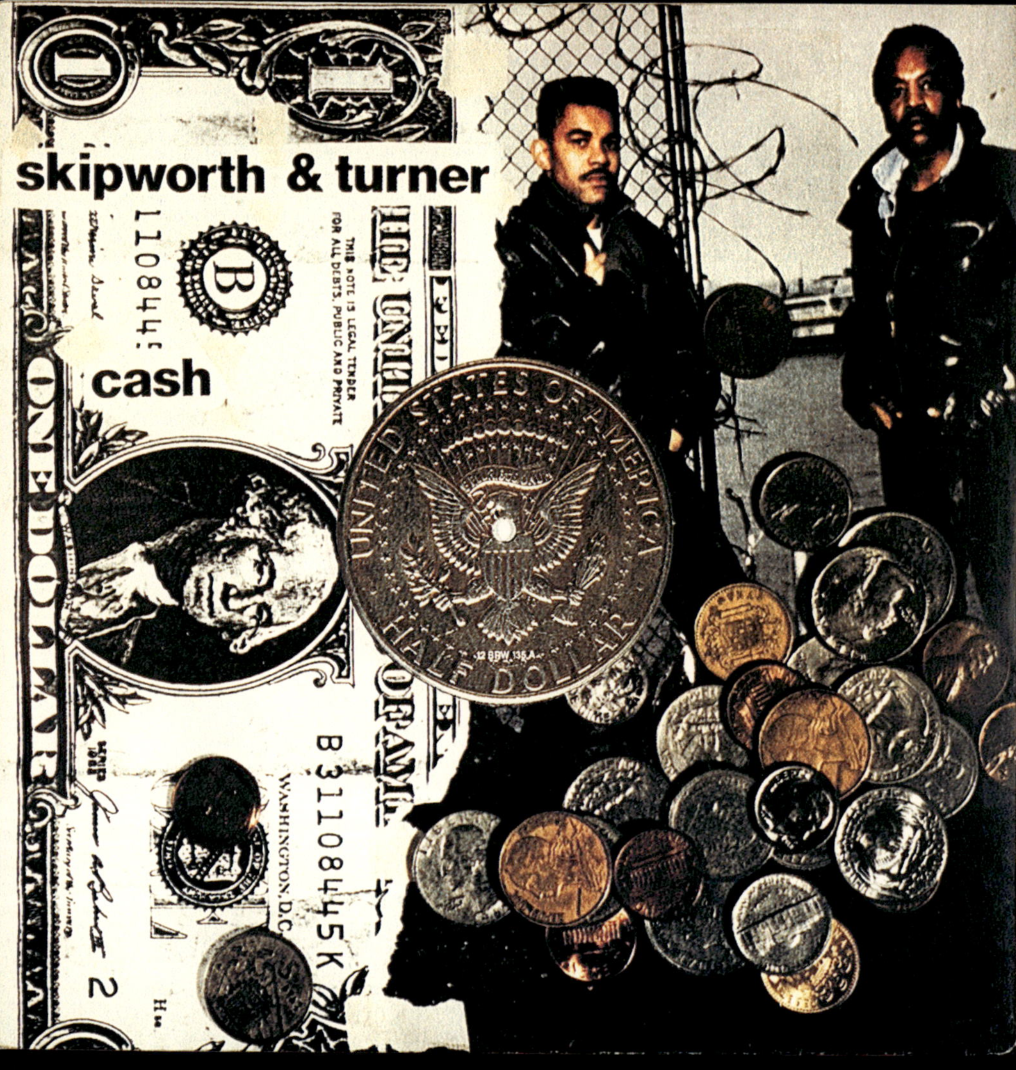

 Artist Skipworth and Turner Title Cash Record Label Island Recods Date 1989

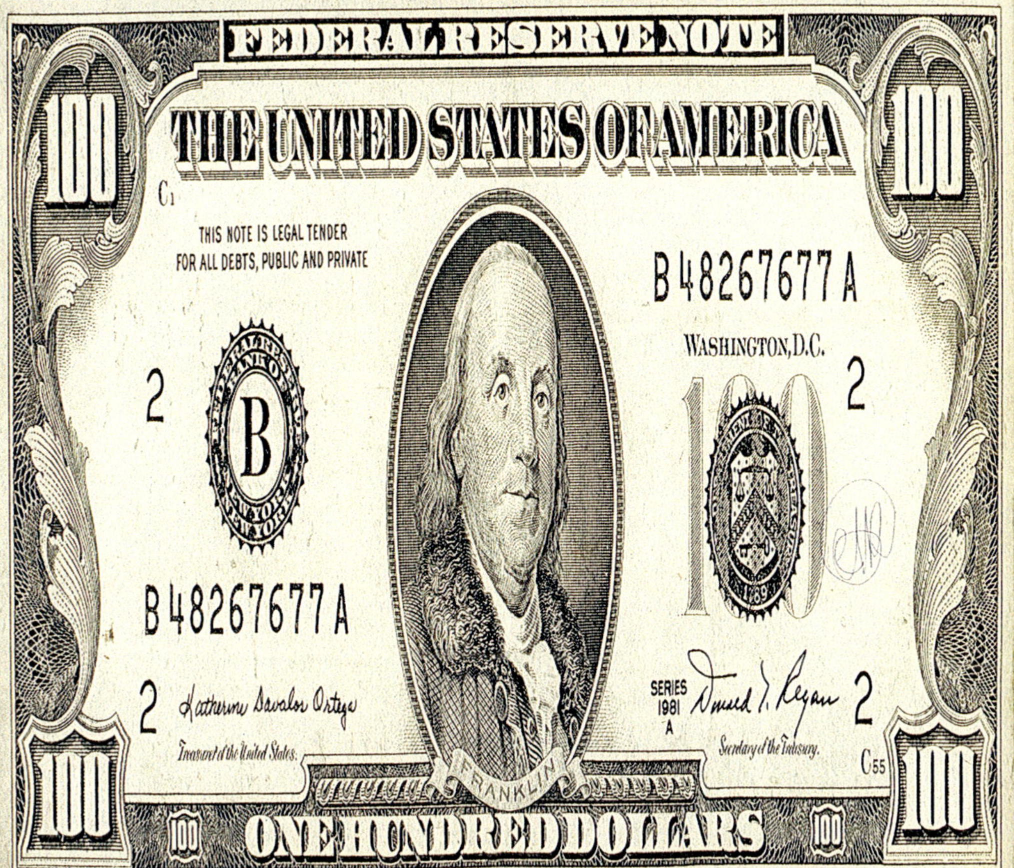

ERIC B. & RAKIM "PAID IN FULL"
(SEVEN MINUTES OF MADNESS —
THE COLDCUT REMIX)
FEDERAL RESERVE NOTE
THE UNITED STATES OF AMERICA
100
100
THIS NOTE IS LEGAL TENDER
FOR ALL DEBTS, PUBLIC AND PRIVATE
B 48267677 A
WASHINGTON, D.C.
2
B
2
100
B 48267677 A
2
Katherine Davalos Ortega
Treasurer of the United States.
SERIES
1981
A
Donald T. Regan
Secretary of the Treasury.
2
FRANKLIN
ONE HUNDRED DOLLARS
100
100
ERIC B. & RAKIM "PAID IN FULL"   ERIC B. & RAKIM "PAID IN FULL"   ERIC B. & RAKIM "PAID IN FULL" ERIC B. & R

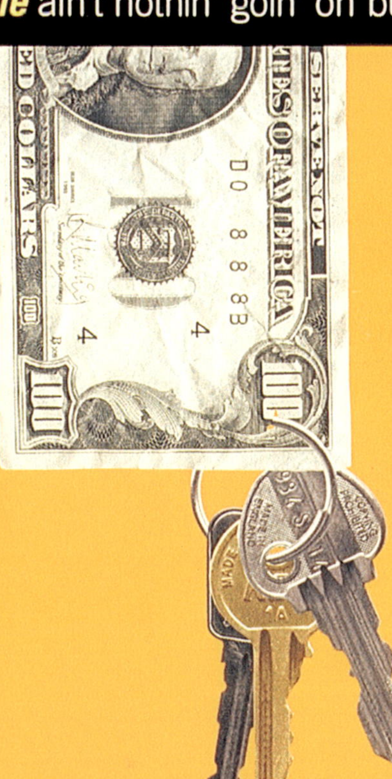
1993 remix
gwen guthrie ain't nothin' goin' on but the rent

THE ADVENTURES OF
STEVIE V.
FEATURING NAZLYN
DIRTY CA$H

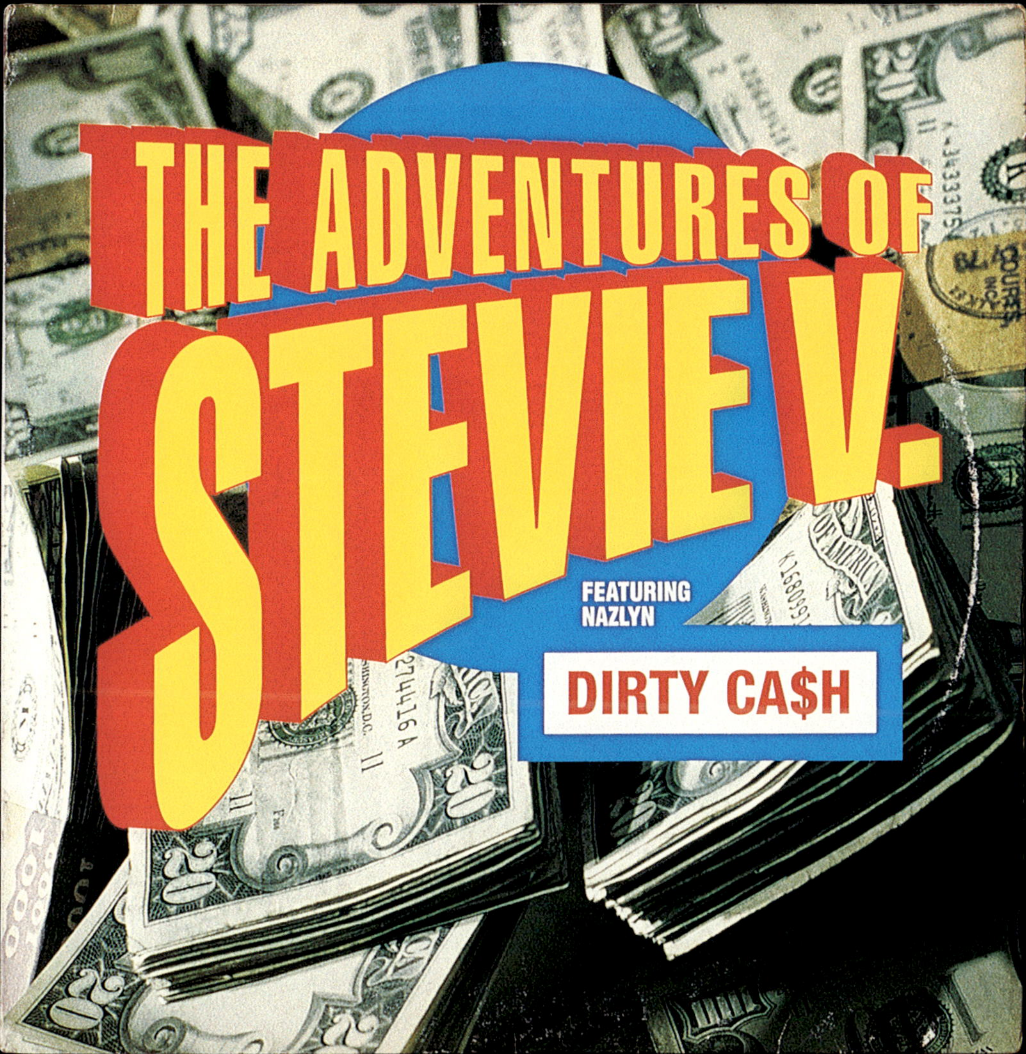

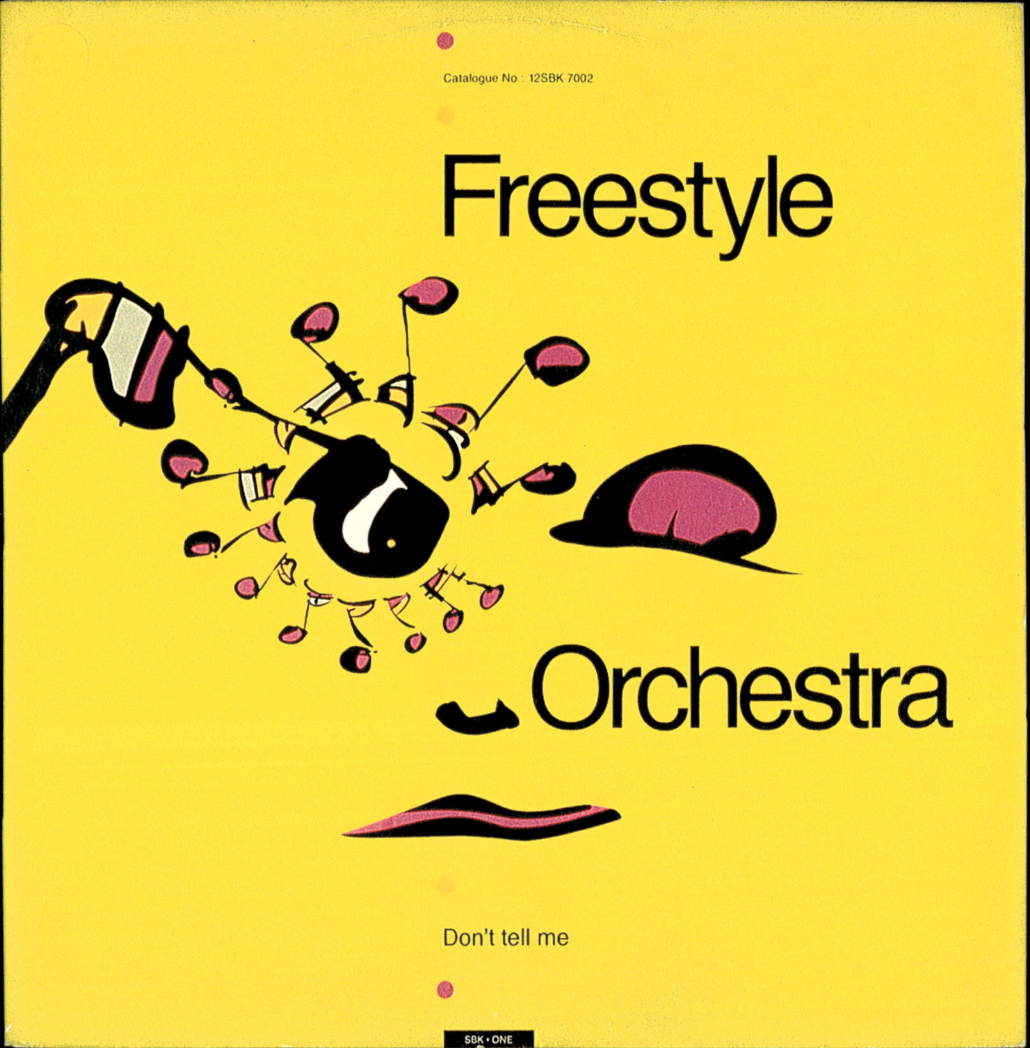

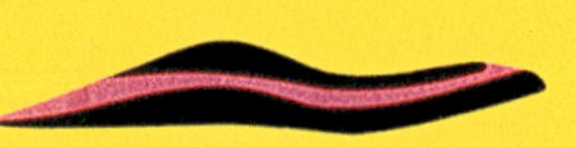

Catalogue No.: 12SBK 7002

Freestyle

Orchestra

Don't tell me

SBK • ONE

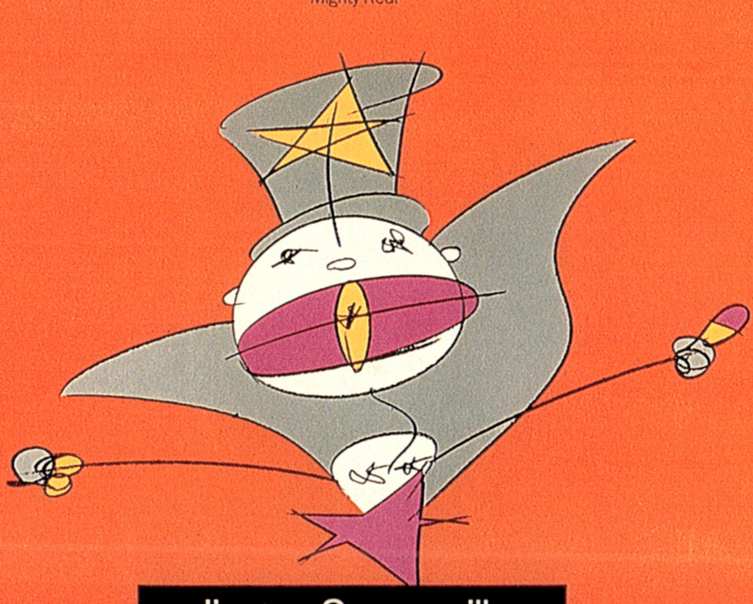
Mighty Real
Jimmy Somerville

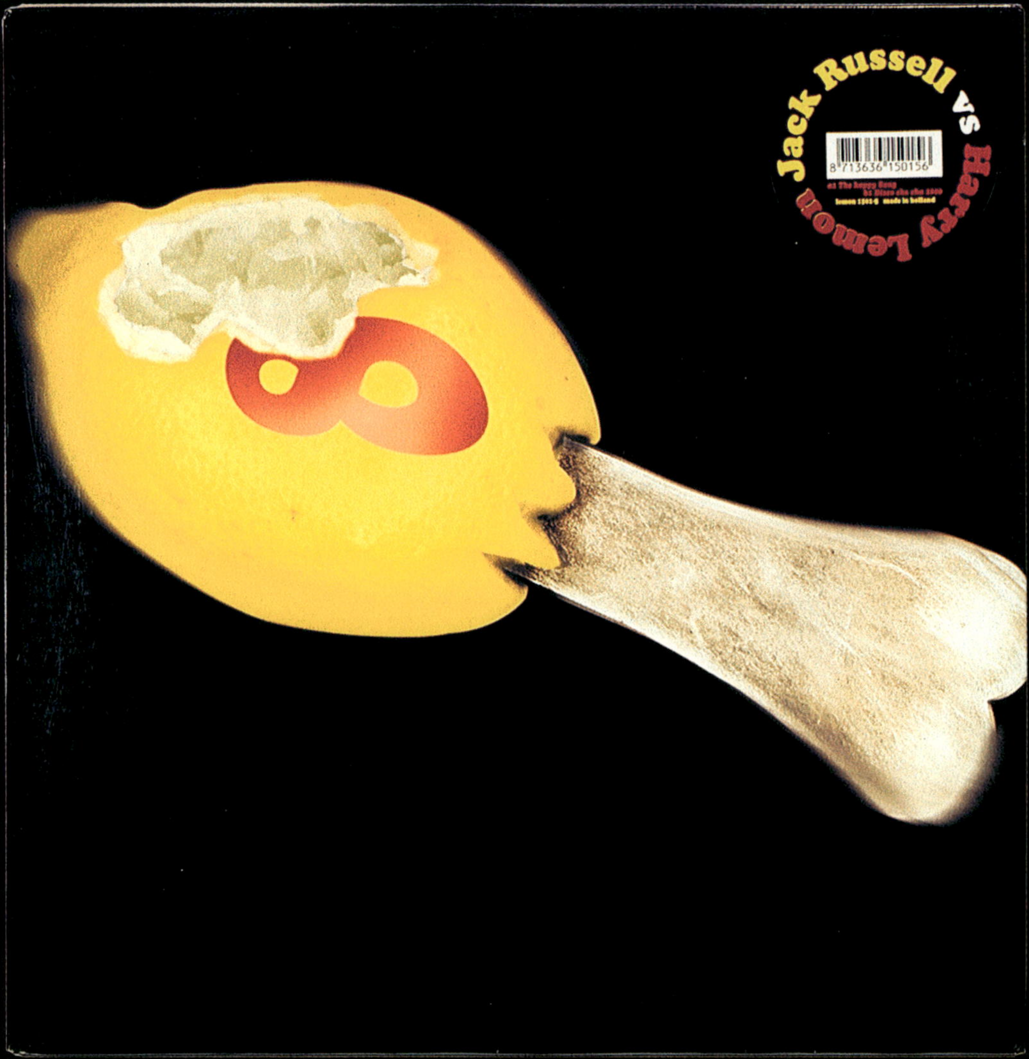

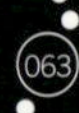

Artist Jack Russell vs Harry Lemon Title The Happy Song Record Label Basic Beat Date 1999

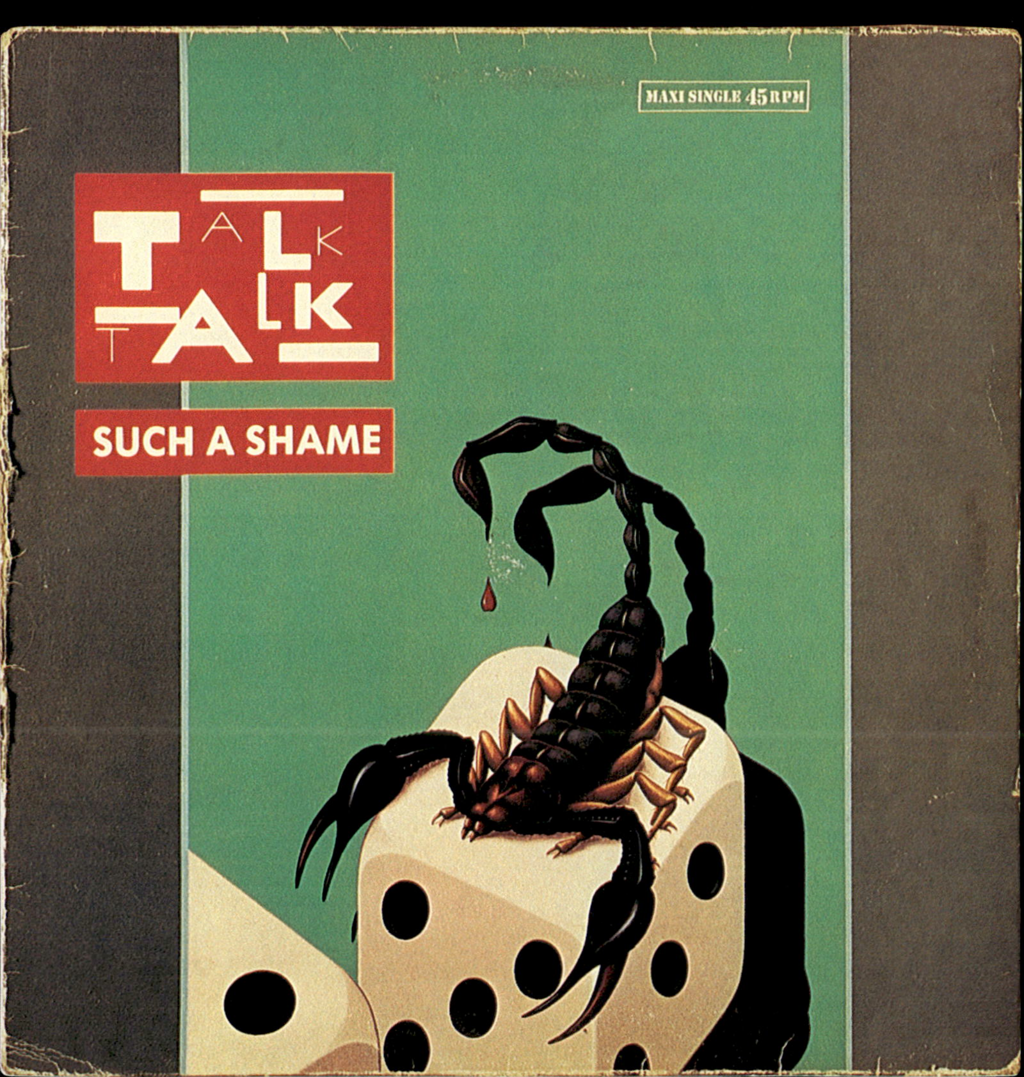
MAXI SINGLE 45 RPM
TALK
TALK
SUCH A SHAME

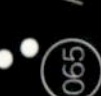

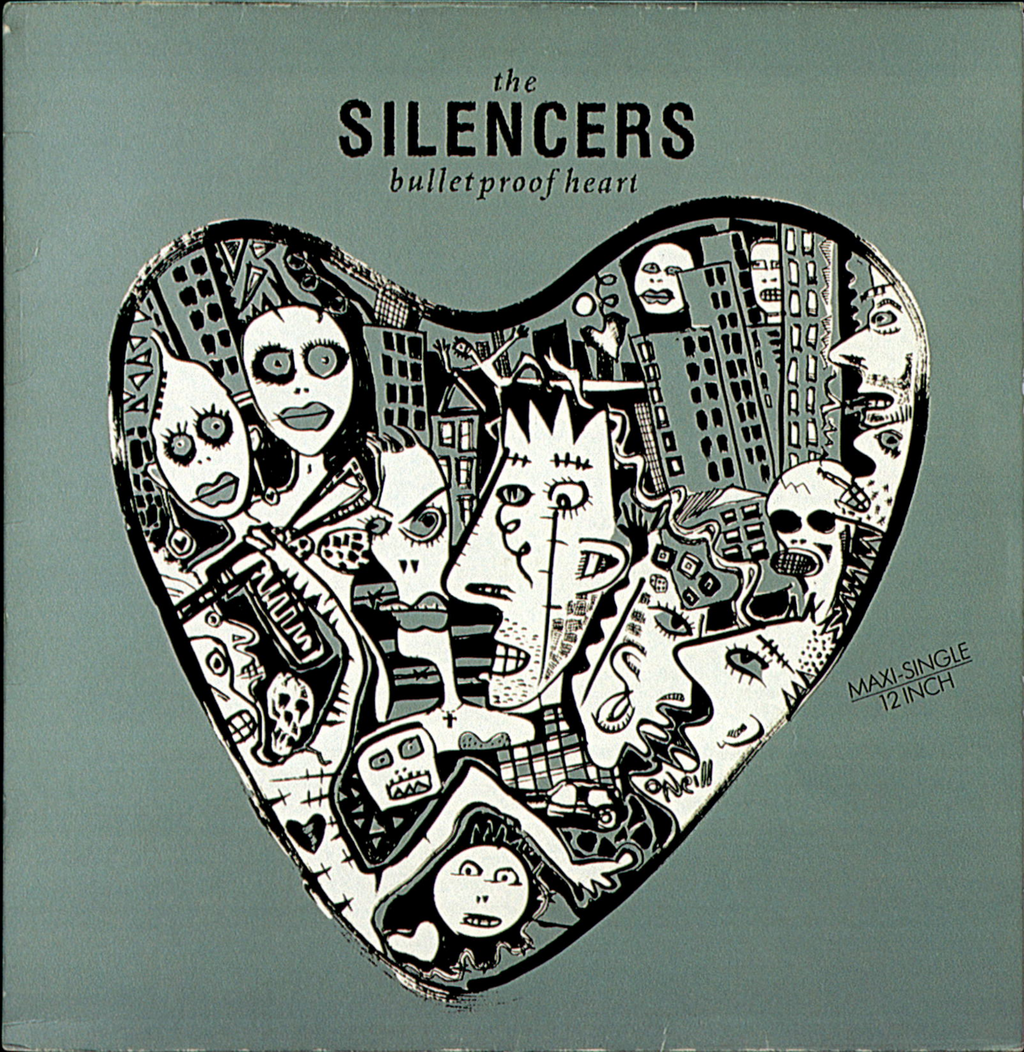

the SILENCERS
bulletproof heart

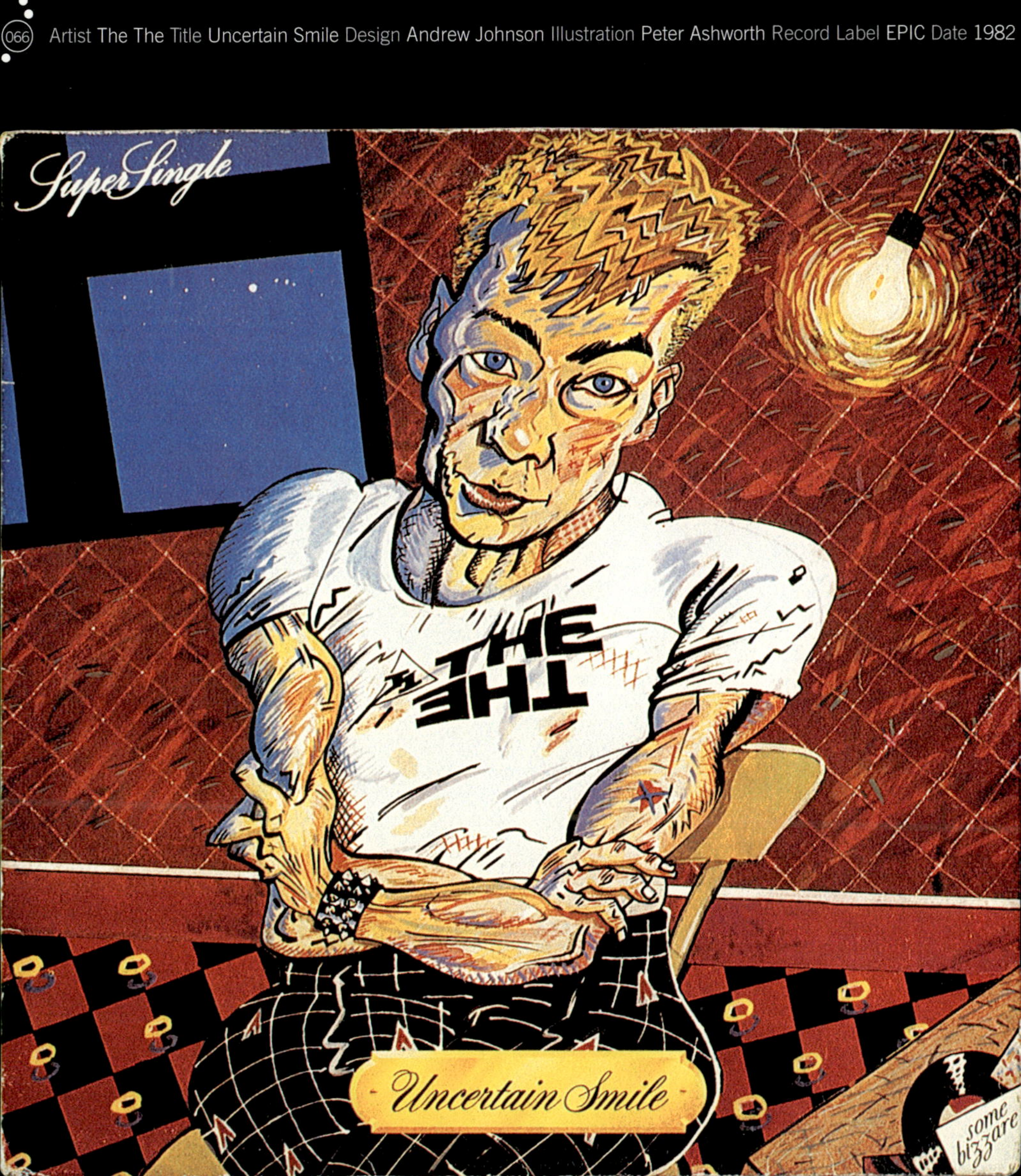
Super Single
THE
THE
Uncertain Smile
some bizzare

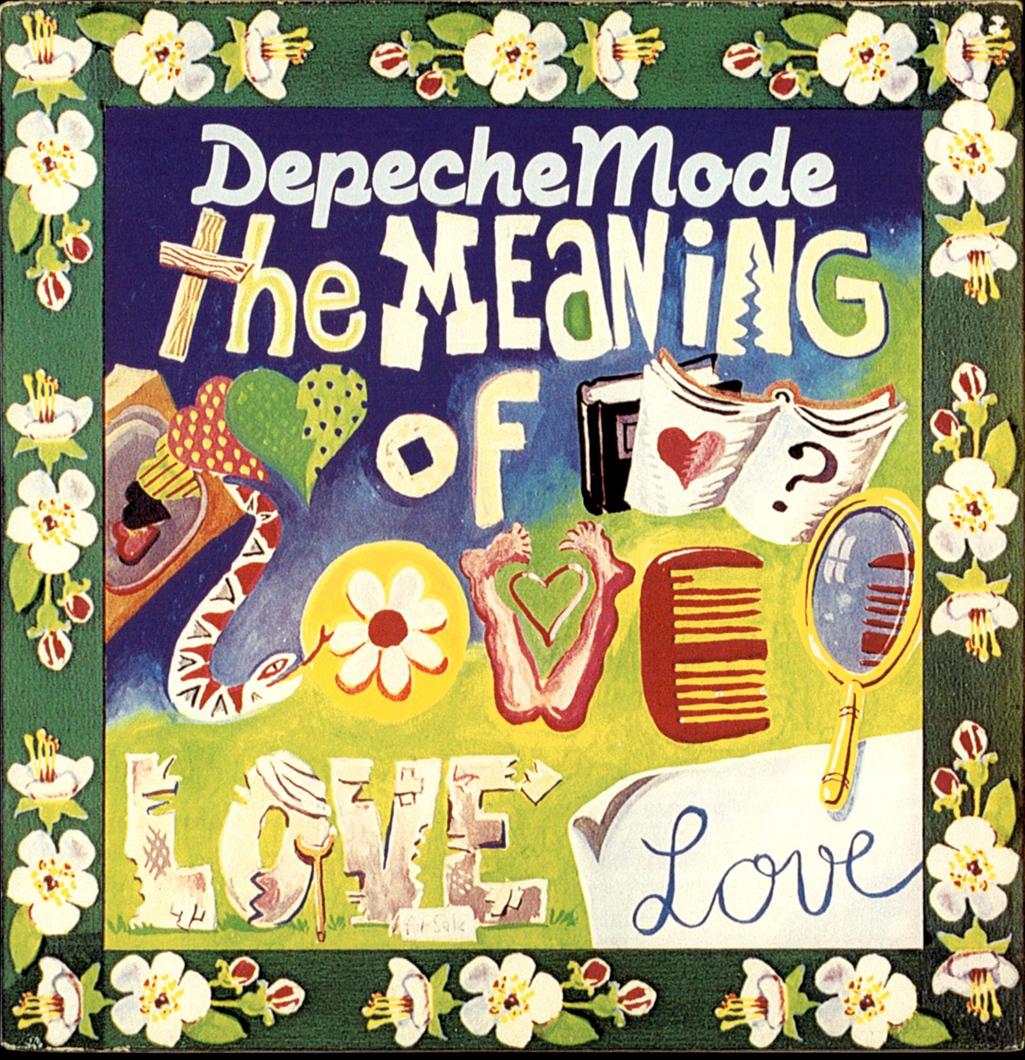

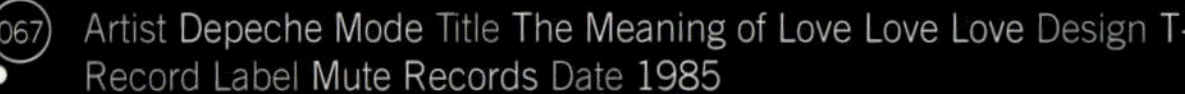

Artist Depeche Mode Title The Meaning of Love Love Love Design T+CP Illustration Tamara Capellaro
Record Label Mute Records Date 1985

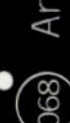

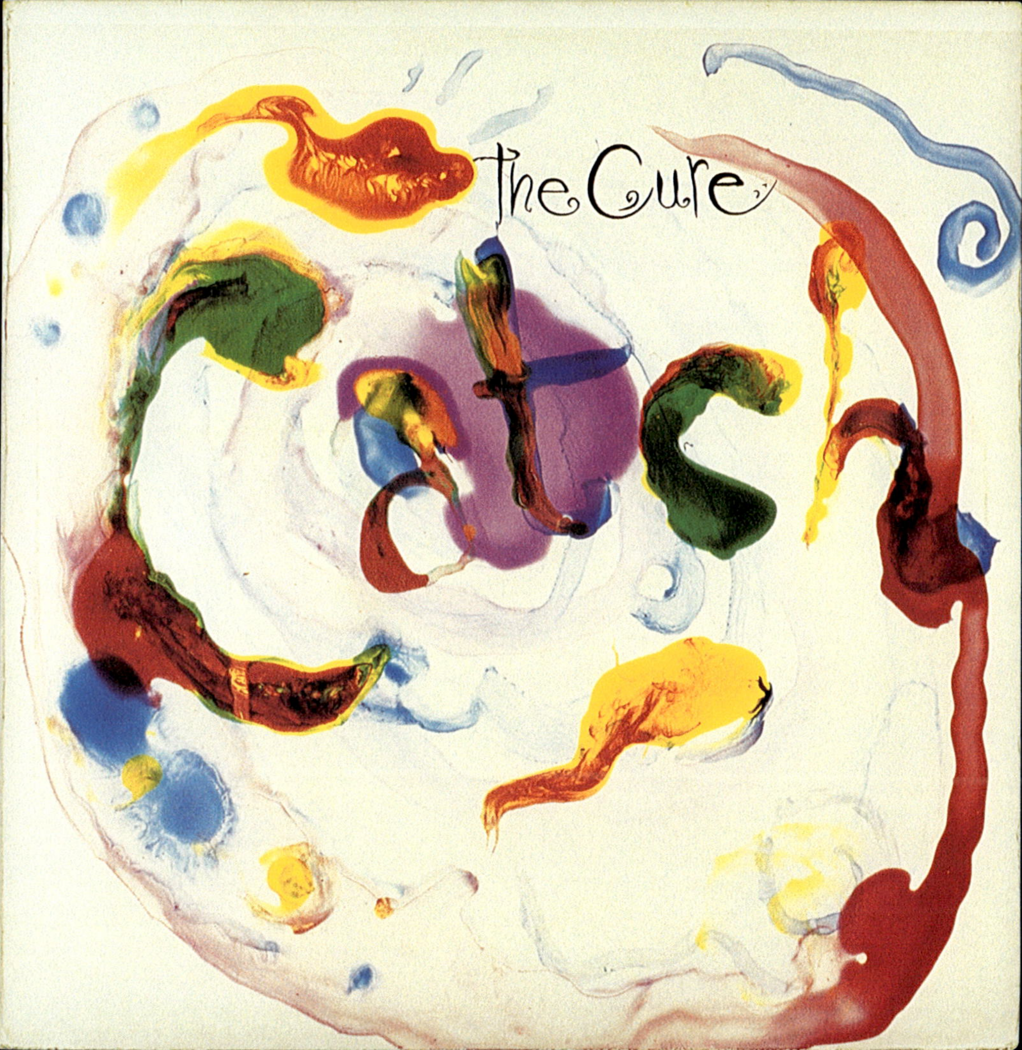

The Cure

Catch

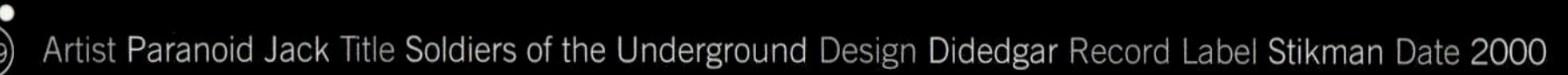
paranoid jack
Soldiers of the Underground

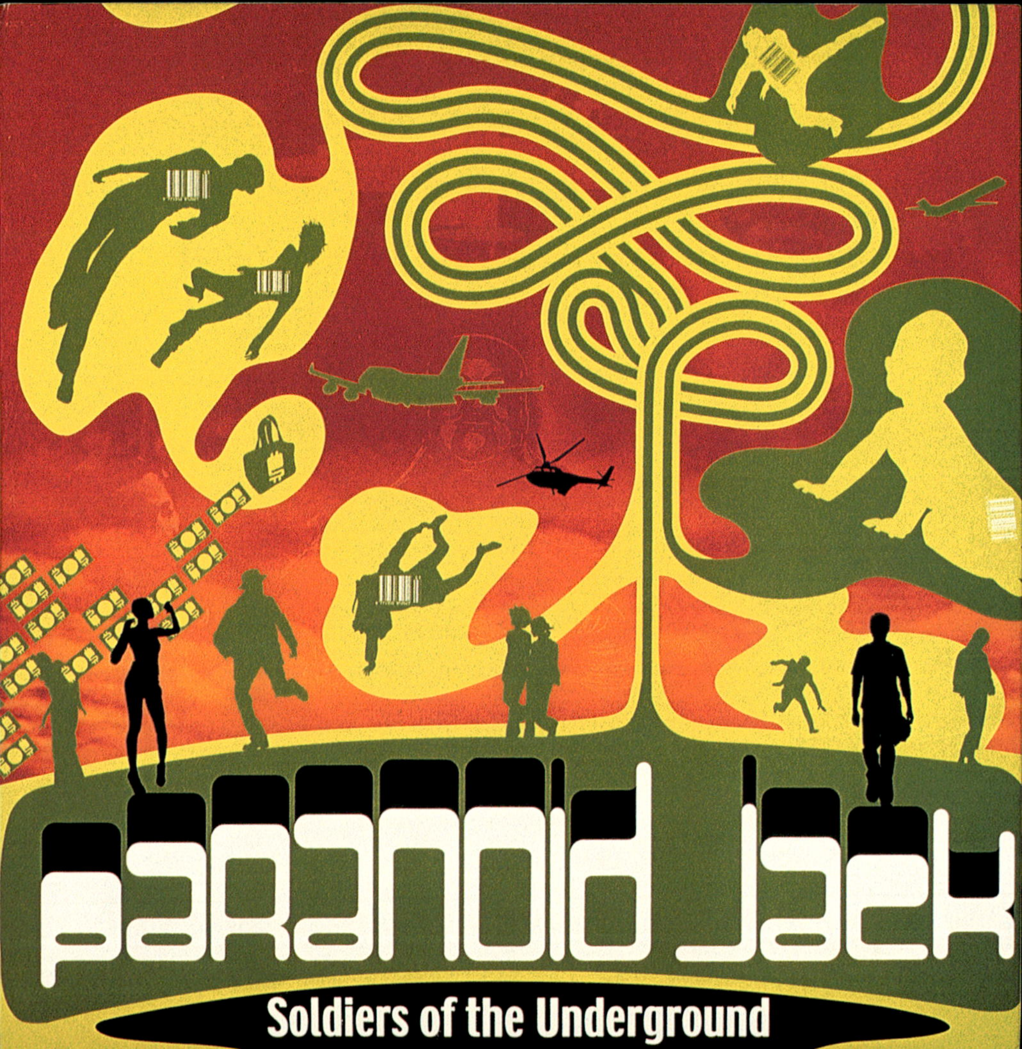

walk out to winter
aztec camera

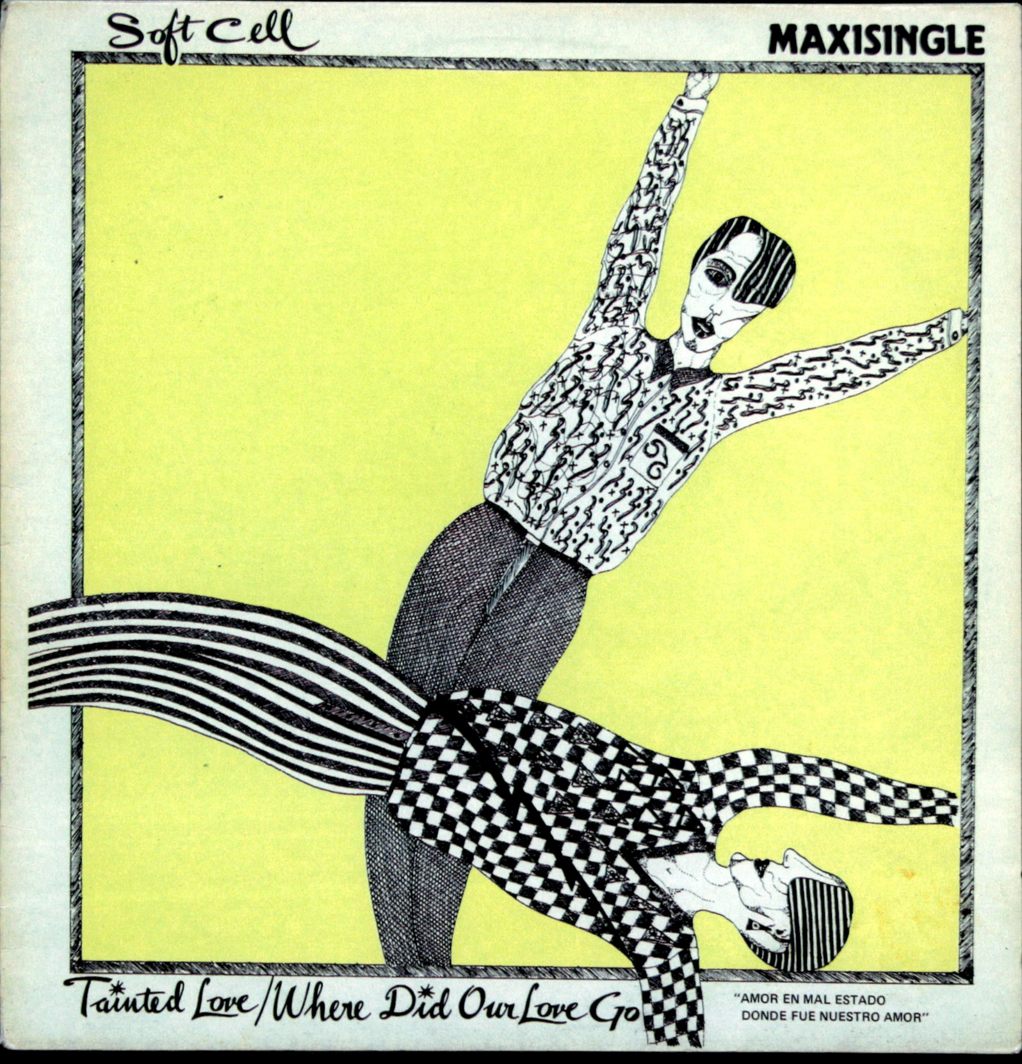

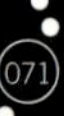
SOFT CELL
MAXISINGLE
Tainted Love / Where Did Our Love Go
"AMOR EN MAL ESTADO
DONDE FUE NUESTRO AMOR"

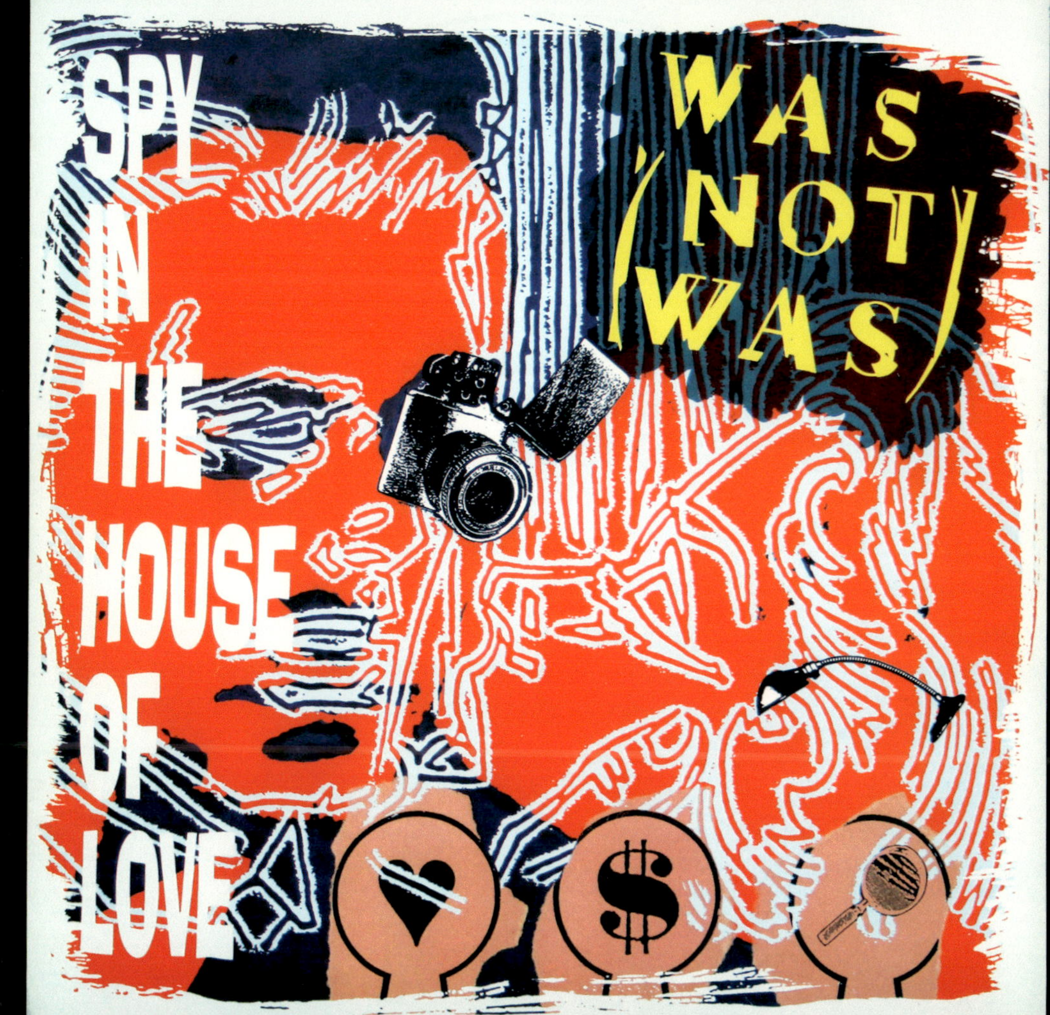
SPY
IN
THE
HOUSE
OF
LOVE
WAS
(NOT)
WAS

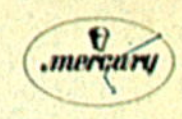

Da da da I don't love you
You don't love me aha aha aha
Ja Ja Ja
Sabine Sabine Sabine

TRIO

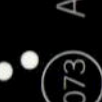

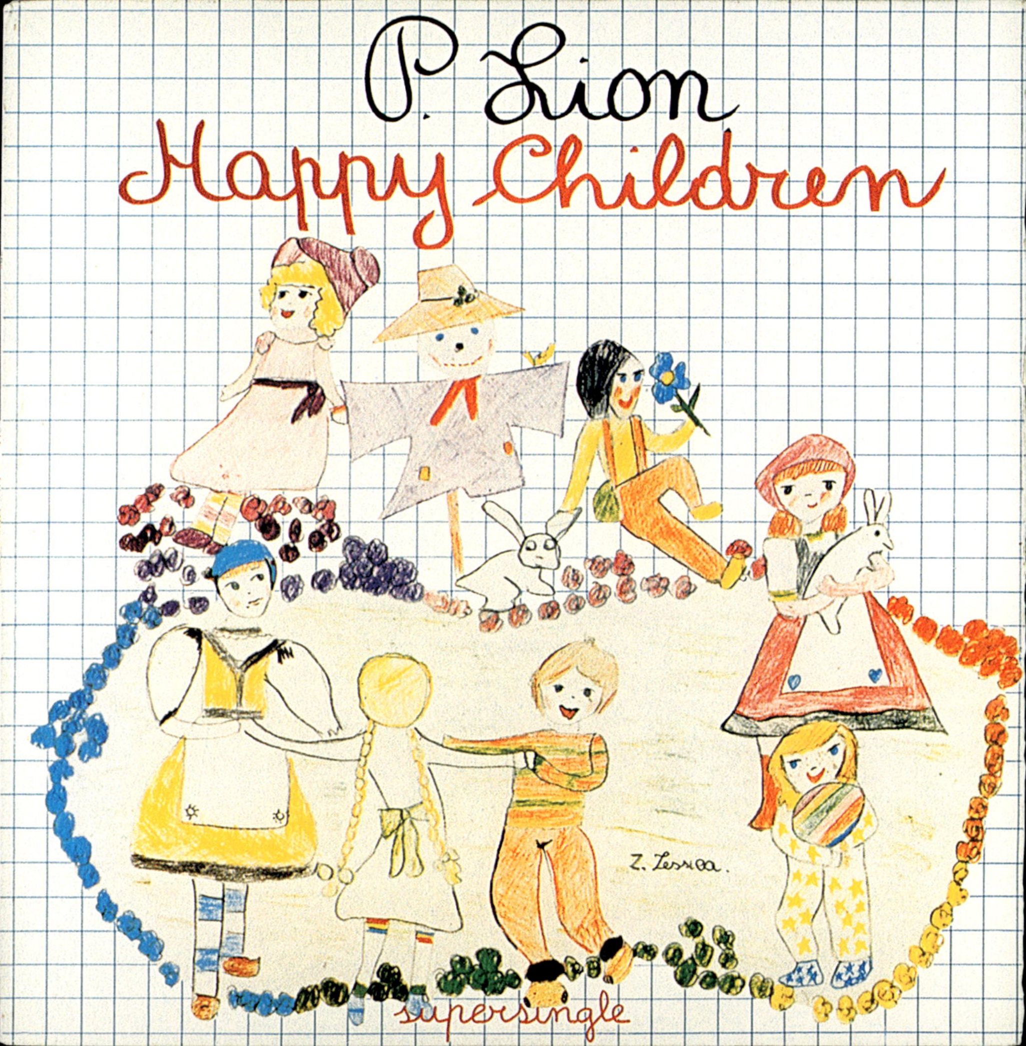
P. Lion
Happy Children
Z. Lessoa.
supersingle

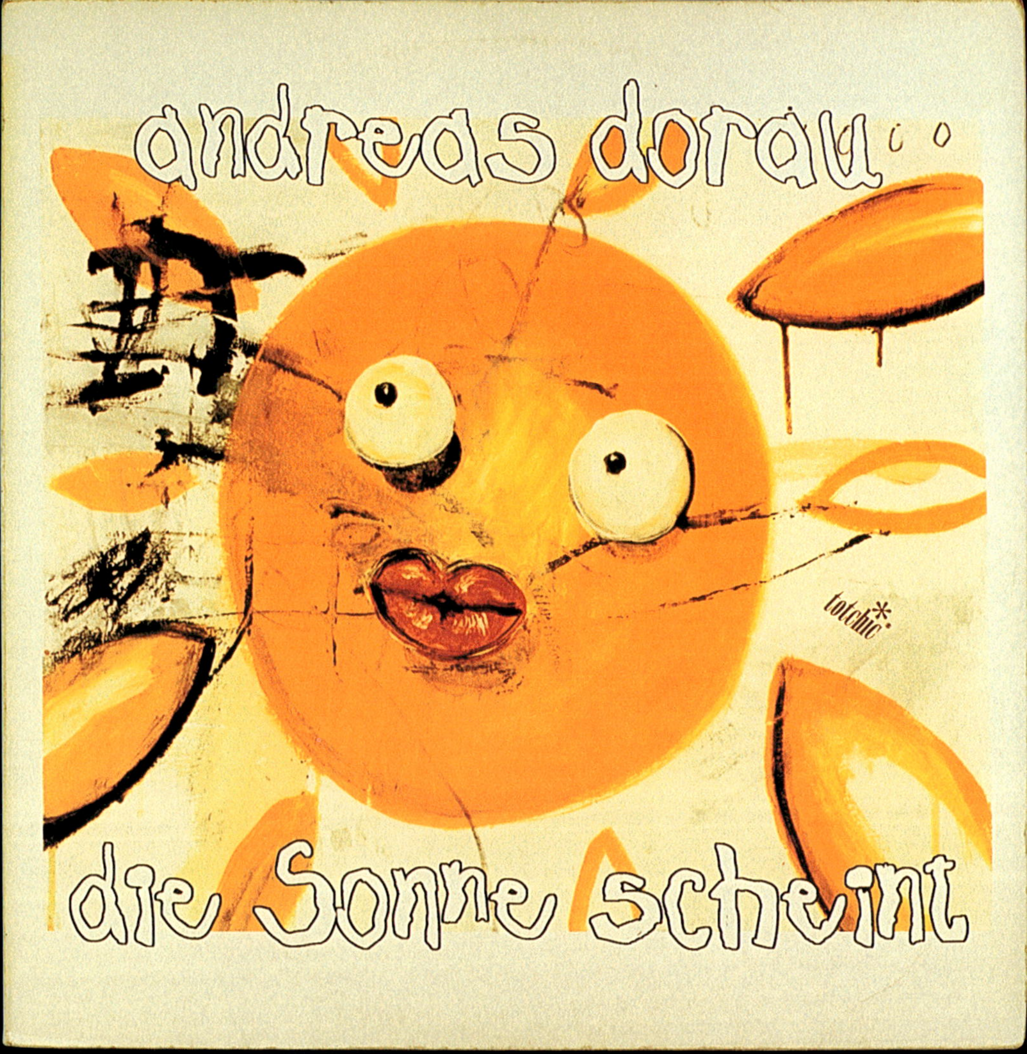

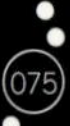

andreas dorau
die Sonne scheint

The TOM TOM Club
MAXI-SINGLE 45 r.p.m.
THE MAN WITH THE 4 WAY HIPS

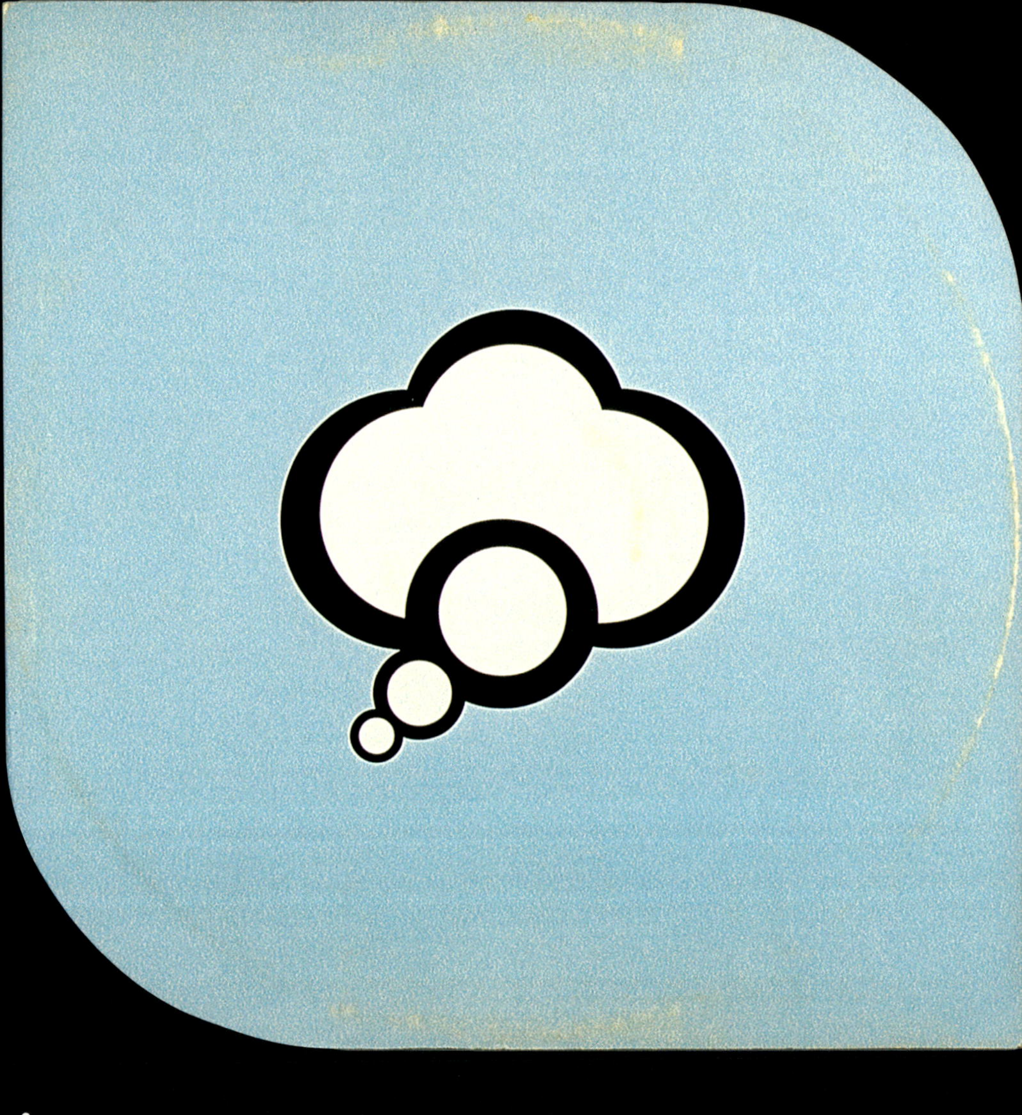

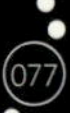

  Artist Garbage Title When I Grow Up Record Label Mushroom Date 1998

Artist Moby Title Why Does My Heart Feel So Bad? Design Ysabel Knyphausen, Slim Smith
Record Label Mute Records Date 1999

MOBY WHY DOES MY HEART FEEL SO BAD?

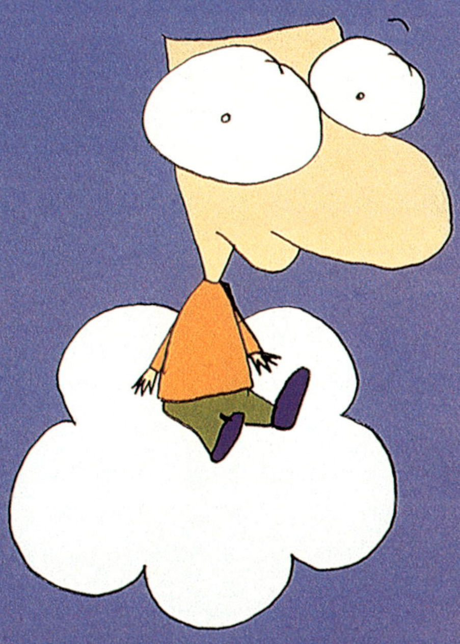

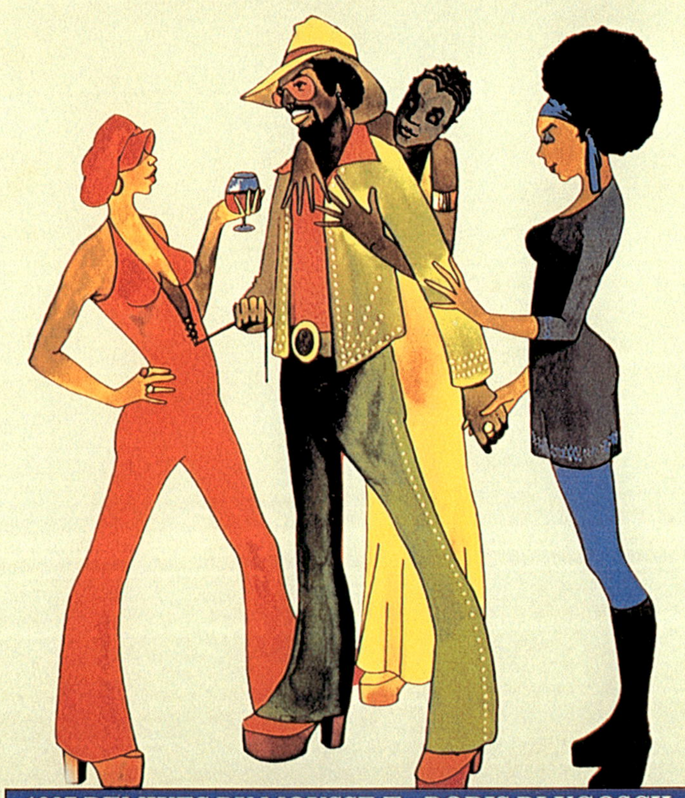
First Choice
The Player (1997 New Remixes)
1997 REMIXES BY MOUSSE T - BORIS DLUGOSCH

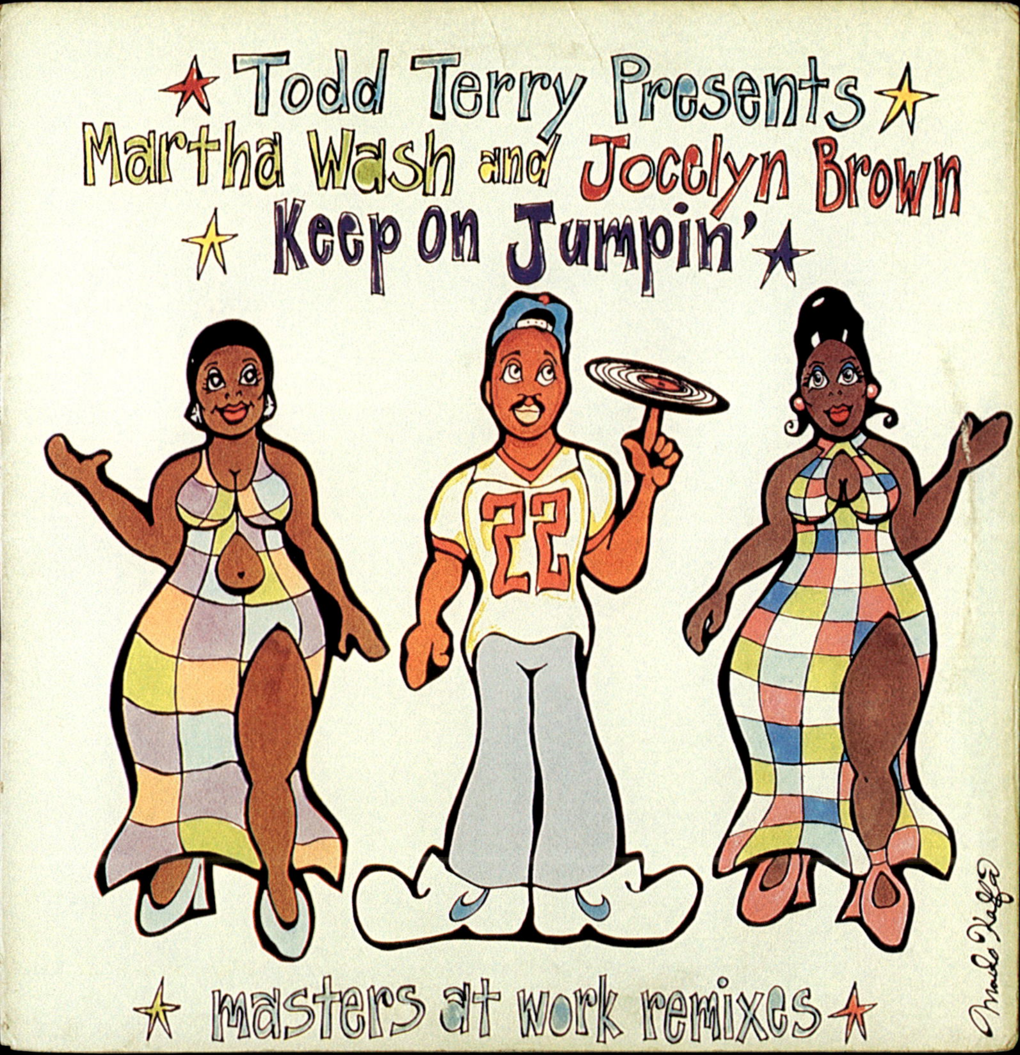

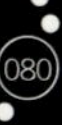

★ Todd Terry Presents ★
Martha Wash and Jocelyn Brown
★ Keep on Jumpin' ★
22
★ masters at work remixes ★

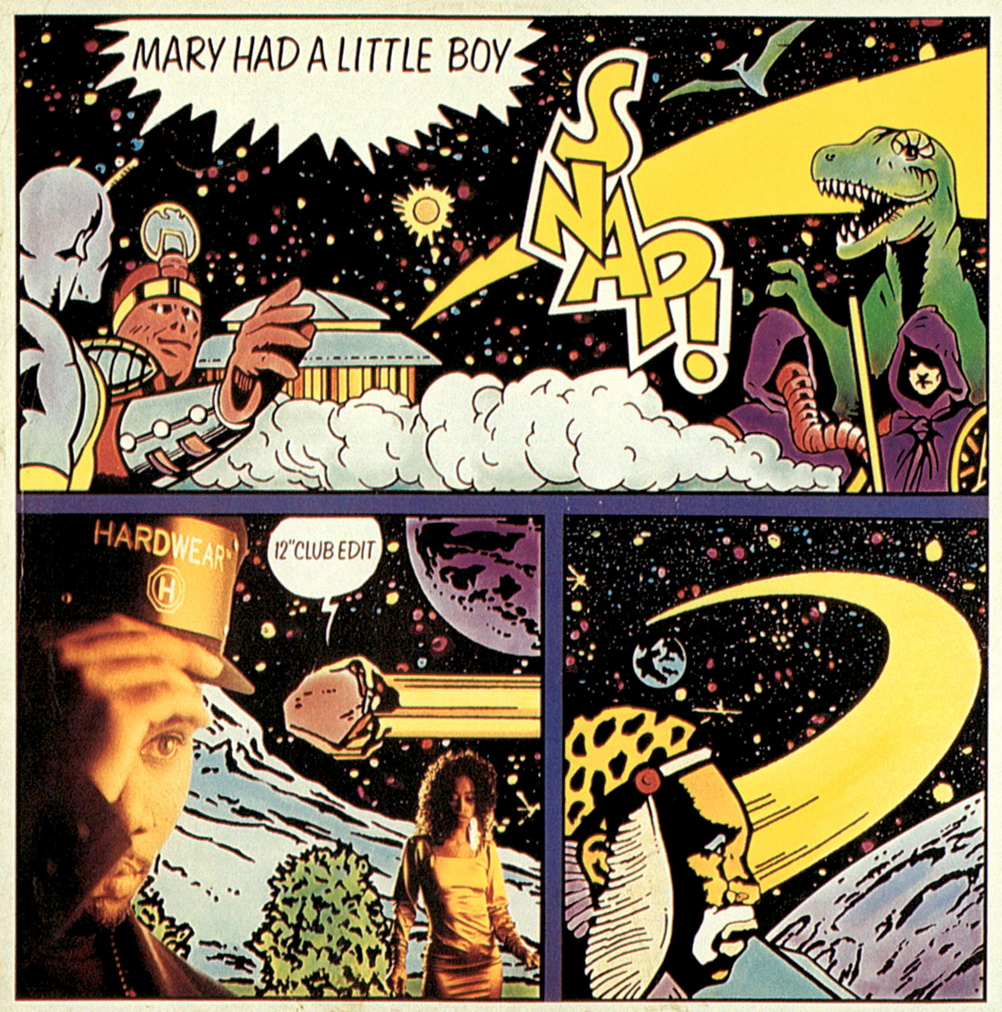

MARY HAD A LITTLE BOY
SNAP!
HARDWEAR
H
12"CLUB EDIT

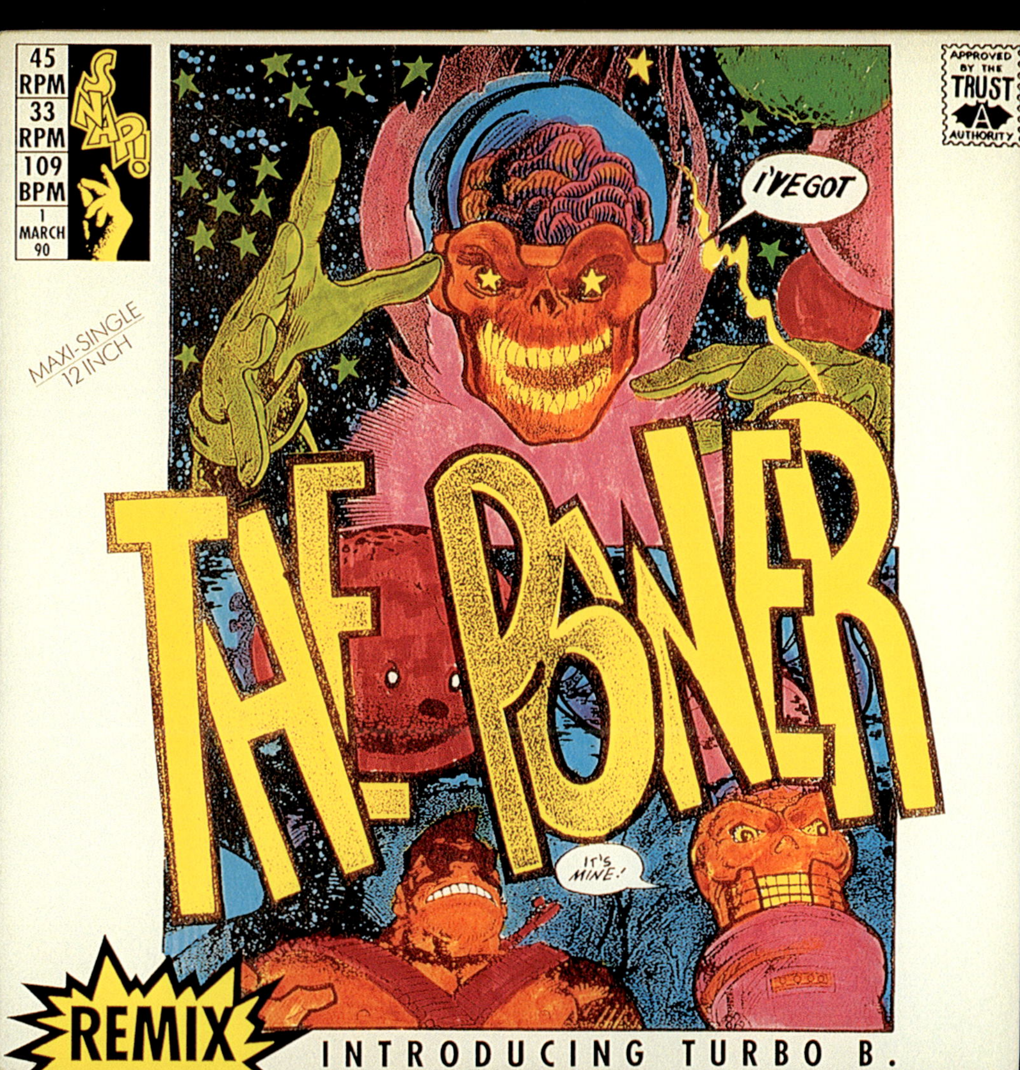
45 RPM
33 RPM
109 BPM
1 MARCH 90
SNAP!
MAXI-SINGLE 12 INCH
APPROVED BY THE TRUST AUTHORITY
I'VE GOT
THE POWER
IT'S MINE!
REMIX
INTRODUCING TURBO B.

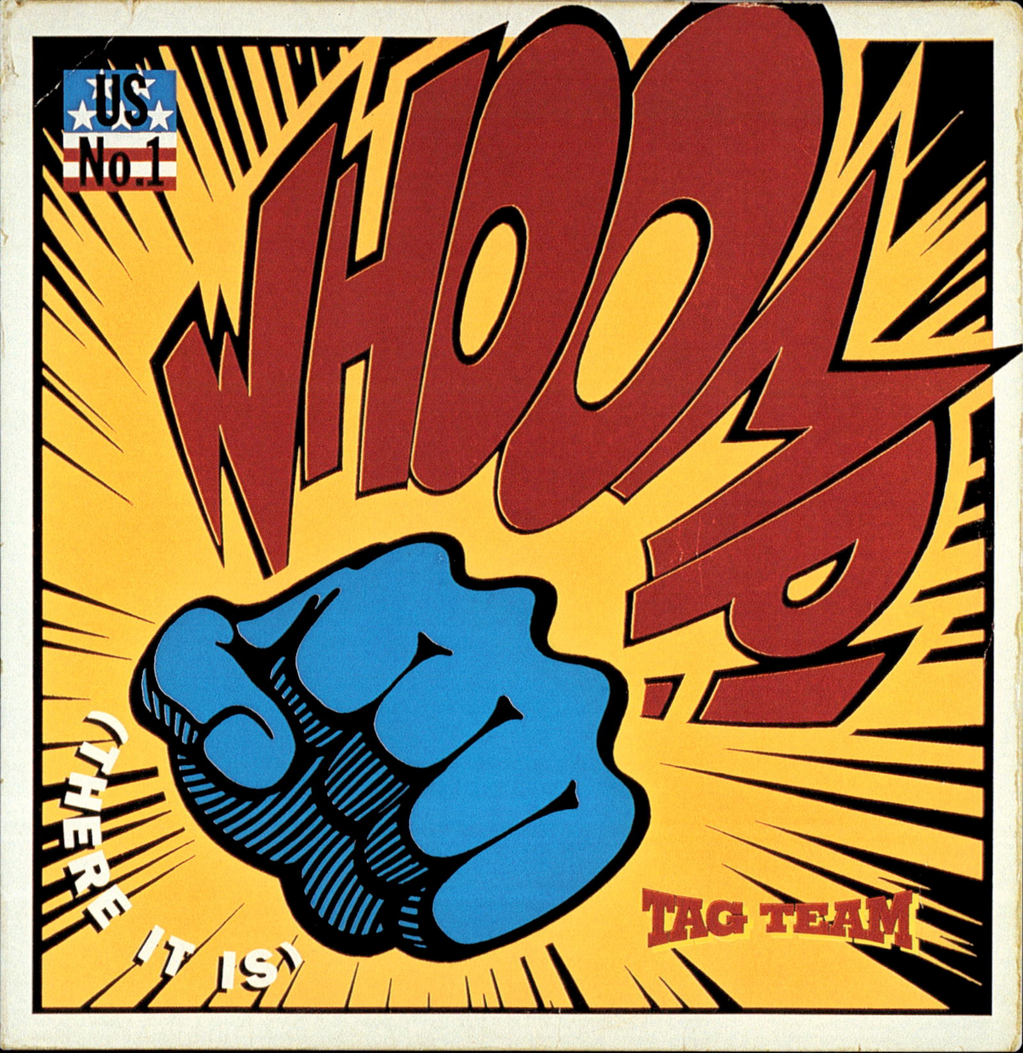

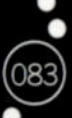

Artist Tag Team Title There It Is Design Gerhard Schröder Record Label Edel Date 1994

ROBBIE RIVERA PRES.
RHYTHM BANGERS
BANG
Artist Robbie Rivera Pres. Title Rhythm Bangers Record Label Vendetta Date 2000
084

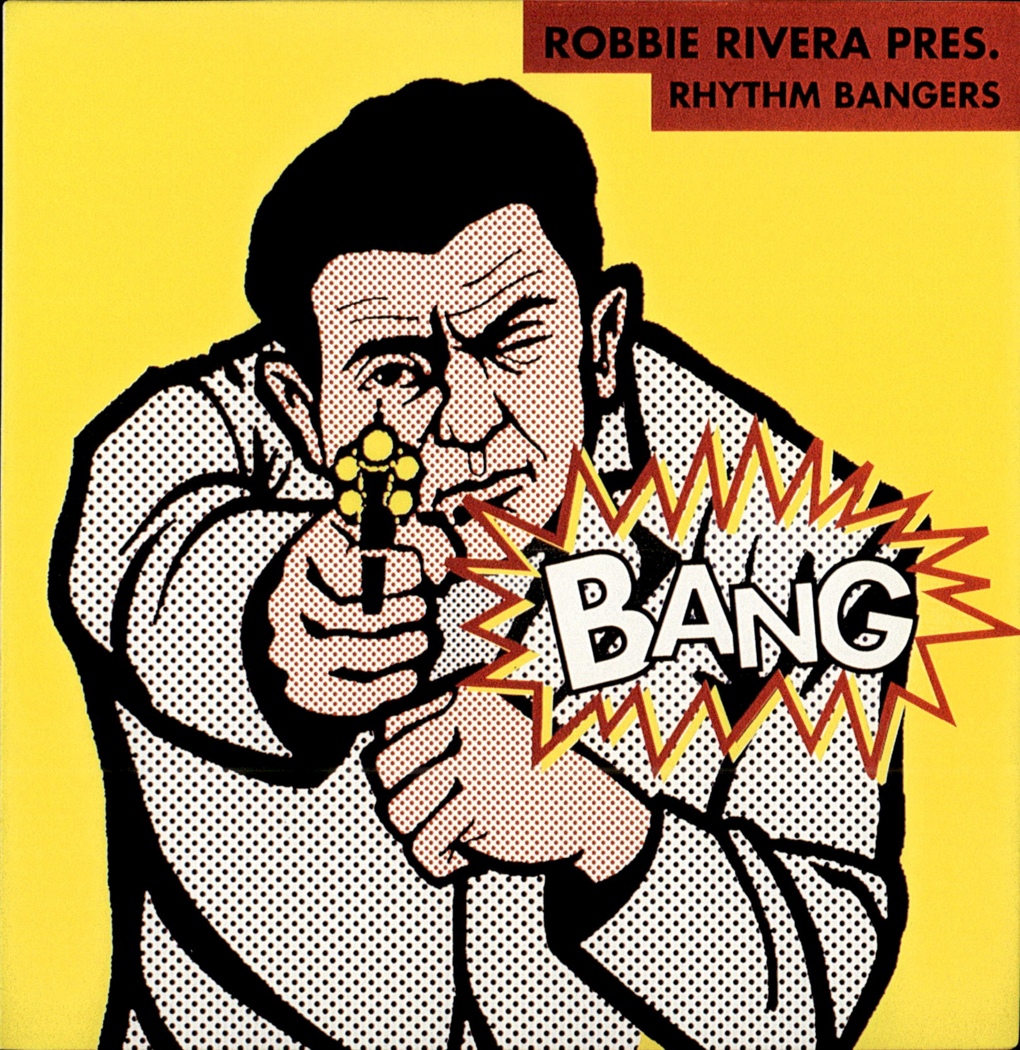

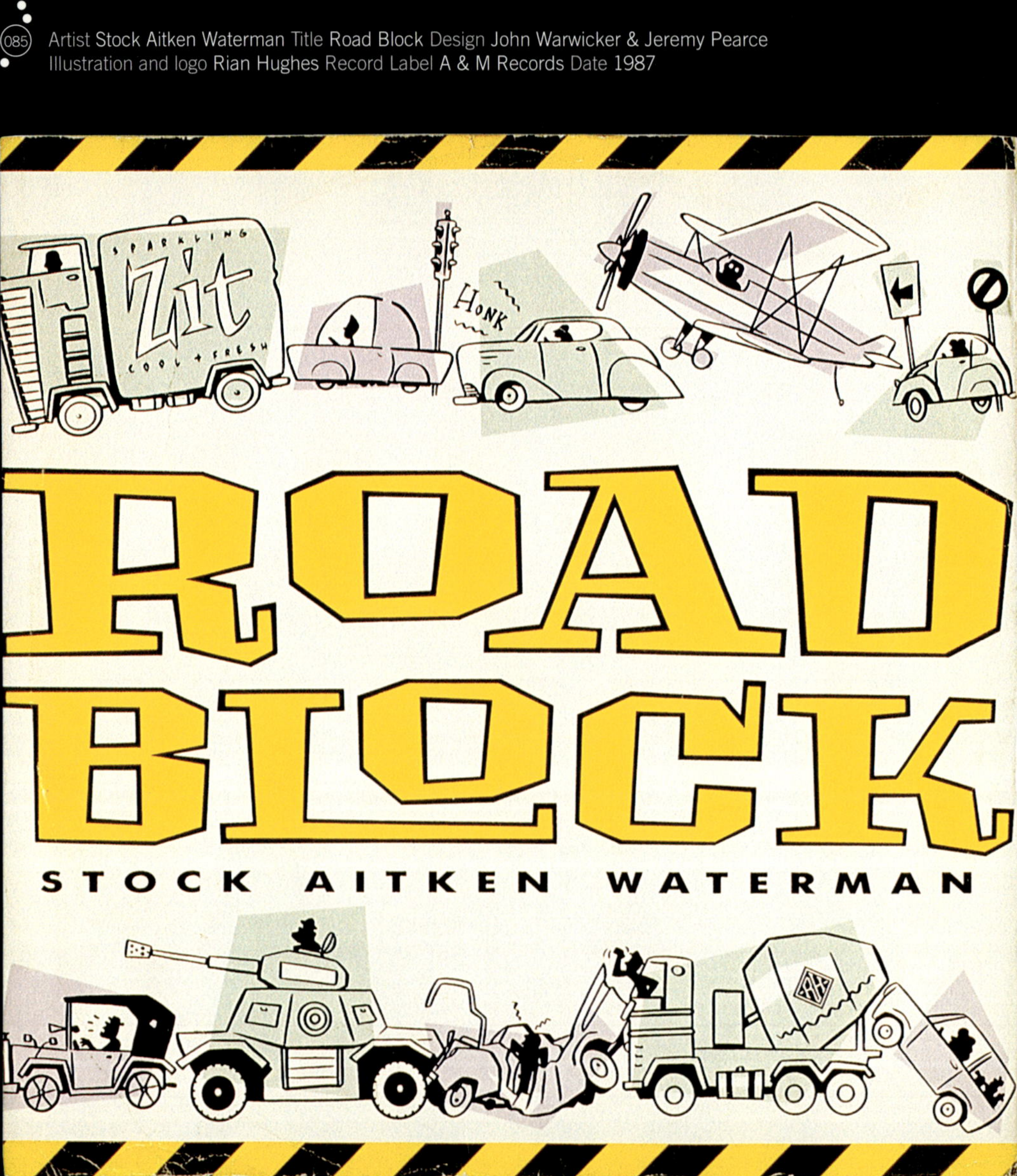

SPARKLING
Zit
COOL + FRESH
HoNK
ROAD
BLOCK
STOCK AITKEN WATERMAN

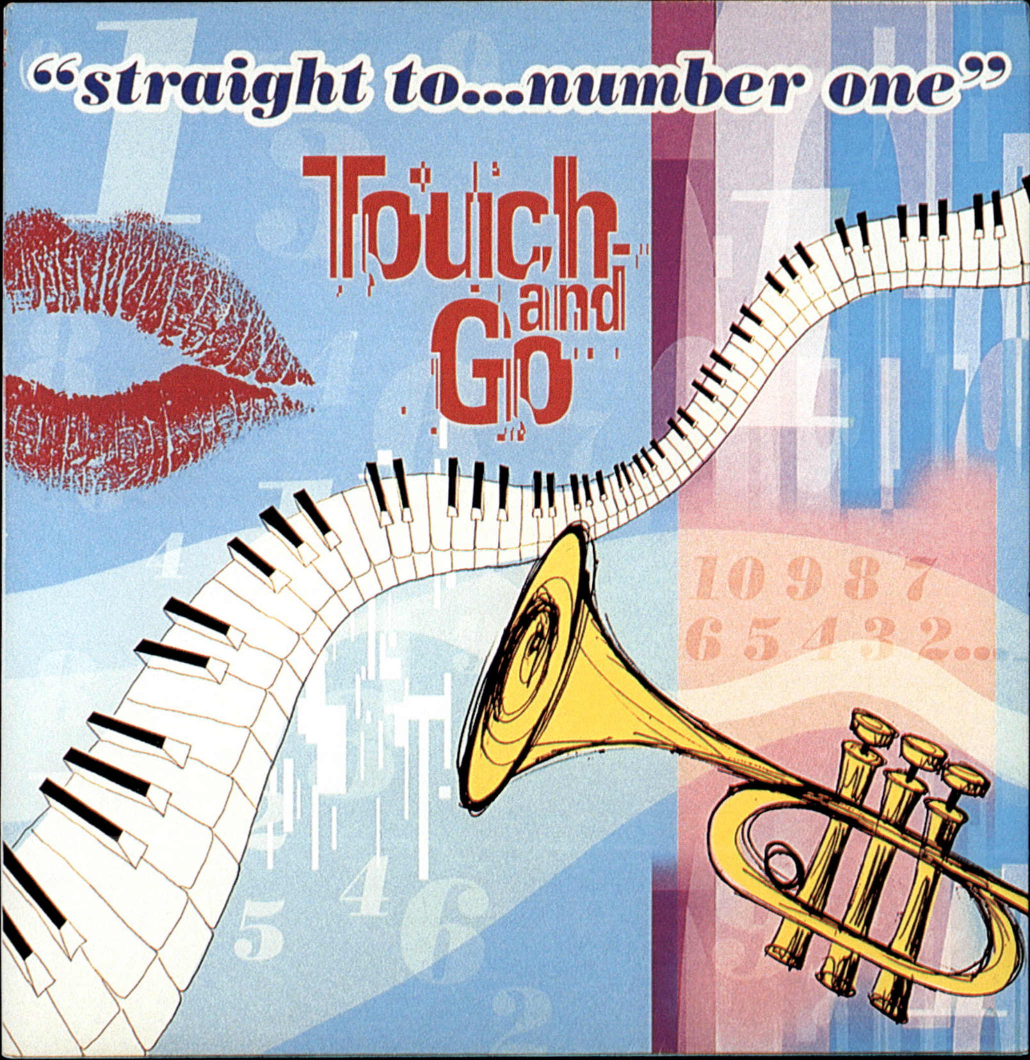

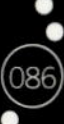

Artist Touch & Go Title Straight To... Number One Design Satellite Record Label U2 Music Limited Date 1999

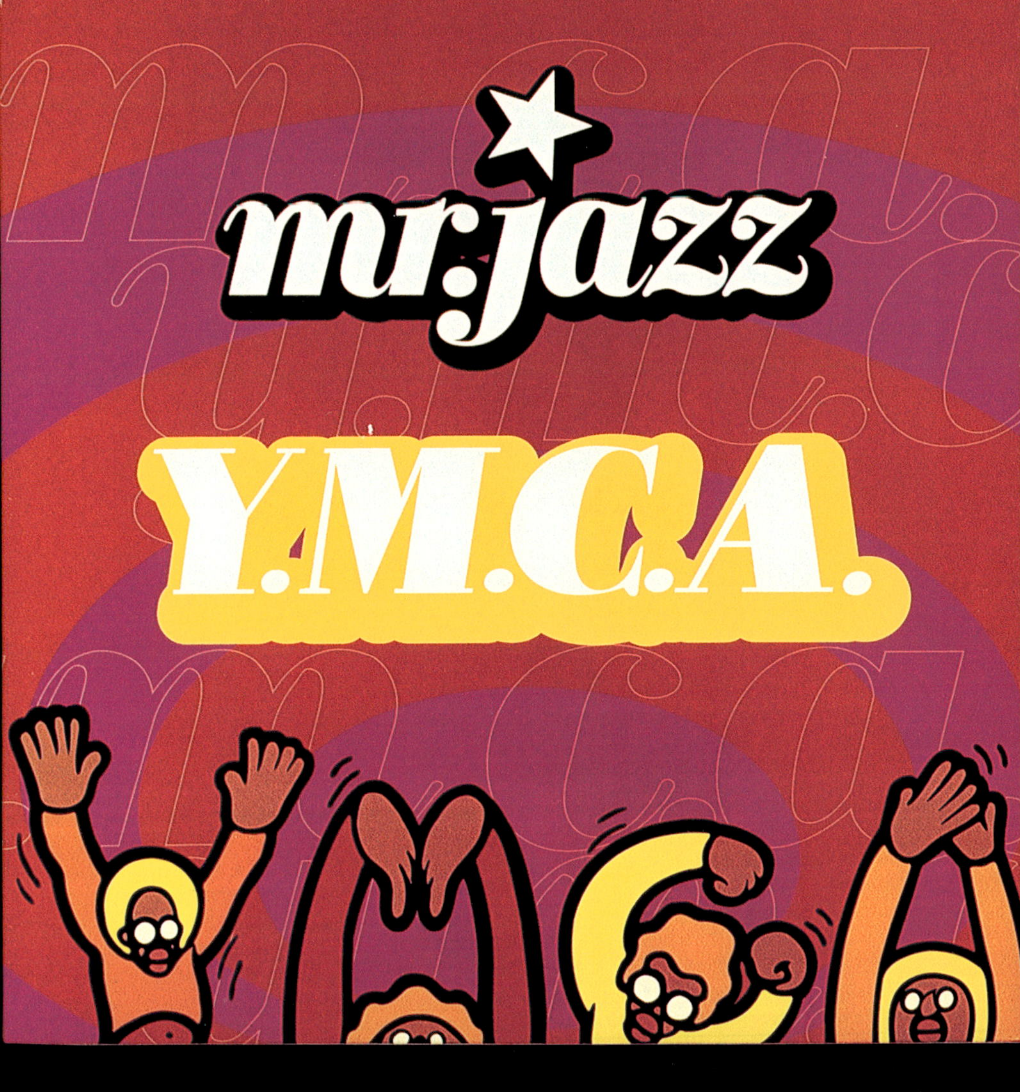

 Artist Mr. Jazz Title Y. M. C. A. Record Label Zafiro Date 1996

produced by 20 fingers
A'LISA B
I'm in love

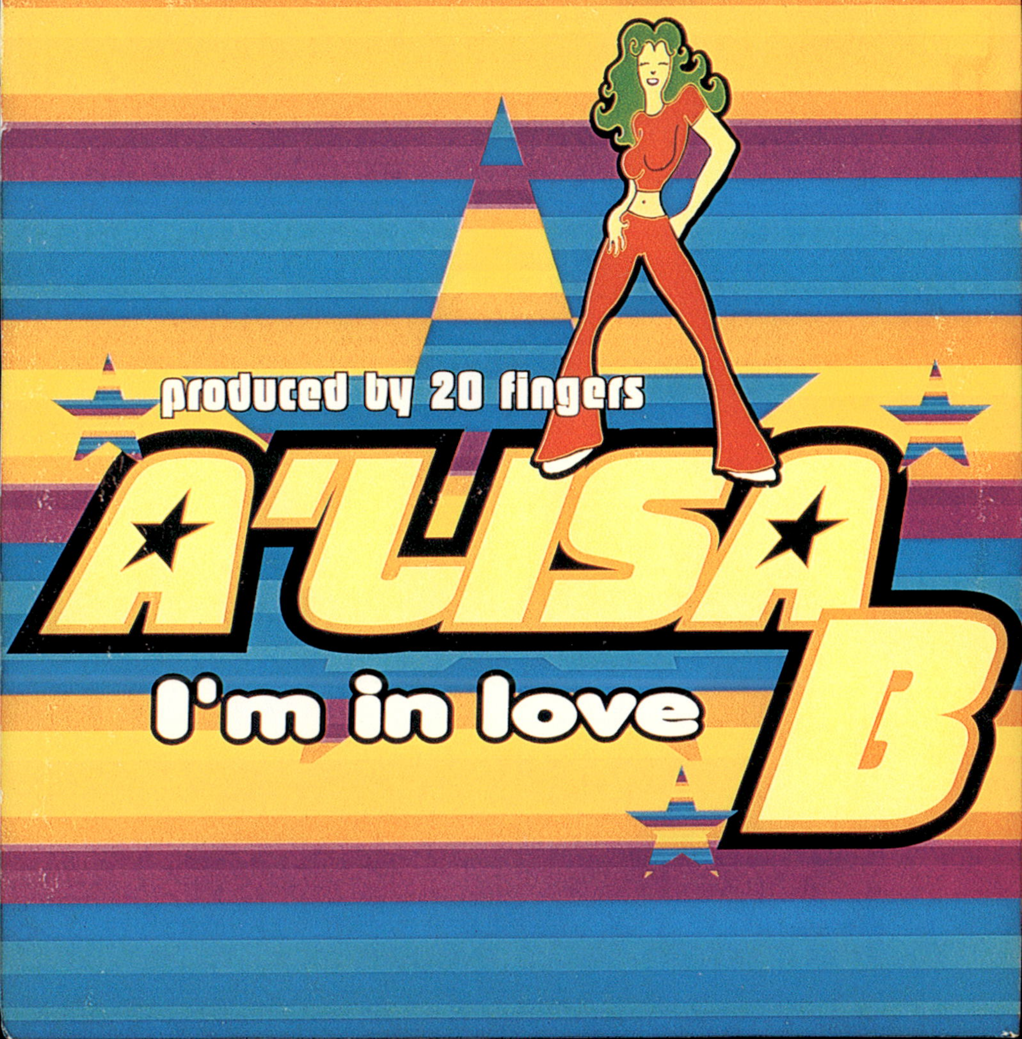

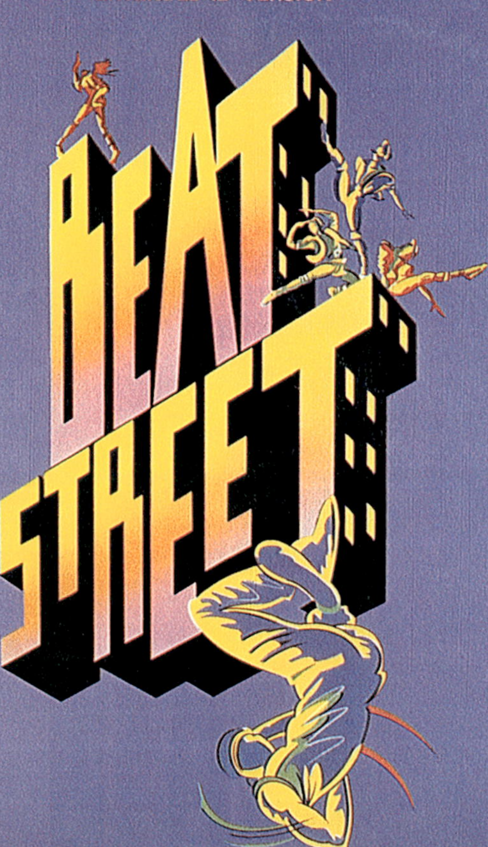
Juicy
BEAT STREET STRUT
EXTENDED 12" VERSION
BEAT
STREET

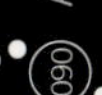

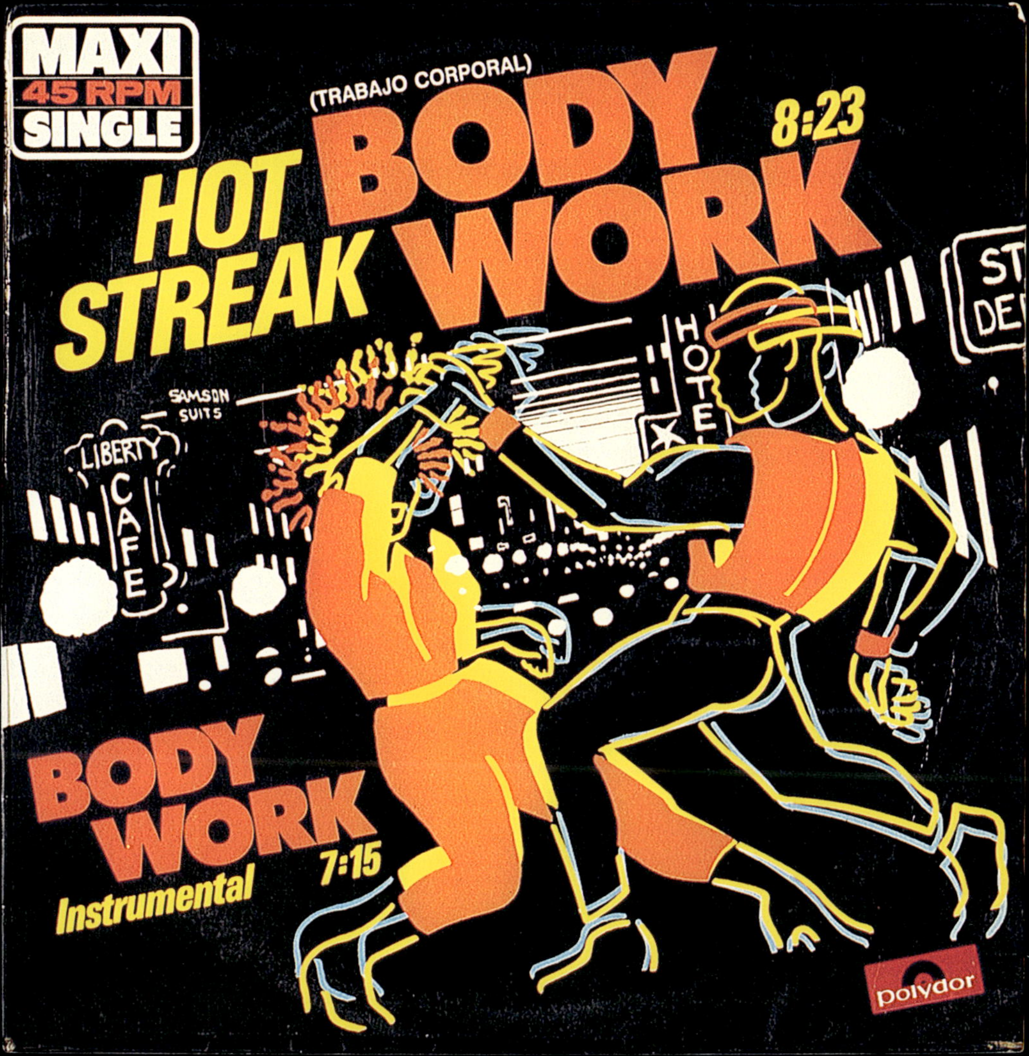

MAXI
45 RPM
SINGLE
(TRABAJO CORPORAL)
HOT STREAK
BODY WORK
8:23
SAMSON SUITS
LIBERTY CAFE
HOTEL
ST DE
BODY WORK
Instrumental
7:15
Polydor

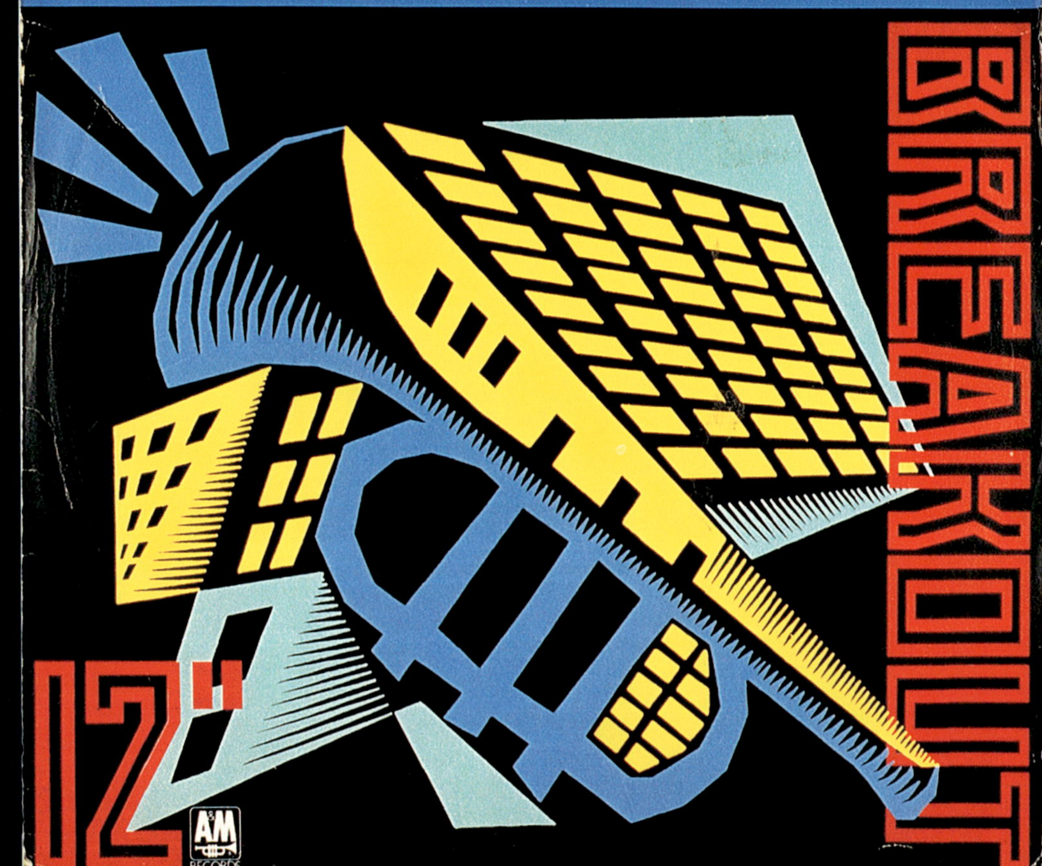
THE BRAT PACK
SO MANY WAYS
BREAKOUT
12"
A&M
RECORDS

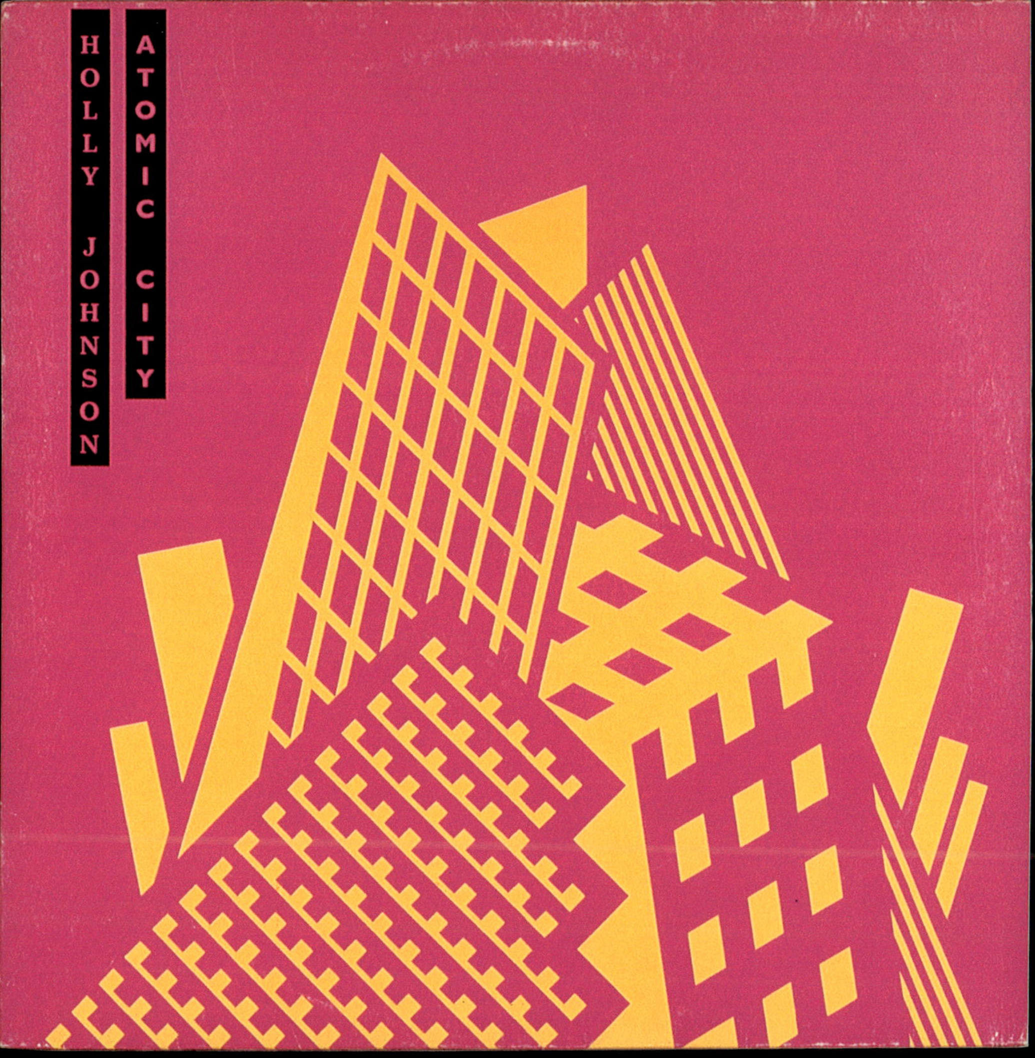

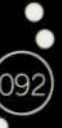

 Artist Holly Johnson Title Atomic City Design Accident Record Label MCA Records Date 1989

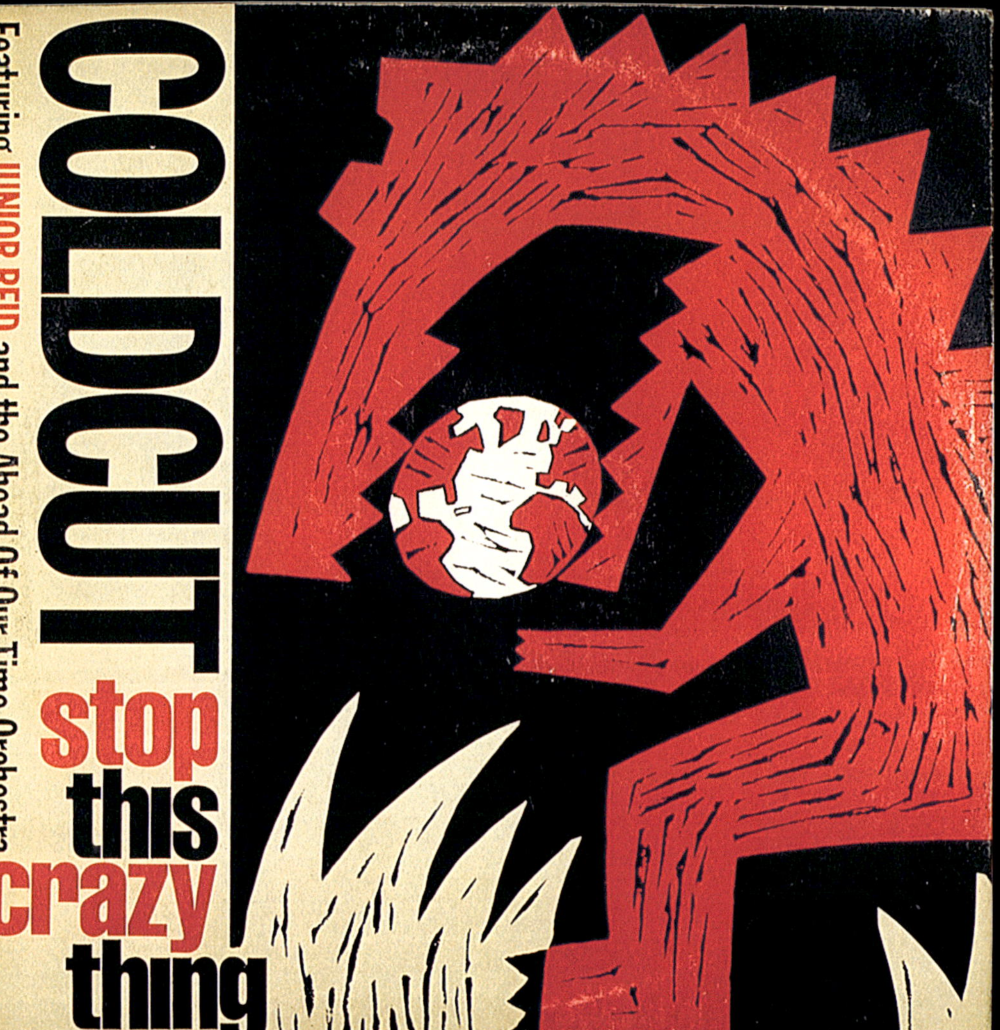
Featuring JUNIOR REID and the Ahead Of Our Time Orchestra
COLDCUT
stop this crazy thing

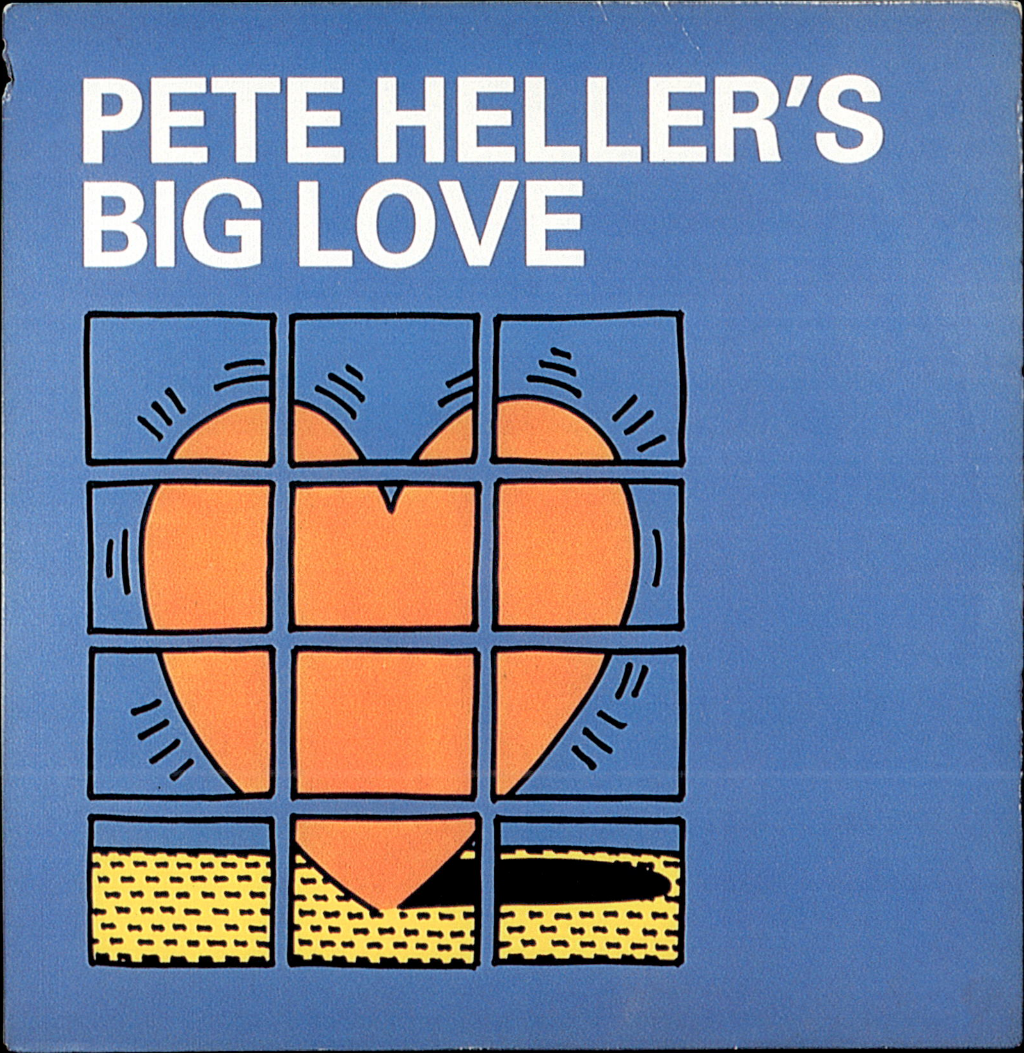

PETE HELLER'S BIG LOVE

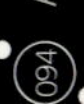

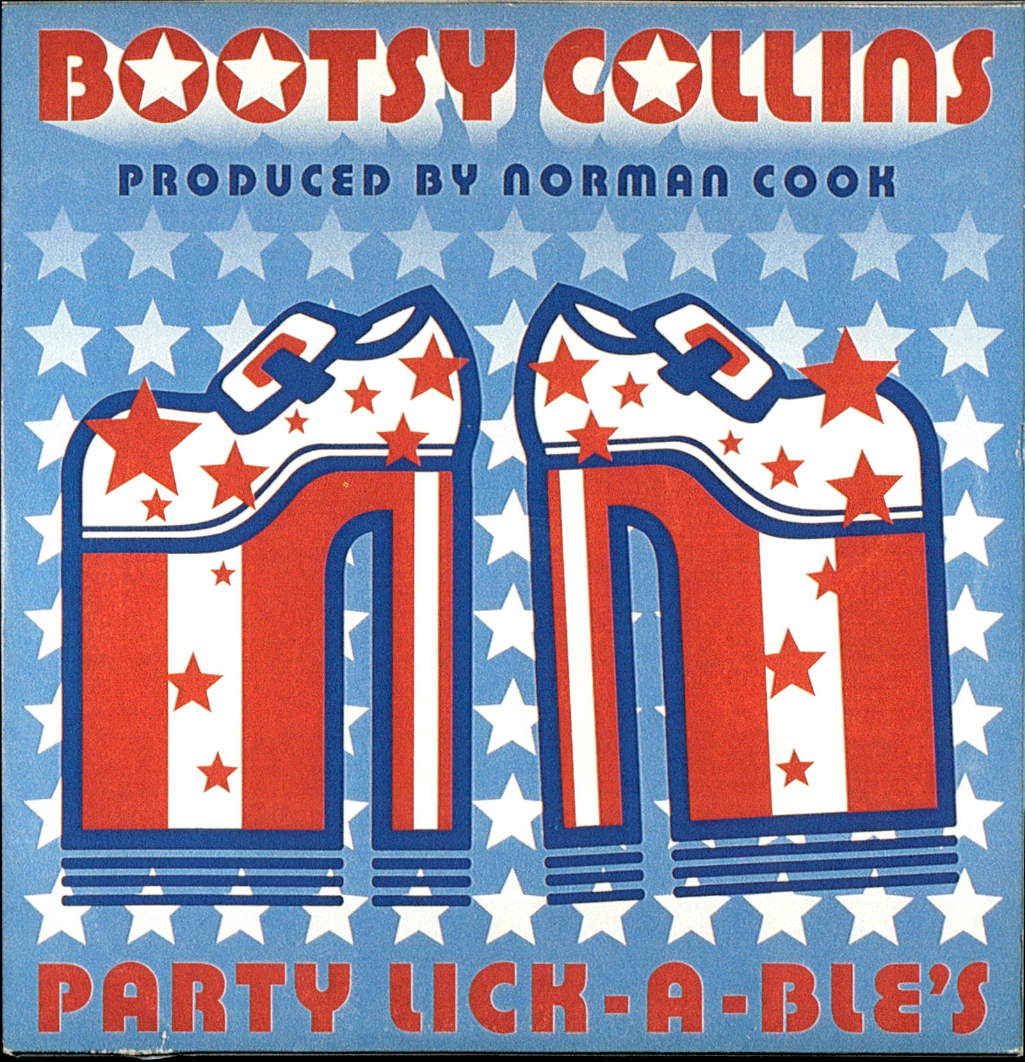

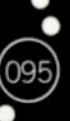

BOOTSY COLLINS
PRODUCED BY NORMAN COOK
PARTY LICK-A-BLE'S

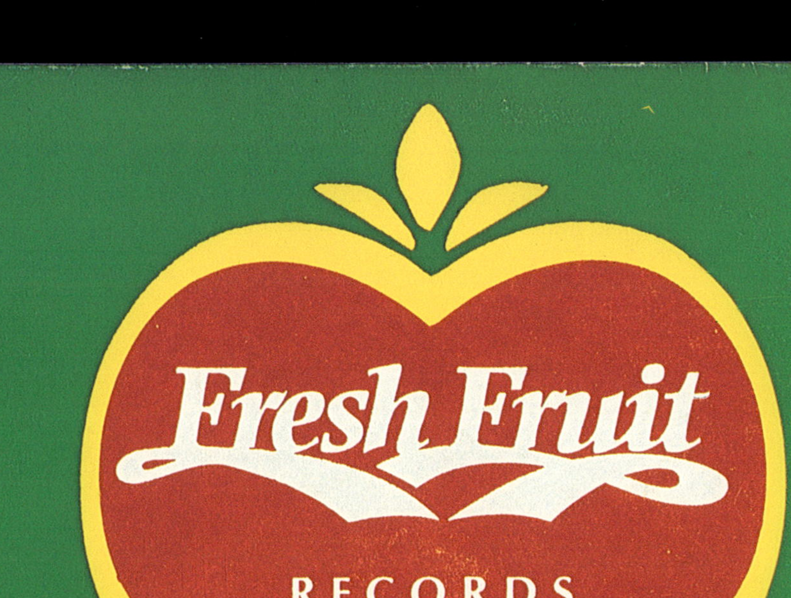
Fresh Fruit
RECORDS
The Good Men

Artist Bob Sinclar feat. Salomé de Bahia Title Eu So Quero Um Xodo Design The Dream Factory
Record Label Sony Music Date 1997

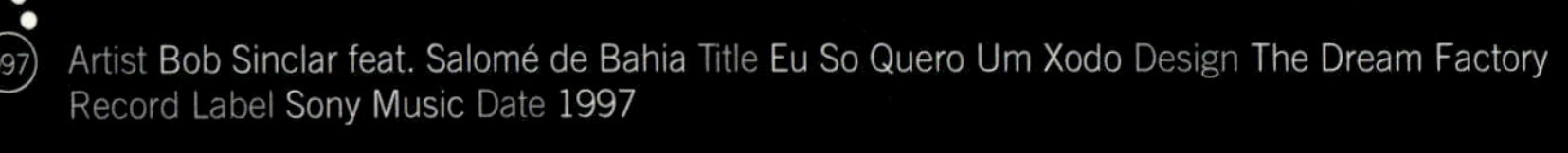

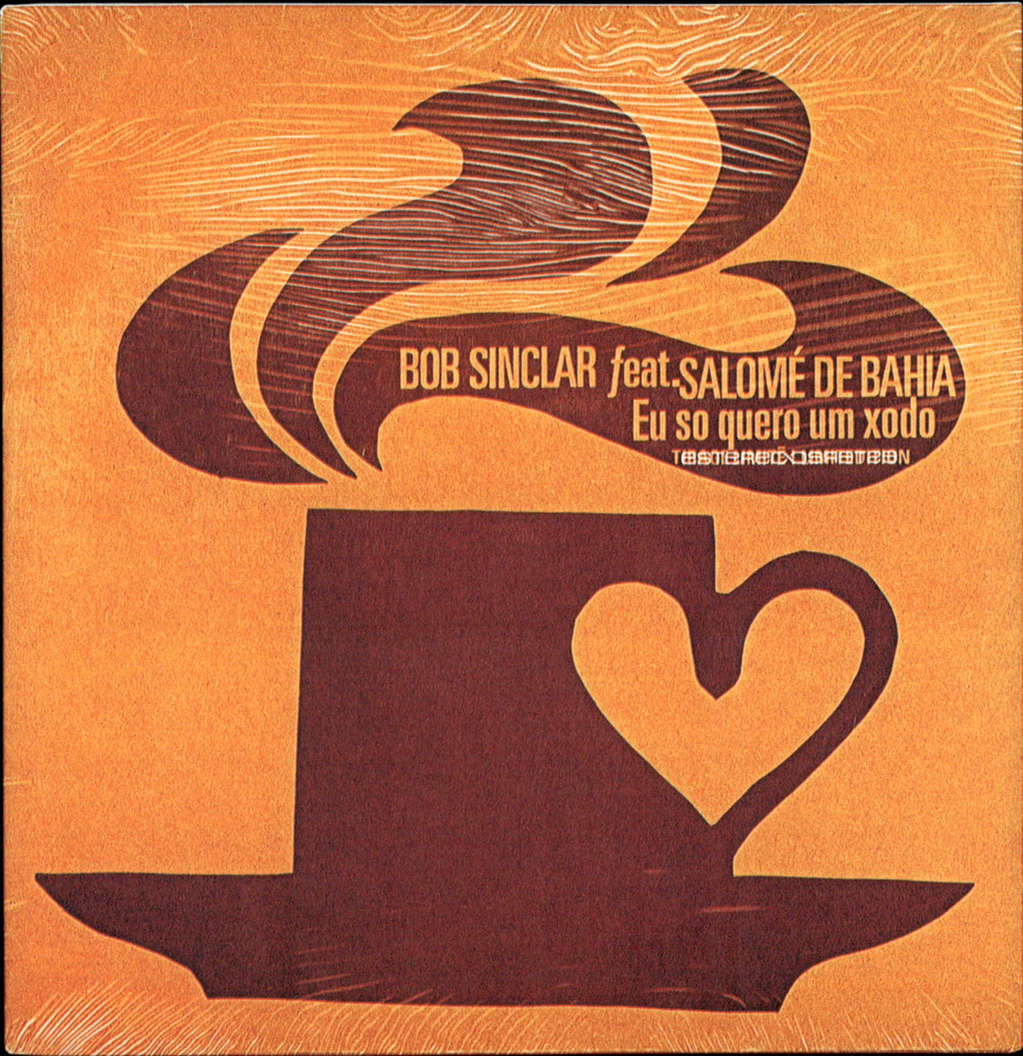

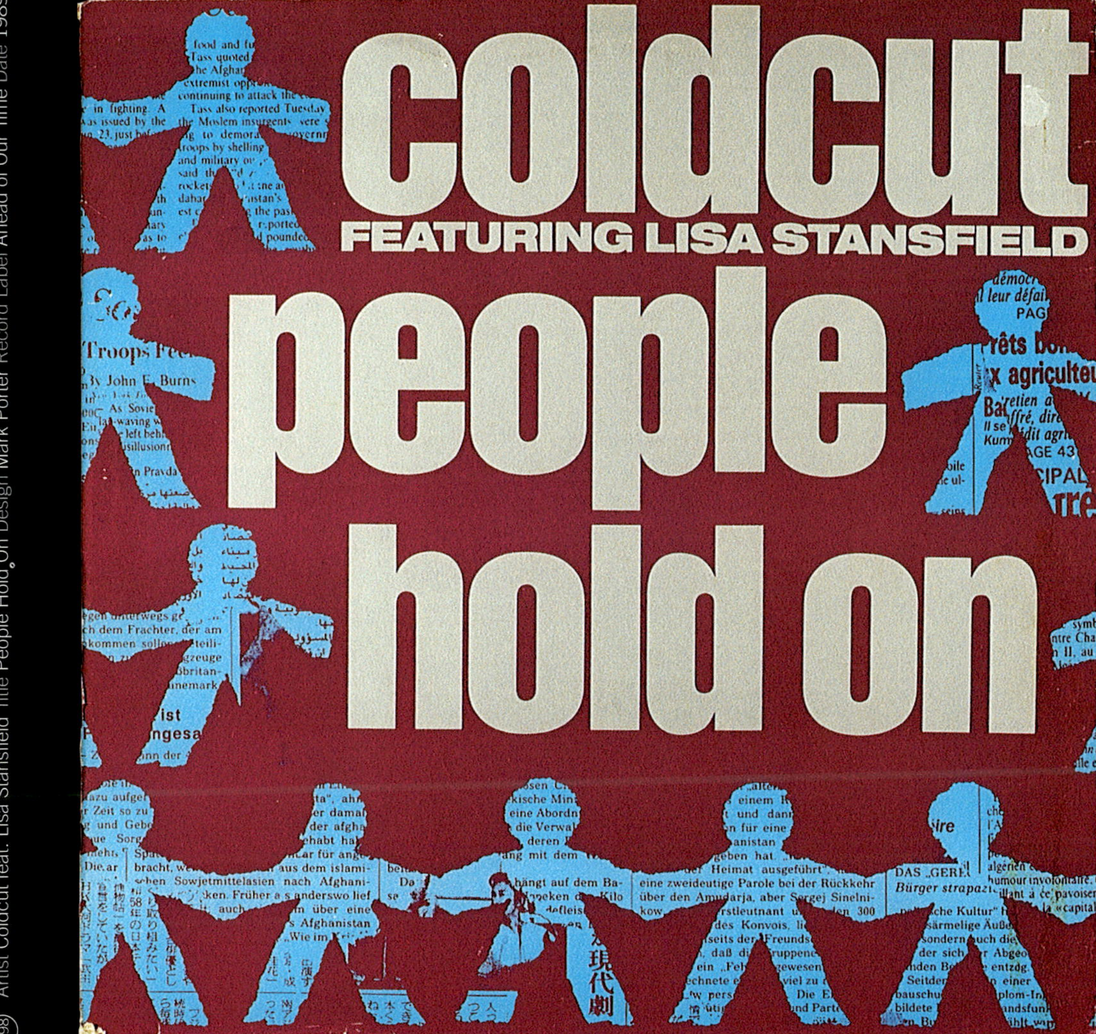

coldcut
FEATURING LISA STANSFIELD
people
hold on

Tom Jones and Mousse T.
Sex Bomb

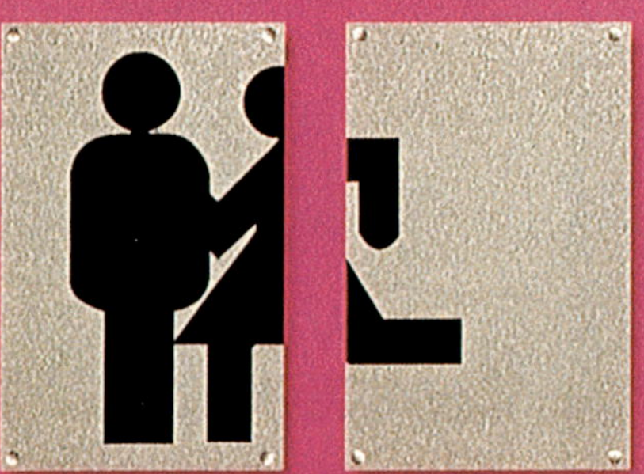

Artist Tom Jones & Mousse T. Title Sex Bomb Design Fresh Produce Photography Julian Bigg Record Label Gut Records Date 1999

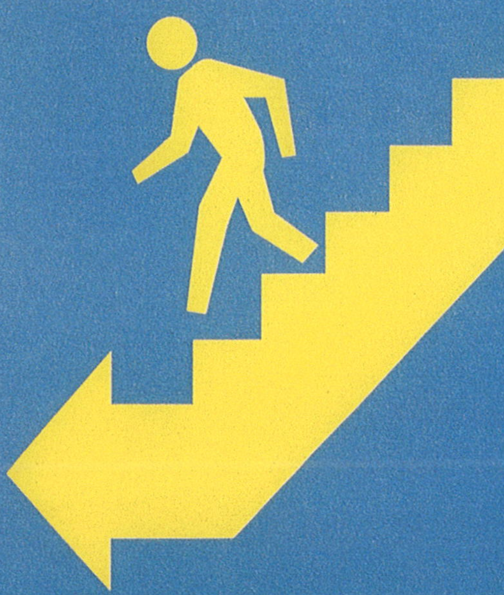

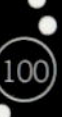

100 Artist Paul Johnson Title Get Get Down Design Peat Design Record Label Legato Date 1999

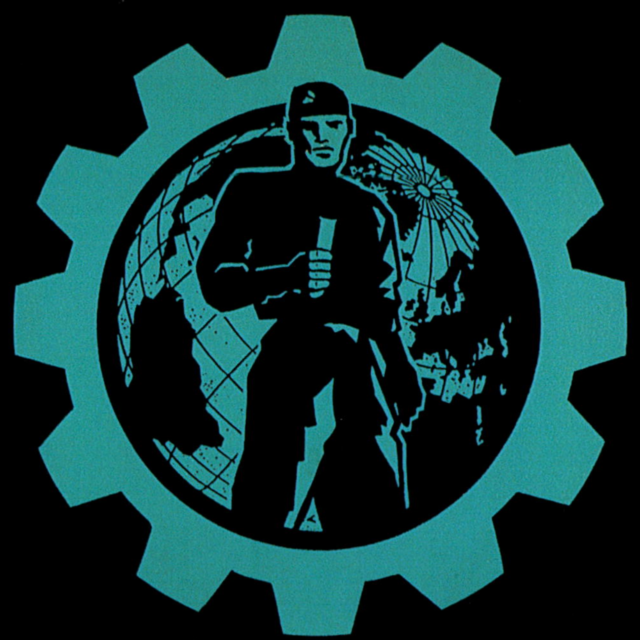

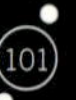
101 Artist Technolyt Title Trax Volume One Design Dominator Record Label ZYX Date 1991

POwER

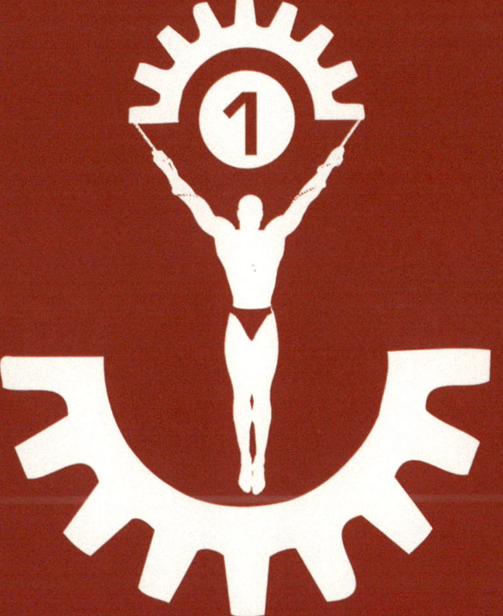

JULIO POSADAS

STATE OF MIND • THIS IS IT

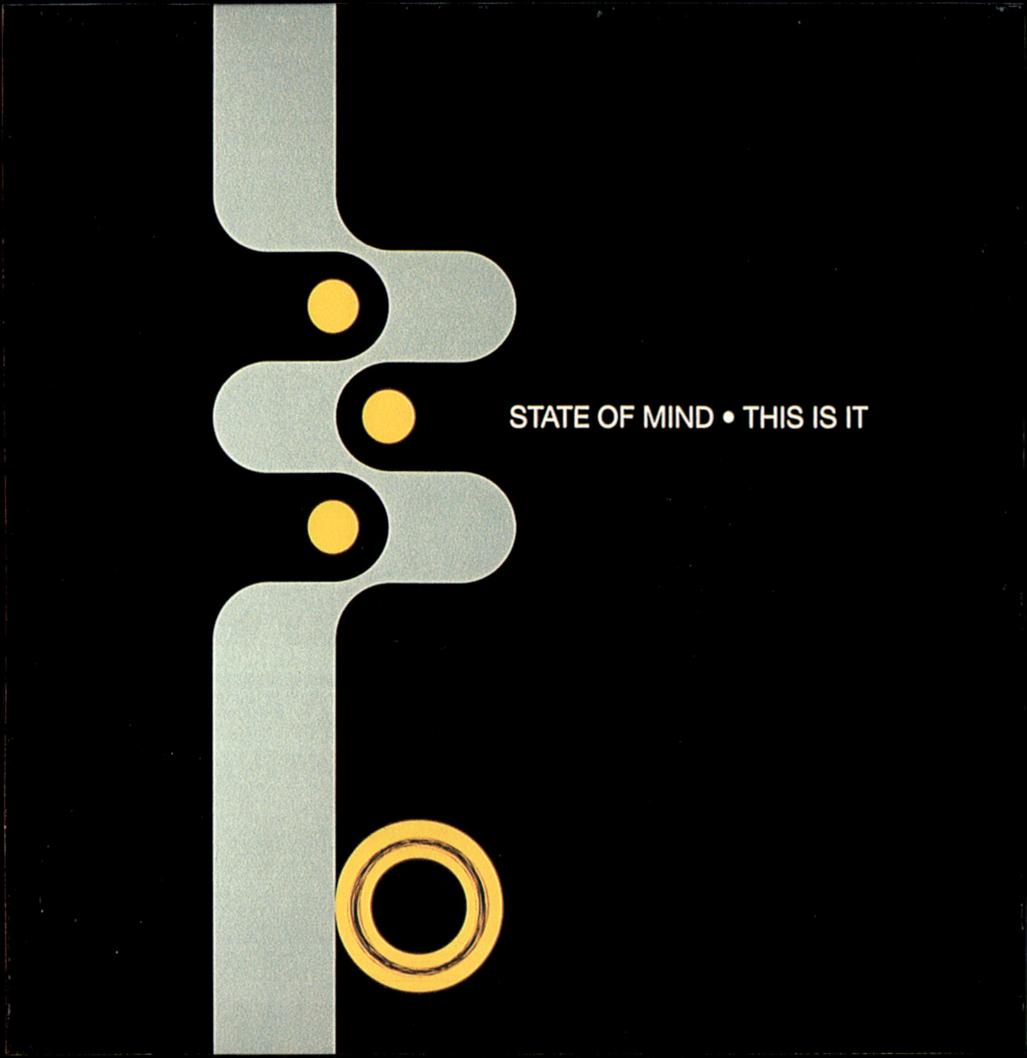

problem boy
self control

Camisra
clap your hands
CLAP
YOUR HANDS

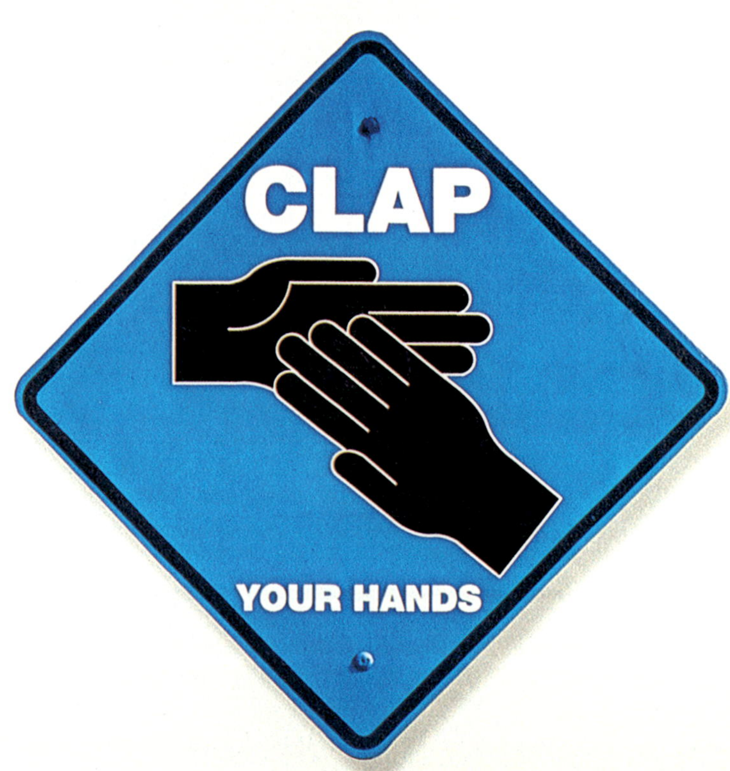
CLAP
YOUR HANDS

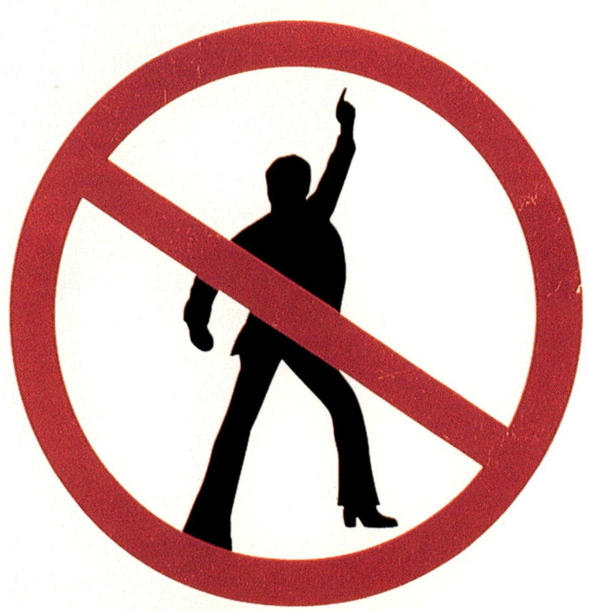

n-trance
featuring Ricardo Da Force
Stayin' Alive

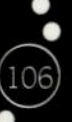

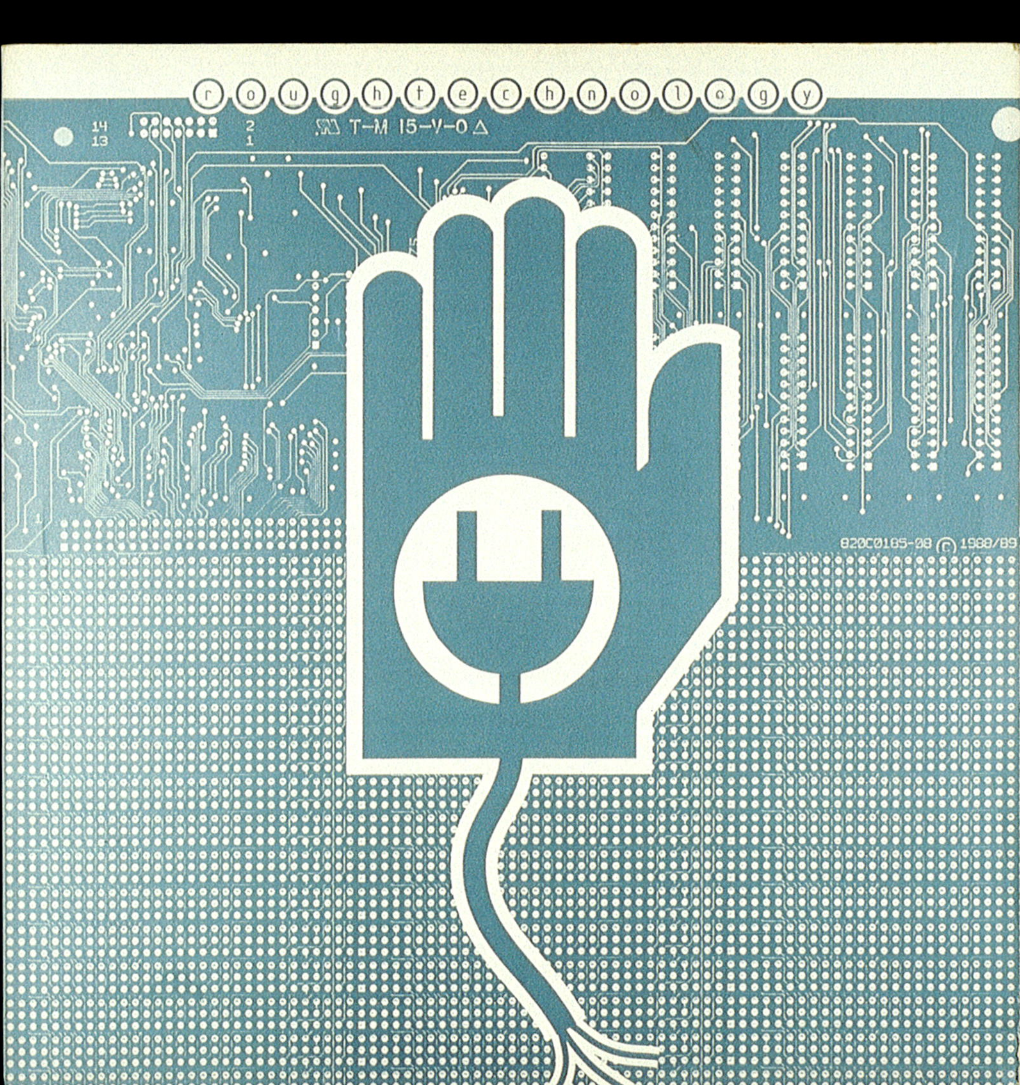
roughtechnology
T-M 15-V-0
14
13
2
1
820C0185-08 © 1988/89

Artist Freak Power Title Turn On, Tune In, Cop Out Record Label 4th B'Way Date 1993

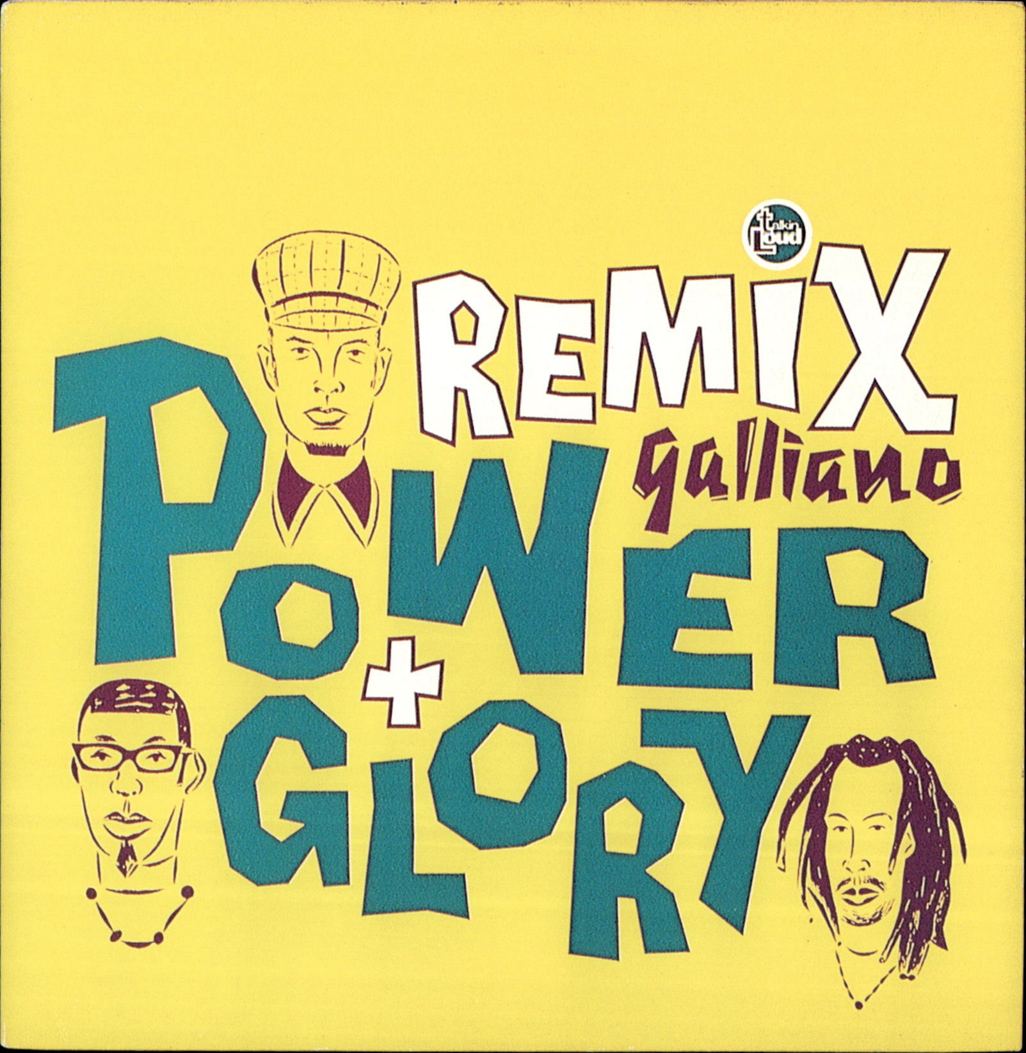

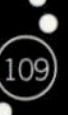

Artist Galliano Title Power & Glory Design Swifty Glory Illustration Chris Long Record Label Talkin Loud Date 1990

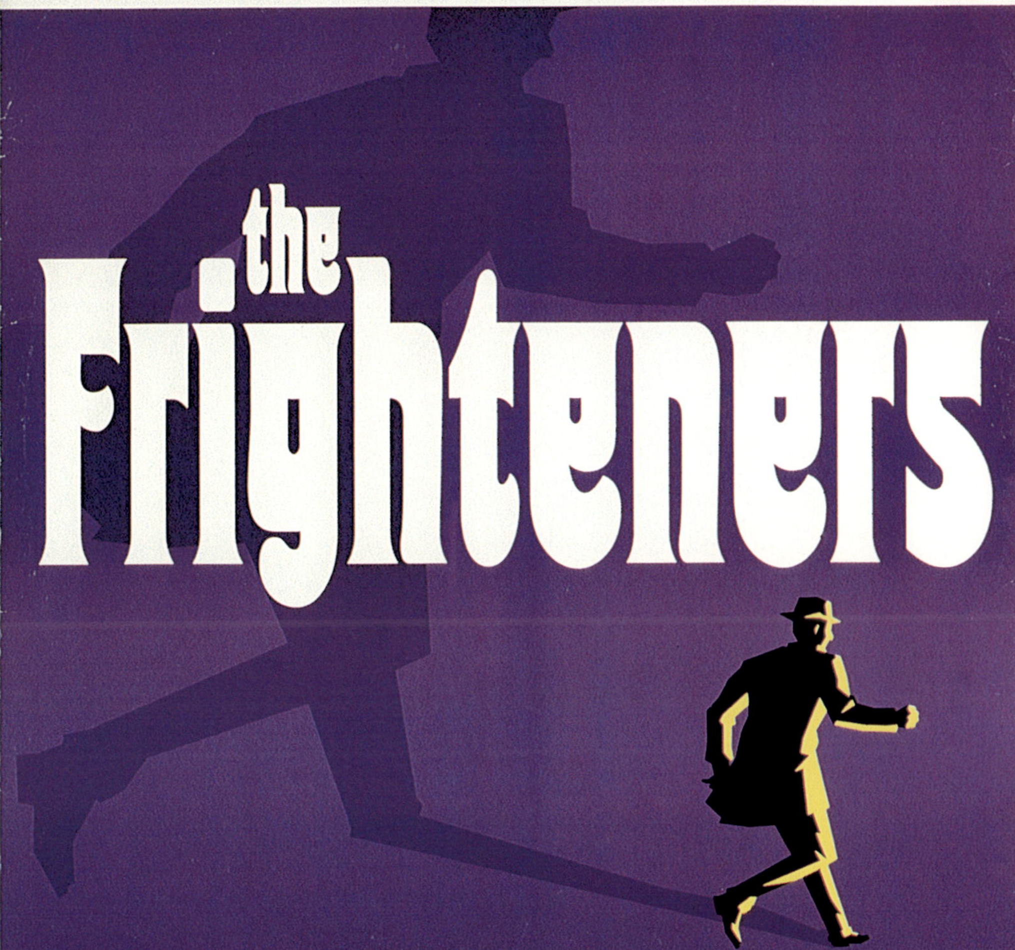
CORDUROY
ACID JAZZ
the Frighteners

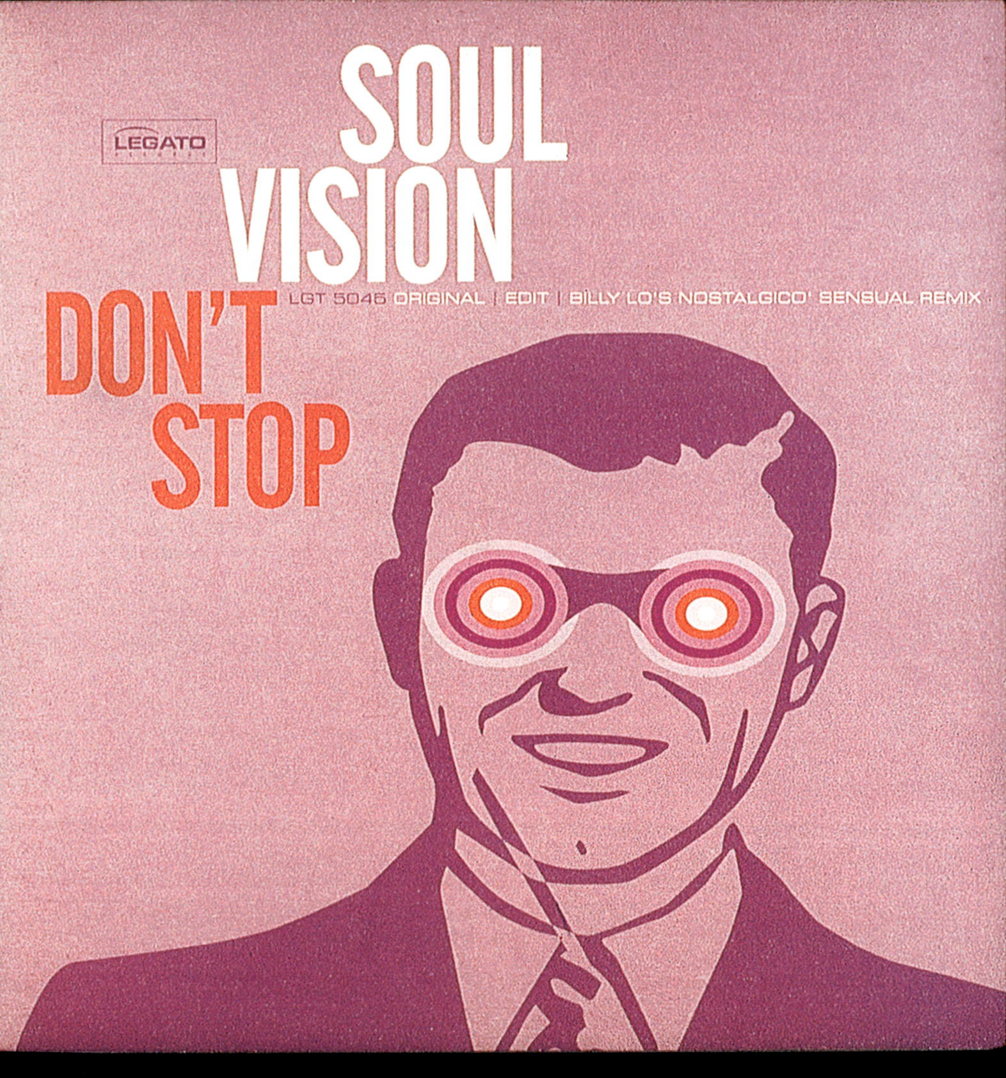

LEGATO
SOUL VISION
DON'T STOP
LGT 5046 ORIGINAL | EDIT | BILLY LO'S NOSTALGICO' SENSUAL REMIX

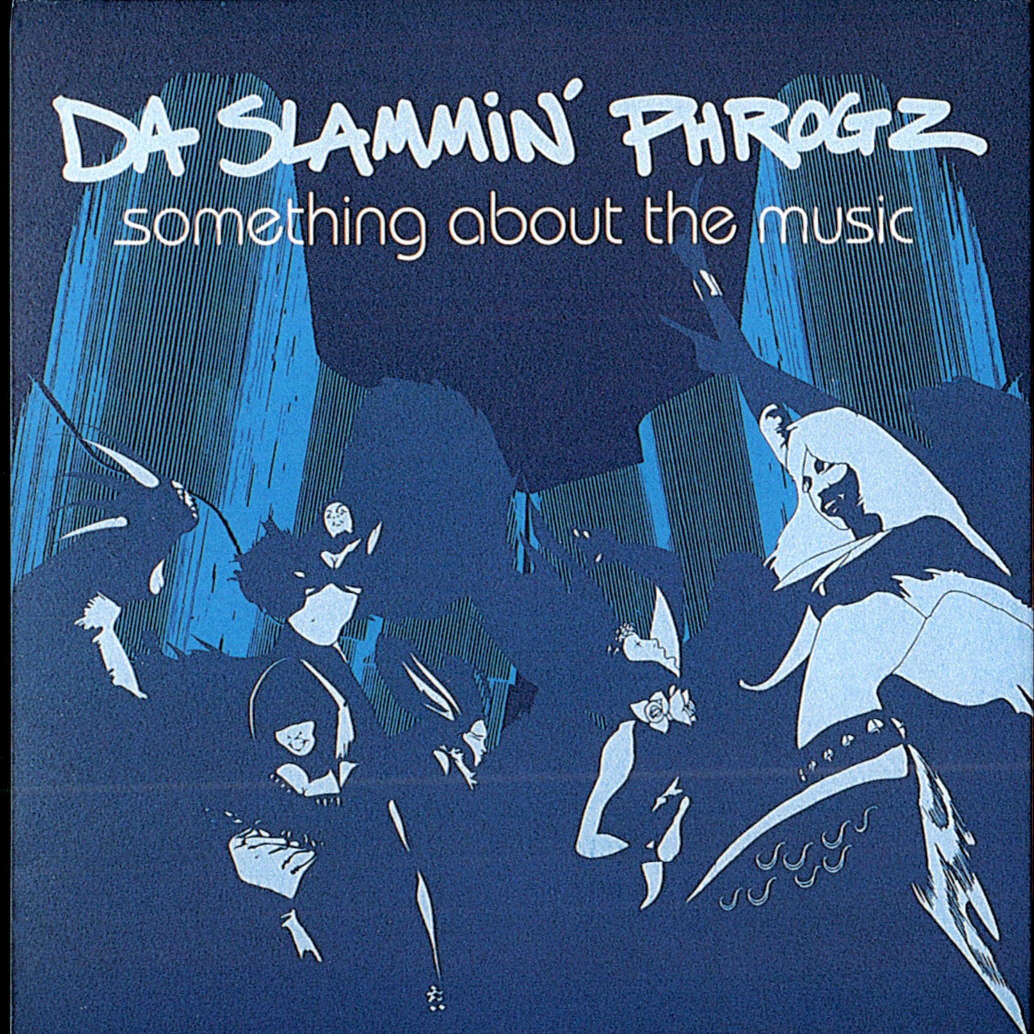

Artist Da Slammin' Phrogz Title Something about the Music Design Edward Bettison Illustration Kristian Russell Record Label Warner Music / Fresh Fish Date 1999

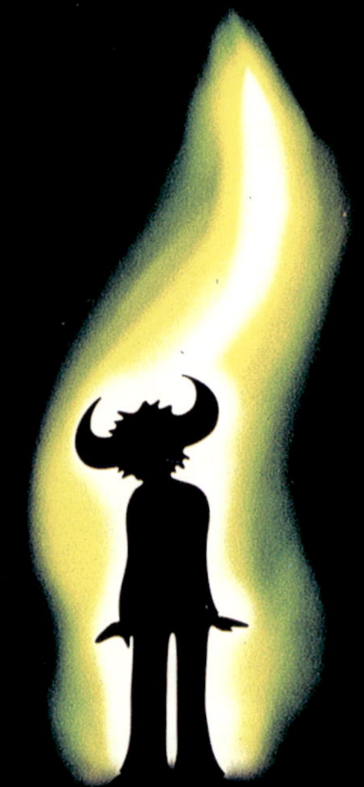

113 Artist Jamiroquai Title Deeper Underground Design Blue Record Label Sony Music Date 1998

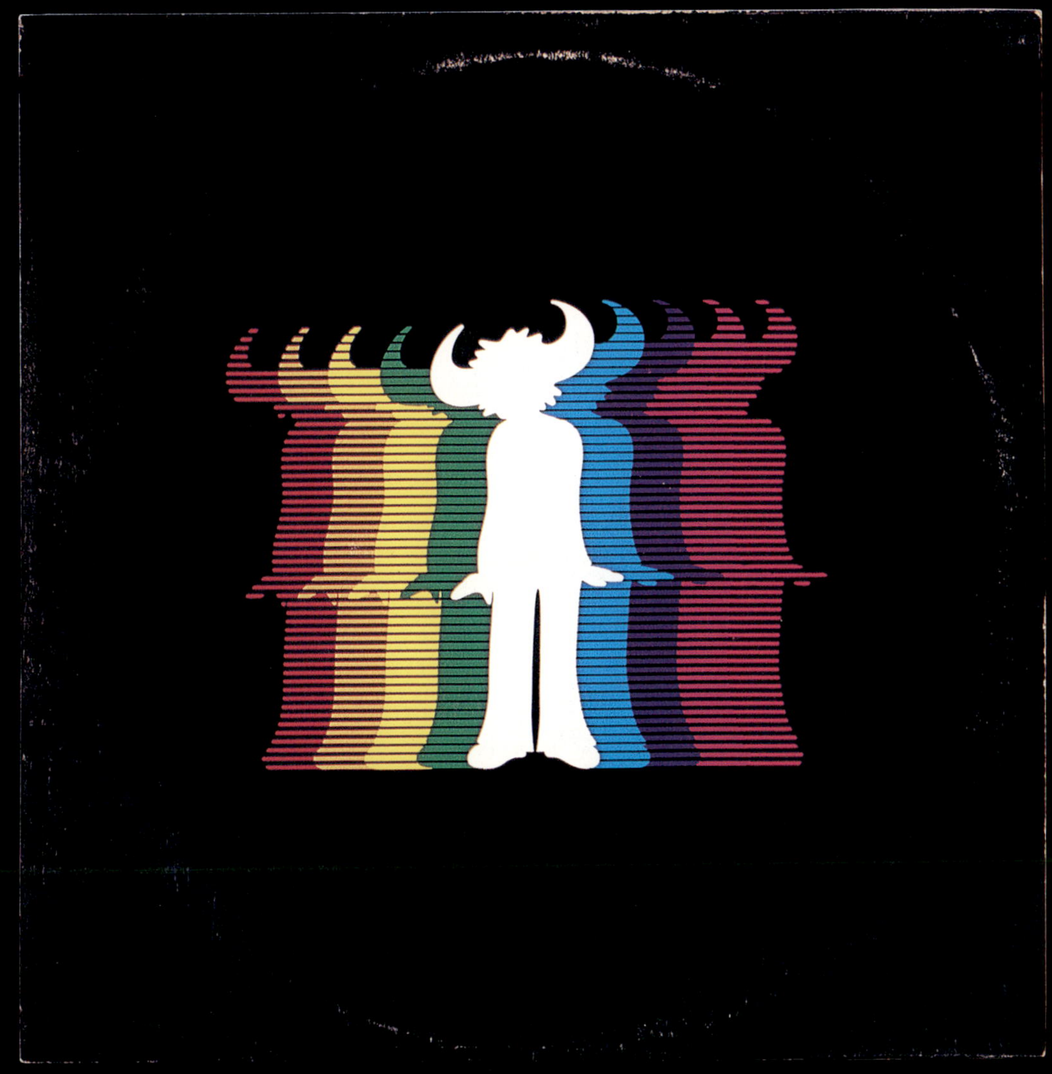

Artist Jamiroquai Title High Times Design Blue Record Label Sony Music Date 1997

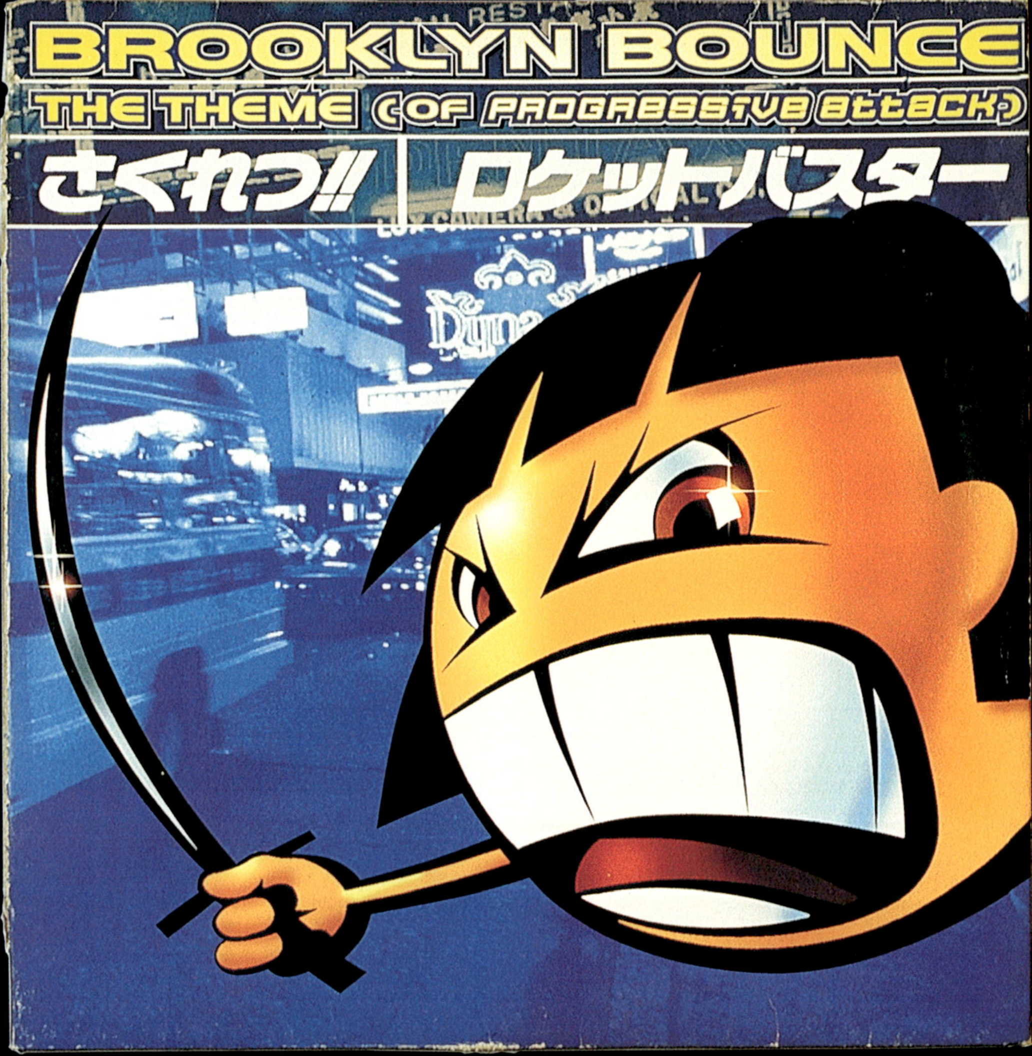

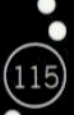

 Artist Brooklyn Bounce Title The Theme (Of Progressive Attack) Record Label Club Tools Date 1996

Right Here,
Right Now
Jacko

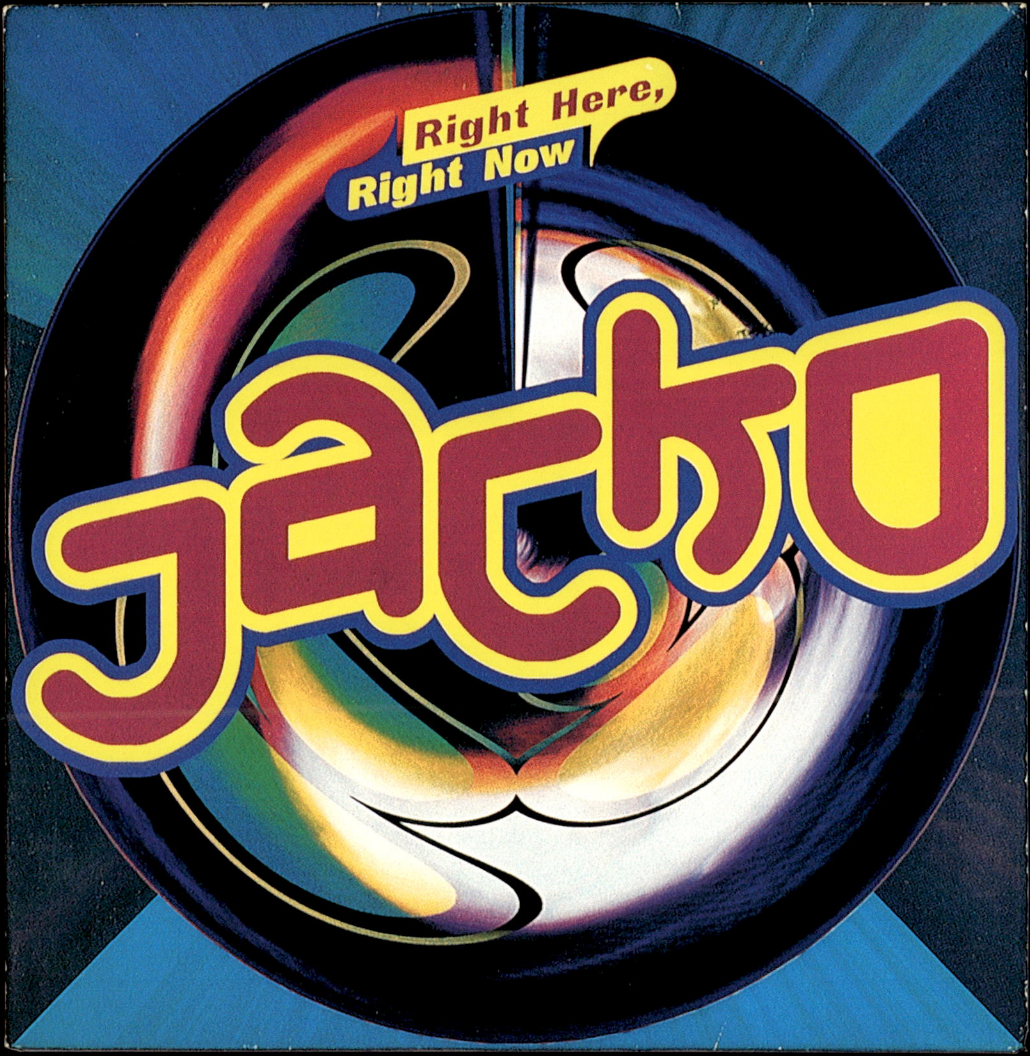

TOKYO GHETTO PUSSY
TGP
I KISS YOUR LIPS GROOVECULT'S MASTERCUTS REMIX
I KISS YOUR LIPS MUSIC FOR THE GIRLIES EXTENDED
I KISS YOUR LIPS CLUB MIX

The
スプーン
ジャム
I KISS YOUR LIPS

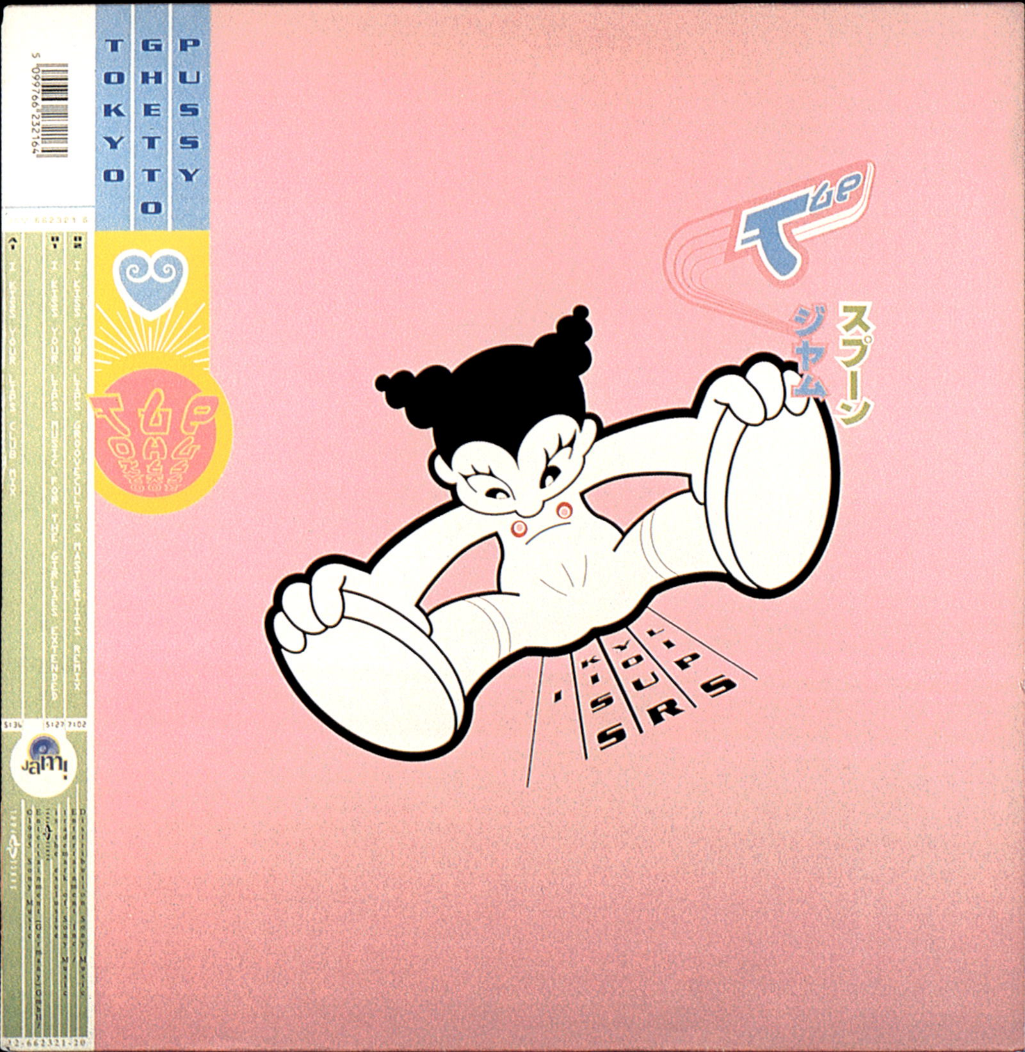

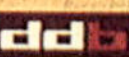

118

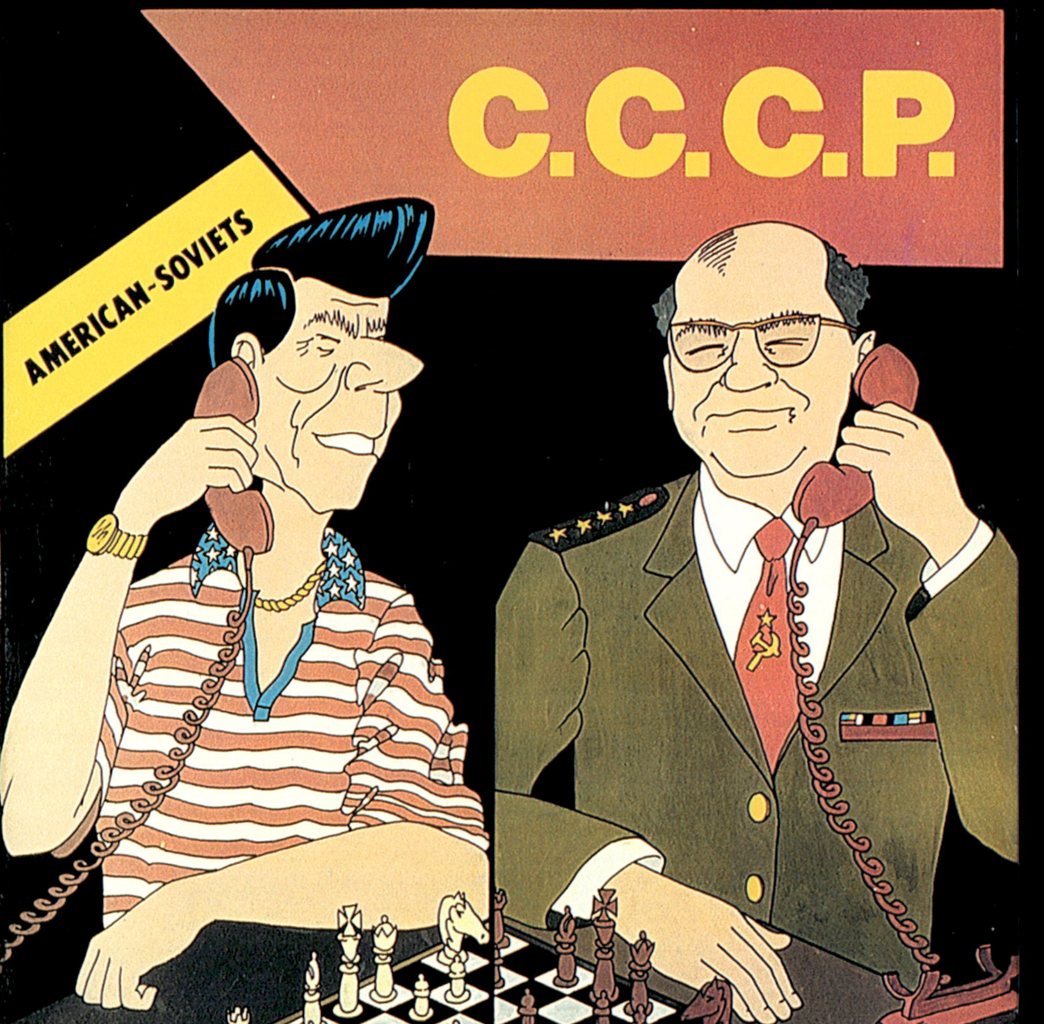

119
Artist C.C.C.P. Title American-Soviets Design René De Versailles Illustration Fred Schomberg
Record Label Raya Records Date 1987

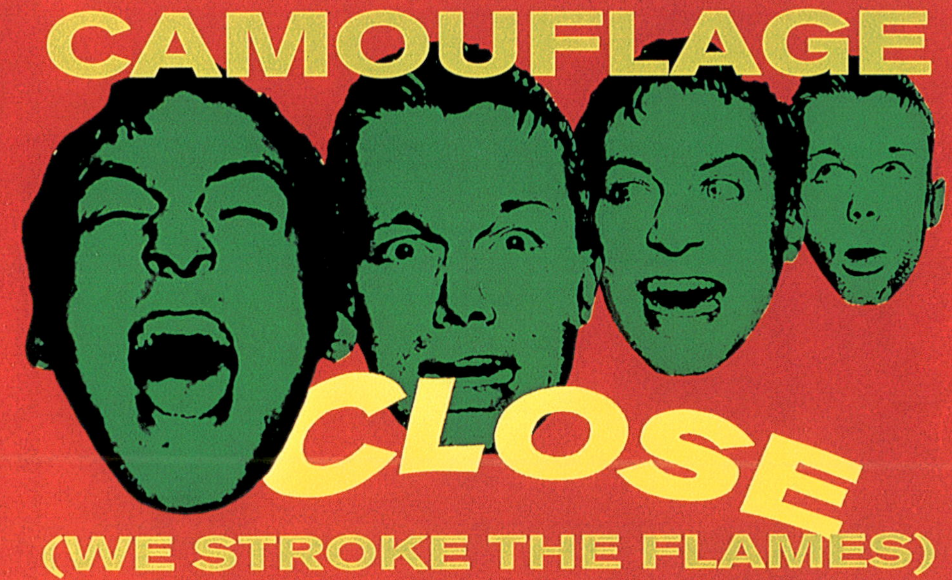
CAMOUFLAGE
CLOSE
(WE STROKE THE FLAMES)

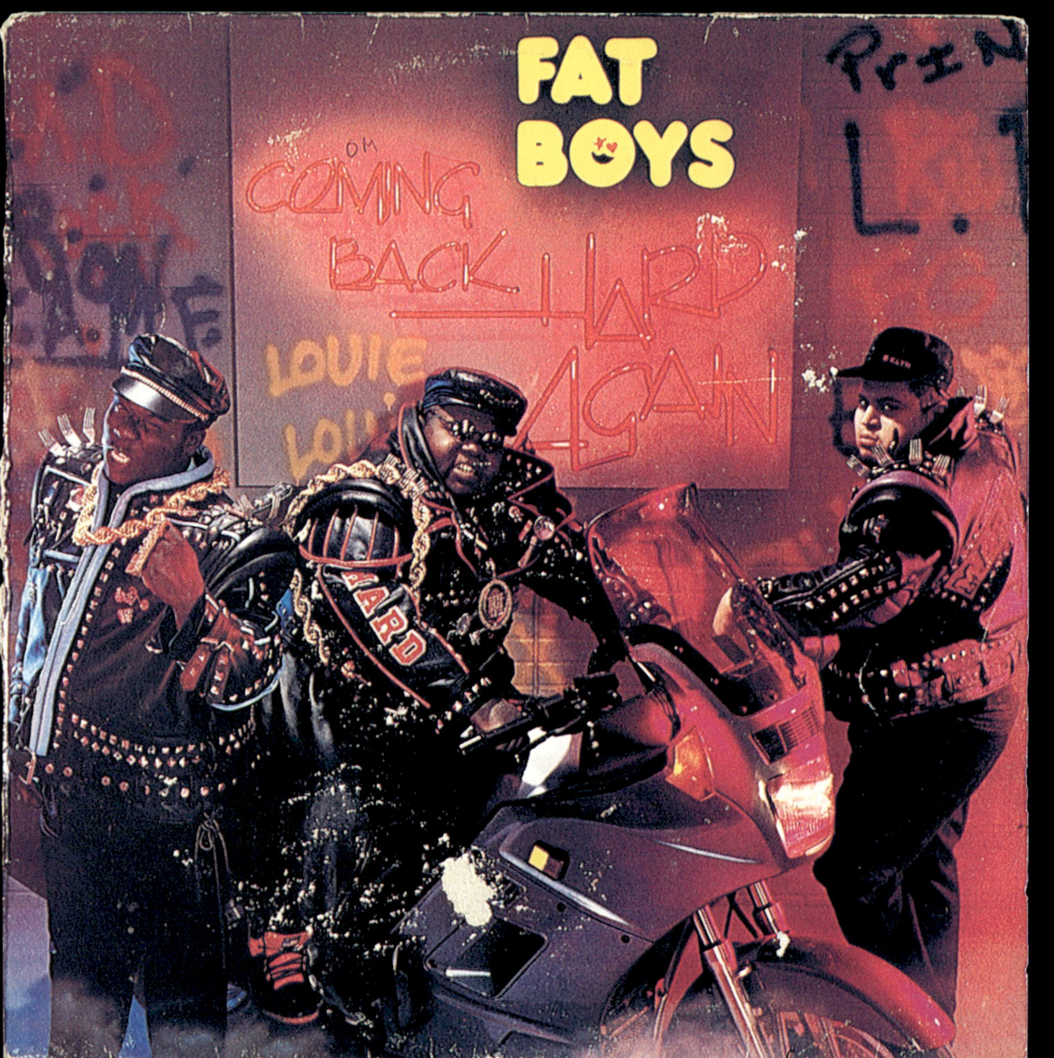

FAT BOYS
COMING BACK HARD AGAIN
LOUIE
HARD

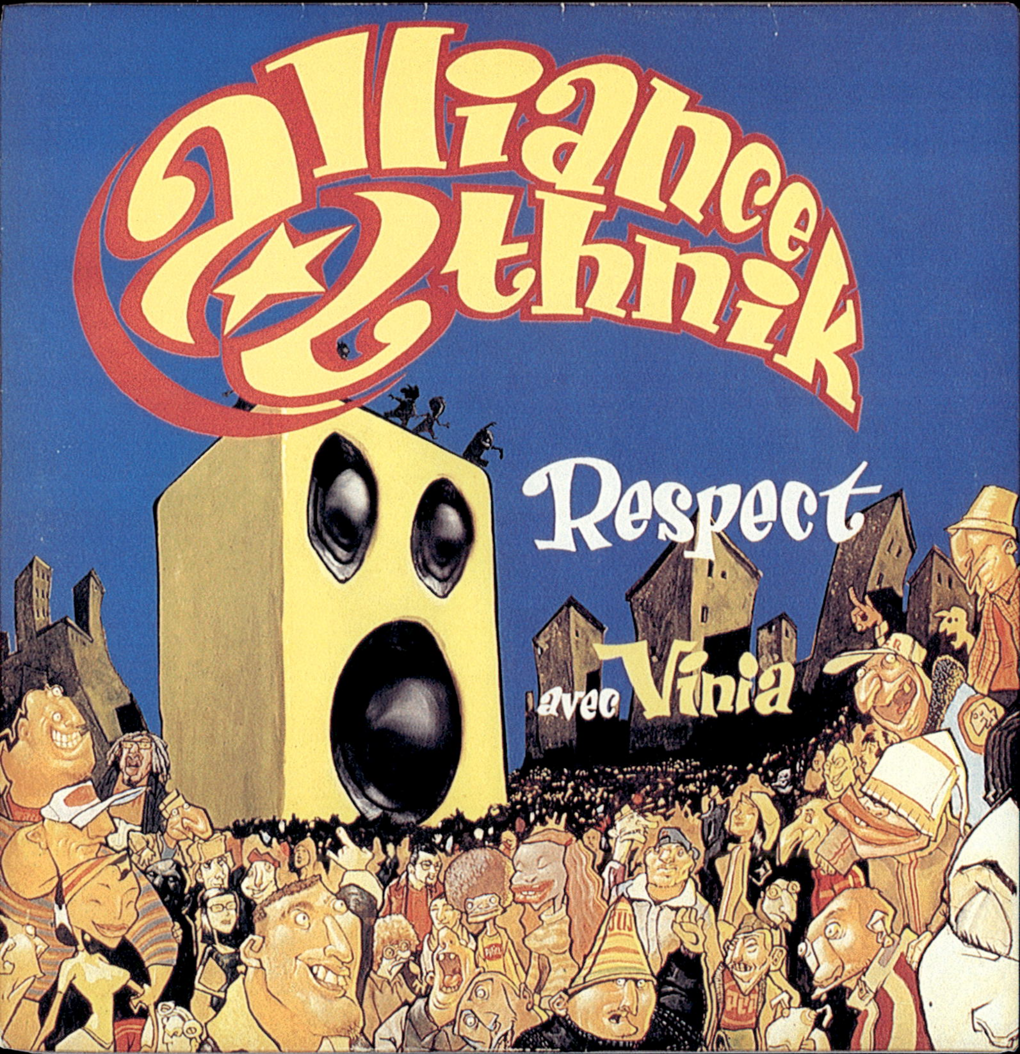

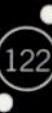

Artist Alliance Ethnik Title Respect Design T. Badin, P. Budestschu Illustration Numero 6 & LN
Record Label Delabel Date 1995

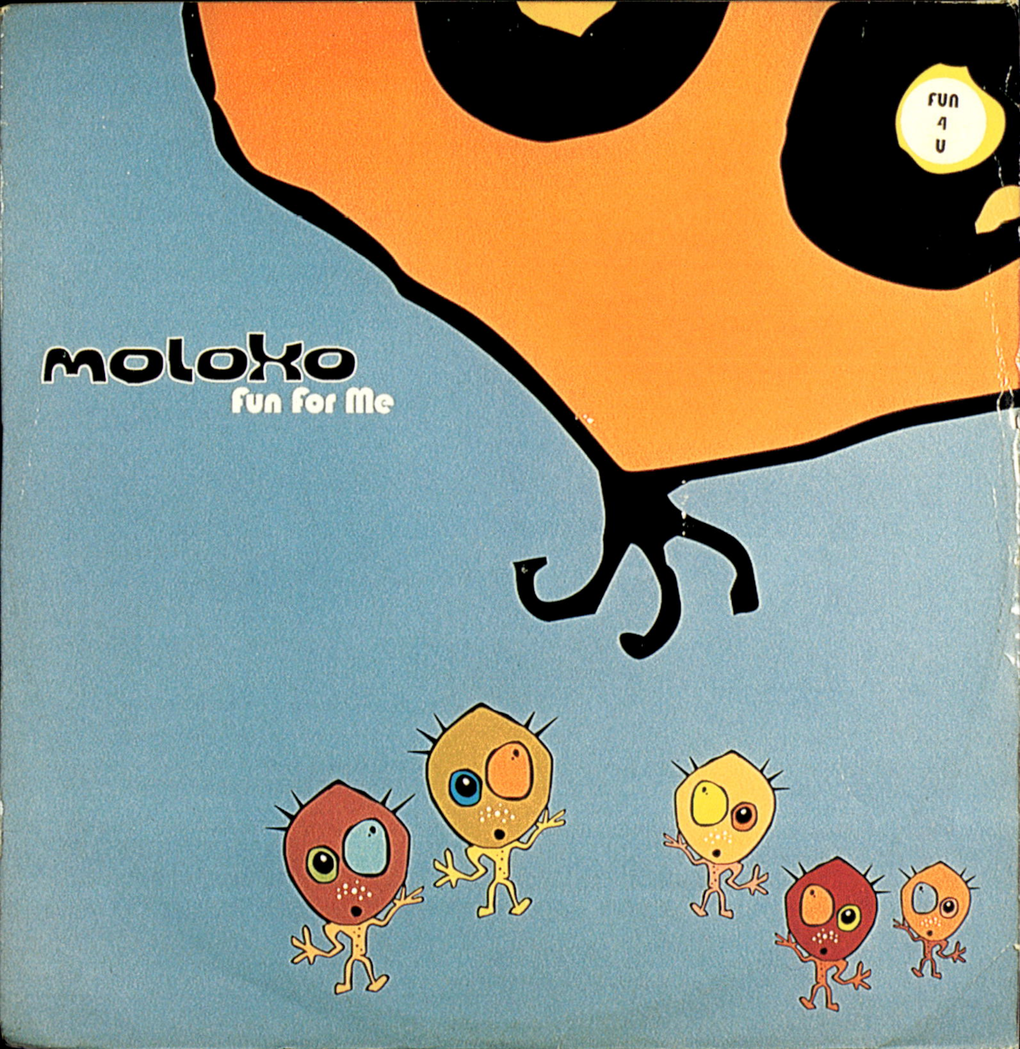

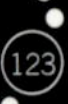 Artist Moloko Title Fun For Me Design Republic Record Label The Echo Label Ltd. Date 1996

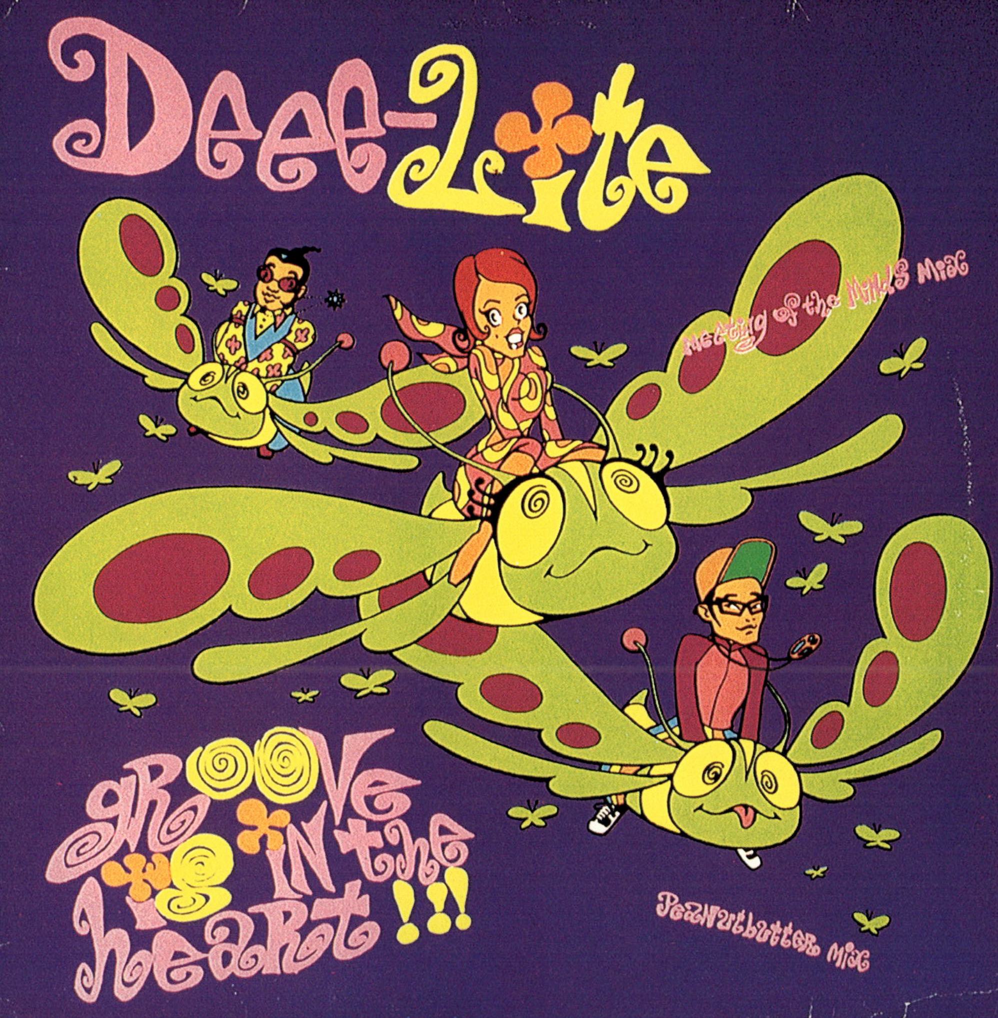
Deee-Lite
Meeting of the Minds Mise
Peanutbutter Mise
groove is in the heart !!!

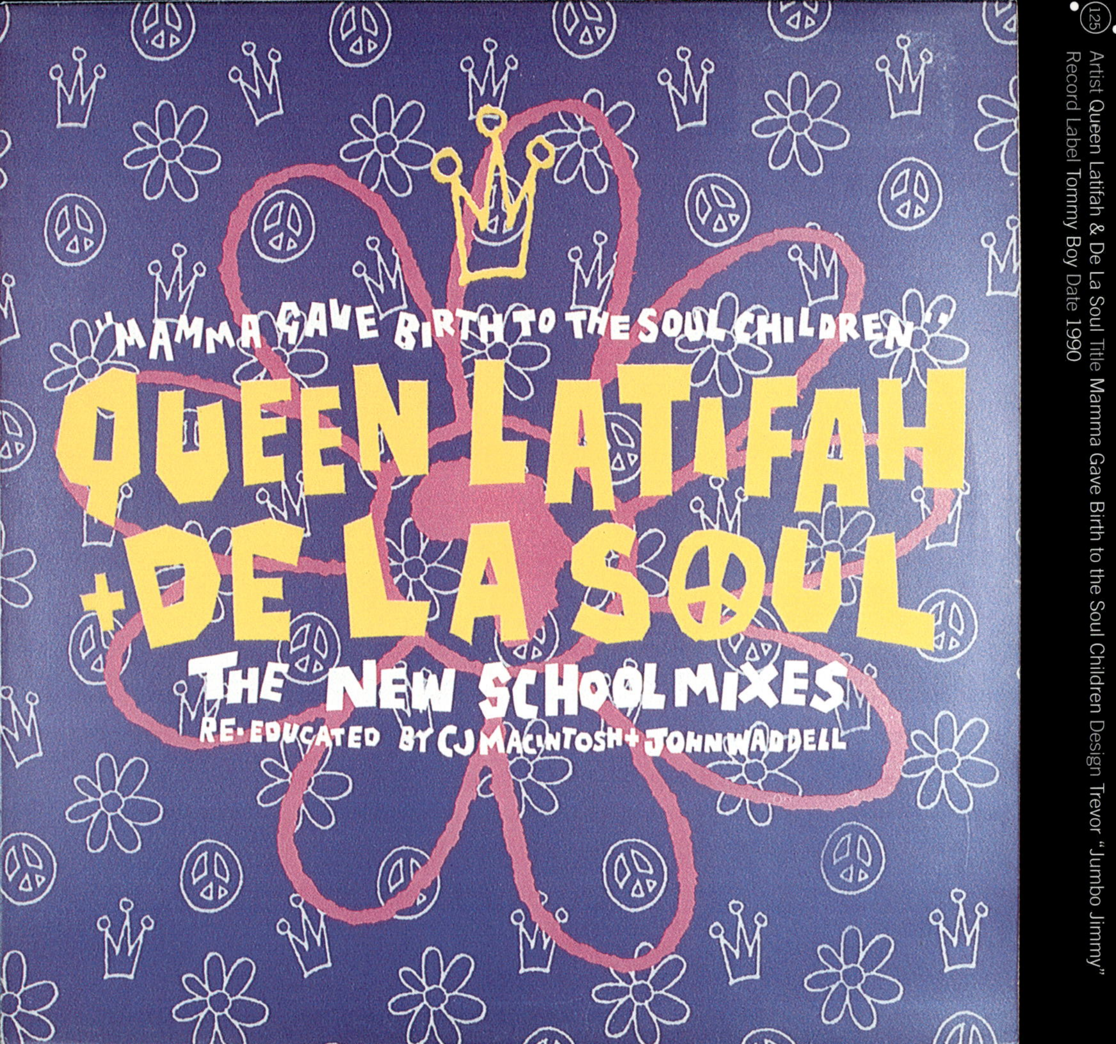

Artist Queen Latifah & De La Soul Title Mamma Gave Birth to the Soul Children Design Trevor "Jumbo Jimmy" Record Label Tommy Boy Date 1990

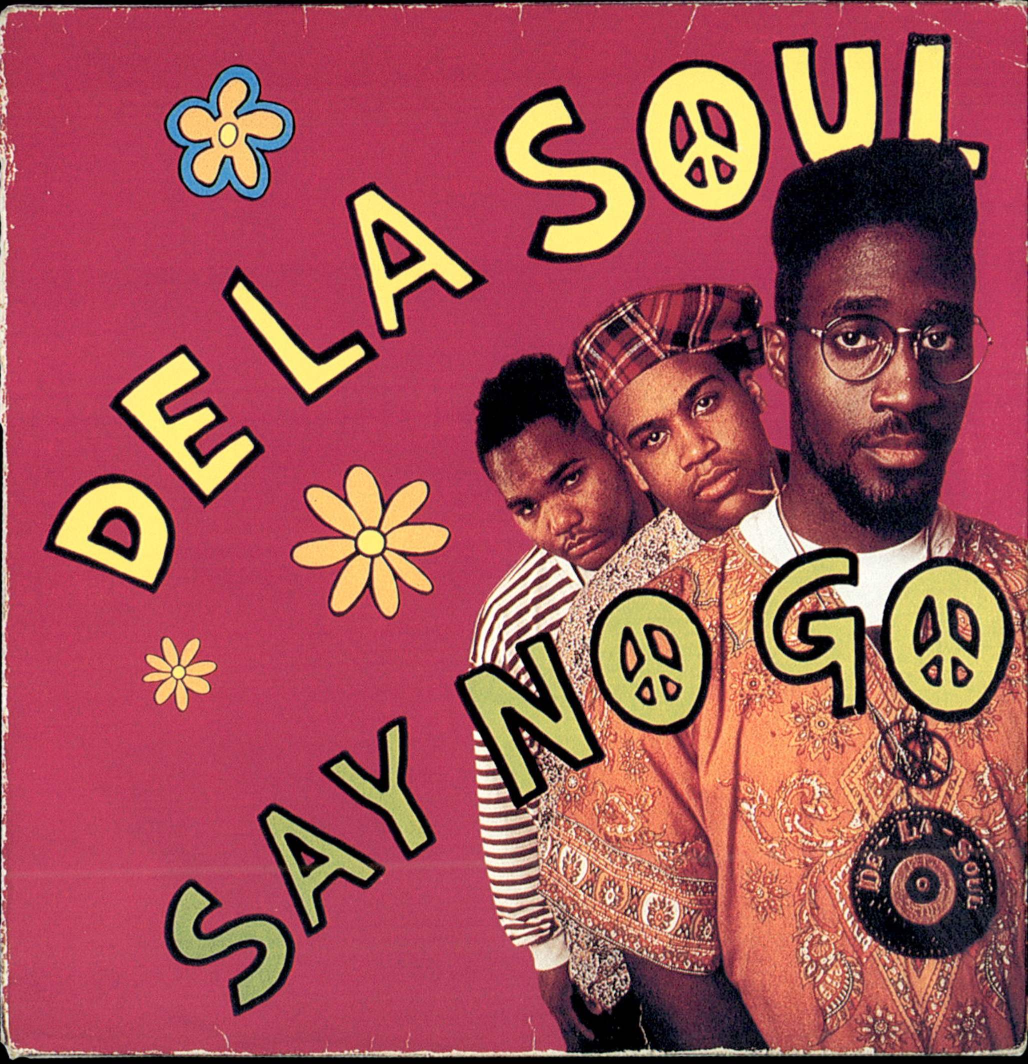

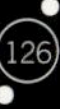

Artist De La Soul Title Say No Go Design Designland Photography Johnnie Miles
Record Label Big Life / Tommy Boy Date 1988

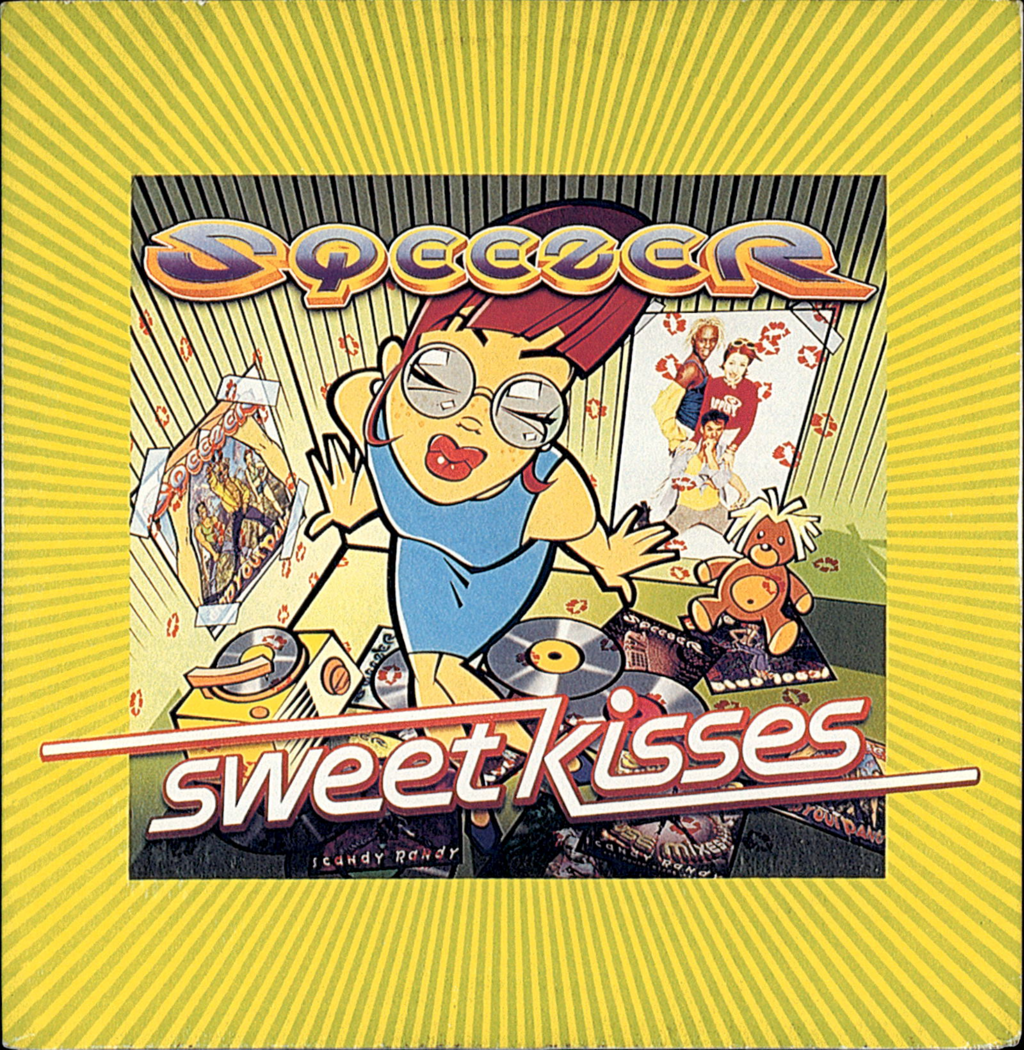

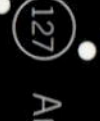

Artist Sqeezer Title Sweet Kisses Design Fantasy Factory Frankfurt Record Label Max Music Date 1996

Artist Alien Nation Title Lovers of the World Design Narodnipodnik, Marc Schlkowski
Record Label Boy Records Date 1992

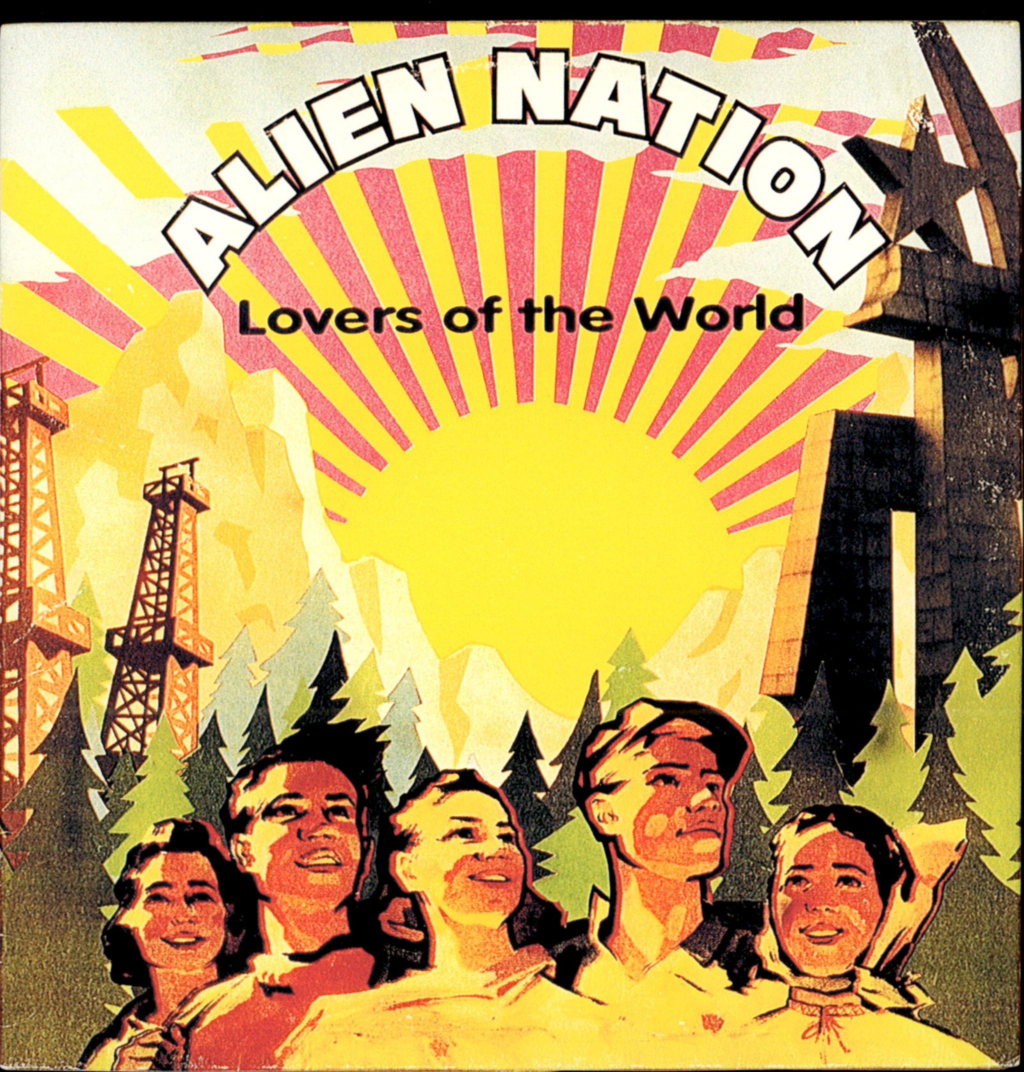

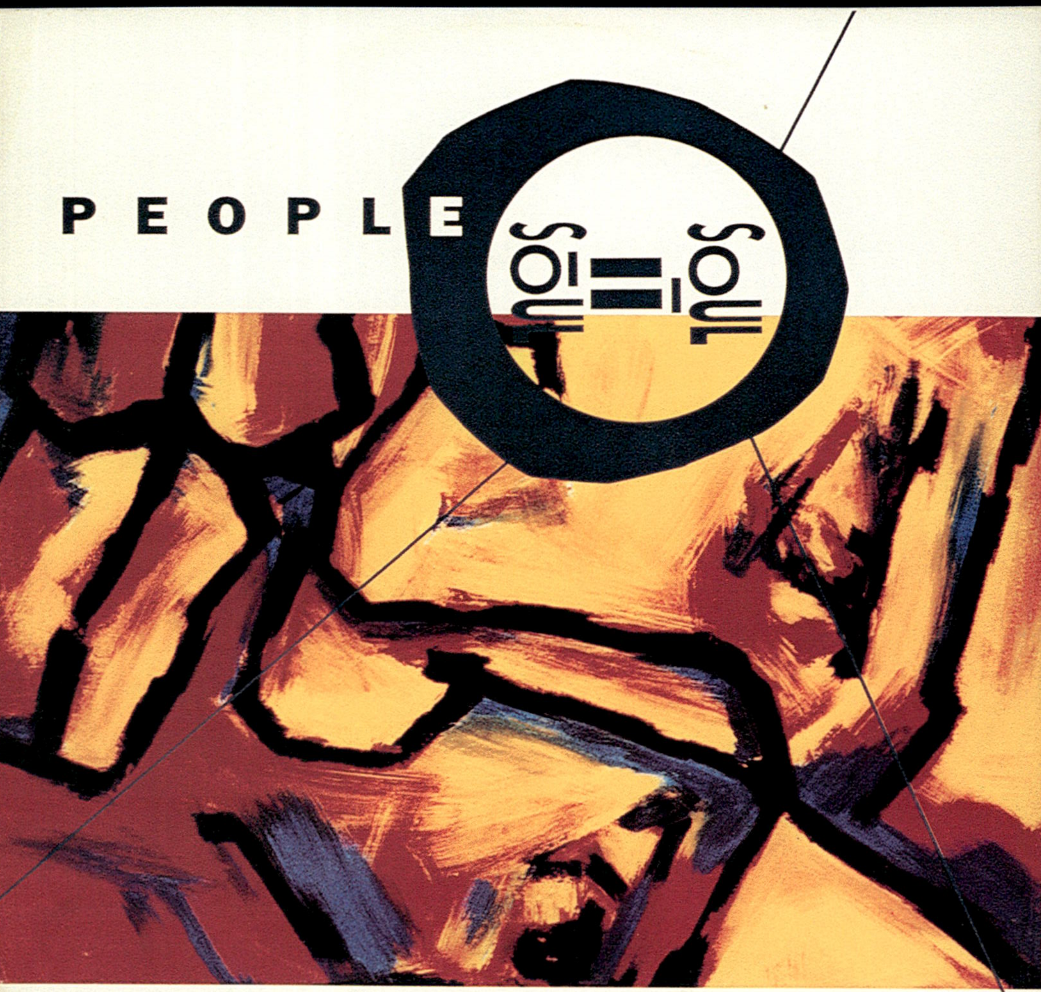

PEOPLE
SOUL II SOUL

Artist **Soul II Soul** Title **Get a Life** Design **Simon Taylor & The Thunder Jockeys** Illustration **Derek Yates**
Record Label **Ten Records** Date **1989**

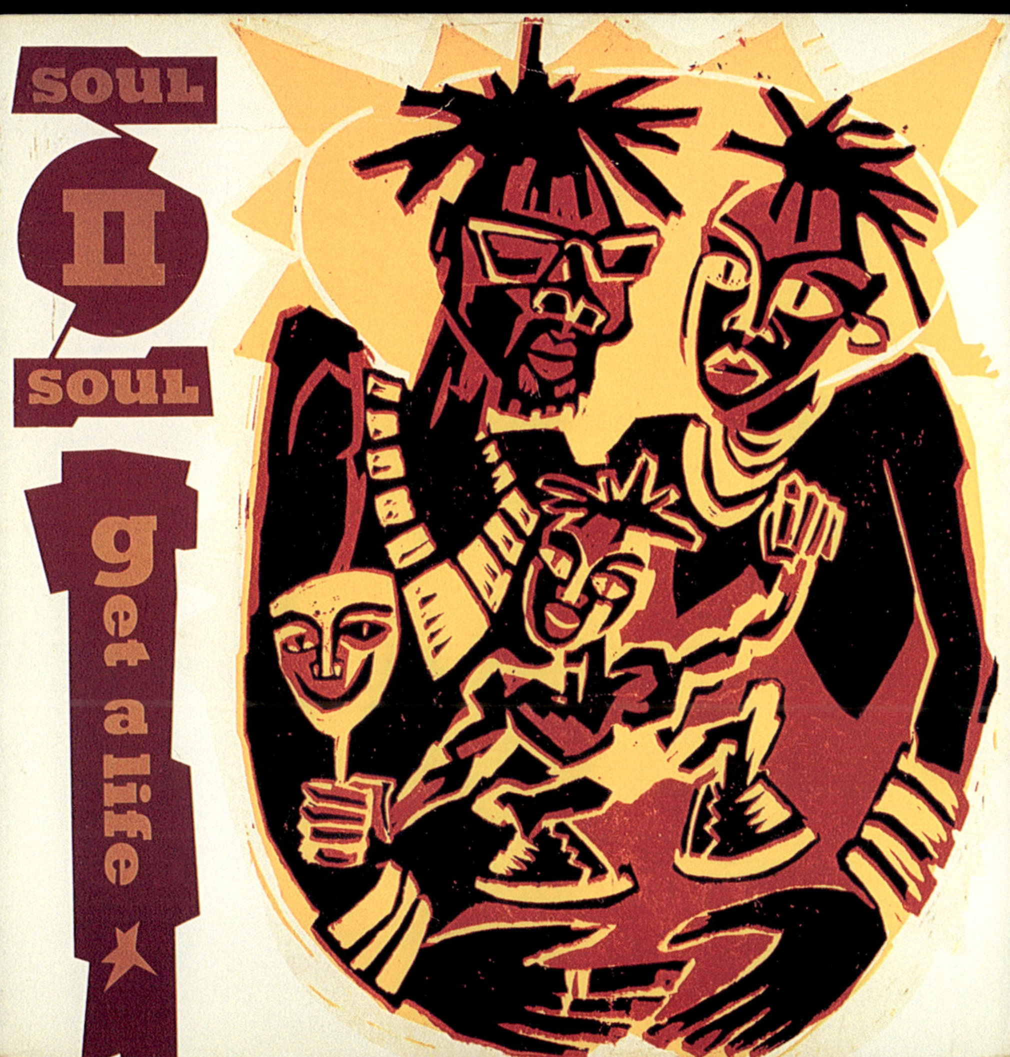

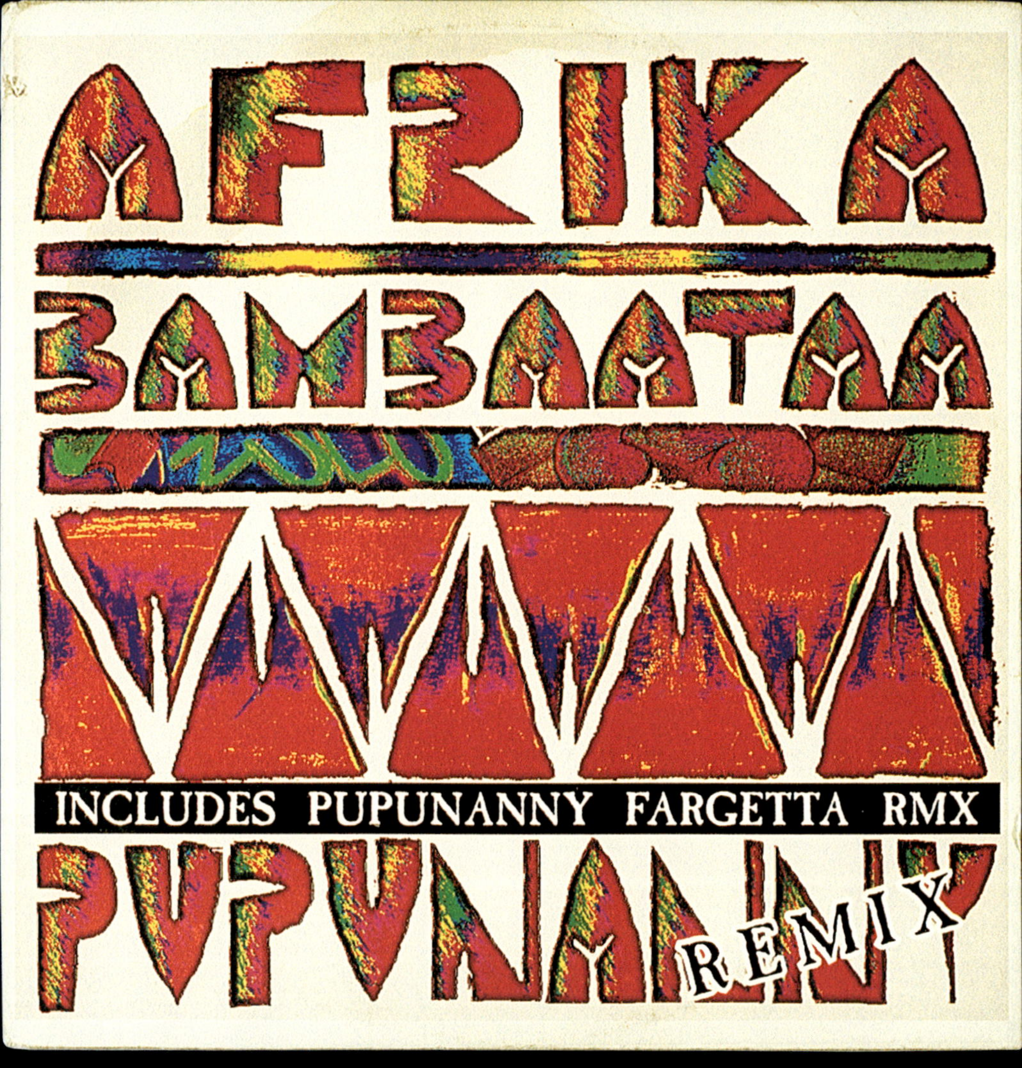

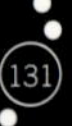

 Artist Afrika Bambaataa Title Pupunanny Design Oscar B. Record Label DFC Date 1994

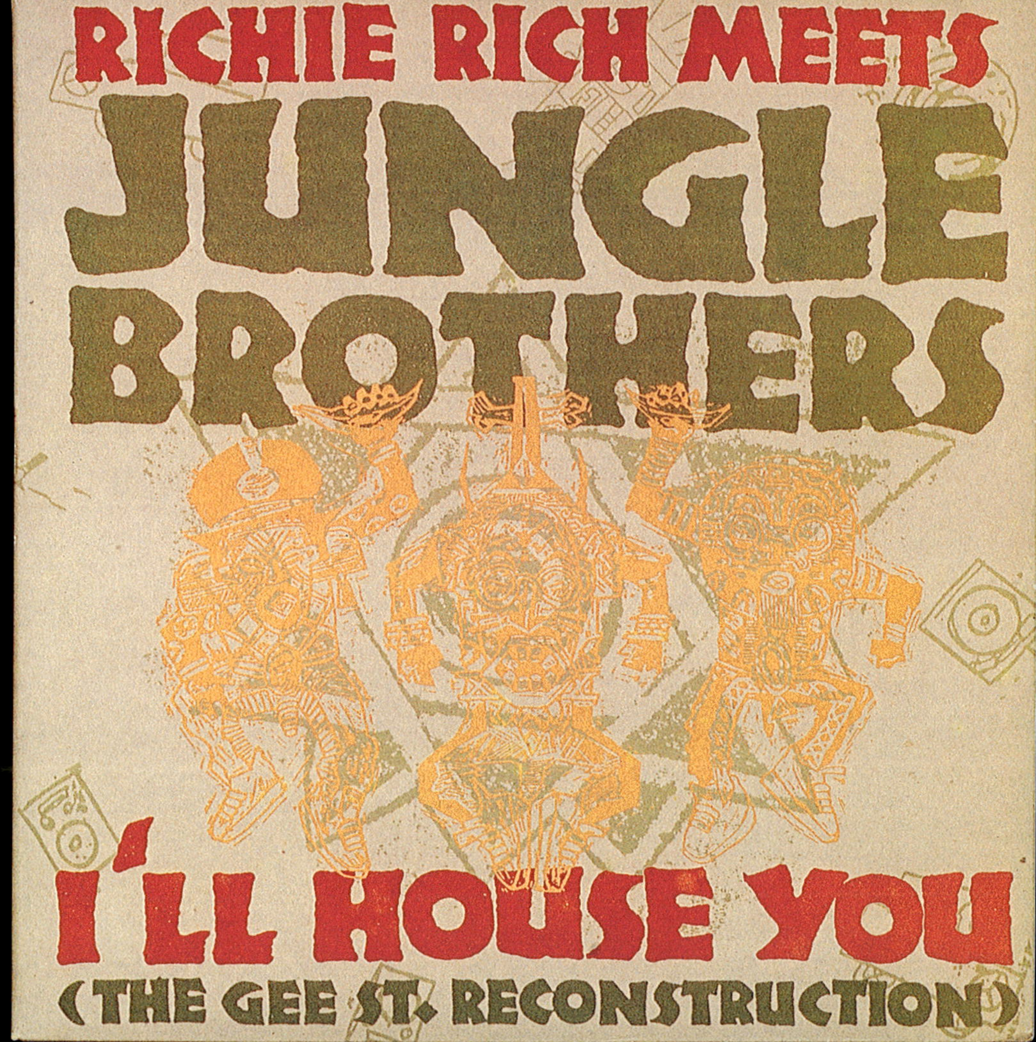

RICHIE RICH MEETS
JUNGLE BROTHERS
I'LL HOUSE YOU
(THE GEE ST. RECONSTRUCTION)

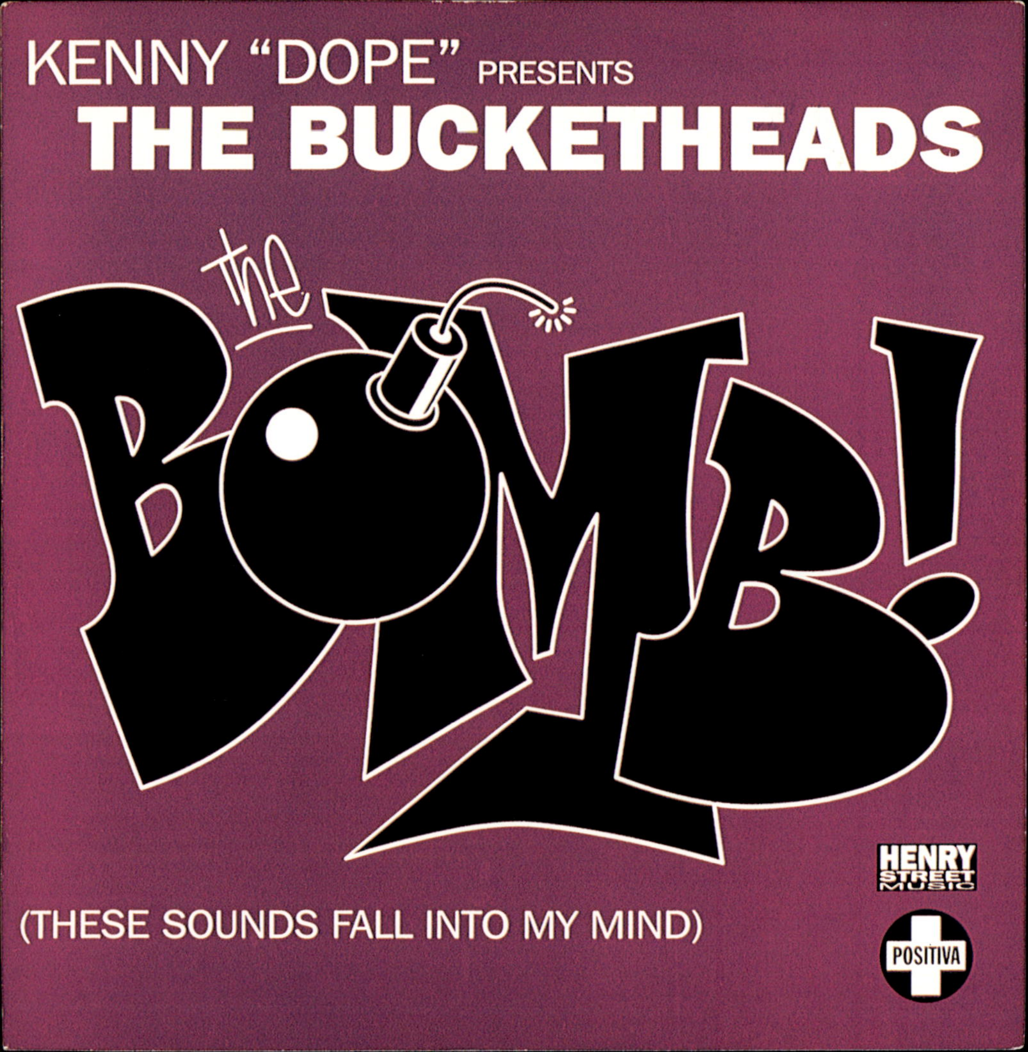

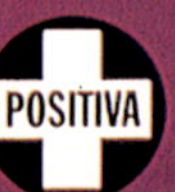

KENNY "DOPE" PRESENTS
THE BUCKETHEADS
THE BOMB!
(THESE SOUNDS FALL INTO MY MIND)
HENRY STREET MUSIC
POSITIVA

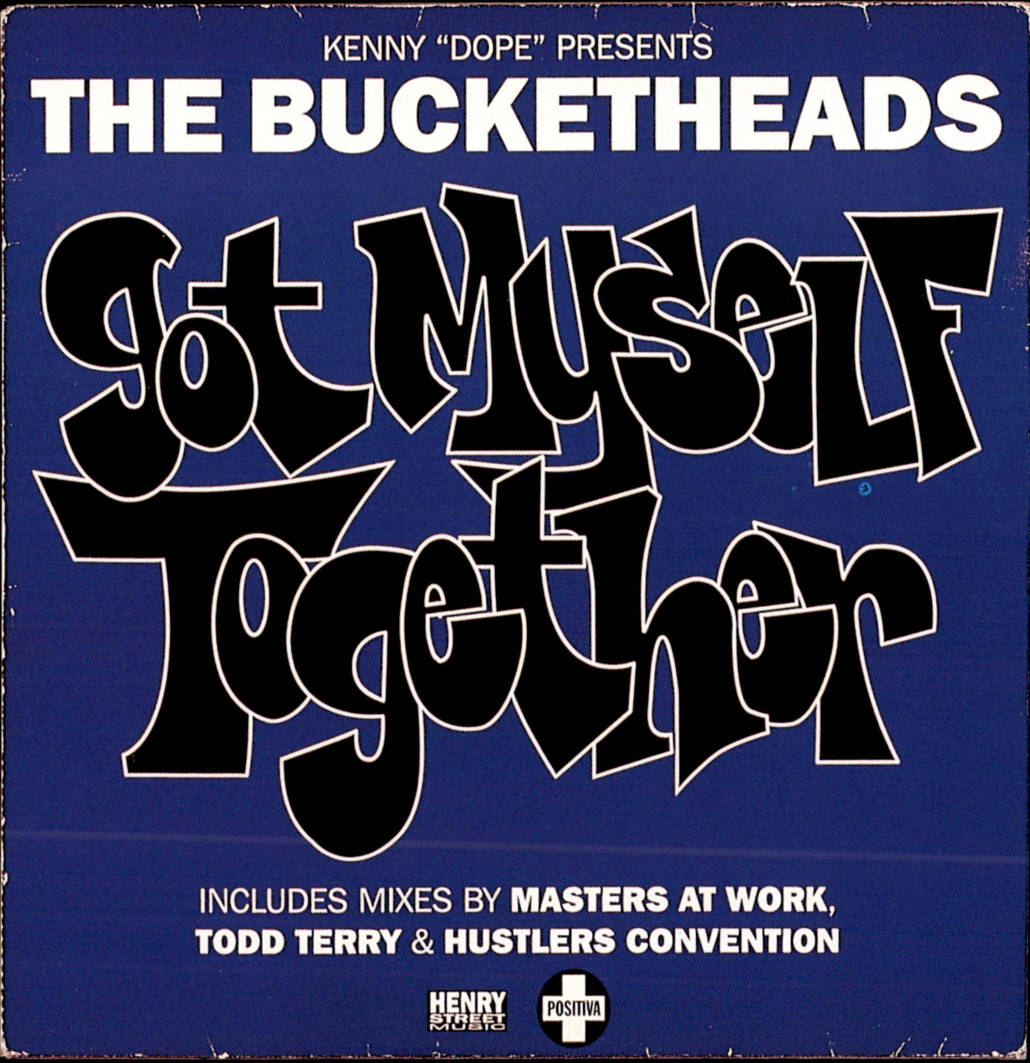

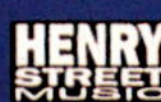
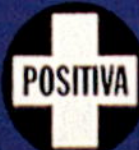

KENNY "DOPE" PRESENTS
THE BUCKETHEADS
got Myself Together
INCLUDES MIXES BY MASTERS AT WORK,
TODD TERRY & HUSTLERS CONVENTION
HENRY STREET MUSIC
POSITIVA

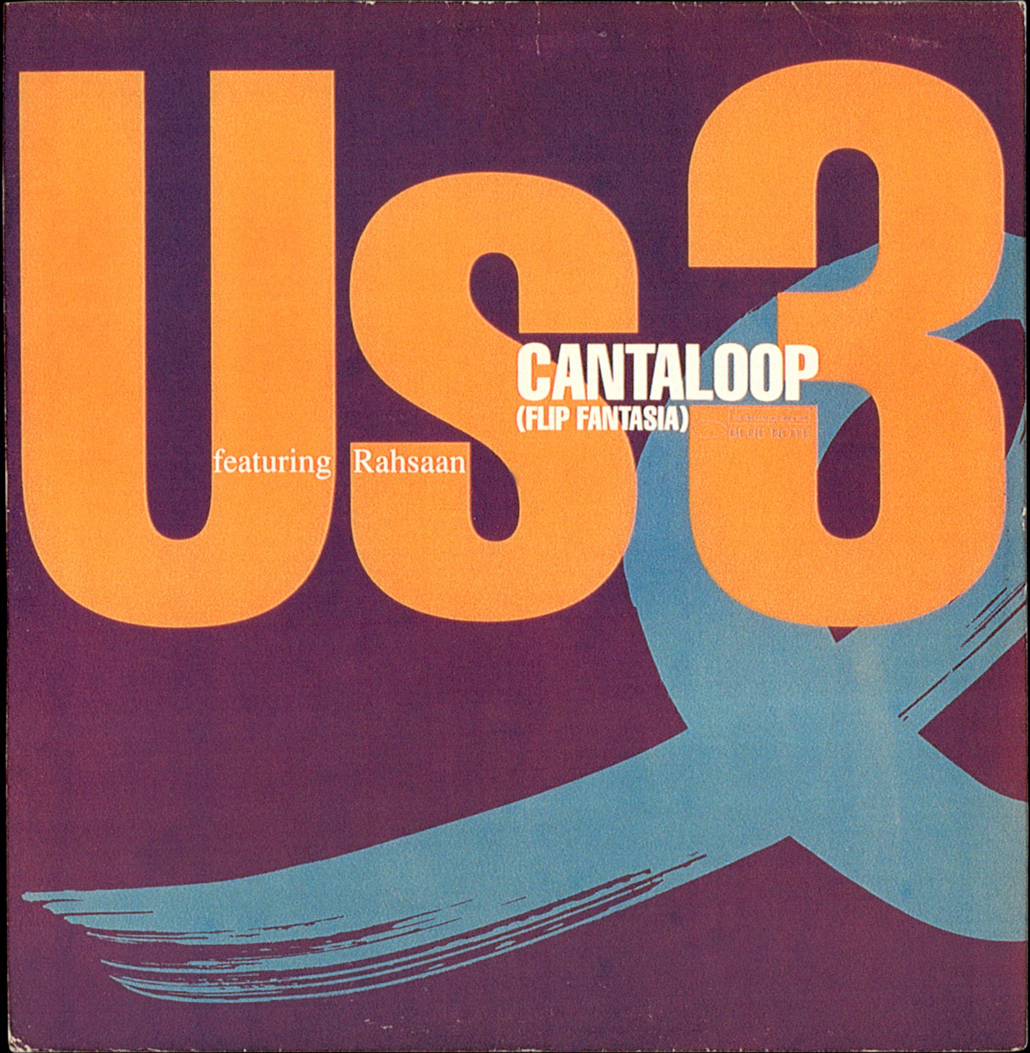

US3
featuring Rahsaan
CANTALOOP
(FLIP FANTASIA)
BLUE NOTE

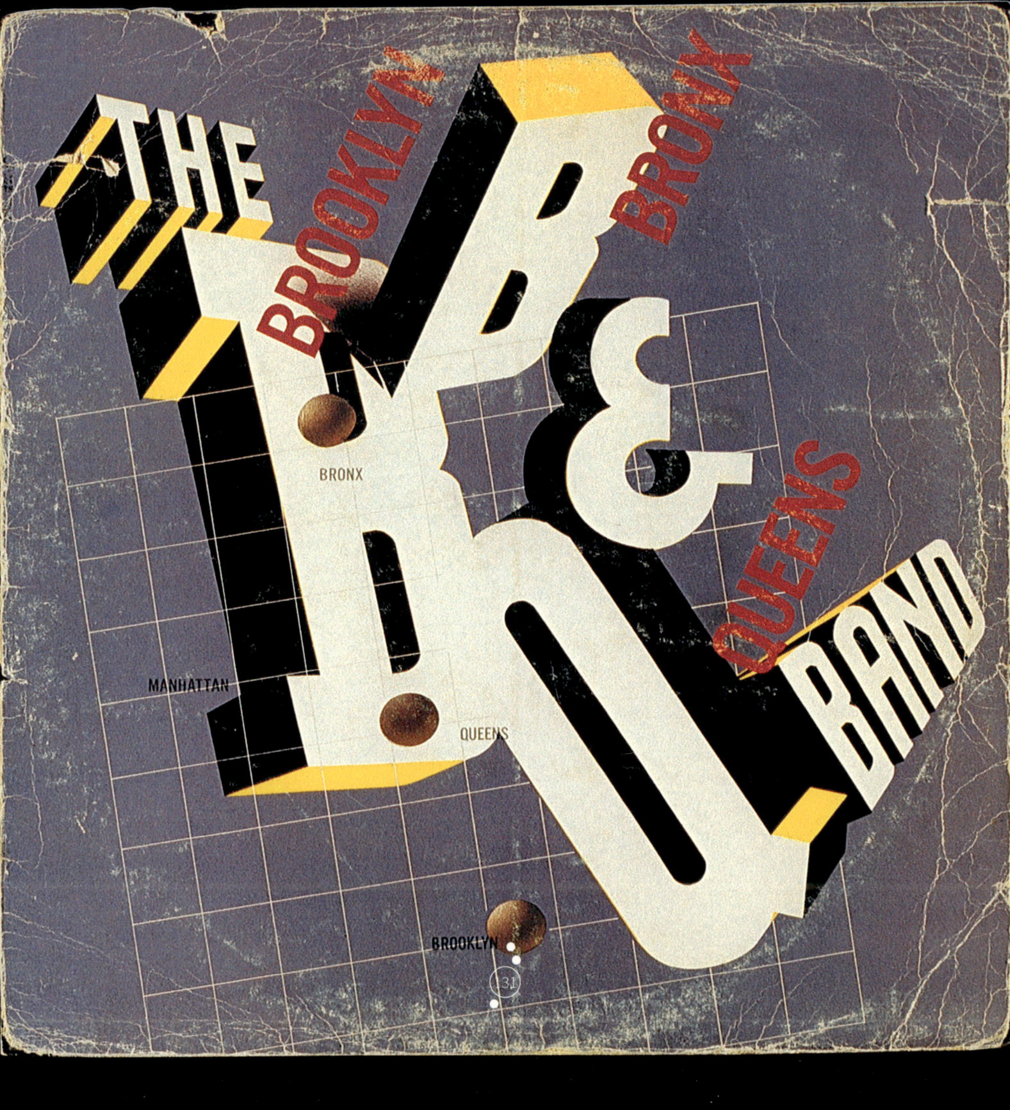

 Artist The Brooklyn, Bronx & Queens Band Record Label Capitol Records Date 1981

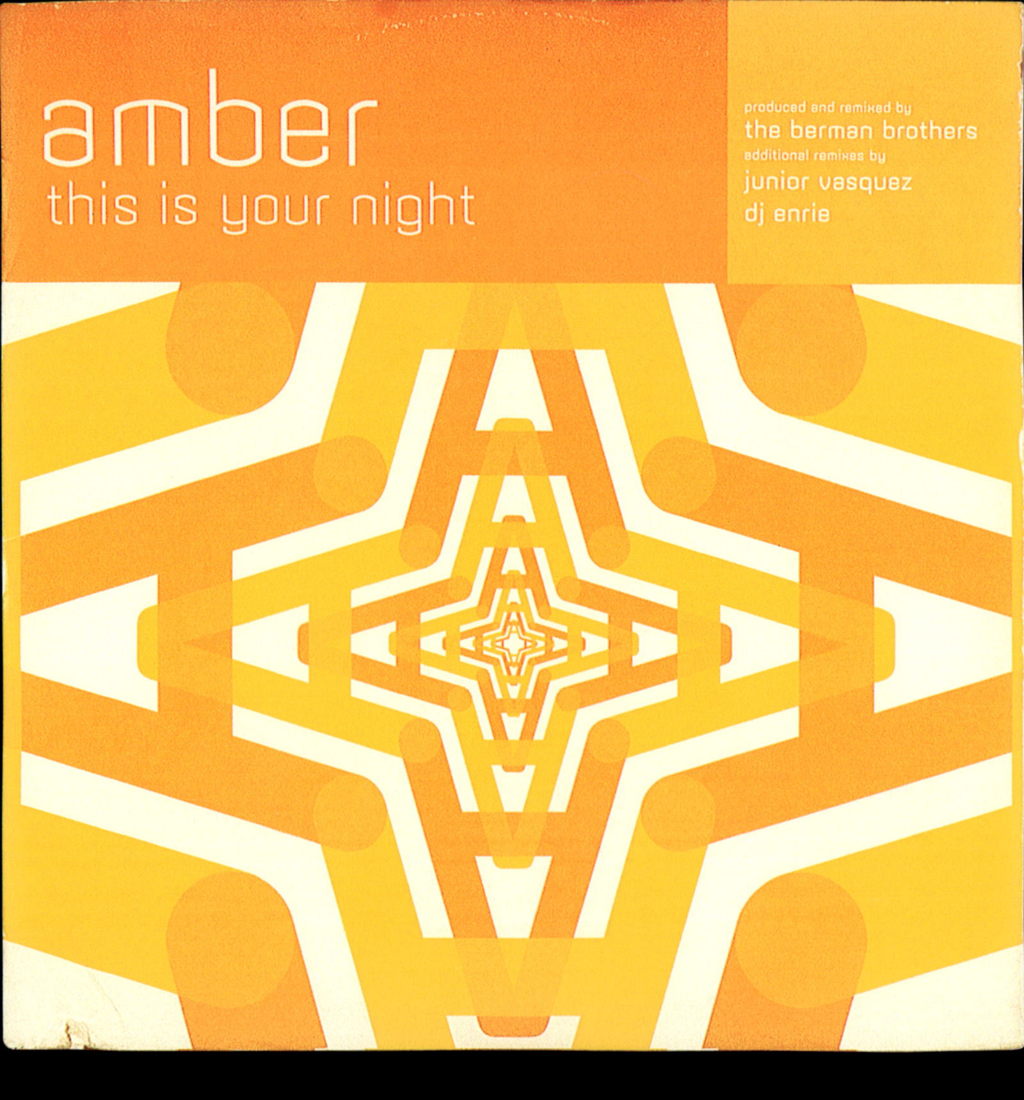

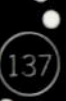

Artist Amber Title This Is Your Night Record Label Tommy Boy Date 1996

HYPER LOGIC

ONLY ME

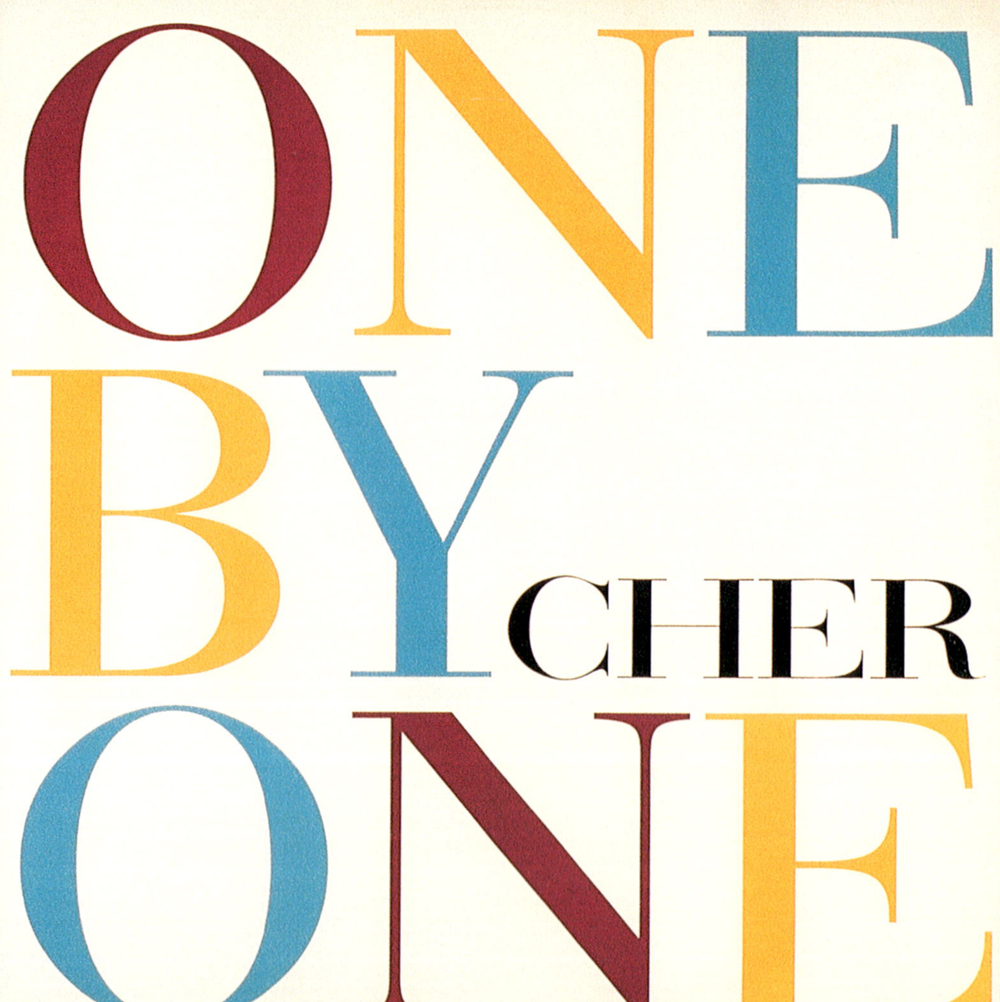
ONE
BY
ONE
CHER

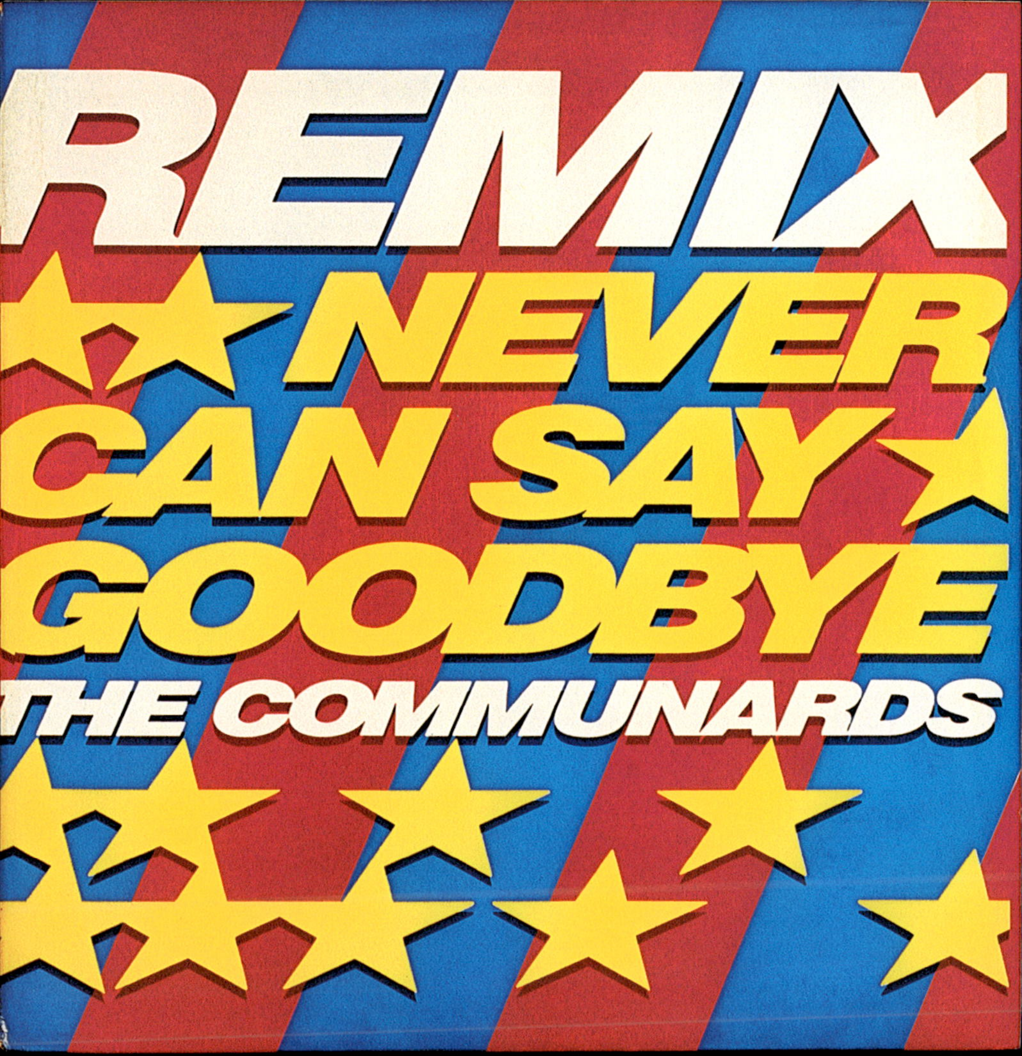

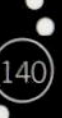

 Artist The Communards Title Never Can Say Goodbye Design DKB Record Label London Records Date 1987

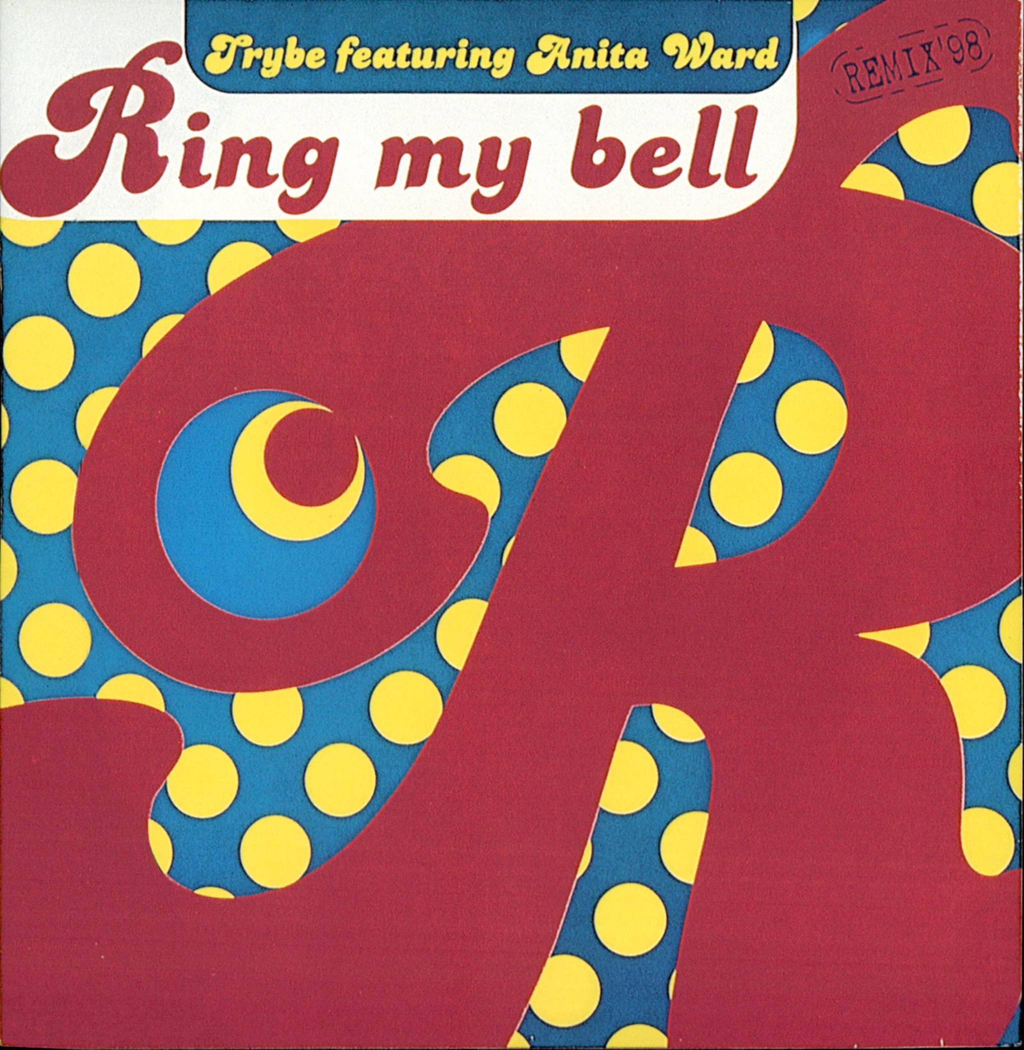

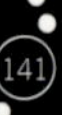

Artist Tribe feat. Anita Ward Title Ring My Bell Design Microfoam Record Label Max Music Date 1998

SUPER DISCO 45 R P.M.
TWIST (ROUND & ROUND)
OOS-603
CHILL
FAC-TORR

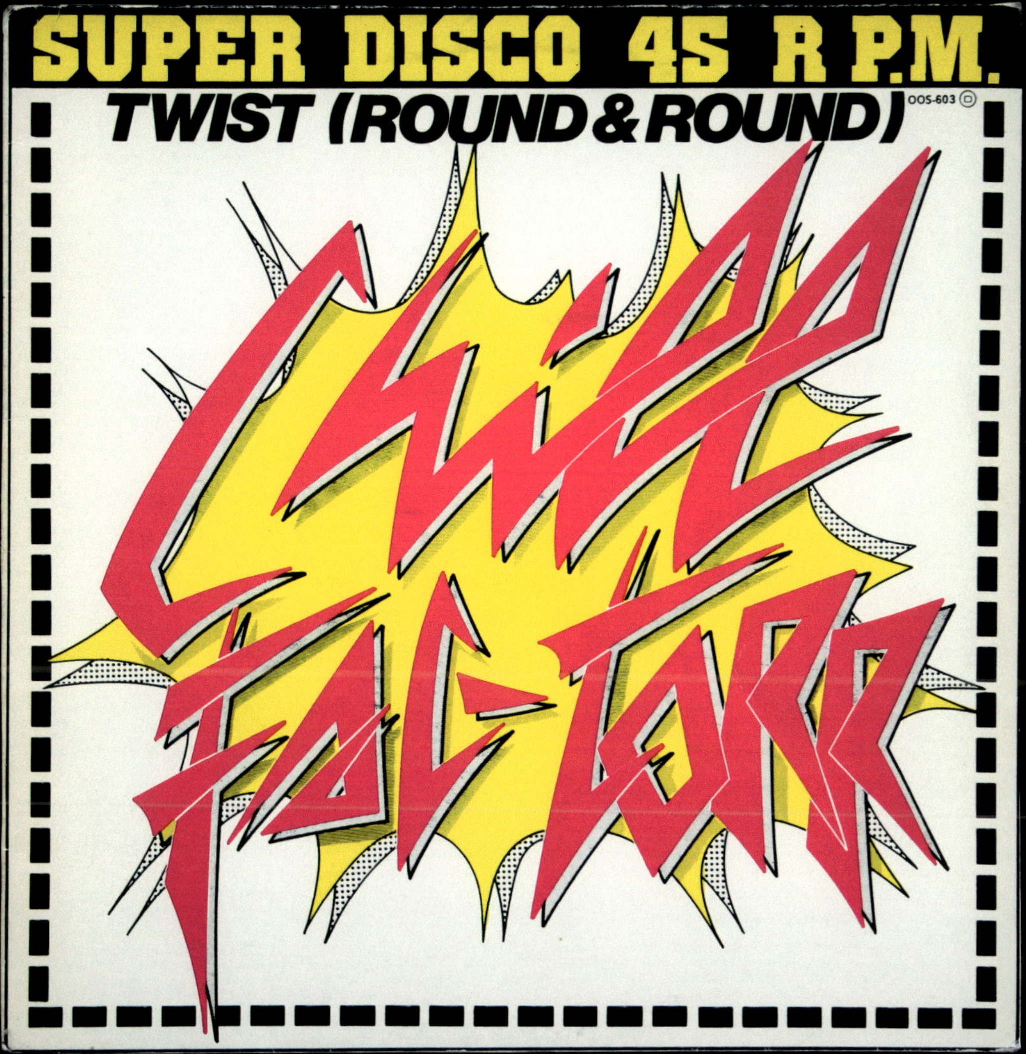

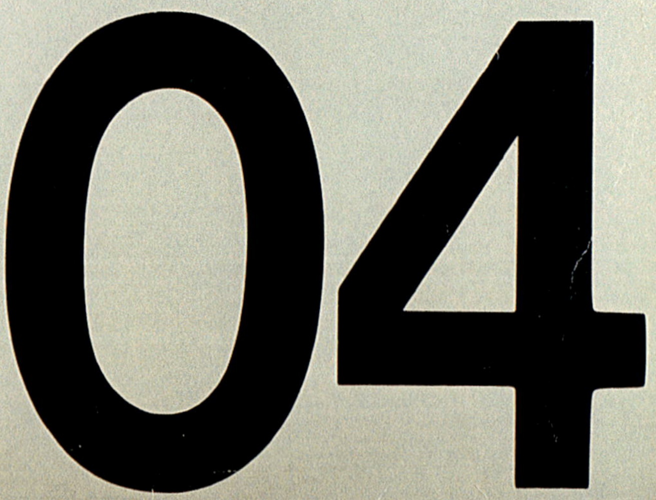

Artist Nitzer Ebb Title Let Your Body Learn Record Label Mute Records Date 1986

KILLEREMIX
ADAMSKI

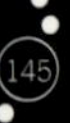

Artist Steve "Silk" Hurley & The Voices of Life Title The Word Is Love Design Dsign>OEL 180°
Record Label Vendetta Date 1998

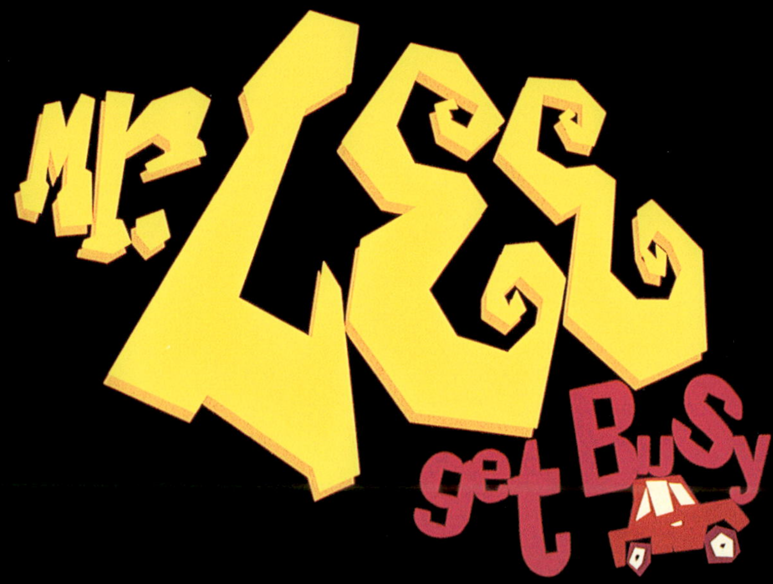

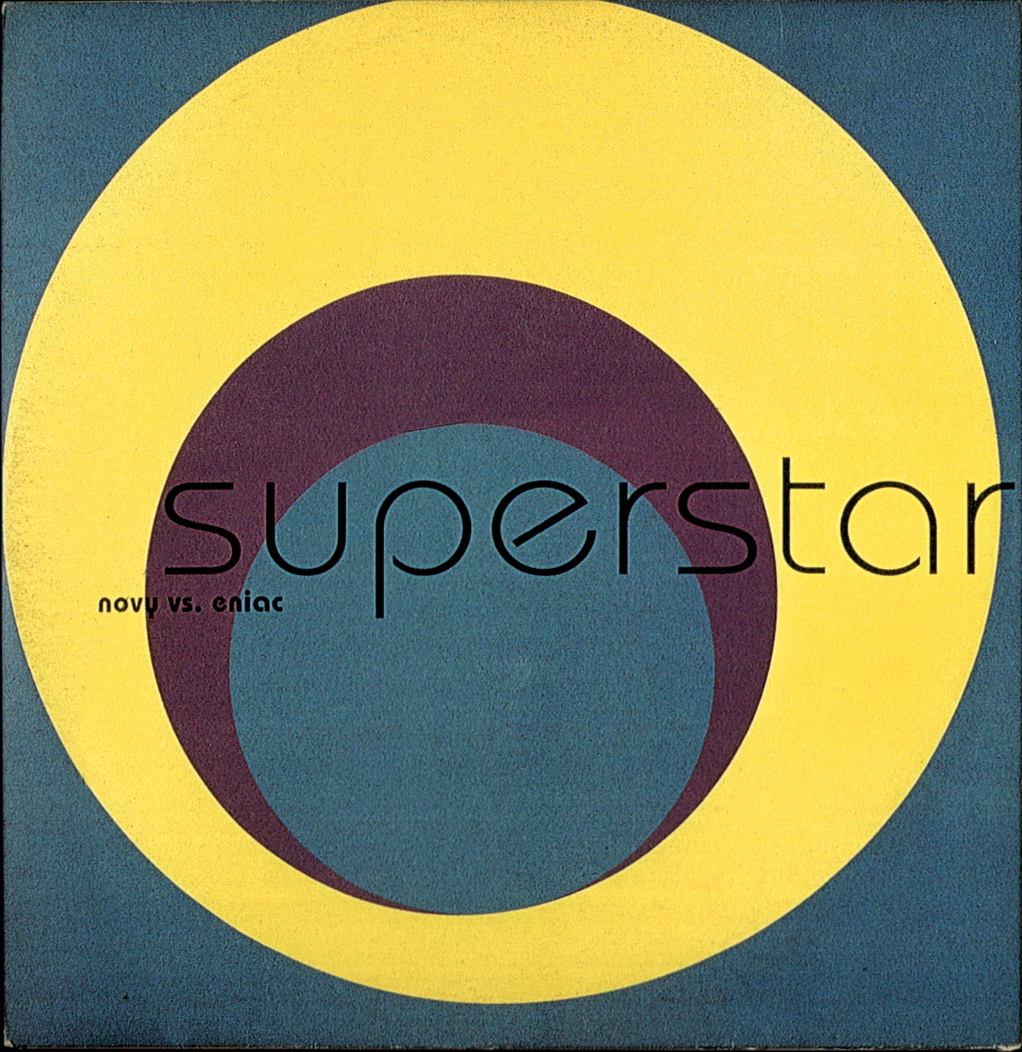

Artist Novy vs. Eniac Title Superstar Record Label Kosmo Date 1997

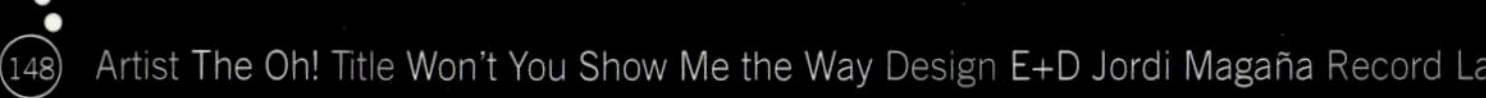

the oh!
won't you show me the way

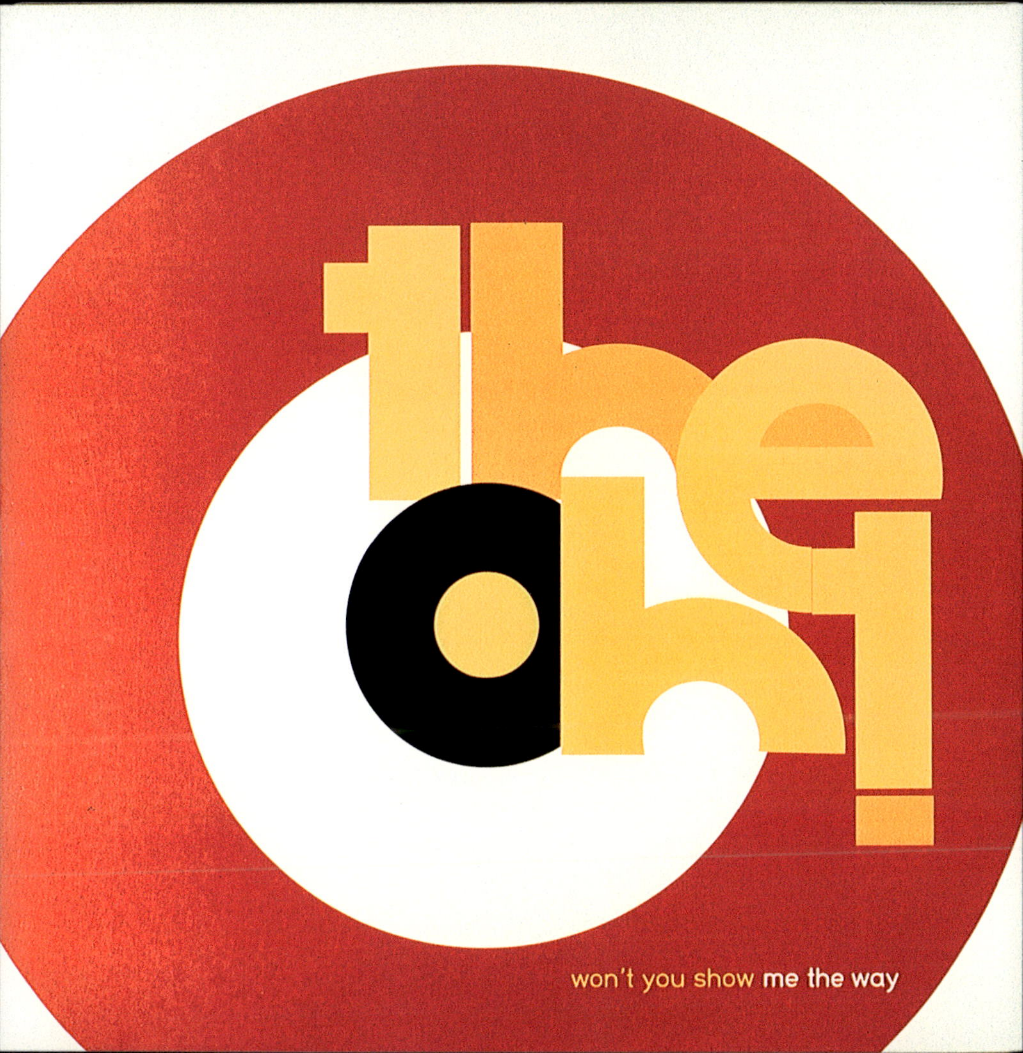

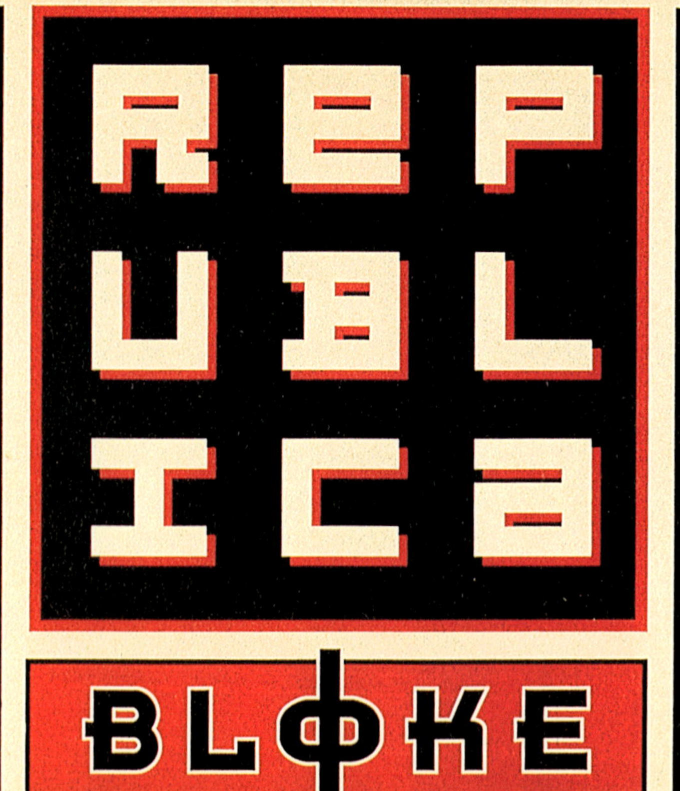
REPUBLICA
BLOKE
A1. EXTENDED MIX B1. BLAME IT ON THE VODKA MIX B2. JACK DANIELS MIX

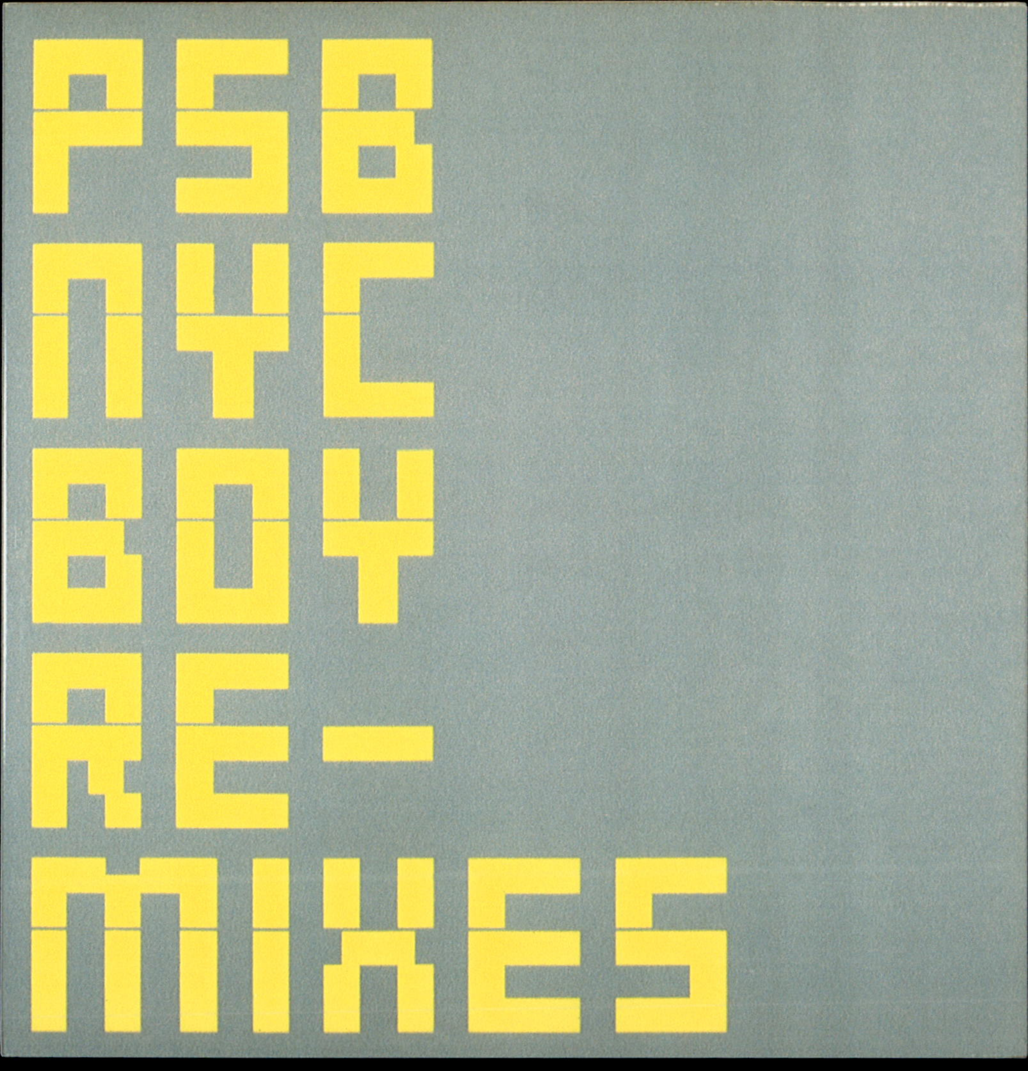

PSB NYC BOY RE-MIXES

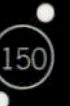

 Artist Pet Shop Boys Title New York City Boy Design Ian MacNeil Record Label EMI Date 1999

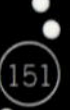

 Artist The Style Council Title Promised Land Design TSC/SJH Record Label Polydor Date 1989

THE WEE PAPA GIRL RAPPERS
HEAT IT UP
FEATURING
2 MEN AND A DRUM MACHINE

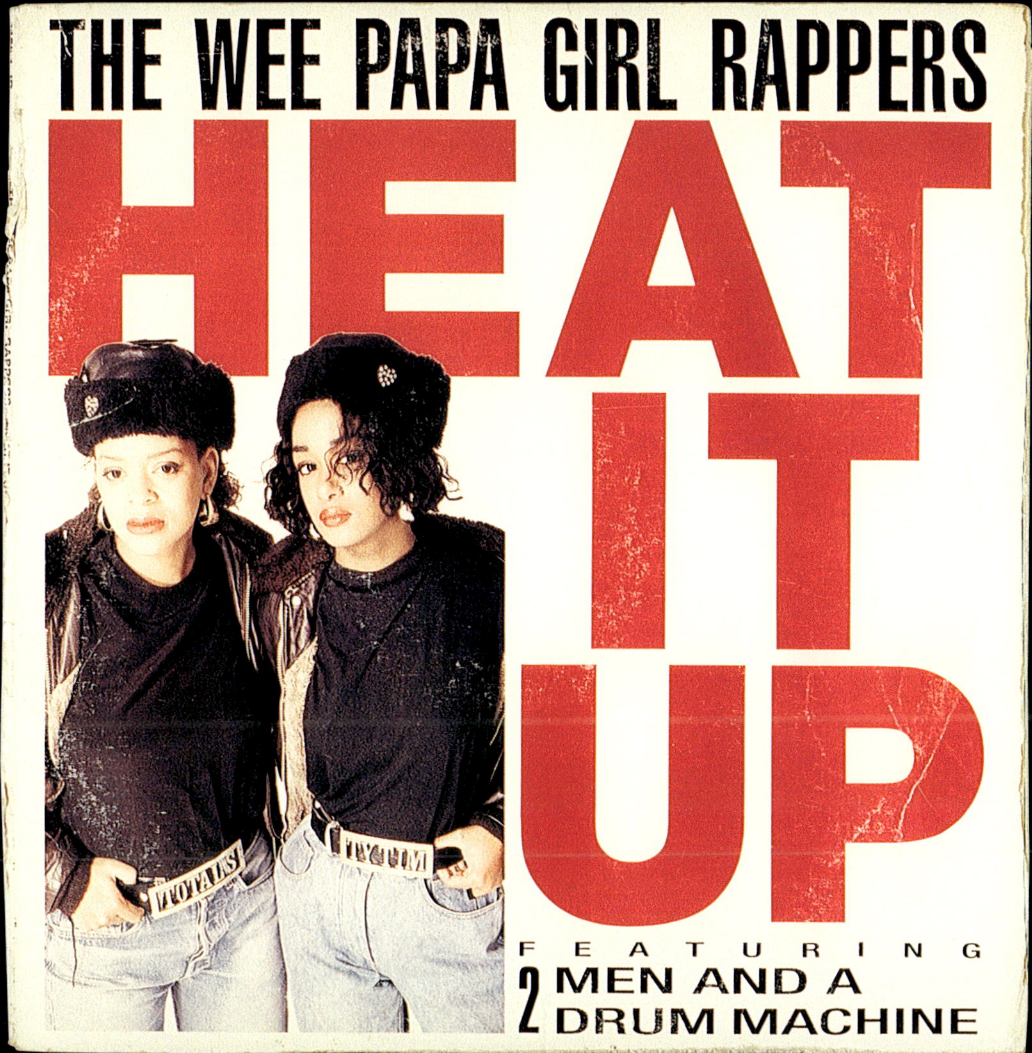

Artist Simply Red Title Ain't That a Lot of Love Design @ Peacock Record Label East West Date 1999

remixes by:
CLUB 69 / Johnny Vicious / Phats & Small
desert eagle discs / Jimmy Gomez

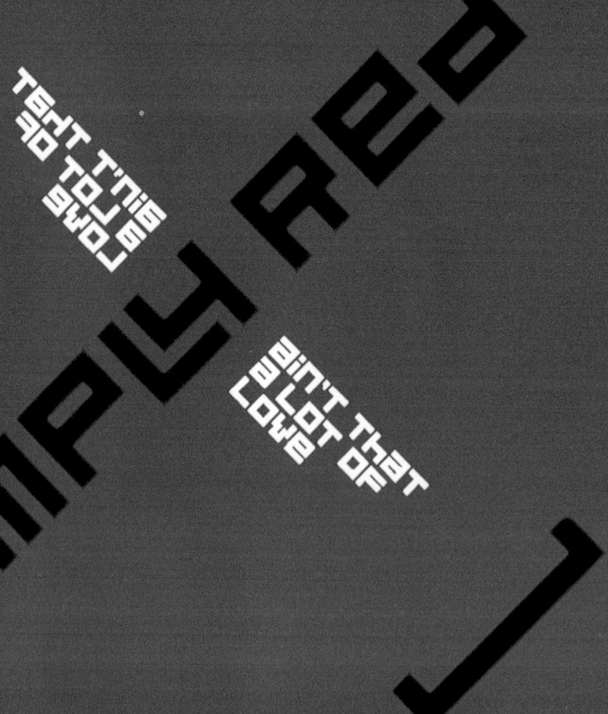

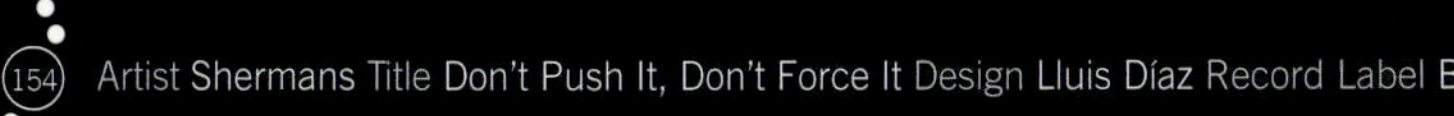
ЗHЕRMAИЗ
SHERMANS
DON'T PUSH IT, DON'T FORCE IT
AGGRESSORS
527th AS

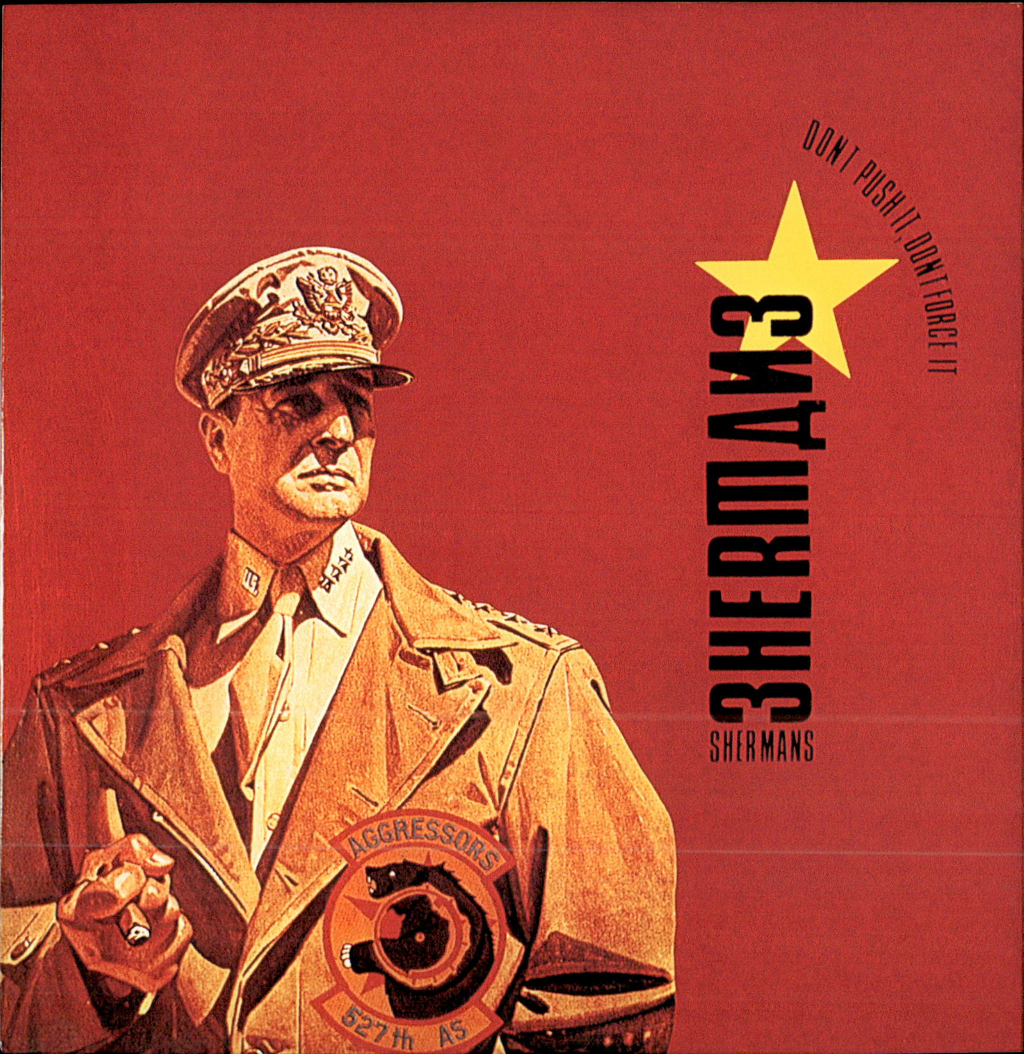

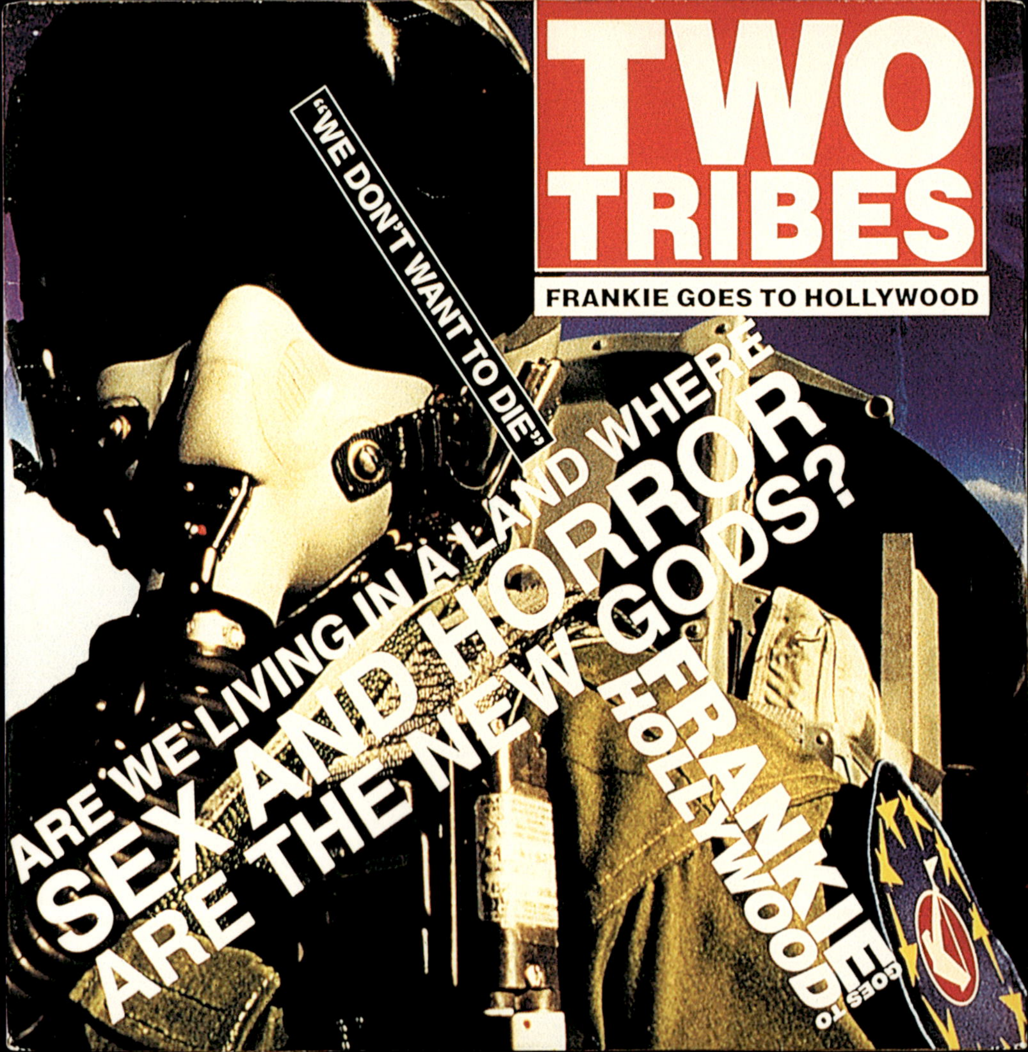

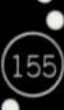

Artist Frankie Goes to Hollywood Title Two Tribes Design Me Company Record Label ZTT Records Date 1984

Artist Frankie Goes to Hollywood Title Two Tribes Mixes

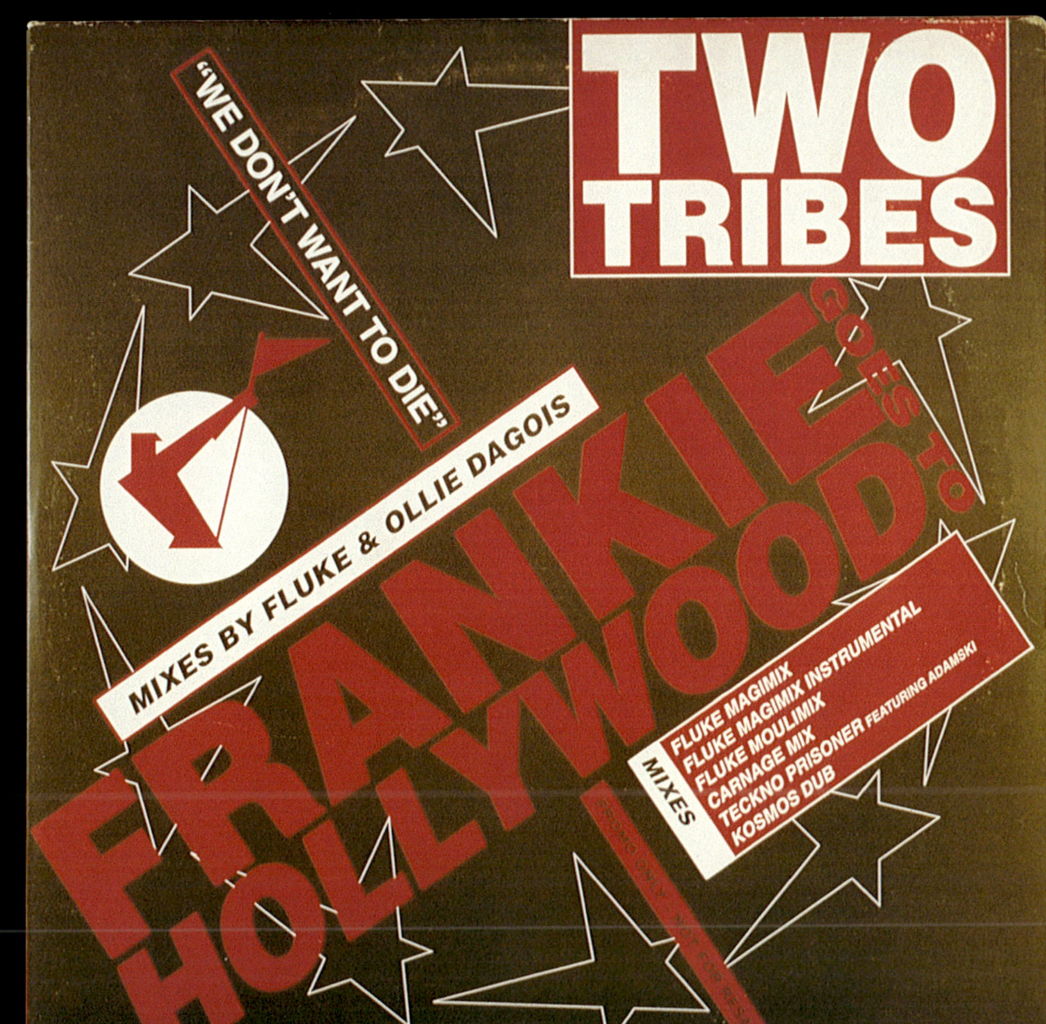

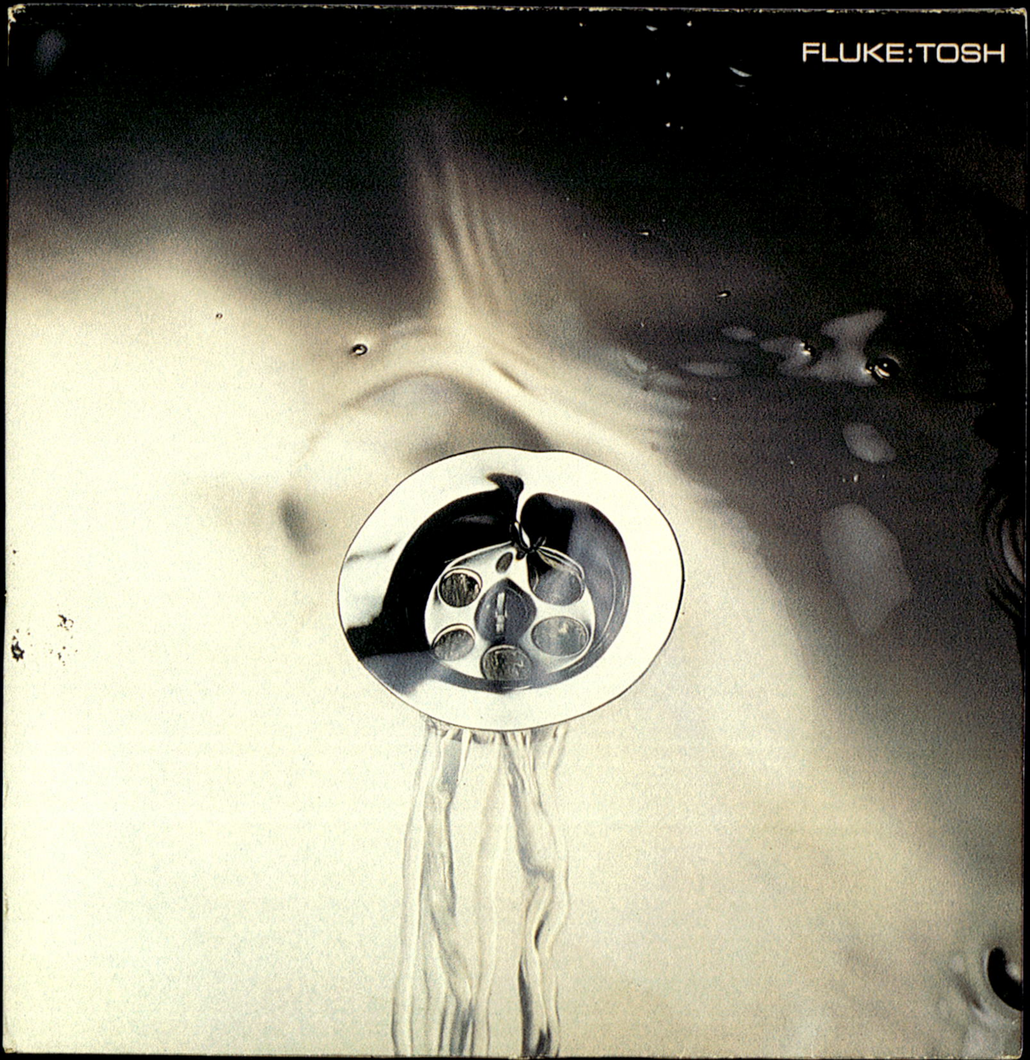

FLUKE:TOSH
Artist Fluke Title Tosh Record Label Circa Records Date 1995

157

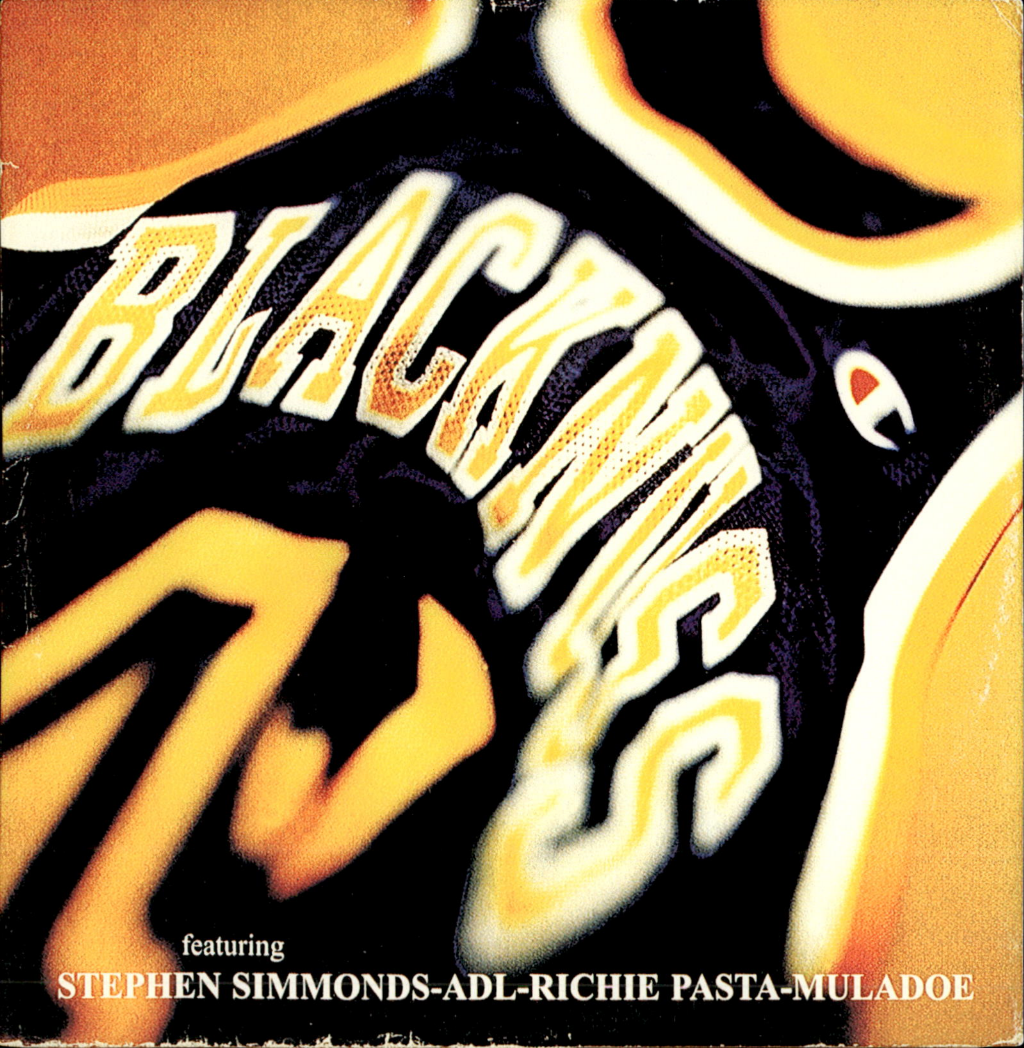

BLACK MUSIC
featuring
STEPHEN SIMMONDS-ADL-RICHIE PASTA-MULADOE

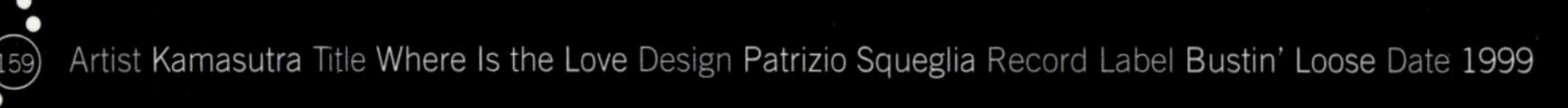
kamasutra where is the love
k

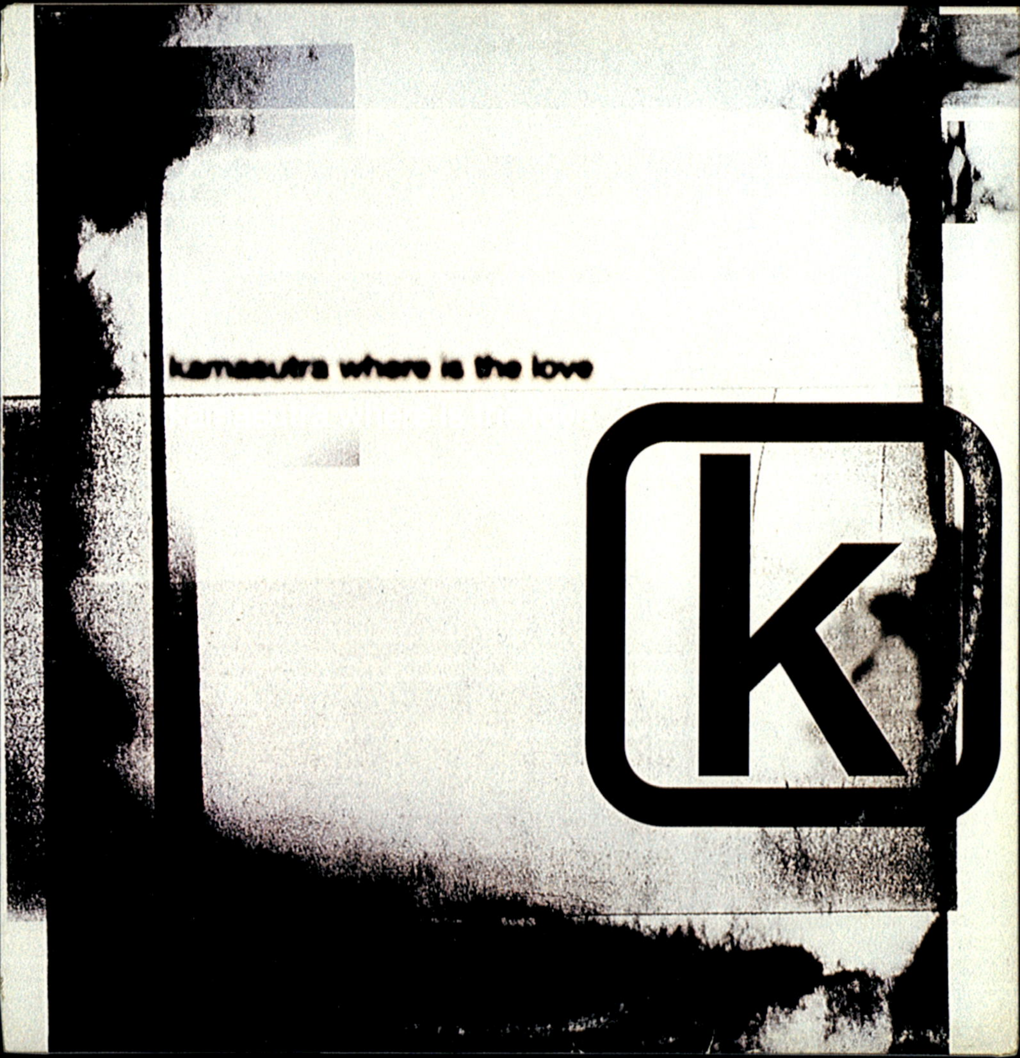

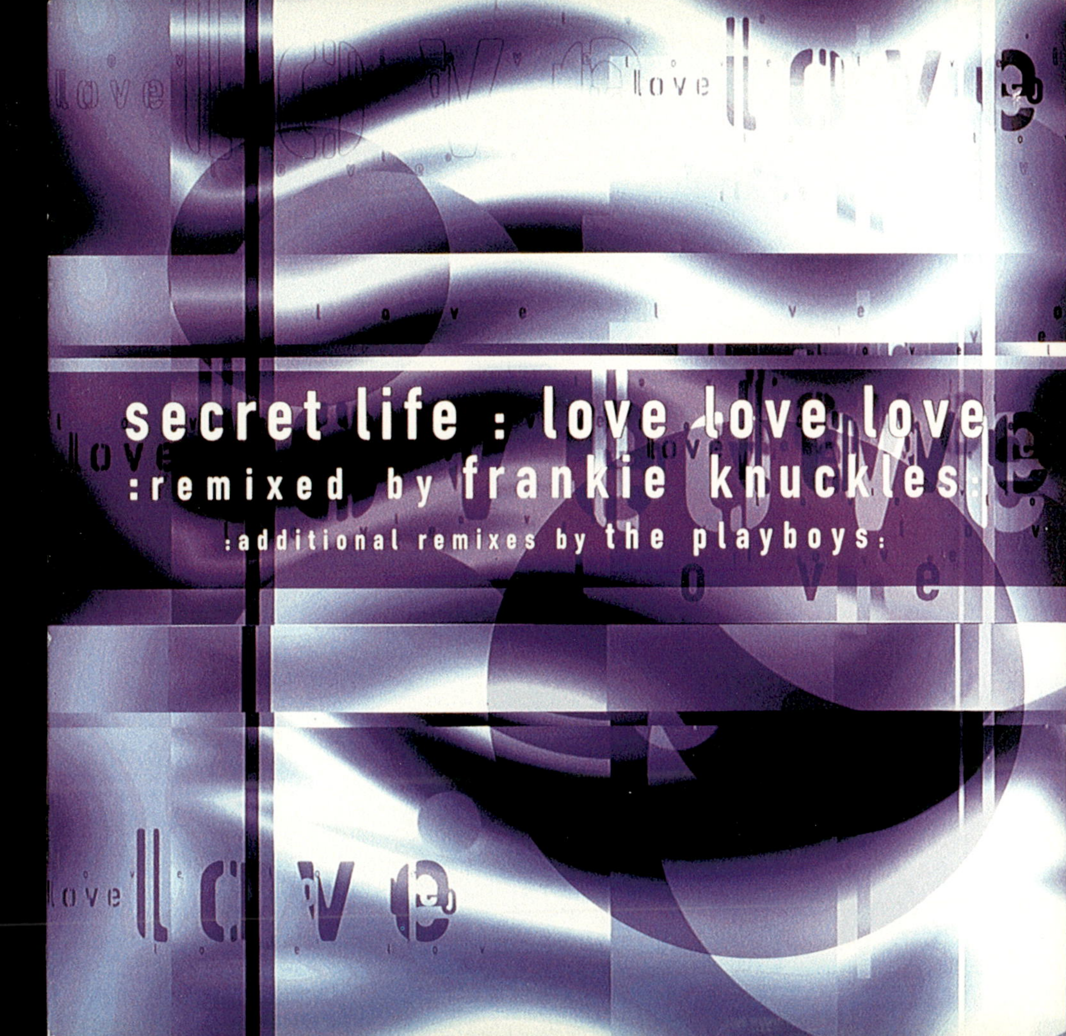

secret life : love love love
:remixed by frankie knuckles:
:additional remixes by the playboys:

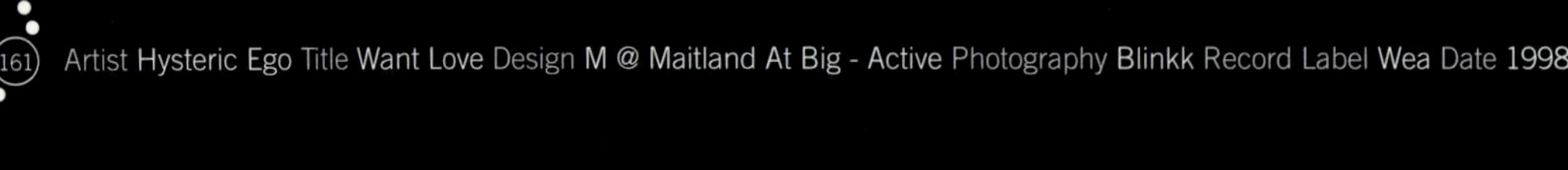

want love   the remixes
hysteric ego
REMIXES BY THE TIMEWRITER, SOL BROTHERS, LES VISITEURS DU SOIR AND HYSTERIC EGO.

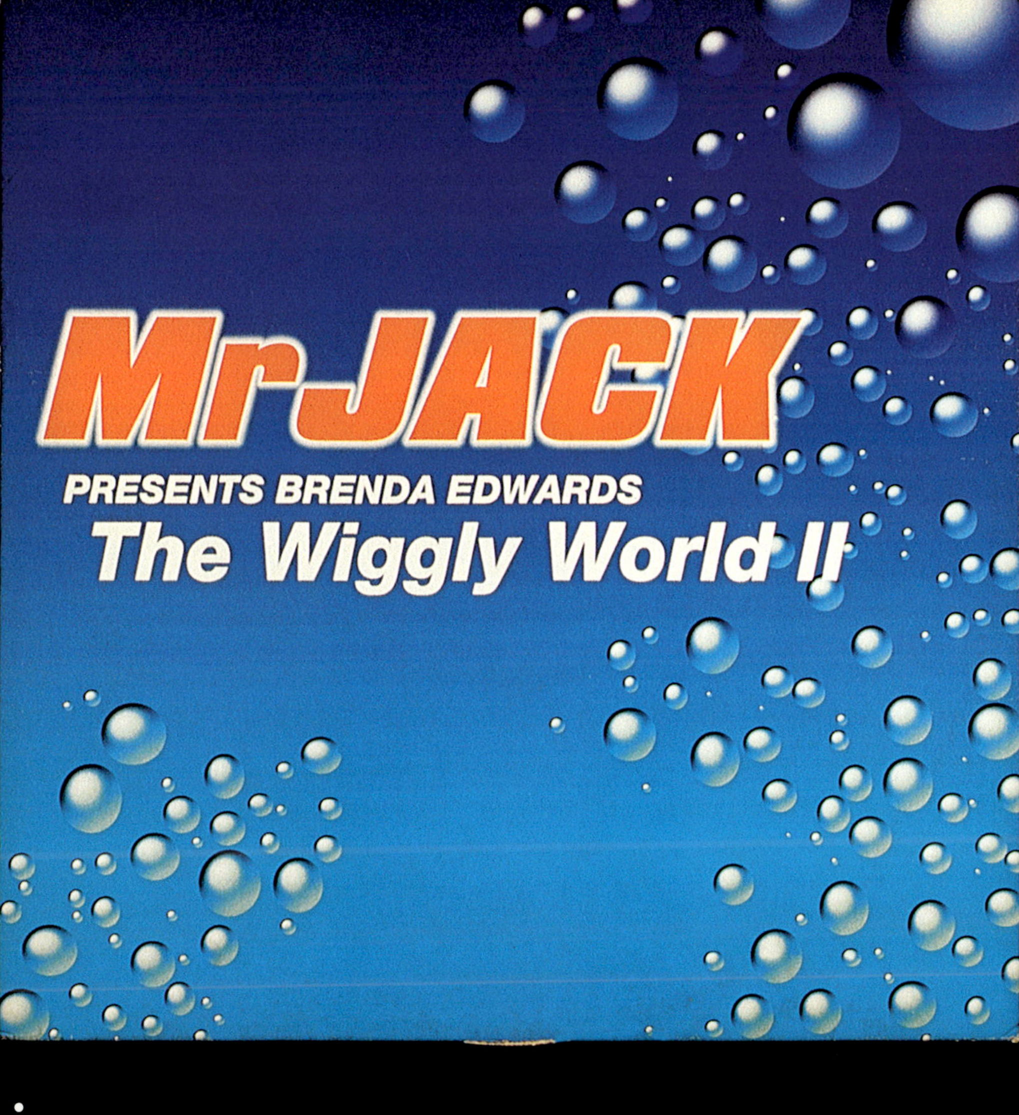

Artist Mr. Jack presents Brenda Edwards Title The Wiggly World II Record Label Noise Traxx Date 1997

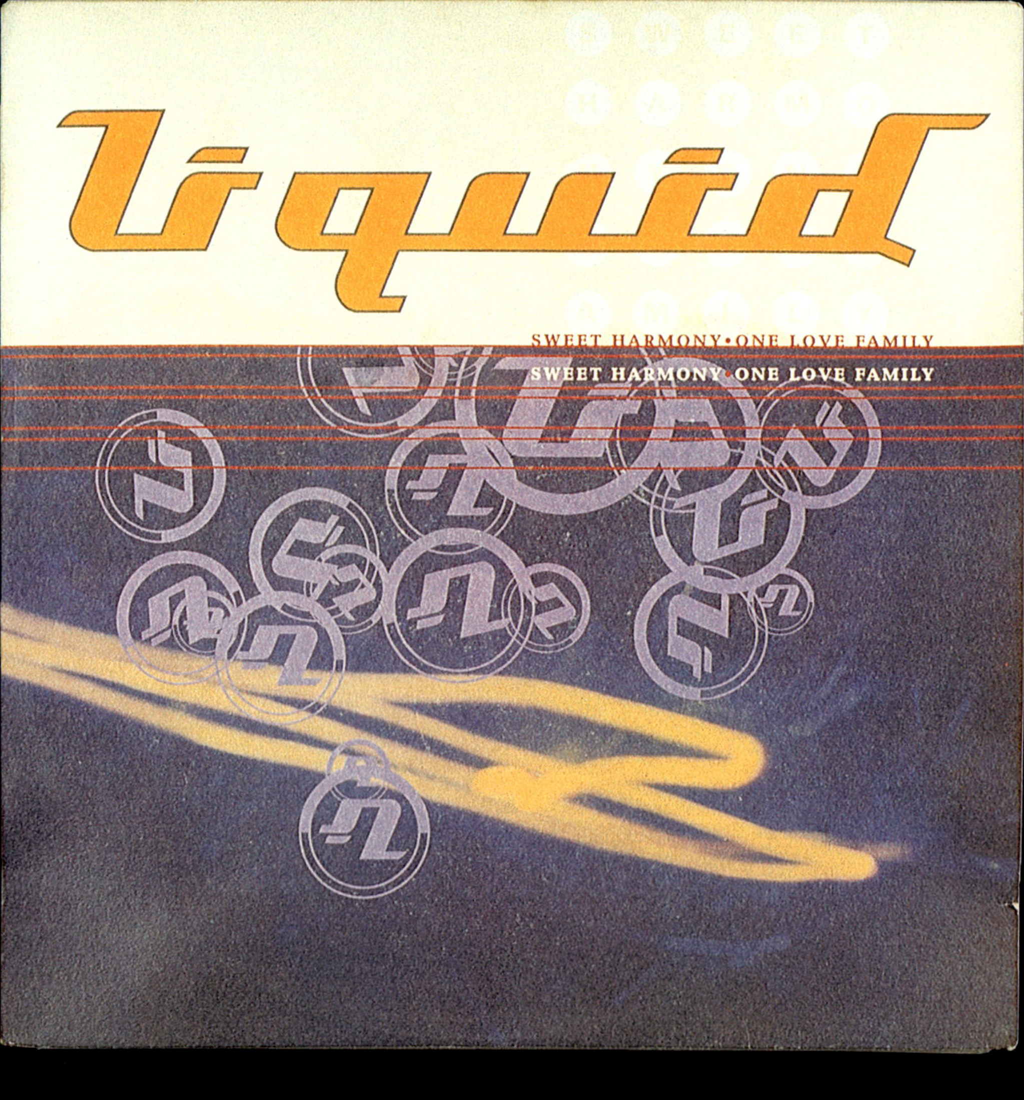

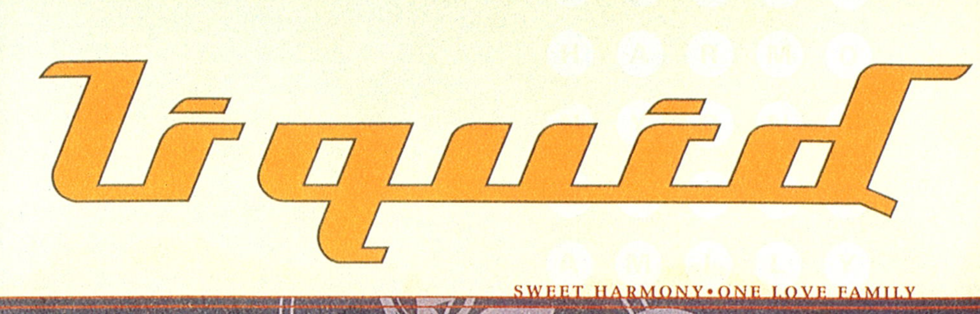

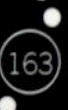

163 Artist Liquid Title Sweet Harmony Design Paul McMenamin At V23 Record Label XL Recordings Date 1995

Liquid

A1
LIQUID LOVE
original mix (6.20)
WRITTEN PRODUCED AND MIXED BY AME ENGINEERED BY MICKY MULLIGAN AT DUBBING THEATRE 1 PUBLISHED BY MOMENTUM MUSIC LIMITED MADE IN ENGLAND ALL RIGHTS RESERVED

A2
INTERFERENCE
original mix (5.45)
WRITTEN PRODUCED AND MIXED BY AME ENGINEERED BY MICKY MULLIGAN AT DUBBING THEATRE 1 PUBLISHED BY MOMENTUM MUSIC LIMITED MADE IN ENGLAND ALL RIGHTS RESERVED

AA1
LIQUID IS LIQUID

L O
AND ADDITIONAL PRODUCTION BY RED JERRY PUBLISHED BY MOMENTUM MUSIC LIMITED MADE IN ENGLAND ALL RIGHTS RESERVED

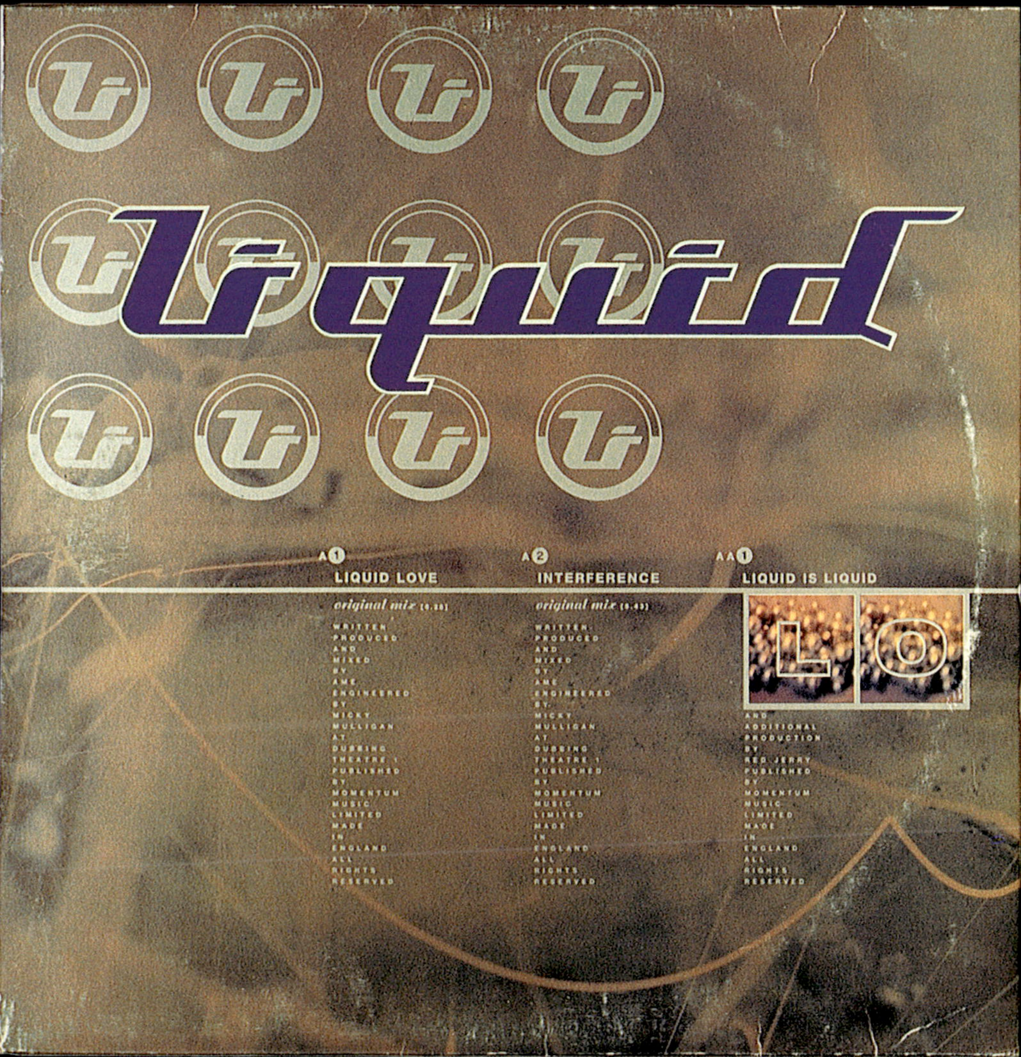

D-LAY:H-MUSIC

_Original_Deep Mix_Impulse Mix

Artist D-Lay Title H-Music Design Think Design Record Label Suck Me Plasma Date 1995

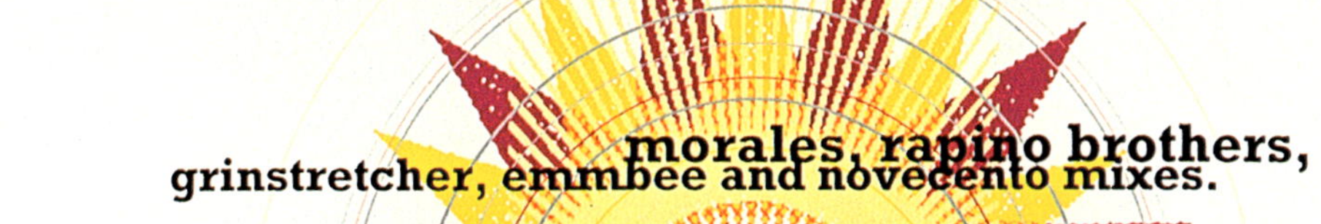

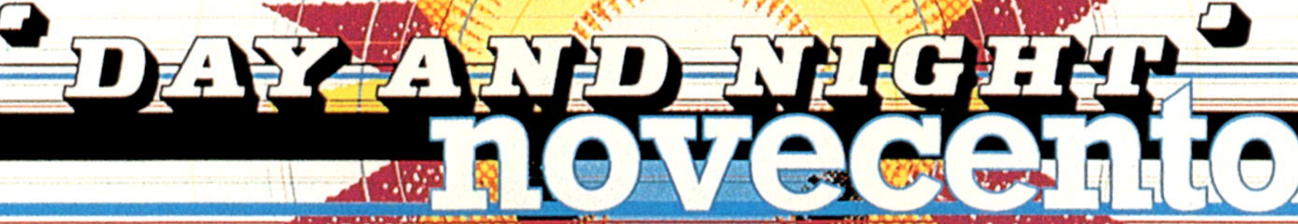

Artist Novecento Title Day & Night Design A Blue Source Photography Tim France
Record Label ZTT Records Date 1995

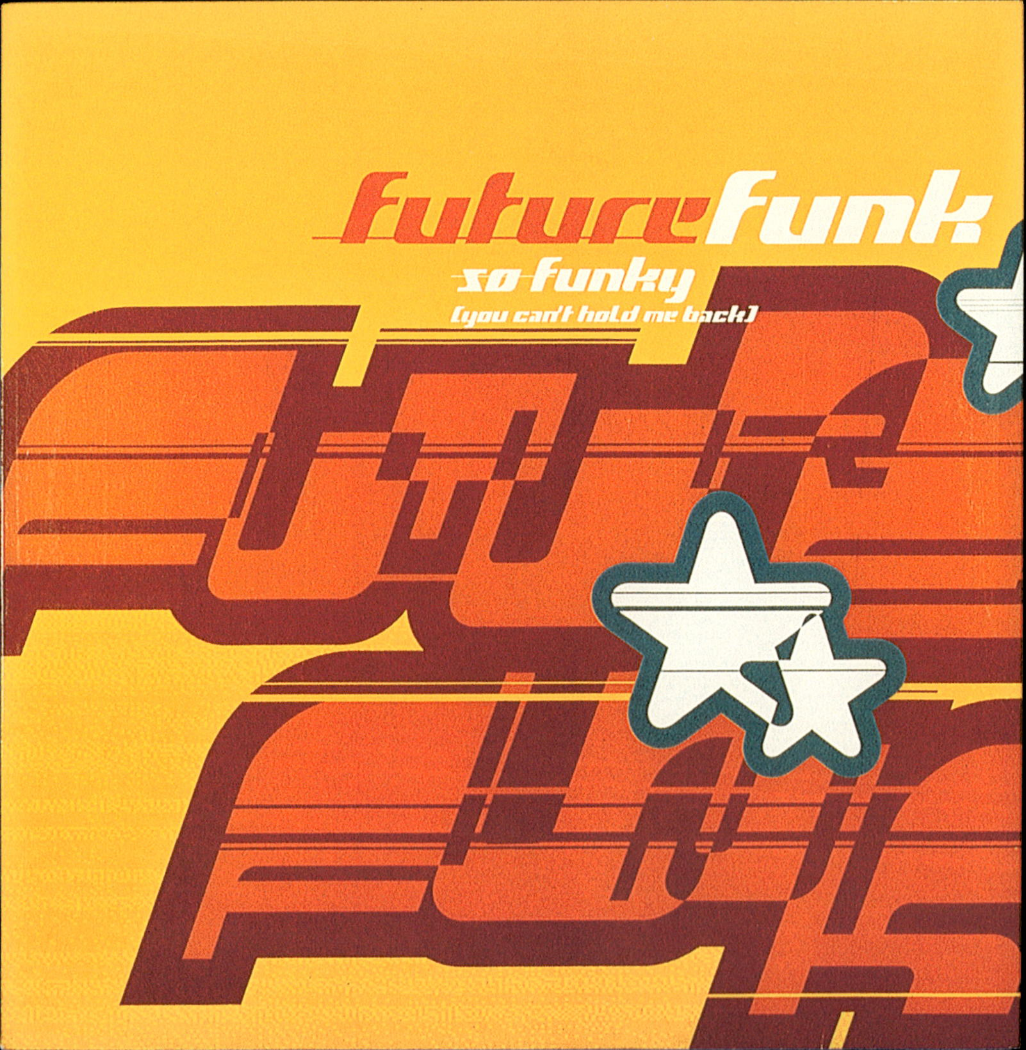

future funk
so funky
(you can't hold me back)

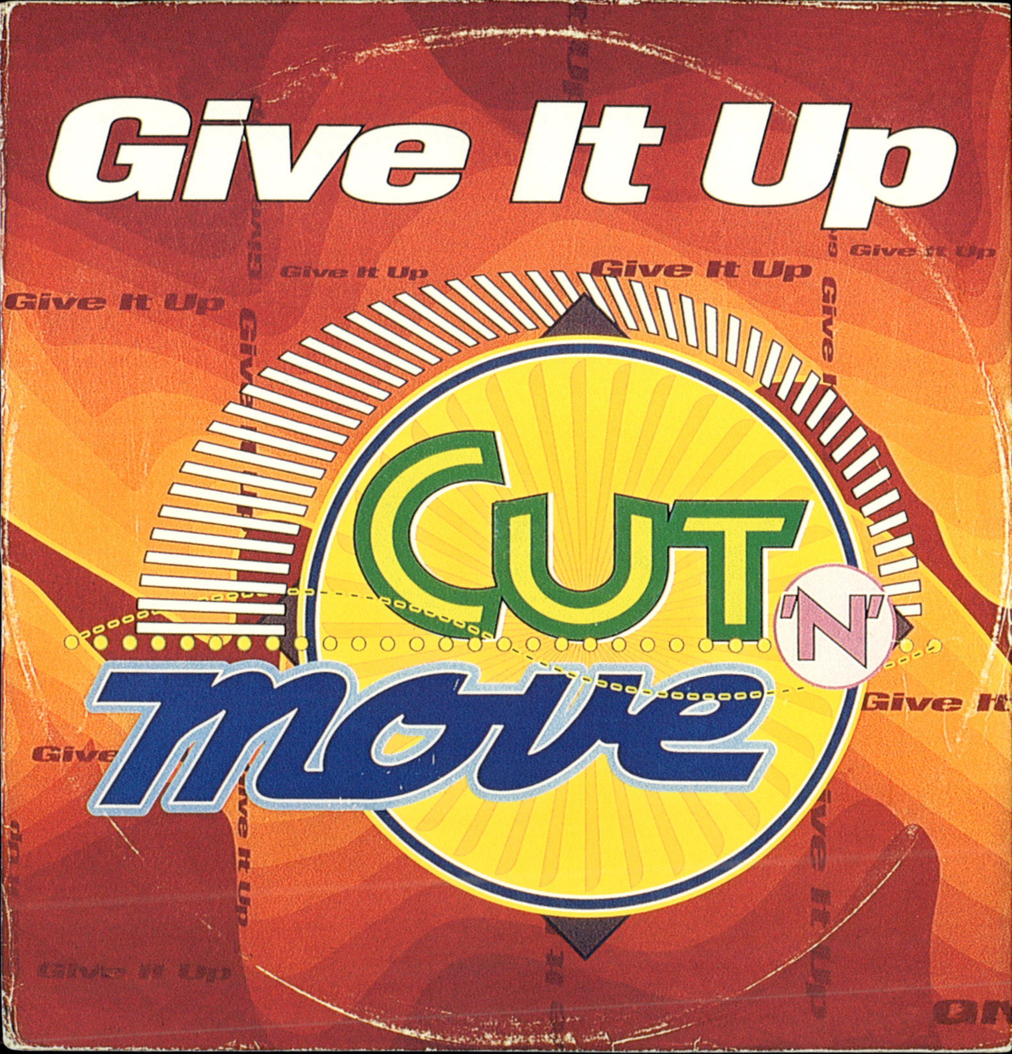

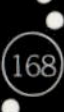

 Artist Cut 'N' Move Title Give It Up Record Label EMI Date 1993

Hannah Jones.
No One Can Love You More Than Me
Mixes by: Stonebridge, Age of Entropy, Discotek and Illusive.

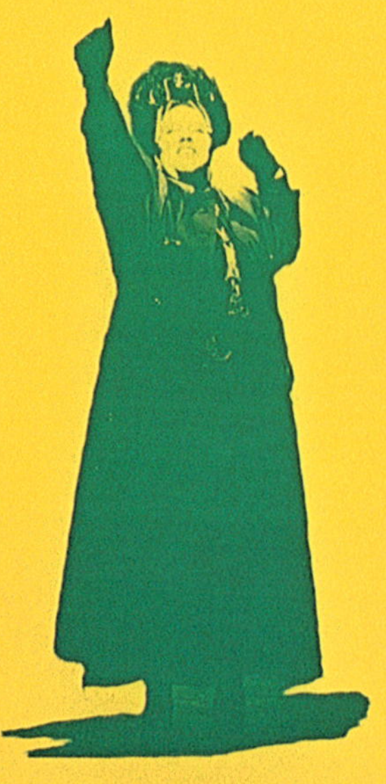

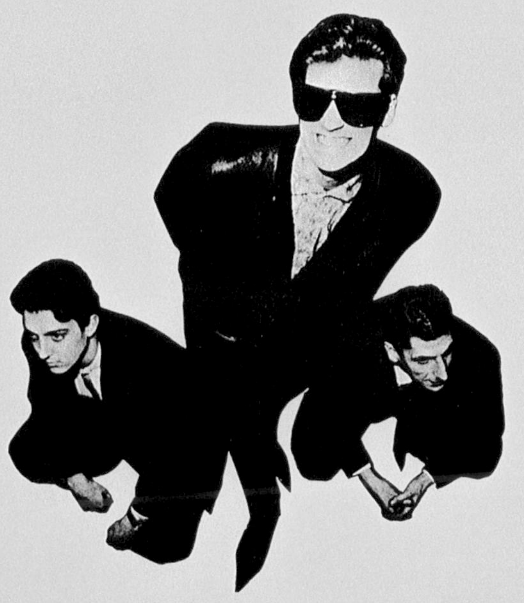

Artist Beat Freaks Title The National Anthem Photography Ronnie McGuigan Date 1986

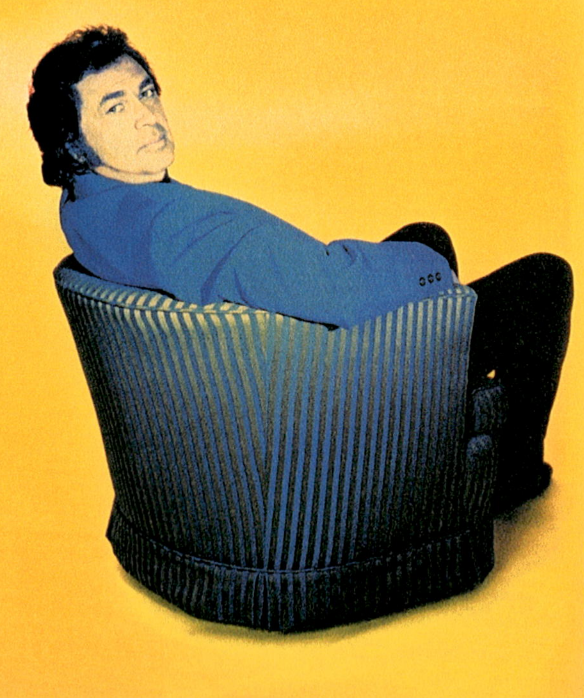

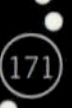
171 Artist Engelbert Humperdinck Title Release Me Gotta Get Release Record Label Arcade Date 1998

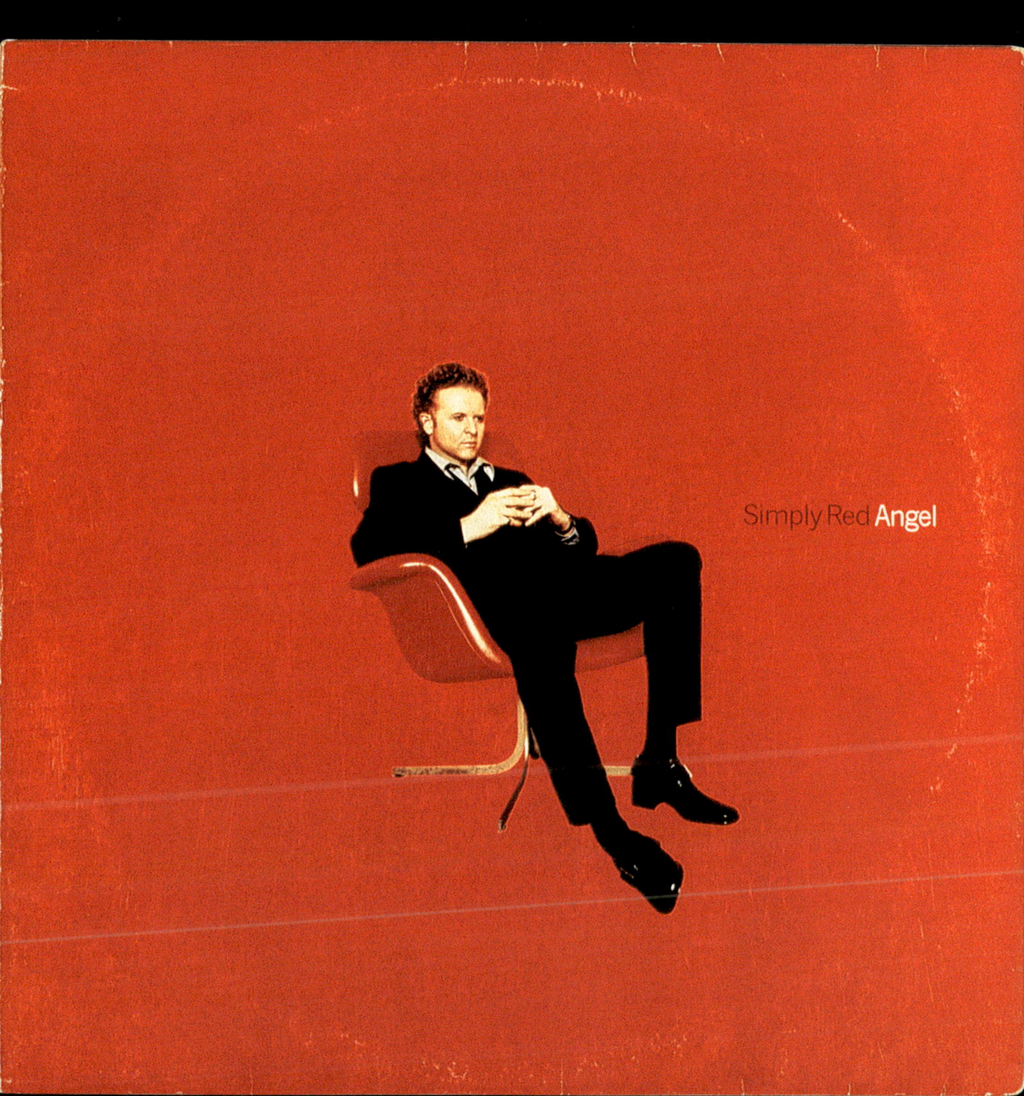
Simply Red Angel

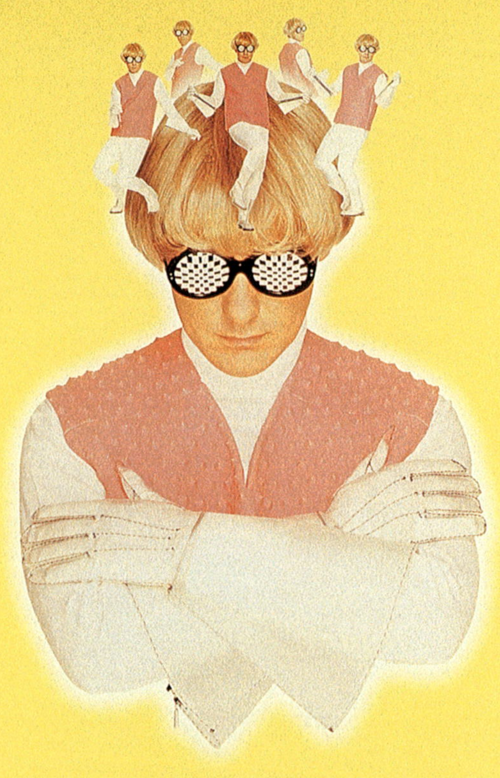

Artist Pet Shop Boys Title I Wouldn't Normally Do This Kind of Thing Design Farrow - PSB Photography Andy Earle Record Label Parlophone Date 1993

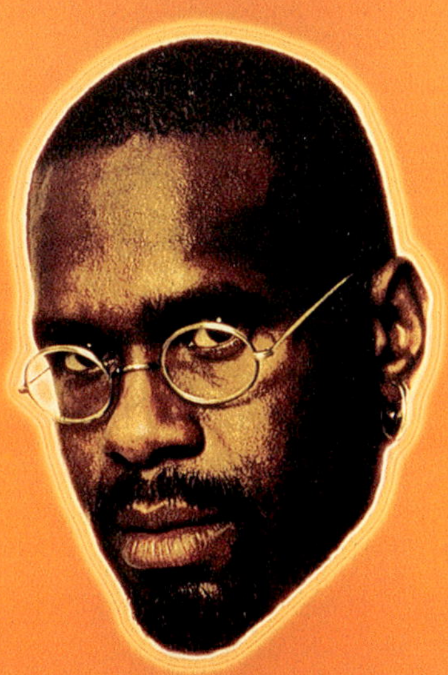

the original
b 2 gether

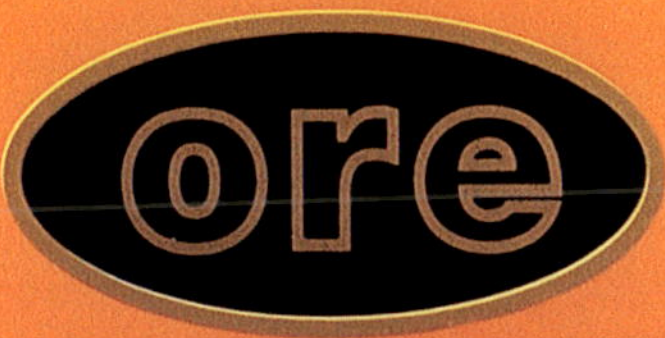

ore

174

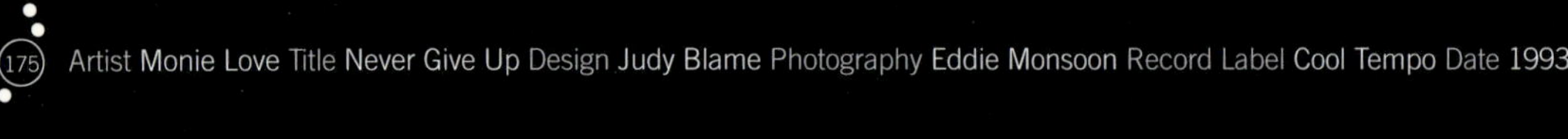
monie love
never give up

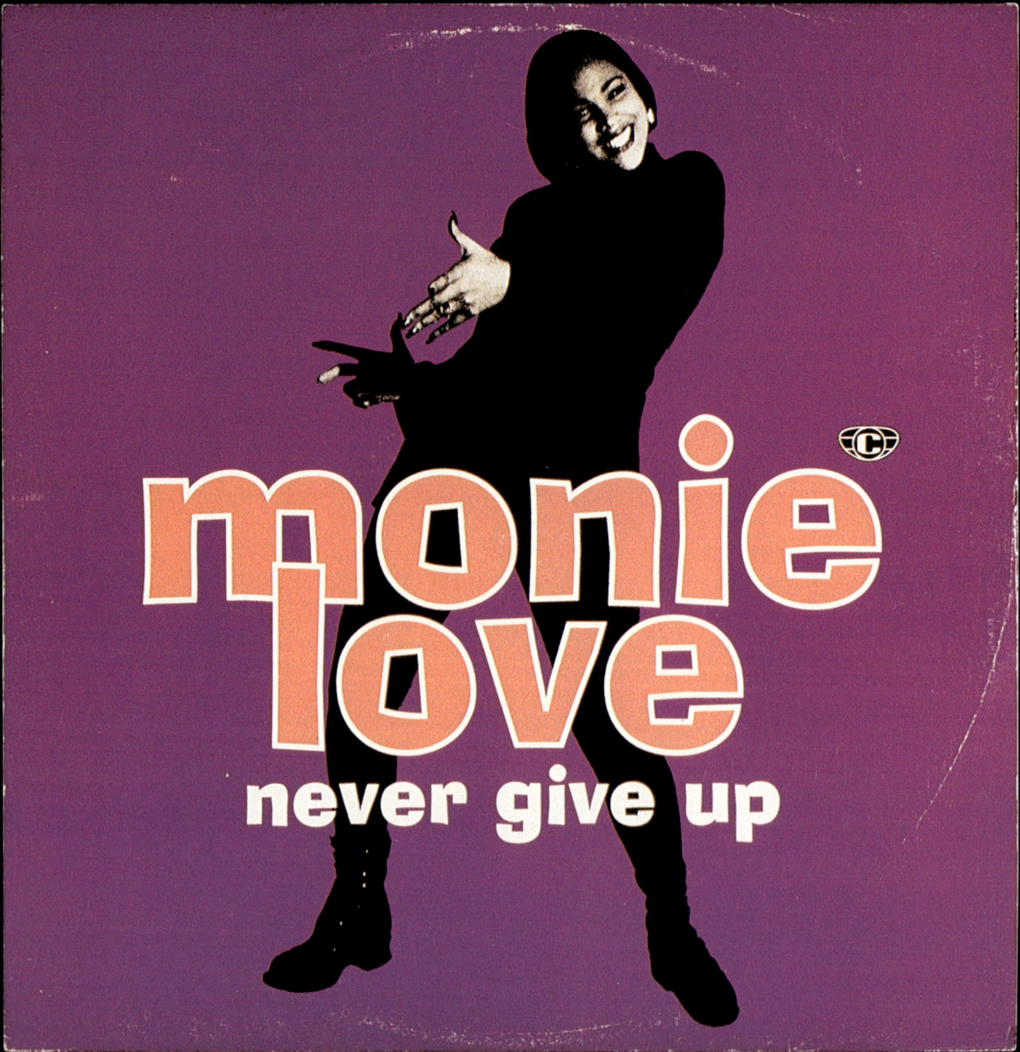

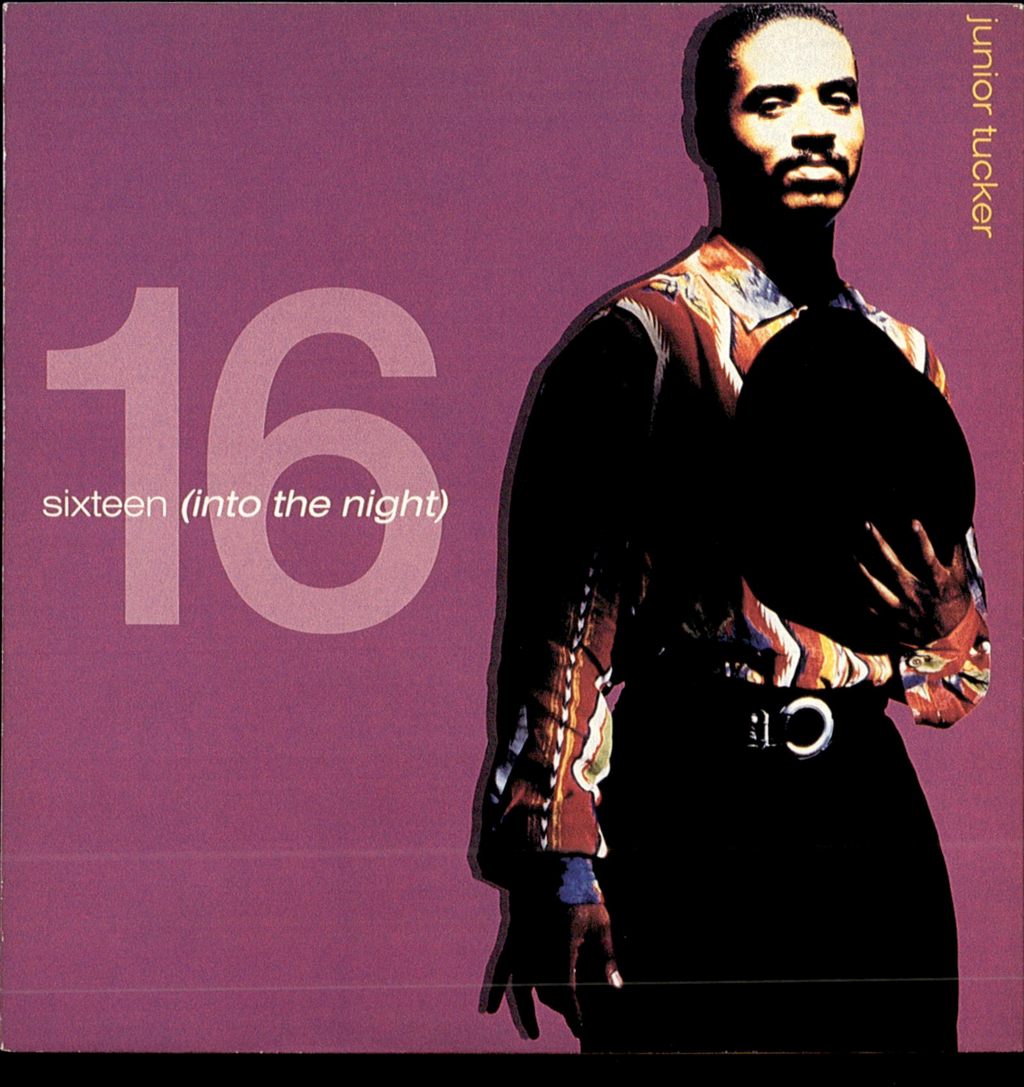

16

sixteen *(into the night)*

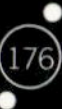

Artist Junior Tucker Title Sixteen (Into the Night) Design Stylorouge Photography Rusell Young
Record Label Ten Records Date 1990

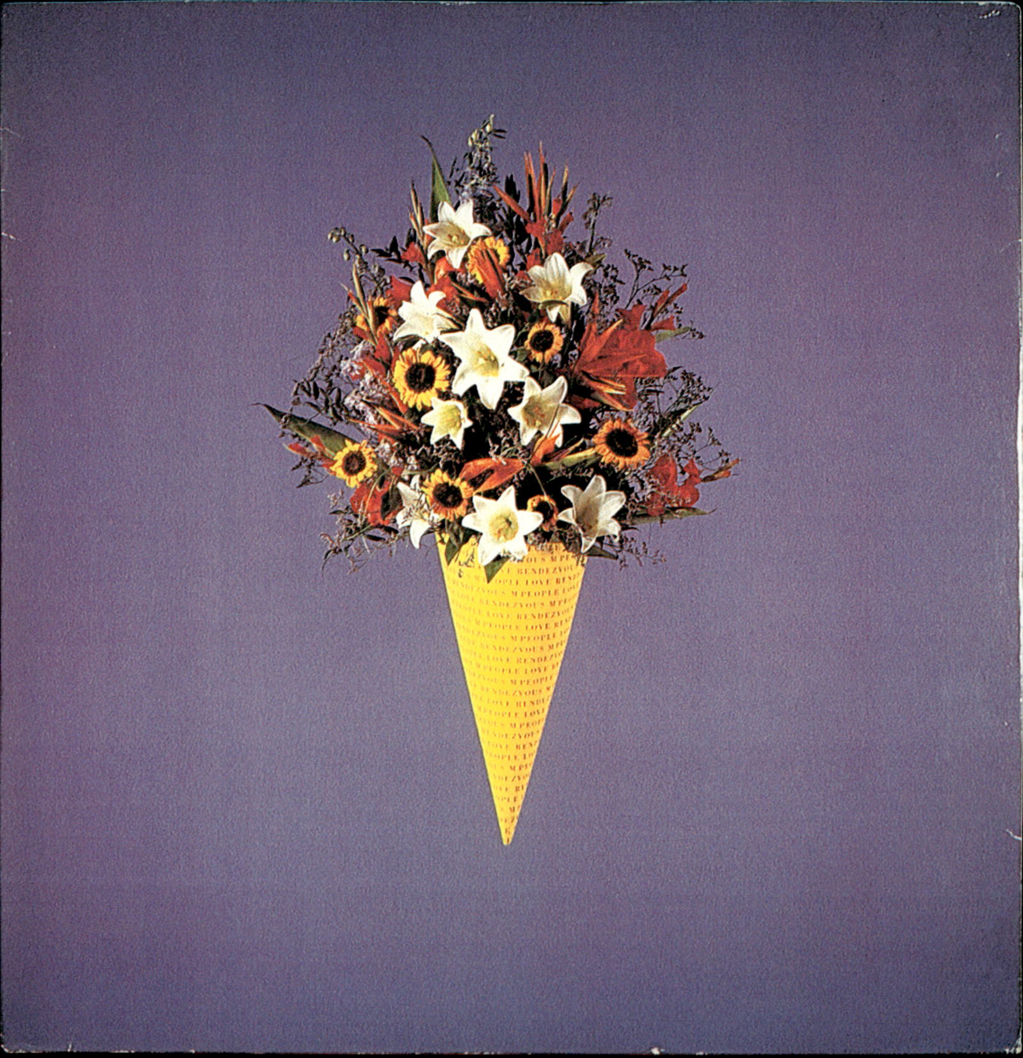

 Artist M People Title Love Rendezvous Design Farrow Design Photography Jason Tozer
Record Label Deconstrution Date 1995

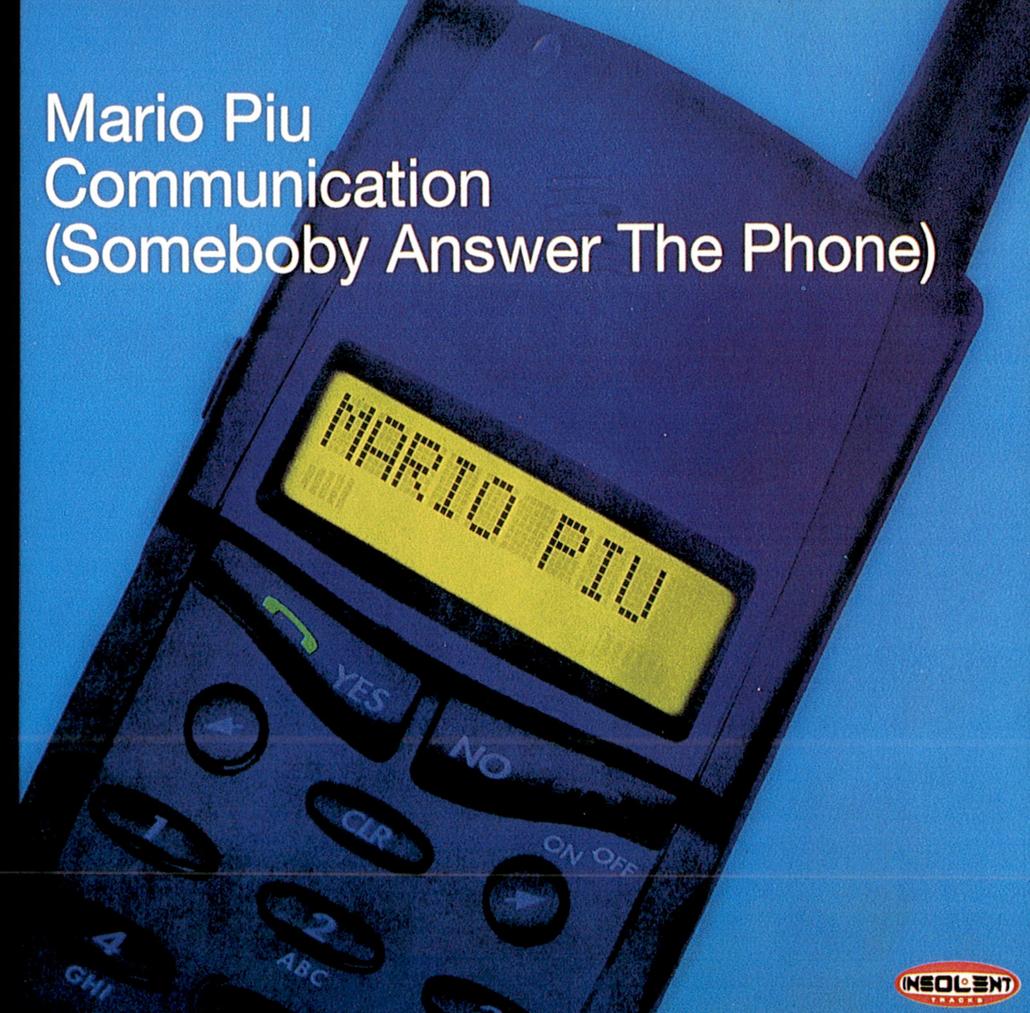

Mario Piu
Communication
(Someboby Answer The Phone)
MARIO PIU
YES
NO
ON OFF
CLR
1
2 ABC
4 GHI
INSOLENT TRACKS
Artist Mario Piu Title Communication Design Design @ The Unknown.Conk Photography Clifton Hall
Record Label Insolent Date 1999
178

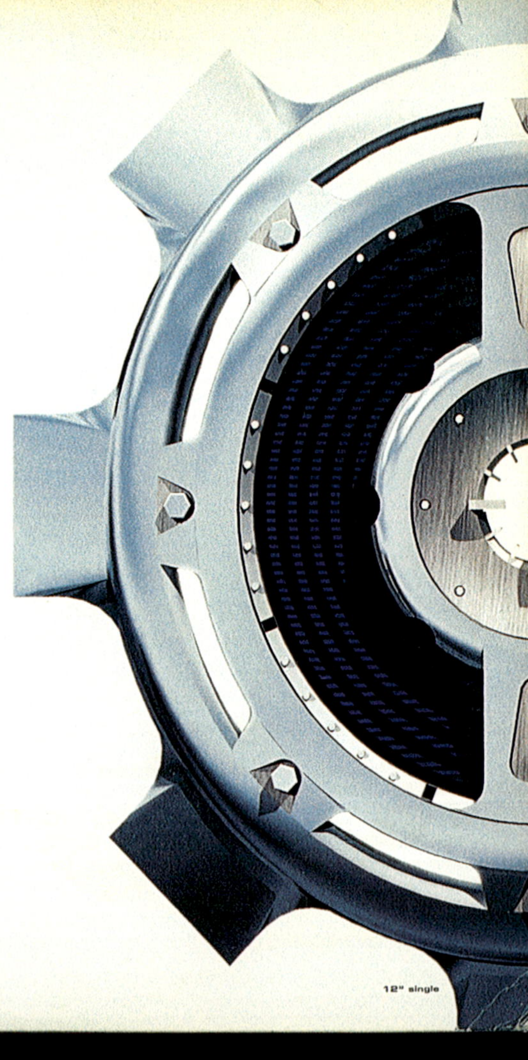
C+C MUSIC FACTORY
I'LL ALWAYS
BE AROUND
12" single

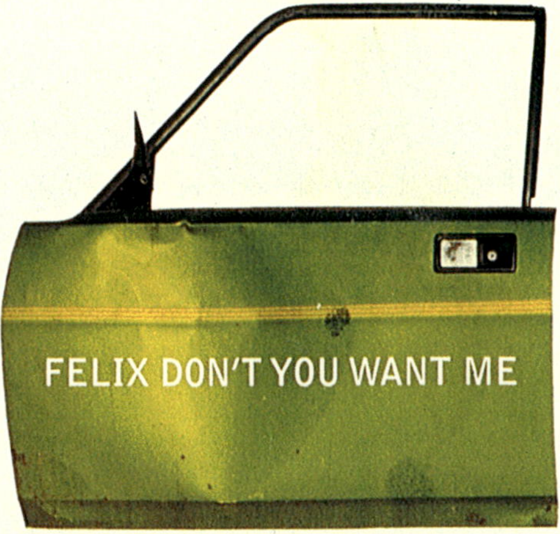

Artist Felix Title Don't You Want Me Design Mark Farrow Photography Christopher Griffiths
Record Label Deconstruction Classics Date 1995

180

ramirez
La musica tremenda RMX.98

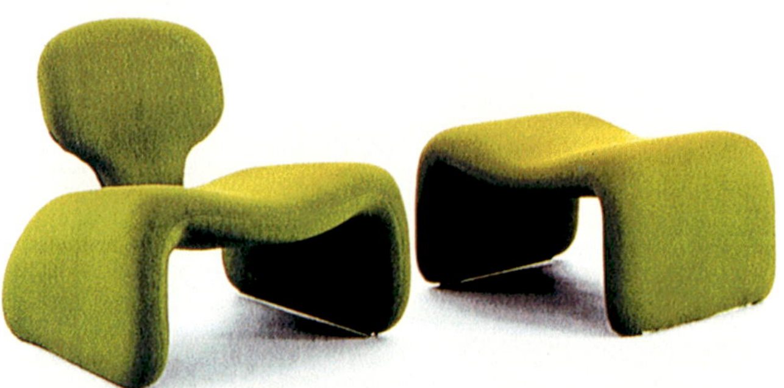

Artist Ramirez Title La Musica Tremenda Record Label Insolent Tracks / Blanco y Negro Date 1998

Prophets of Sound

High

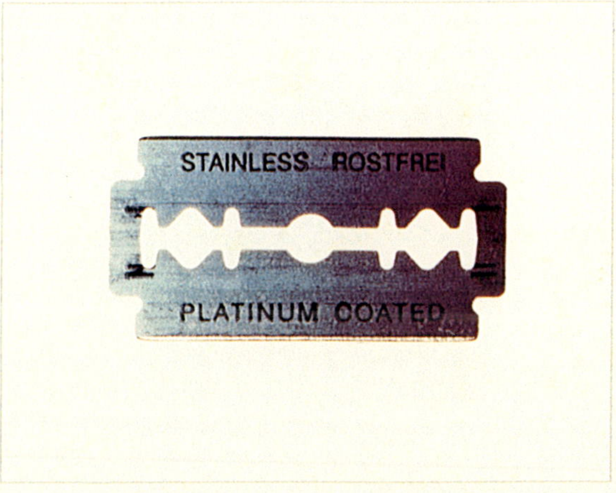

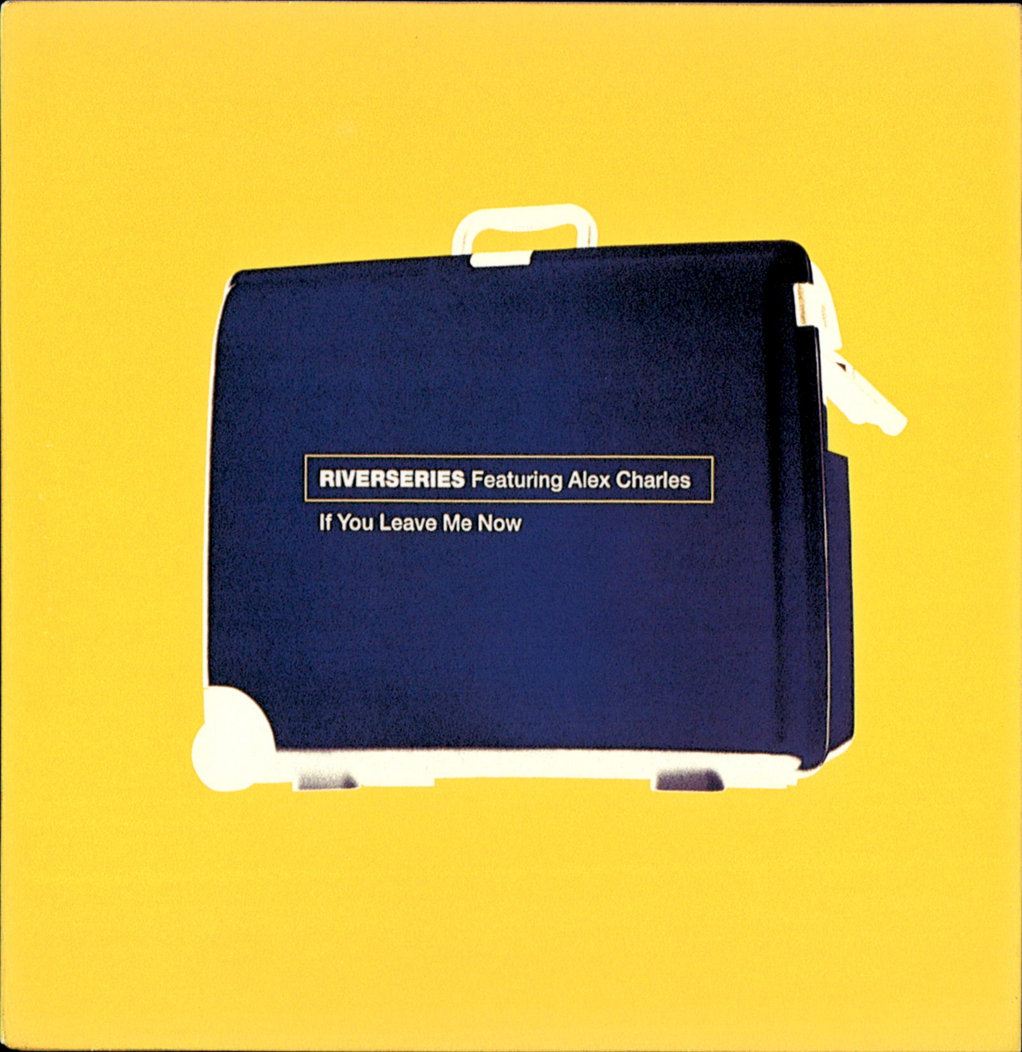

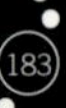

183 Artist Riverseries feat. Alex Charles Title If You Leave Me Now Record Label Dance Pool Date 1995

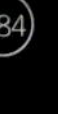

Artist **Moby** Title **Natural Blues** Design **Ysabel Knyphause** Photography **Henrik Bonnevier**
Record Label **Mute Records** Date 2000

MOBY
NATURAL BLUES

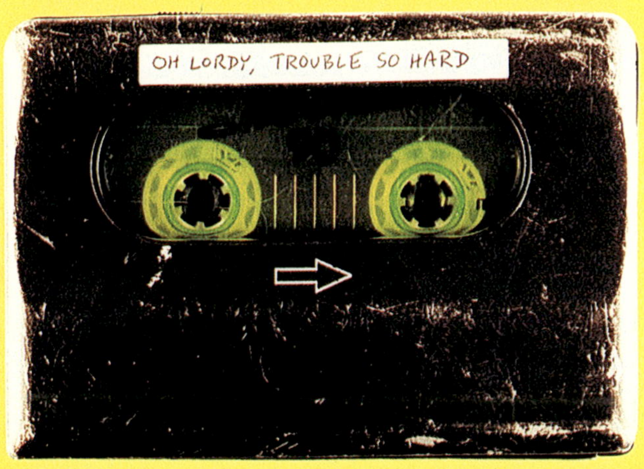

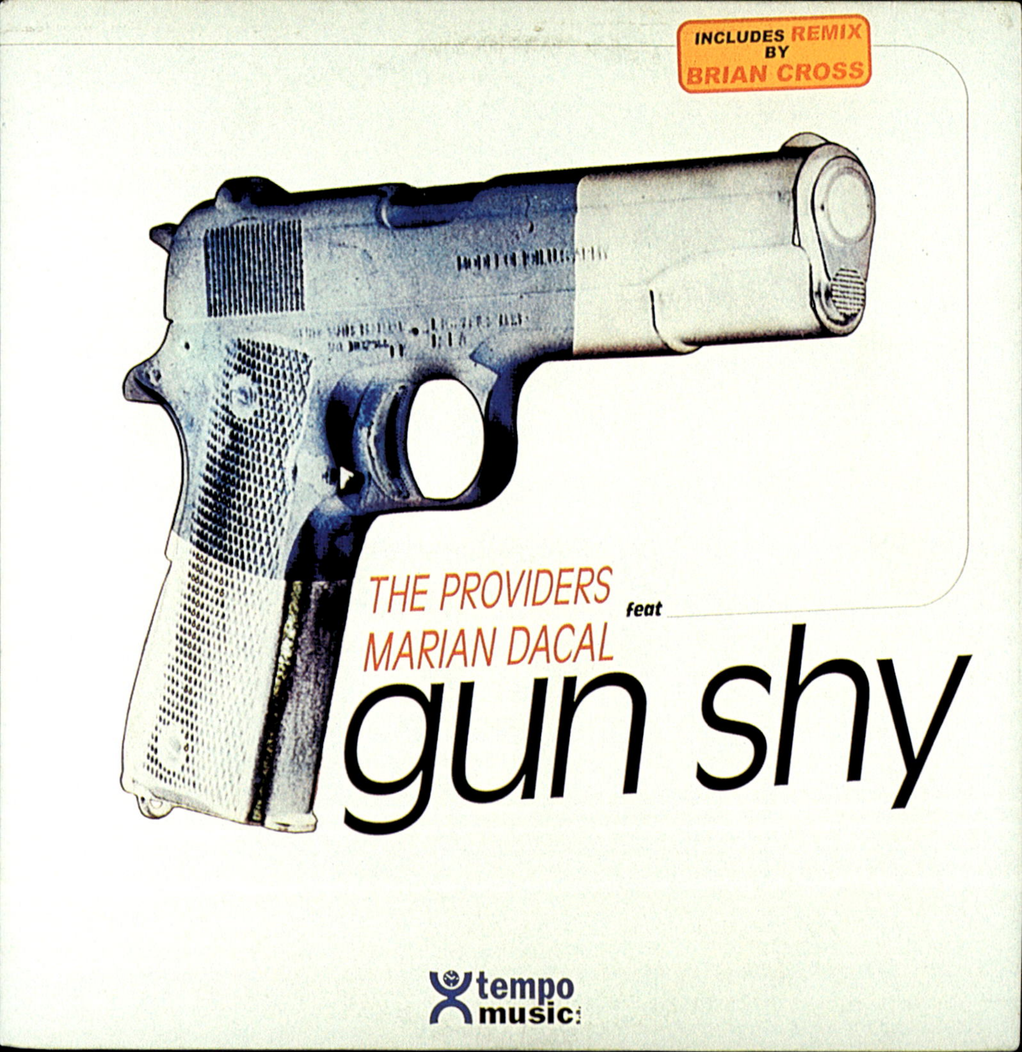

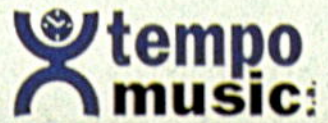

INCLUDES REMIX
BY
BRIAN CROSS

THE PROVIDERS feat
MARIAN DACAL
gun shy

tempo
music

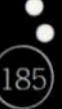

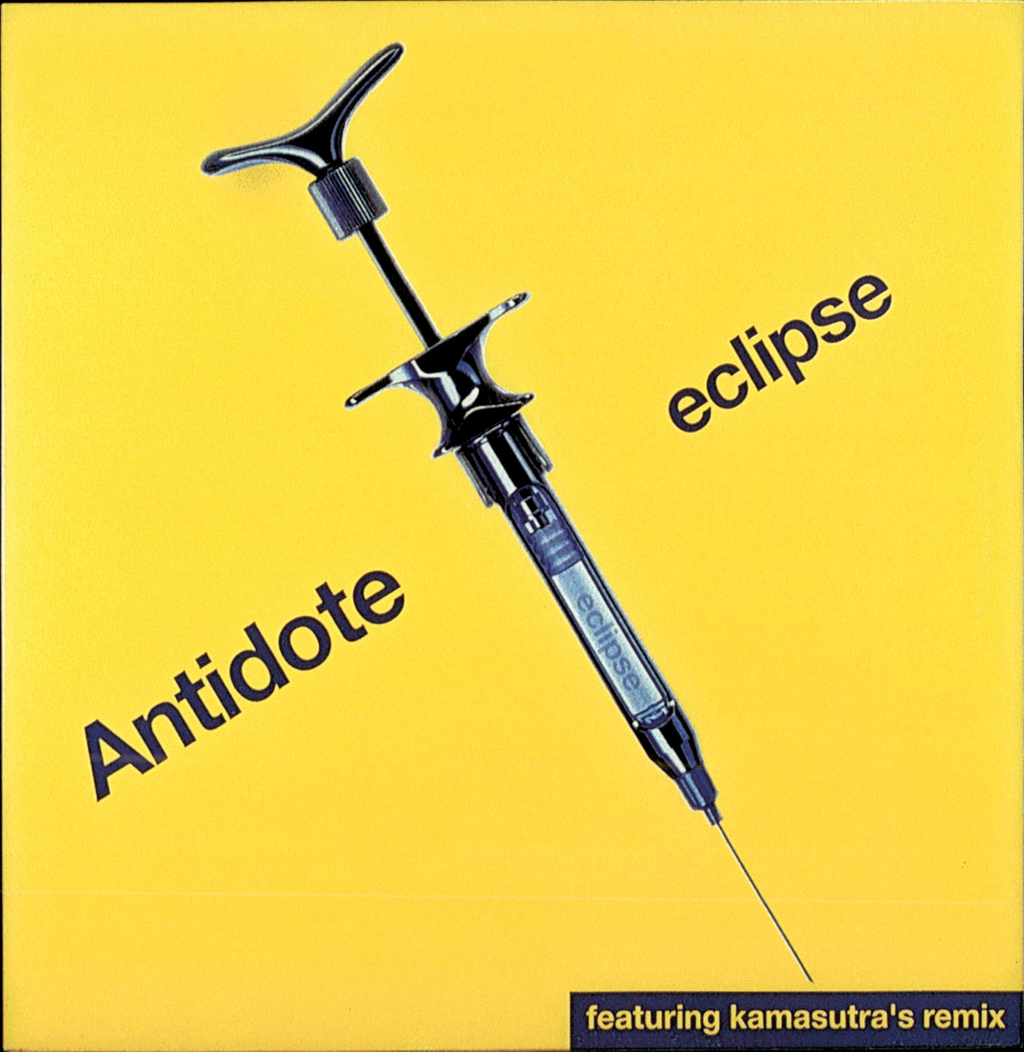

186

eclipse

Antidote

eclipse

featuring kamasutra's remix

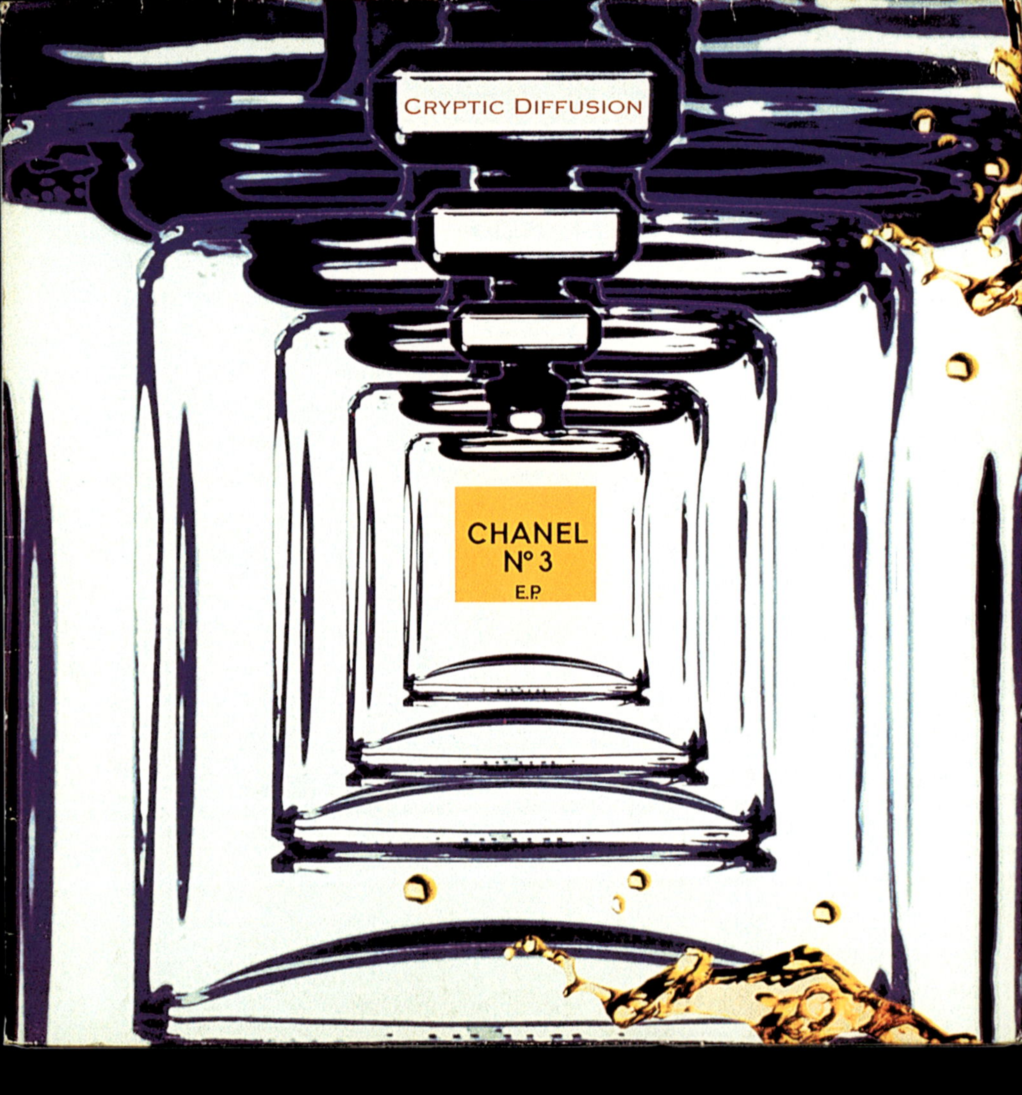

Artist Cryptic Diffusion Title Chanel N°3 E.P. Design Hype Graphics Photography Tijai Record Label Suck 42

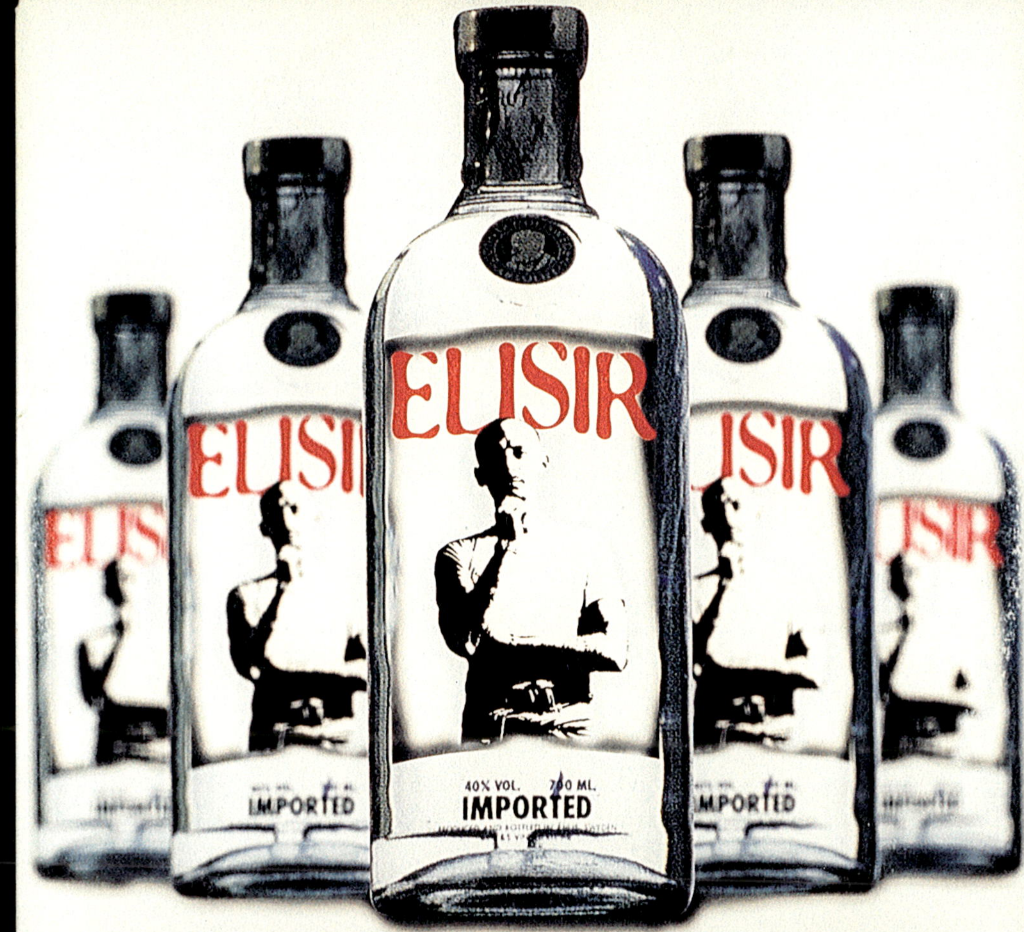

ELISIR
40% VOL.   700 ML.
IMPORTED
GIGI D'AGOSTINO

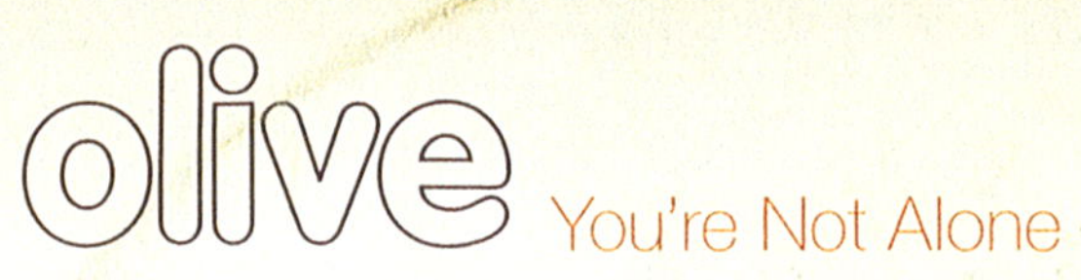

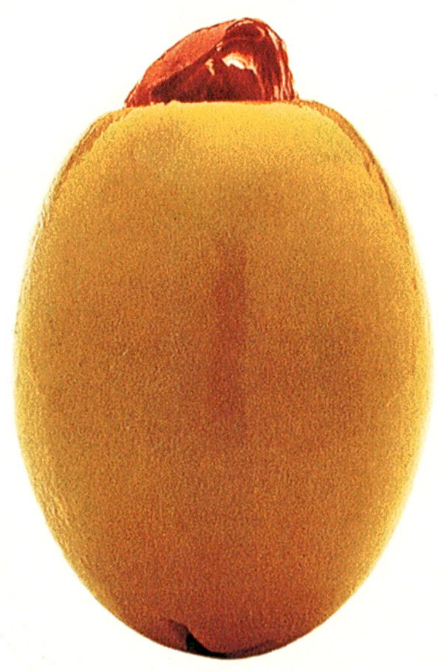
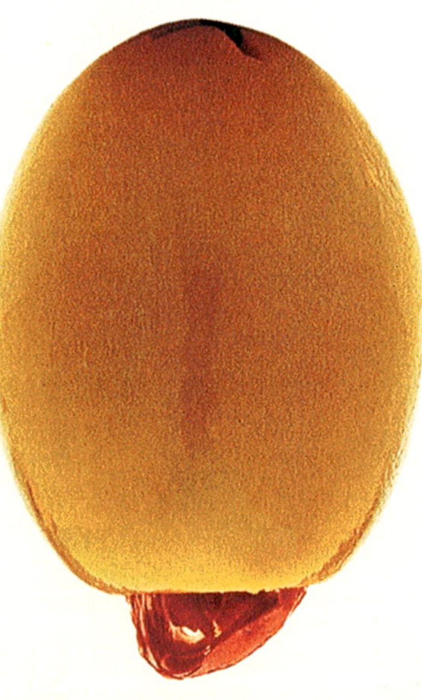

Artist **Olive** Title **You're Not Alone** Design Peter For Zip Design Photography Matthew Donaldson Record Label BMG Date 1996

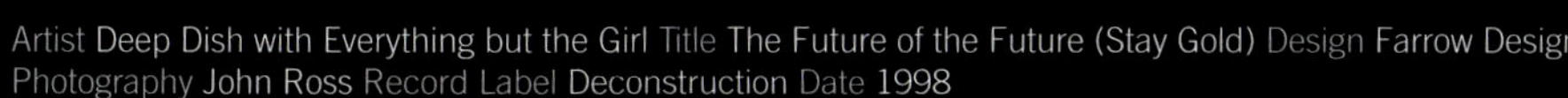

— deep dish
with everything but the girl
— the future of the future (stay gold)

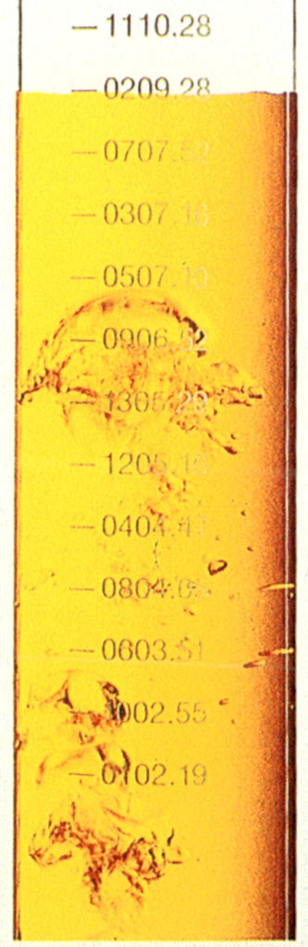

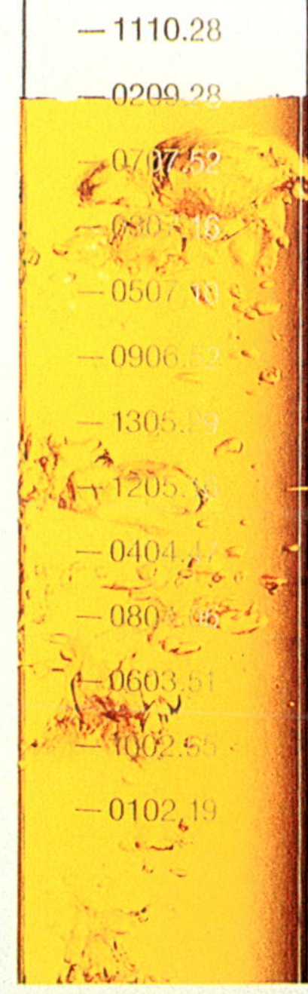

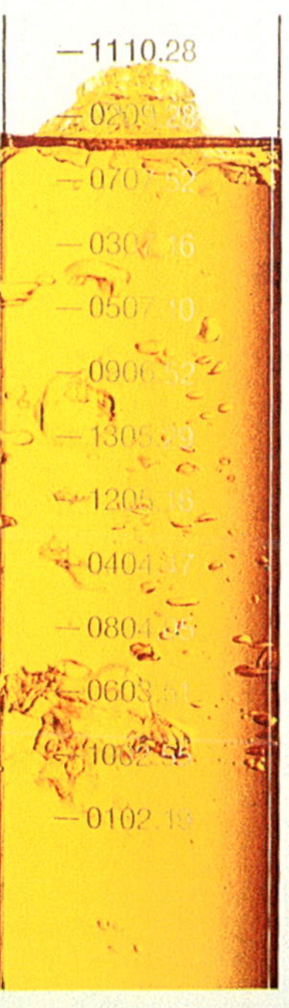

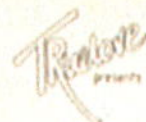
the source featuring candi staton
YOU GOT THE LOVE

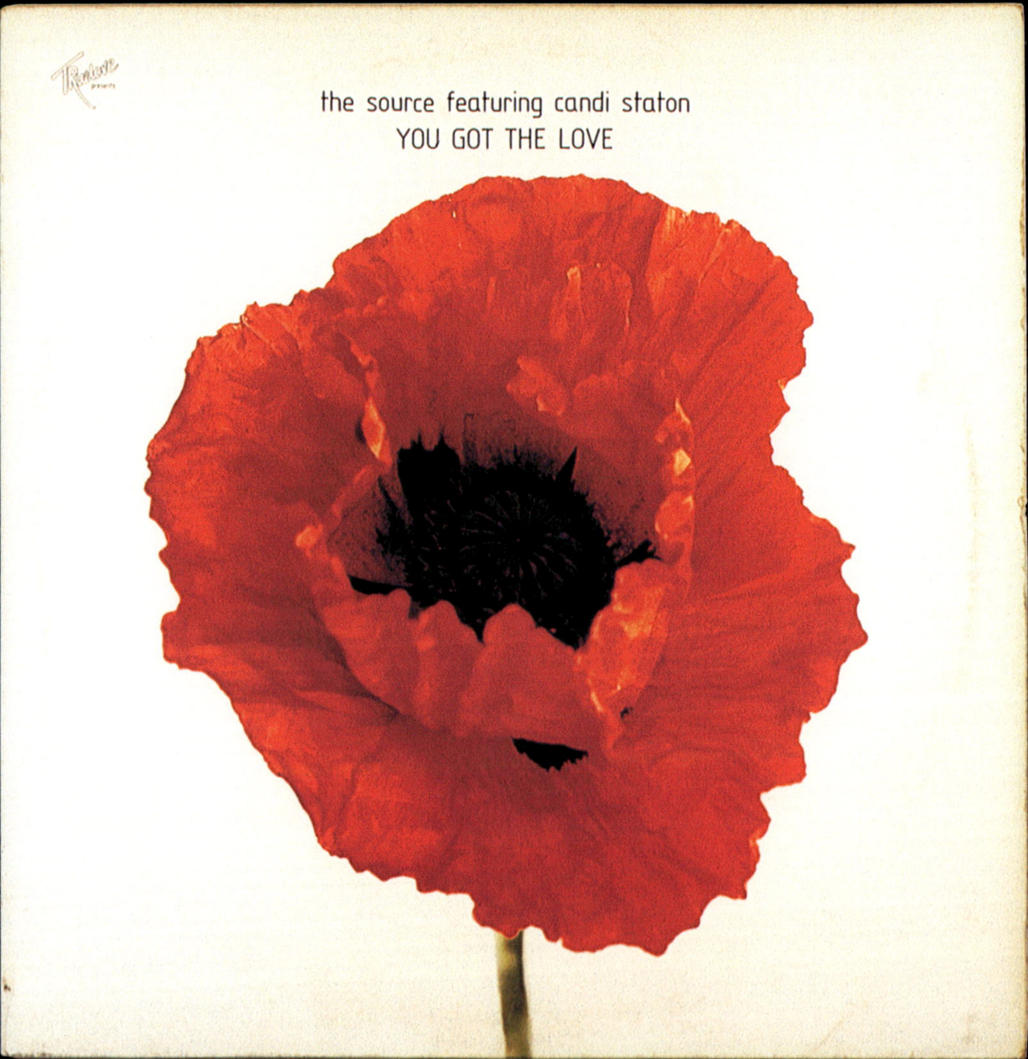

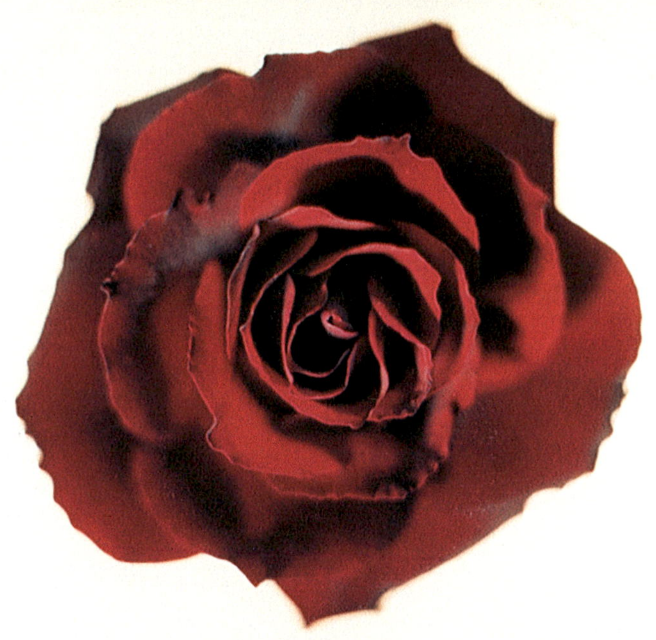

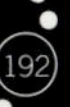
192 Artist Loveland feat. Rachel McFarlane Title I Need Somebody Design Wink Photography Lewis Mulatero Record Label Eastern Bloc Date 1994

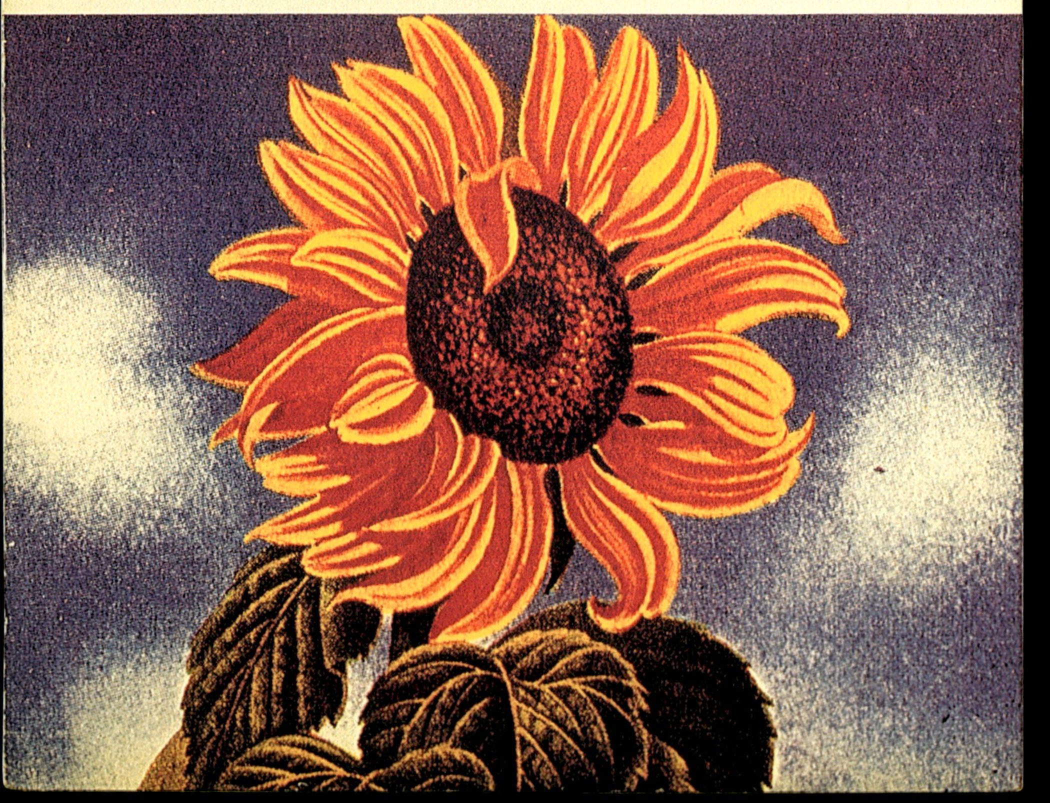
FEELING GROOVY Woodstock play
the 59th Bridge Street Song featuring
the Rhythm Quest powerflower remix

193 Artist Woodstock Title 59th Bridge Street Song (Feeling Groovy) Design Groovy Twins Record Label VC Records Date 1992

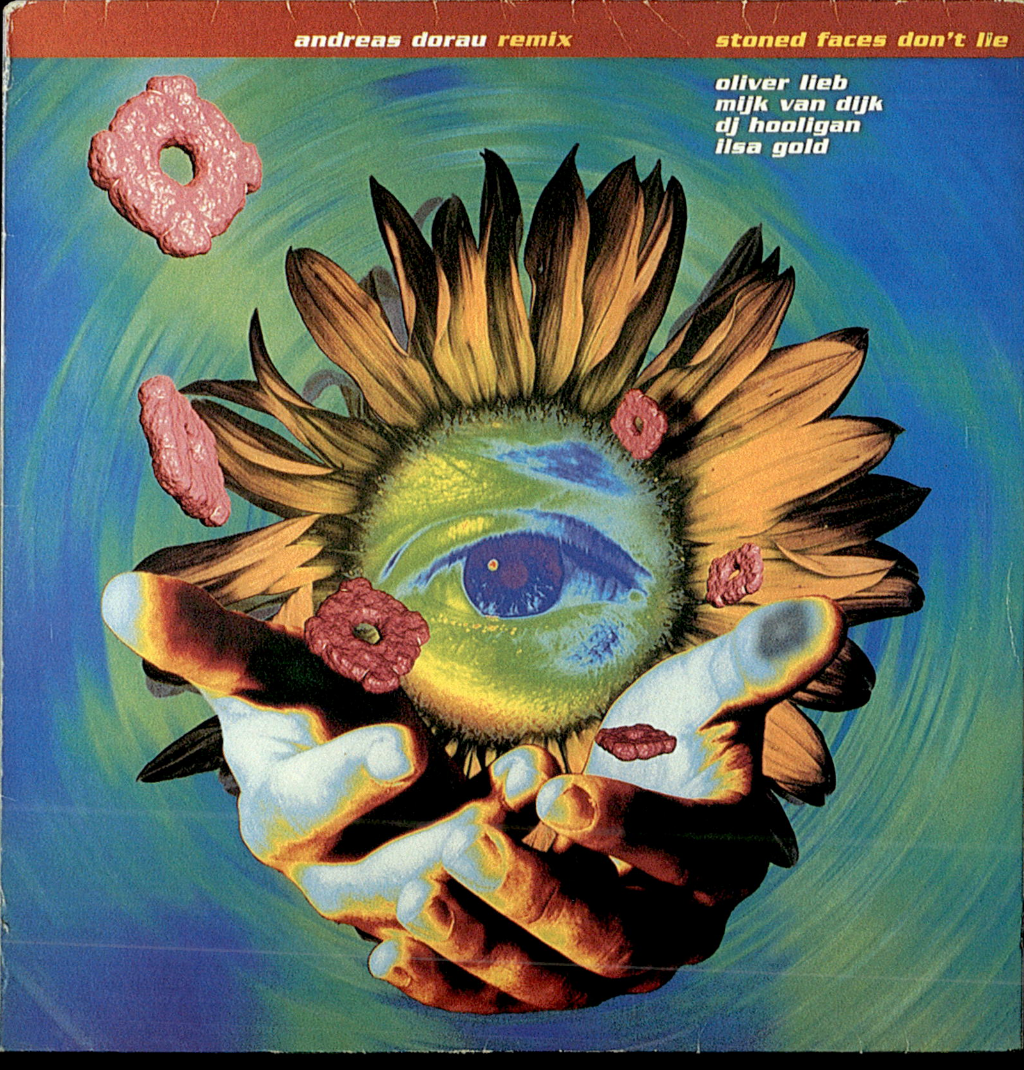
andreas dorau remix
stoned faces don't lie
oliver lieb
mijk van dijk
dj hooligan
ilsa gold

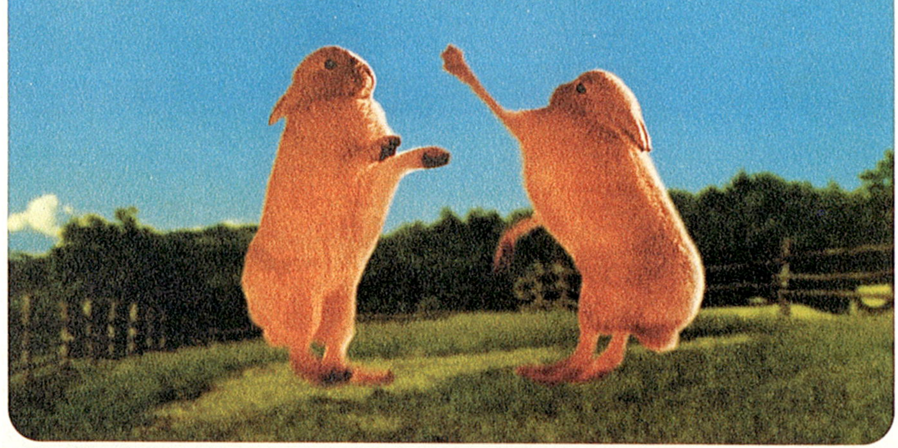

tomy or zox
my desire
a1: long desire
a2: hard desire
aa1: santos space funk desire
aa2: santos space desire dub
blanco y negro
8 421597 019978
BLANCO Y NEGRO MUSIC Llacuna, 11 - 08005 Barcelona - Spain - Tel.: 93 225 44 00 - FAX:93 225 41 01/93 225 46 00 - http://www.blancoynegro.com / E-mail:mail@blancoynegro.com

plaxmen
The Top
a1: blue nitro extended
a2: piano cut mix
b1: piano extended
b2: blue nitro cut mix
mtr 2085
8 014360 208541
Mantra Vibes is a label of: Expanded Music srl
via Romagnoli 3/b I-40010 Bentivoglio (BO)
tel+39 51 6643711 fax+39 51 6643766
expanded@expandedmusic.com
distributed by Self Distribuzione spa
via Quintiliano 5 I-20138 Milano tel+39 2 50901.1
fax italy+39 2 58014633 fax export+39 2 58015741

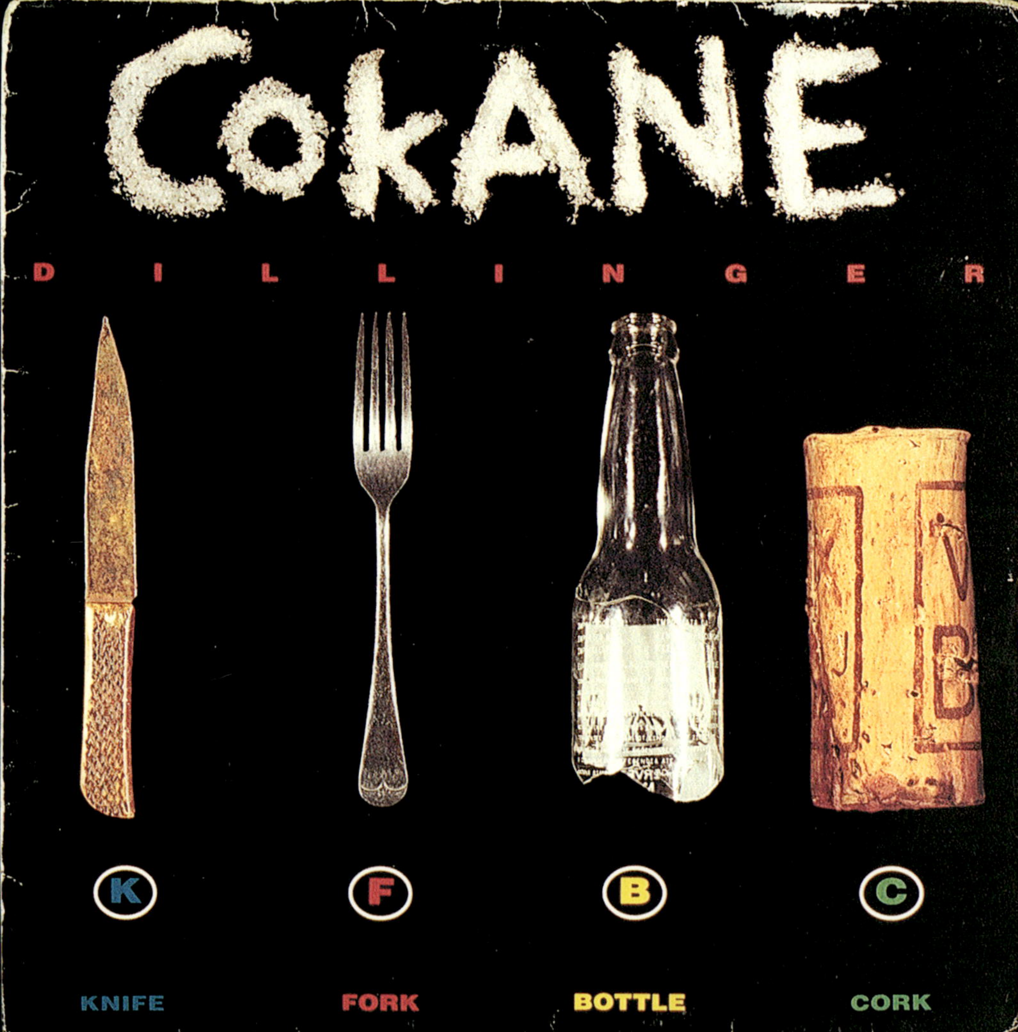

Artist Dillinger Title Cokane In My Brain Design Cally Record Label Island Records Date 1992

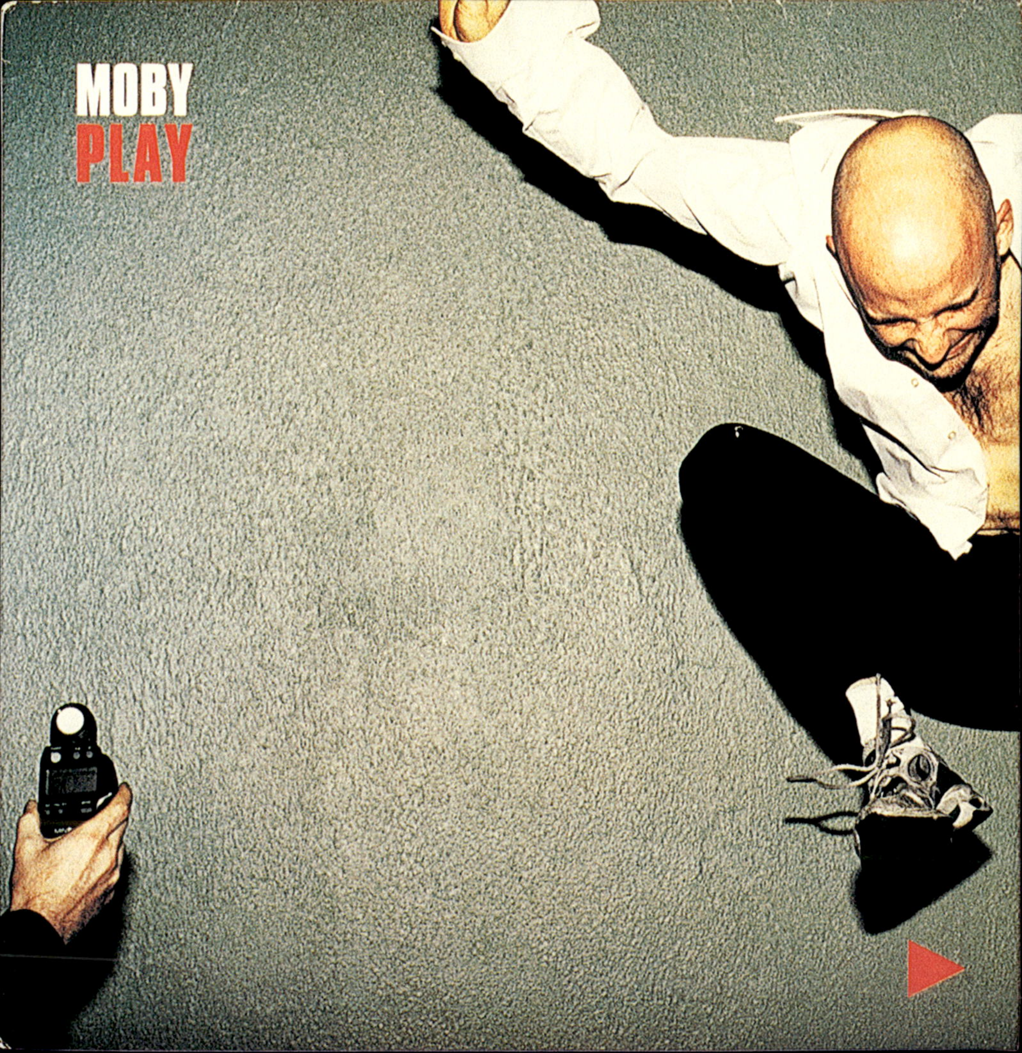

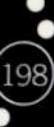

Artist Moby Title Play Design Ysabel Zu Innhausen & Knyphausen Photography Corinne Day
Record Label Mute Date 1999

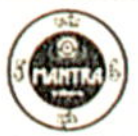

dealers de funk
new jersey

a1:   new jersey mix
a2:   da filter mix
b1:   santos state of funk re-edit
b2:   new jersey by night mix

mtr 2079

8 014360 207940

Mantra Vibes is a label of Expanded Music srl
via Romagnoli 3/b I-40010 Bentivoglio (BO)
tel+39 051 6643711 fax+39 051 6643766.
expanded.music@newtech.it
distributed by Self Distribuzione spa
via Quintiliano 5 I-20138 Milano
tel+39 02 50901.1 fax italy+39 02 58014633
fax export+39 02 58015741
Fabrizio Schiavi Design: www.agonet.it/fabrizioschiavi

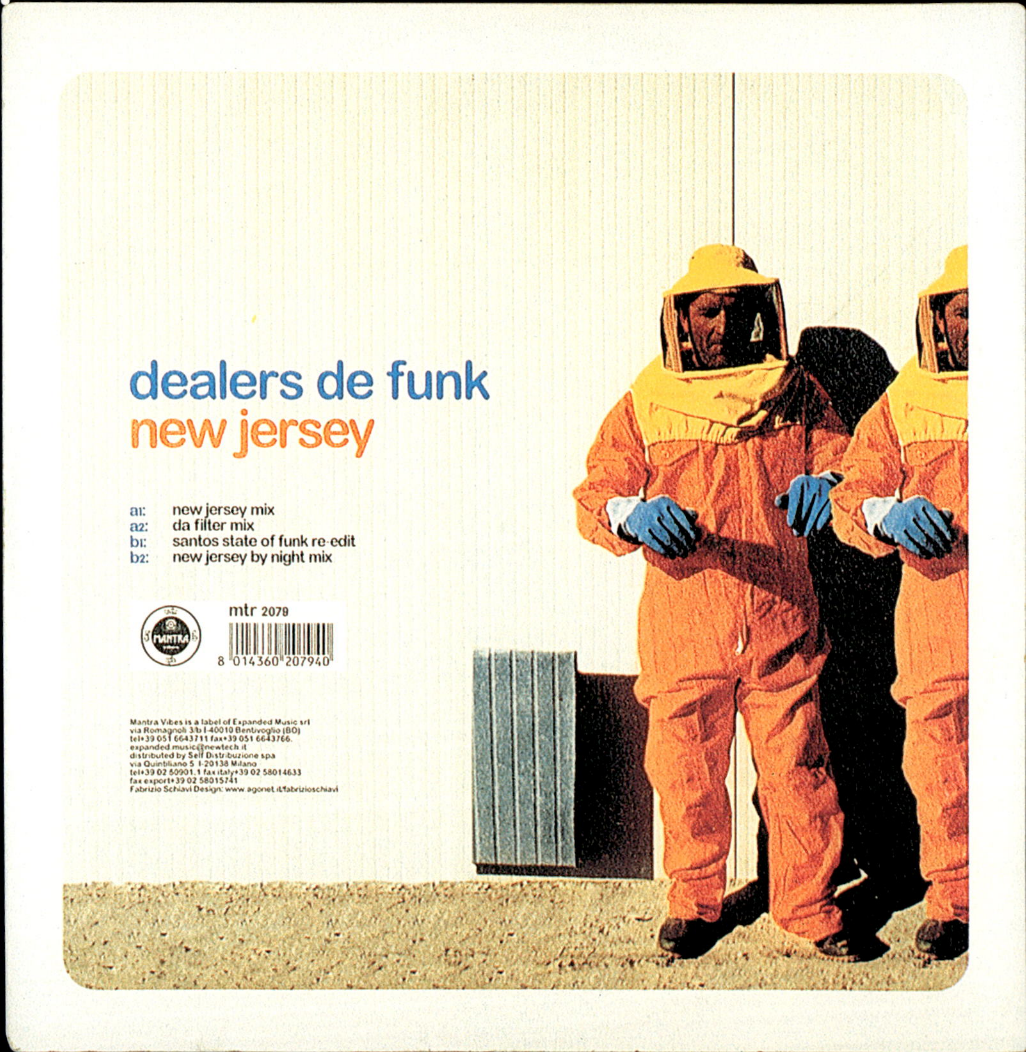

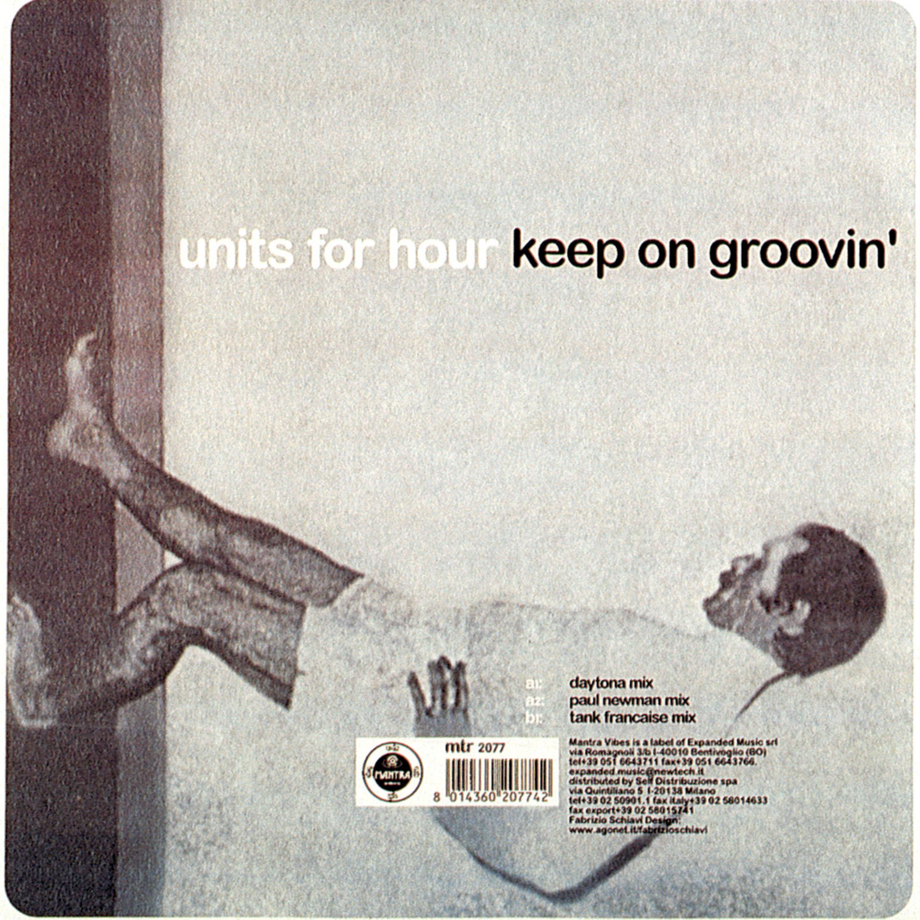

units for hour keep on groovin'

a1:   daytona mix
a2:   paul newman mix
b1:   tank francaise mix

mtr 2077

8 014360 207742

Mantra Vibes is a label of Expanded Music srl
via Romagnoli 3/b I-40010 Bentivoglio (BO)
tel+39 051 6643711 fax+39 051 6643766.
expanded.music@newtech.it
distributed by Self Distribuzione spa
via Quintiliano 5 I-20138 Milano
tel+39 02 50901.1 fax italy+39 02 58014633
fax export+39 02 58015741
Fabrizio Schiavi Design:
www.agonet.it/fabrizioschiavi

Artist Oliver Moldan Title Pulp Design Factor Product Photography Von Denis Pernath Record Label Kosmos

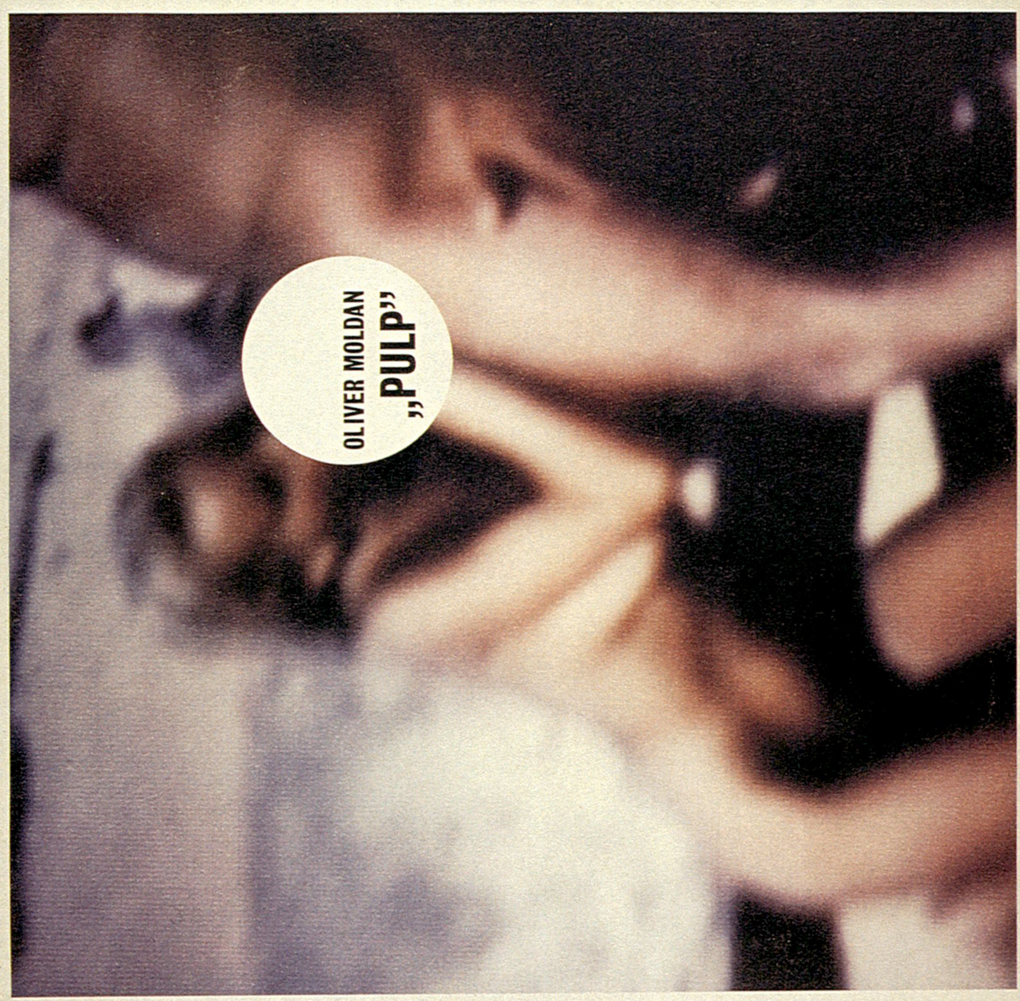

Bob Sinclar

Ultimate funk

 Artist Bob Sinclar Title Ultimate Funk Record Label Yellow Date 1998

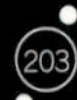

Artist **Fidelfatti with Ronnette** Title **Just Wanna Touch Me** Record Label Service / Magic

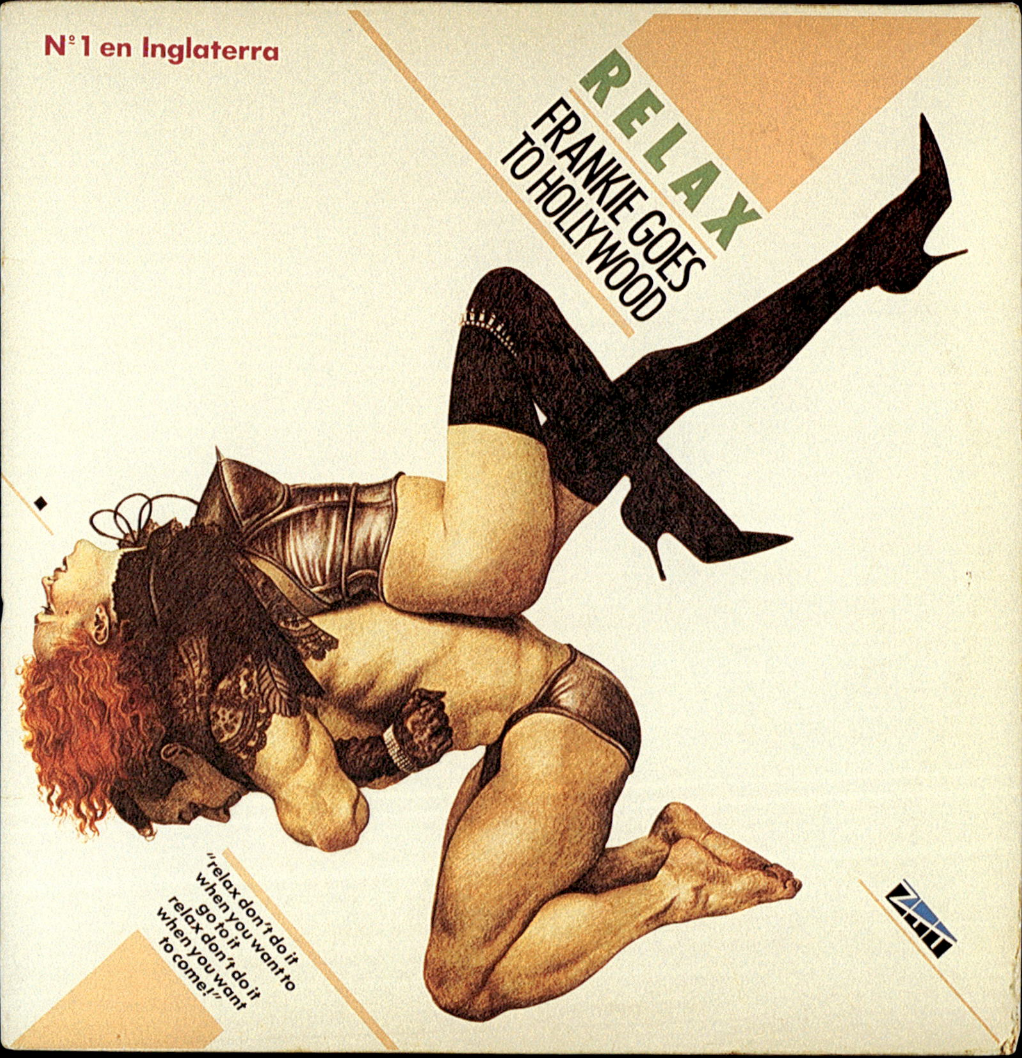

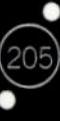

205 Artist **Frankie Goes to Hollywood** Title **Relax** Design **XL ZTT** Illustration **Anne Yvonne Gilbert**
Record Label **ZTT** Date **1984**

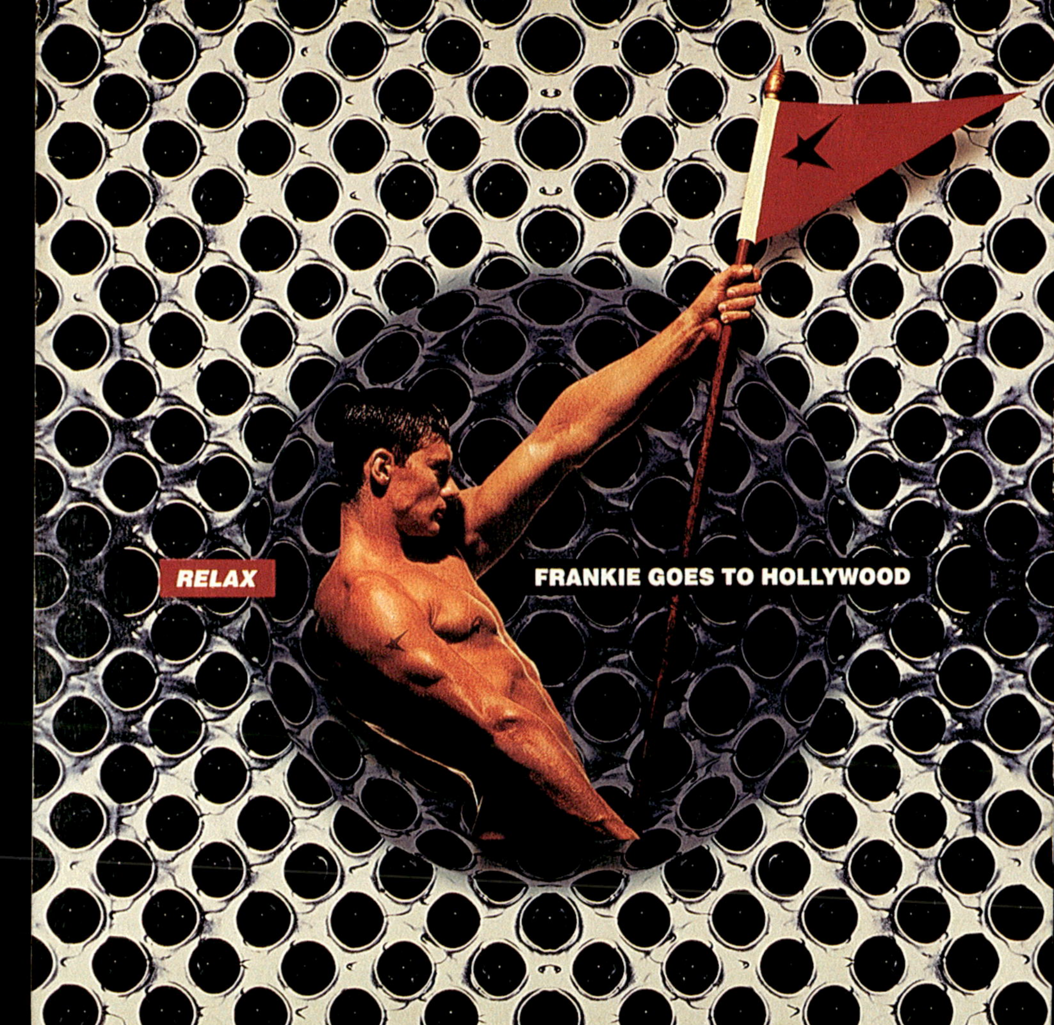

Artist Frankie Goes to Hollywood Title Relax Design Me Company Photography Mark Liddell Record Label ZTT Date 1993

206

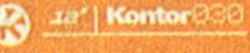
12" | Kontor030

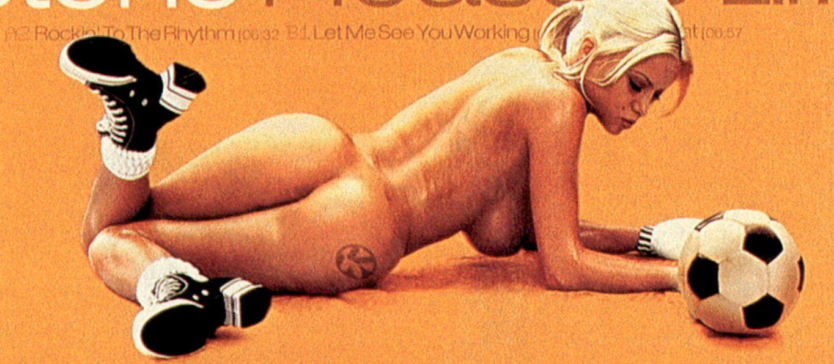
Caba Kroll presents
C.J Stone Pleasure E.P.
A1 Mothers Bass (06:30) A2 Rockin' To The Rhythm (06:32) B1 Let Me See You Working (06:57)

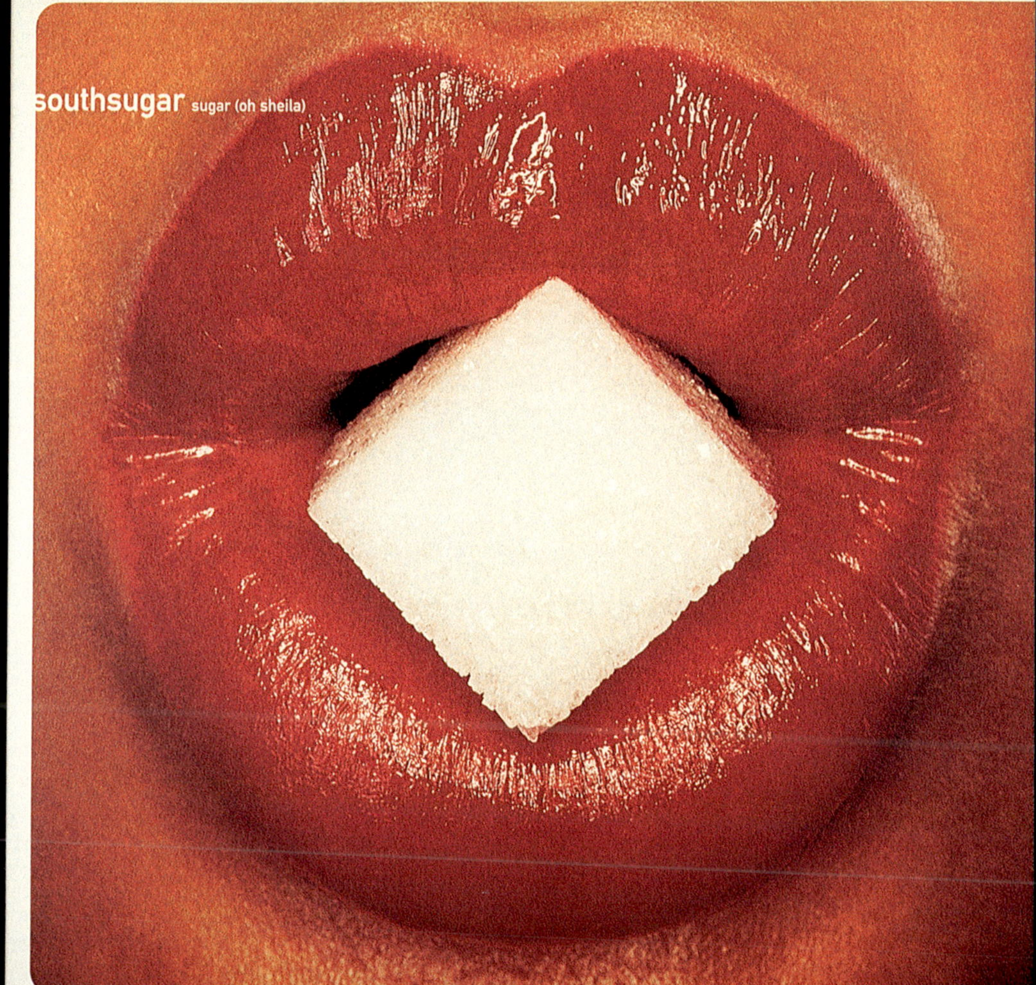
southsugar sugar (oh sheila)

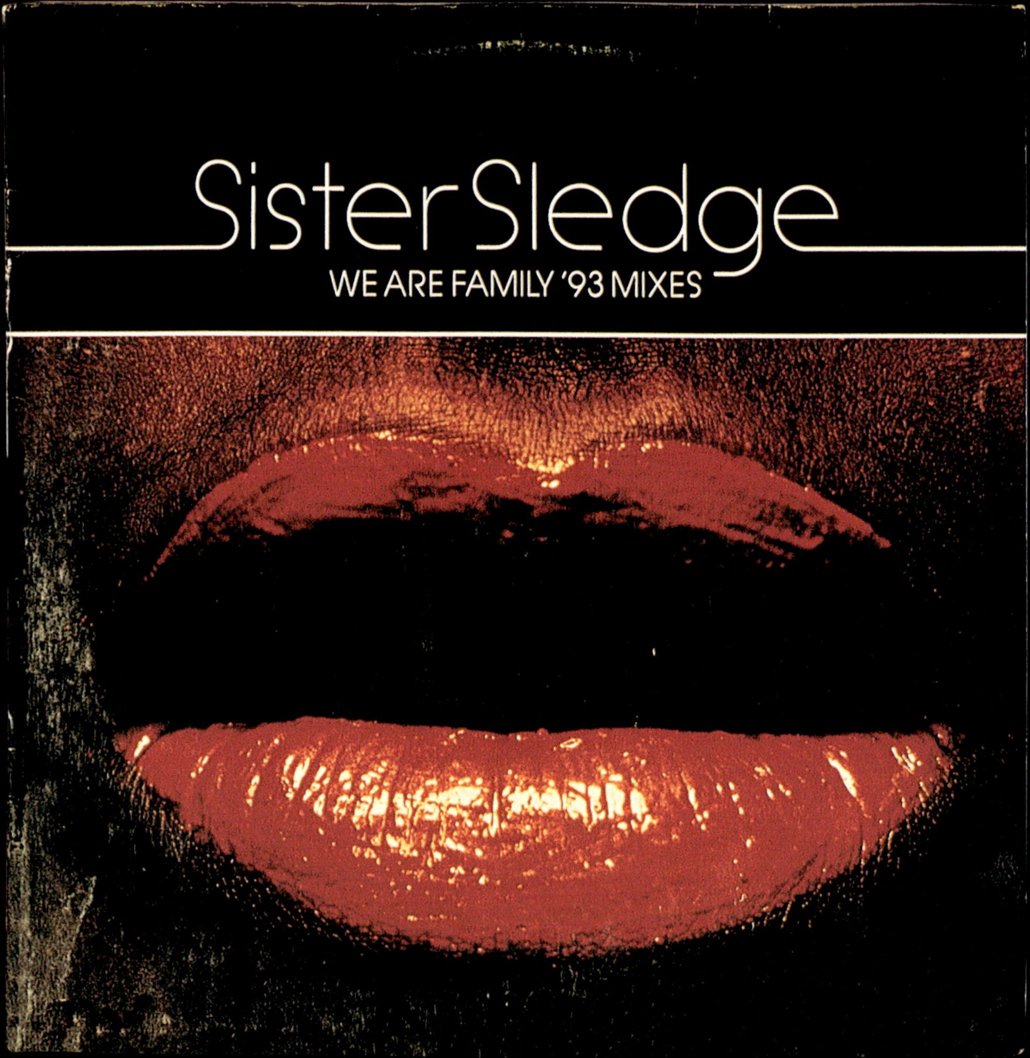

SisterSledge

WE ARE FAMILY '93 MIXES

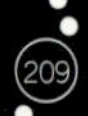

209 Artist Sister Sledge Title We Are Family Design David James Associates Photography Pete Turner
Record Label Atlantic Date 1993

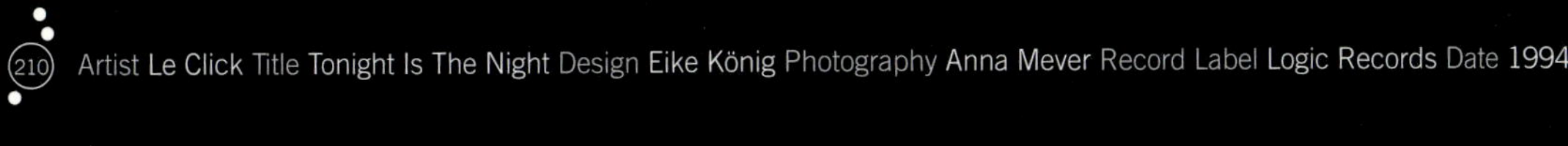

LE CLICK
tonight is the night

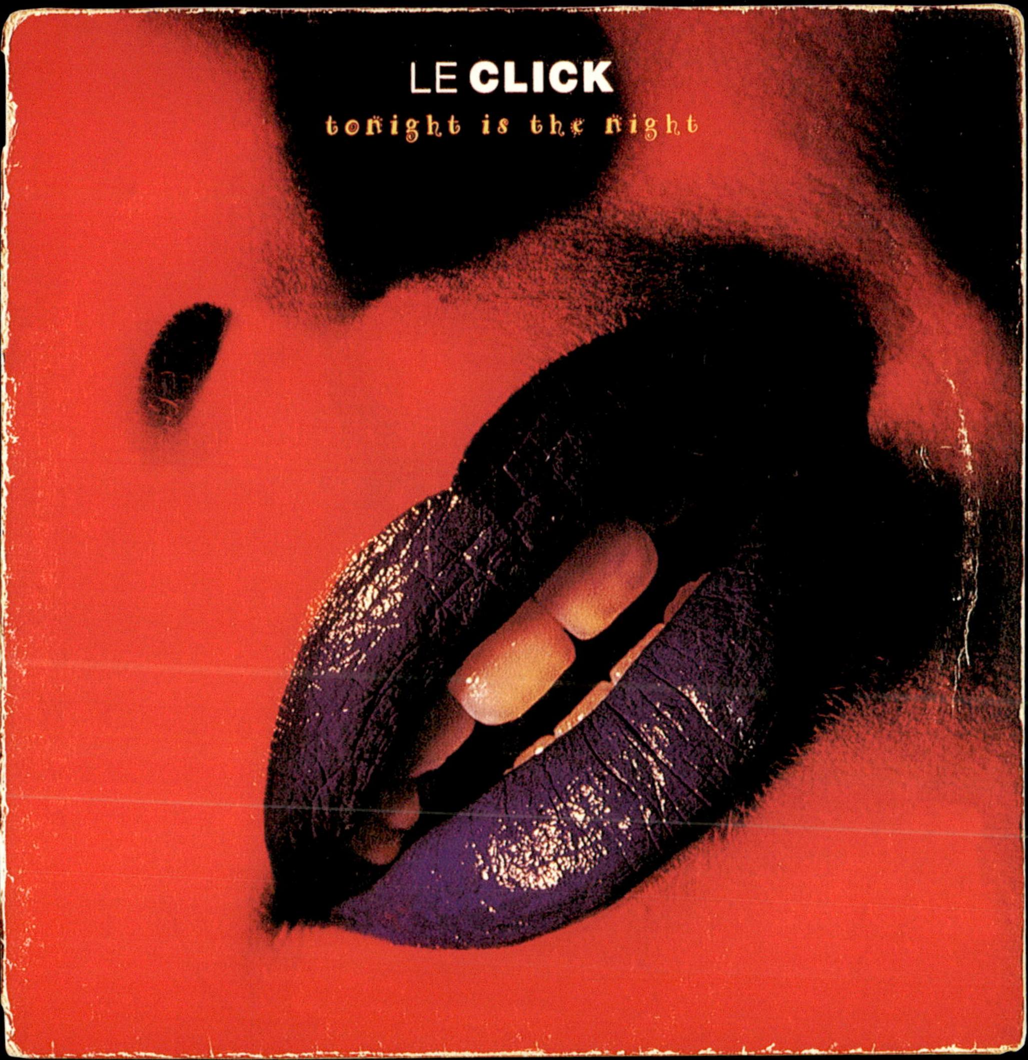

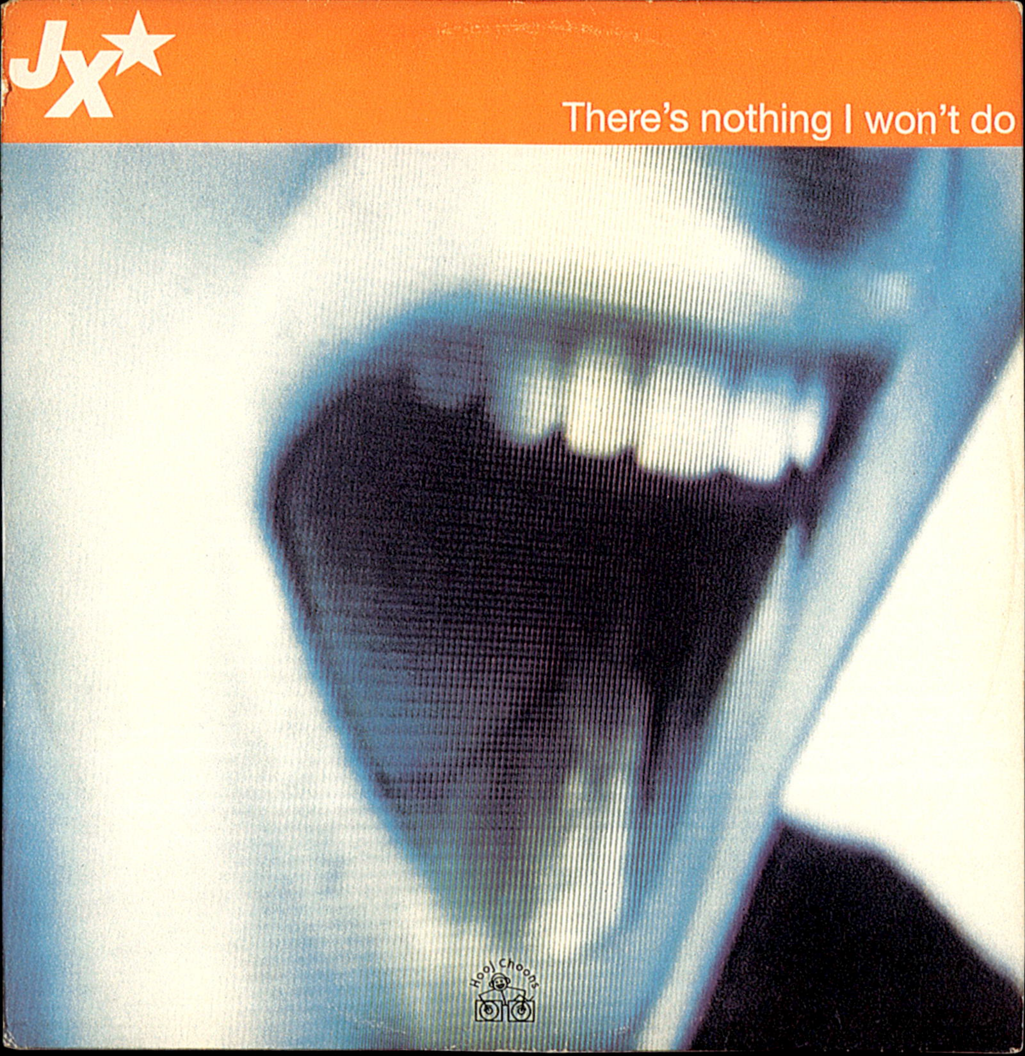

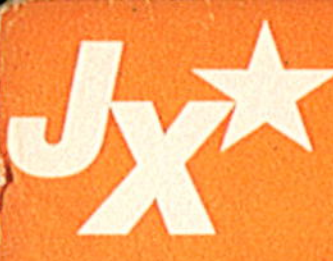

JX
There's nothing I won't do
Hool Choons

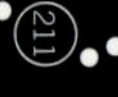

(21)
Artist JX Title There's Nothing I Won't Do Design Mouthco Design Record Label Freedom Date 1996

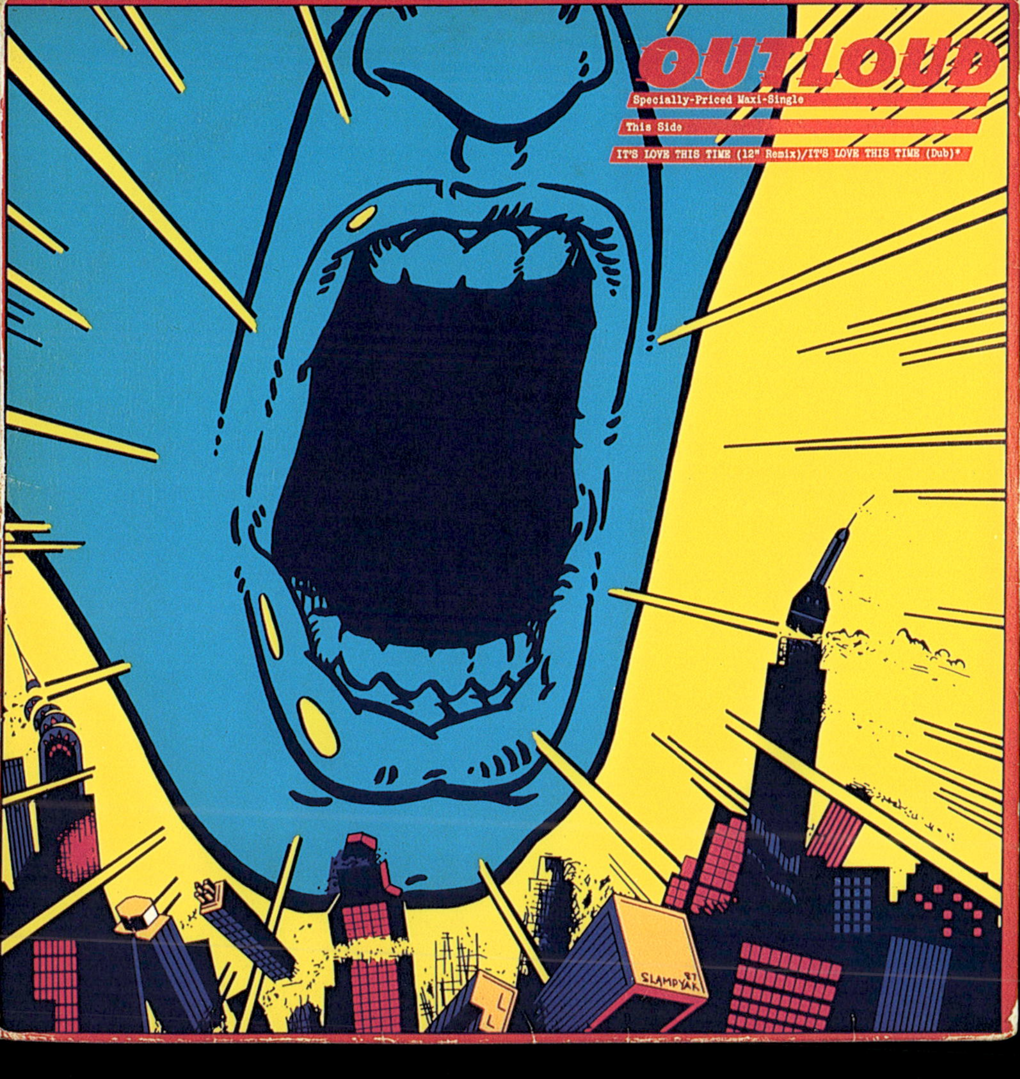

 Artist Outloud Title It's Love This Time Design Peter Corriston Record Label Warner Bros Date 1987

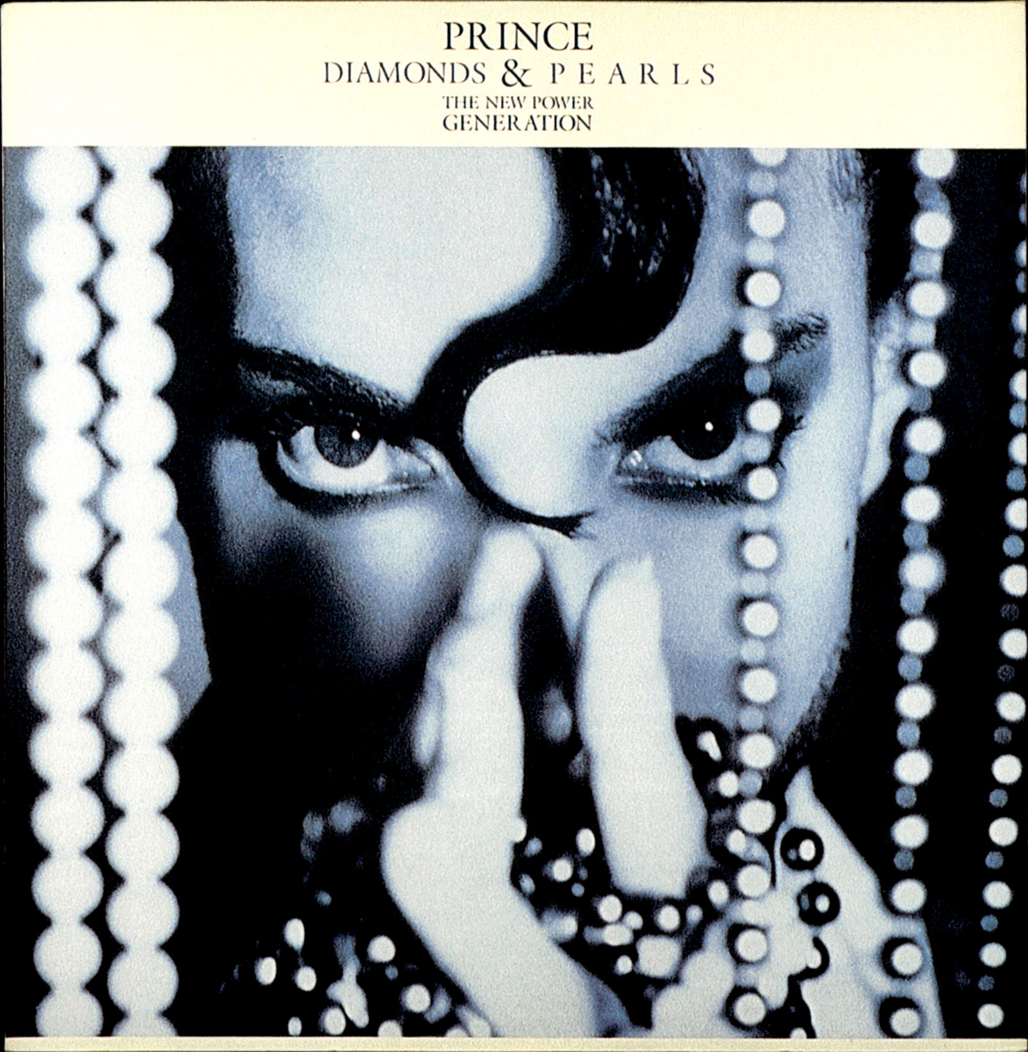

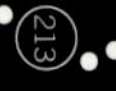

Artist Prince & The New Power Generation Title Diamonds & Pearls Photography Randee St. Nicholas Record Label Paisley Park Records Date 1991

214 Artist Sister Sledge Title Thinking of You Design David James Assoc. Photography Graeme Montgomery Record Label Atlantic Date 1993

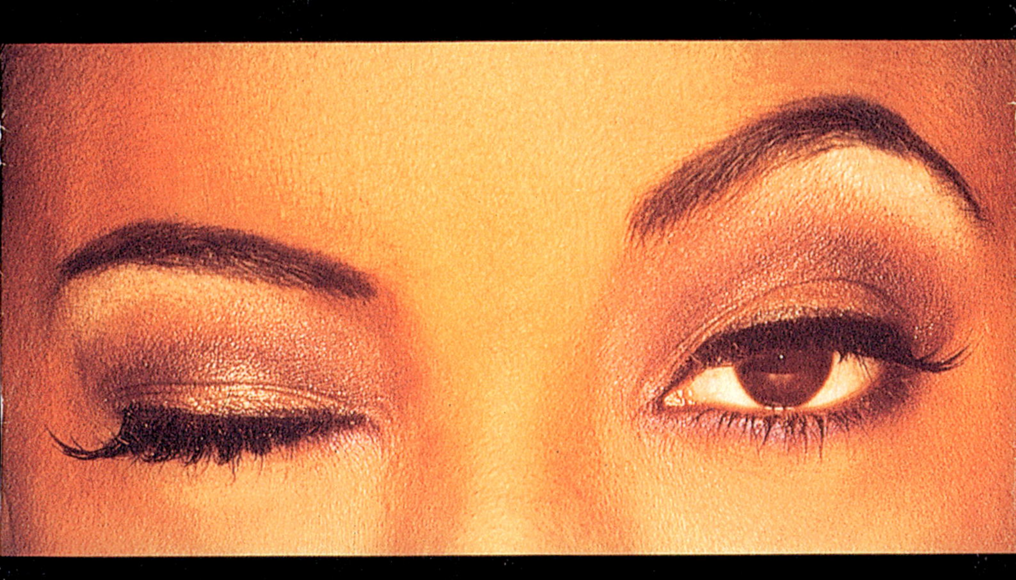

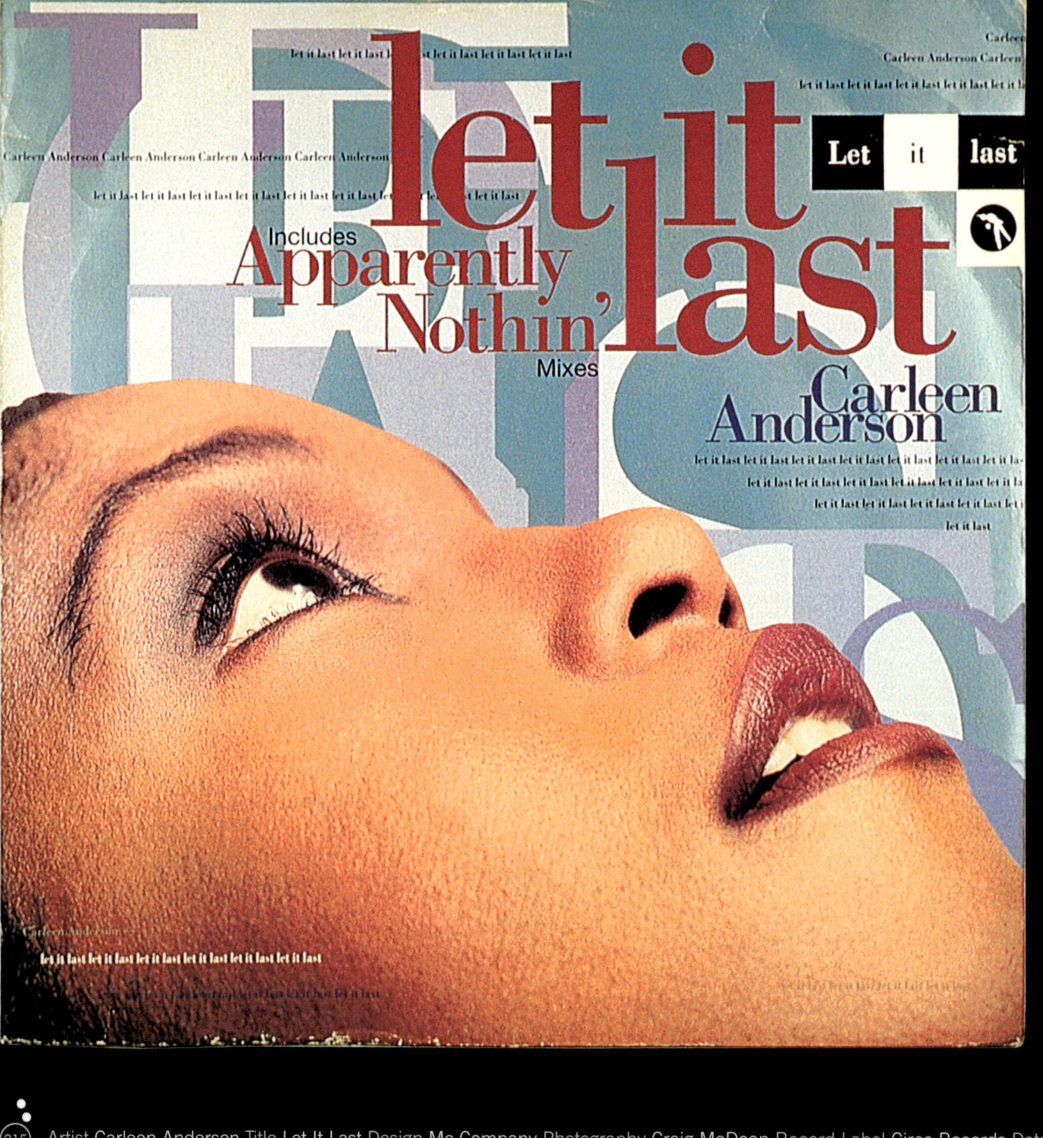

 Artist Carleen Anderson Title Let It Last Design Me Company Photography Craig McDean Record Label Circa Records Date

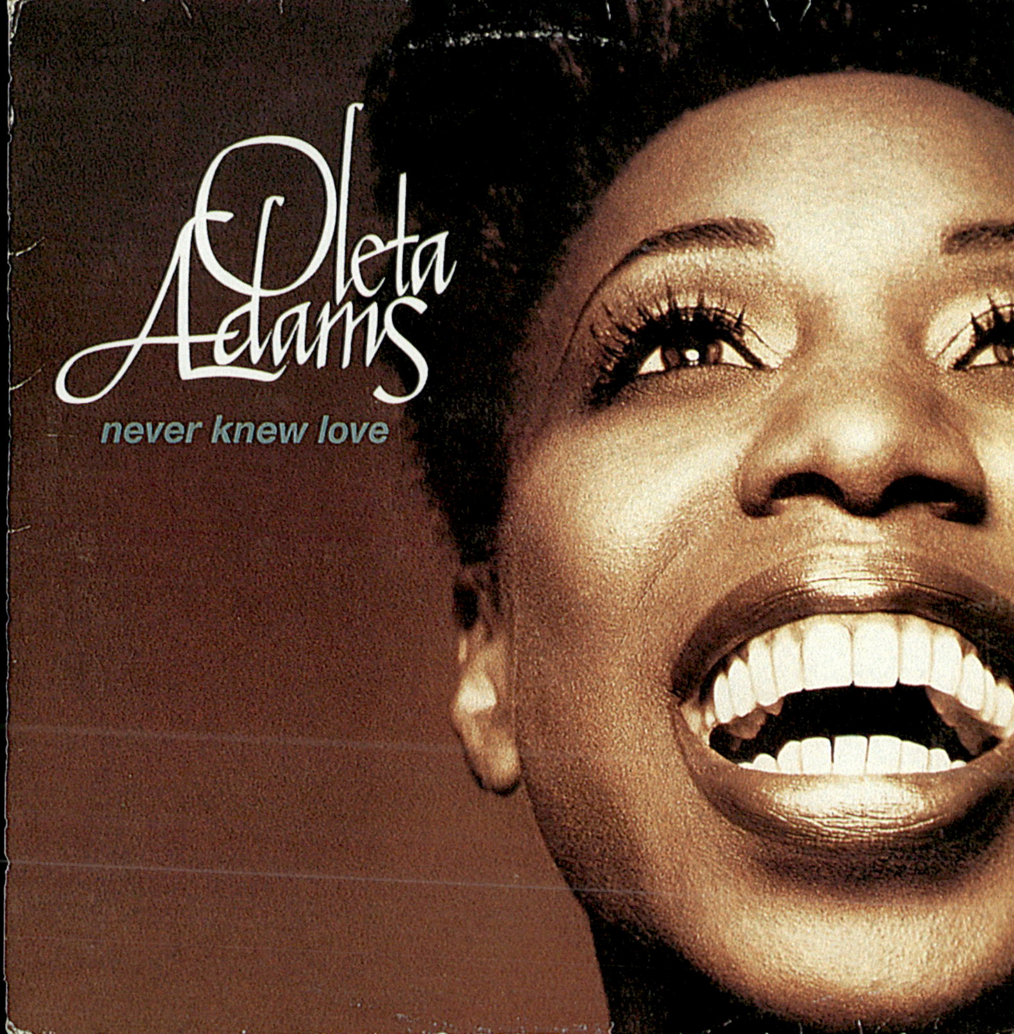

Oleta Adams
never knew love
Artist Oleta Adams Title Never Knew Love Design Mercury Art Photography Michel Comte
Record Label Fontana / Mercury Date 1995
216

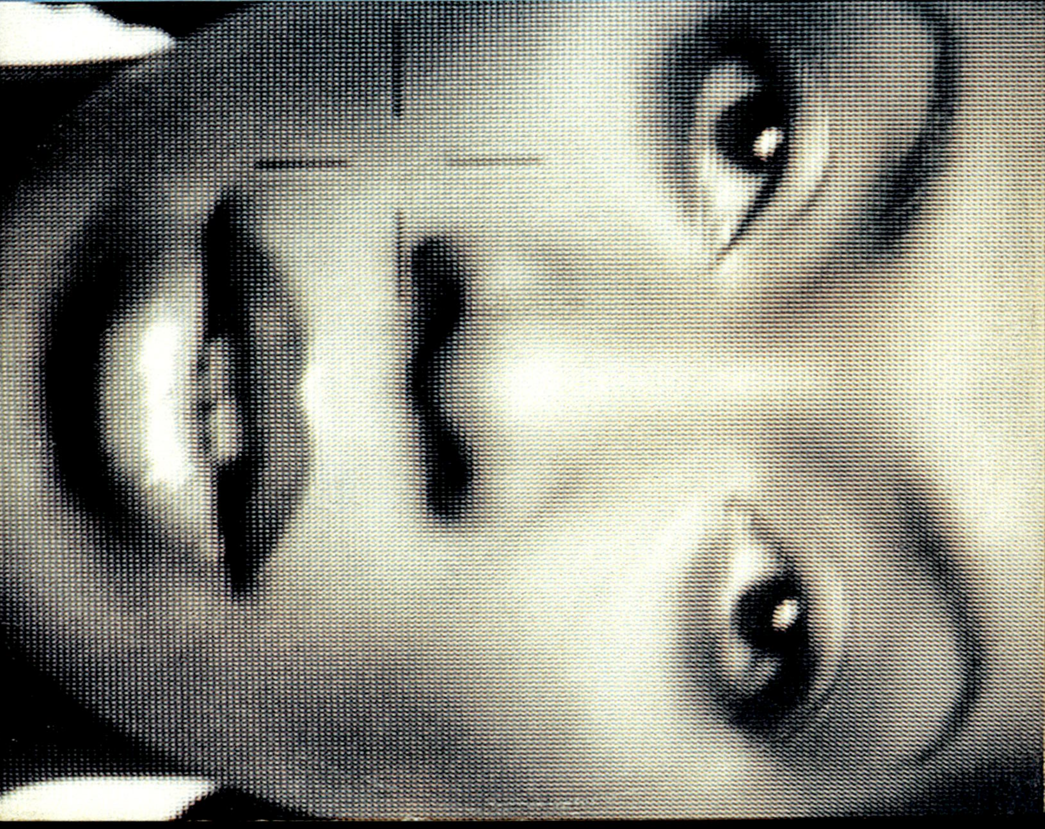

lovestationteardrops
Artist Teardrops Title Lovestation Photography Larry Dunstan Record Label Fresh Records Date 1998

faith
evans
love like this

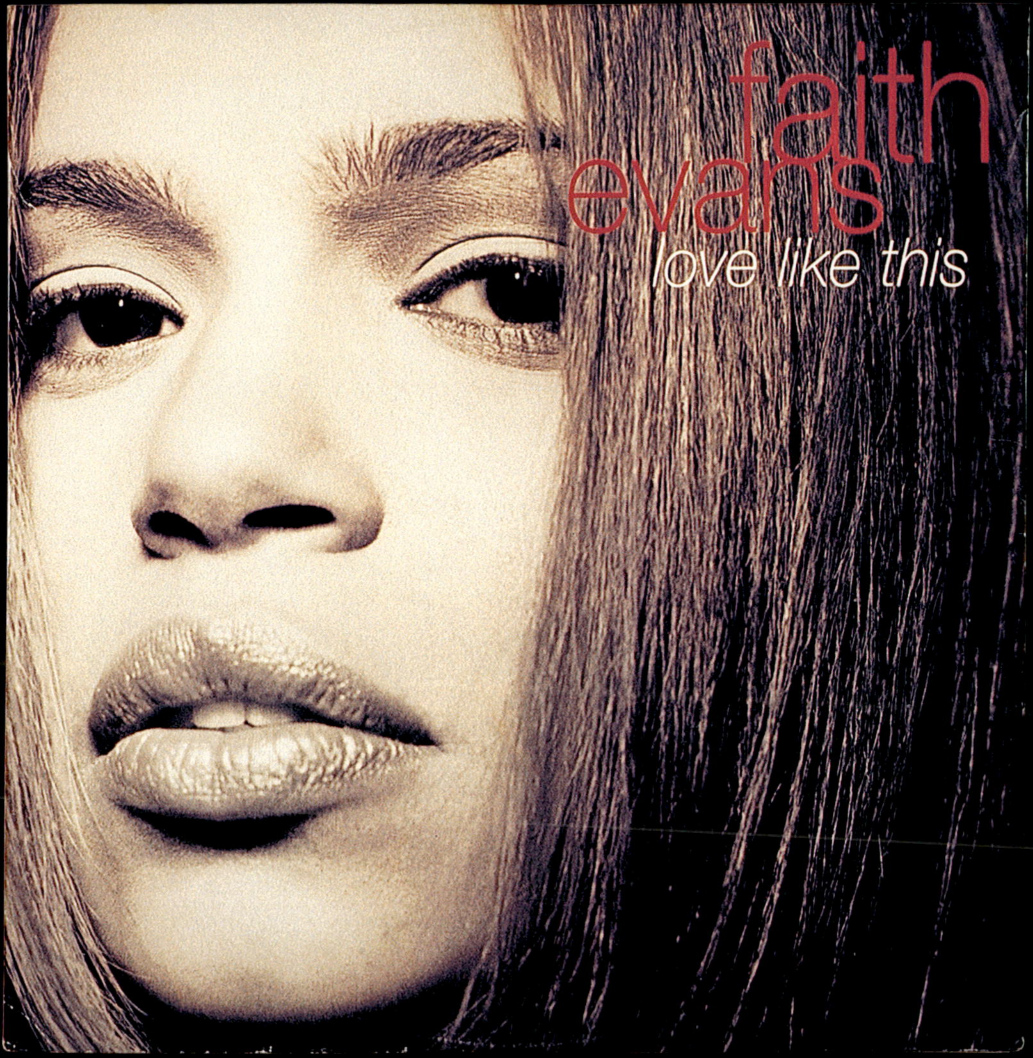

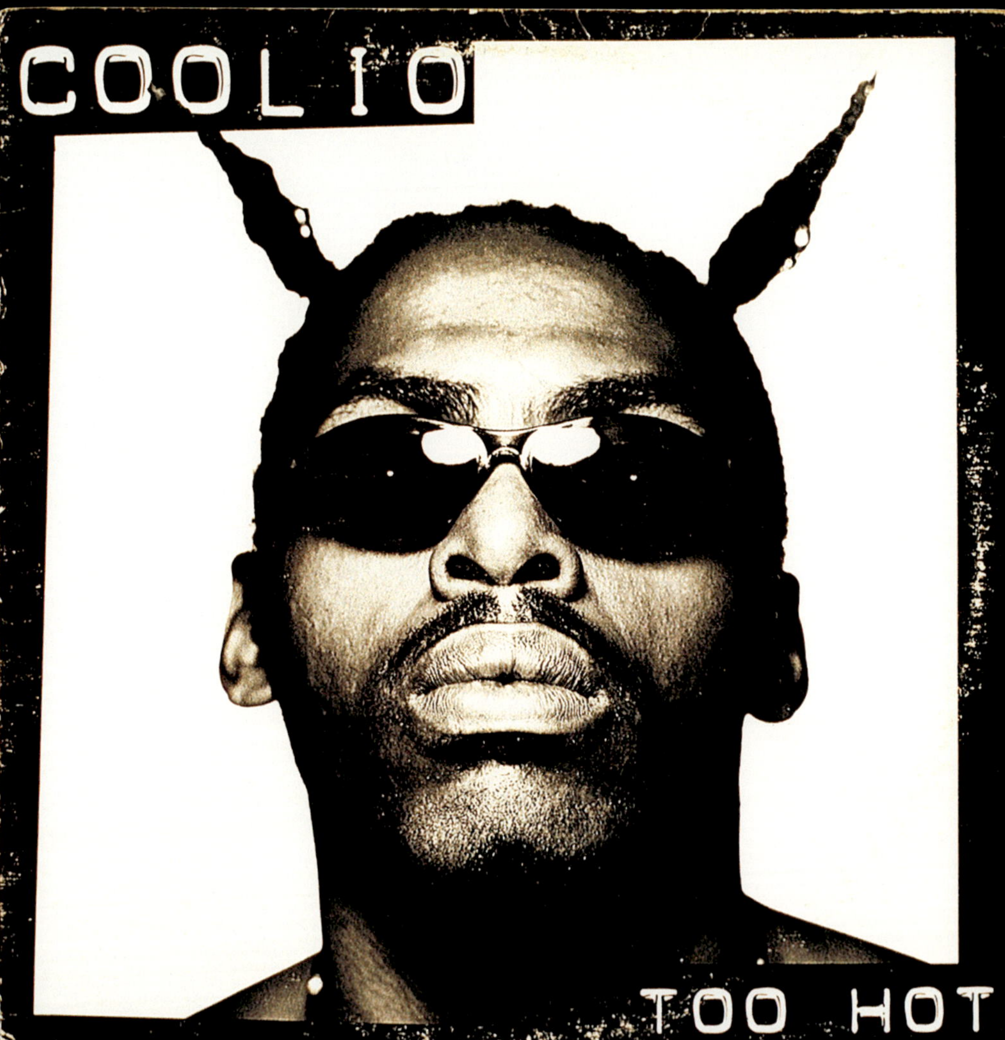
COOLIO
TOO HOT

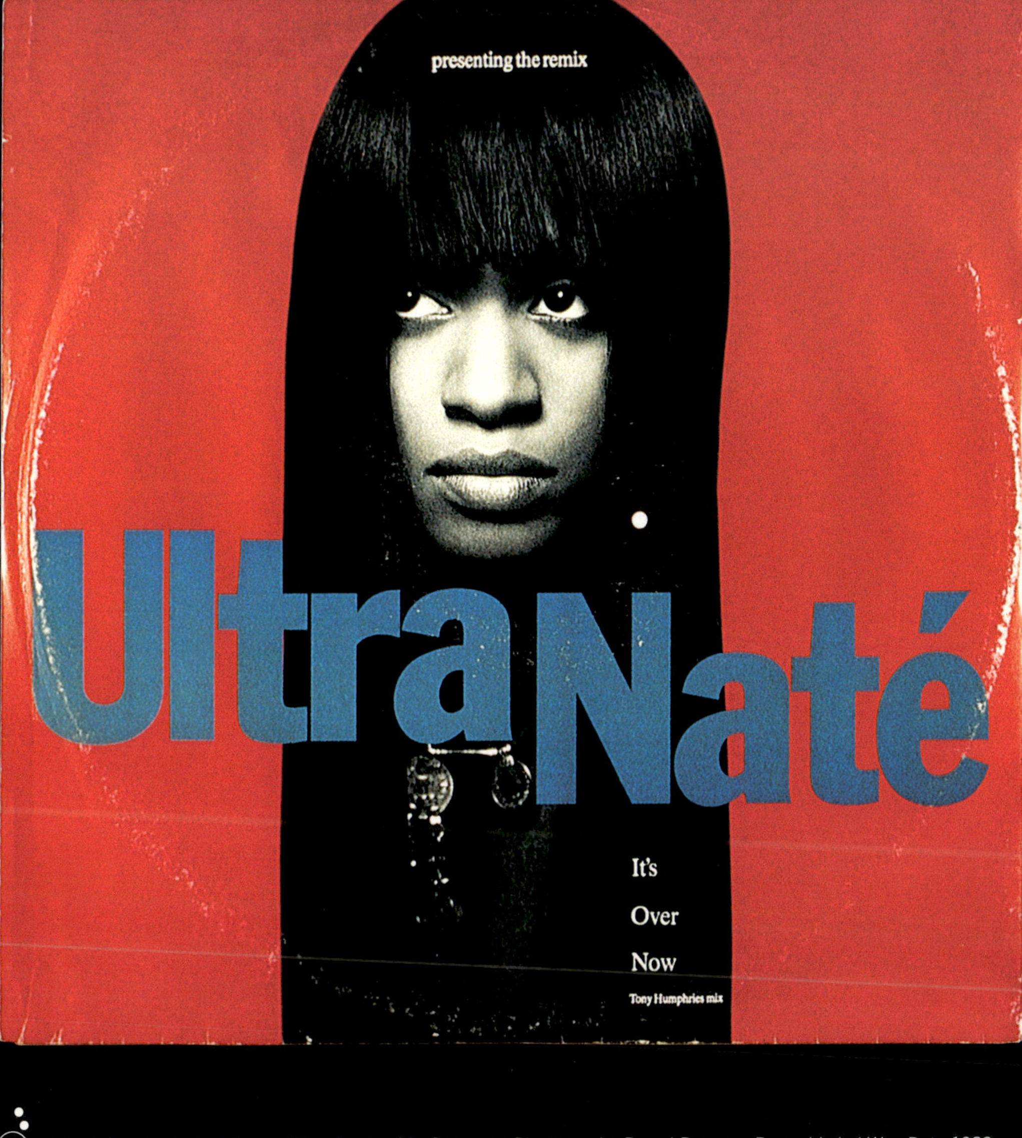

Artist Ultra Naté Title It's Over Now Design Me Company Photography Brand Branson Record Label Wea Date 1989

ADEVA!
I THANK YOU

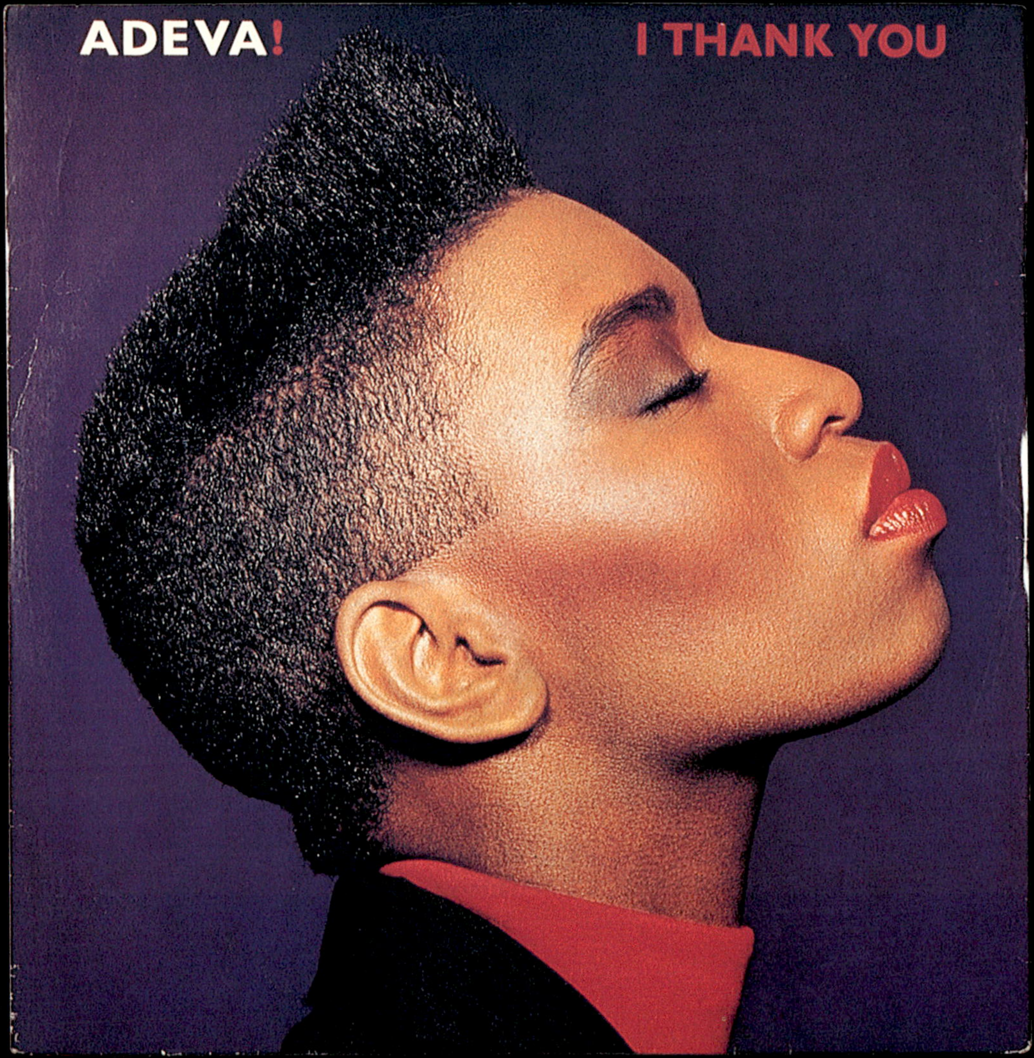

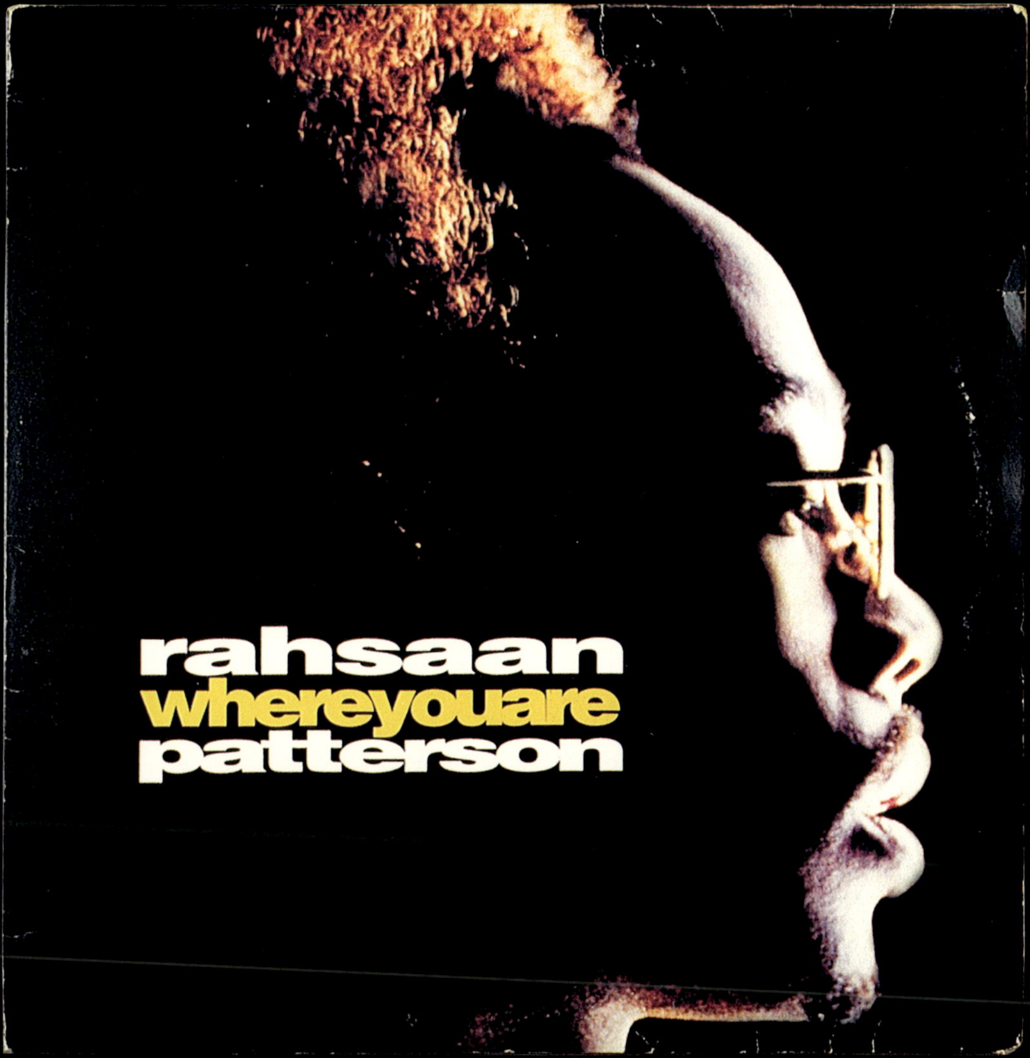

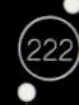

Artist Rahsaan Patterson Title Where You Are Design Same Photography Drew Fitzgerald Record Label MCA Date 1998

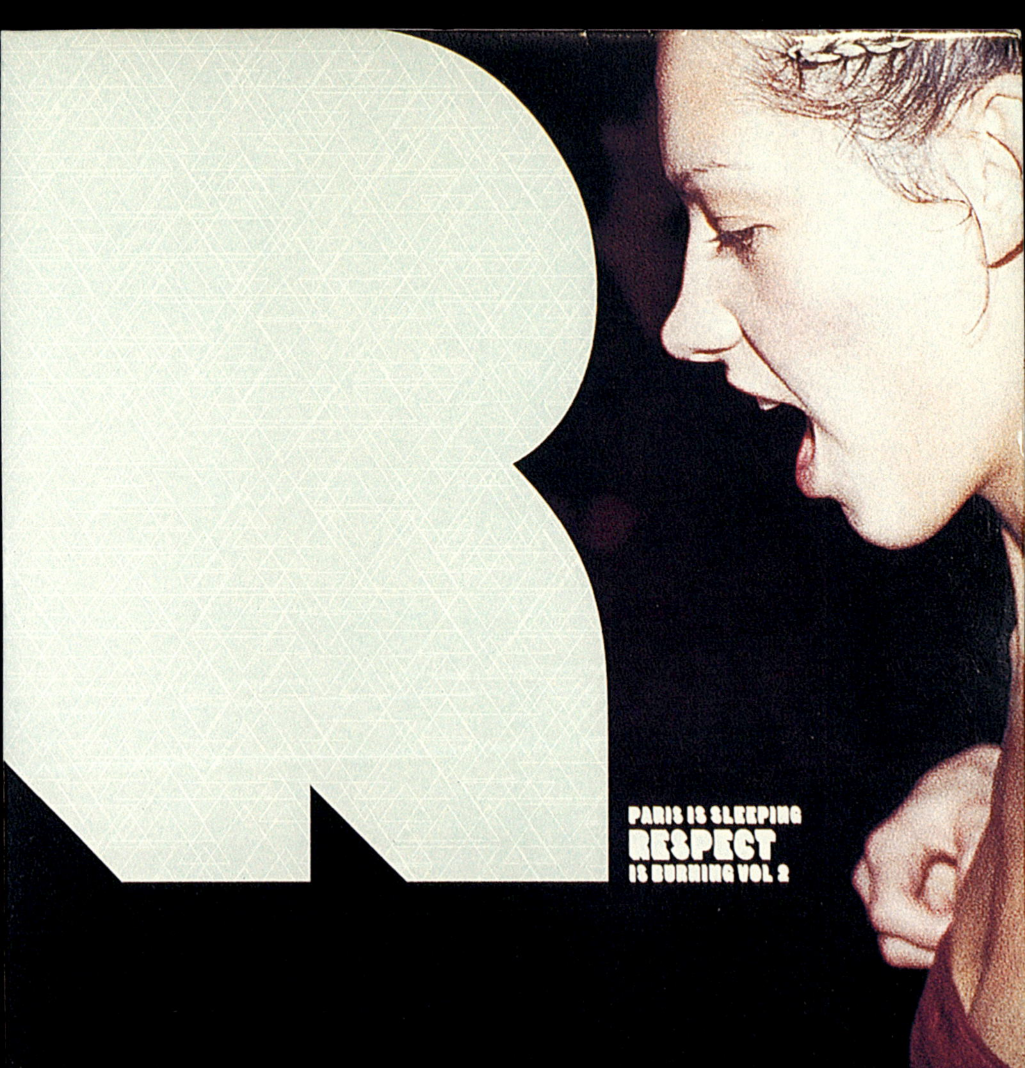

PARIS IS SLEEPING
RESPECT
IS BURNING VOL. 2

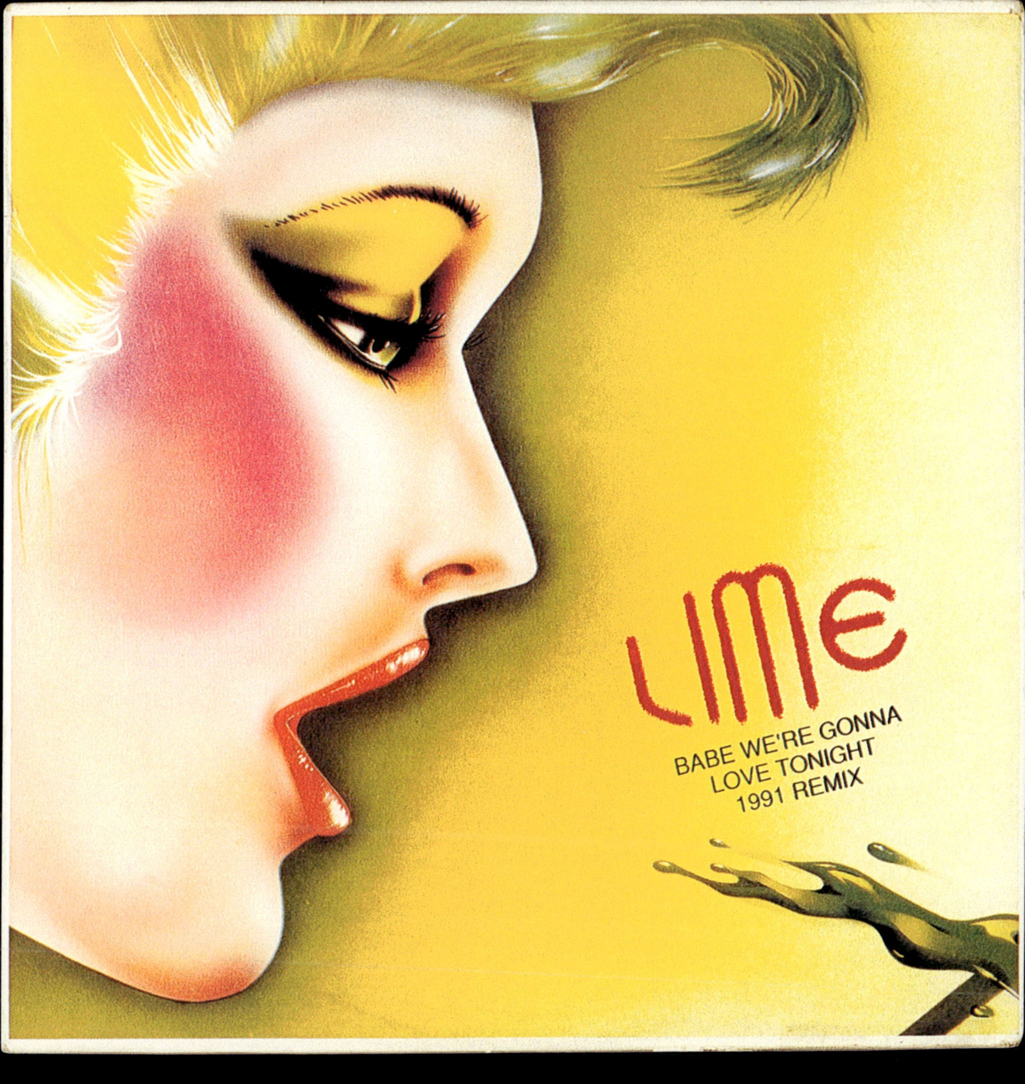

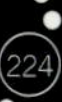

Artist Lime Title Babe We're Gonna Love Tonight (Remix) Record Label Blanco y Negro Date 1991

Artist Armand Van Helden Title You Don't Know Me Record Label FFRR Date 1999

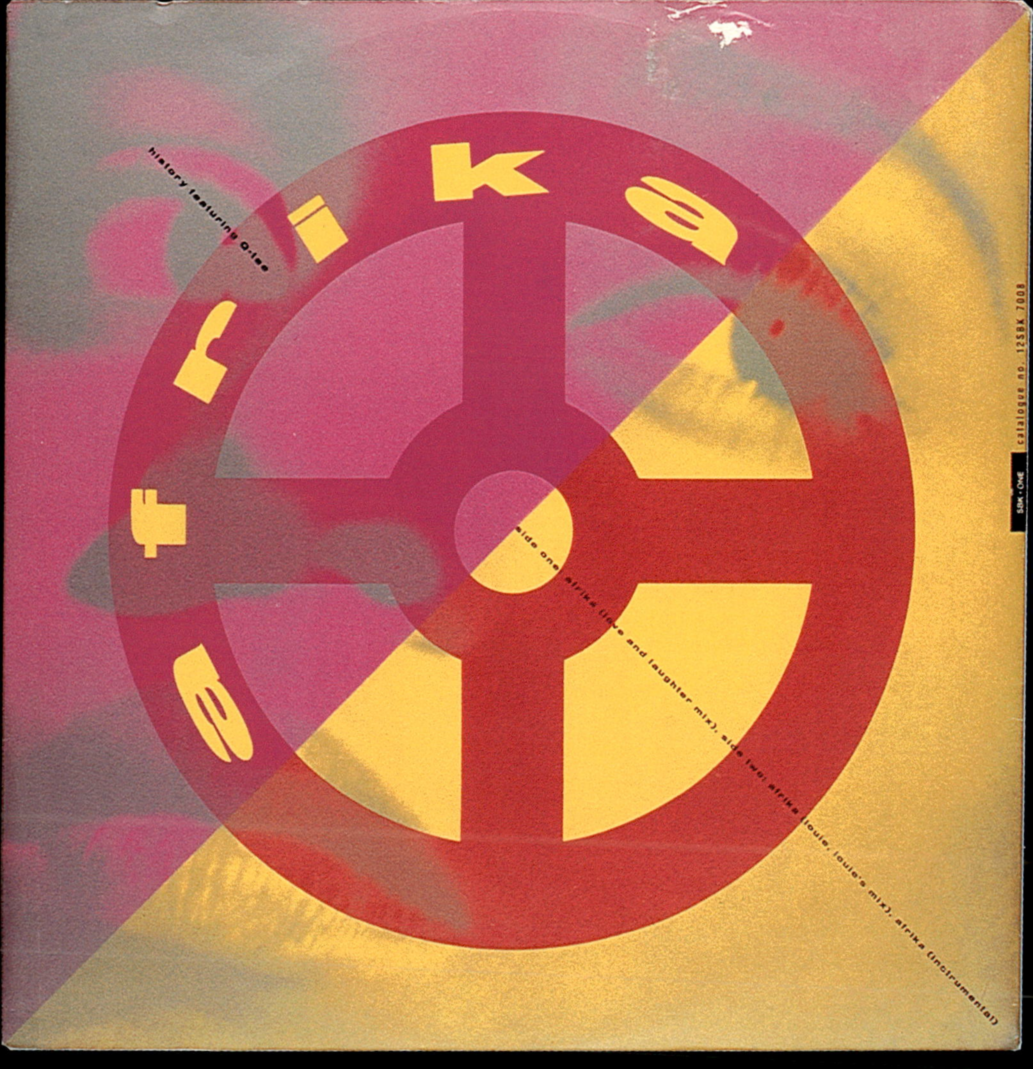

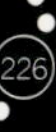

Artist History feat. Q-Tee Title Afrika Design Me Company Photography Peter Ashworth
Record Label SBK Records Date 1990

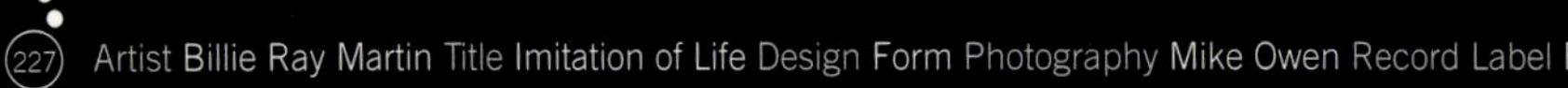

bRM
"Passing the time
So many lies, yes
All of it mine, all of the time
Imitation of life
And the days go by..."
BillieRayMartin
Imitation Of Life

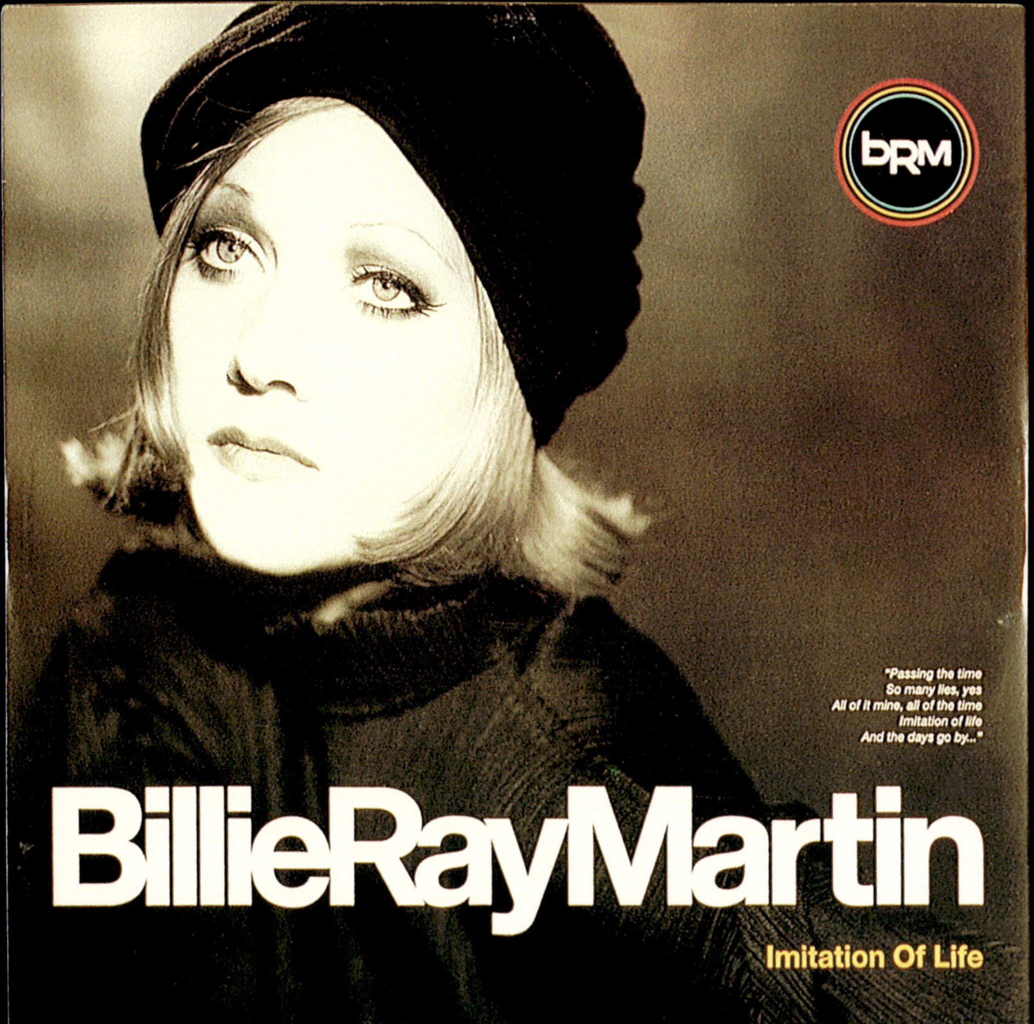

I CAN'T SEE
NICOLE RAY

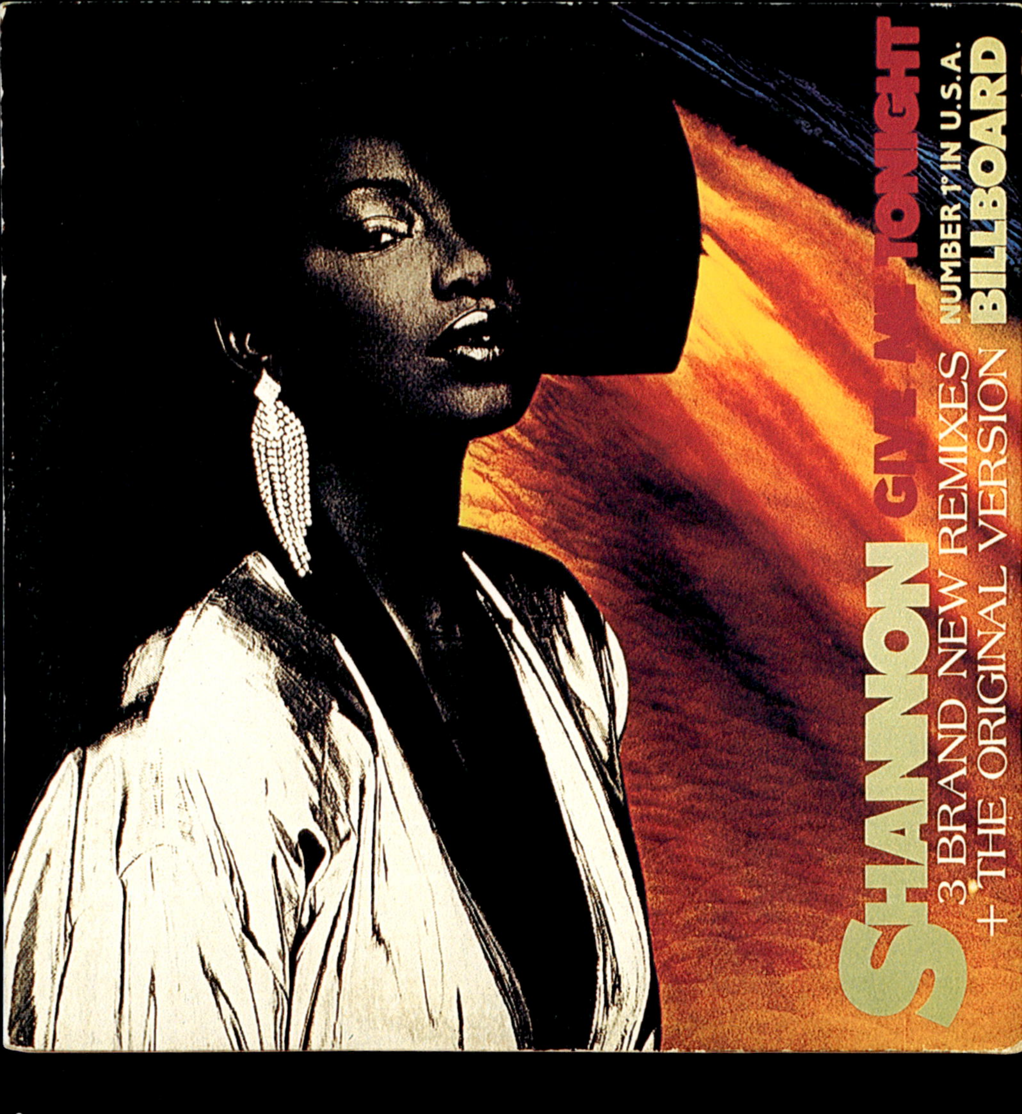

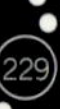

Artist Shannon Title Give Me Tonight Design P. Squeglia Photography Roy Volkman Record Label Flying Date 1990

YAZZ   TREAT ME GOOD

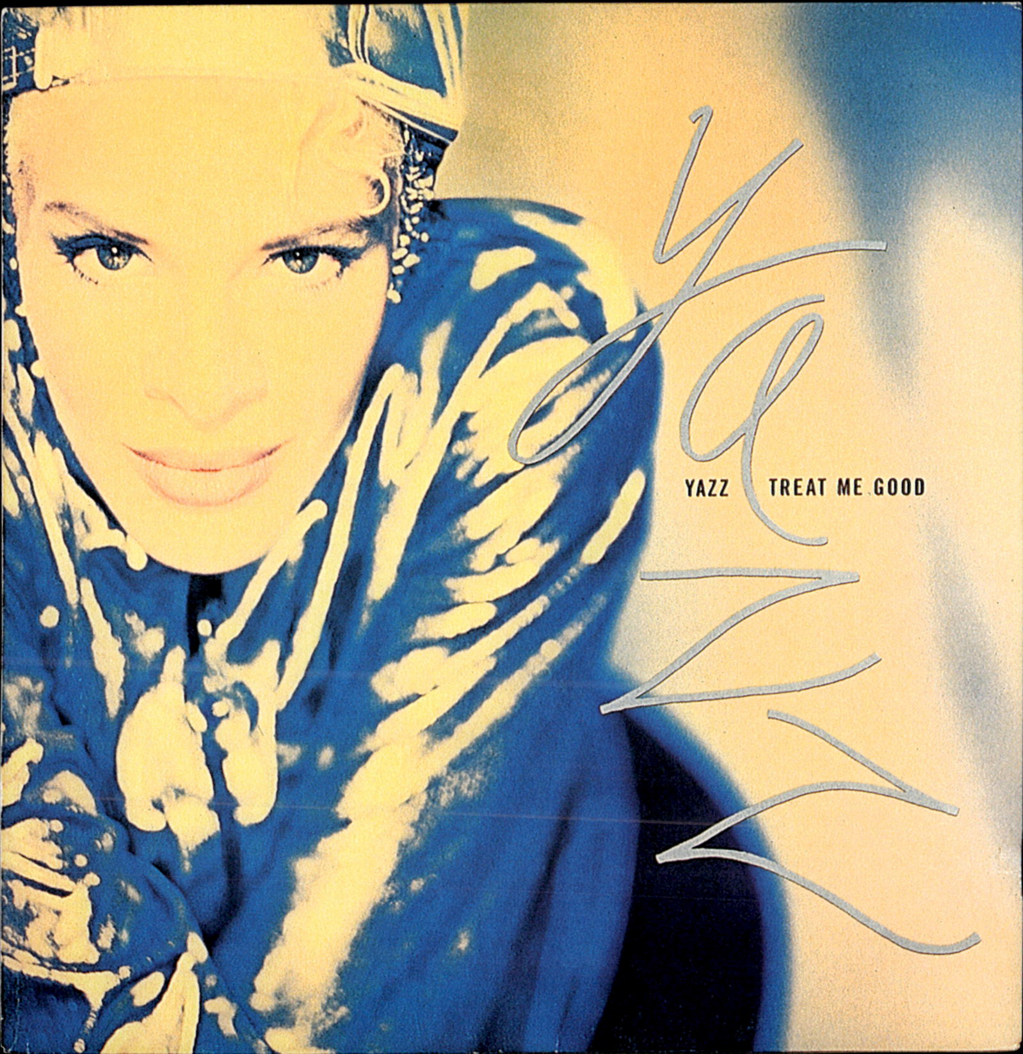

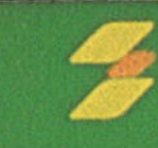

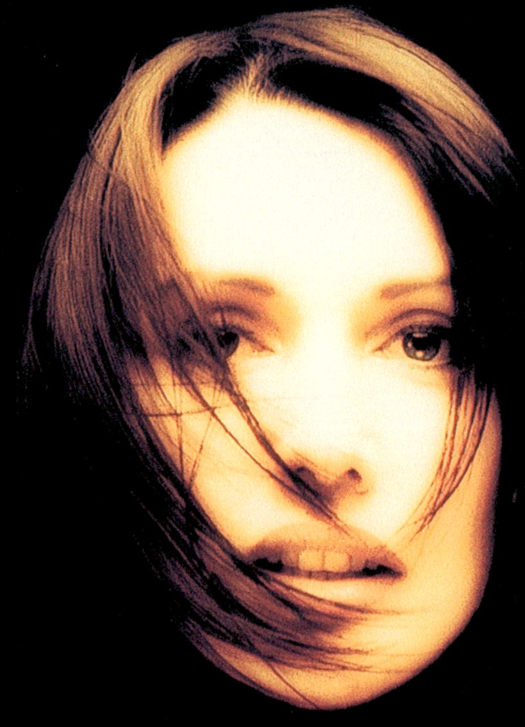

231 Artist **Essence** Title **The Promise** Record Label **Virgin** Date **1998**

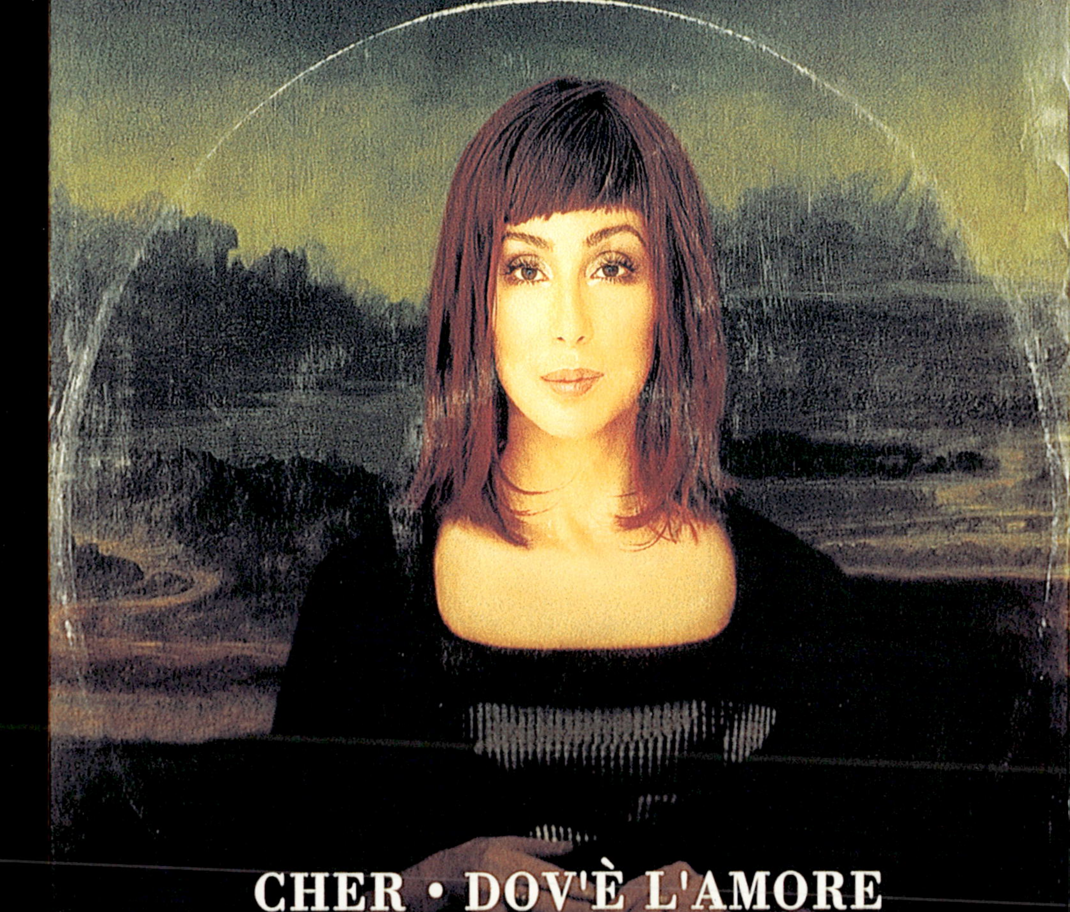

CHER • DOV'È L'AMORE

Cher Title Dov'è l'amore Design Ryan Art Record Label Wea Date 1999

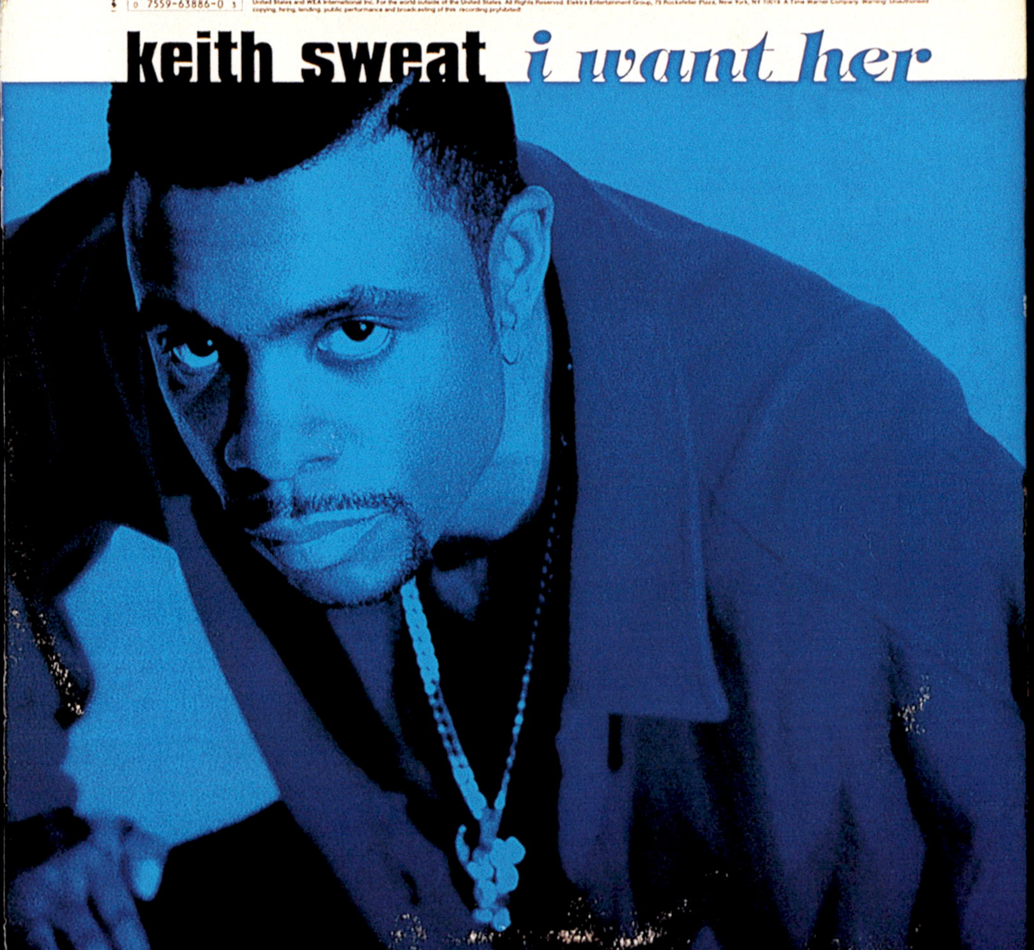
1:01. femi fem's master mix   1:02. femi fem's instrumental   1:03. funky di remix
2:01. dubaholics vocal dub mix   2:02. dubaholics deep club dubb
0 7559-63886-0 3
7559-63886-0 • E3627T • • ℗ & © 1997 Elektra Entertainment Group for the United States and WEA International Inc. For the world outside of the United States. All Rights Reserved. © 1997 Elektra Entertainment Group for the United States and WEA International Inc. For the world outside of the United States. All Rights Reserved. Elektra Entertainment Group, 75 Rockefeller Plaza, New York, NY 10019. A Time Warner Company. Warning: Unauthorized copying, hiring, lending, public performance and broadcasting of this recording prohibited!
keith sweat i want her

233

Includes "Lost Souls" featuring Jamiroquai
GURU
JAZZMATAZZ Vol. II The New Reality
FEEL THE MUSIC

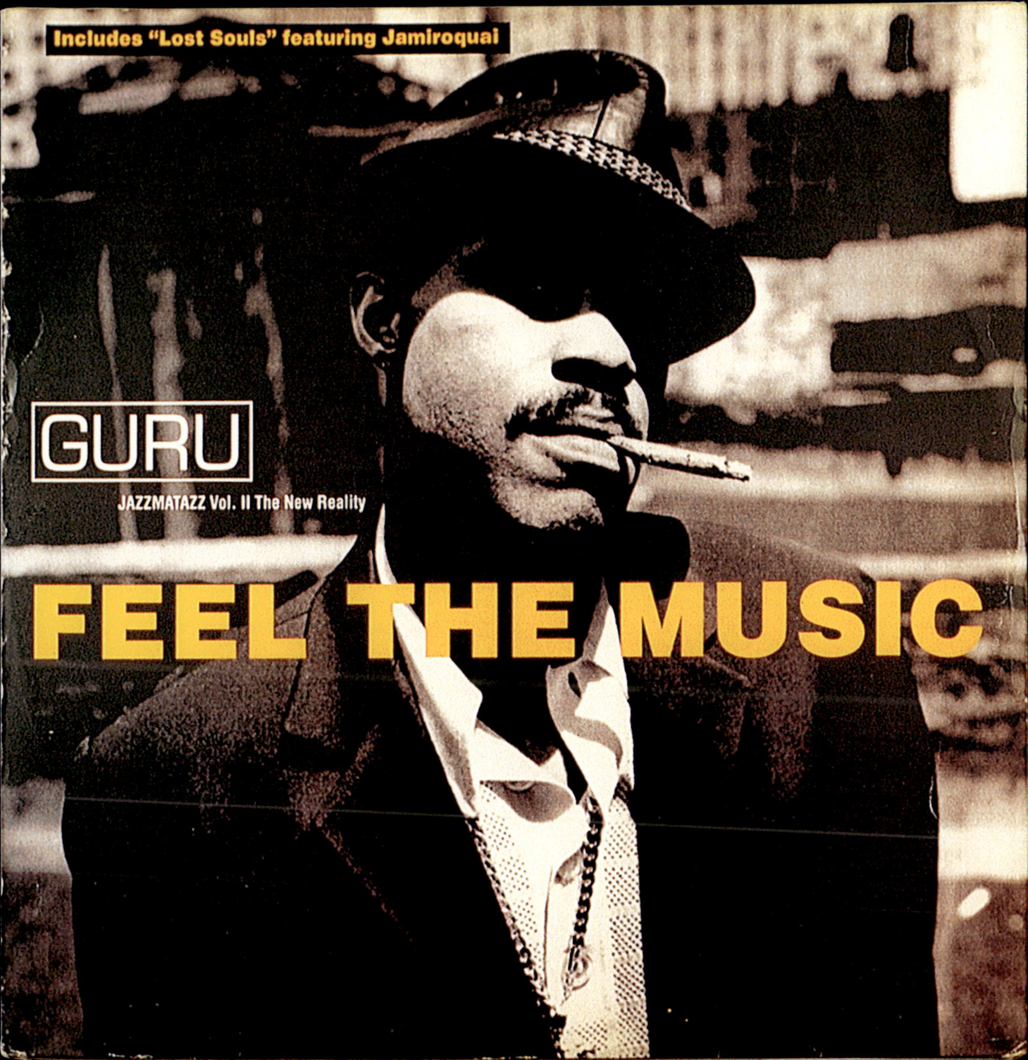

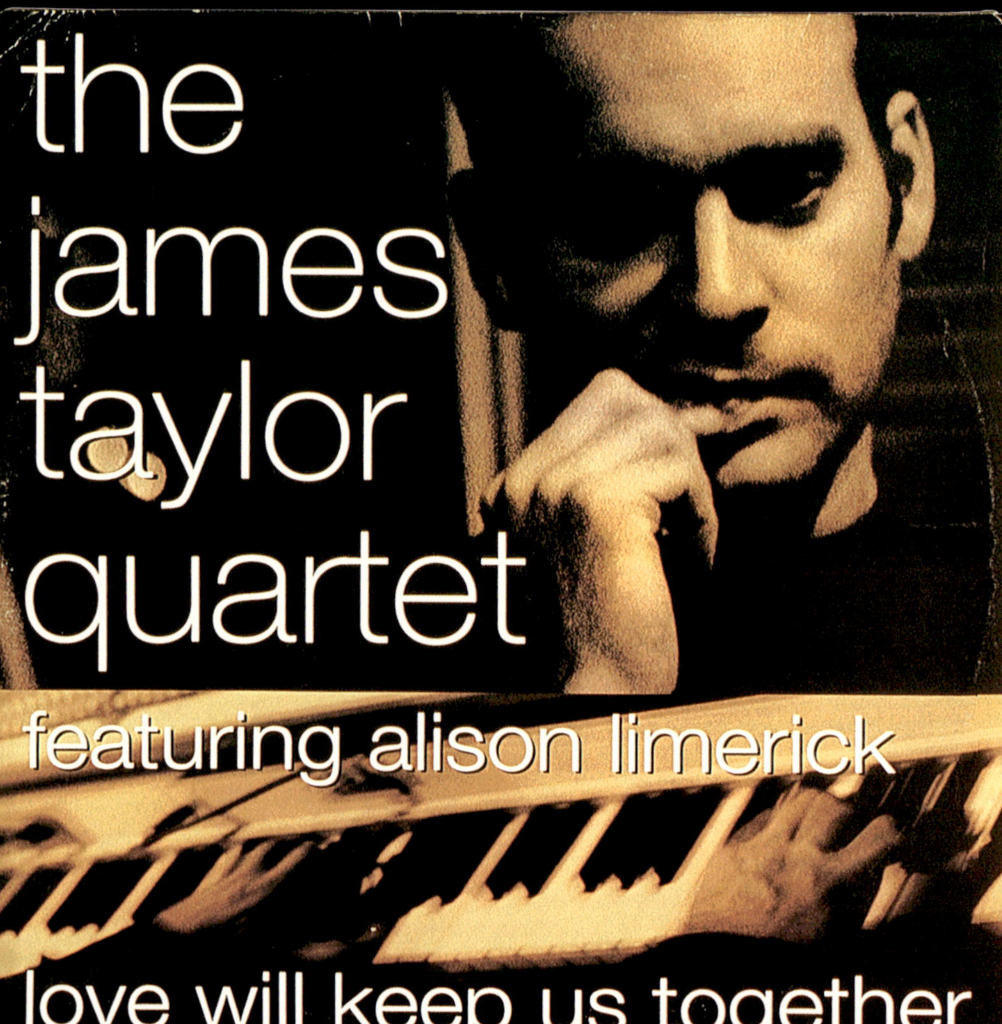

the james taylor quartet
featuring alison limerick
love will keep us together

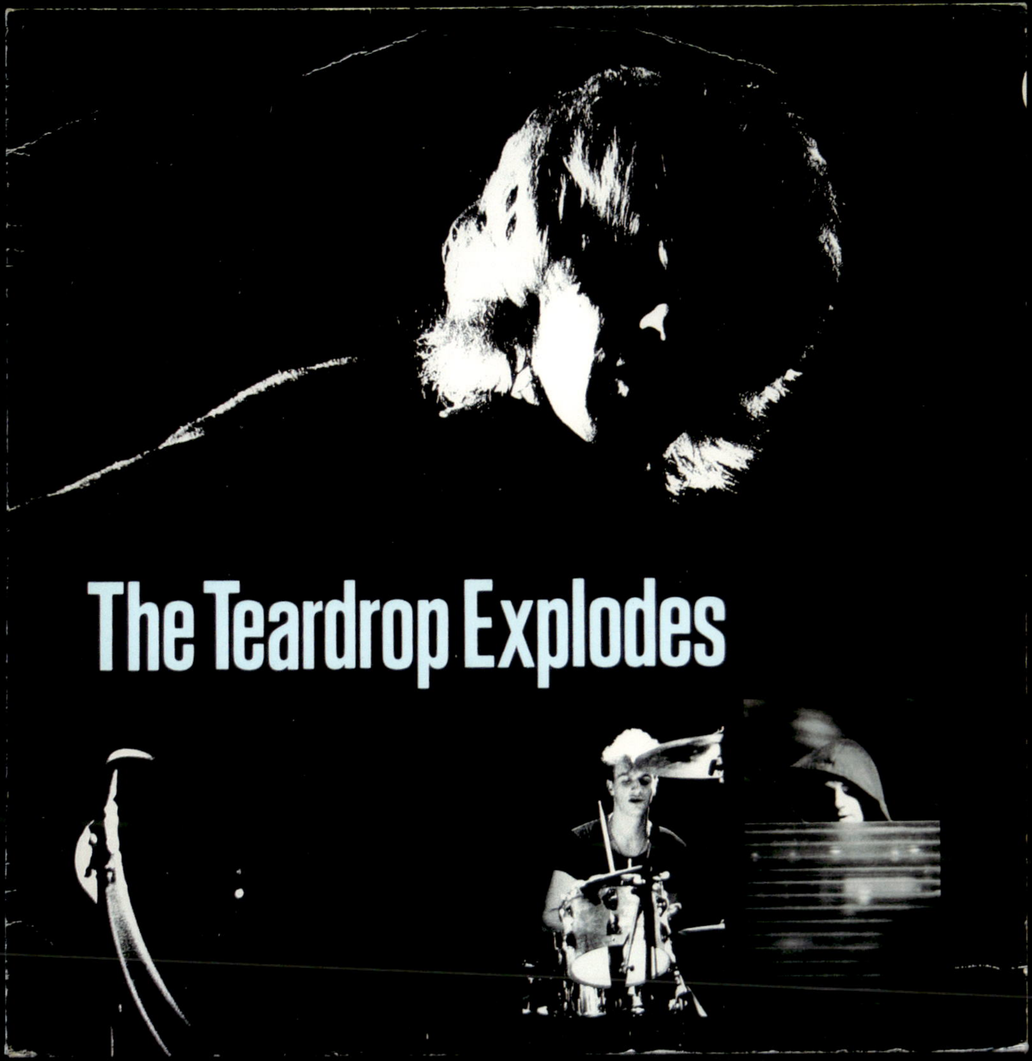

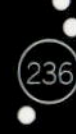

Artist The Teardrop Explodes Design Julian and Julian Photography Antoine Moonen and Bryn Jones
Record Label Phonogram

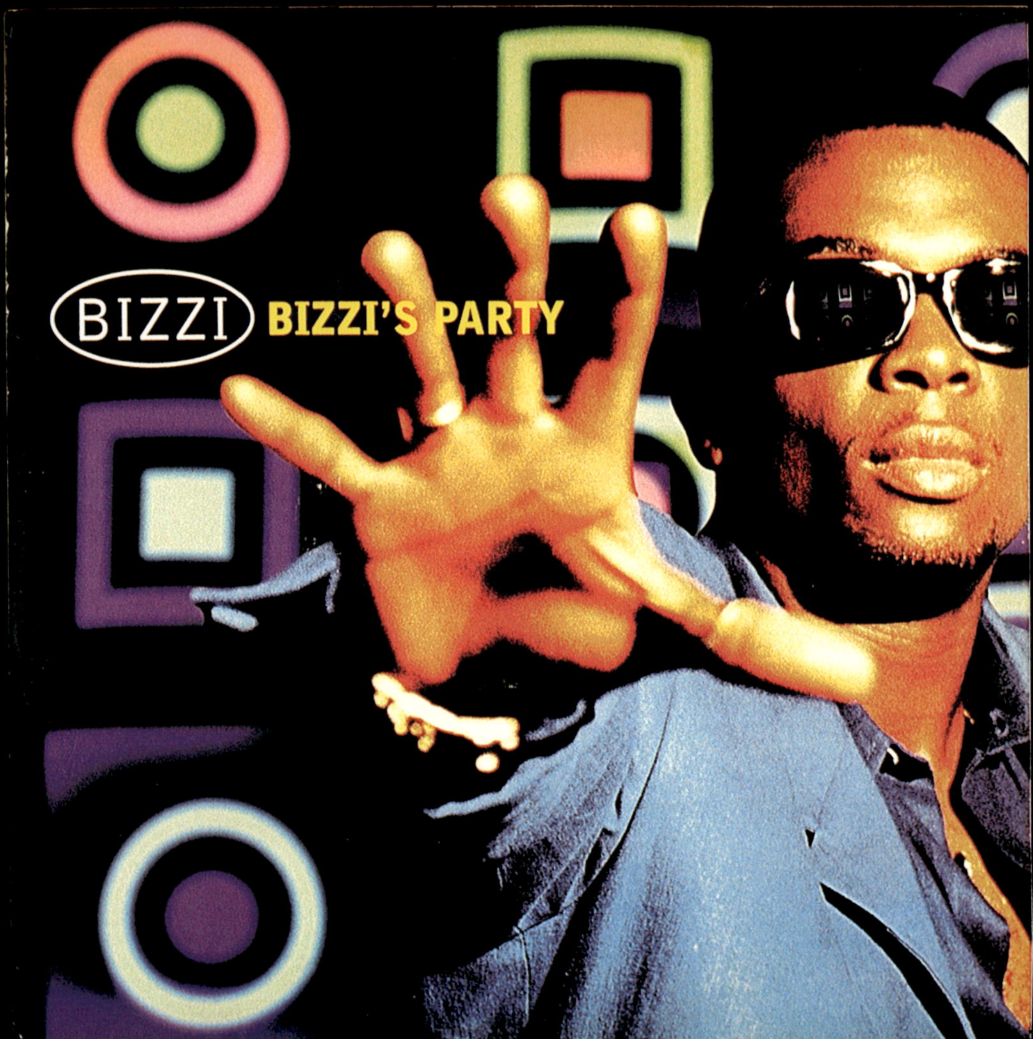
BIZZI
BIZZI'S PARTY

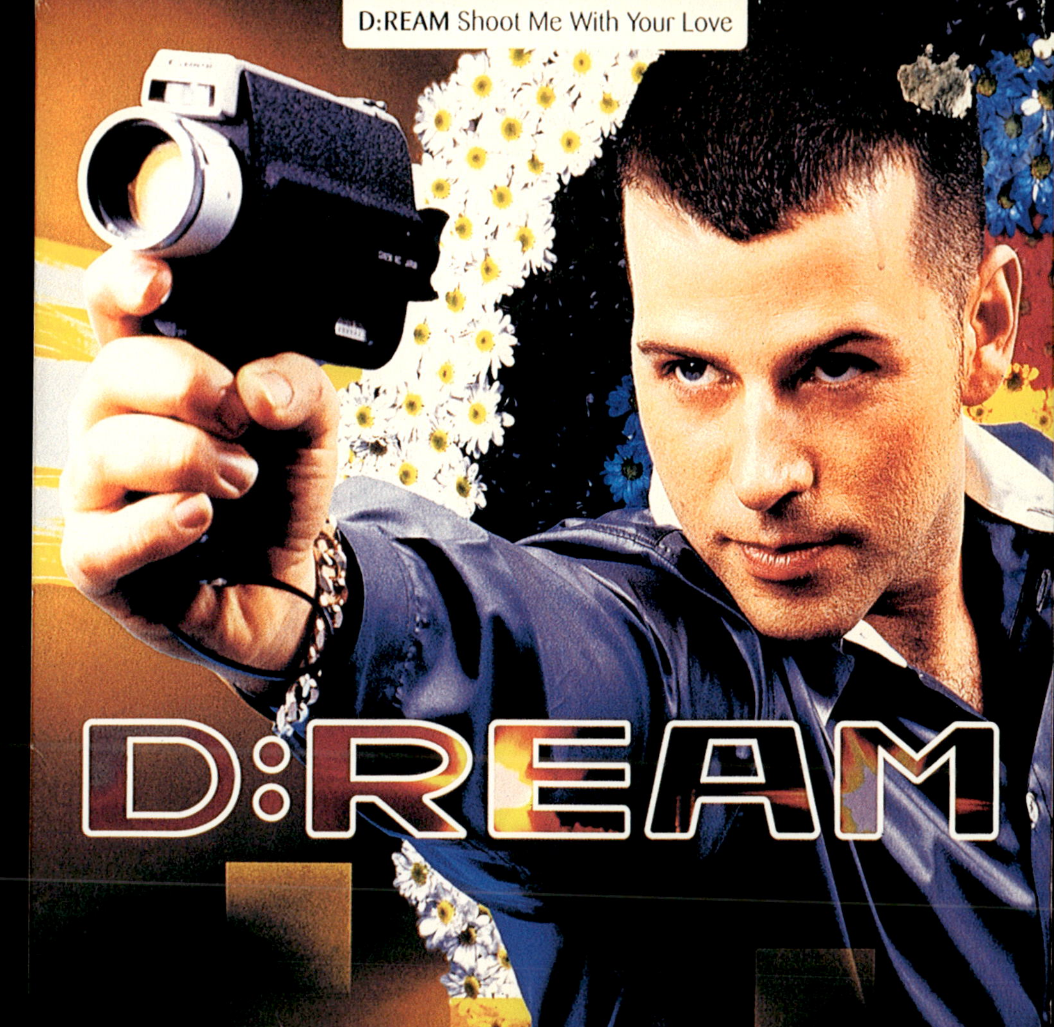

D:REAM Shoot Me With Your Love
D:REAM
Artist D: Ream Title Shoot Me With Your Love Photography Mike Diver Record Label Warner Music Date 1995
238

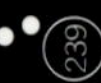

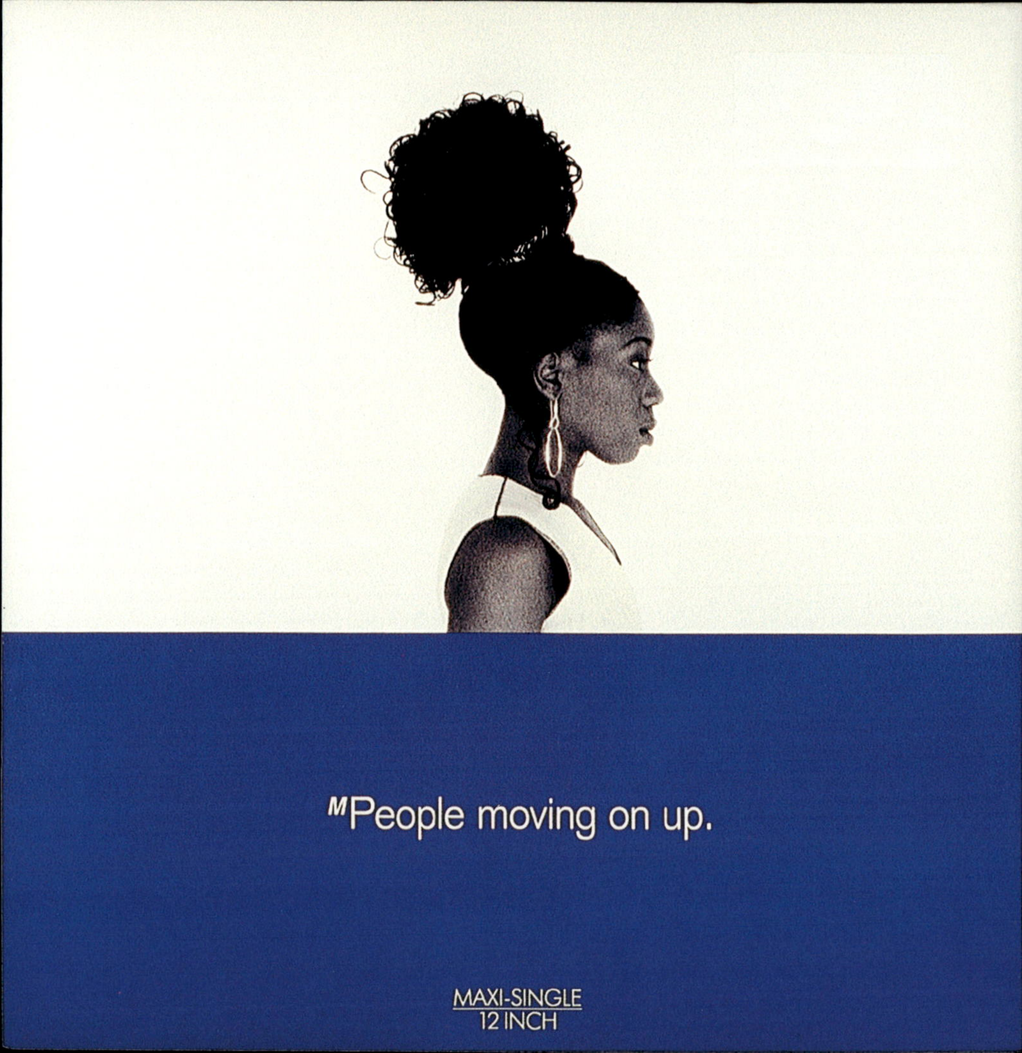

ᴹPeople moving on up.
MAXI-SINGLE
12 INCH

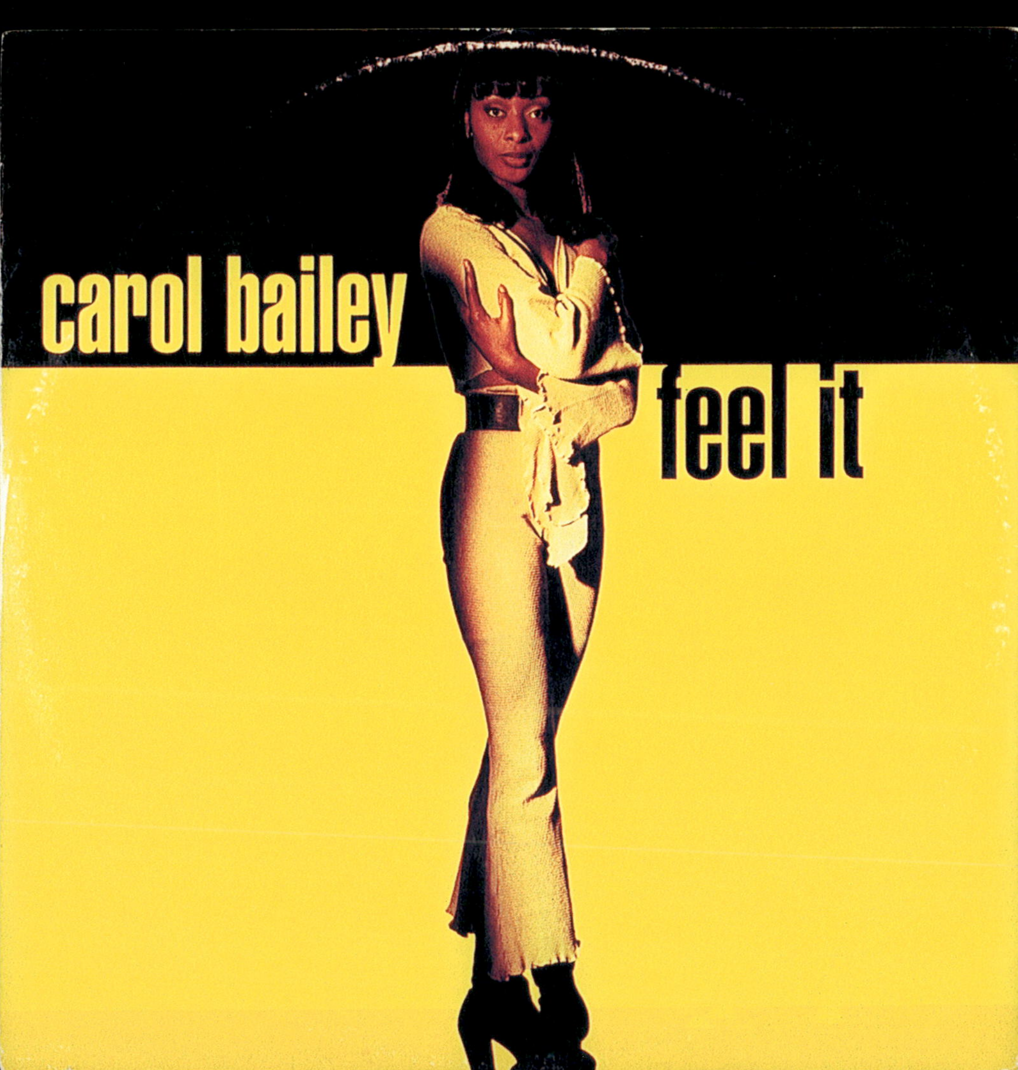
carol bailey
feel it

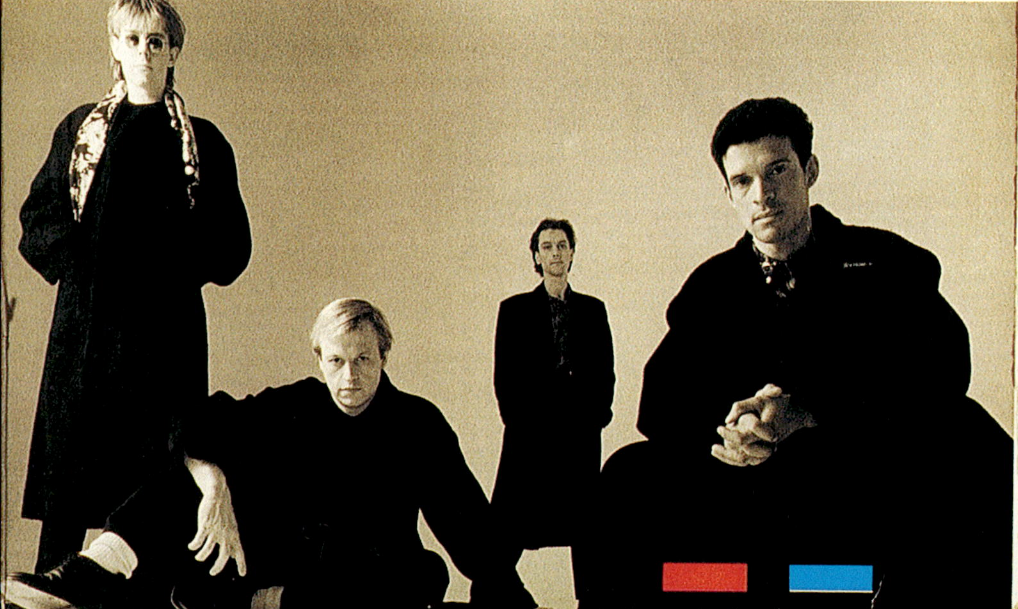
LEVEL
42
LESSONS
IN LOVE
(EXTENDED VERSION)

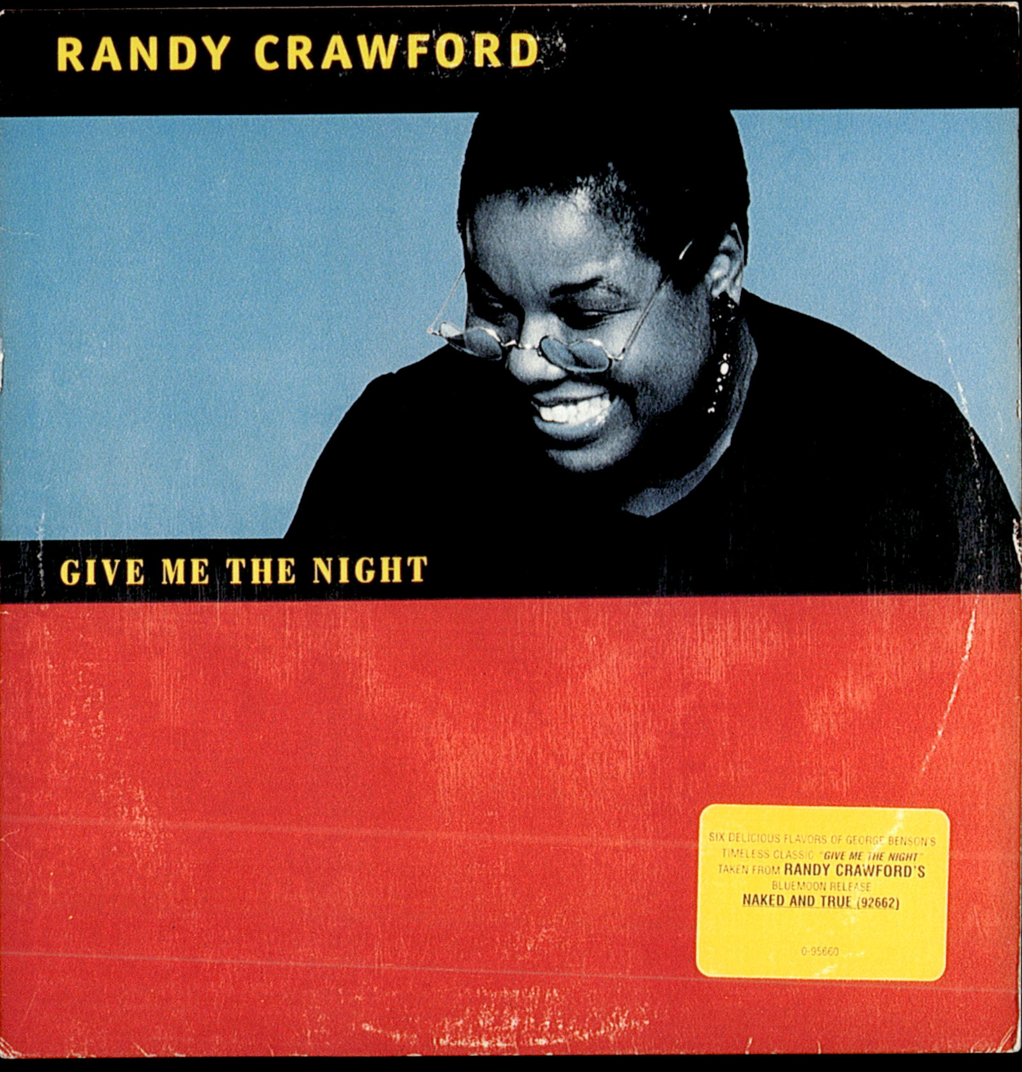

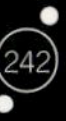

Artist Randy Crawford Title Give Me The Night Design Sheila Michel Molnar / Hair & Make Up
Photography André Fichte Record Label Wea Date 1995

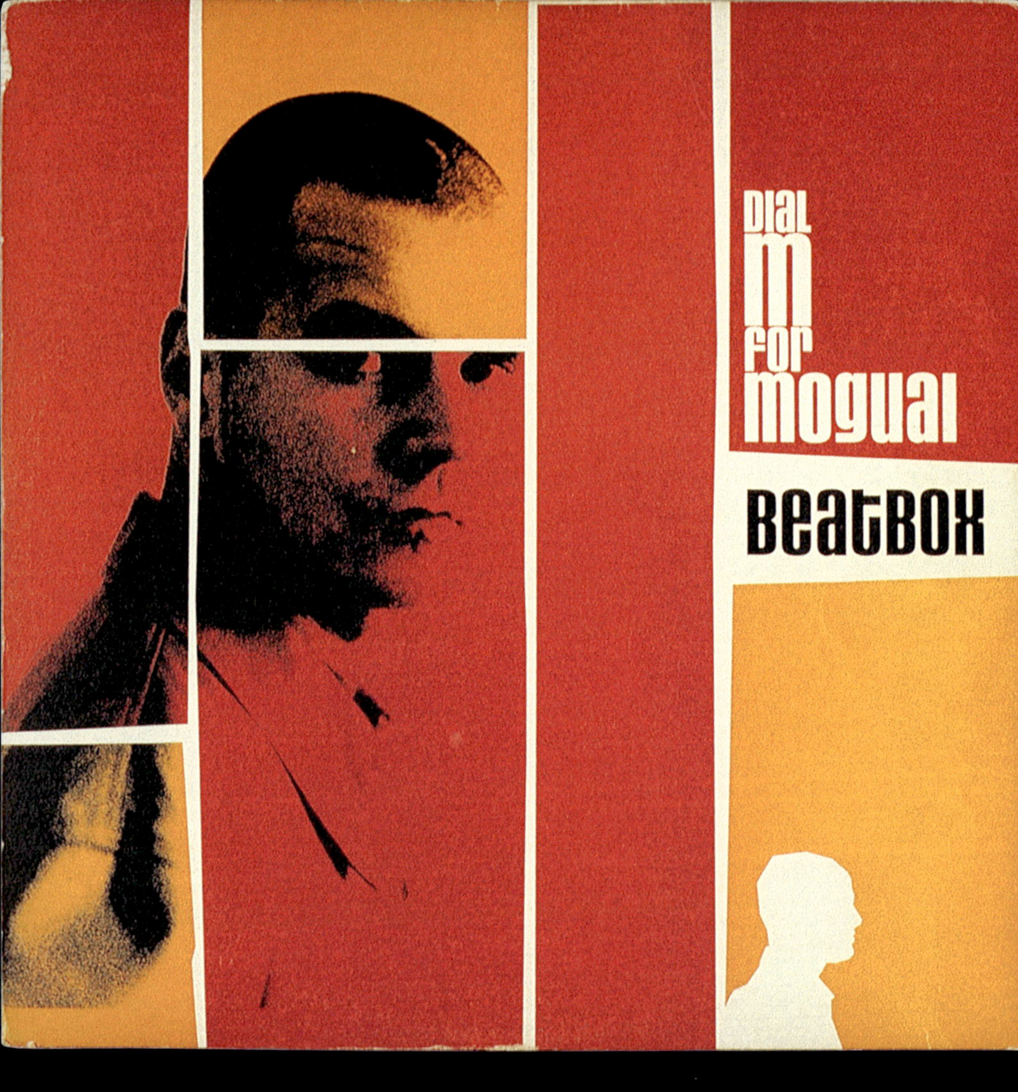

Artist Dial M for Moguai Title Beat Box Design Factor Produc, München Record Label Kosmos Records Date 1999

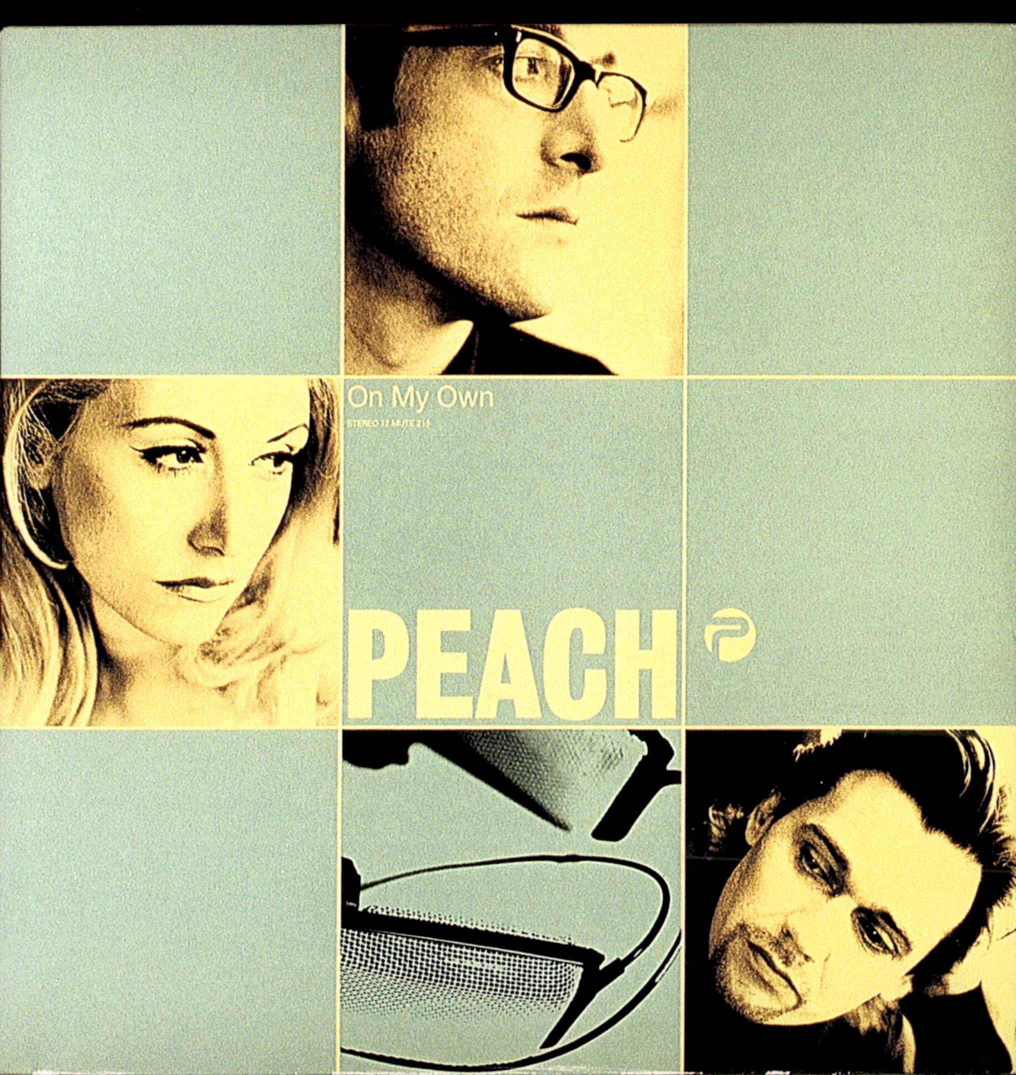
On My Own
STEREO 12 MUTE 216
PEACH

PETER
BROWN
THEY
ONLY
COME
OUT AT
NIGHT
B/W THEY ONLY COME OUT AT NIGHT
(INSTRUMENTAL)
12" SINGLE
DANCE MIX

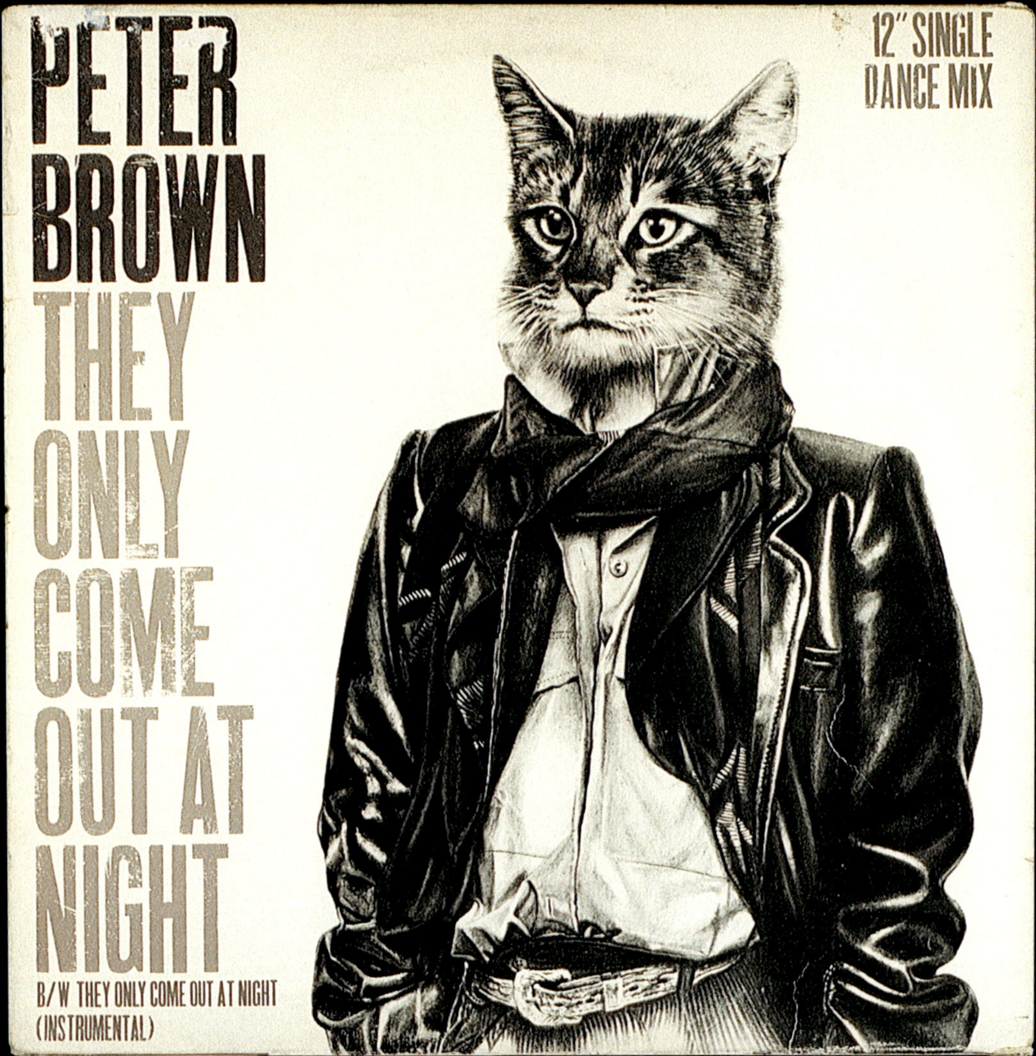

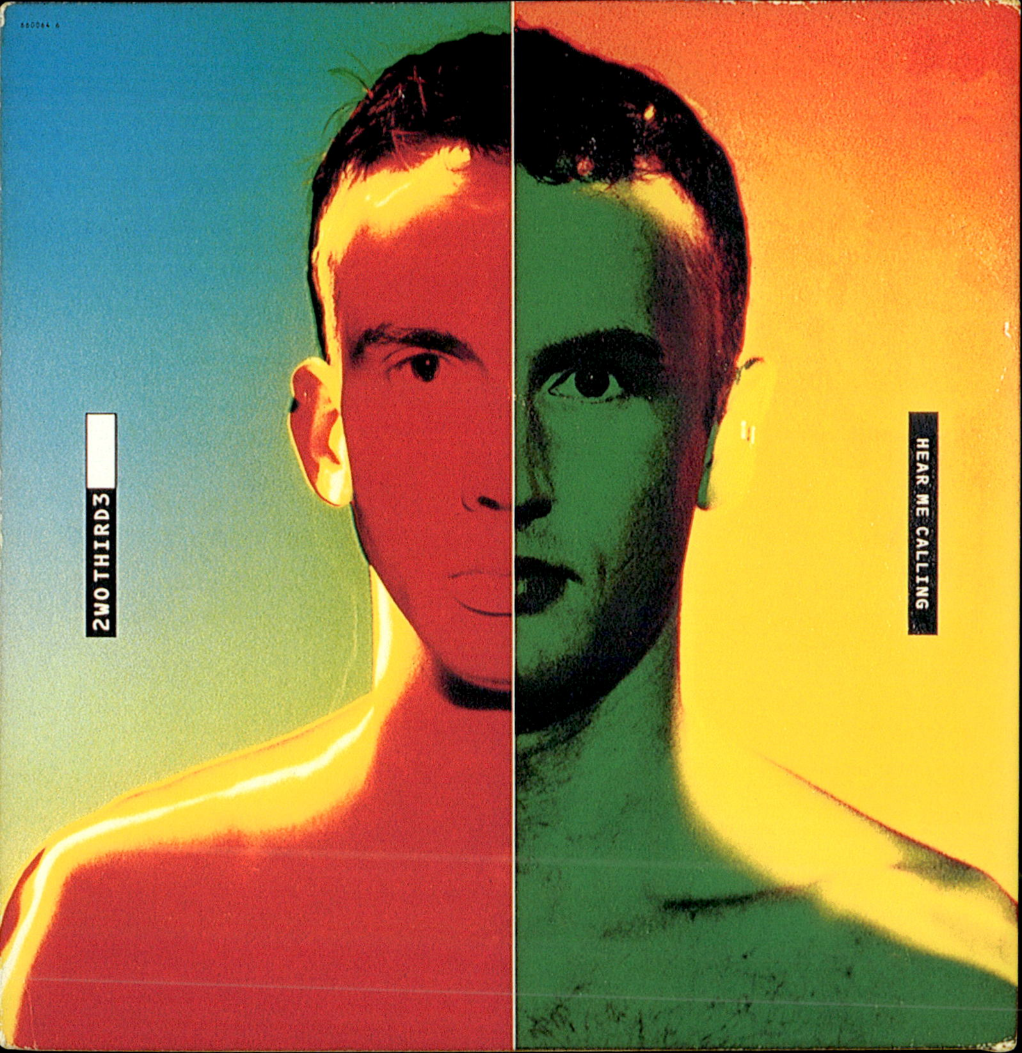

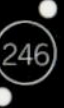

 Artist 2Wo Third3 Title Hear Me Calling Design Form Photography Spiros Record Label Sony Music Date 1994

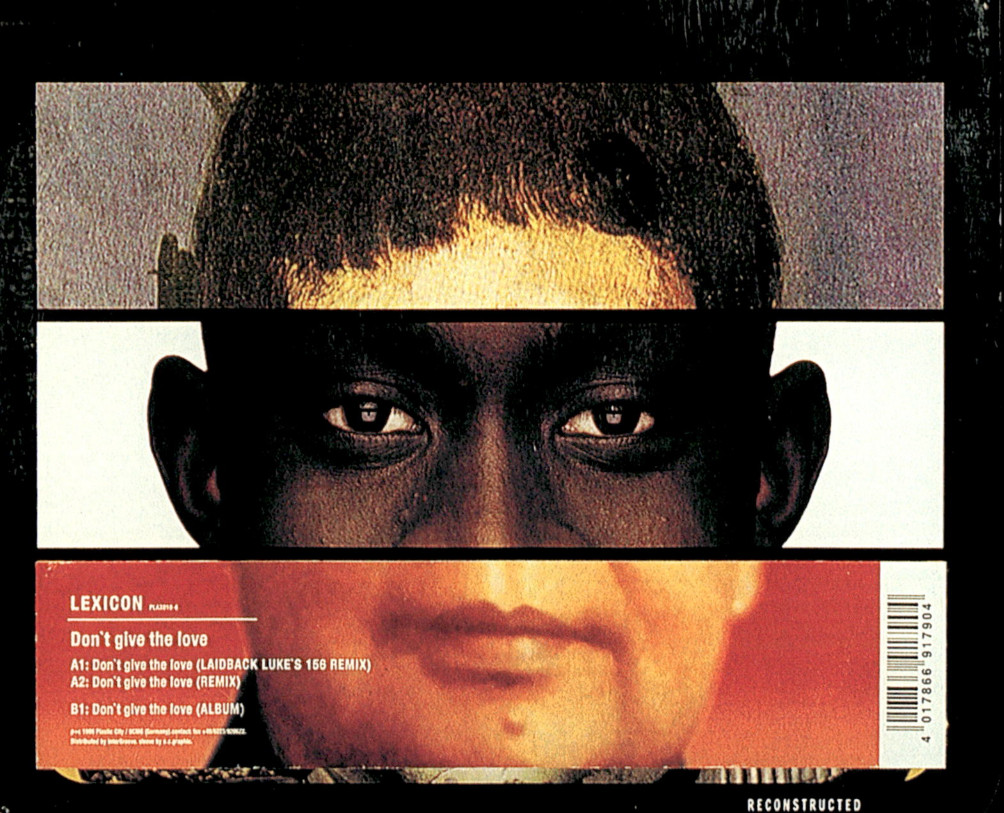

LEXICON PLA3919-4
Don't give the love
A1: Don't give the love (LAIDBACK LUKE'S 156 REMIX)
A2: Don't give the love (REMIX)
B1: Don't give the love (ALBUM)
p+c 1999 Plastic City / SCNS (Germany). contact. fax +49/6223/920622.
Distributed by InterGroove. sleeve by s.c.graphic.
RECONSTRUCTED
Don't Give The Love Design U.C. Graphic Record Label Plastic City Date 1999

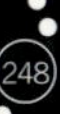

Lexicon
Why Don't You?

Written and produced by Joel Gelsacher
and DJ La Monde. Published by UCM Music
Publishing / EMI Songs. P+C Plastic City
America 1999. sleeve by a.i.graphic.

b1: Why Don't You?
(Jadenty's Pad Edit)

b2: Why Don't You?
(Tech house Arcade Mix)

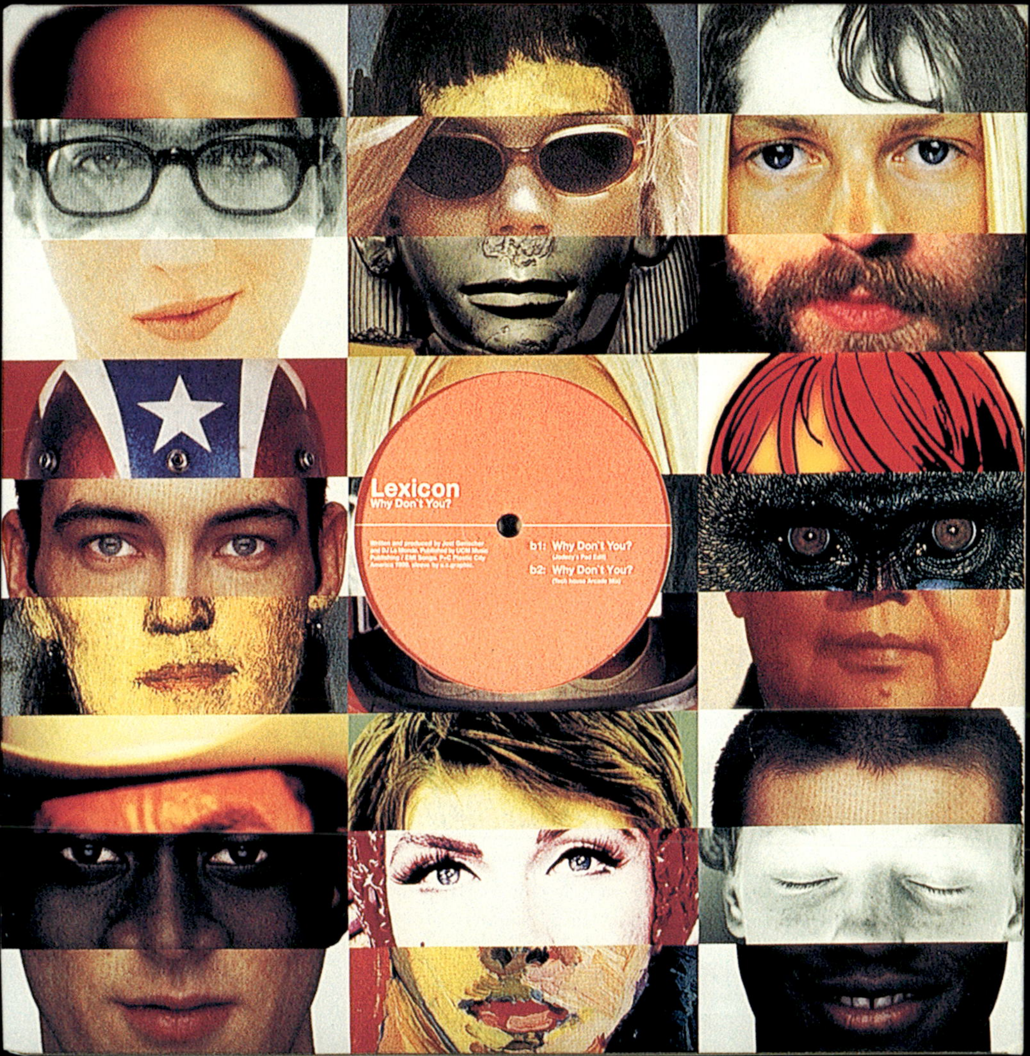

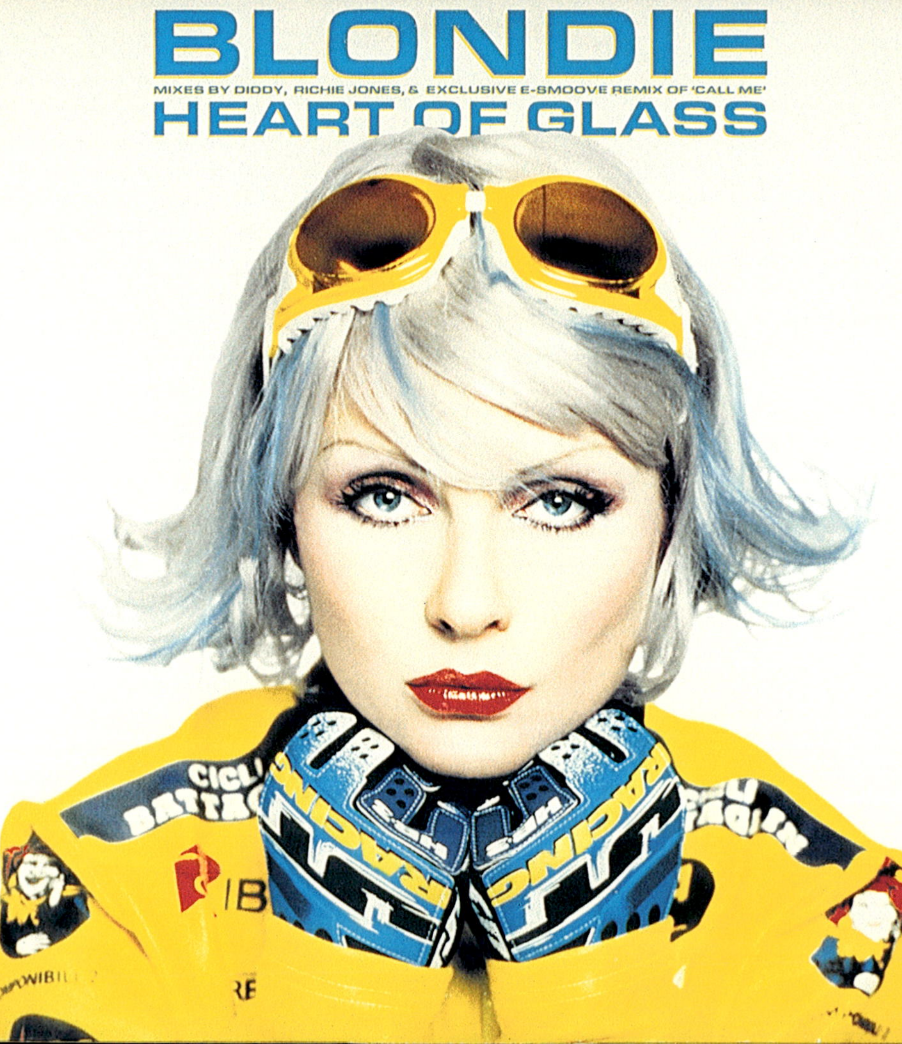

BLONDIE
MIXES BY DIDDY, RICHIE JONES, & EXCLUSIVE E-SMOOVE REMIX OF 'CALL ME'
HEART OF GLASS

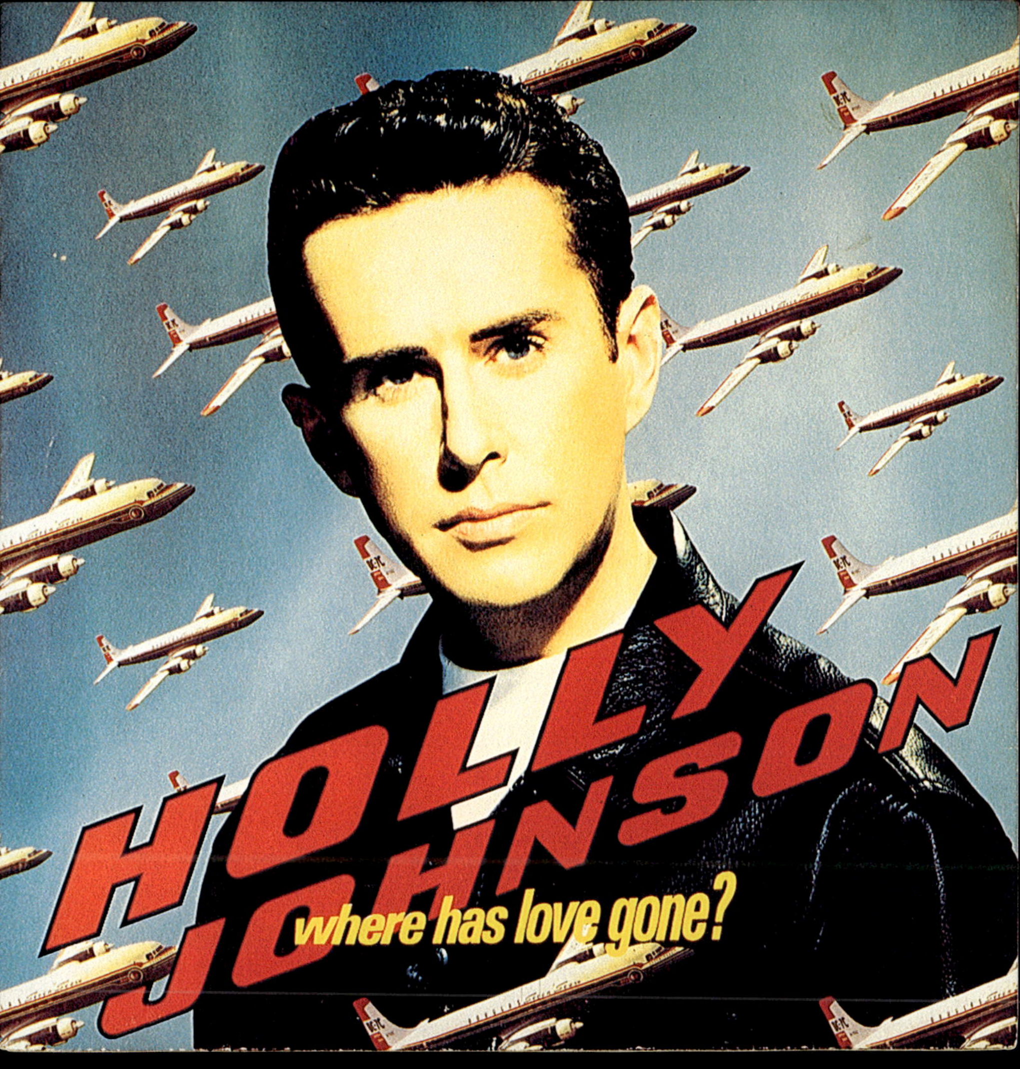

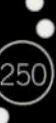

250 Artist Holly Johnson Title Where Has Love Gone? Design Me Company Photography Richard Houghton
Record Label Funky Date 1990

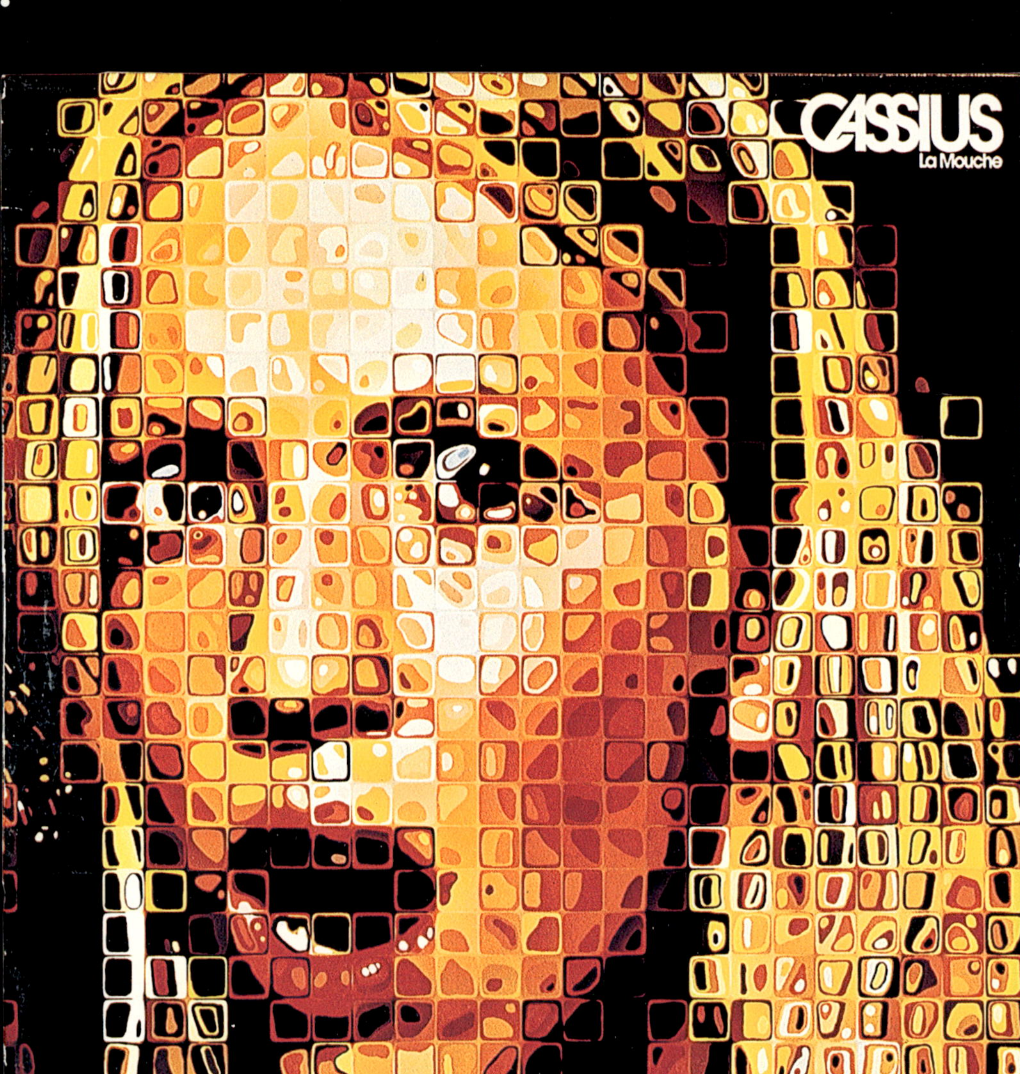
CASSIUS
La Mouche

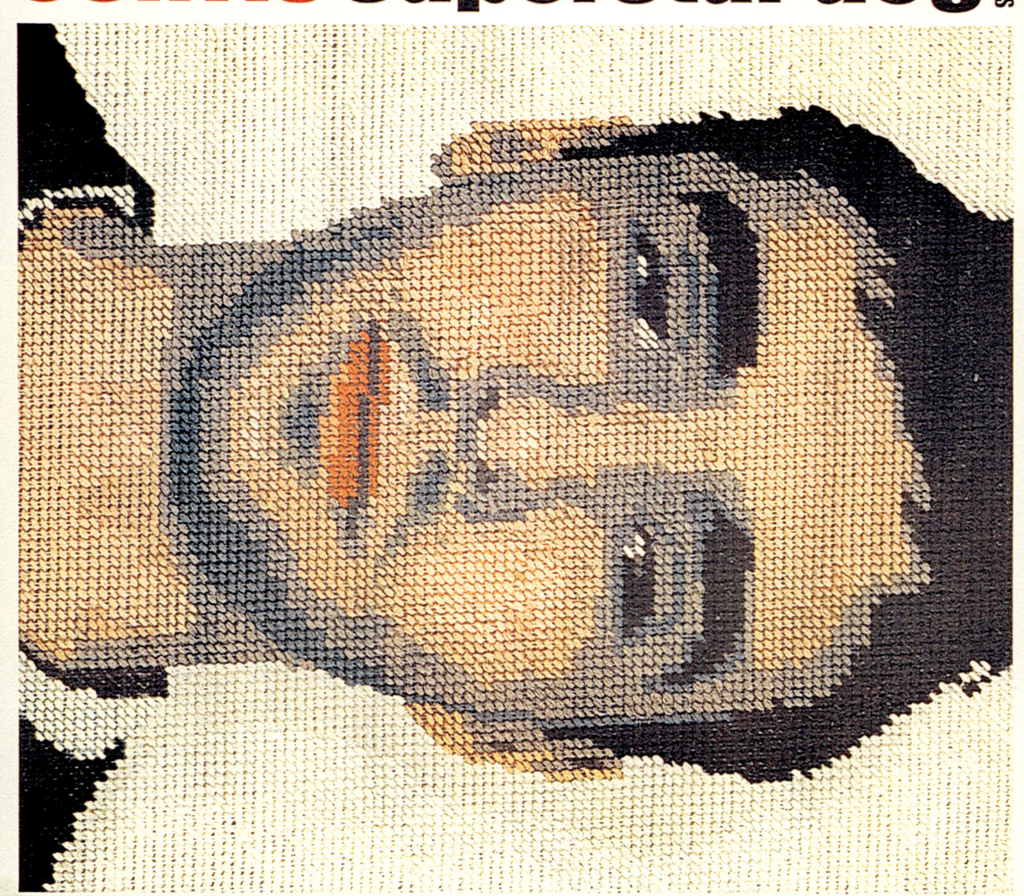

CURTIS superstar dog REMIXES

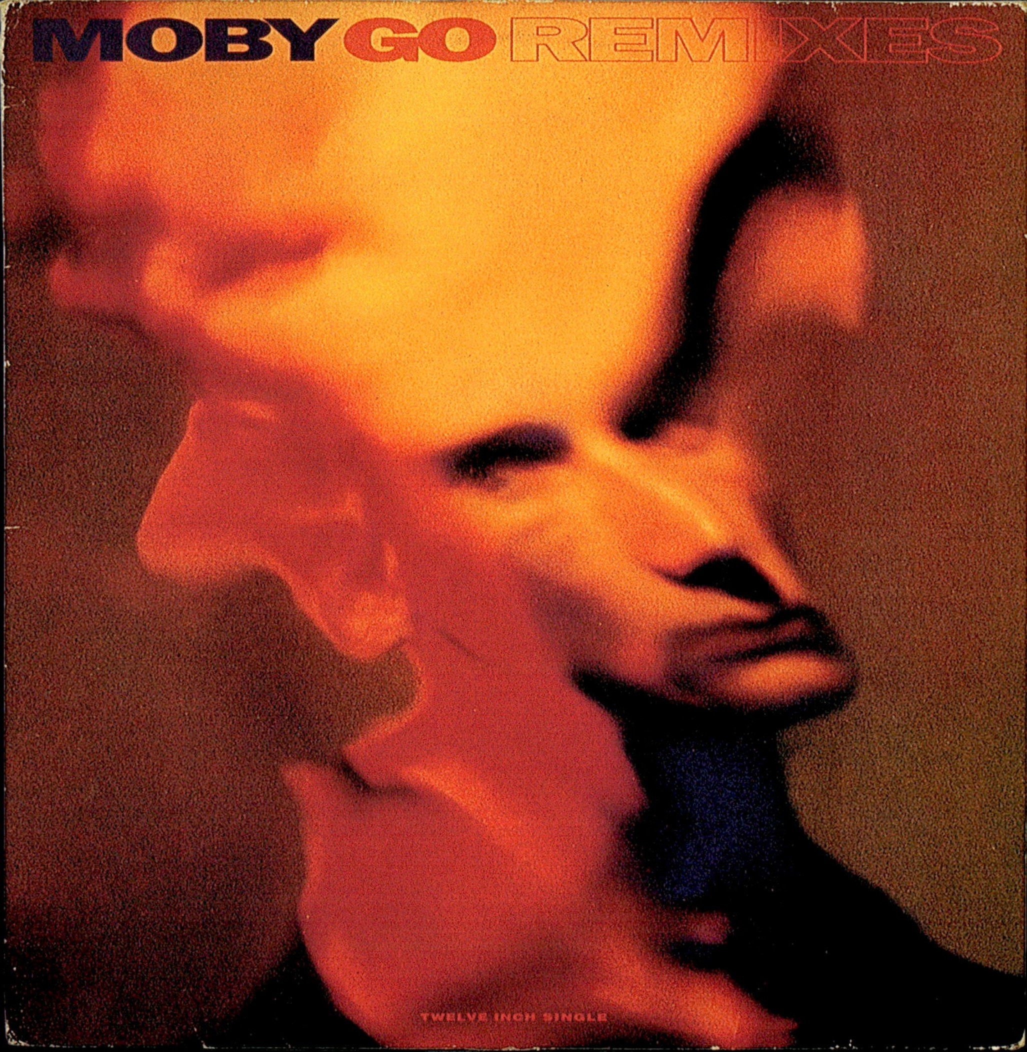

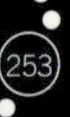

Artist Moby Title Go. Remixes Design Dave Brubaker Photography Jill Greenberg Record Label Instinct Date 1991

Pet Shop Boys DISCO

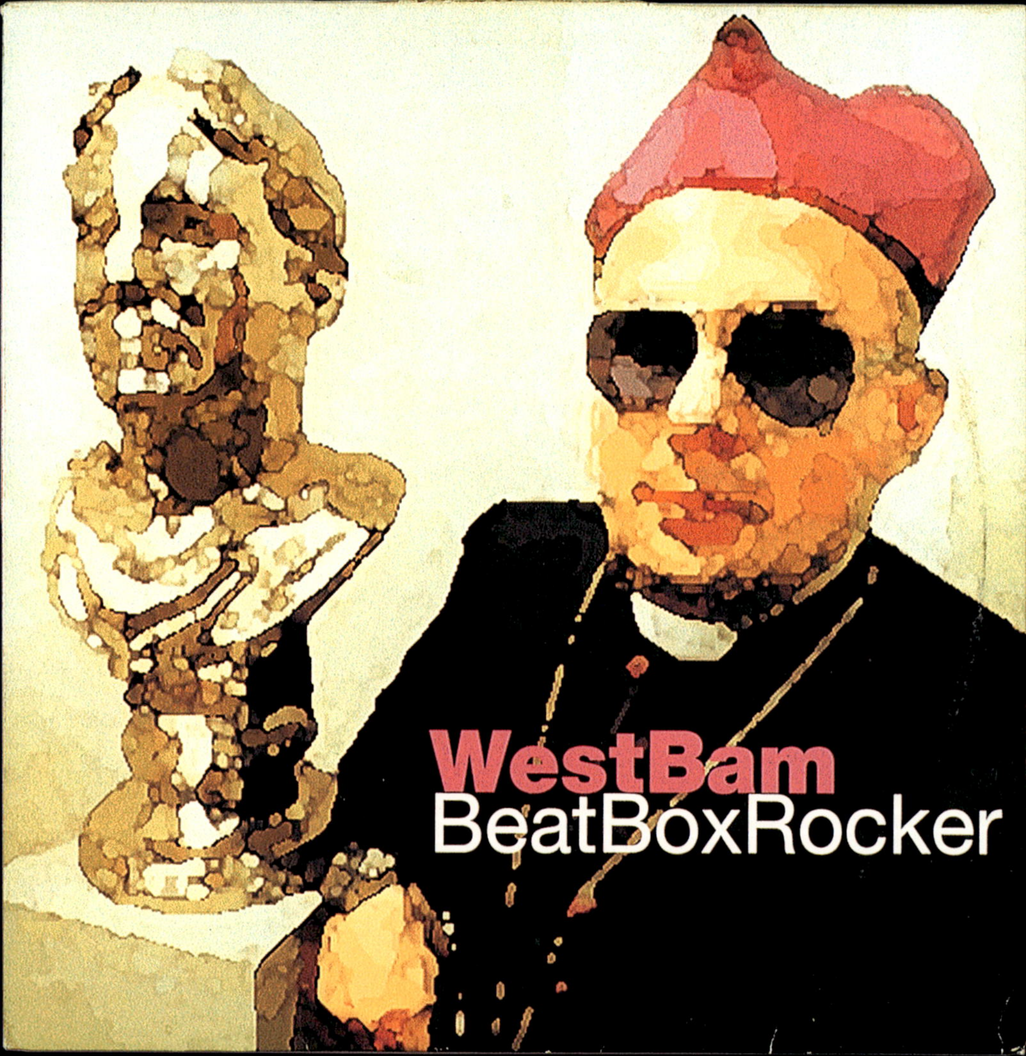

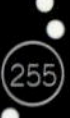

WestBam
BeatBoxRocker

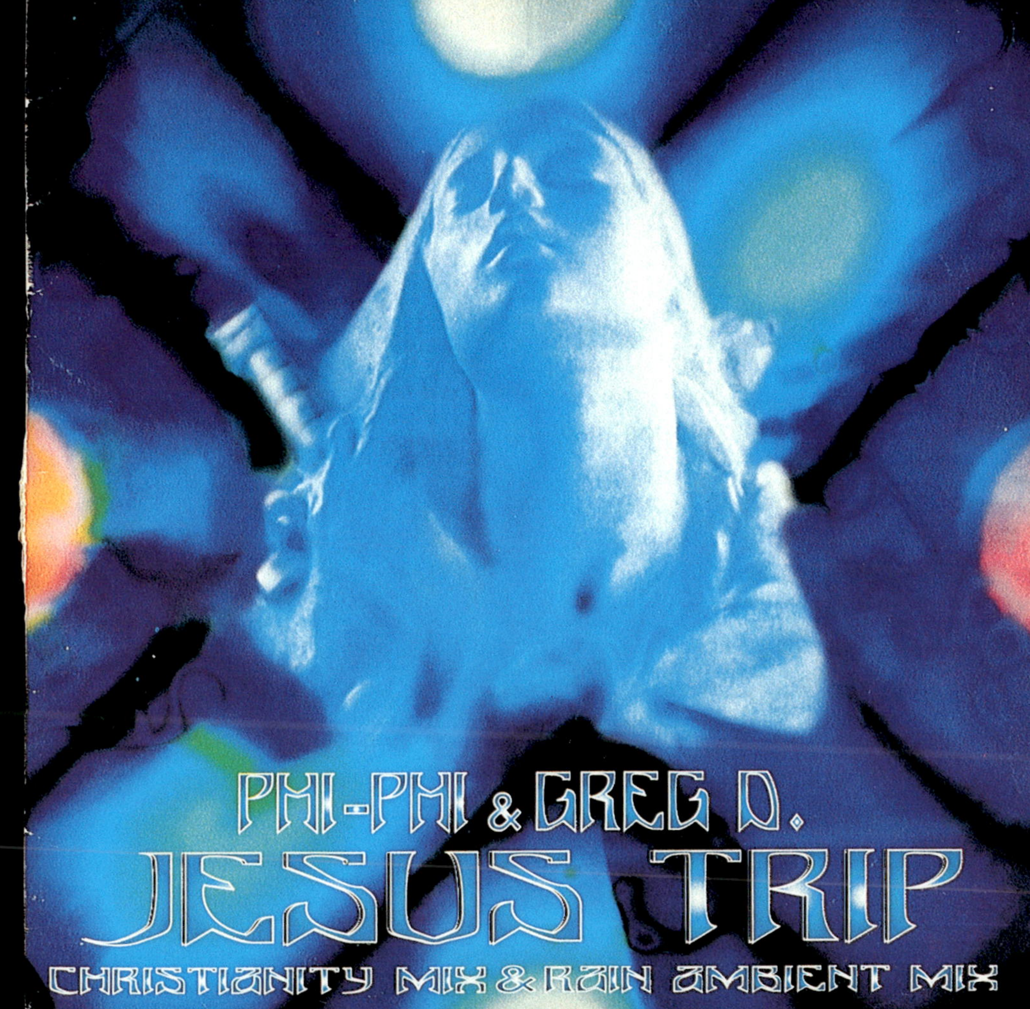
PHI-PHI & GREG D.
JESUS TRIP
CHRISTIANITY MIX & RAIN AMBIENT MIX

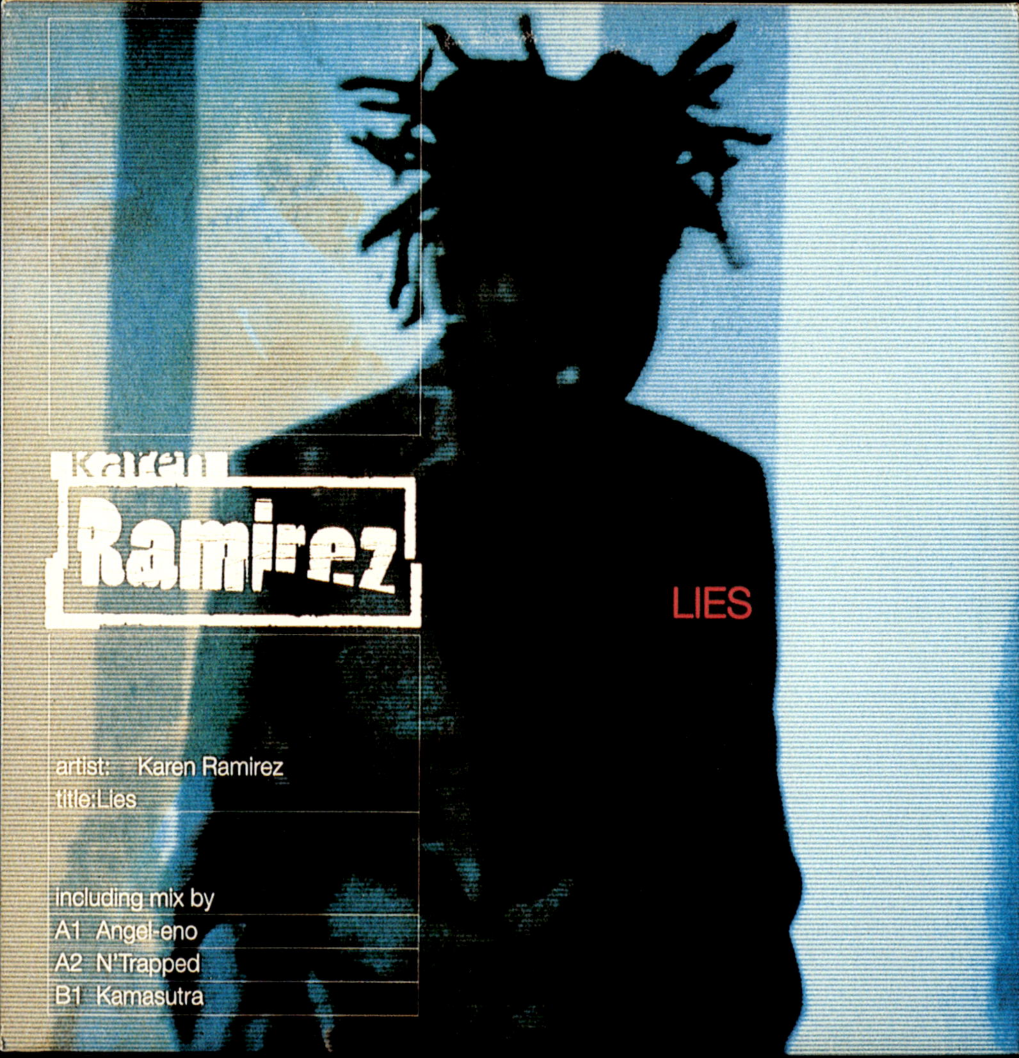

Karen

Ramirez

LIES

artist: Karen Ramirez
title:Lies

including mix by
A1 Angel-eno
A2 N'Trapped
B1 Kamasutra

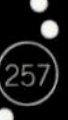

 Artist Karen Ramirez Title Lies Design Patrizio Squeglia Record Label Bustin Loose Date 1999

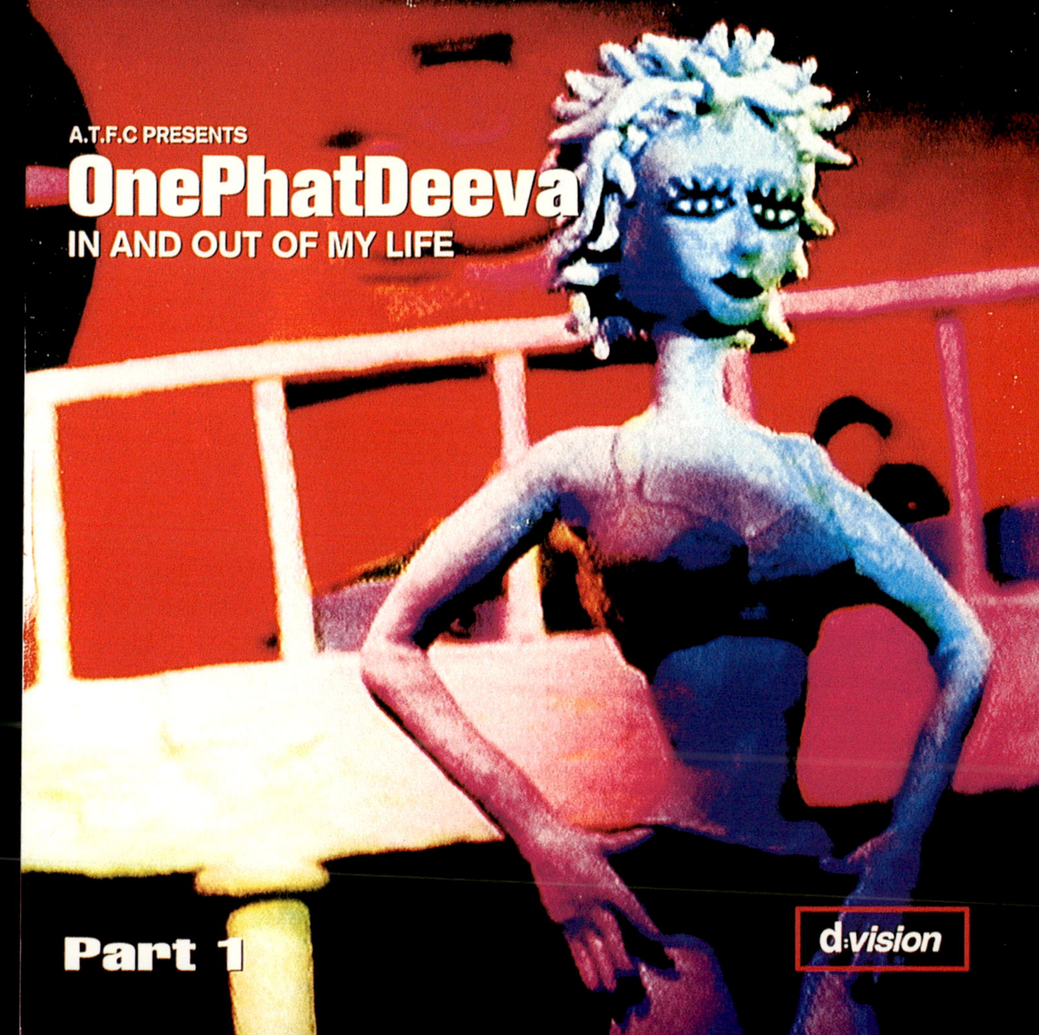
A.T.F.C PRESENTS
OnePhatDeeva
IN AND OUT OF MY LIFE
Part 1
d:vision

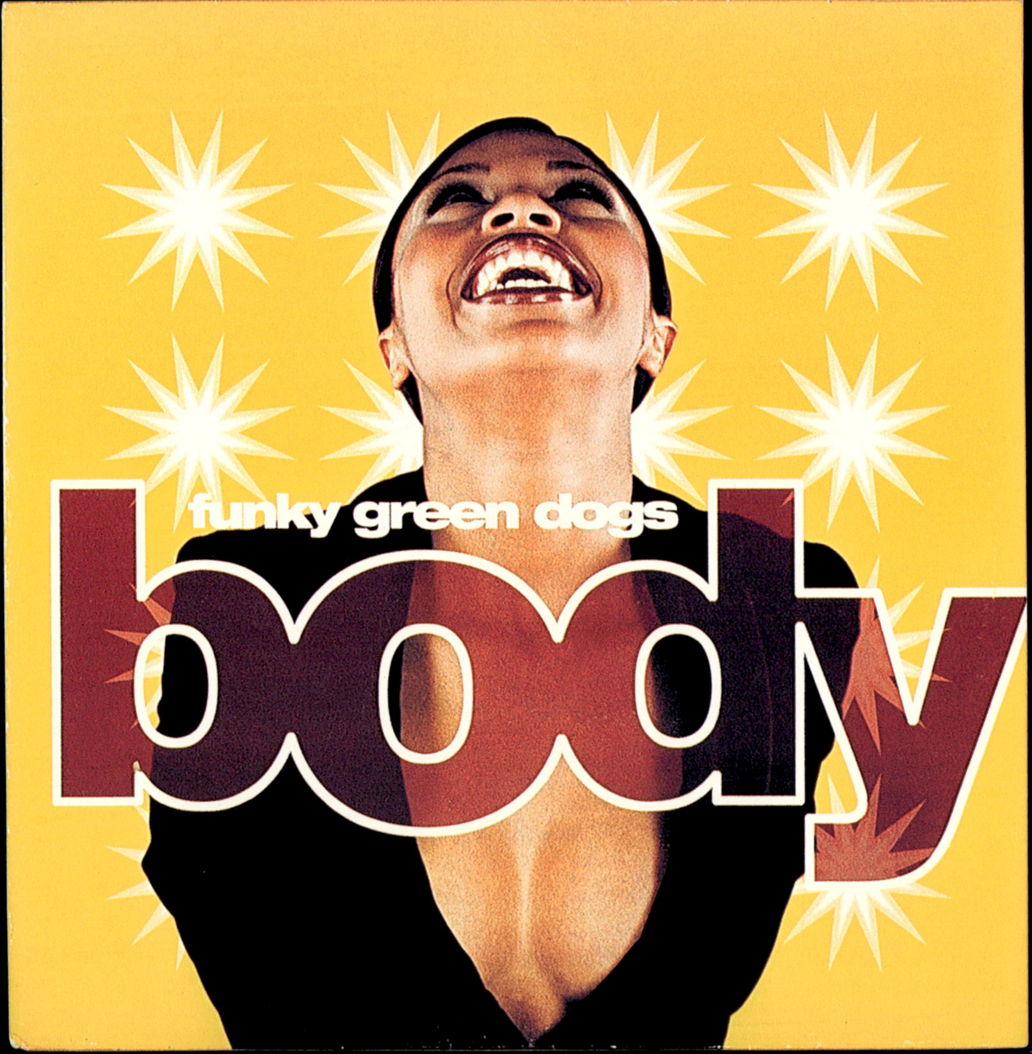

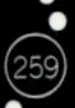

Artist Funky Green Dogs Title Body Design Steve Newman Photography Benoit Peverelli Record Label Twisted Date 1999

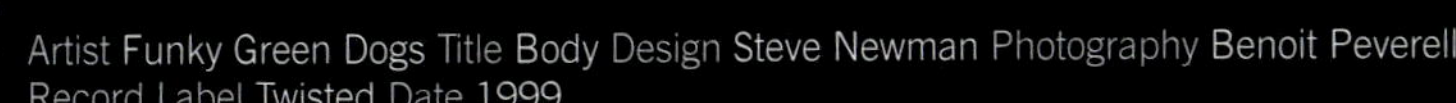

funky green dogs
body

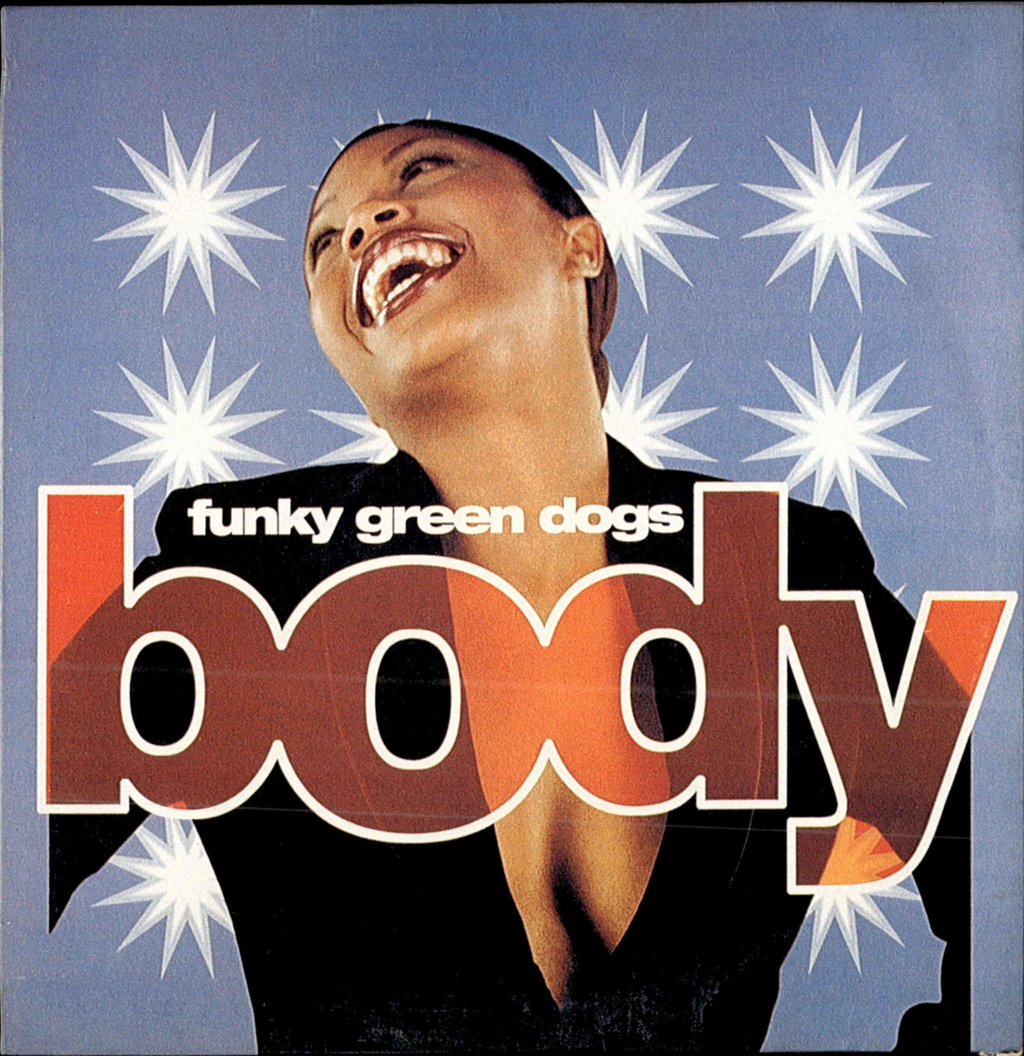

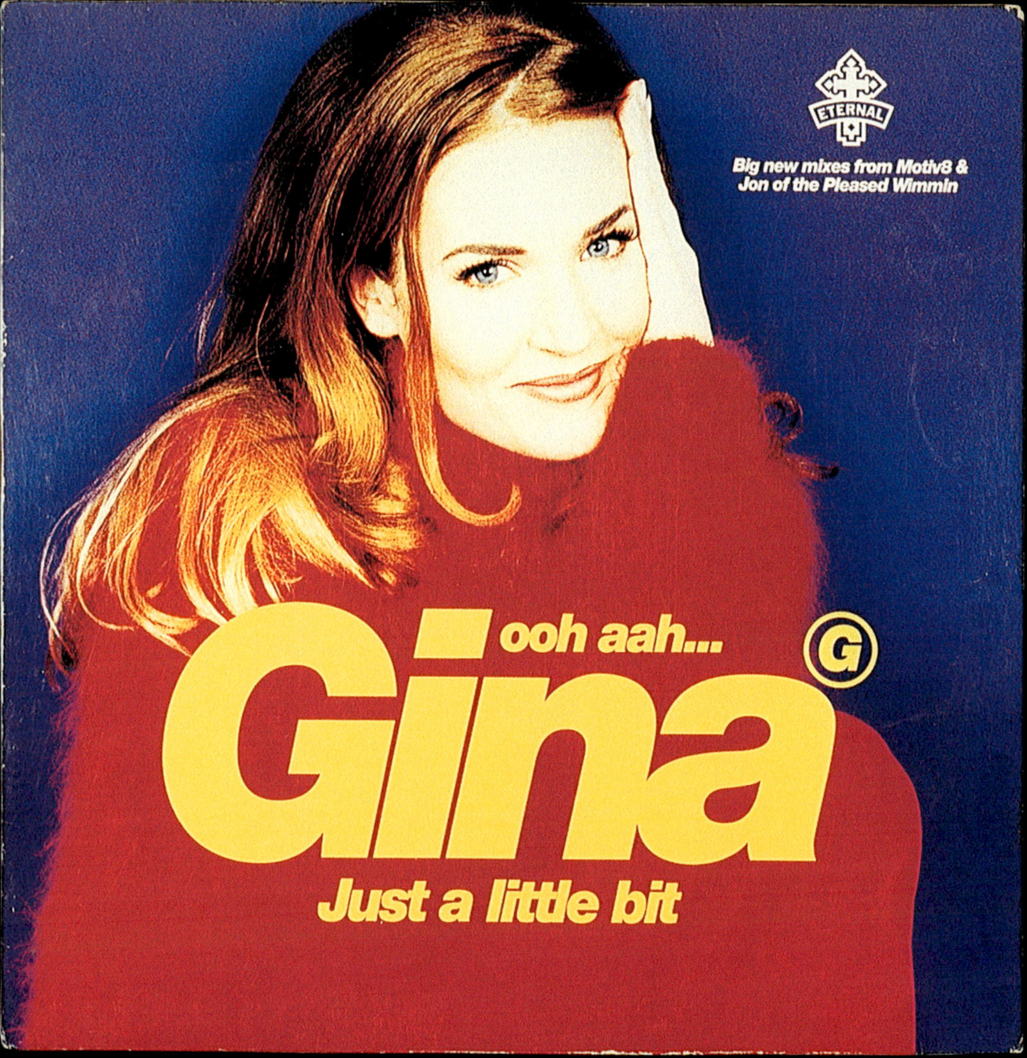

Artist Gina Title Just a Little Bit Design M@ Maitland for the Church Photography Lorenzo Agius Record Label Eternal Date

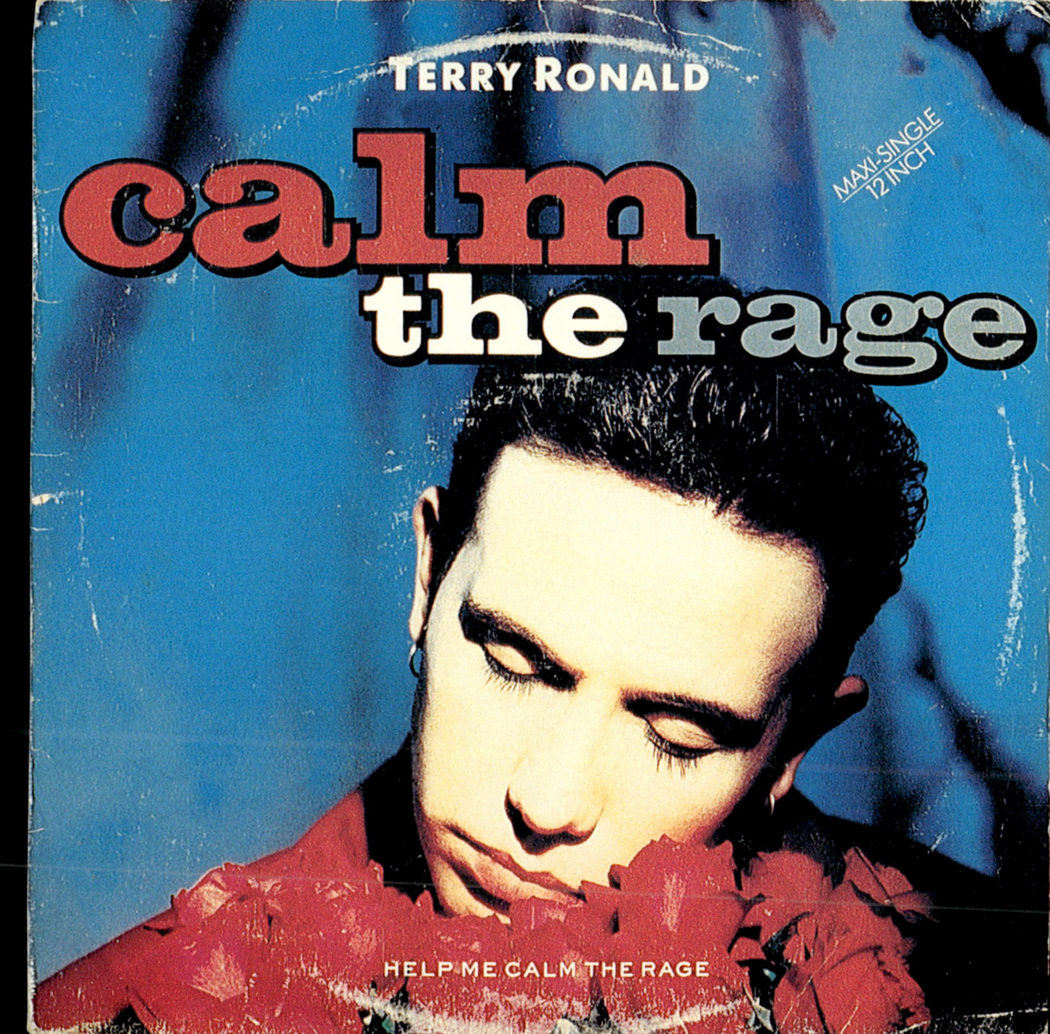

TERRY RONALD
calm
the rage
MAXI-SINGLE
12 INCH
HELP ME CALM THE RAGE

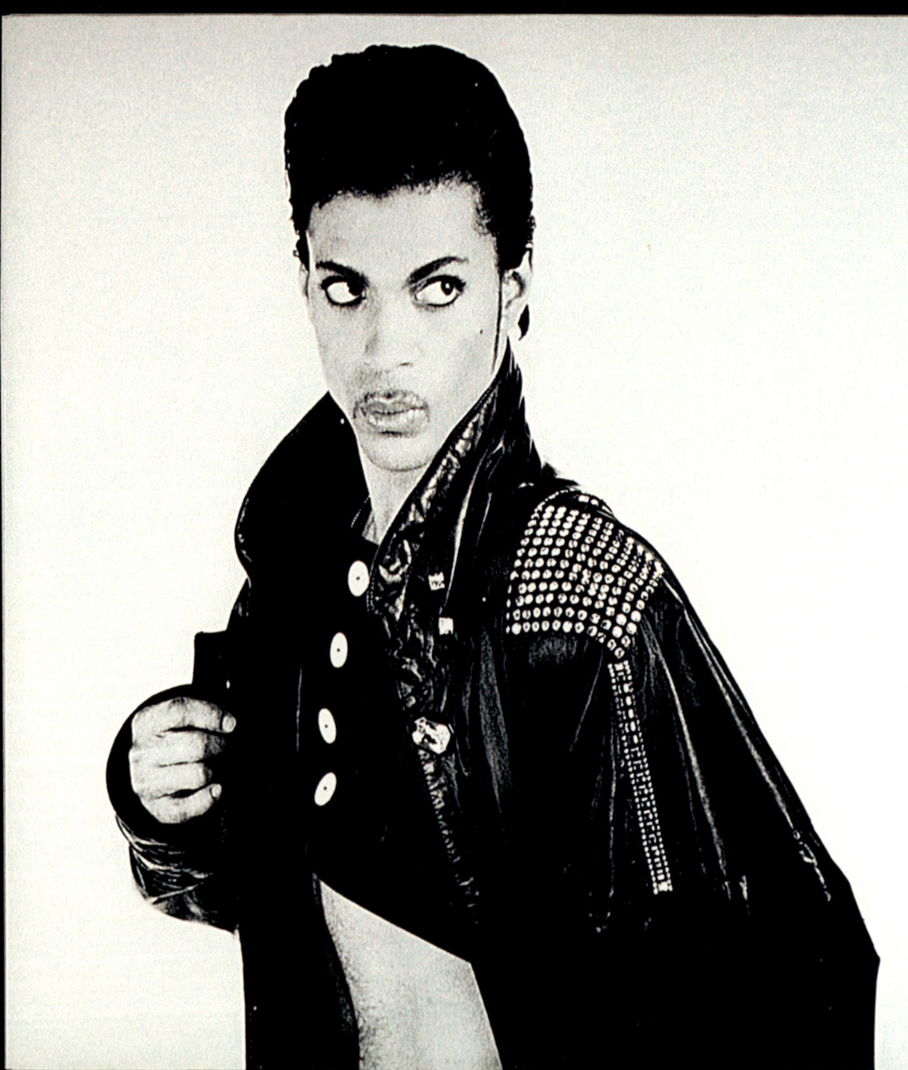
PRINCE AND THE REVOLUTION/KISS

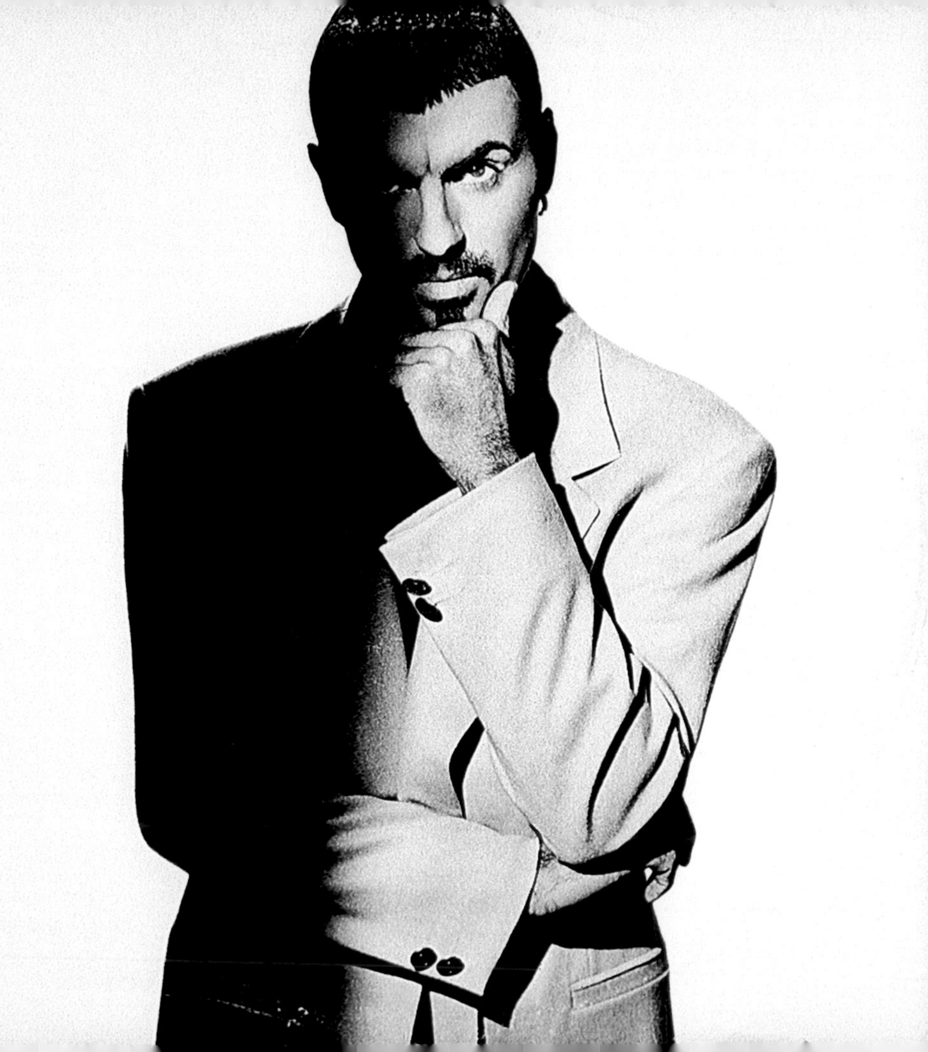

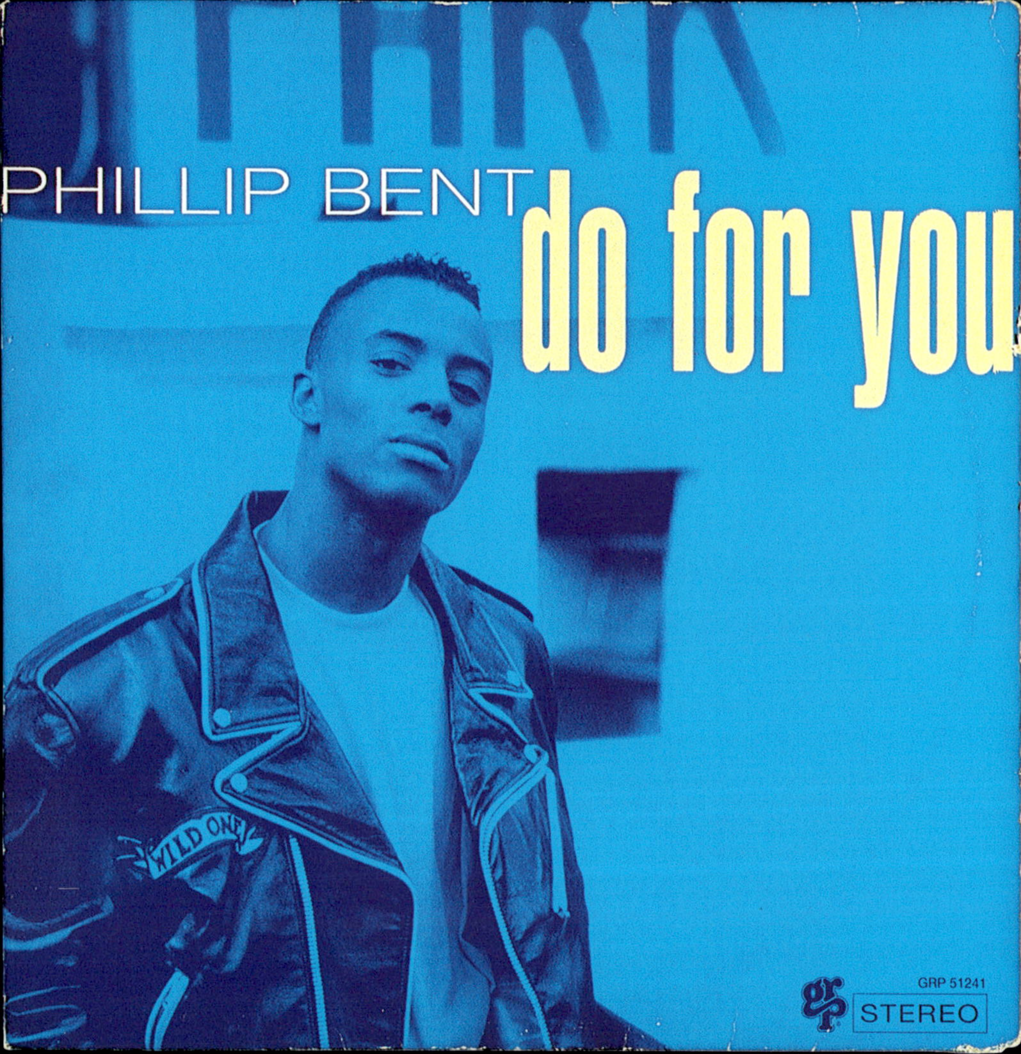

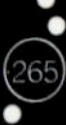

Artist Phillip Bent Title Do For You Design David Palmer & Peter Kelsey Photography Carol Weinberg
Record Label GRP Date 1993

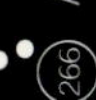

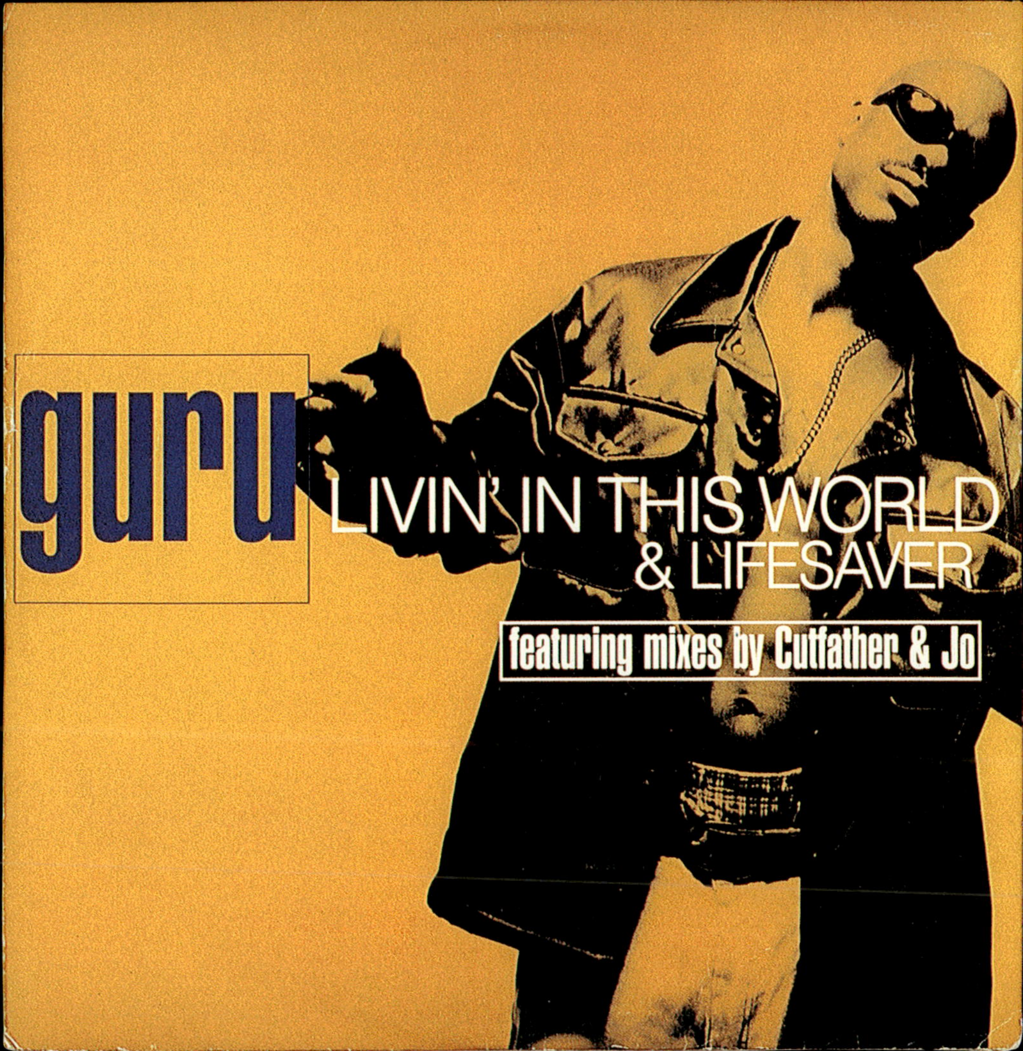

guru
LIVIN' IN THIS WORLD
& LIFESAVER
featuring mixes by Cutfather & Jo

267 Artist Soul II Soul Title I Care Photography Philknott Record Label Virgin Date 1995

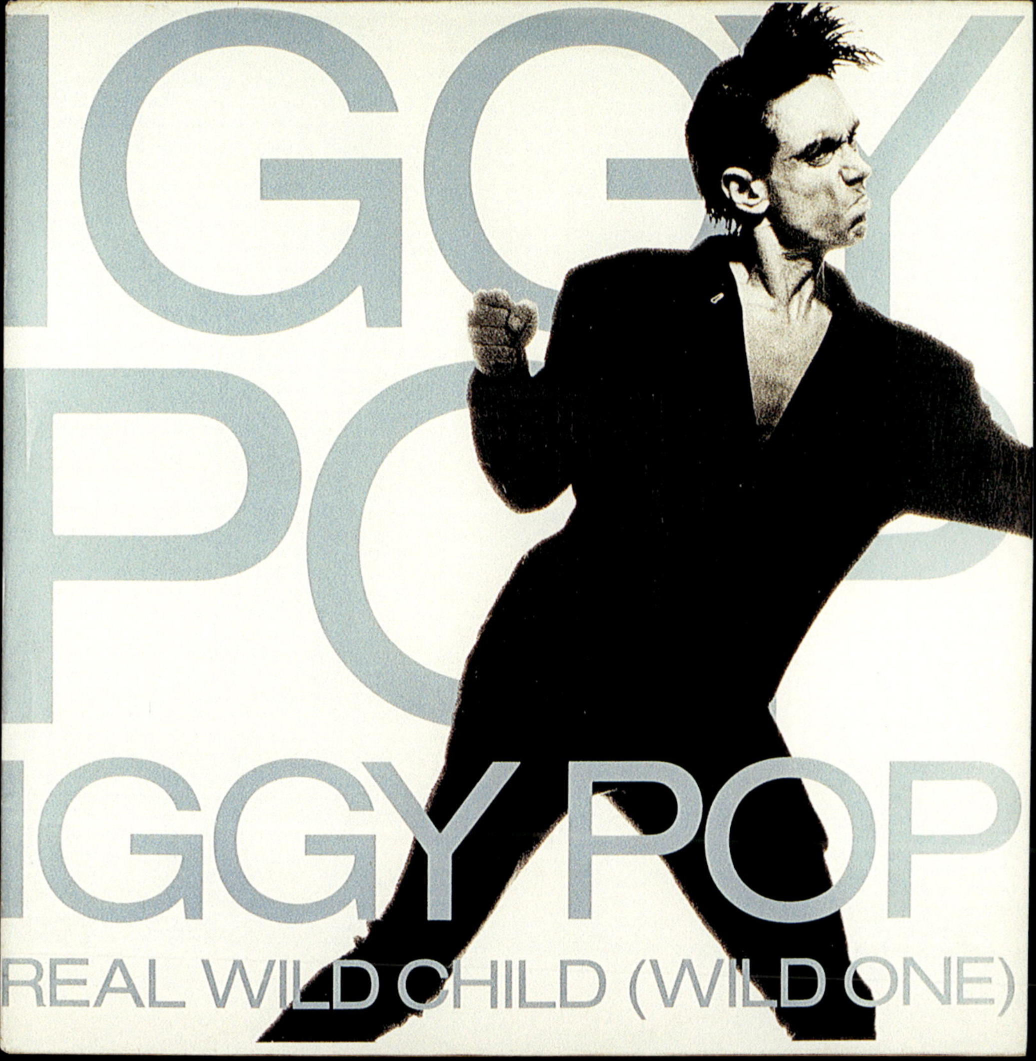

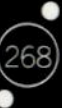

IGGY
POP
IGGY POP
REAL WILD CHILD (WILD ONE)

Artist **Jermaine Stewart** Title **Don't Talk Dirty to Me** Design **Bill Smith Studio** Photography **Christof G. Stalder**
Record Label **Siren** Date **1988**

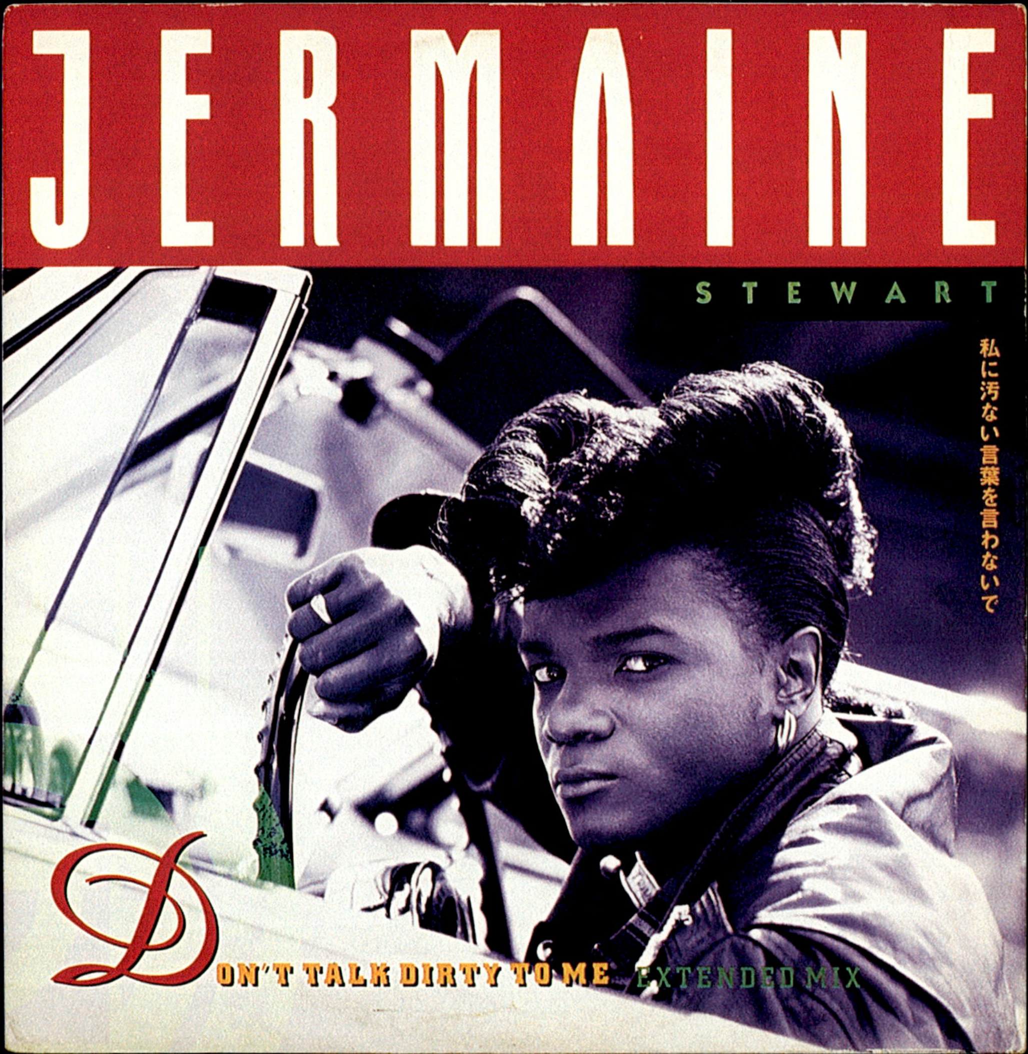

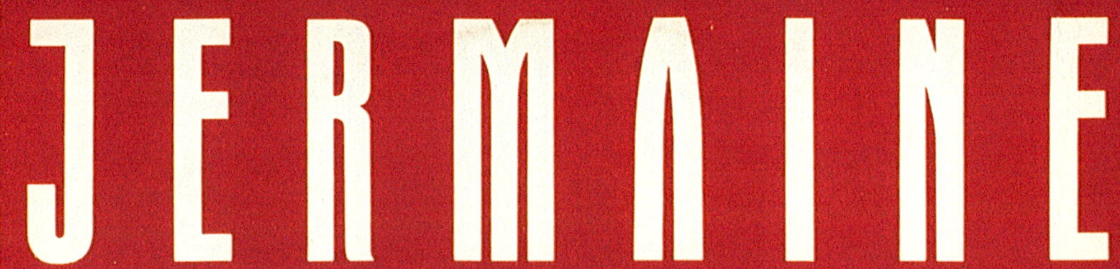

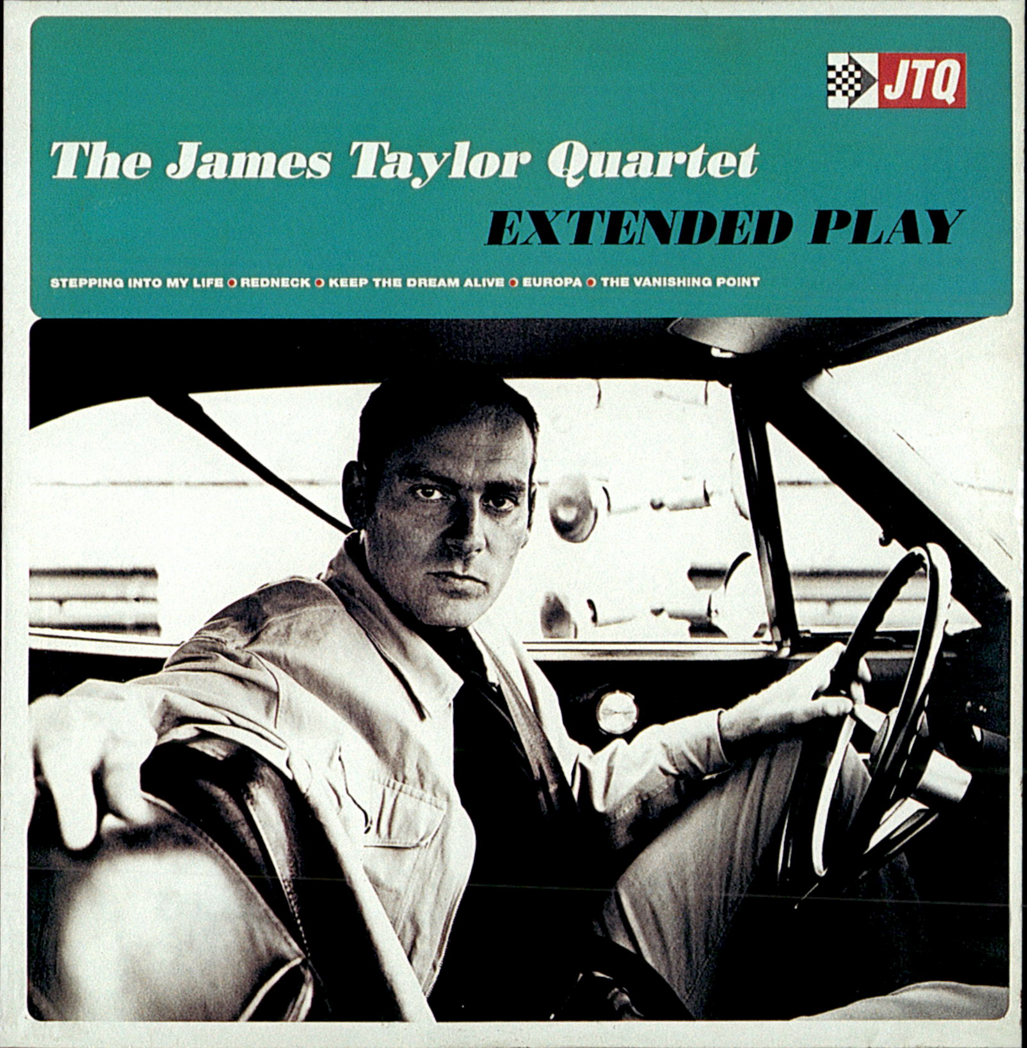

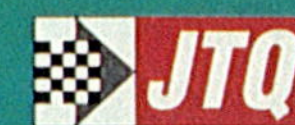

JTQ
The James Taylor Quartet
EXTENDED PLAY
STEPPING INTO MY LIFE • REDNECK • KEEP THE DREAM ALIVE • EUROPA • THE VANISHING POINT

270
Artist The James Taylor Quartet Title Stepping Into My Life Design Vegas Photography Steve Hall
Record Label Acid Jazz Date 1994

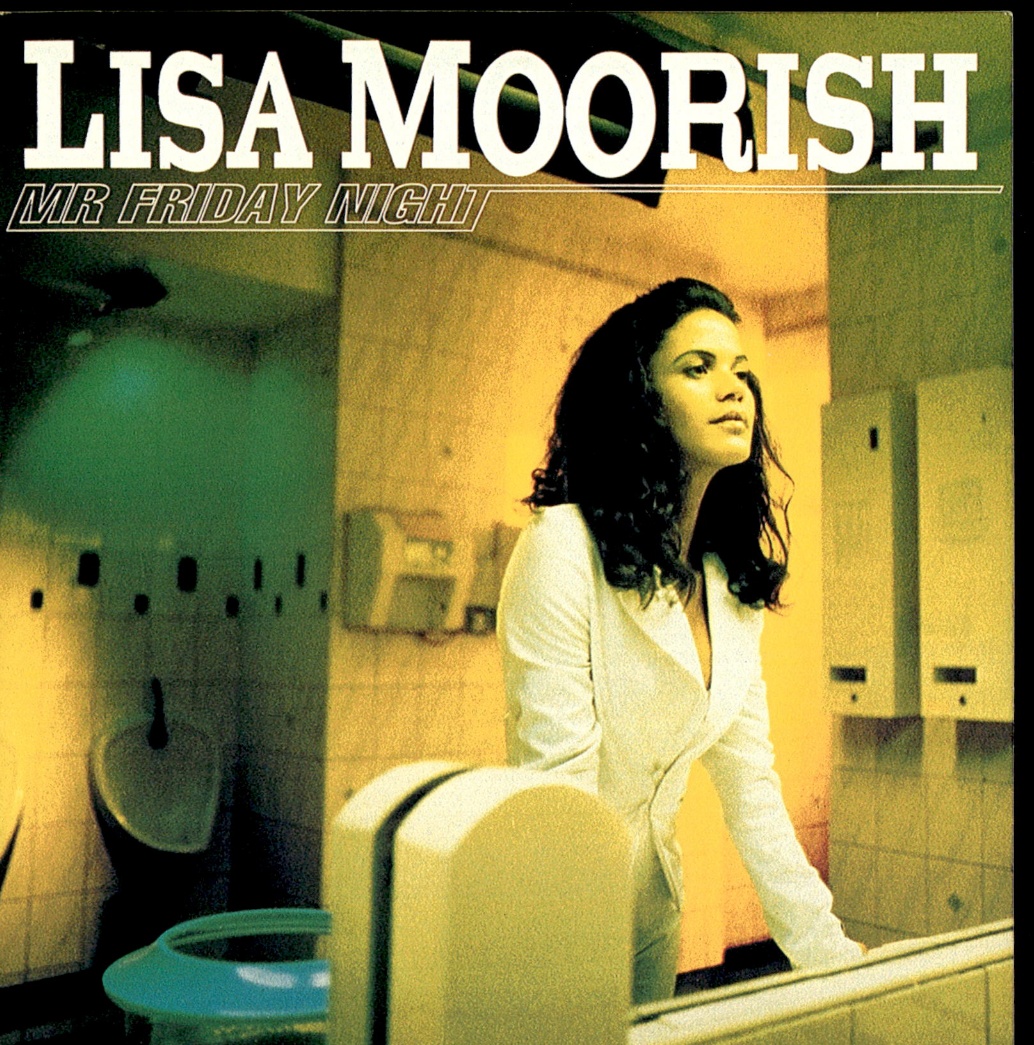

LISA MOORISH
MR FRIDAY NIGHT

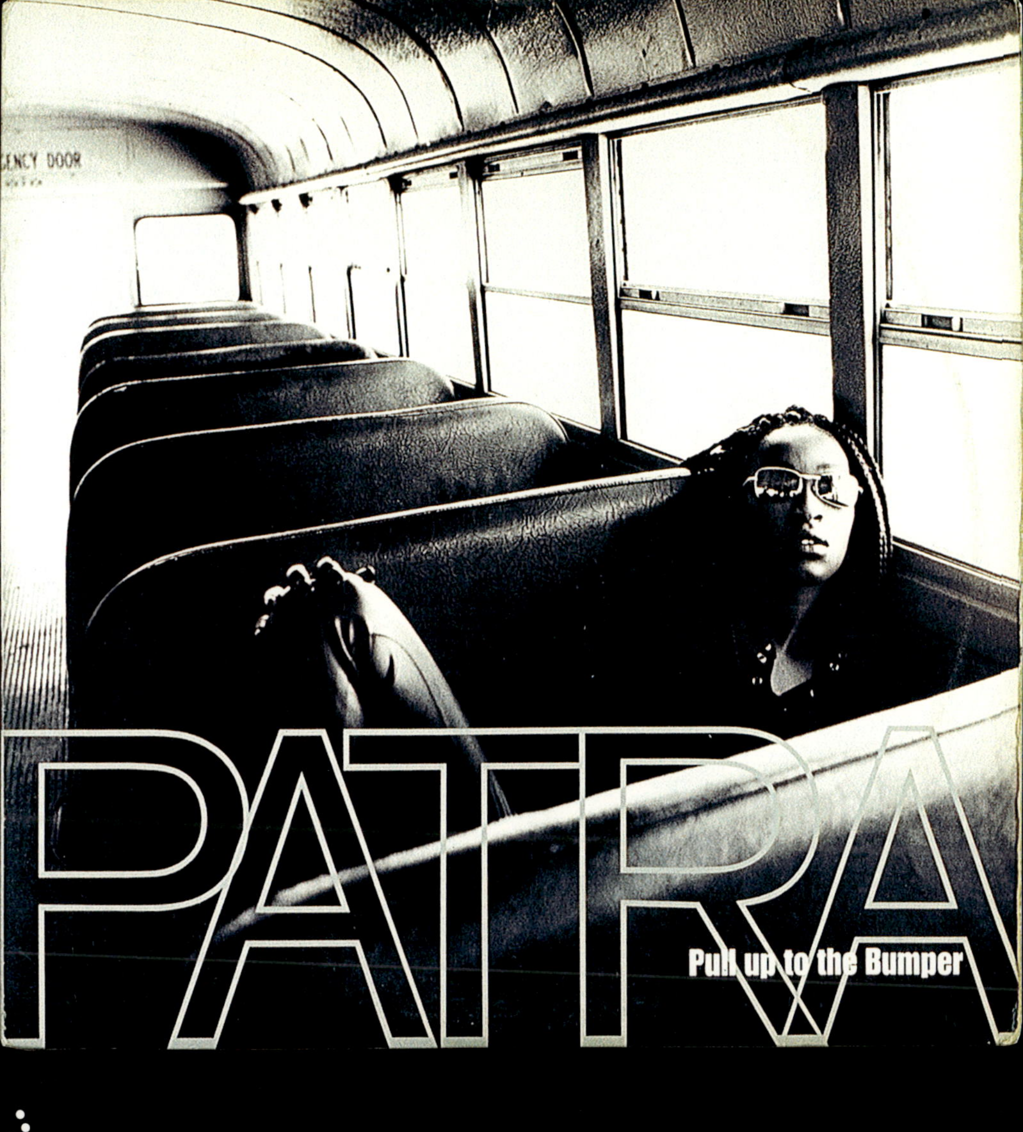

Artist Patra Title Pull Up to the Bumper Design Tony Sellari Photography Eric Johnson Record Label Sony Date 1995

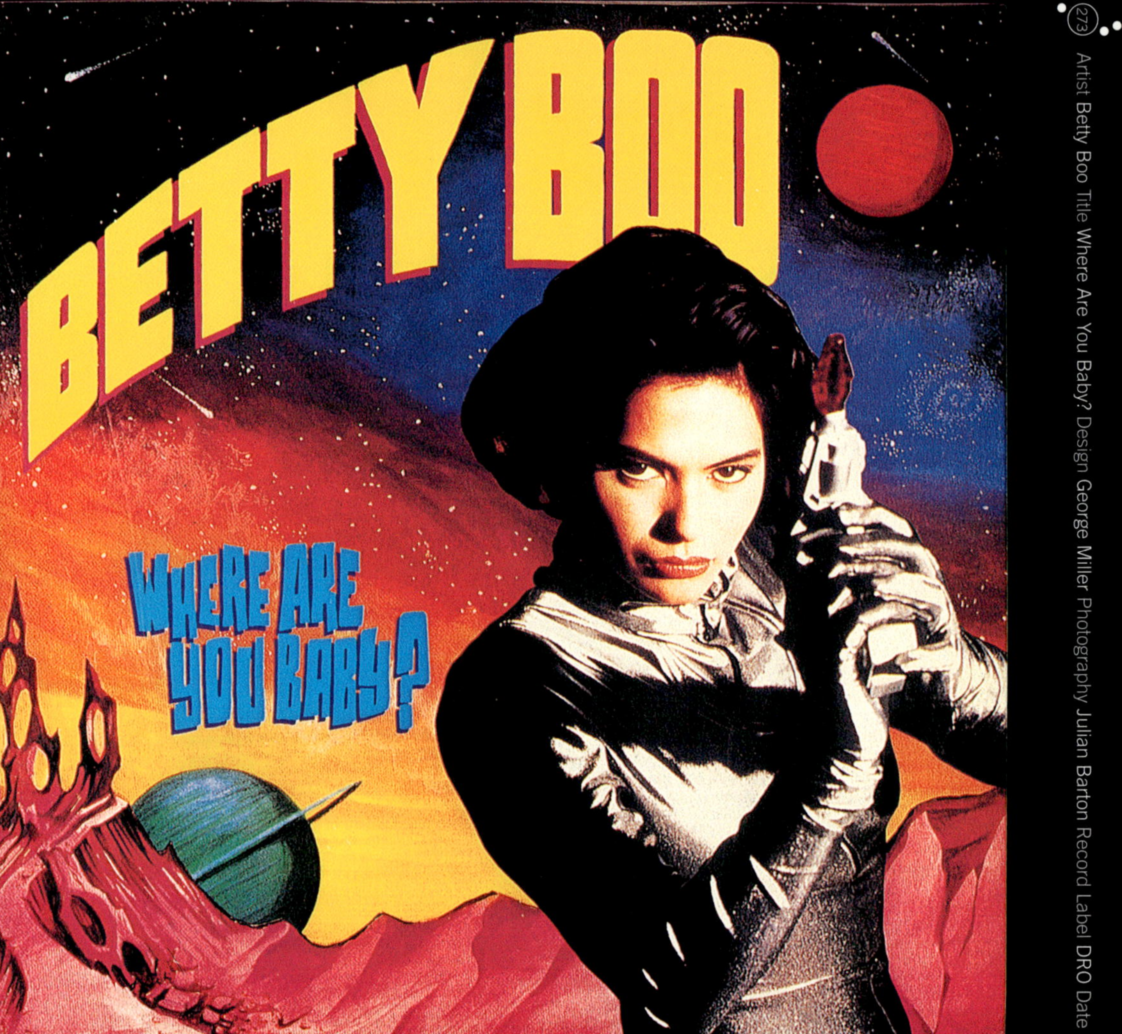

BETTY BOO
WHERE ARE YOU BABY?

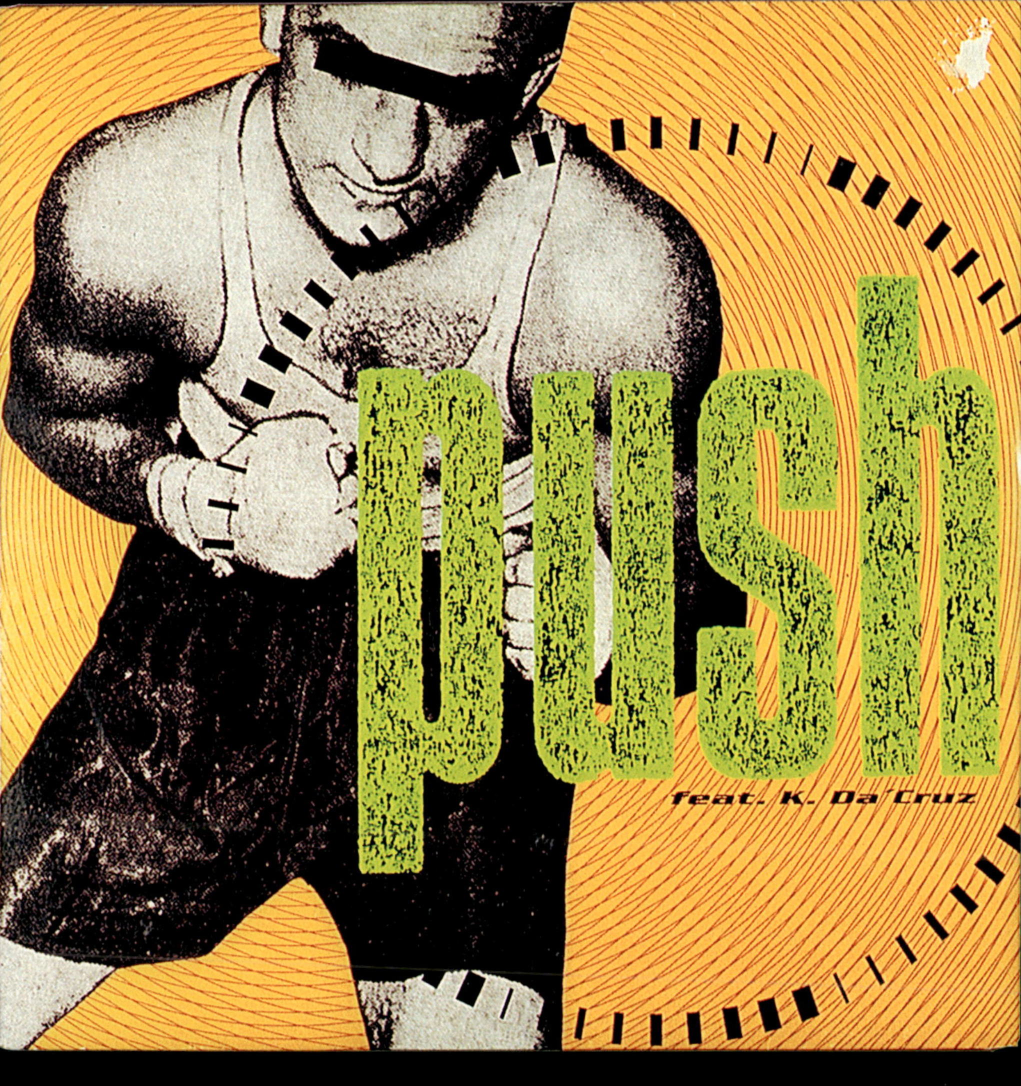

 Artist Push feat. K. Da Cruz Title Push Design Goutte Record Label Polydor Date 1993

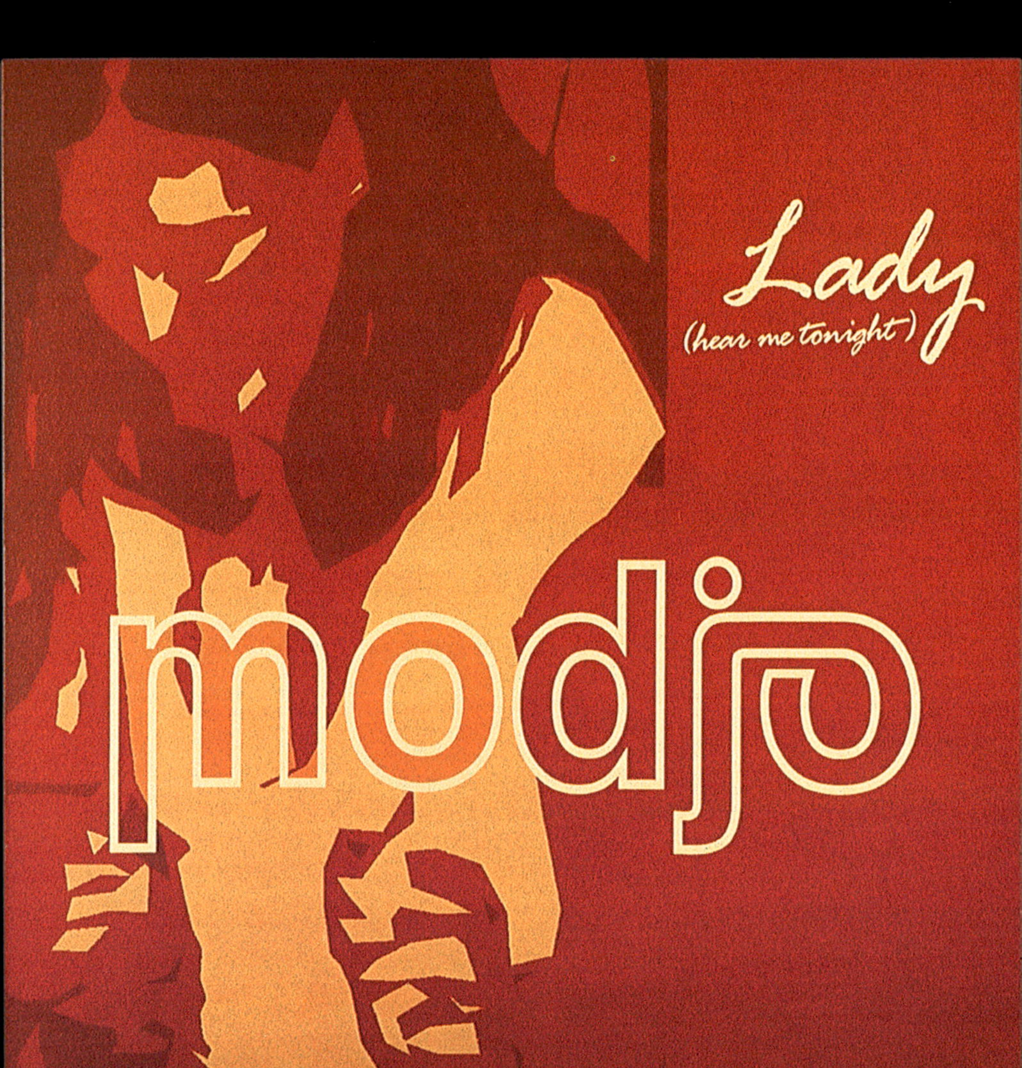
Lady
(hear me tonight)
modjo

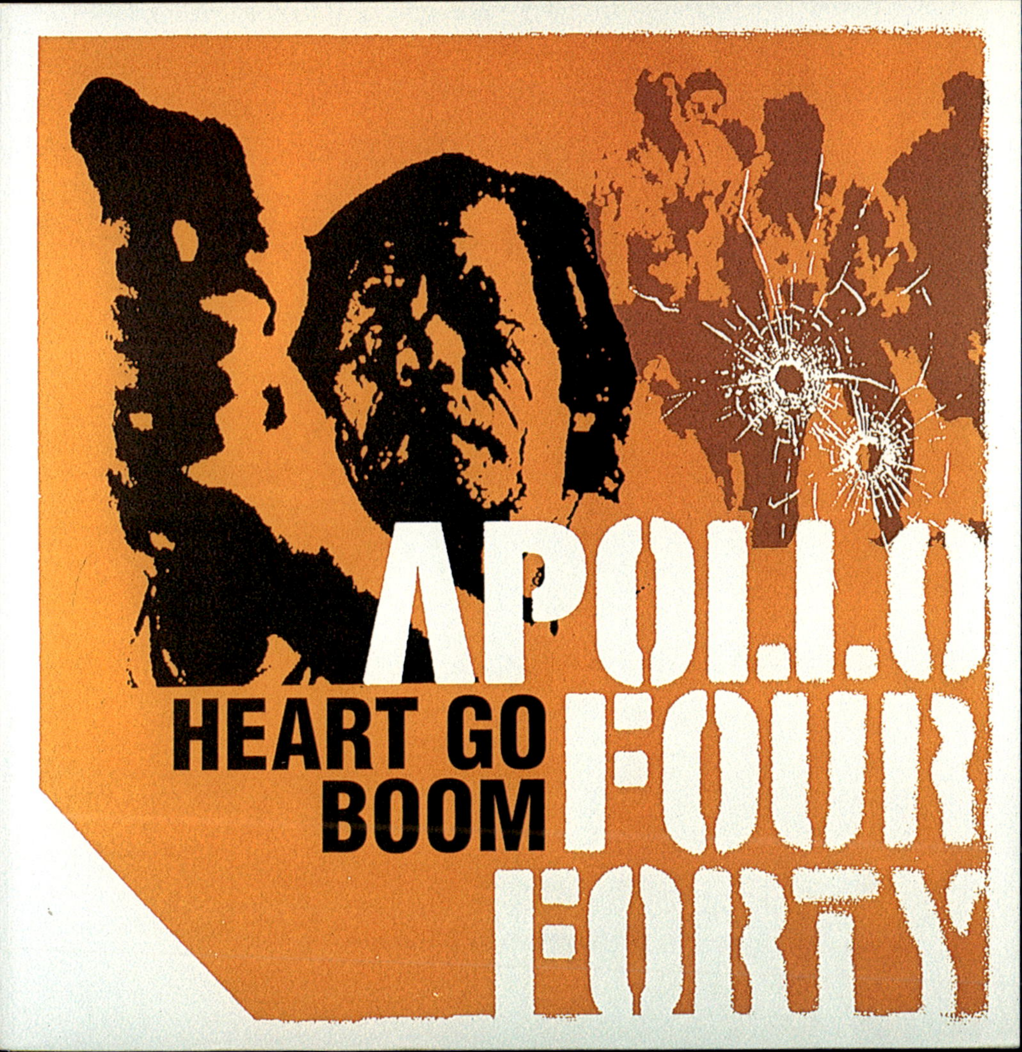

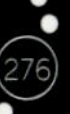

Artist Apollo Four Forty Title Heart Go Boom Design Think 1 Record Label Sony Music Date 1999

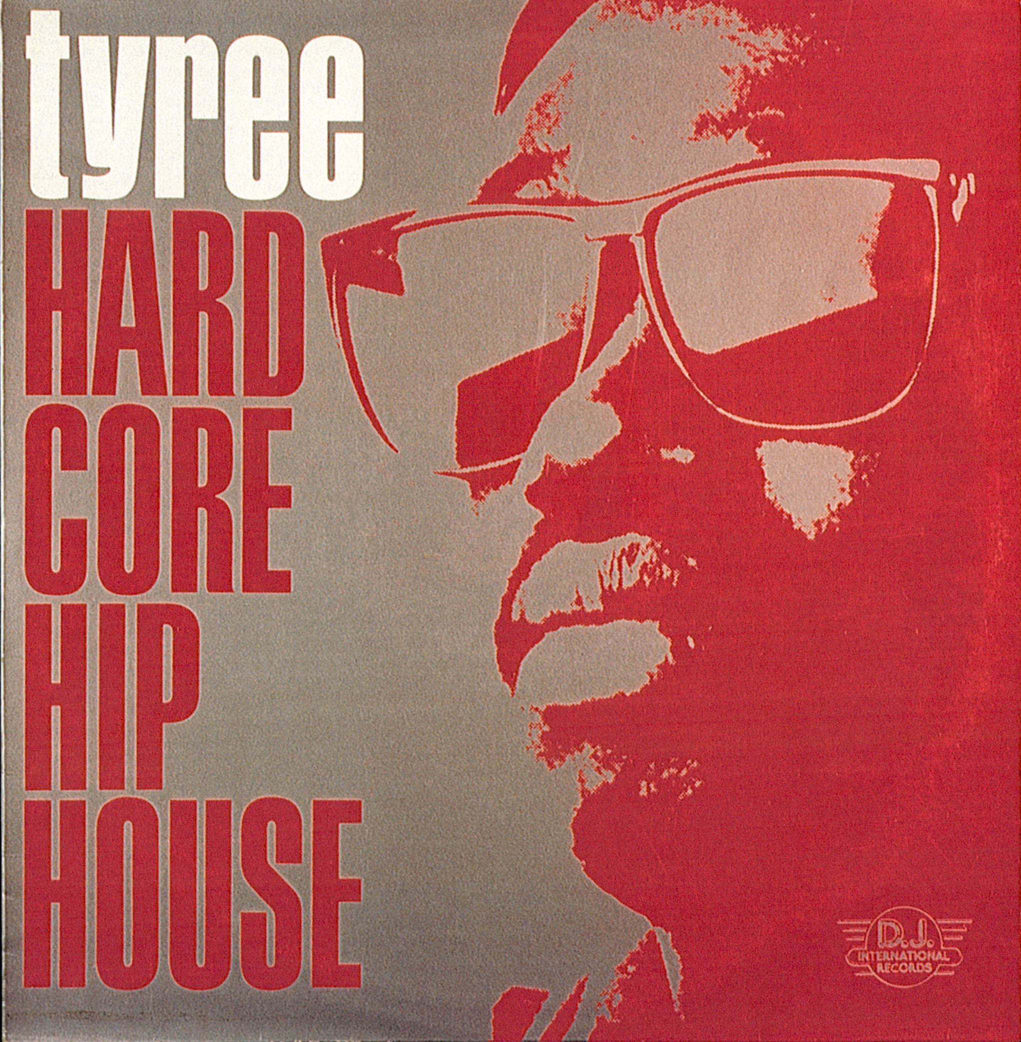
tyree
HARD
CORE
HIP
HOUSE
D.J.
INTERNATIONAL
RECORDS

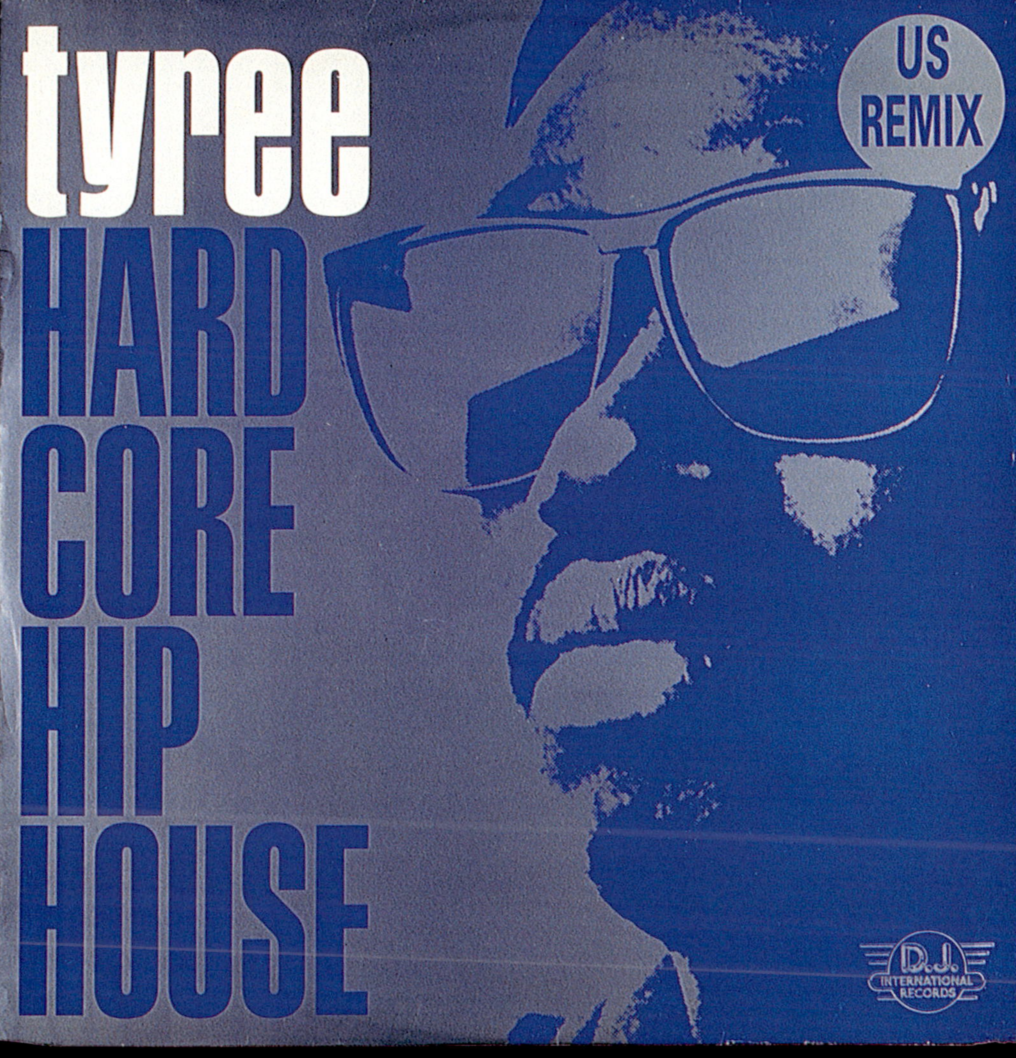

 Artist Tyree Title Hard Core Hip House Design Idest Photography James Alexander Newbury

RAVEN MAIZE
FOREVER TOGETHER

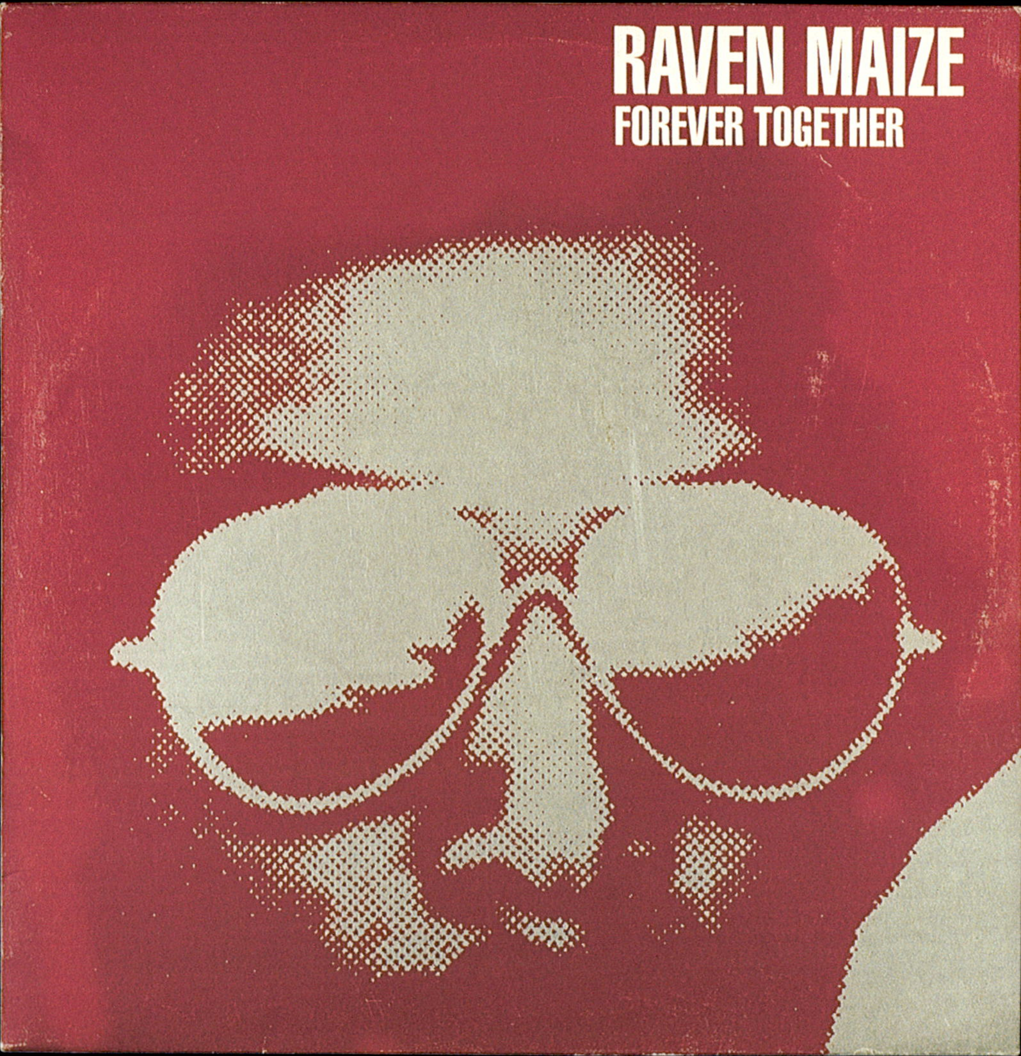

Full Intention

'Everybody Loves
The Sunshine'

sugar daddy records

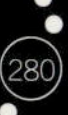

 Artist Full Intention Title Everybody Loves the Sunshine Record Label Sugar Daddy Date 1998

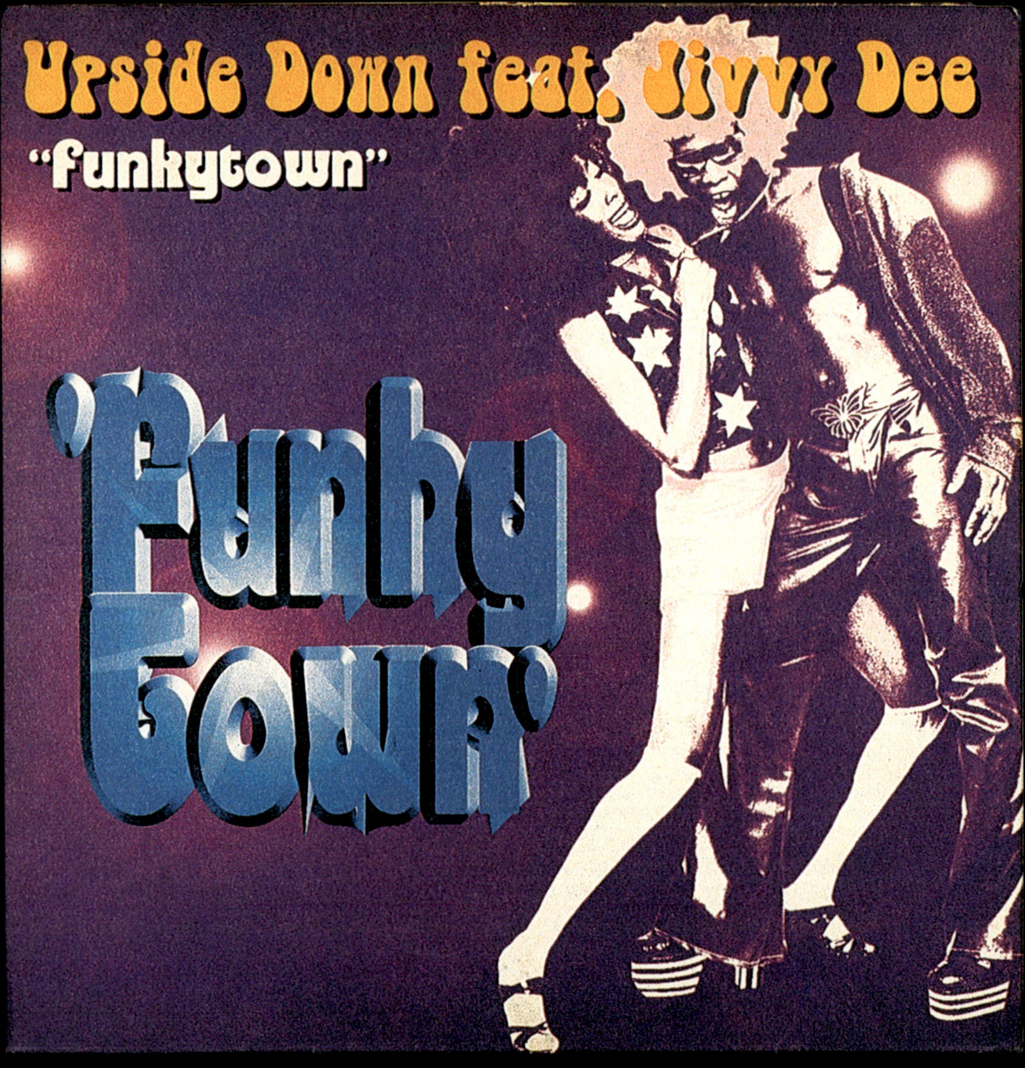

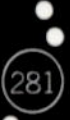

Upside Down feat. Jivvy Dee

"funkytown"

'Funky Town'

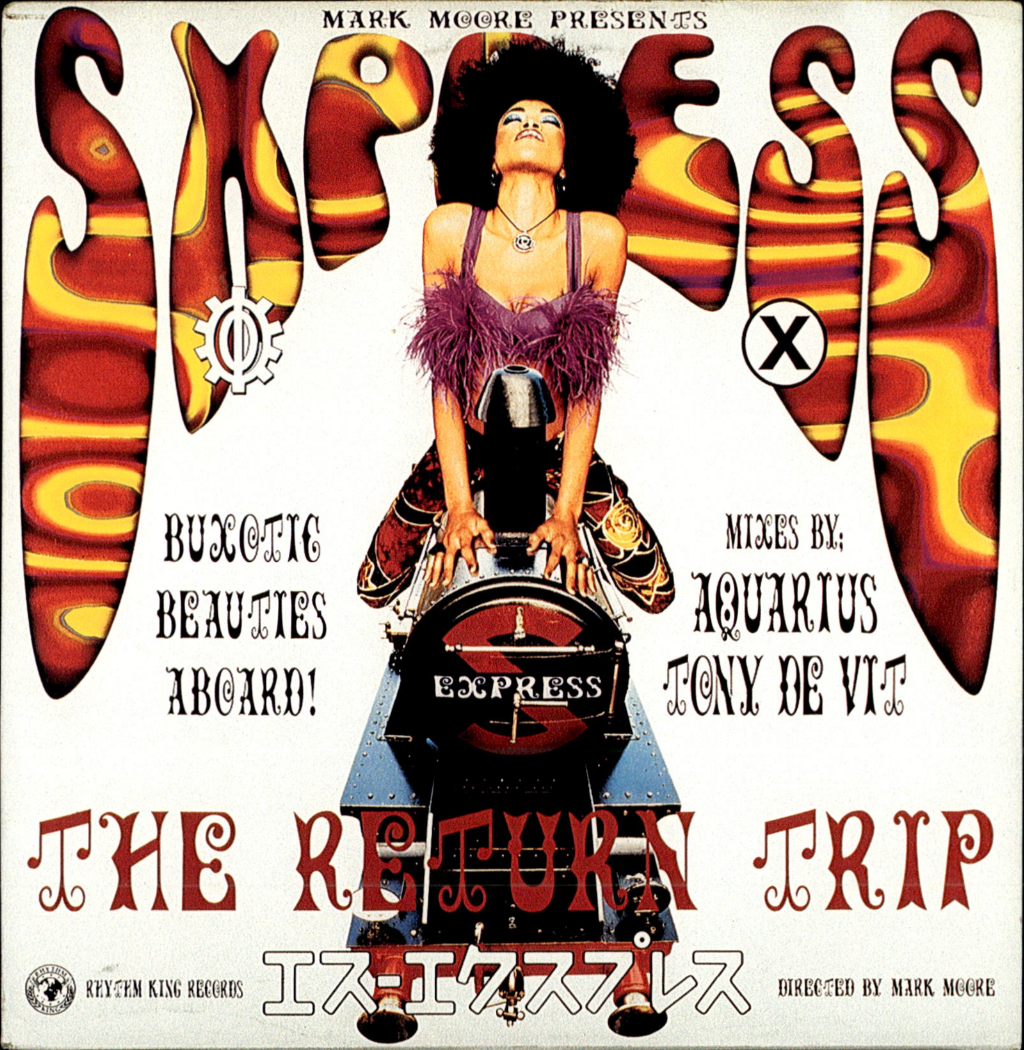

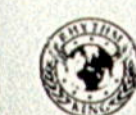
282

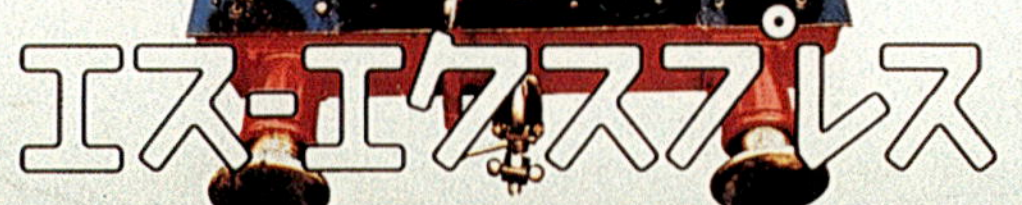
MARK MOORE PRESENTS
S XPRESS
BUXOTIC BEAUTIES ABOARD!
MIXES BY:
AQUARIUS
TONY DE VIT
EXPRESS
THE RETURN TRIP
エス・エクスプレス
RHYTHM KING RECORDS
DIRECTED BY MARK MOORE

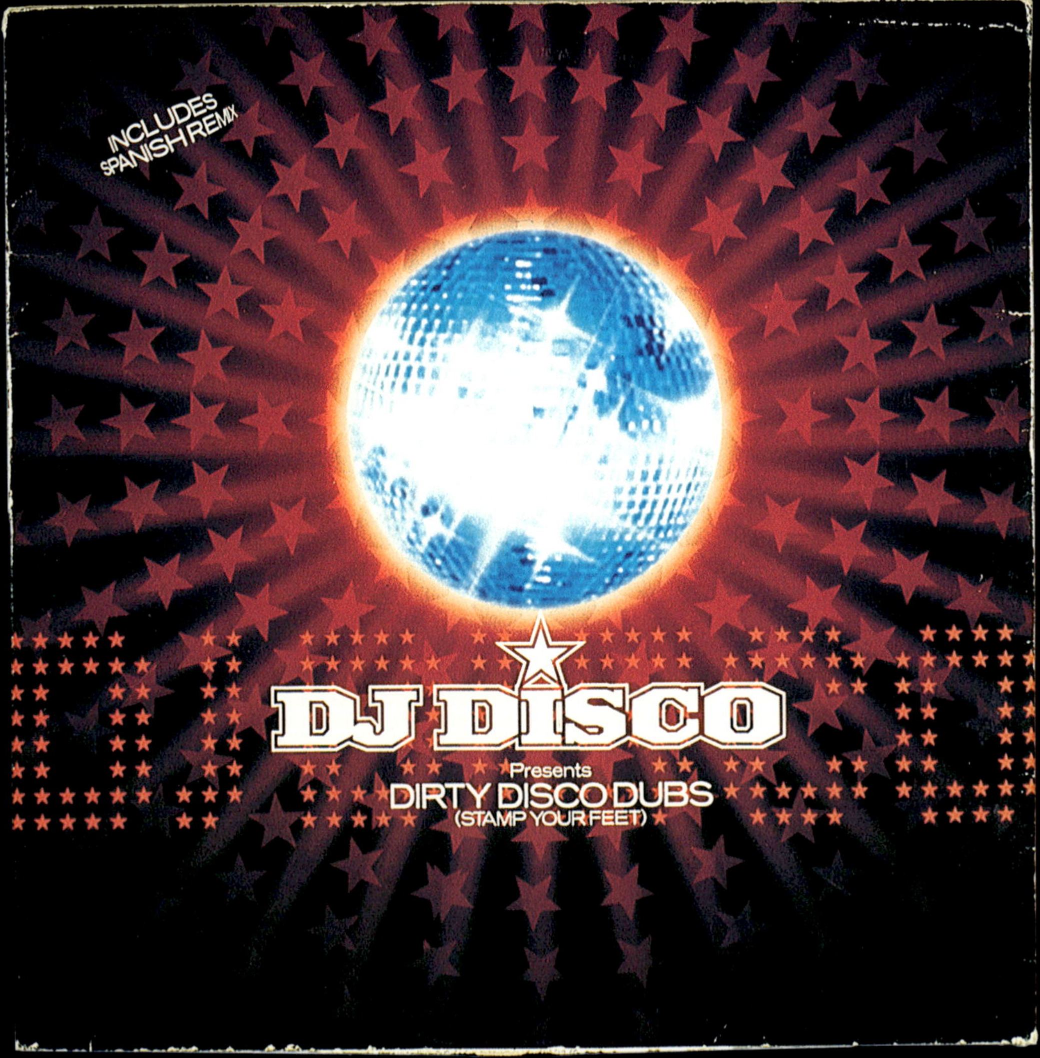

INCLUDES
SPANISH REMIX

DJ DISCO
Presents
DIRTY DISCO DUBS
(STAMP YOUR FEET)

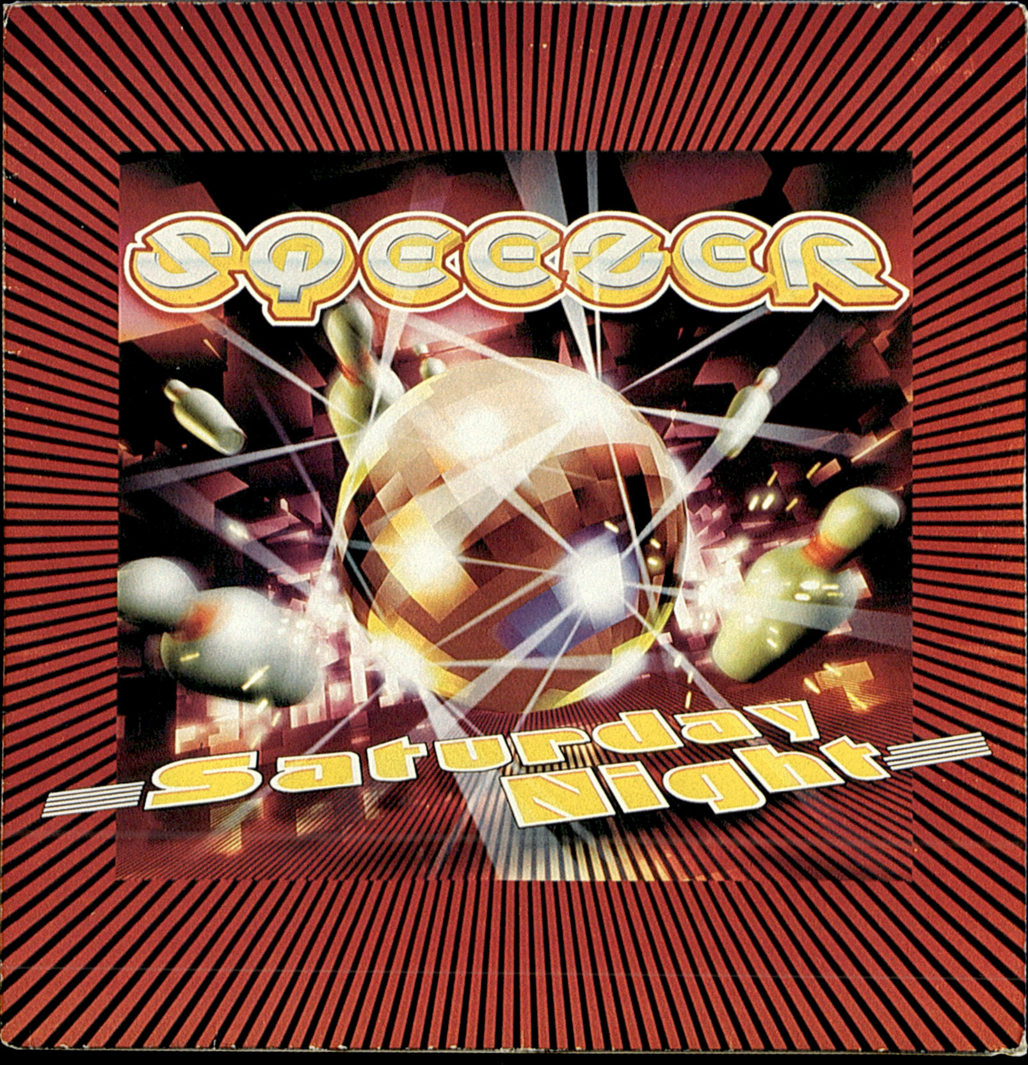

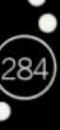

Artist Sqeezer Title Saturday Night Photography Fantasy Factory Record Label Max Music / Cologne Dance Label
Date 1997

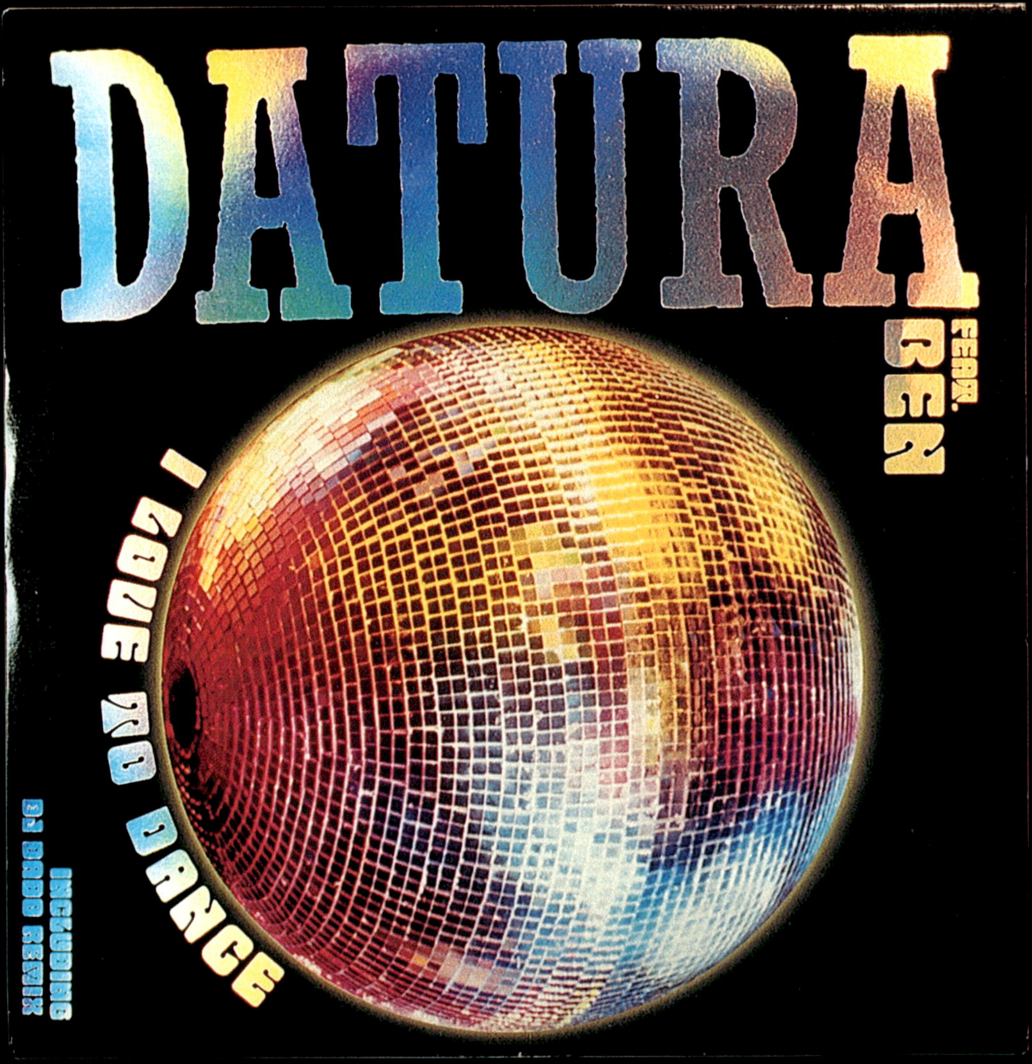

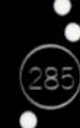

Artist Datura feat. Ben Title I Love To Dance Record Label Time Date 1999

WHIRLPOOL PRODUCTIONS FROM: DISCO TO: DISCO

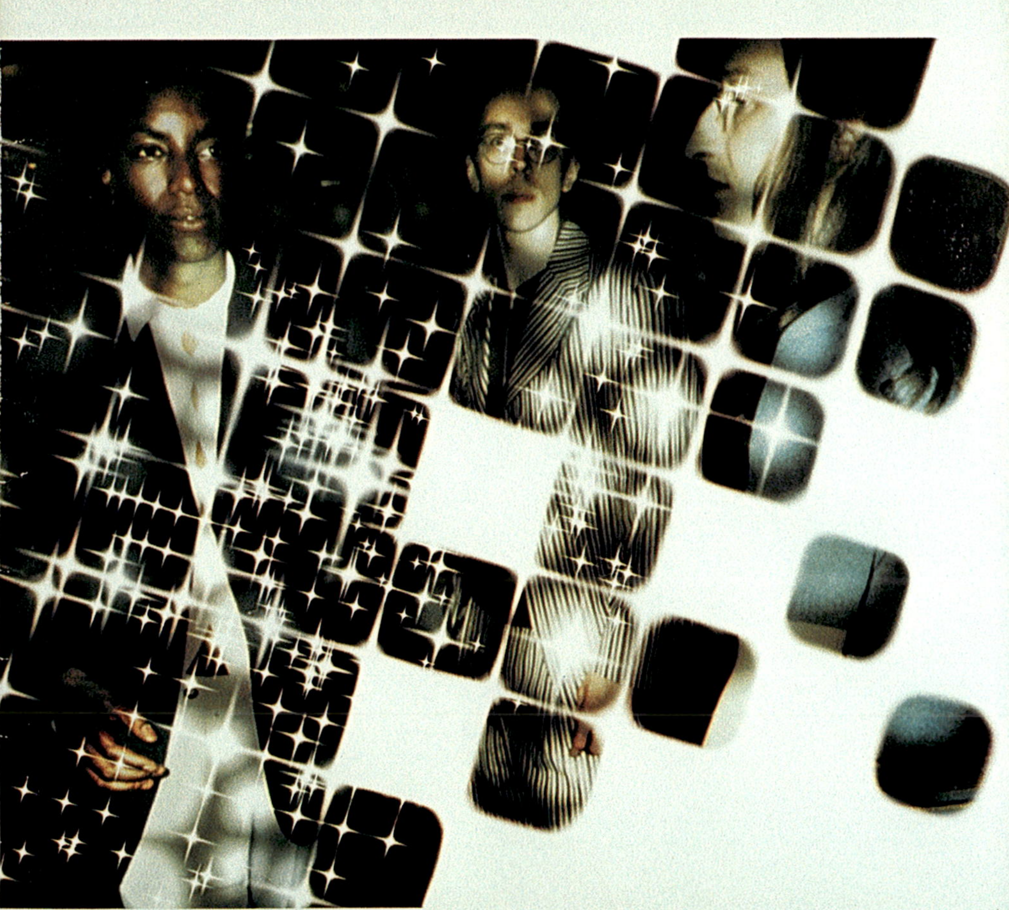

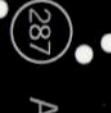

cardenia · passion
cardenia
passion

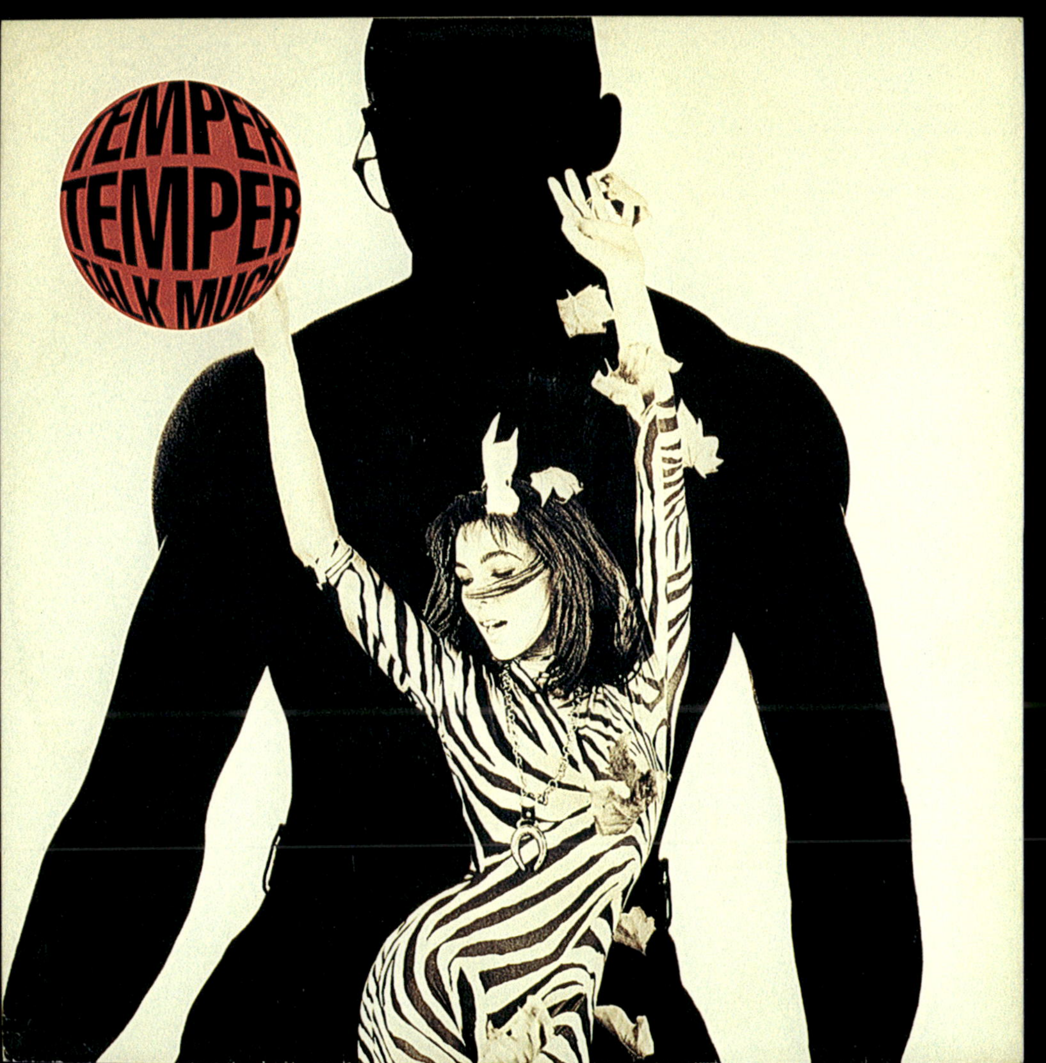
TEMPER
TEMPER
TALK MUCH

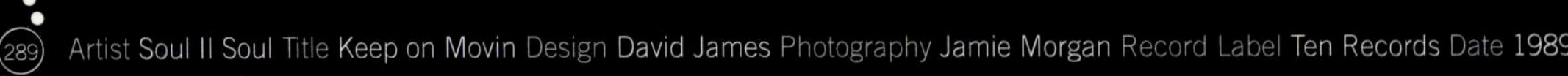
Soul II Soul
Keep on movin

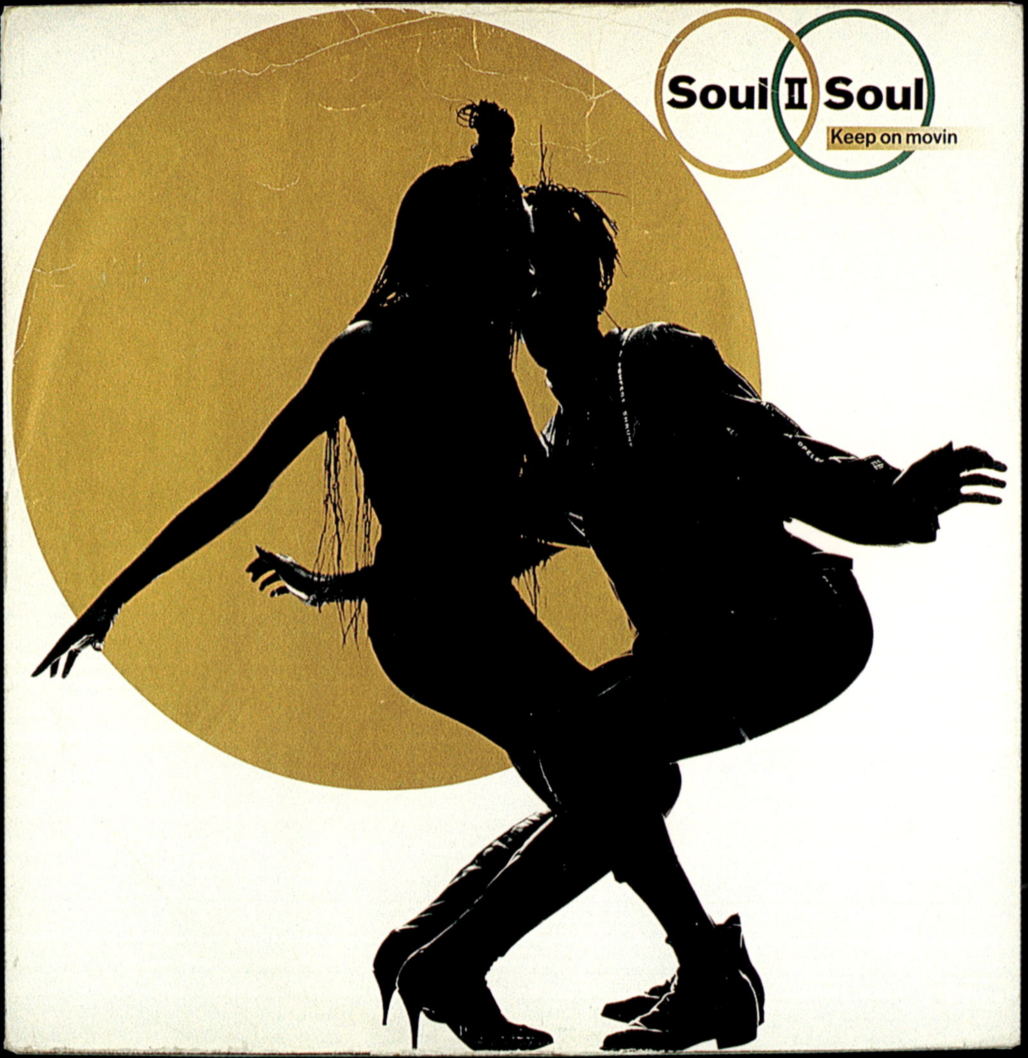

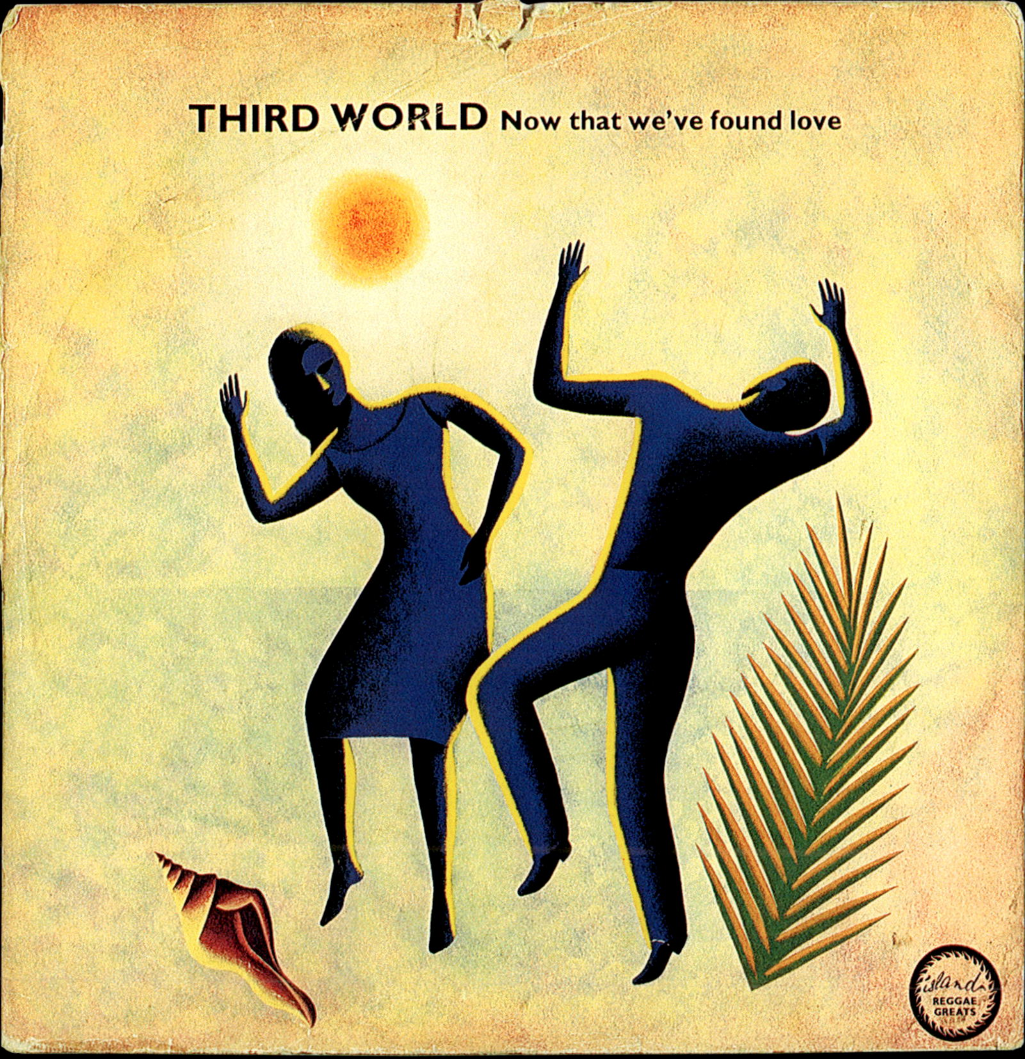

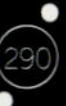

THIRD WORLD Now that we've found love

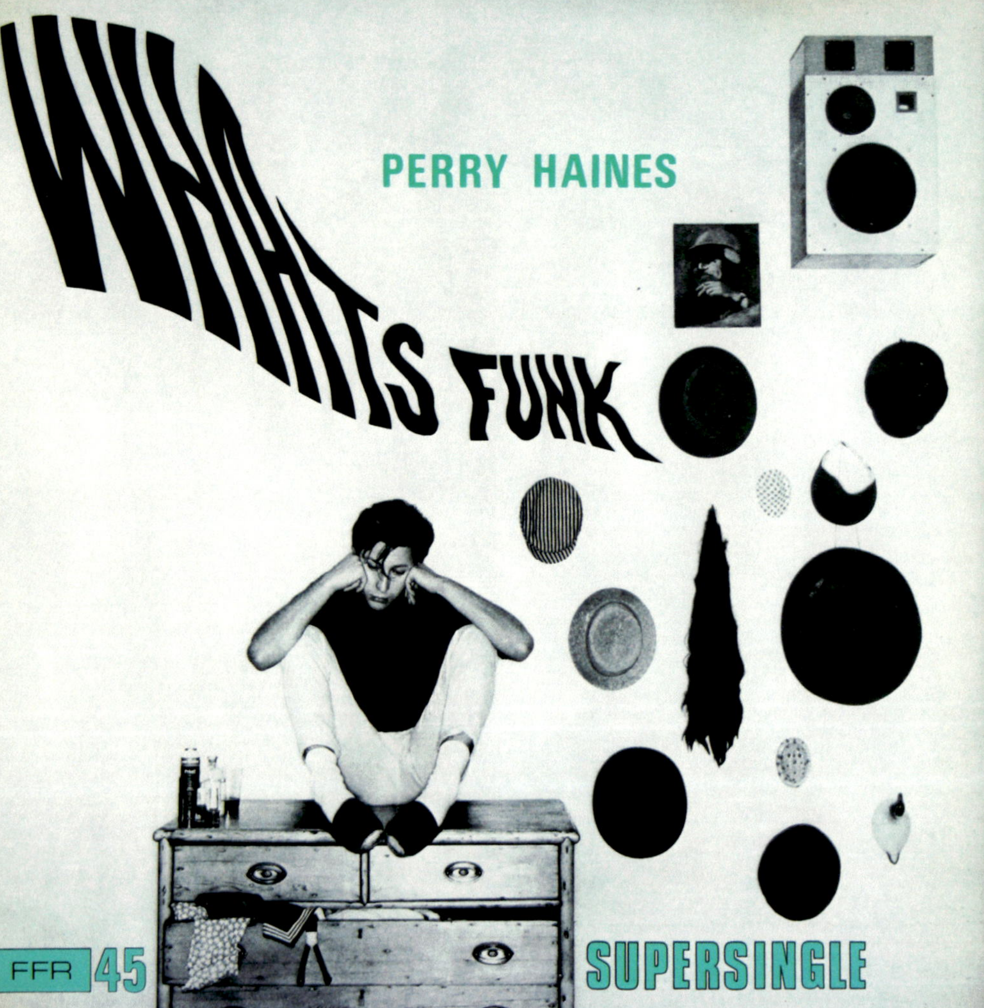

PERRY HAINES
WHATS FUNK
FFR 45
SUPERSINGLE

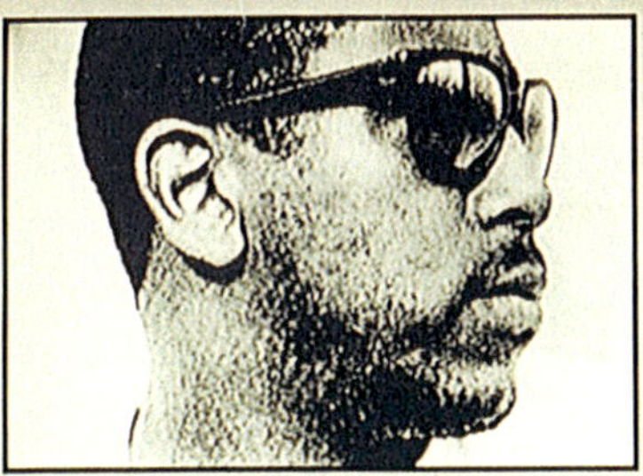

TONE-LŌC
"WILD THING"
MAXI-SINGLE
12 INCH

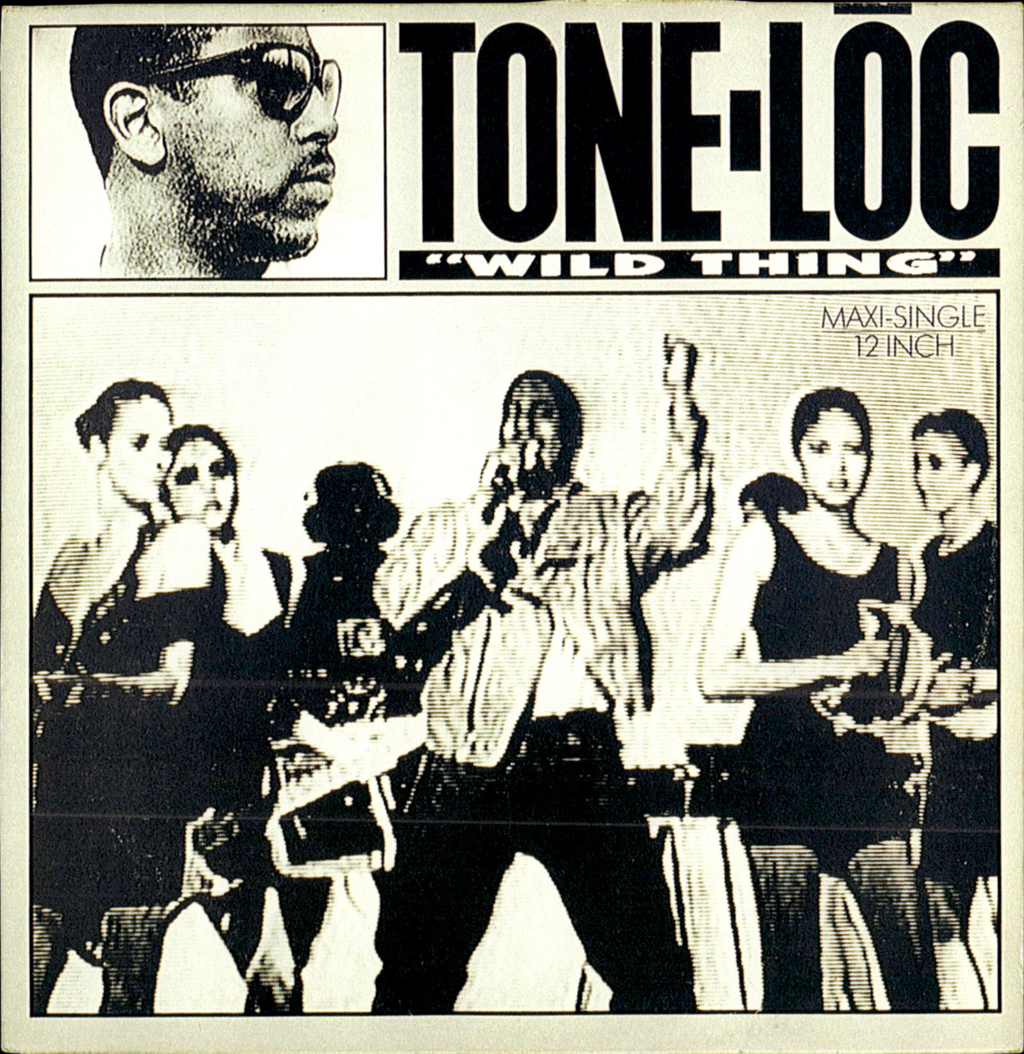

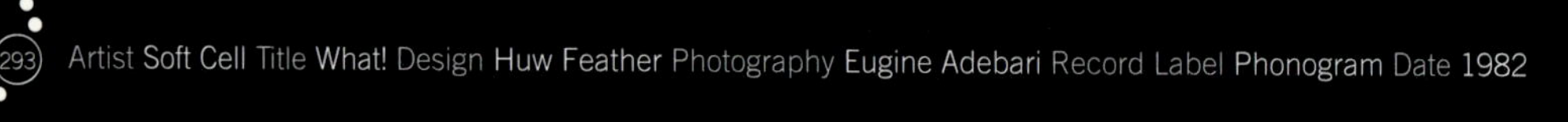

WHAT!
Soft Cell
¡QUE!
12"45

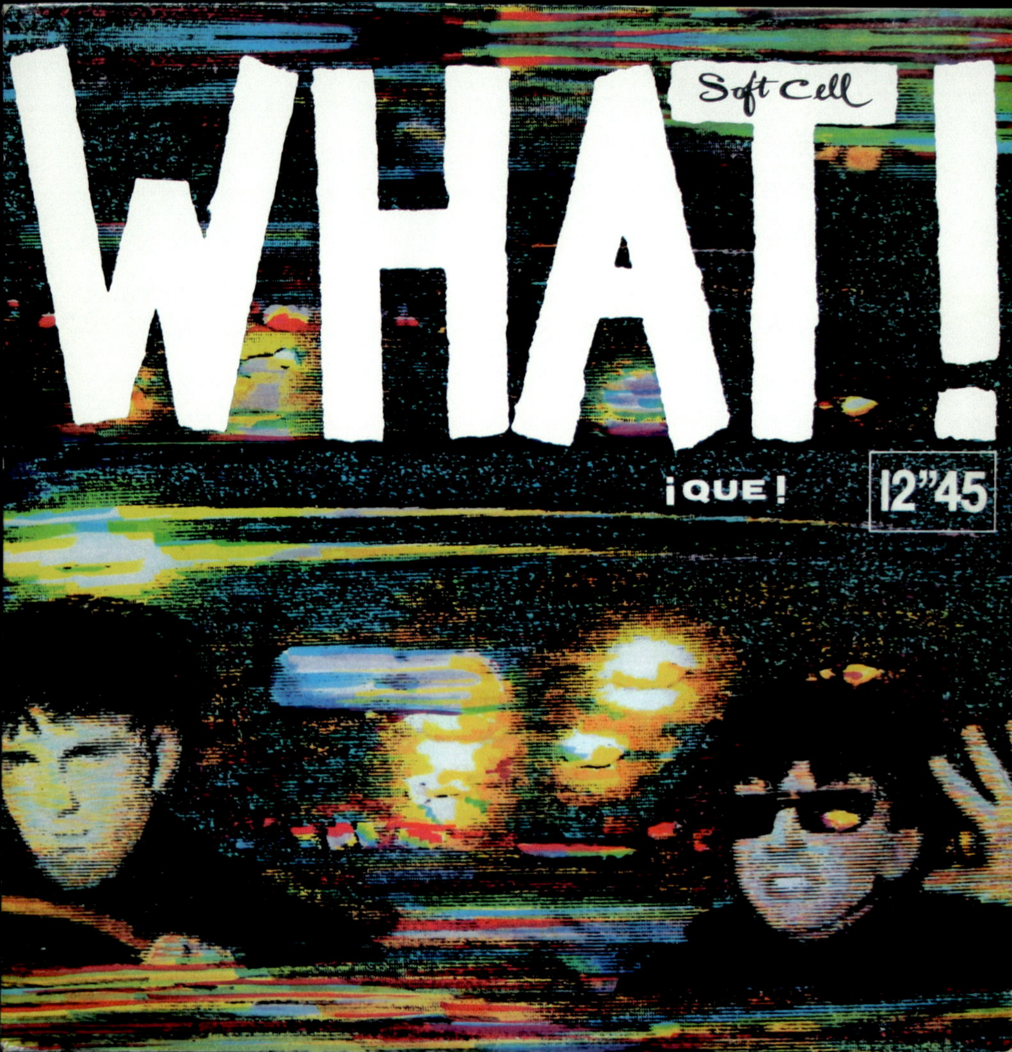

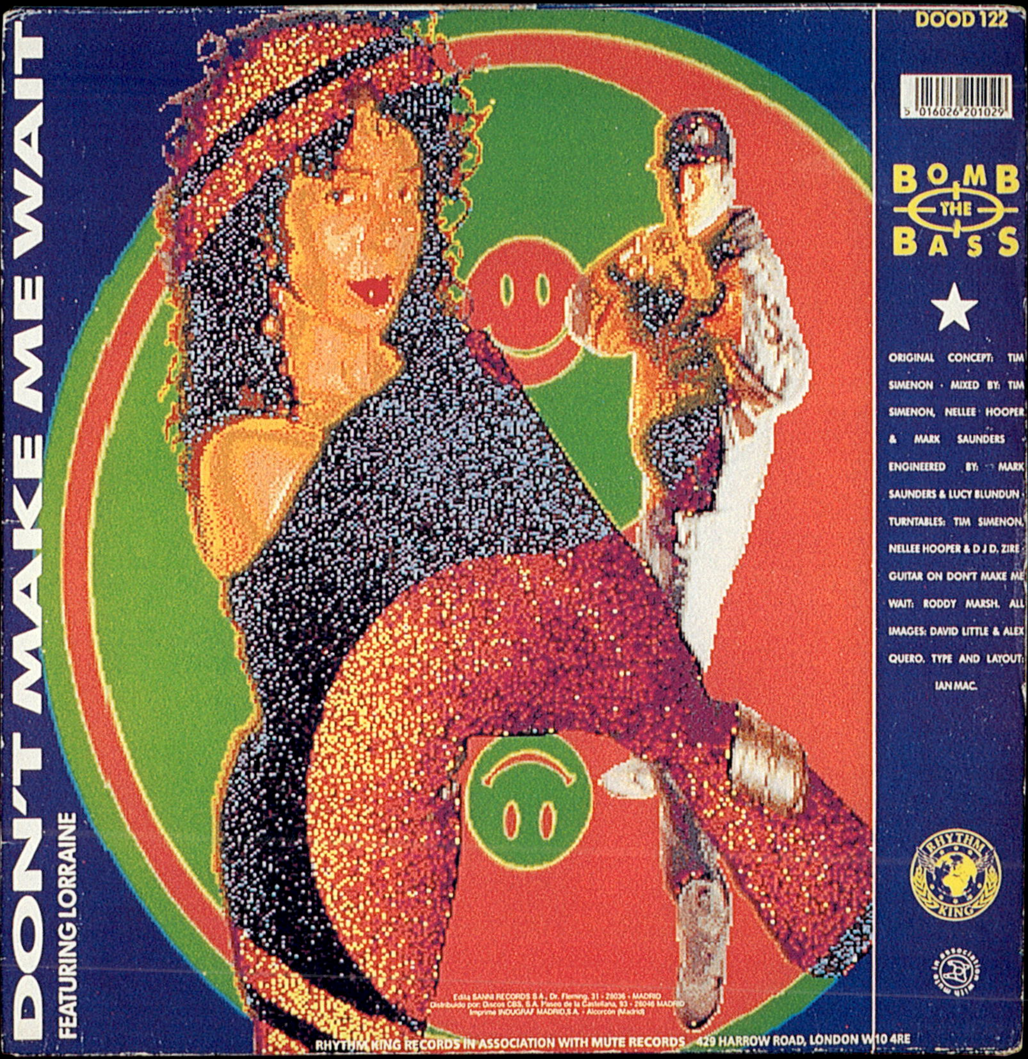

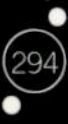

Artist Bomb The Bass feat. Lorraine Title Don't Make Me Wait Design Ian Mac. Photography David Little & Alex Quero Record Label Mute Records Date 1988

DISCO
DEUTSCHLAND
MONKEY SAY MONKEY DO
LOW SPIRIT
4th WESTBAM DISCO RIOT

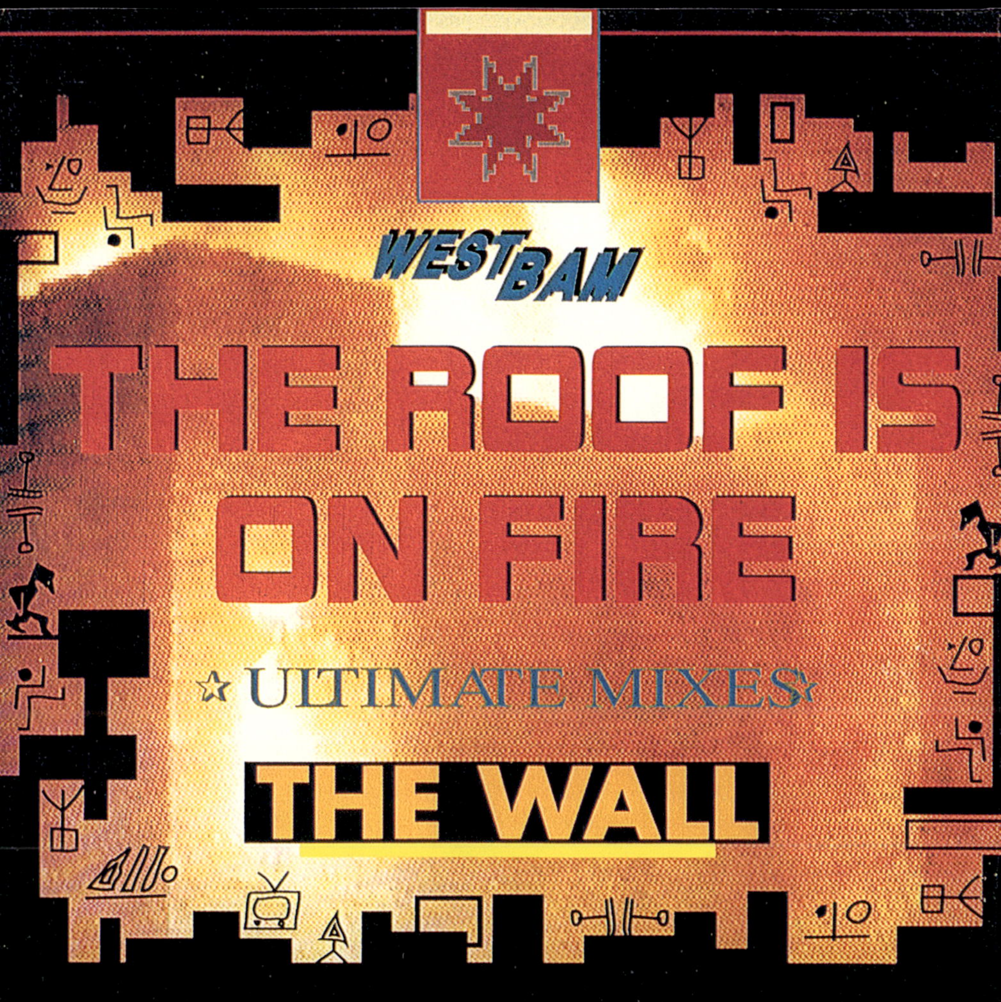
WESTBAM
THE ROOF IS ON FIRE
ULTIMATE MIXES
THE WALL

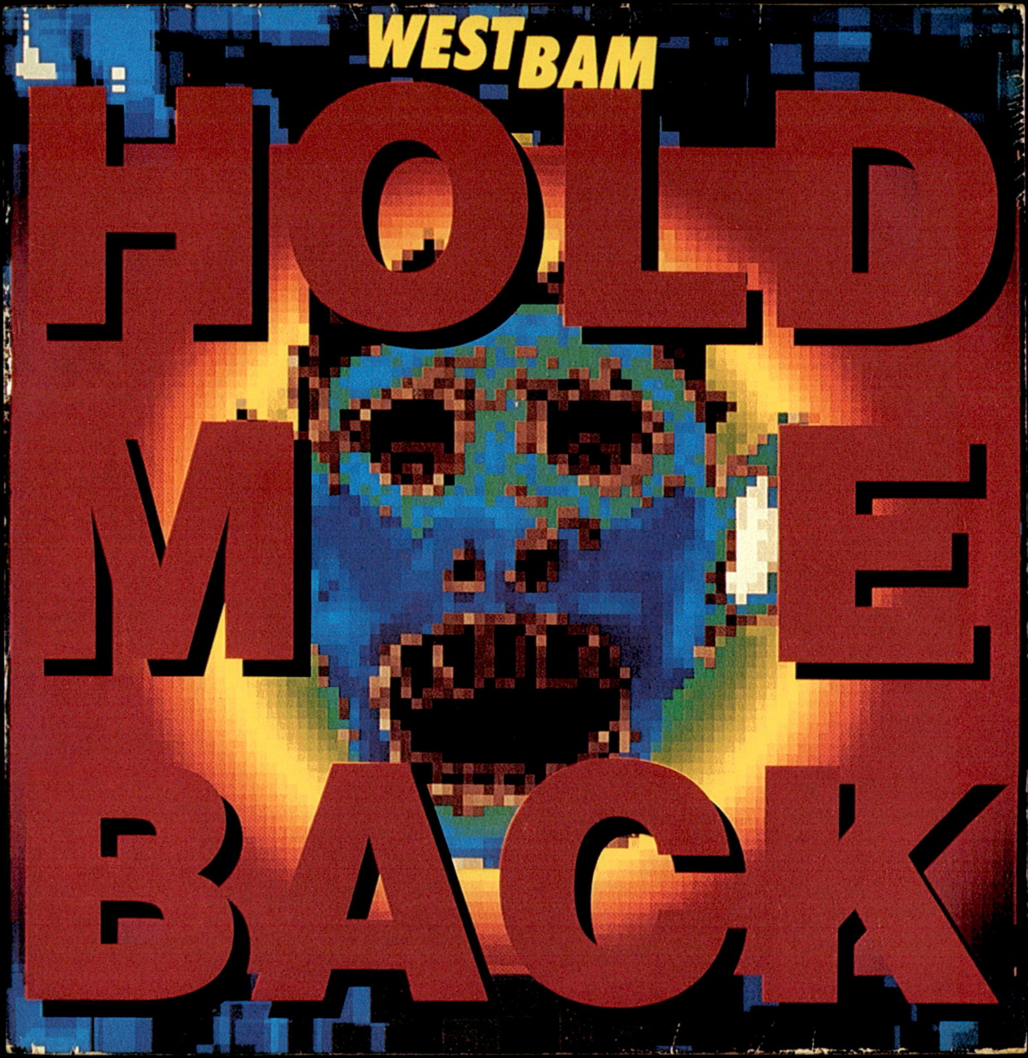

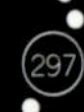

 Artist WestBam Title Hold Me Back Record Label Low Spirit Date 1990

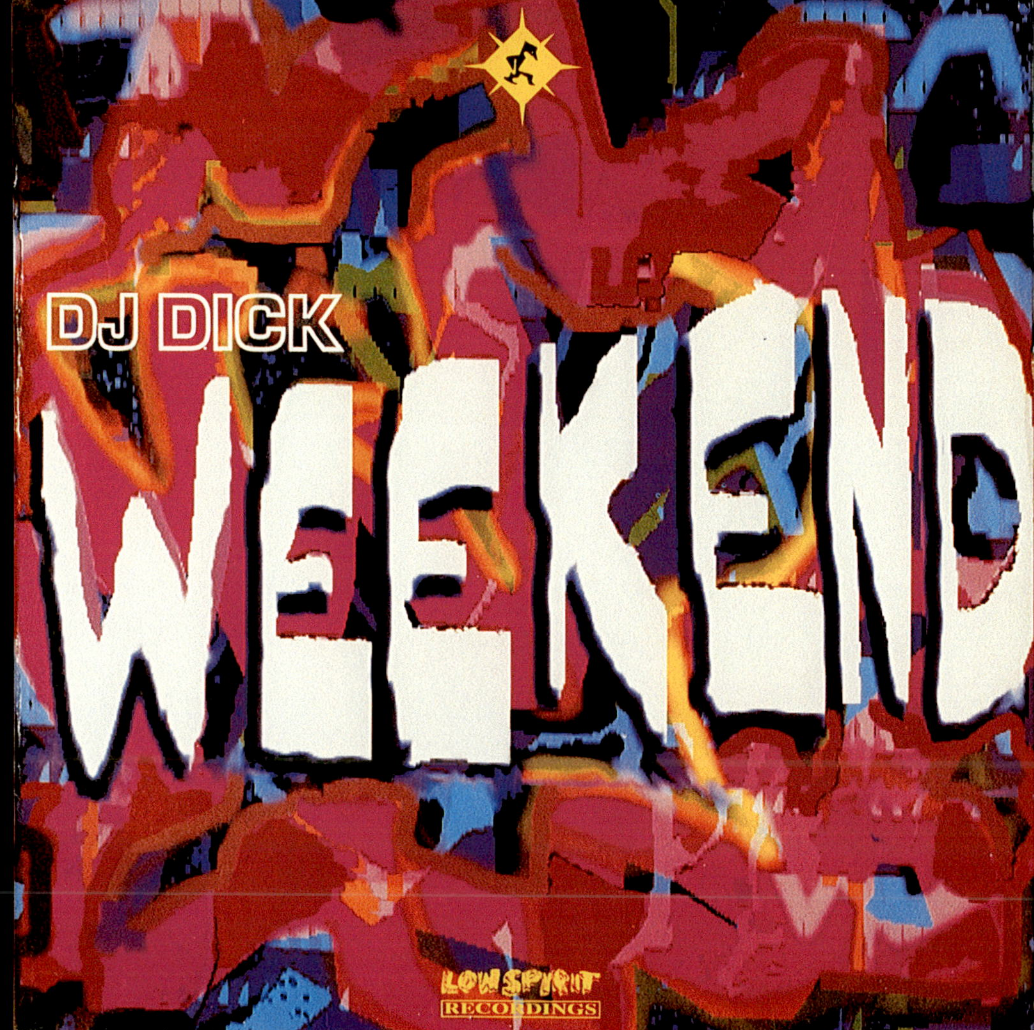
DJ DICK
WEEKEND
LOW SPIRIT
RECORDINGS

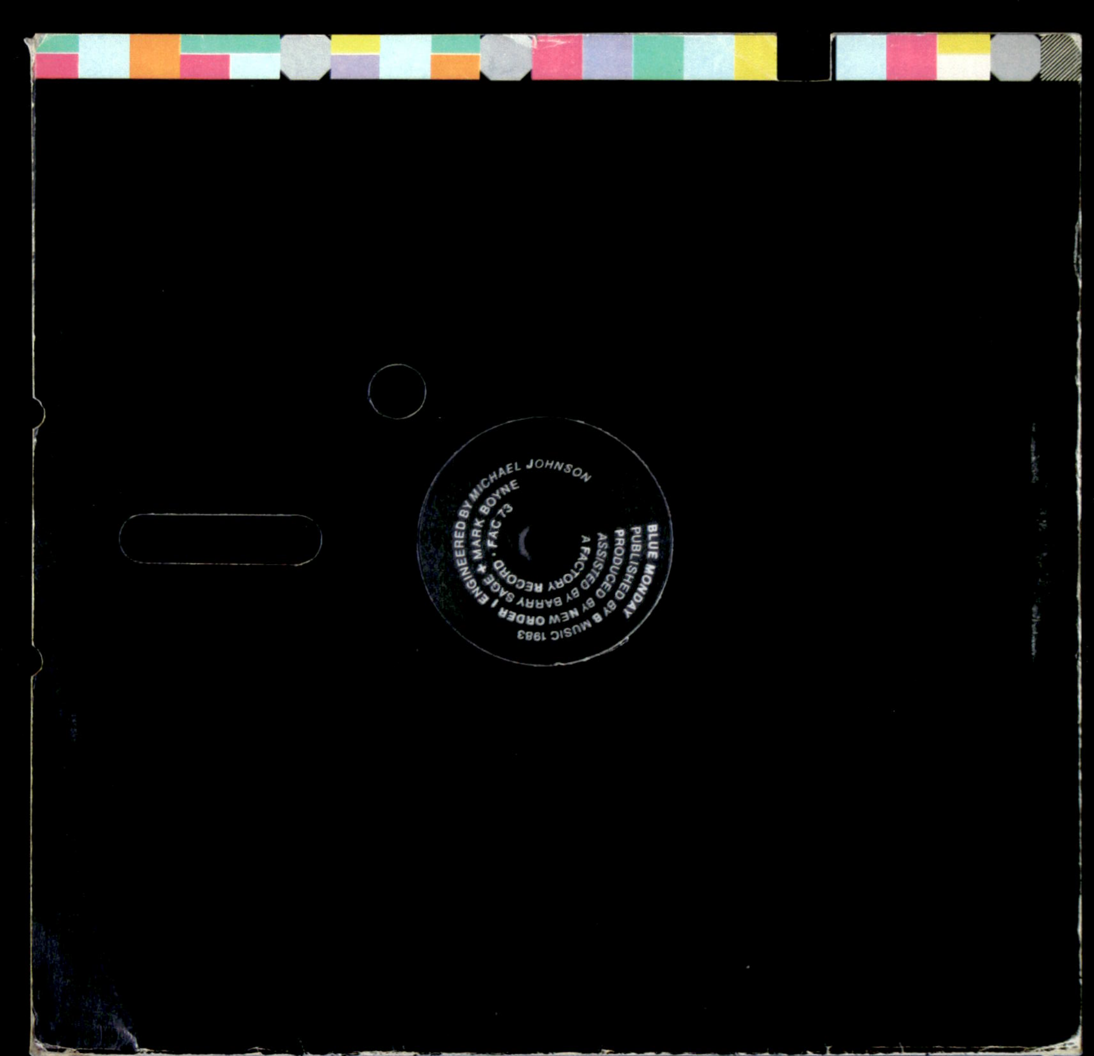
ENGINEERED BY MICHAEL JOHNSON
★ MARK BOYNE
FAC 73
BLUE MONDAY
PUBLISHED BY B MUSIC 1983
PRODUCED BY NEW ORDER
ASSISTED BY BARRY SAGE
A FACTORY RECORD

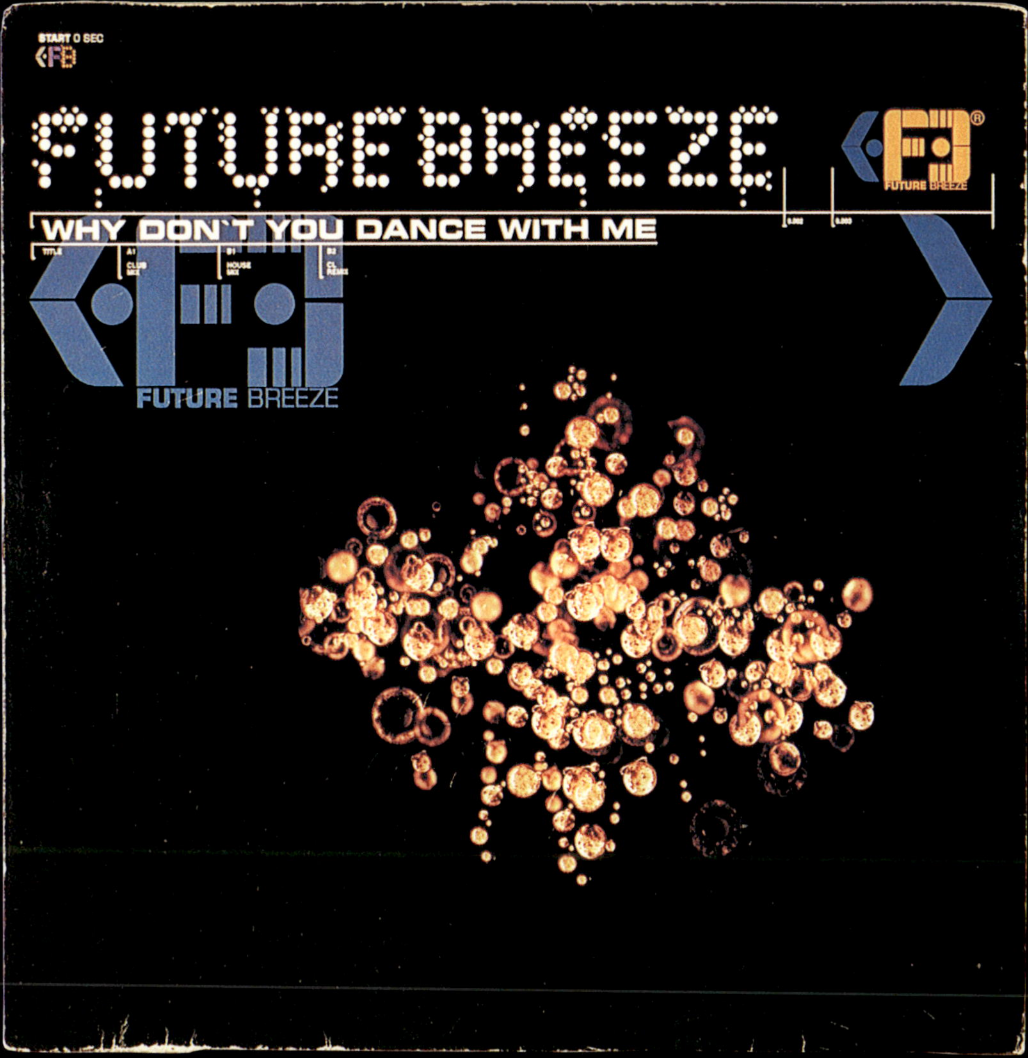

START 0 SEC
FB
FUTURE BREEZE
FUTURE BREEZE
WHY DON`T YOU DANCE WITH ME
TITLE
A1 CLUB MIX
B1 HOUSE MIX
B2 CL REMIX
FUTURE BREEZE

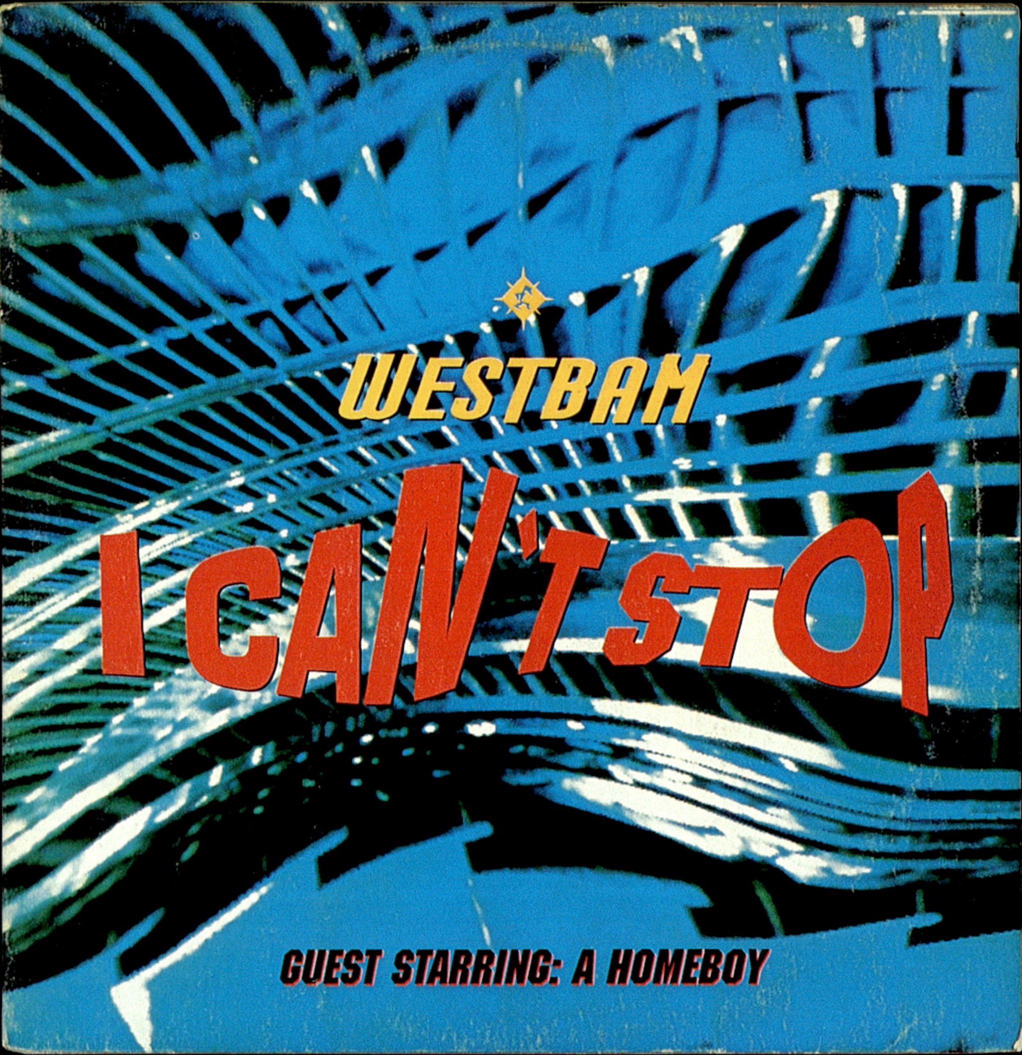

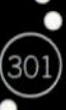

 Artist WestBam Title I Can't Stop Design Style: Fabian L.D. Record Label Low Spirit Date 1991

THE SHAMEN • BOSS DRUM • TPLP42
SHAMEN
BOSS DRUM

remix
remixed by PERPLEXER • STAR WASH • MIKE INK. • SENSORAMA • DANIEL KLEIN
andreas dorau
das telefon sagt du

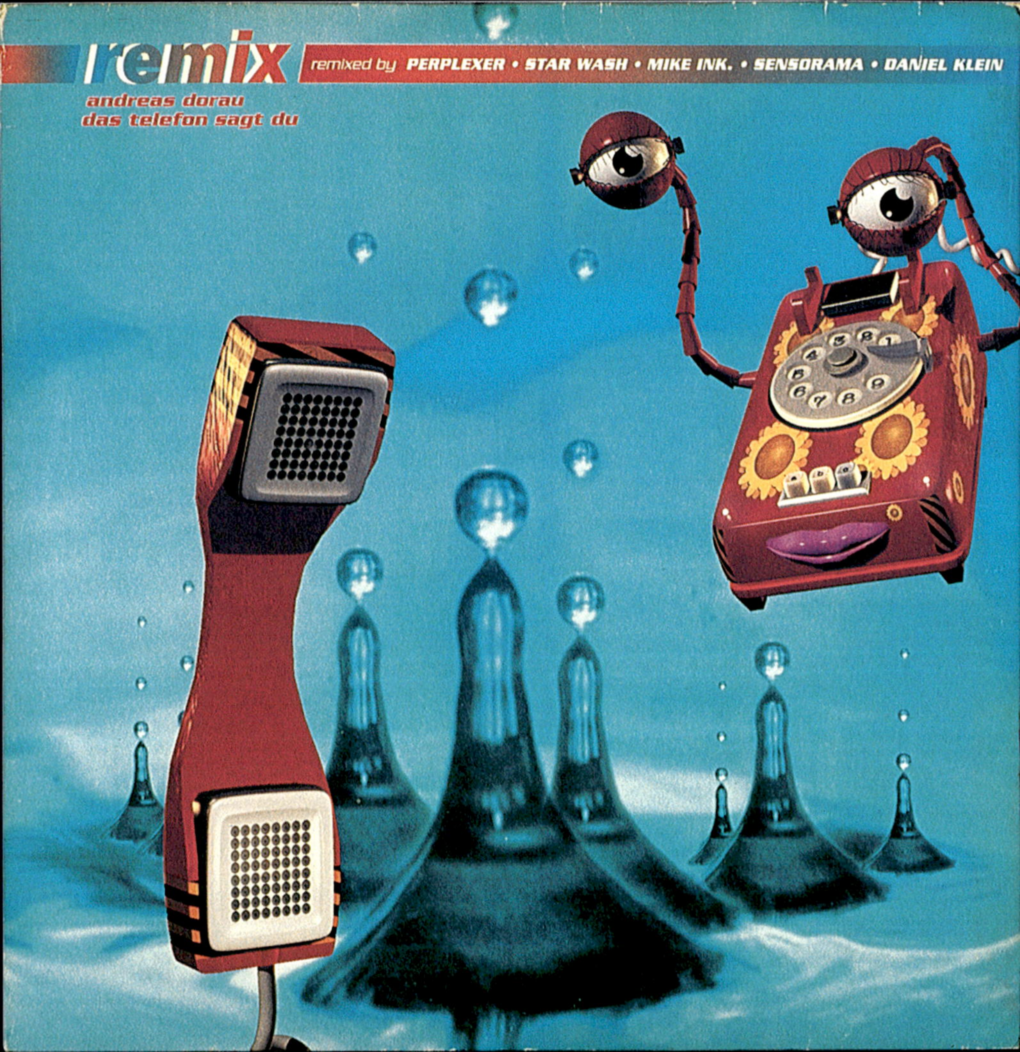

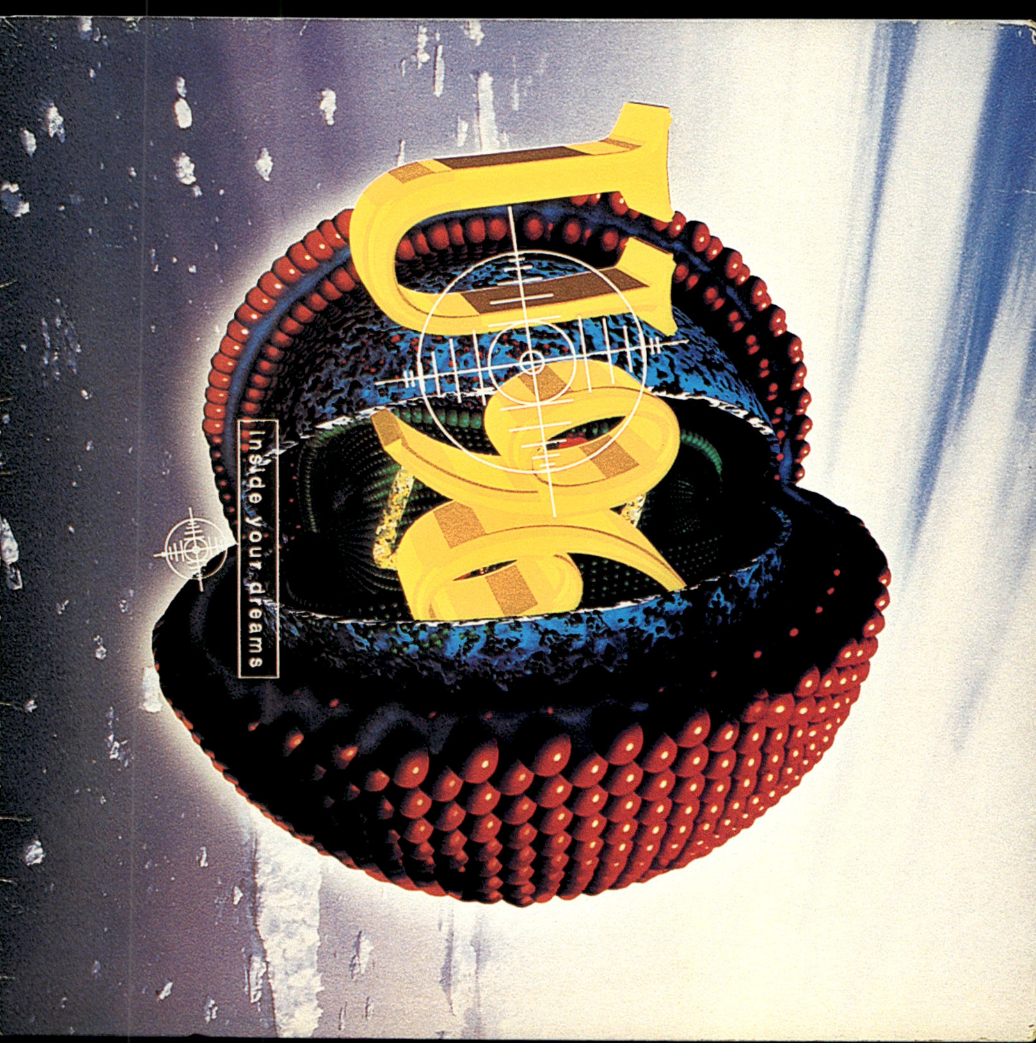

U96
inside your dreams

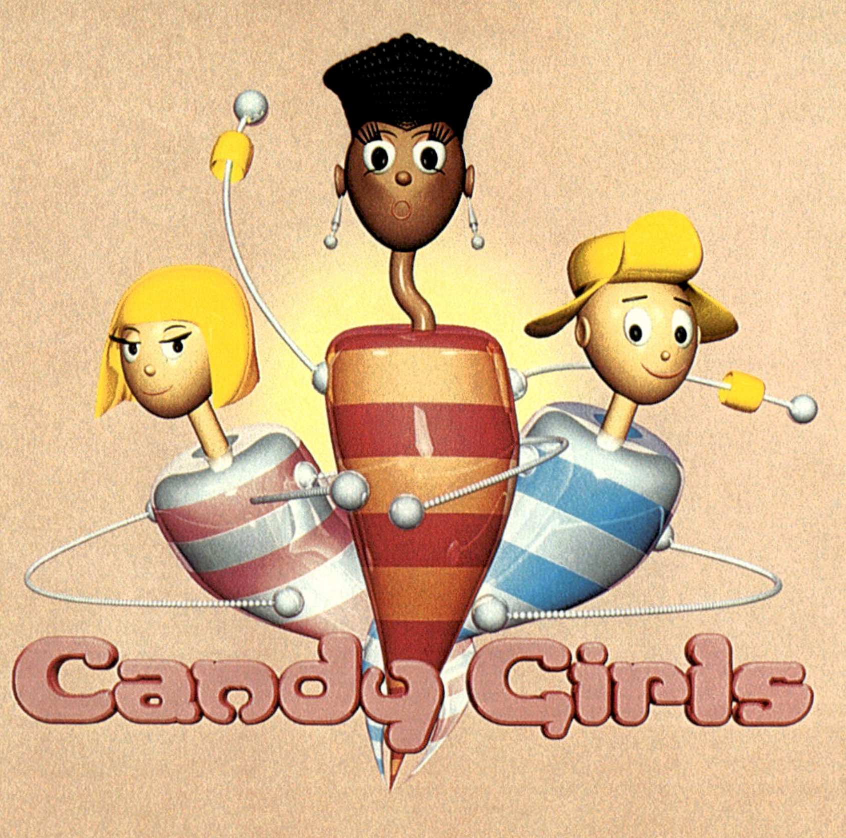
Wham Bam
Candy Girls
featuring Sweet Pussy Pauline

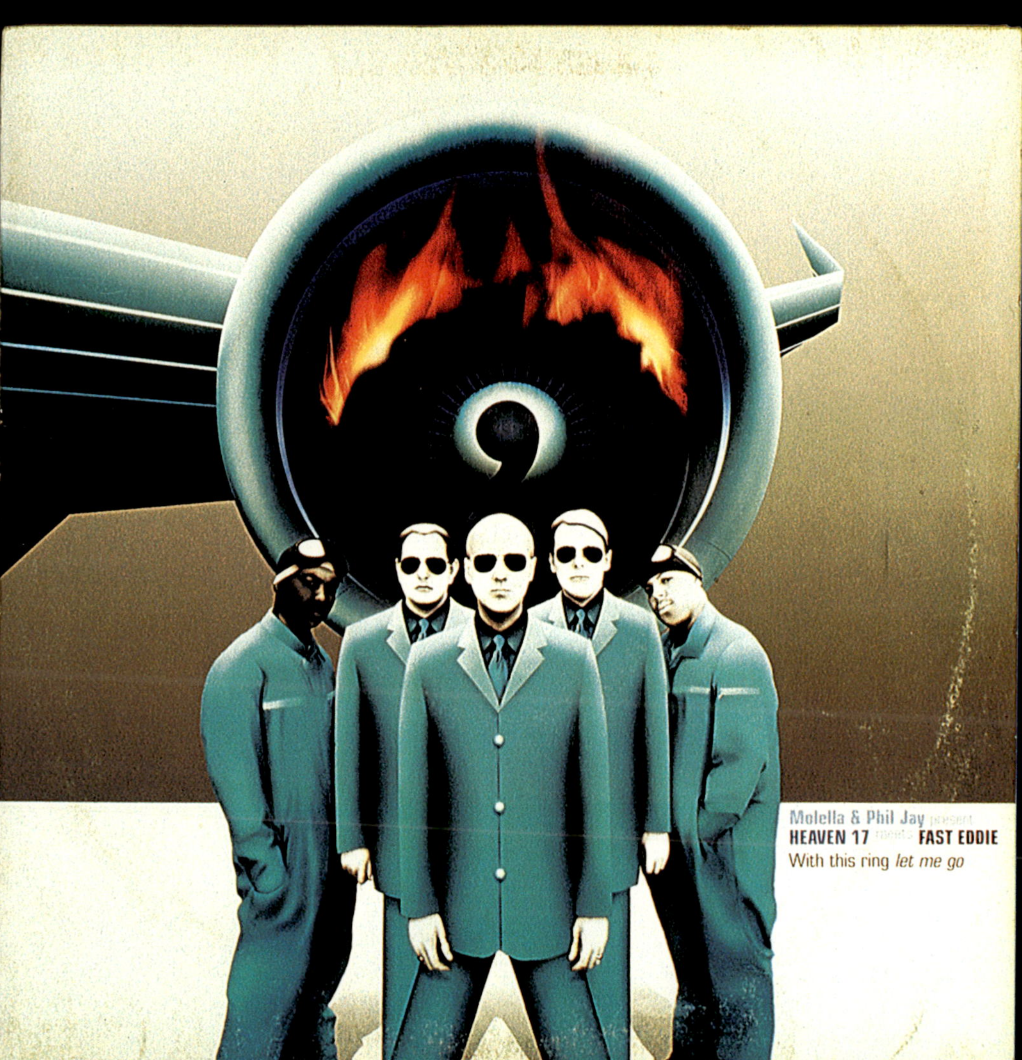
Molella & Phil Jay present
HEAVEN 17 meets FAST EDDIE
With this ring let me go

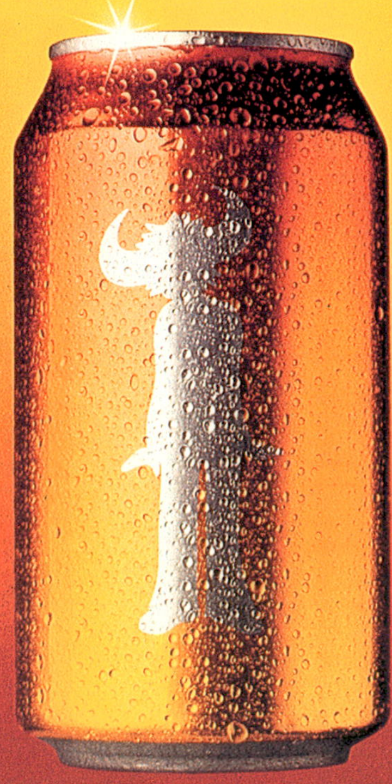
jamiroquai
CANNED HEAT

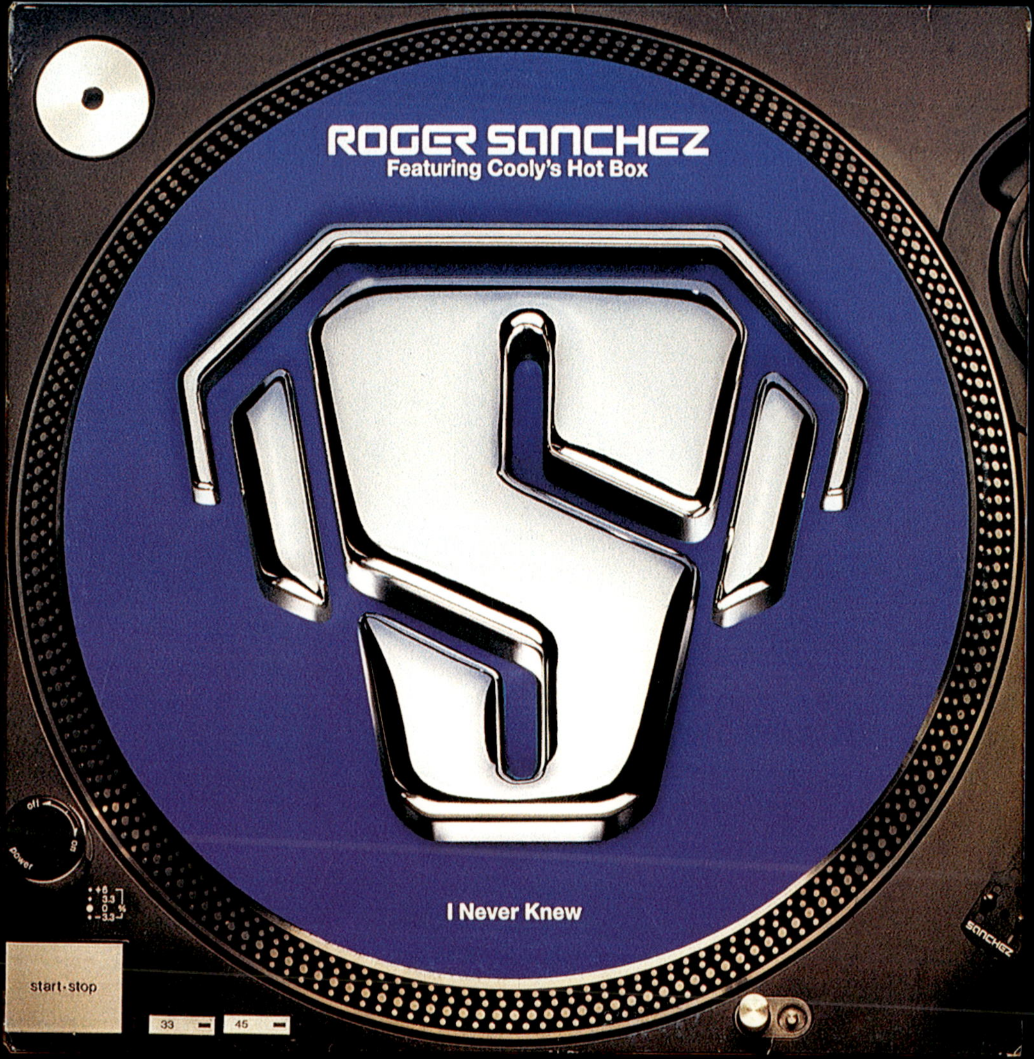

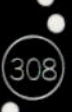

308 Artist Roger Sanchez feat. Cooly's Hot Box Title I Never Knew Record Label Sony Music Date 1999

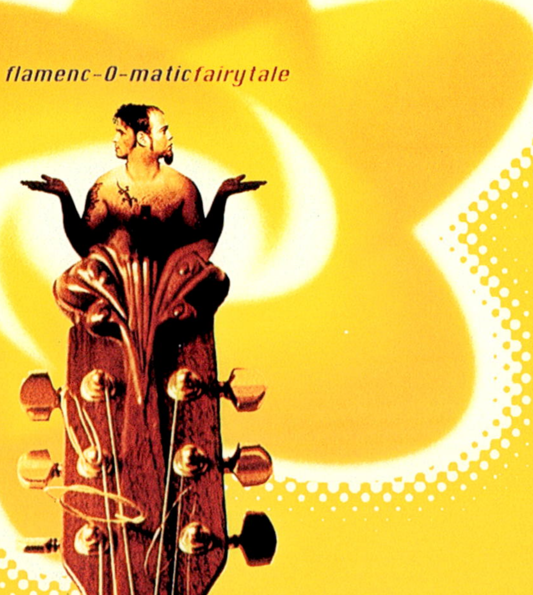

jam & spoon
RiGht iN the Night
(fall in love with music)
flamenc-0-maticfairytale

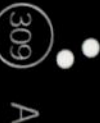

309

jam & spoon
featuring
PLAVKA
find me
ODYSSEY TO ANYOONA

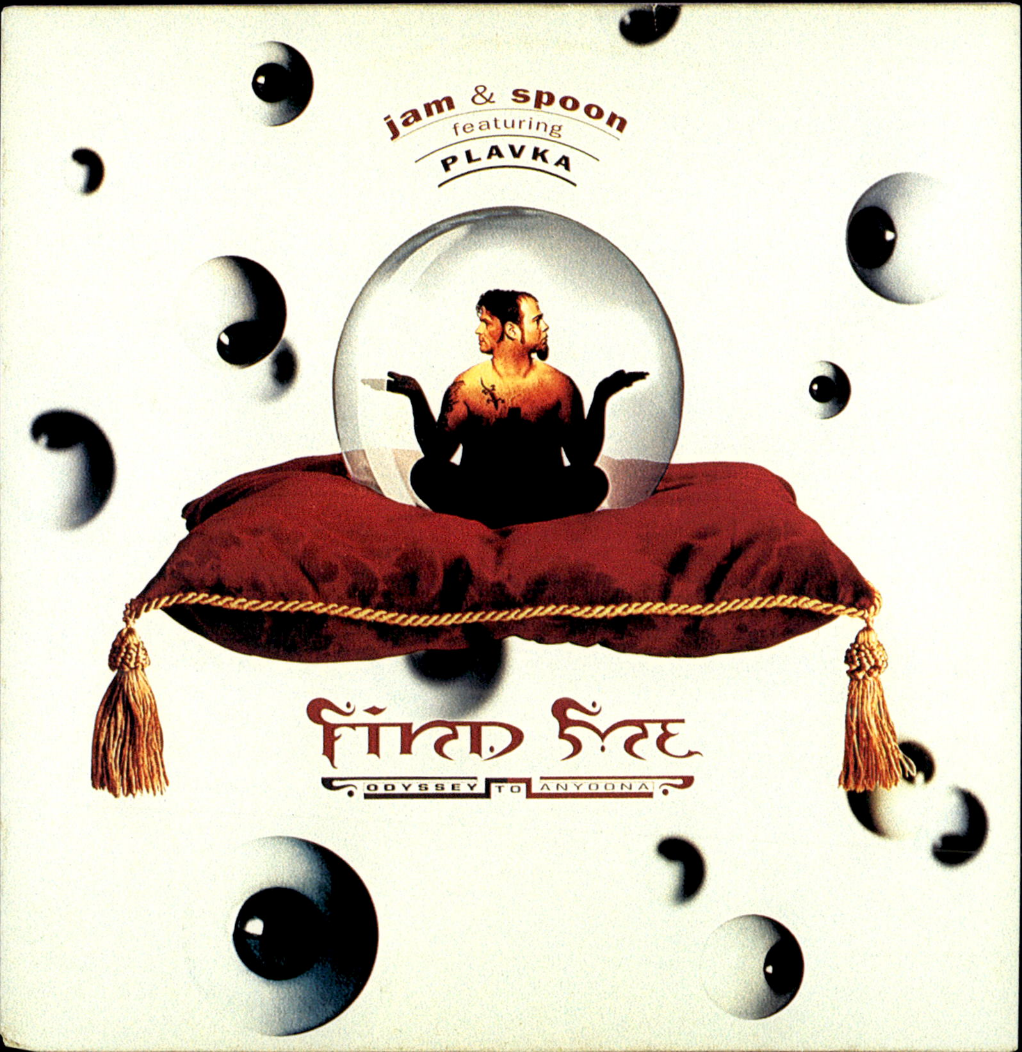

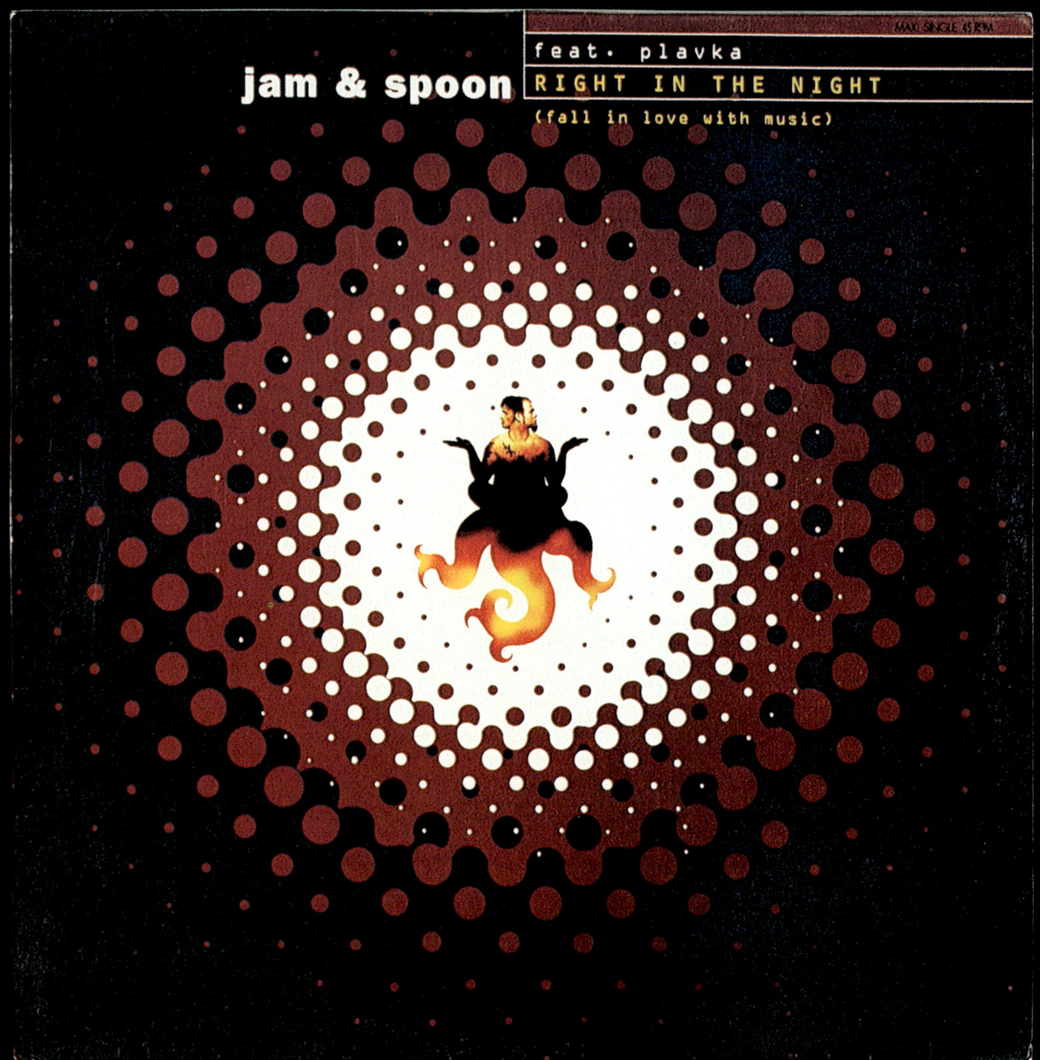

311 Artist Jam & Spoon feat. Plavka Title Right in the Night Design KM7 At Trust Record Label Sony Music Date 1993

U 9 6
U96
LOVE RELIGION

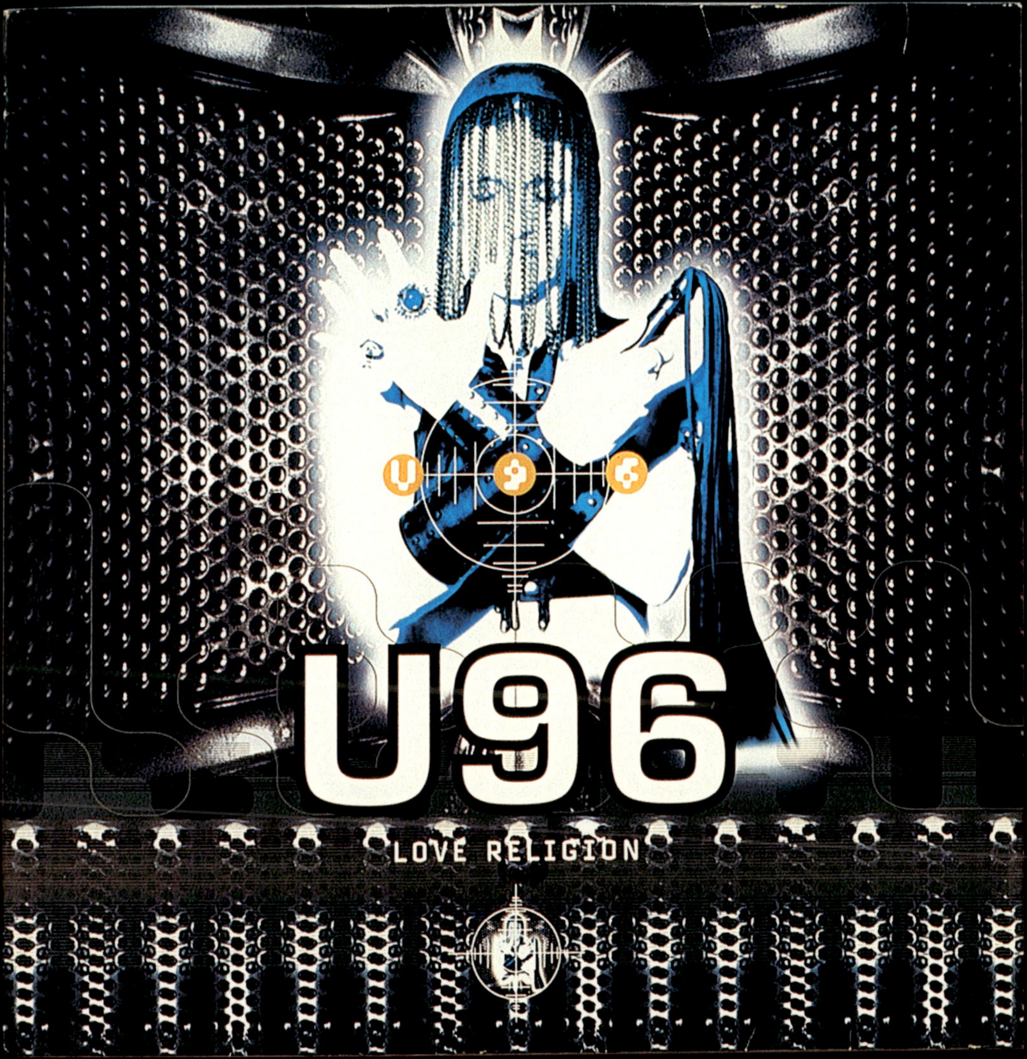

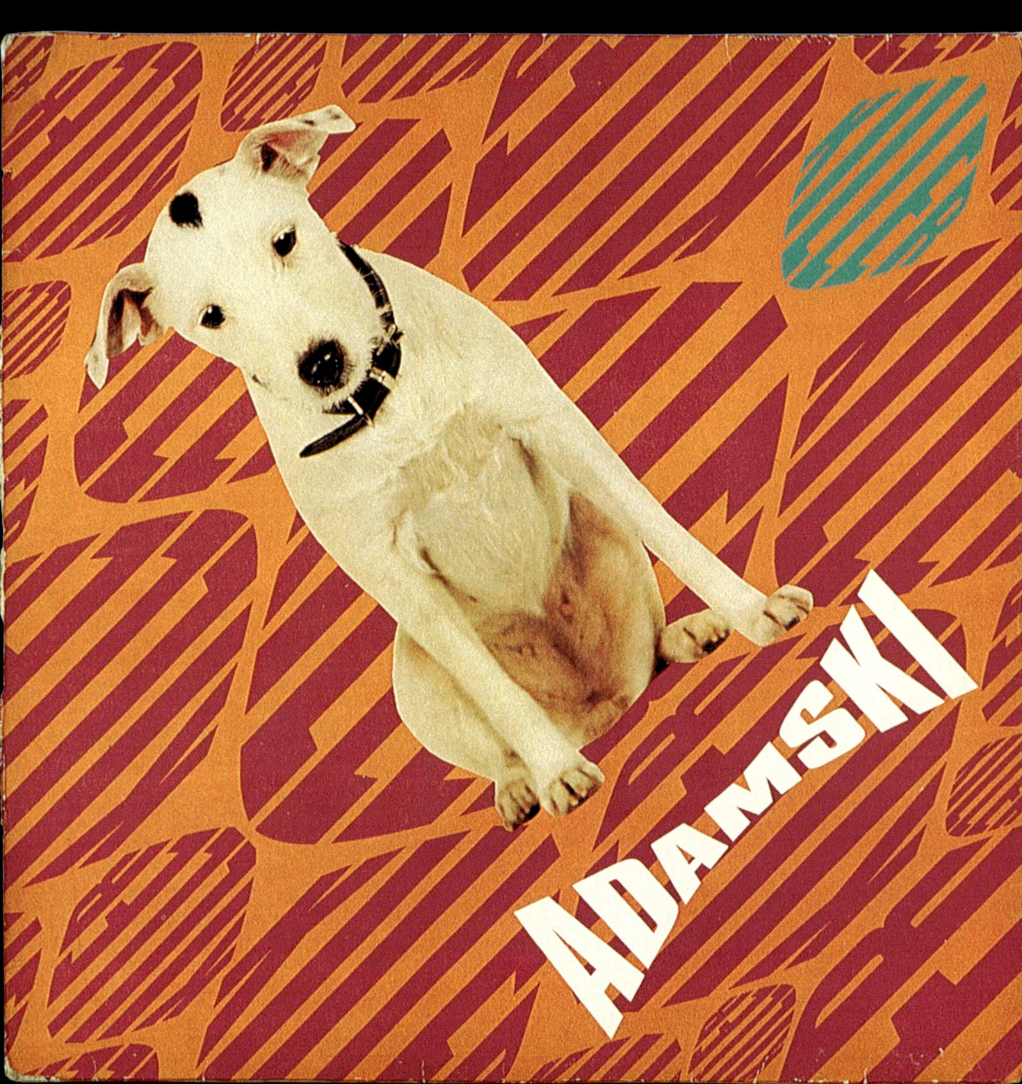
ADAMSKI

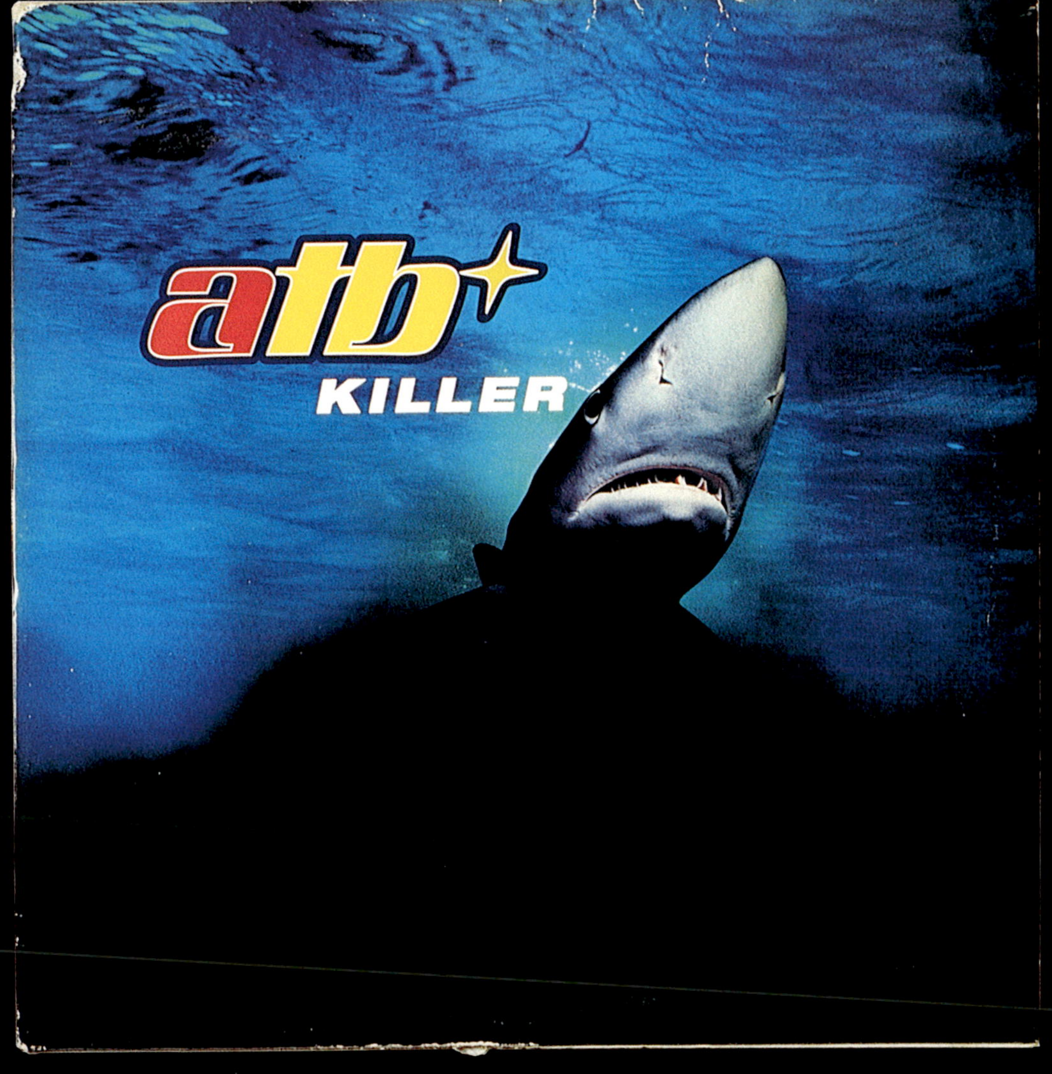

Artist ATB Title Killer Record Label Urban / Kontor Date 1999

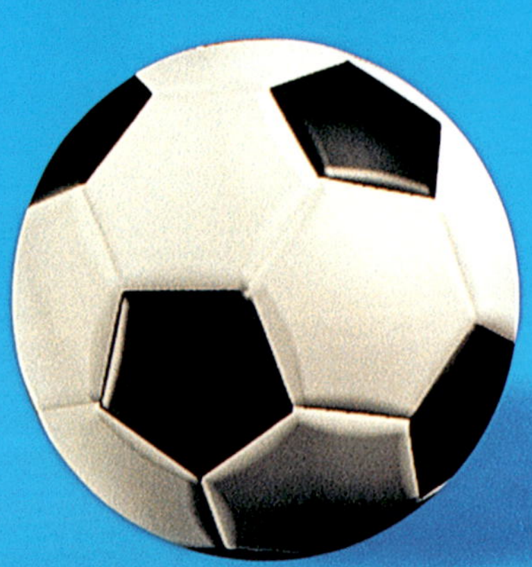

DJデロ
DjDero
BatucadaN°3
Showtime

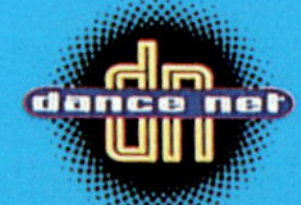

dance net

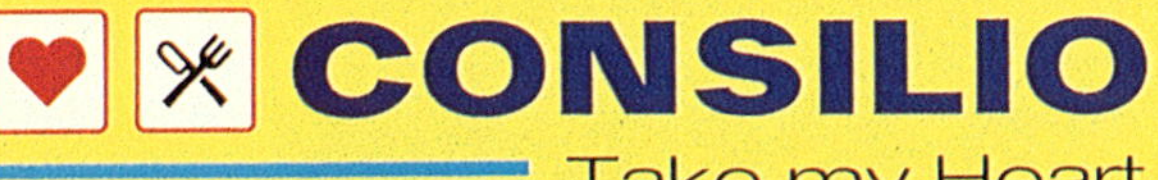
CONSILIO
Take my Heart

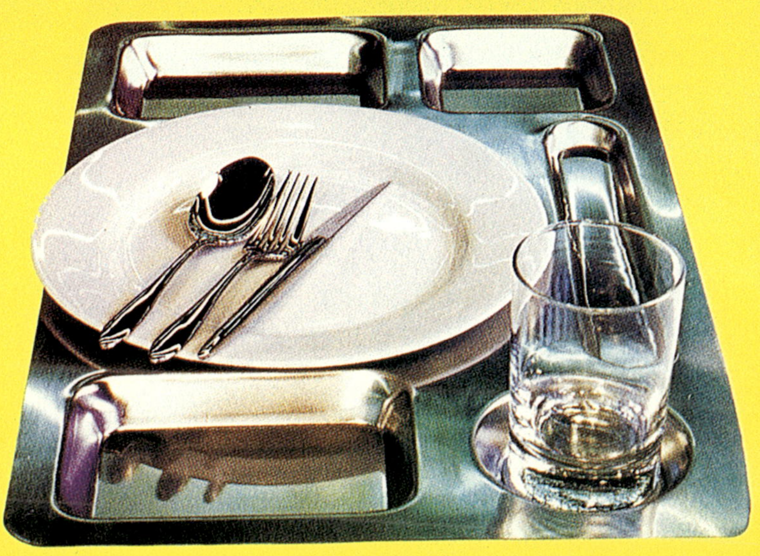

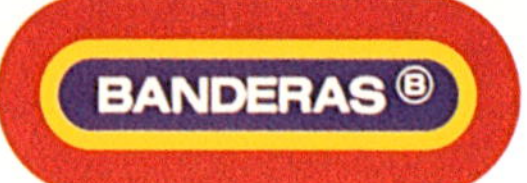
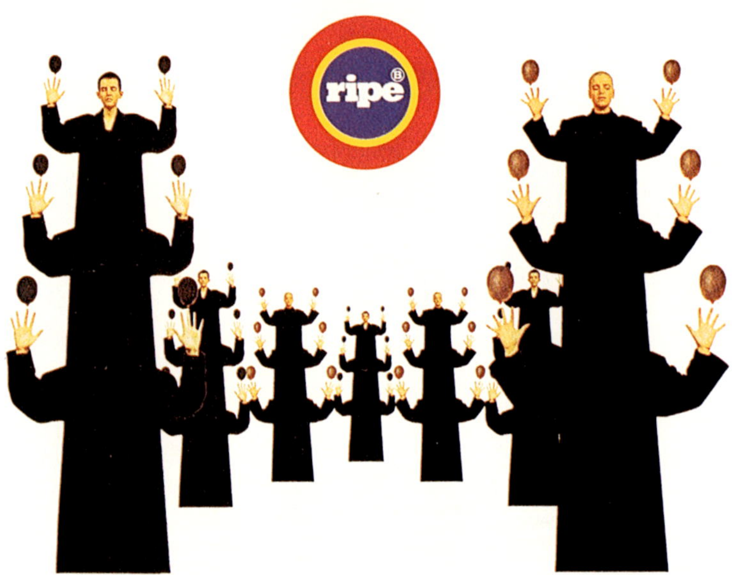

BANDERAS
ripe

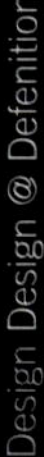

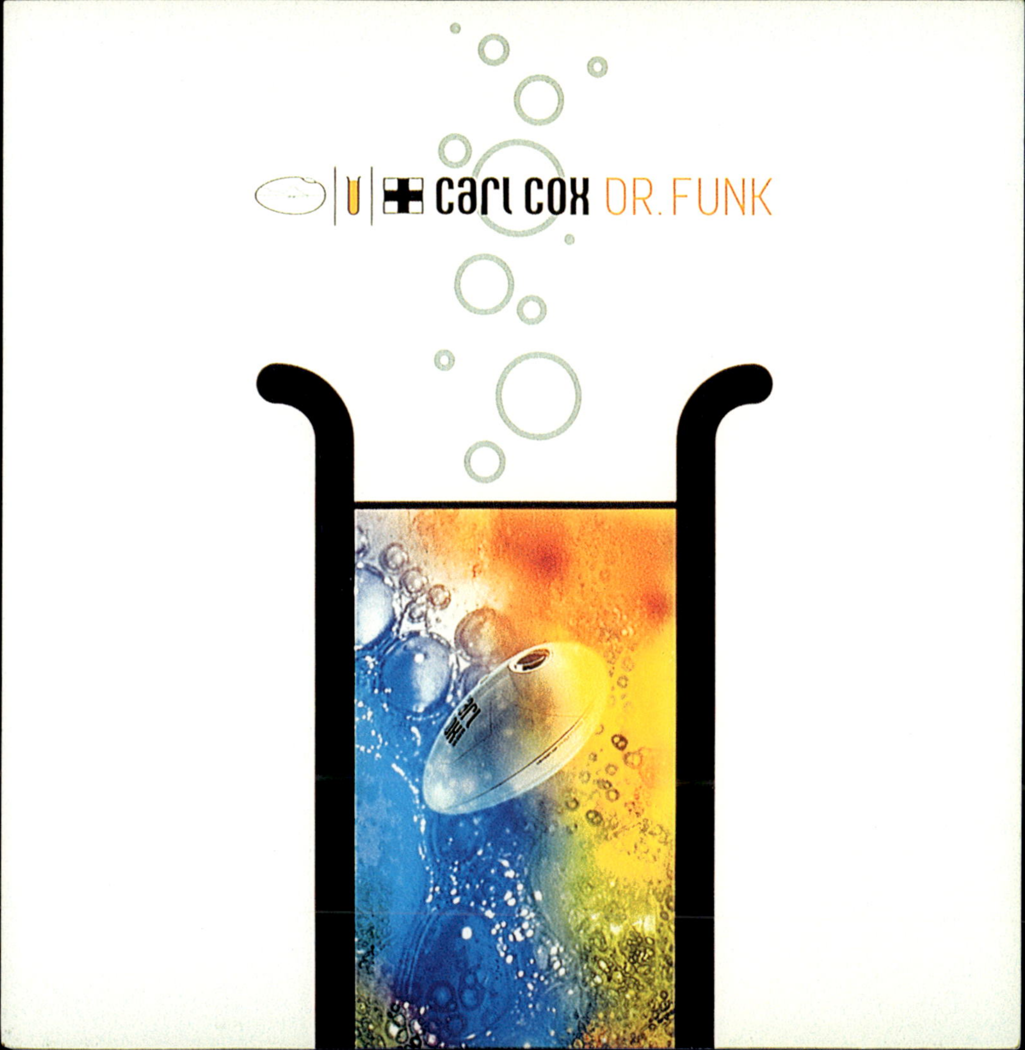

carl cox DR. FUNK

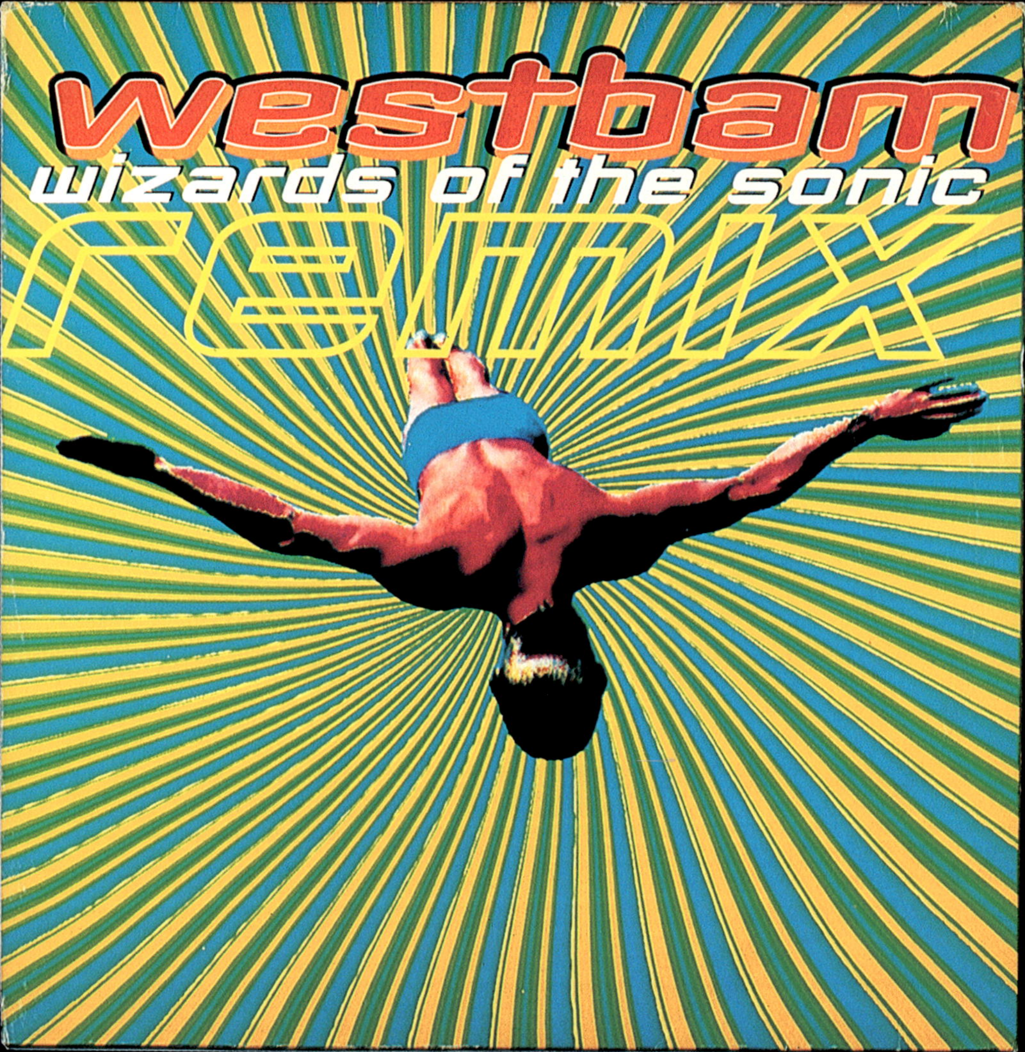

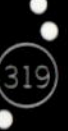

westbam
wizards of the sonic
remix

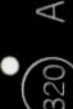

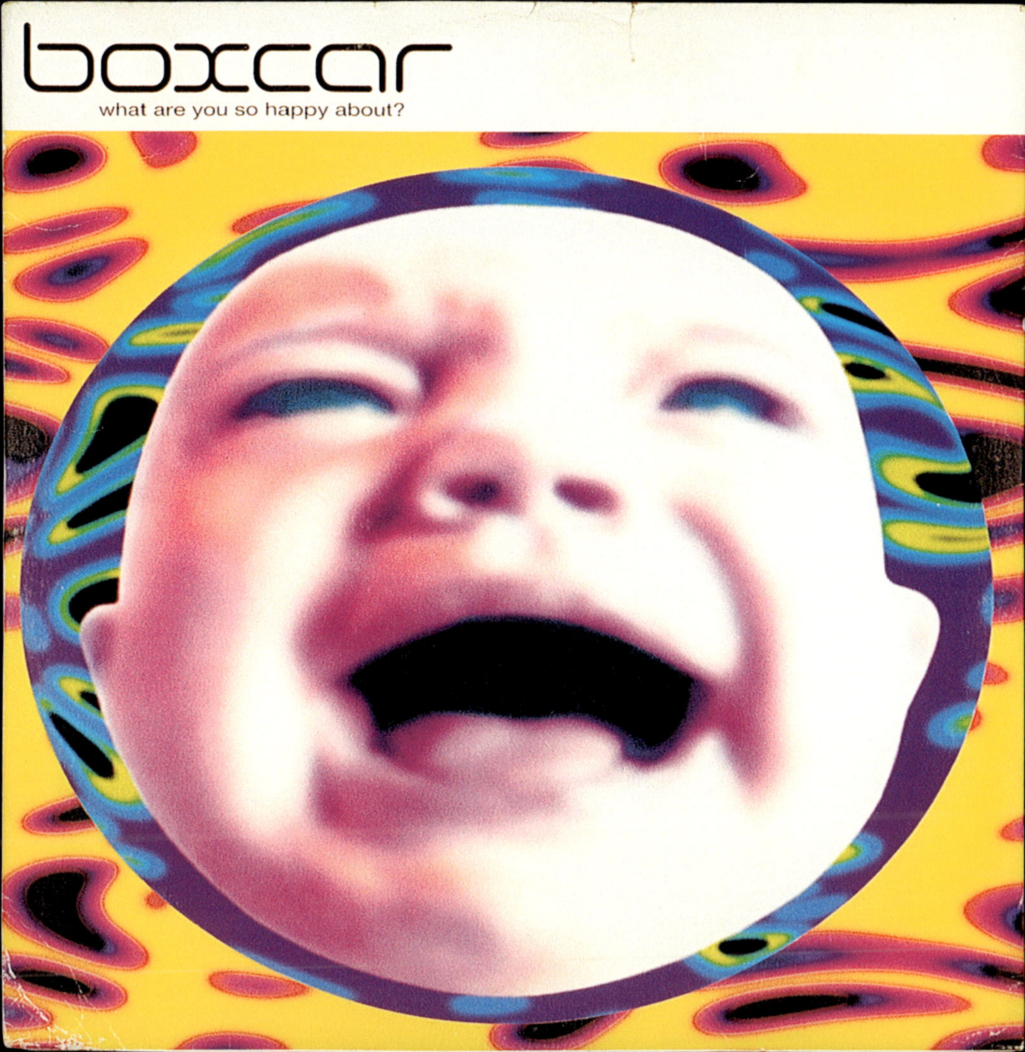

boxcar

what are you so happy about?

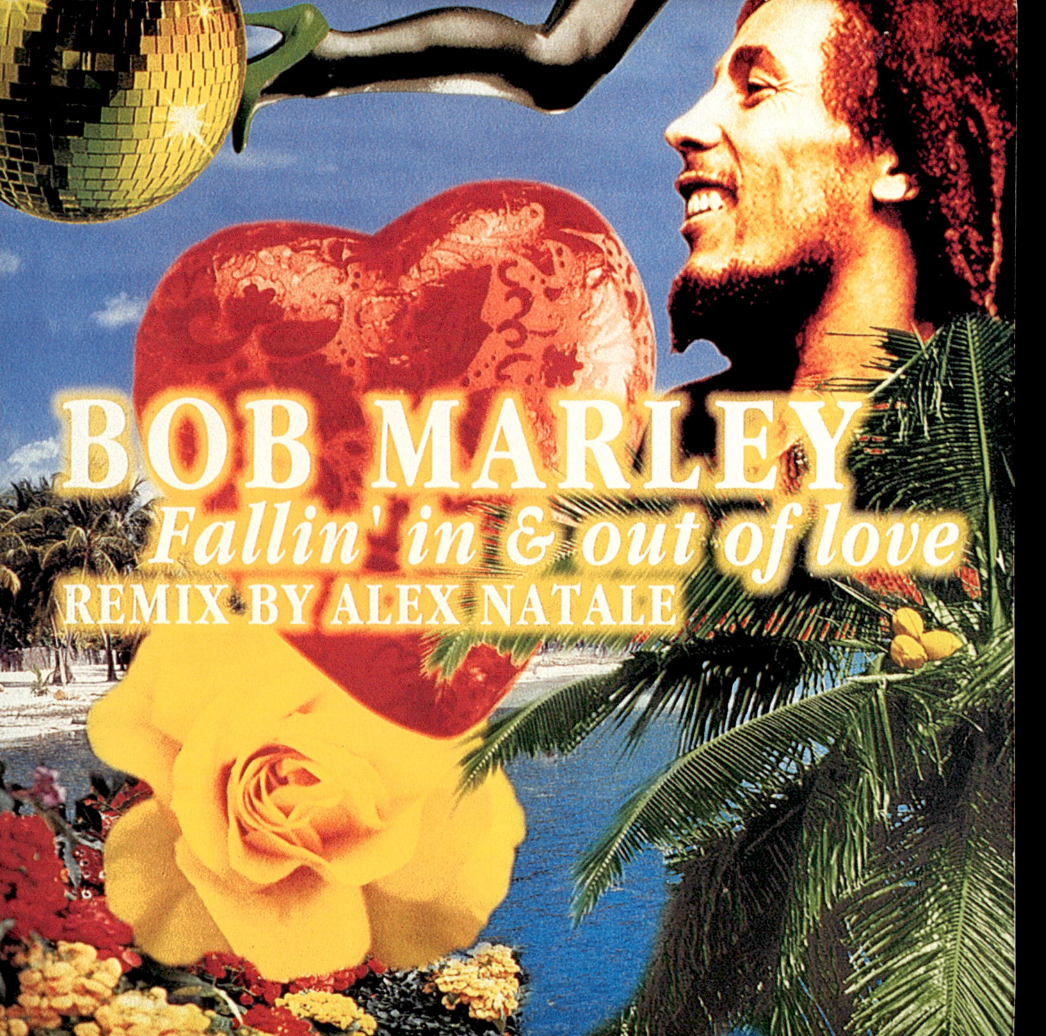
321
Artist Bob Marley Title Fallin' In & Out of Love Computer Graphics Andrea Cappelletti Design Giuseppe Spaba
Record Label Dance Factory Date 1997
BOB MARLEY
Fallin' in & out of love
REMIX BY ALEX NATALE

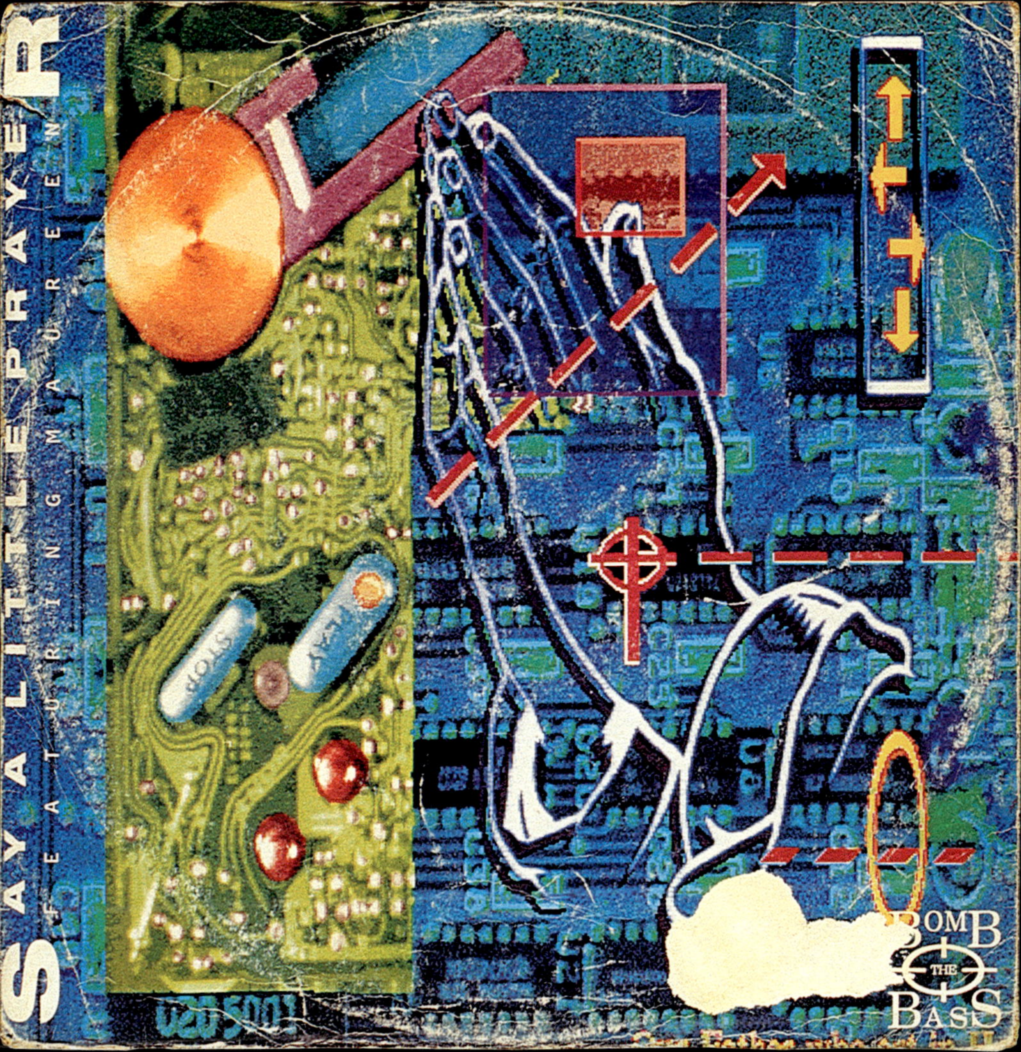

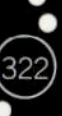

Artist Bomb The Bass feat. Maureen Title Say a Little Prayer Design Ian Mac Photography David Little, Alex Quero Record Label Rhythm King Date 1989

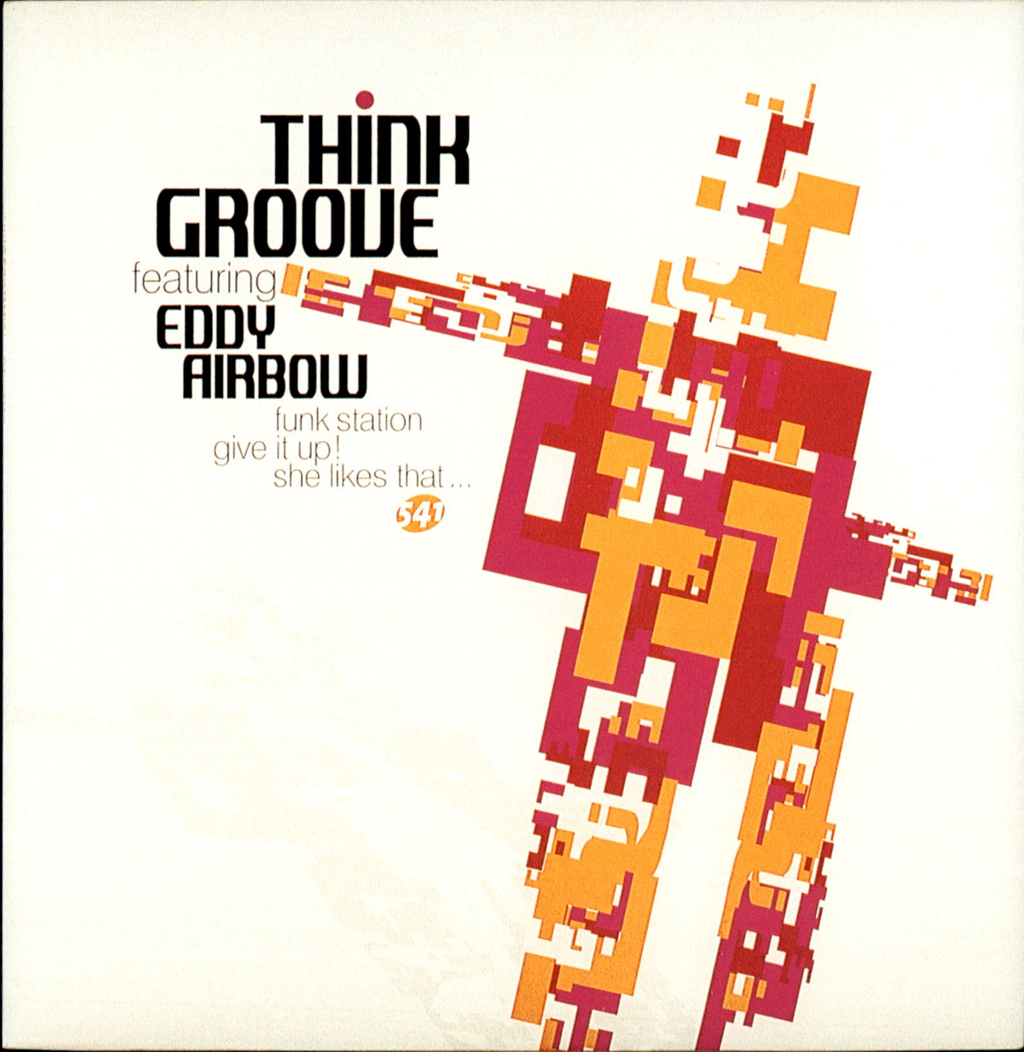

THINK
GROOVE
featuring
EDDY
AIRBOW
funk station
give it up!
she likes that ...
541

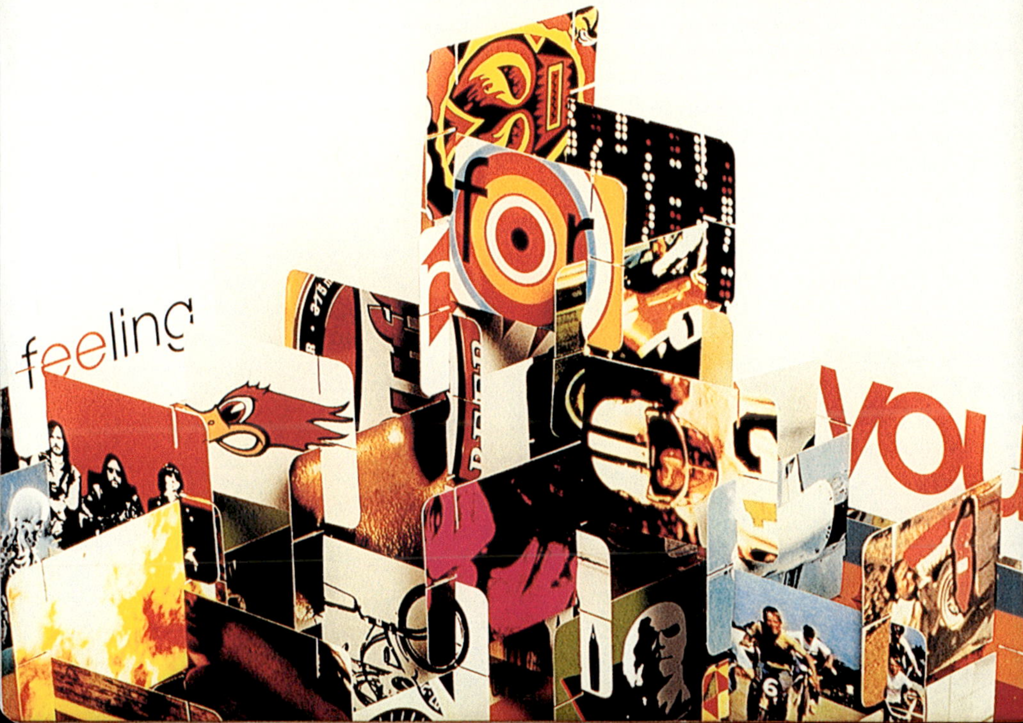
CASSIUS
feeling
you

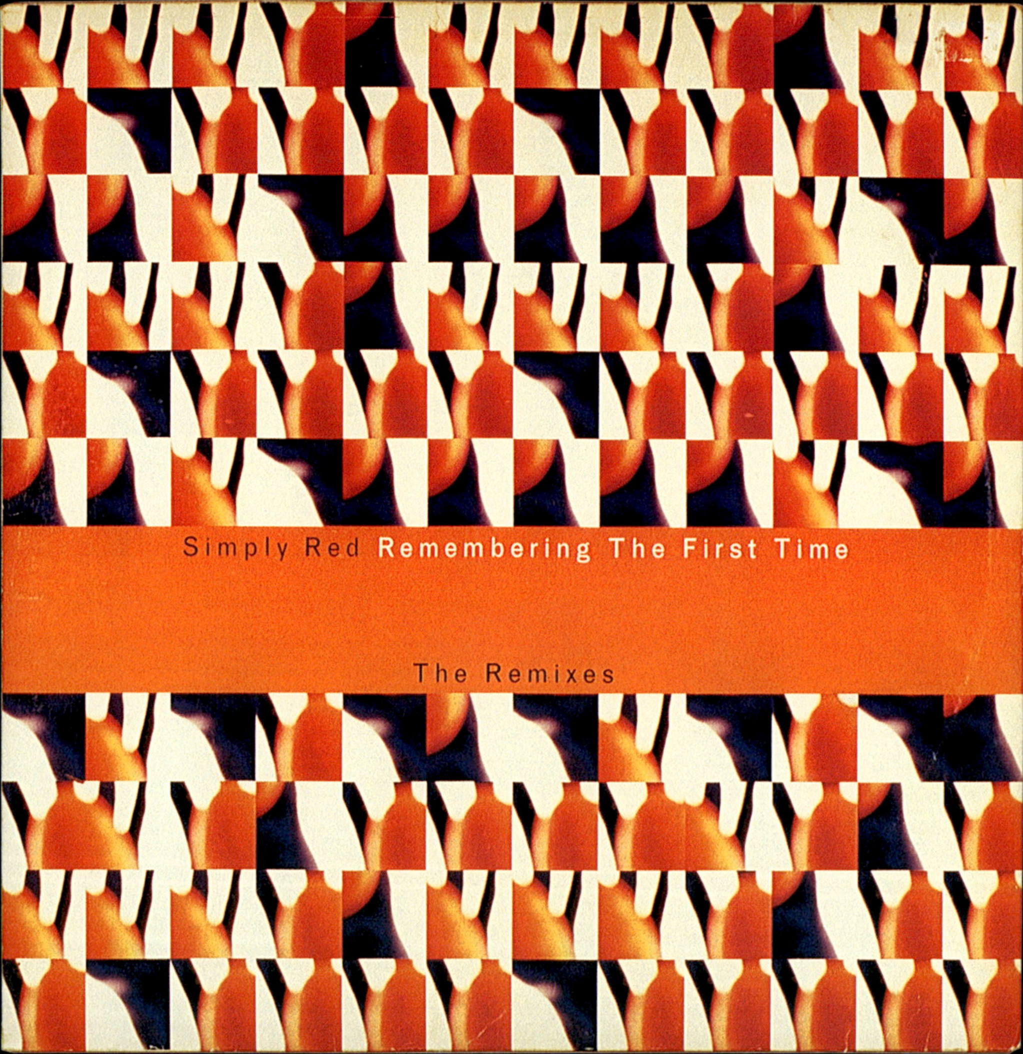

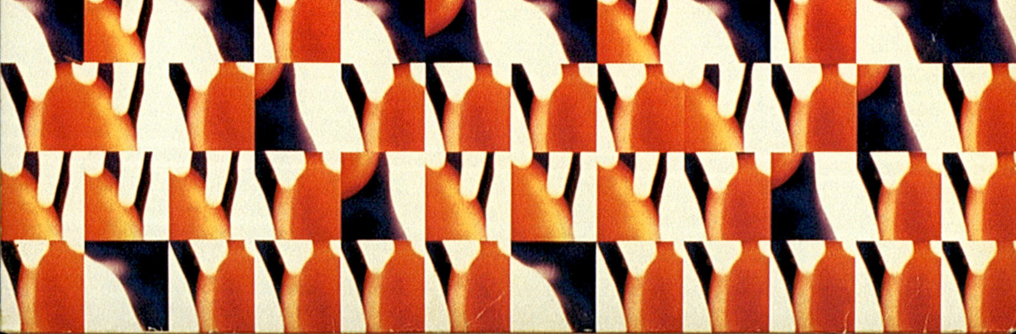

Simply Red Remembering The First Time
The Remixes

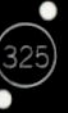

FREAK POWER • RUSH

Artist Freak Power Title Rush Design Island Records Record Label Island Records Date 1994

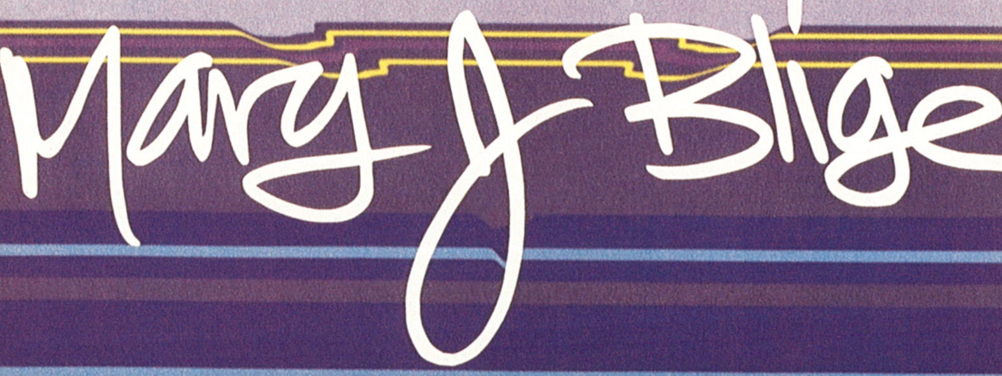

Mary J. Blige

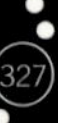

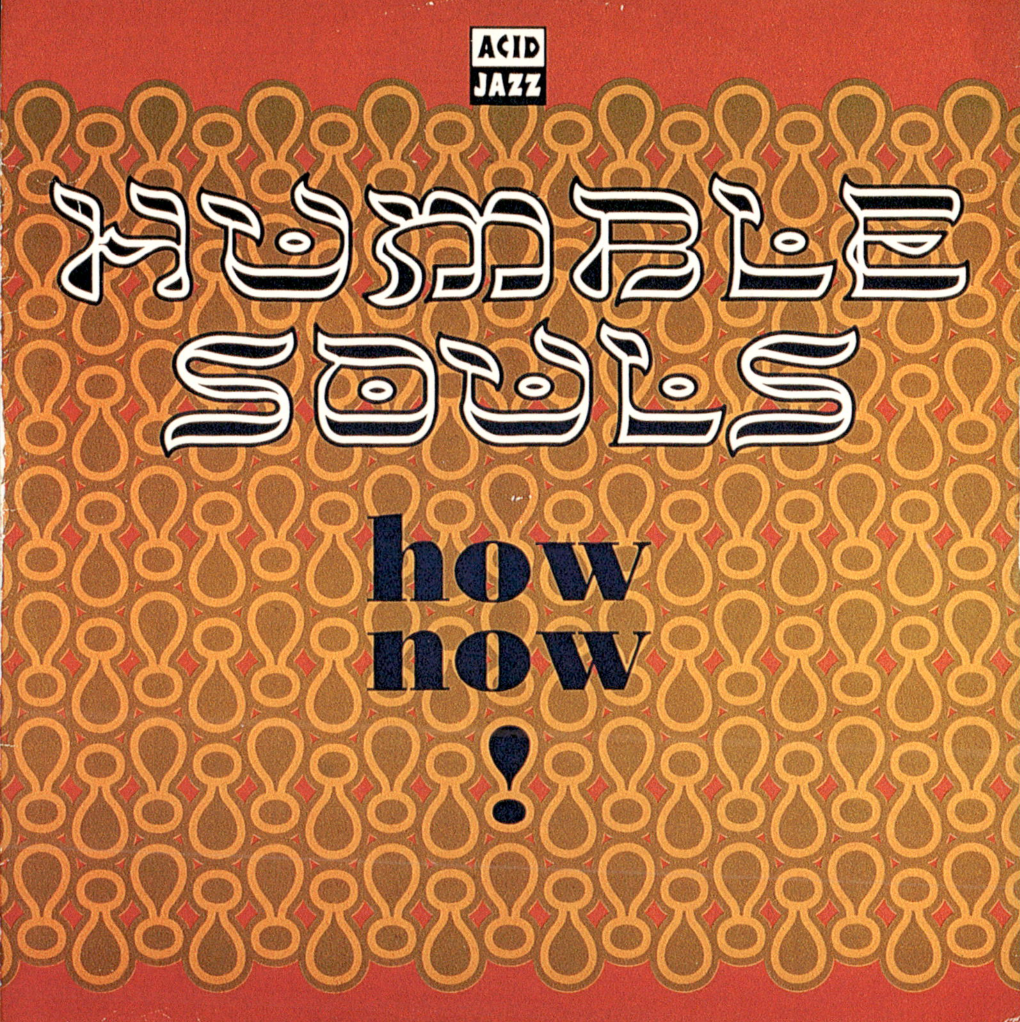
ACID
JAZZ
HUMBLE
SOULS
how
now
!

U2
mysterious WAYS

U2 LEMON
REMIXES
Artist U2 Title Lemon Record Label Island Records Date 1993
330

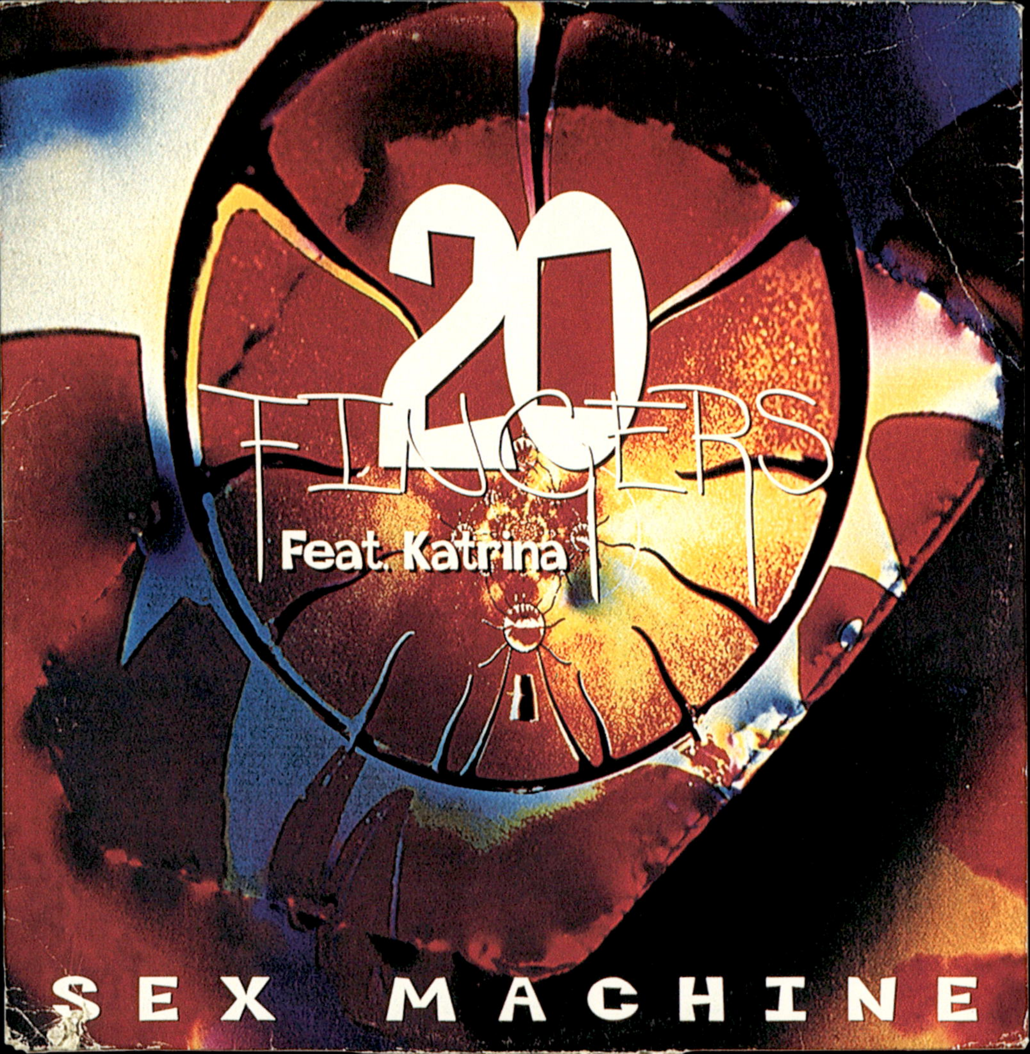

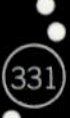

20
FINGERS
Feat. Katrina
SEX MACHINE

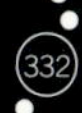

Depeche Mode
Songs of faith
and devotion
LIVE

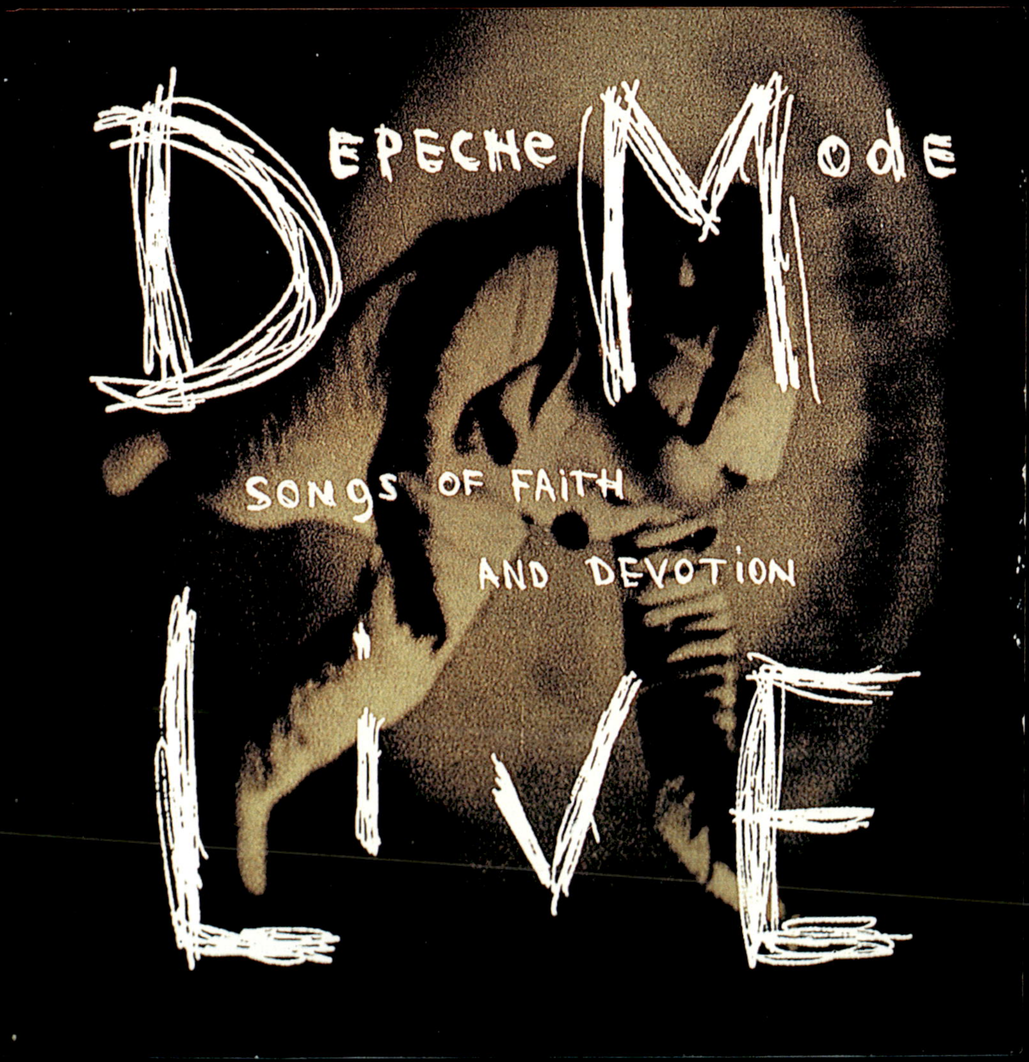

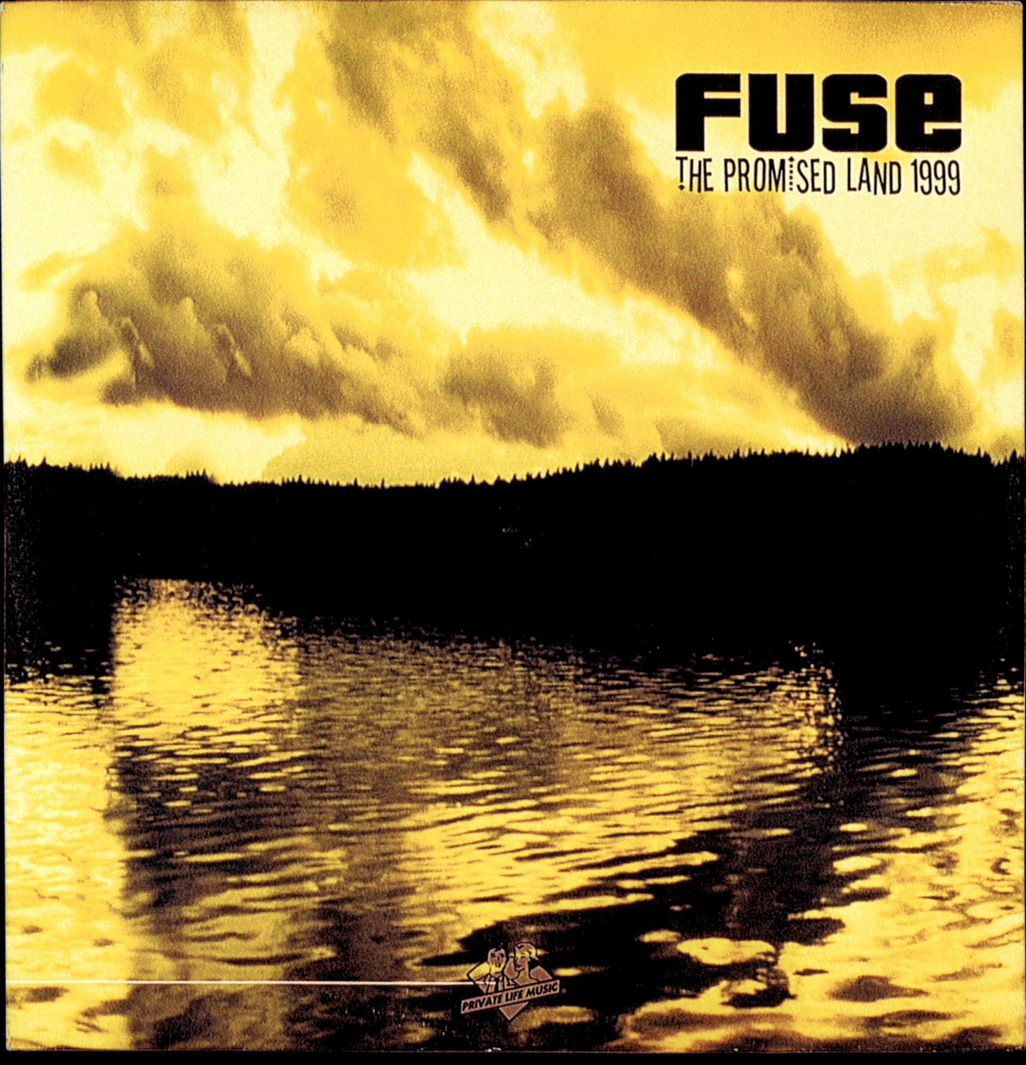

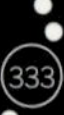

Artist Fuse Title The Promised Land 1999 Record Label Private Life Music Date 1999

Artist Brooklyn Funk Essentials Title The Creator Has a Master Plan Design Stuart Patterson At Hygiene Photography Andrea C. Davis Record Label Groovetown Date 1995

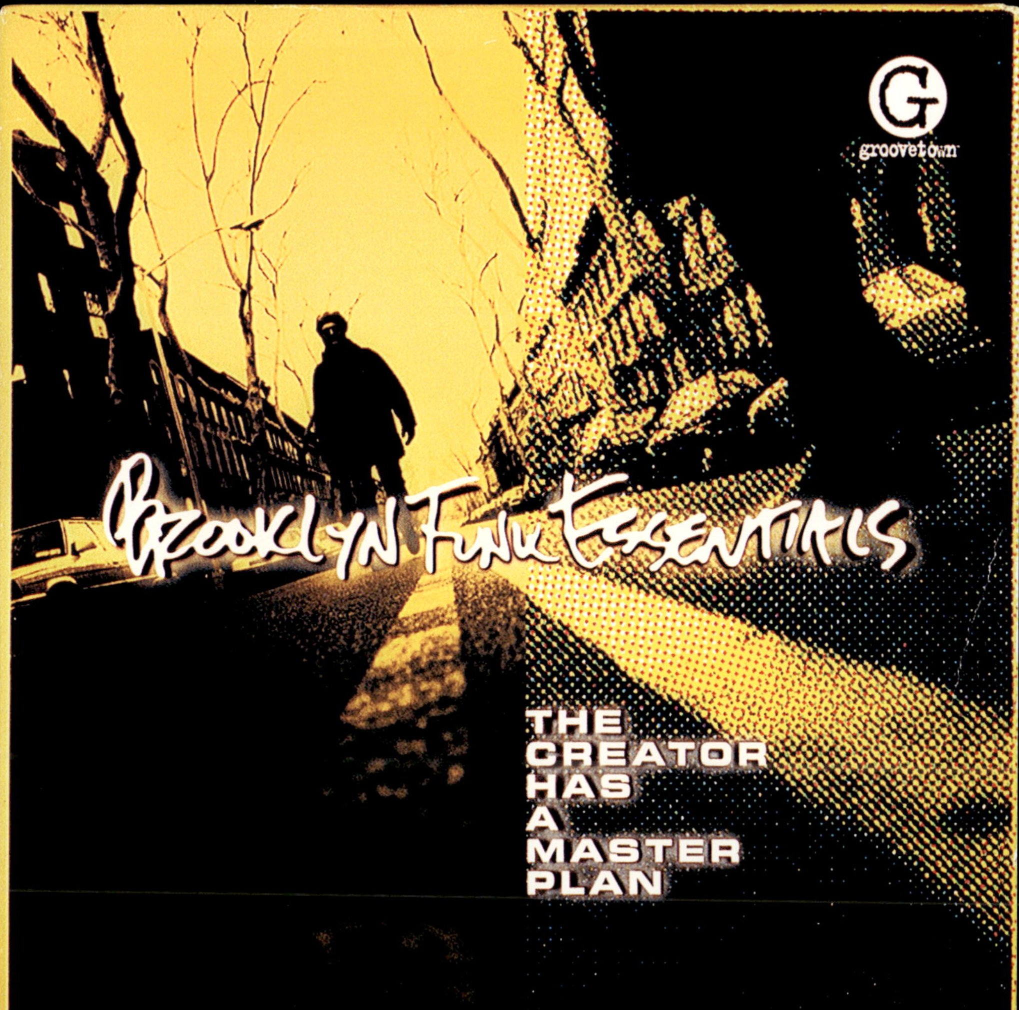

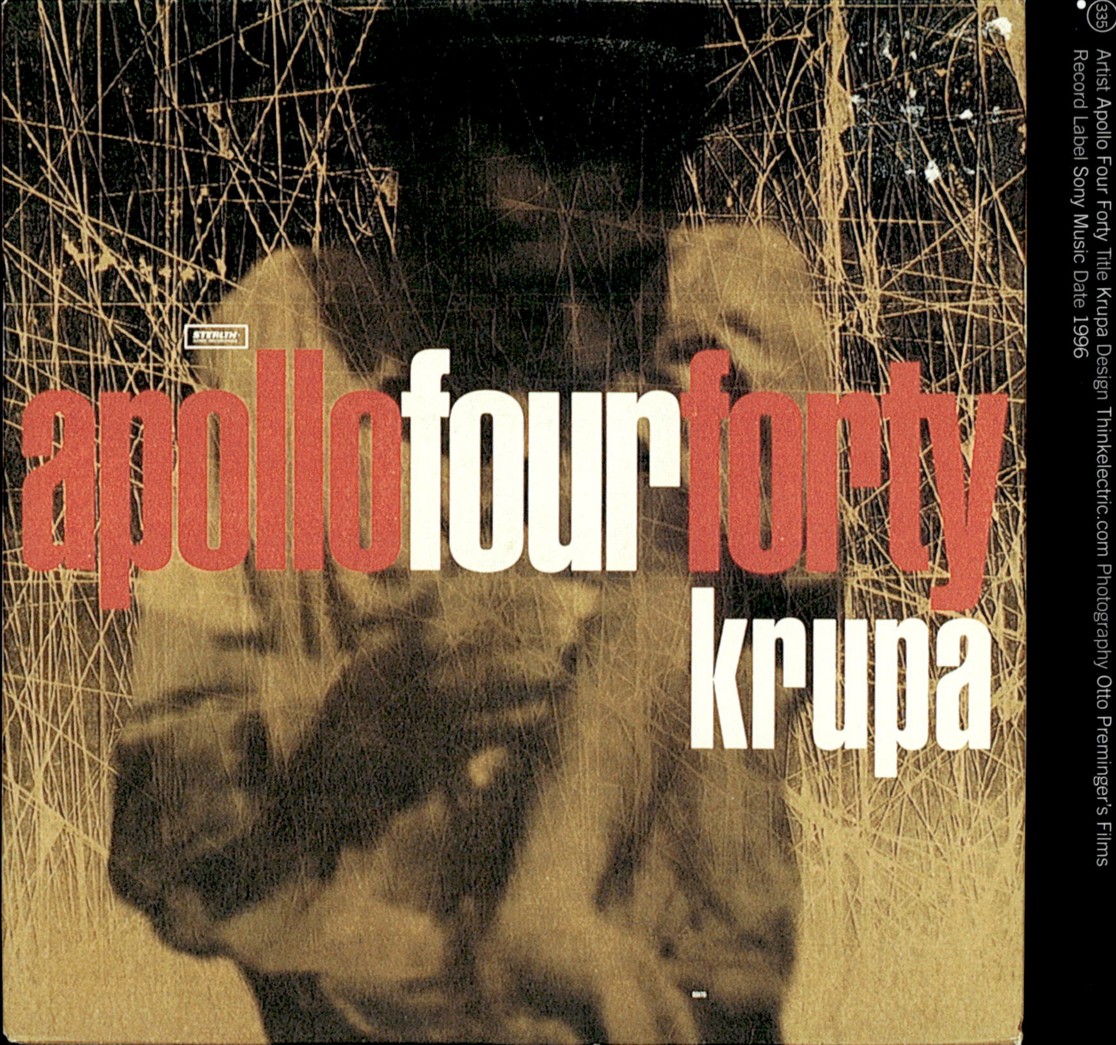

335
Artist Apollo Four Forty Title Krupa Design Thinkelectric.com Photography Otto Preminger's Films
Record Label Sony Music Date 1996

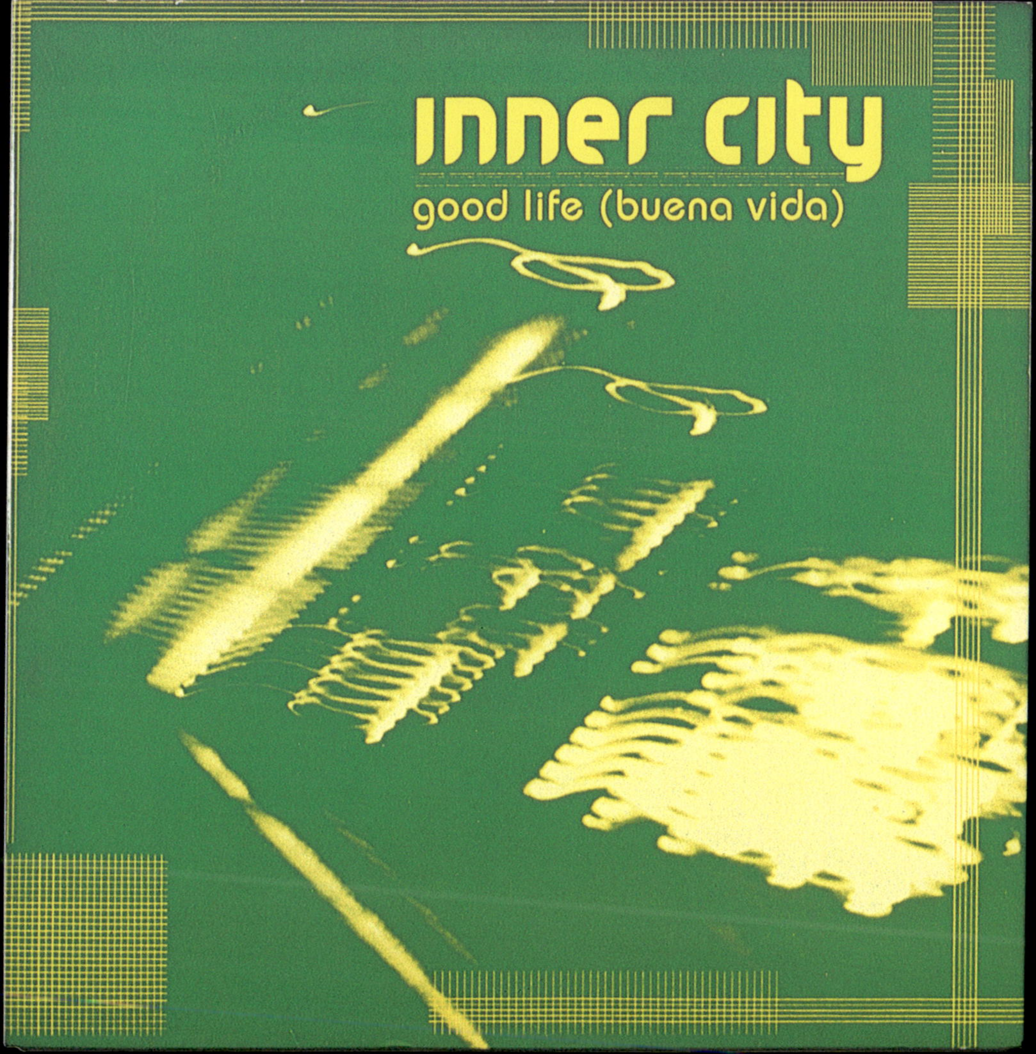

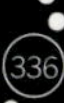

inner city
good life (buena vida)

Artist **Oasis** Title **Live Forever** Design **Brian Cannon** for **Microdot** Photography **Michael Spencer Jones**
Record Label **Creation Records** Date **1994**

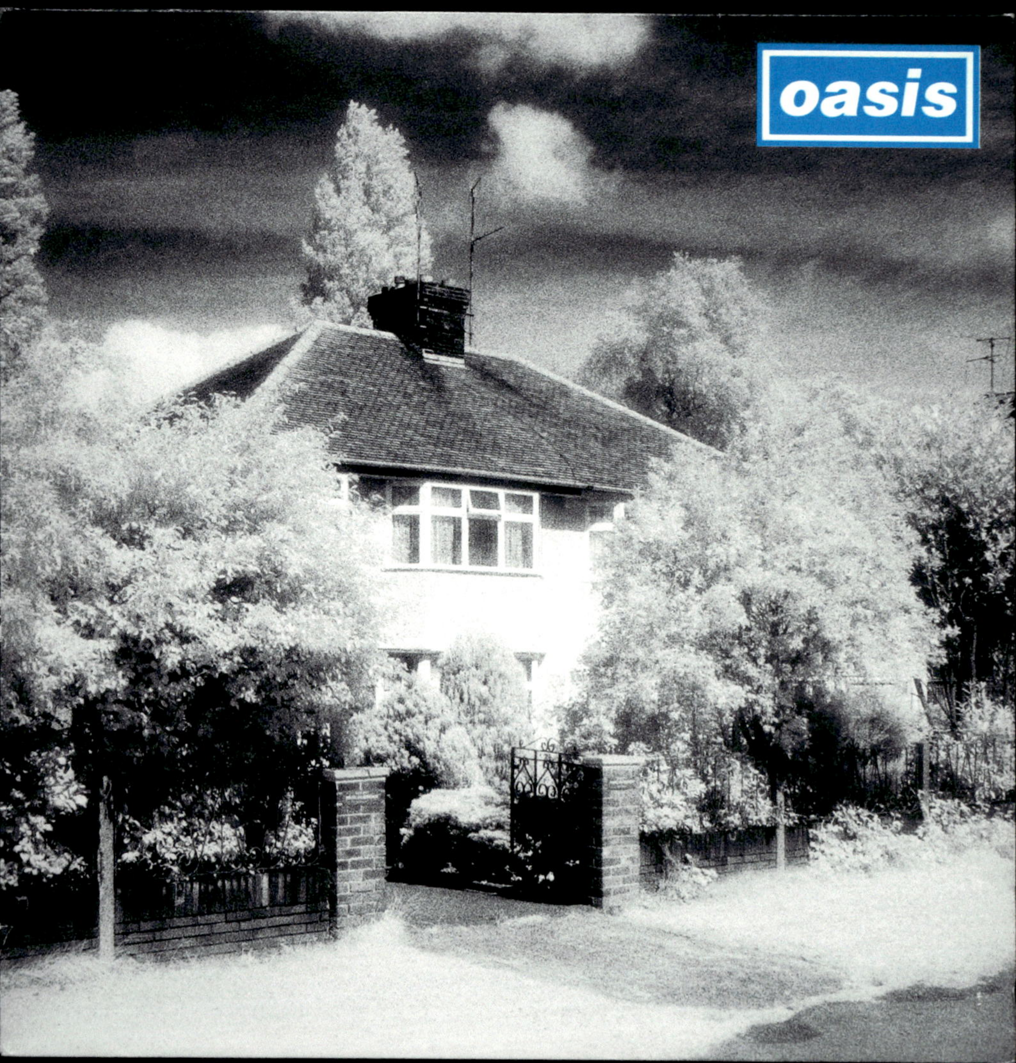

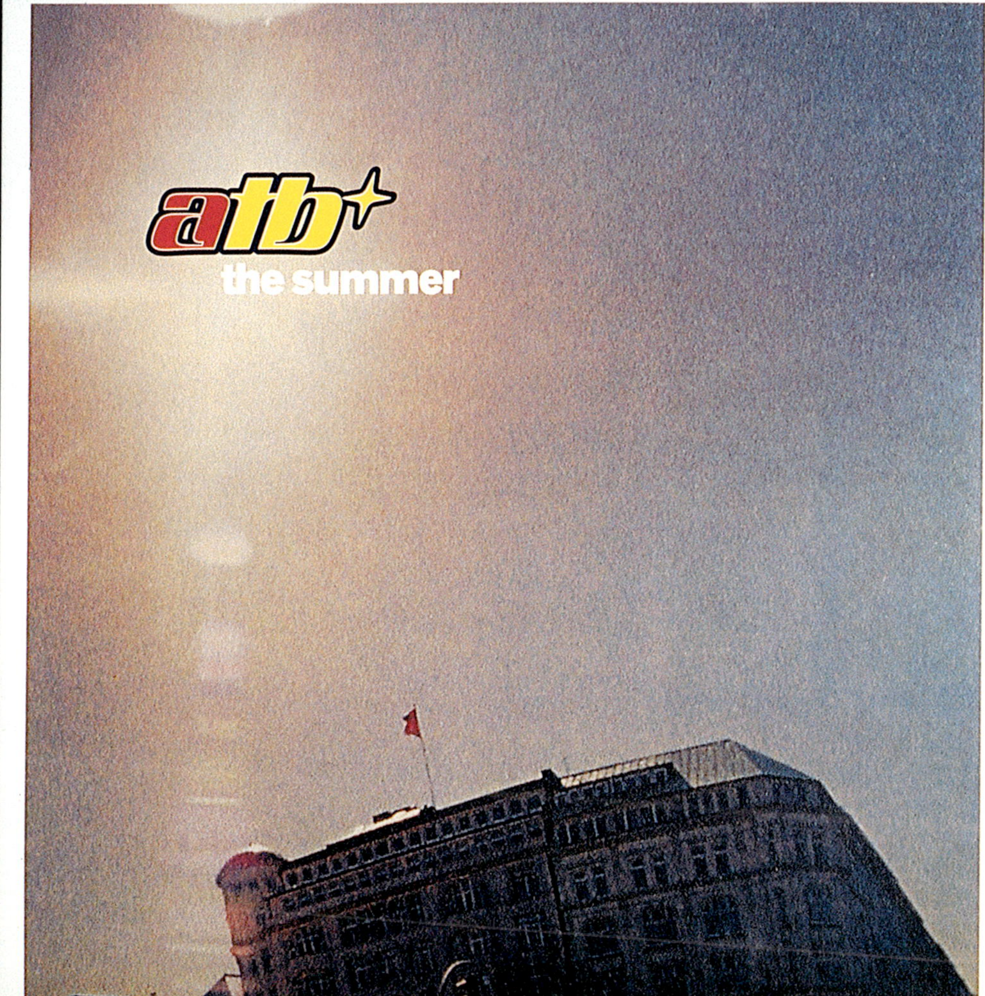

atb
the summer

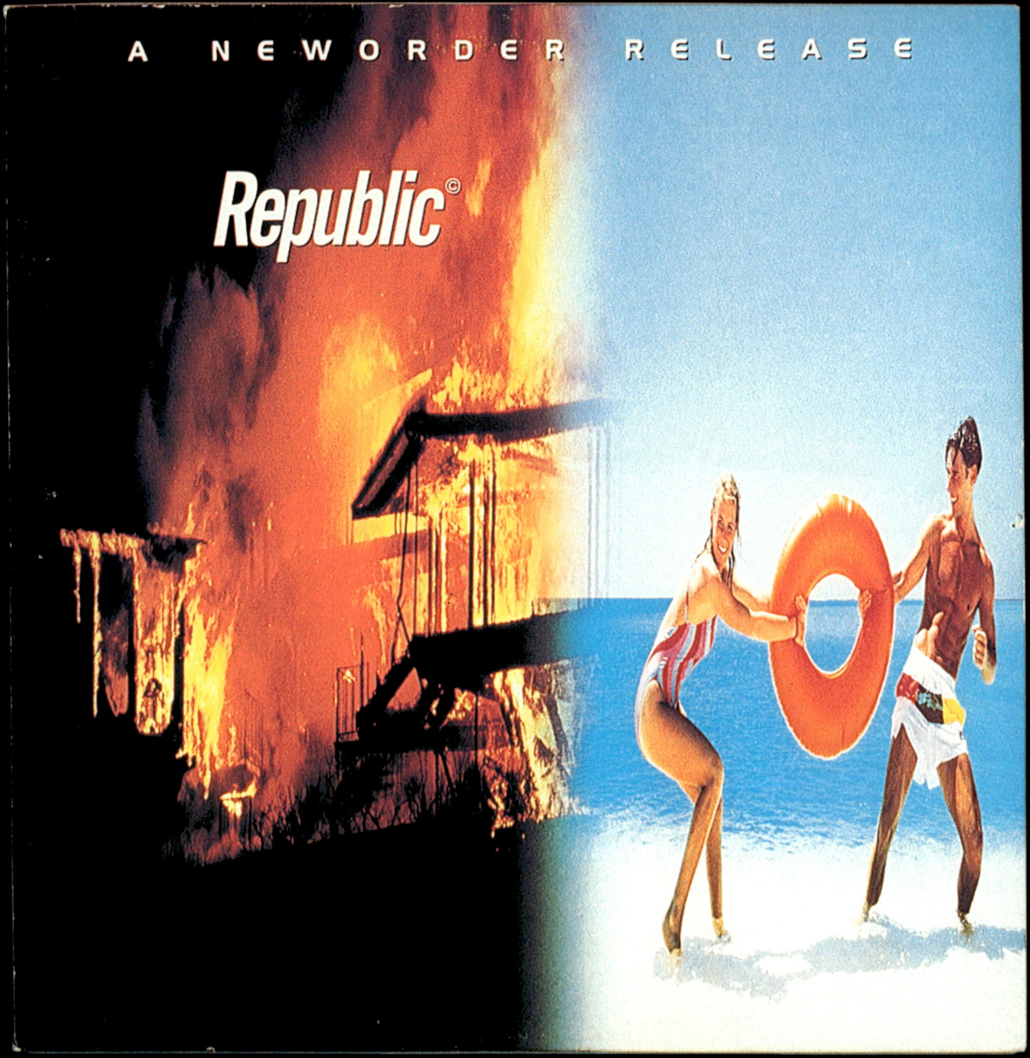

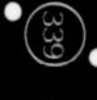

A NEW ORDER RELEASE
Republic©

Artist New Order Title Republic Record Label London Recordings Date 1993

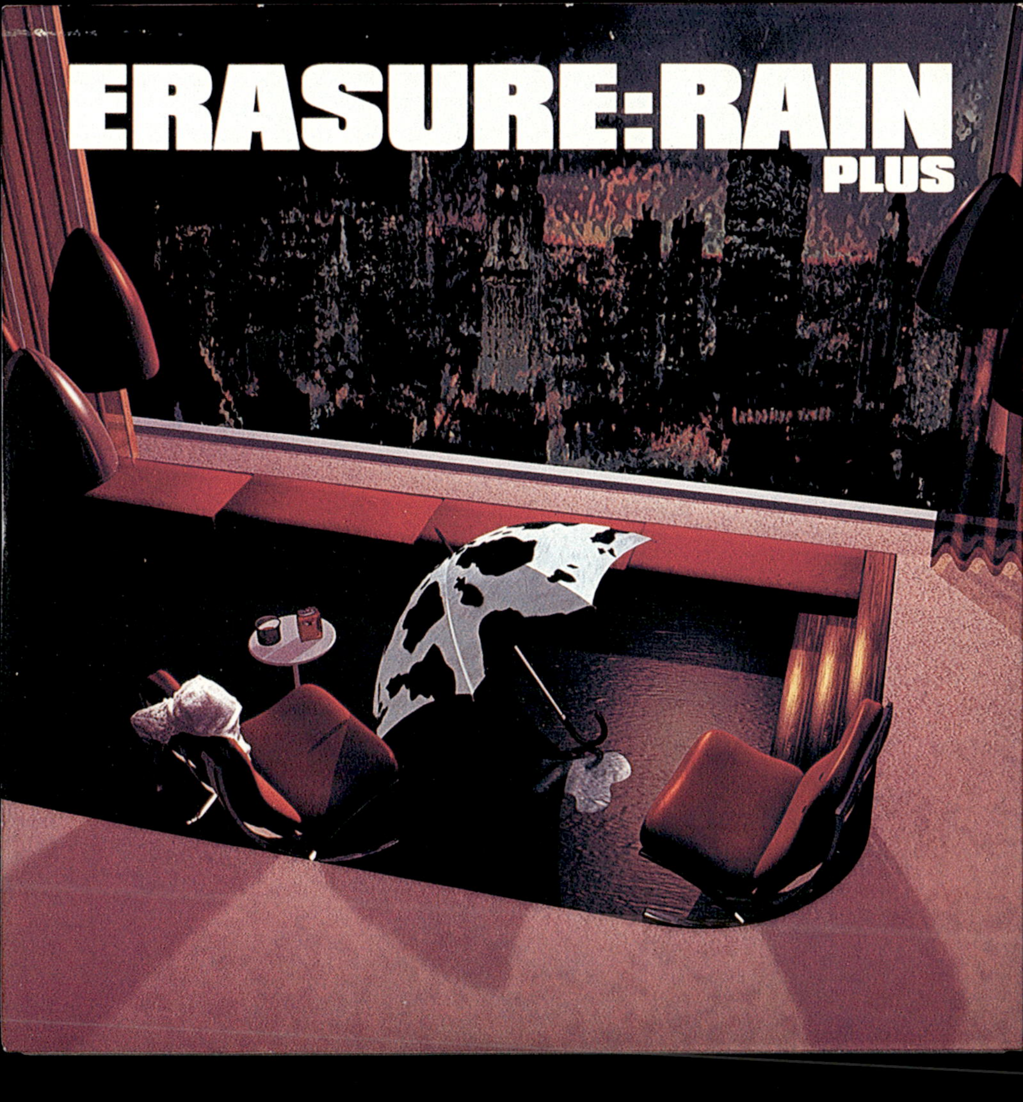

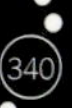

  Artist Erasure Title Rain Plus Record Label Mute Date 1997

The publishers and the author would like to thank the record labels for allowing their maxi-single covers to be reproduced in this book, and the graphic designers, illustrators and photographers, whose work has made this book what it is.

La editorial y el autor agradecen a las discográficas el permiso para reproducir las portadas de los maxi-singles, y a los diseñadores gráficos, ilustradores y fotógrafos, sin cuyo trabajo este libro no hubiera sido posible.

Record labels / Discográficas

2E Records, 4th B'Way, A & M Records, Acid Jazz, Activ Records, Ahead of Our Time, Arcade, B Music, Basic Beat, Big Life, Black Culture, Blanco y Negro, BMG Ariola, BMS Records, Boy Records, Breakout, Bustin' Loose, Capitol, CBS, CFE, Chrysalis, Circa Records, Club Tools, Cologne Dance Label, Compact Listeners, Cook, Cooltempo, Creation Records, D.J. International, D: Vision, Dance Net, Dance Pool, Deconstruction, Delabel, Delicious Vinyl, DFC, Downtown, DRO, Duke, East Side Records, East West, Eastern Bloc, Edel, Eight Ball Records, Elektra, Elektro Motor, EMI, Enfasis, EPIC, Essential Recordings, Eternal, Eve Records, Fetish Records, FFRR, Fiction Records, Flying, Fontana, Freedom, Fresh Fish, Fresh Fruit Records, Fresh Records, Funky, Go Beat, Go Discs, Groovetown, GRP, Gut Records, Hey Babe, Hispavox, Insolent Tracks, Instinct, Island Records, Jam Records, JBO, Jive, Junior, Kontor, Kosmos Records, Le Club, Legato, Let It Shine, Logic Records, London Recordings, Low Spirit, Magic, Mantra, Max Music, Mercury, Metronome, More Vinil, Motor Music, Mushroom, Music Master, Mute Records, N.E.W.S., New Music International, Noise Traxx, Orange, ORE, P.R.T. Records, Paisley Park Records, Parlophone, Peppermint Jam Records, Philips, Phonogram, Pias Recordings, Plastic City, Plastic Records, Platinum, Polydor, Positiva, Pulse 8, RCA, React Music, Recordings for the Connoisseur, Rhythm King, Rise, Rough Trade, Royal Records, SBK Records, Service, Siren, Six 6, Sony Music, Stikman, Stream, Suck 42, Suck Me Plasma, Sugar Daddy, Sugar Hill Records Ltd, Systematic, Talkin Loud, Tempo Music, Ten Records, The Echo Label Ltd., Time, Tommy Boy, Twisted, U2 Music Limited, United Recordings, Universal Music, Urban, Vale Music, VC Records, Vendetta, Victoria, Virgin, Volition Records, Warner Music, Wea, XL Recordings, Yellow, Zafiro, ZTT Records, ZYX Records

Graphic designers, photographers and illustrators / Diseñadores gráficos, ilustradores, fotógrafos
@ Peacock, 3 Points, A Blue Source, A Design League Sleeve, Accident, Agnes Dahan, AK, Alex Courtes, Alex Quero, Alex Strehl, Alistair Thain, An Unknown, André Fichte, Andrea C. Davis, Andrea Cappelletti, Andrew Johnson, Andrew Levy & Troy, Andrew MacPherson, Andy Earle, Anna Mever, Anne Yvonne Gilbert, Antoine Moonen, Anton Corbijn, APE, Arnarson, Cooke, Wright, ATB & Marc Schilkowski, Benoit Peverelli, Bernard Benant, Bill Smith Studio, Blinkk Record, Blue, Blue Source, Brand Branson, Brian Cannon, Bryn Jones, Cally, Carol Weinberg, Chris Clunn, Chris Craymer, Chris Long, Chris Nash, Christof G. Stalder, Christopher Griffiths, Clifton Hall, Corduroy, Corinne Day, Craig McDean, D. Rudolph, D. Storey, Dave Brubakers, David Band, David James Associates, David Little, David Palmer & Peter Kelsey, Derek Yates, Design @ Definition, Designed At The ES-P, Designland, Didedgar, DKB, Dominator, Drew Fitzgerald, Dsign>OEL 180º, E+D Jordi Magaña, Eddie Monsoon, Edward Bettison, Eidologic, Eike König, Eikes Grafischer, Eikman, Elestudio, Eric Haze, Eric Johnson, ES-Ps, Eugine Adebari, Fabian L.D., Fabrice Destagnol, Factor Product, Fantasy Factory, Form, Fresh Produce, Gaby Gerster, Garuso and Ausenda, George Du Bose, George Michael, Peter B. & Simon Halfon, George Miller, Gerhard Schröder, Get Wet, Giuseppe Spaba, Goutte, Graeme Montgomery, Groovy Twins, Groupe, Guy Debord, Henrik Bonnevier, Hothouse, Huw Feather, Hype Graphics, Ian Mac, Ian MacNeil, Idest, Ingrid Albrecht, Introdesign, Island Records, J. Plumb @ Sonicon, James Alexander, James Fry, James Marsh, James R1221, Jamie Morgan, Jason Tozer, Jeremy Pearce, Jill Greenberg, John Pasche, John Ross, John Warwicker, Johnnie Miles, Jon Barraclough and Vicky Andrew for the Unknown, Jörgen Brennicke, Judy Blame, Julian and Julian, Julian Barton, Julian Bigg, Kate Garner, Kay Graphics, Keith Breeden, Kenny Cowburn, Kevin Westenberg, KM7, Kris Neat, Kristian Russell, Larry Dunstan, Lawrence Watson, Leo Para Elestudio, Leonard Freed, Lewis Mulatero, LIN 21, Lluis Díaz, Lorenzo Agius, Lynda West, M @ Maitland At Big – Active, M@ Maitland for the Church, Marc Shilkowski, Mark America, Mark Farrow, Mark Humphreys, Mark Porter, Marko Kalfa, Mat Cook, Matthew Donaldson, Me Company, Meco @ Meco. Demon.Co.Uk, Mercury Art, Michael Bartalos, Michael Economy, Michael Gray, Michael Nash Assoc., Michael Spencer Jones, Michel Comte, Mick Deluxe, Microdot, Microfoam, Mika Väisänen, Mike Diver, Mike Owen, Momis, Moogly, Mouthco Design, Nacy Brown, Narodnipodnik, Marc Schlkowski, Nick Knight, Numero 6 & LN, O'Neill, Olivier Teepe, Oscar B., P. Budestschu, P. Cox, Paolo Portuesi, Patrizio Squeglia, Paul Leith, Paul McMenamin At V23, Peat Design, Pete Turner, Peter Ashworth, Peter Barret, Andrew Biscomb, Peter Corriston, Peter For Zip Design, Phil Ward, Philknott, Prodesign, Randee St. Nicholas, Rankin, Ray @ Intro, Red Ranch, Reiner Pfisterer, Republic, Restez Vivants, Rian Hughes, Richard Houghton, Rick Guests, Robert Erdmann, Ronnie McGuigan, Roy Volkman, Rusell Young, Ryan Art, Same, Satellite, Sheila Michel Molnar, Silhouettes: Pat Redding, Silver Haze, Simon Taylor for Faction 2D, Slim Smith, Spin, Spiros, Stefano Coletti, Steve Hall, Steve Newman, Stuart Dace, Stuart Patterson At Hygiene, Studio Monty Shadow, Stylorouge, Swifty Glory, T. Badin, T+CP, Tamara Capellaro, The Dream Factory, The Funky Morgan Penn, The Swinging Michael Heissner, The Thunder Jockeys, Think 1, Think Design, Thinkelectric.com, Tijai, Tim France, Tim Harrison, Tom Bouman, Tom Pitts, Tom Record, Toni Rubio, Tony Chiumento, Tony Sellari, Tow, Trevor "Jumbo Jimmy", Trust, TSC/SJH, U.C. Graphic, Ute Klaphake, Vegas, Von Denis Pernath, Wilie Ryan, Wink, Work Associates, XL ZTT, Youri Lenquette, Ysabel Knyphause, Zak Ove, Zanna

Published by / Publicado por
ACTAR

Editor and Graphic Design
Autor y diseño gráfico
Toni Rubio
Toni@dissenyrubio.com

Text / Texto
Jaume Pujagut

Printed by / Impresión
Ingoprint S.A.

Distributed by / Distribución
ACTAR D
Roca i Batlle 2
E-08023 Barcelona
office@actar-d.com
Tel: +34 93 417 49 93
Fax: +34 93 418 67 07

ISBN 84-95951-94-0
DL B-24618-05

Printed and bound in the European Union
Impreso y encuadernado en la Unión Europea

Acknowledgements / Agradecimientos
Ramon Prat, Anna Tetas, Angelito,
Pep Garcés (Plastic), Debla Aladren,
Oscar Munt, Metropol Records,
Mario García, José Luis Hernández.